D1401683

ALCOHOL PROBLEMS IN WOMEN

THE GUILFORD ALCOHOL STUDIES SERIES

Howard Blane and Donald Goodwin, Editors

Alcohol Problems in Women: Antecedents, Consequences, and Intervention
Sharon C. Wilsnack and Linda J. Beckman, Editors

Drinking and Crime: Perspectives on the Relationships between Alcohol Consumption and Criminal Behavior
James J. Collins, Jr., Editor

Alcohol Problems in Women

Antecedents, Consequences, and Intervention

Edited by

SHARON C. WILSNACK
University of North Dakota School of Medicine
and
LINDA J. BECKMAN
School of Medicine
University of California, Los Angeles

The Guilford Press
New York   London

© 1984 The Guilford Press
A Division of Guilford Publications, Inc.
200 Park Avenue South, New York, N.Y. 10003

Printed in the United States of America

LIBRARY OF CONGRESS CATALOGING IN PUBLICATION DATA
Main entry under title:

Alcohol problems in women.

(The Guilford alcohol studies series)
Bibliography: p.
Includes index.
1. Women—Alcohol use—Addresses, essays, lectures. 2. Women—Alcohol use—Treatment—Addresses, essays, lectures. I. Wilsnack, Sharon C. II. Beckman, Linda J. III. Series.
[DNLM: 1. Alcoholism. 2. Women. WM 274 A354]
HV5137.A4 1984 362.2′92′088042 82-21059
ISBN 0-89862-164-X

CONTRIBUTORS

Hortensia Amaro, PhD, Department of Psychiatry, School of Medicine, Neuro-psychiatric Institute, University of California, Los Angeles, California. Current affiliation: School of Public Health, Boston University, Boston, Massachusetts

Linda J. Beckman, PhD, Department of Psychiatry, School of Medicine, Neuro-psychiatric Institute, University of California, Los Angeles, California

Harriet B. Braiker, PhD, Clinical Psychologist in private practice, Los Angeles, California

David D. Celentano, ScD, Department of Behavioral Sciences, School of Hygiene and Public Health, The Johns Hopkins University, Baltimore, Maryland

Cynthia H. Ervin, PhD, Department of Psychology, University of Puget Sound, Tacoma, Washington

Roberta G. Ferrence, MA, Addiction Research Foundation, Toronto, Ontario, Canada, and Department of Sociology, Queen's University, Kingston, Ontario, Canada

Kaye Middleton Fillmore, PhD, Alcohol Research Group, Institute of Epidemiology and Behavioral Medicine, Medical Research Institute of San Francisco, Berkeley, California, and School of Public Health, University of California at Berkeley, Berkeley, California

Irene Hanson Frieze, PhD, Department of Psychology, University of Pittsburgh, Pittsburgh, Pennsylvania

Edith S. Lisansky Gomberg, PhD, School of Social Work, University of Michigan, Ann Arbor, Michigan

Shirley Y. Hill, PhD, Western Psychiatric Institute and Clinic, and Department of Psychiatry, University of Pittsburgh School of Medicine, Pittsburgh, Pennsylvania

Lorraine V. Klerman, DPH, Department of Public Health, Florence Heller Graduate School for Advanced Studies in Social Welfare, Brandeis University, Waltham, Massachusetts

Joy Leland, PhD, Desert Research Institute, University of Nevada, Reno, Nevada

Judith M. Lisansky, PhD, Department of Human Ecology, Cook College, Rutgers—The State University, New Brunswick, New Jersey

Ruth E. Little, ScD, Alcoholism and Drug Abuse Institute, University of Washington, Seattle, Washington

David V. McQueen, ScD, Research Unit in Health and Behavioural Change, University of Edinburgh, Scotland

Patricia Cooney Schafer, BS, Department of Psychology, University of Pittsburgh, Pittsburgh, Pennsylvania

Kevin M. Thompson, MA, Department of Sociology, University of Arizona, Tucson, Arizona

Marsha Vannicelli, PhD, Appleton Treatment Center, McLean Hospital, Belmont, Massachusetts, and Department of Psychiatry, Harvard Medical School, Boston, Massachusetts

Carol N. Williams, PhD,Center for Alcohol Studies, Brown University, Providence, Rhode Island

Richard W. Wilsnack, PhD, Department of Sociology, University of North Dakota, Grand Forks, North Dakota

Sharon C. Wilsnack, PhD, Department of Neuroscience, University of North Dakota School of Medicine, Grand Forks, North Dakota

ACKNOWLEDGMENTS

Many individuals have made important contributions to this book. We are especially grateful to the chapter authors, who took time from busy and demanding schedules to prepare their reviews, in many cases involving data that were dispersed, fragmented, and not previously organized.

We appreciate the enthusiasm and encouragement of Seymour Weingarten, Editor-in-Chief of The Guilford Press; the advice and consultation of Howard T. Blane and Donald W. Goodwin, Editors of Guilford's Alcohol Studies Series; and the efficient editorial management of Jean Ford throughout the publication process.

Invaluable help with library research, copyediting, proofreading, and other aspects of manuscript preparation was provided by Virginia Anderson, Cathey Heron, and Janice Danielski. We also appreciate the contributions of the Department of Neuroscience, University of North Dakota School of Medicine, and the Department of Psychiatry and Biobehavioral Sciences, UCLA School of Medicine, including their support of the many lengthy cross-country telephone calls needed to successfully complete this volume.

Finally, we are particularly grateful for the understanding and continuing support of our families—Dan Beckman, Richard Wilsnack, and Joel, Brian, Peter, Kirsten, and Jonathan Wilsnack.

SCW
LJB

PREFACE

Until quite recently women received little specific attention in research on alcohol problems. In a search of the literature published between 1929 and 1970, Sandmaier (1980) found only 28 English-language studies of alcoholic women. Higher rates of problem drinking and alcoholism among men than women, underrepresentation of women in popular clinical research settings (e.g., VA or state hospitals), and lack of any special interest in women's alcohol problems on the part of predominantly male researchers may all have contributed to the neglect of women as subjects of alcohol-related research.

The past 12 years have seen increasing public awareness and concern about alcohol problems in women. One source of this awareness has undoubtedly been the women's movement in this country and others, which has focused attention on women's issues in general. A second source may have been the widespread publicity surrounding research on the fetal alcohol syndrome (FAS) and other fetal alcohol effects, dramatic evidence that women and their offspring are not immune to the harmful effects of alcohol. A third factor that stimulated and reinforced public concern about women's drinking was a variety of reports, in both the popular and scientific literature of the 1970s, that drinking and drinking problems were increasing markedly among women. As discussed in chapters by Fillmore (Chapter 1) and by Thompson and Wilsnack (Chapter 2), there appears to have been little scientific evidence for major increases in female drinking in the 1970s. Rather, the claims may have reflected a delayed reaction to earlier changes in women's drinking, or a general societal anxiety about changing roles and statuses of women and their possible negative consequences.

Through much of the 1970s scientific research on women lagged behind public concern about the "women's alcohol problem." In fact, in 1975 an interdisciplinary group of researchers defined the area of alcohol and drug abuse in women as a "nonfield," with few acknowledged experts and virtually no specialized literature (Kalant, 1980). In the absence of empirical data on women and alcohol, myths and assumptions abounded. Arising from cultural stereotypes and anecdotal clinical reports, common beliefs about alcoholic women included the notions that they were primarily white middle-class housewives who successfully hid their drinking from others (including family, friends, and survey researchers); that most were sexually promiscuous, especially when drinking; that they were "sicker" or more psychologically disturbed than male alcoholics; and that they had poorer treatment outcomes than their male counterparts. Interestingly, as discussed by Fillmore (Chapter 1) and by Vannicelli (Chapter 13), certain false assumptions about alcoholic women persisted even when contradictory evidence became available, perhaps because the beliefs served important social and political ends.

The state of the art of research on women and alcohol has improved considerably since the mid-1970s. A growing number of researchers from diverse disciplines have become interested in the antecedents and consequences of women's alcohol use, and how women's alcohol problems differ from those of men. Many (but by no means all) of these researchers have been women, as reflected in the predominance of women contributors to this volume. In 1978 the National Institute on Alcohol Abuse and Alcoholism (NIAAA) sponsored a working conference of approximately 25 American and Canadian scientists active in research on women and alcohol. Conference participants reviewed the state of the art of research on various aspects of women's alcohol problems and developed a number of methodological and substantive recommendations to guide future research efforts (NIAAA, 1980). Dissemination of these recommendations helped to stimulate additional interest in women's issues among alcohol researchers, as did the announcement of a new federal initiative giving special attention to the problem of alcoholism in women by the U.S. Secretary of Health, Education, and Welfare in May 1979.

Although they are still greatly out of proportion to research on men, published studies and funded research on women and alcohol are steadily increasing. In 1982, the *Journal of Studies on Alcohol* abstracted 49 empirical studies of drinking, problem drinking, or alcoholism among women (excluding FAS research and studies paying only minor attention to gender differences), more than the sum of studies published in English between 1929 and 1970. Between 1971 and 1976 NIAAA funded three research projects with a specific focus on women drinkers or alcoholics, excluding studies of pregnancy outcome. From 1976 to 1984, NIAAA funded 18 such projects, as well as additional projects that use women as comparison groups in studies of gender differences. Clearly empirical data are beginning to accumulate in this new area of alcohol studies. The present volume is an attempt to organize the emerging data on alcohol problems in women, to critically review their methodological adequacy and substantive implications, and to identify major continuing gaps in knowledge and directions for future research.

As indicated by its title, the book is concerned with a range of specific alcohol problems experienced by women. These problems include—and some chapters focus primarily on—the clinical syndrome of alcoholism, characterized by alcohol dependence and negative consequences of drinking in multiple life areas. However, attention is also given to a variety of other alcohol-related problems that may be experienced both by alcoholic women and by nonalcoholic women in the general population, including various health consequences of heavy alcohol consumption, FAS and other fetal alcohol effects, alcohol–drug interactions, and alcohol-related family problems, marital violence, and sexual dysfunction.

The book is organized in four sections. Section I, Patterns of Alcohol Use and Alcohol Problems in Women, reviews epidemiological and other evidence regarding rates and correlates of drinking and drinking problems in adolescent and adult women, ethnic differences in women's drinking, and patterns of multiple substance abuse among women. Section II, Biological and Psychosexual Aspects of Alcohol Use in Women, summarizes findings on gender differences in biomedical consequences of chronic alcohol abuse, reviews current knowledge about the etiology of and intervention with one specific alcohol problem of women—FAS and other fetal alcohol effects— and analyzes available information relating alcohol use and sexual functioning in women.

Section III, Antecedents and Consequences of Alcohol Problems in Women, provides an overview of research on biological, psychological, and sociocultural risk factors for alcohol problems in women and considers two special consequences of women's alcohol abuse: effects on the family, and relationships to marital violence. Section IV, Treatment and Prevention of Alcohol Problems in Women, contains chapters on barriers to women's utilization of alcoholism treatment, psychotherapeutic issues with alcoholic women, outcome of alcoholism treatment for women, and approaches to preventing alcohol problems in women. The 14 contributed chapters represent, to our knowledge, the most comprehensive empirical reviews to date of research in their areas.

Although this book is intended primarily as a contribution to the research literature on women and alcohol, we believe that it will also be of interest to persons other than researchers who are concerned about understanding and alleviating women's alcohol problems. We have tried in two major ways to bridge the gap that often exists between research findings and clinical applications. First, we have devoted approximately one-fourth of the book (Section IV) to issues directly relevant to prevention and treatment. Second, we have asked the authors of all chapters to consider, where possible, the potential implications for prevention and treatment of the research findings they review. We hope these efforts have been successful in enhancing the book's usefulness to treatment and prevention practitioners, both as a source of empirical data that may help guide clinical and programmatic interventions and as a source of hypotheses that can be tested further by systematic clinical observation and rigorous clinical research.

In attempting to present a comprehensive overview of major research areas, we are aware of a number of topics that could have been given more detailed attention. Among these are acute physiological effects of ethanol in women and certain specific hypothetical antecedents of women's drinking, including life stress, affective disorders, and sex-role conflicts. Although individual authors address a number of subgroups of women drinkers, including ethnic minority women, female adolescents, multiple substance abusers, and lesbians, there are other important subgroups that might have been discussed in greater detail, for example, older problem-drinking women.

The tone of this introduction is cautiously optimistic, finding grounds for encouragement in the increasing numbers of researchers who are becoming interested in gender differences and women's alcohol problems, and in the empirical data that are beginning to accumulate. Despite this optimism, great disparities still exist in the relative attention given to women and men by alcohol researchers and in the proportions of funded studies and published reports that deal with women as compared with men. Critical methodological issues still face the researcher on women and alcohol, including questions of definition and measurement (e.g., should the same or different criteria be used for defining heavy drinking, alcohol problems, and alcoholism in women as in men?) and practical matters of data analysis and reporting (e.g., how can researchers be encouraged to conduct and report cross-gender comparisons in data sets that include both women and men?). Many substantive issues of major theoretical and clinical significance have barely begun to be addressed. Some particularly important questions posed by authors in this book are the complex interactions among biological and psychosocial antecedents of women's drinking, probable differences in etiology and consequences of alcohol problems across demographic and other subgroups of women, and the contribution of various social influences to women's alcohol problems, including gender-specific drinking norms, family and occupational roles, the behavior of heavy-drinking partners, and characteristics of the alcohol treatment system. In addition to documenting progress in research on women and alcohol to date, we hope the present volume will stimulate further research that will help answer these questions and ultimately will help prevent or ameliorate the significant personal and social costs of alcohol problems in women.

Sharon C. Wilsnack
Linda J. Beckman

REFERENCES

Kalant, O. J. (Ed.). *Research advances in alcohol and drug problems* (Vol. 5: *Alcohol and drug problems in women*). New York: Plenum, 1980.

National Institute on Alcohol Abuse and Alcoholism. *Alcoholism and alcohol abuse among women: Research issues* (NIAAA Research Monograph No. 1, U.S. Department of Health, Education, and Welfare Publication No. ADM-80-835). Washington, D.C.: U.S. Government Printing Office, 1980.

Sandmaier, M. *The invisible alcoholics: Women and alcohol abuse in America.* New York: McGraw-Hill, 1980.

CONTENTS

ALCOHOL PROBLEMS IN WOMEN

PATTERNS OF ALCOHOL USE AND ALCOHOL PROBLEMS IN WOMEN

The first four chapters discuss patterns of alcohol and other drug use among adult women and female adolescents. In Chapter 1 Fillmore reviews epidemiological literature of the past 4 decades and concludes that, although the proportion of women who drink rather than abstain has increased since the 1940s, rates of heavy drinking and drinking problems among women have remained relatively constant during the period. Despite this constancy, researchers and writers in the 1940s and 1950s chose to minimize the extent of women's drinking, while recent reports have raised alarms about increased drinking by women converging with that of men. Fillmore suggests several historical and political determinants of the shift from minimization to maximization of women's alcohol problems. These include the impact of Wet–Dry politics on scholarly estimates of women's drinking in earlier decades; efforts of the modern alcoholism movement and of a new federal alcohol agency, the National Institute on Alcohol Abuse and Alcoholism, to "sell" alcoholism as a major health and social problem requiring expanded resources for treatment and prevention; and current social unease about possible consequences of women's liberation from traditional sex roles.

Fillmore goes beyond this provocative historical analysis to present new findings from a cohort analysis of data from three national surveys conducted in 1964, 1967, and 1979. Contrary to earlier conclusions regarding lack of change in heavier drinking in the general female population, she finds some evidence for increased heavy–frequent drinking among women in the youngest (ages 21–29) age cohort, particularly among younger women who are employed. If the patterns reported by Fillmore are replicated in other surveys, they may signal a modest recent increase in heavier drinking among young adult women, which may extend to older groups as these young women age.

As Fillmore does for adult women, Thompson and Wilsnack in Chapter 2 evaluate evidence among adolescents for the so-called "convergence hypothesis"—that rates of drinking and drinking problems are increasing among female adolescents and approaching or equaling rates for male adolescents. Thompson and Wilsnack find some support in regional and national survey data for the convergence of boys' and girls' drinking. However, four qualifications are noted: (1) the greatest increases in girls' drinking occurred between the 1940s and 1970s, with few changes since the late 1970s; (2) converging rates of boys' and girls' drinking appear to reflect both increases in girls' drinking and some stabilization or decline in boys' drinking; (3) what has increased the most among girls is drinking, as opposed to abstaining; while (4) heavy drinking and drinking-related problems are still considerably more common among adolescent boys than among adolescent girls.

One reason why many alcohol researchers are particularly interested in the convergence hypothesis, as explicated by Fillmore and by Thompson and Wilsnack, is that it may seem to bear directly on the question of biological versus psychosocial determinants of drinking behavior. If drinking by women and girls remains relatively stable during a historical period characterized by major changes in women's roles and life experiences, might this imply an important biological contribution to gender differences in drinking behavior? To answer this question, we would need to specify carefully both the time period over which changes are observed and the actual changes in women's roles and statuses during that period. Certainly there were major changes in women's employment and family roles between the 1940s and early 1970s, accompanied by increased rates of drinking among both adult and adolescent women. It may be that further changes in sex roles during the past decade have been more modest, or have occurred only for certain subgroups of women. If so, associated changes in drinking behavior might be very small or nonexistent or apparent only within specific demographic subgroups, as Fillmore's findings suggest may be the case. In any event, both theoretical and social policy considerations make it important to continue to monitor time trends in drinking behavior of women and girls. Such monitoring should include attention to subgroup differences and use measures that are sensitive to possible special characteristics of female drinking.

At times the public and scientific interest in whether female drinking is converging with male drinking may distract attention from other important considerations. For example, Thompson and Wilsnack point out that large absolute numbers of female adolescents engage in at least occasional episodes of heavy drinking, regardless of whether these numbers equal comparable rates among males. A striking statistic from a 1978 national survey of high school seniors is that 30% of the young women surveyed reported having had 5 or more drinks on at least one occasion in the past 2 weeks, a slight increase from 26% in 1975. Such data may be possible grounds for concern that the patterns or contexts of girls' drinking are changing in such a manner that occasional episodes of drunkenness or extremely heavy drinking could become typical and acceptable behavior among adolescent girls as well as boys.

Thompson and Wilsnack comprehensively review the research on correlates of adolescent drinking, including demographic characteristics, parental and peer influences, personality attributes, and others. Among the gender differences noted is the possibility that parental drinking behavior influences girls' drinking more than boys', perhaps because boys have more and earlier peer models of drinking than do girls. Unfortunately, many researchers present their data for boys and girls combined, making it impossible to tell if various influences affect girls any differently than boys. Thompson and Wilsnack believe that attention to possible gender differences in future research may be particularly important in determining whether some of the traditional cultural barriers to girls' drinking are weakening, for example, restricted drinking opportunities, gender-specific drinking norms, and traditional feminine values.

Not only do many epidemiological and clinical studies fail to analyze gender differences but, as Leland observes in Chapter 3, many of these studies also neglect possible ethnic differences, and gender–ethnicity interactions, if indeed the samples even include adequate numbers of ethnic group representatives to permit such analyses. Despite these difficulties, Leland has gathered a wide variety of published and unpublished data concerning drinking patterns of white, black, Hispanic, and Native American women. Data sources include national and regional surveys of adults and adolescents, national health consequences statistics, unpublished treatment outcome data from federally funded ethnic alcoholism treatment programs, and anthropological studies of drinking within various ethnic subcultures, including Leland's own research on drinking among Native American women.

One general conclusion of Leland's chapter is that the problem consequences of drinking for ethnic women may be more severe than their rates of heavy drinking in general population surveys would predict. Particularly striking is the high rate of cirrhosis of the liver among Native American women. Leland also uses the available empirical data to evaluate certain stereotypes about ethnic drinking, including the notions that a black "matriarchy" is responsible for relatively high rates of heavy drinking among black women drinkers, and that traditional sex roles of "machismo" and "marianismo" underlie strongly gender-differentiated drinking behavior among Hispanic men and women.

Leland's analysis of data from federally funded ethnic treatment programs raises several important questions. Although not broken down by gender, treatment outcome was poorer for ethnic minority men and women combined than for nonethnic clients. There is some suggestion elsewhere in her data that lack of culture-specific programming and absence of support system involvement may be associated with poorer outcomes. Do these influences operate similarly or differently for ethnic minority women and men? For example, might support system involvement be particularly important for women, and lack of it perhaps help to explain the underrepresentation of Hispanic women alcoholics in treatment?

In addition to its substantive contributions, comparing drinking patterns and problems of women of different ethnicity, Leland's chapter underscores the need to take into account ethnic and cultural factors in interpreting the findings of alcohol research in general. For example, many studies of biological aspects of alcohol use do not describe the ethnic composition of their samples, although the elevated rates of health consequences Leland reports for Native Americans suggest that ethnic differences in biomedical consequences may be present. In psychological and social research, cultural and ethnic variations in social roles of men and women and in gender-specific drinking contexts and drinking patterns suggest the need for great caution in using personality or social-role measures or drinking measures developed within one ethnic group (generally non-Hispanic whites) with members of other ethnic populations.

Some questions raised by Leland cannot be answered with available data, due to the small numbers of ethnic women studied. For example, do Hispanic women have relatively high rates of alcohol problems, as suggested by a 1979 national survey, or lower rates, as suggested by a 1974 California study? How do patterns of drinking and drinking problems among Native American women nationwide compare with those of other ethnic groups? How does drinking among Asian-American women compare with drinking among Asian-American men and among women of other ethnic groups? It is to be hoped that the high rates of alcohol problems within certain ethnic subgroups will encourage future researchers, including those conducting general population surveys, to consider oversampling ethnic minorities to ensure adequate numbers of ethnic respondents—by gender and by drinking classification—to permit reliable parameter estimates and statistical comparisons.

The final chapter in Section I raises a critical issue for the study of women and alcohol, namely, that many women abuse both alcohol and other psychoactive drugs. In Chapter 4 Celentano and McQueen argue that for such women separate discussion of, research on, and treatment or prevention of "alcohol problems" on the one hand and "drug problems" on the other not only is artificial and arbitrary but also is unlikely to lead to fruitful conclusions or interventions.

Although few alcohol researchers or clinicians would dispute the preceding statements, Celentano and McQueen find that surprisingly little research is available to answer important questions about the prevalence and correlates of multiple substance abuse in women. Several clinical studies suggest that women alcoholics in treatment are more likely than men alcoholics to have abused tranquilizers and other prescription drugs. Most general population surveys, on the other hand, (1) have asked only about alcohol use *or* about use of other drugs, (2) have asked about both alcohol and other drug use but have analyzed and reported each type of use separately, so that percentages of women who use *both* alcohol and other drugs cannot be determined, or (3) have reported rates of concurrent alcohol and drug use but have not separately analyzed data from women and men. Reasons for the neglect of research on multiple substance abuse in women are unclear. Celentano and McQueen speculate that contributing factors may include the separation of alcohol and drug funding agencies on a federal level and the specialization of researchers in either "alcohol problems" or "drug problems," often with little knowledge of the other domain.

Critically reviewing the data available, Celentano and McQueen conclude that multiple substance abuse may be more common among women problem drinkers than among men problem drinkers, given the higher rates of prescription drug use among women in the general population and clinical findings that women alcoholics are more likely than men alcoholics to abuse prescription tranquilizers and sedatives. They discuss a number of social influences that may contribute to women's multiple substance abuse, including media advertising, economic incentives encouraging drug production, and cultural values of pleasure and escape. They urge that treatment and prevention personnel adopt a more "holistic" perspective that encompasses both alcohol and other drug problems, and call for increased education of persons in treatment and referral positions with regard to the pharmacological interactions of alcohol and other drugs most often used by women.

Celentano and McQueen believe that there is reason to expect improved research on multiple substance abuse in women in the near future. Calling for greater collaboration between alcohol and drug researchers, they point to one potential source of data for such collaboration. A series of Epidemiological Catchment Area Studies presently being supported by the National Institute of Mental Health will soon provide data on multiple concurrent substance use in a number of urban samples. The female samples should be large enough and the drug histories detailed enough to permit answers to many of the critical questions raised in this chapter.

1

"When Angels Fall": Women's Drinking as Cultural Preoccupation and as Reality

KAYE MIDDLETON FILLMORE
Medical Research Institute of San Francisco and University of California at Berkeley

INTRODUCTION

There have been so many reviews of the epidemiological literature on women's drinking in recent years that it may seem redundant to approach still one more. To state one more time that the sex ratio for alcoholism indicates that men have a higher proportion of alcohol problems than women, that the ratio is contingent on the population under study (one clinical sample versus another, one set of mortality statistics versus another and so on) or that one sex may come to the attention of treatment or social statistics more than the other would be to repeat the essence and conclusions of much work which precedes this review (see, e.g., Ferrence, 1980; Wechsler, 1980).

This review starts from a different perspective and attempts to address a puzzle that surrounds findings from epidemiological research comparing the drinking behaviors of men and women. The evidence for the last 40 years has strongly indicated that female drinking patterns in this country have remained fairly consistent. However, during this 40-year stretch, the scholarly literature has treated these findings in dramatically different ways—sometimes these findings have been overstated while at other times they have been understated. The first portion of this chapter attempts to understand why women's drinking patterns have been deemed important or unimportant over the last 40 years. Historically tracing the epidemiological findings regarding drinking patterns and problems among women, it suggests that researchers have differentially used these findings because of a number of influences including the status of women, the status of the alcohol research, the changing image of the alcoholic in America and the threat to the society of perceived role shifts among women. The focus of the investigation in this paper is to examine the contemporary claim or the hypothesis that drinking styles are converging between the sexes. The first portion of the chapter is a review and discussion around this issue, and the second portion is devoted to a quantitative examination of this hypothesis. Using age cohorts in the general population as well as trend data over the last 15 years, we test some elements of the convergence hypothesis.

THE REITERATION OF THE CONVERGENCE HYPOTHESIS

Concern about alcohol problems among women has for the most part been relatively rare. Even during the American Temperance Movement, women were rarely the target of interest primarily because temperance ideology was organized around the issue of men's drinking (Levine, 1980). When women did use alcohol, they were often seen as occupying exceptionally low statuses such as prostitute or were, at the very least, seen as promiscuous (Clarke, 1917; Morella, 1974). Barrington, Pearson, and Heron (1910) in a study of alcoholics at the turn of the century could conclude that "it is probable that in the lowest grade of prostitution all with scarcely an exception are alcoholic" (p. 20).

As in current times, some scholars were interested in documenting the social characteristics of institutionalized alcoholics. Lender (1981) reports six studies between 1883 and 1912 that presented data on the sex ratio of inebriates in a number of institutions. As in the present day, the ratio varied markedly (from 9:1 to 3:1), as a function of the type of institution and the socioeconomic status of the patients. Lender reports that because most researchers of the period found the ratio to be between 4:1 and 9:1, it was concluded that about 10% of American alcoholics were women (Hultgen, 1909, p. 122).

We have been able to locate only two reports from the last century which suggested that alcohol problems were increasing among women. T. D. Crothers (1892), then superintendent of the Walnut Lodge Hospital in Hartford, Connecticut, addressed the issue but concluded that "the emancipation of women from slavery of caste and ignorance and the steady upward movement in mental and physical development, will prevent any general increase of alcoholism or inebriety" (p. 735). While Crothers's conclusion reflected the temperance ideology of the times in America, Kerr's observations in England in 1894 were not so optimistic. As President of England's Society for the Study of Inebriety, he reported his own observations of drunkenness among women.

> Twenty years ago I rarely ever saw a female drinking at the bar of a public-house or beerhouse. Now I see numbers so engaged from an early hour in the morning, not a few of these early risers and early drinkers having had an infant at the breast, and giving the child a share of the morning dram. (p. 158)

There are very clear similarities between this earlier literature on female drinking and the literature emerging from the first years of the modern alcoholism movement. First, the epidemiological evidence suggested that the incidence of alcoholism among women was considerably lower than that among men and, second, alcoholism was so widely considered a "man's disease" that women were rarely the object of scholarly investigation. However, the space of half a century created changes in the status of women and saw the sharp decline of the Temperance Movement and the repeal of Prohibition. Although it is not documented by methods that would allow researchers to project the extent of drinking among women, this period saw some changes in their drinking patterns. Reports from the clinical literature in the 1930s indicated that the numbers of women admitted to treatment for alcoholism were increasing among hospitalized samples (Curran, 1937) and reports from the press indicated the same.

Modern interest in alcohol problems may be dated to the 1940s with the creation of the Yale Center of Alcohol Studies (later to be located at Rutgers University) and the success and publicity given to the self-help group, Alcoholics Anonymous.[1] Central to the scholarly work of the period were the formulations, theoretical and empirical, of E. M. Jellinek at Yale. Among his many contributions to this early literature, Jellinek developed the first prevalence estimates of alcoholism, based primarily on cirrhosis mortality data. The formula for determining the sex ratio was developed in a public atmosphere of alarm and concern over the changing drinking patterns of women. Although, as indicated previously, there did seem to be some support for the notion that greater numbers of women were being institutionalized for alcoholism, Jellinek (1947) rejected this notion by stating that "female alcoholism is by no means 'a sign of the times'" (p. 41). Jellinek's formula for determining the sex ratio of alcoholism dominated the literature between the late 1940s and the early 1950s when the ratio hovered between 5:1 and 6:1. By the middle 1950s the formula was suffering from increasing attacks in the scholarly literature (Brenner, 1959, 1960; Popham, 1956; Seeley, 1959); however, these criticisms were not specifically aimed at the means by which the sex ratio was determined. Recent evidence has suggested that Jellinek may have underestimated the rate of alcoholism among women given the data available at that period and, had he taken those data into account, the ratio would have been a much narrower one (Roizen & Milkes, 1980). Roizen and Milkes strongly suggest to their readers that "in the present climate of considerable political interest respecting the prevalence of alcoholism among women, it would be unfortunate to encourage readers to believe that the ratio is smaller than it probably is. This would be to repeat Jellinek's error in the other direction" (p. 691).

1. It is worthy of note that, of the 29 personal stories in the first edition of *Alcoholics Anonymous* (1939), only one was written by a woman.

Jellinek, like Crothers some 55 years earlier, minimized the prevalence of alcoholism among women and even the likelihood of an increase in alcohol problems, which is unusual given the data available to him. However, in the spirit of historical speculation, it seems reasonable that he would do so. Jellinek's early work was done during a period in which Wet–Dry politics was still a heated issue. To report that alcoholism was increasing among women during this period would suggest an identification with the politics of the Drys, who regarded the availability of alcohol as directly causative of inebriety. To report that there was virtually no alcoholism would be, first, to disregard social fact and, second, to identify strongly with the Wets. Jellinek's sex ratio presented a middle ground where there was alcoholism among women but it was quite infrequent compared to alcoholism among men.

The underlying question in this discussion, of course, is why would alcoholism among one half of the society's adults be a cause for alarm while for the other half it was regarded as social fact. In response to this question, some authors have suggested that the position women hold in the society implies that they are the upholders of the moral order, that drunkenness or alcoholism may be seen as a relatively crucial symbol of the instability of a society in which women are perceived as taking on the roles of men (Clark, 1964; Gomberg, 1976; Knupfer, 1964; Lisansky, 1957). These reasons may well have played a role in Jellinek's tendency to underemphasize alcoholism among women.

Surveys in the general population, however, did tend to support Jellinek's formula for the sex ratio. A 1946 national survey of drinking practices conducted by the National Opinion Research Center reported that two out of every three adults in postwar America were drinkers while three times as many men as women were "regular" drinkers (Riley & Marden, 1947). In an effort to determine if these findings were indicative of a major social change, Riley and Marden compared their data to a 1940 sample of 10,000 insurance policy holders, acknowledging that the latter sample might bias the comparison. They concluded that drinking per se was on the increase over the 6-year period.

> Not only is the incidence of drinking among both men and women, particularly in the 20's and 30's, characterized by a sharp rise from 1940 to 1946, but the gap between men and women, particularly in the age brackets under 50, is smaller than it was 6 years ago. This narrowing of the gap between the sexes in respect to drinking would appear to be in line with the general trend in our society toward less and less differentiation in the social behavior of men and women. (p. 267)

Finding that well over 50% of the U.S. adult population were drinkers led these analysts to offer a defense of such a finding. Roizen, Clark, and Milkes (1979) suggest that this may have been the first and the last time survey researchers would ever defend themselves for overreporting the prevalence of drinking.

> Doubt in the finding that as many as two-thirds of the adult population drank may well have reflected the continuing role of the Dry–Wet axis of struggle in providing the proximate context for the interpretation of alcohol-related research findings. Given that the prohibition issue had fueled a long and difficult controversy it may have been easy to assume that the popular force on each side of the issue was about equal. That assumption, in turn, would have suggested about an even split in drinkers and nondrinkers in the adult population. The Dry–Wet axis gives us an insight into the special meaning of questions concerning drinking and nondrinking at the time. (Roizen *et al.*, 1979, p. 37)

Also supportive of Jellinek's sex ratio was the Straus and Bacon (1953) study of drinking patterns and problems among college students in the late 1940s and early 1950s. These analysts reported that 39% of their female respondents and 20% of their male respondents abstained from alcohol and, among drinkers, only 1% of the women drank more than 6 cans (3 ounces absolute alcohol) of beer (compared to 9% of the men), less than .5% of the women drank the equivalent amount of wine (compared to 4% of the men) and 7% of the women drank the equivalent amount of hard liquor on an average occasion (compared to 29% of the men). Because the frequency of drinking for women was so low compared to men, Straus and Bacon felt compelled to create a typology for women that had much lower cutpoints than the typology for men.

Continued support for Jellinek's original assumptions concerning the sex ratio came from Keller and Efron's (1955) updated prevalence estimate in which the analysts reported that the "widespread impression that there are more alcoholic women about" (p. 632) was not in fact the case. Although they did find a slight increase in female alcoholism between 1940 and 1953, they attributed the finding to better reporting and to the fact that more "hidden" female alcoholics were coming out of the closet to be counted in social statistics.

> One line of evidence that seems to point against any substantial relative increase of alcoholism among women is the ratio of male to female alcoholics. . . . This ratio has varied only within a narrow range in the time under consideration, never going above 6.3 or below 5.3. Between 1945 and 1953 it has ranged only between 5.5 and 5.8, and in 1953 it was 5.5 to 1. There is no indication of a downward trend in this ratio which would suggest an increase of alcoholism among women in particular. Thus, on the whole, it seems probable that the question whether alcoholism among women is rising relative to alcoholism among men should be answered in the negative. (p. 622)

One study from the clinical literature of the mid-1950s seemed to suggest that alcoholism may have been increasing among women, but the authors interpreted their own data in a different light. Lemere, O'Hollaren, and Maxwell (1956) described the sex ratio from the Shadel Sanitarium over a 20-year period from 1935 to 1955. Although the ratio narrowed from 15 : 1 during 1935–1940 to 5.6 : 1 between 1951 and 1955, the researchers did not ascribe the change to an increase in female alcoholism. Rather, they suggested that their data confirmed Jellinek's 1947 hypothesis that as hospitalization became more acceptable for women the sex ratio would level off among the treatment population.

Very few articles were written on the subject of female drinking and alcohol problems in the 1940s and 1950s, probably because it was so firmly established that alcoholics were primarily men and sex differences were not considered a salient factor. One of the few researchers to be interested in alcoholism among women was Edith Lisansky (Gomberg), who commented in 1957 on the dearth of interest in the subject: "In the literature on psychopathology of alcoholism a focus on the male patient is perhaps to be expected. In all western societies, male alcoholics outnumber women alcoholics" (p. 588).

What little literature there was on alcoholism among women treated the condition in a somewhat different way than it treated the condition among men. This difference in approach may well throw light on the tendency not only to keep women's alcohol problems distinct from men's, but also to continue to see them as less of an epidemiological problem.

While women were regarded as less vulnerable to alcoholism, when it did occur it was seen as much more "deviant" or "abnormal" than in men (Karpman, 1948). In a world where the disease concept of alcoholism played a major role in conceptualizing alcohol problems, it would seem rather odd that alcoholism among women was thought to be different from that among men, as though there were a special measles or mumps for each sex and a special set of causative circumstances as well. The variety of causative explanations clearly reflected the vision of women in the society. Van Amberg (1943) suggested that social drinking among women was in itself conducive to alcohol problems, clearly reflecting a Dry position on the subject. His suggestion implied that the same practice was acceptable among men but unacceptable among women, reflecting perhaps a sexual double standard. Lolli (1949) considered menopause and depression to be major causes of alcoholism (reminiscent of an earlier day when the source of women's problems was believed to center around problems with the womb—see Stage, 1979, for a discussion of this view in the 19th century). Other researchers attributed women's drinking problems to personality disorganization (Hewitt, 1943) or to sexual dysfunction (Levine, 1955). These explanations have not been lost to history (see Lindbeck's 1972 review as an example) and the notion that female alcoholics are somehow different from or more abnormal than male alcoholics is still very much in evidence.

First, a doctor who is faced with a female alcoholic, tries more to find out the reasons for such behavior than he does when he is faced with a man. Why on earth does she drink, he asks himself. The question almost implicitly draws a distinction between habitual, social, almost "normal" drinking that we find in male alcoholism, and female alcoholism which is pathological, abnormal, psycho-neurotic. (Haas, 1975, p. 1)

Lisansky, in 1957, recognized this line of reasoning regarding female alcoholism and articulated its source in the following way:

Alcoholism in women is more disapproved than in men, therefore the woman alcoholic is more poorly adjusted to her social milieu. . . . A variation of this reasoning is that women are subject in our society to more repression than men and therefore build up more tension; when pressure becomes intolerable and the woman loses control of her drinking, her "alcoholism" must be more vehemently expressed, being in proportion to the tension behind it (Karpman, 1948). It follows—an important inference—that women are more difficult to treat. (p. 589)

Little has changed in the last 30 years in the manner in which alcoholism among women is envisioned. Roizen et al. (1979) discern what they regard as a "sort of dimly coherent gestalt" in the literature used to describe the underlying characteristics of alcoholism among women.

It seems that one can weave a good part of the web of this gestalt by beginning with the idea that alcoholism in women is (I) *more frowned upon than alcoholism in men*. From (I) it may follow that (II) women therefore will keep the condition hidden longer, and (III), thus, that it will be more highly developed when it finally comes to the attentions of the agents of social response to alcoholism. Because alcohol misuse is more frowned upon, only women who are (IV) more deviant or more pathologic in the first place may become alcoholics. Thus, (V) women alcoholics may be more difficult to treat. Since heavy drinking (and thus the development of alcoholism as well) may be part of the masculine role for some men, men may develop alcoholism as a matter of course and without specific circumstances or events to prompt it; women, on the other hand (VI), are not expected to be heavy drinkers as a matter of course, and thus will develop alcoholism more often in specific life events or circumstances. Or, because such drinking in women more pointedly demands an account or explanation, (VII) women will be better at retrospectively providing them. (Roizen et al., 1979, p. 55)

That alcoholic women are seen to be stepping out of their feminine roles and into the roles of men has its roots in the 19th century and may also be found in the research of the 1970s (see Beckman 1975, and Wilsnack, 1973b, as examples). While stepping out of the feminine role was seen to be more "abnormal," more "pathological," and associated with other deviant statuses (prostitution and promiscuity) in an earlier day, the latter day interpretations center around "sex-role conflict," which basically means that women have difficulty juggling both feminine and masculine roles. The perceived characteristics of women who were alcoholic may help explain the minimization of the size of the problem in the 1940s and 1950s—not only was heavy or frequent drinking found to be abhorrent among women, but also it represented a major deviation from traditional female roles. Neither the abhorrent behavior nor the deviation from sex roles could be tolerated by the modern alcoholism movement in an era that was still sensitive to Wet–Dry politics. Interestingly, the founders of the modern alcoholism movement were seeking to locate the alcoholic within the spectrum of social classes of the society by changing the stereotype of the male alcoholic from a skid row image to an employed one (see Fillmore & Caetano, 1982, and Fillmore, 1981, in reference to alcoholism and the workplace). Rarely, however, did this change of image include women in the earlier days of the movement. It was only somewhat later that the image of the female alcoholic moved from the prostitute to the housewife, who hid her drinking behind closed doors.

During the 1960s, definitions surrounding alcohol problems began to change in the scholarly literature, and studies including women became more common. While Jellinek's conceptualizations of alcoholism were narrowly defined to include only a small portion of those with alcohol problems, a wider definition of alcoholism (Robinson, 1976) could more readily accommodate an alcoholism specific to women and an alcoholism specific to men. Contributing to this wider definition was the notion of a disaggregation of alcohol problems, which gained prominence in household surveys of alcohol problems in the late 1960s. A disaggregated approach to conceptualizing alcoholism suggested, first, that there were different kinds of alcohol problems and, second, that different problems each have their own predictive or explanatory variables.

While household surveys allowed the researcher to turn away from clinical samples with their attending biases and turn to the possibility of determining prevalence in the untreated "normal" population, these surveys ran into a number of their own difficulties. For one, when surveyors began to ask questions relating to drinking patterns among those who did drink— rather than simply dividing the world into abstainers and drinkers—they found very few women to occupy their heavy drinking category. As mentioned before, Straus and Bacon (1953) solved this problem in their youthful sample by creating a sex-based quantity–frequency typology. While "heavy drinking" clearly varied from survey to survey in terms of its operational definition, quite often the cutpoints would have to be adjusted downward considerably to include enough women for a multivariate analysis.

The problems surrounding the dependent variable may be illustrated by a few examples. Mulford and Miller's (1960) survey, conducted in 1959, used as a definition of heavy drinking, drinking more than once a week and consuming on an average occasion 4 or more bottles of beer, 3 or more drinks of hard liquor or 4 or more glasses of wine; these categories defined 4% of women as heavy drinkers. Knupfer and Room's (1964) more complex definition of the higher levels of drinking identified 13% of women as heavy drinkers. Their definition included the following: a frequency of two or three times a month with a modal quantity of 5 or more drinks, or a frequency of three to five times a week with any modal quantity and a range of 5 or more drinks, or a frequency of every day with any modal quantity and a range of 3 or more drinks. Globetti's 1967 definition included only frequency of drinking, with frequent users being those using two or three times a month; this definition identified 15% of women as frequent users. A 1979 national survey (Clark, Midanik, & Knupfer, 1981) used as an operational definition of heavy drinking 120 drinks or more per month, with 1.6% of women fitting into the category.

In a world where the researcher was expected to look at "deviant" cases (meaning at the very least the heavy–frequent drinkers in the sample), it was difficult indeed to find enough heavy-drinking women in the general population—after having removed at least one-third who abstained altogether. In the case of some researchers the definition became so lenient that many readers would have trouble distinguishing between popular conceptions of "social" drinking and analytical conceptions of "heavy" drinking. In the case of other researchers, the definition became sufficiently tight to exclude the statistical norm of social drinking, but the analysis suffered from too few cases. It is no surprise that when the Social Research Group collected data on their second independent national sample, they confined their data collection to men only, with the explanation that they were "the highest risk group which does much of the heavy drinking, constitutes the majority of the working population and holds a large share of economic and political power in the United States" (Cahalan & Room, 1974, pp. xii–xiii). In view of the findings from general population research, this restriction was understandable. Given a relatively tight definition of heavy or frequent drinking, there were simply too few cases to be found among women.

Compounding the difficulty of finding enough cases of heavy–frequent drinkers among women in the general population was finding women who reported "alcohol problems." For instance, the Social Research Group's 1967 national survey defined 2% of the women as heavy drinkers (drinking 5 or more drinks per occasion of at least two beverage types and drinking more than ten times per month), with less than 5% to none of the 608 women in the sample reporting even minimal negative consequences of drinking (including health, belligerence, problems with friends, job problems, problems with the law or alcohol-related accidents, and problems with spouse) (Cahalan, 1970). What trend data were available from the 1940s through the 1960s indicated that abstention among women (as well as men) was relatively stable and that heavy drinking and problem drinking were relatively rare phenomena among women. Thus, women were not an "interesting" target of study to survey researchers. Furthermore, although Jellinek's (1947) prevalence estimates had been called into serious question by the 1960s, these studies from a general population standpoint continued to support his postulation that women did not experience alcohol problems to nearly as great an extent as men.

The third major difficulty that surveys ran into revolved around their "charge," which was to establish alcoholism prevalence rates among the untreated general population. However, when survey researchers attempted to find respondents in the general population who clearly resembled alcoholics found in clinical populations in terms of aggregation of problems or drinking levels, they found only 1–3% (Armor, Polich, & Stambul, 1976; Room, 1977). In national samples of 2000 people, where half of them, let us assume, are women, this would yield 10 to 30 women meeting the clinical criteria. However, survey researchers quickly found that "adding up" scores from a variety of alcohol problem areas was a less interesting analytic task than looking at respondents who got into different kinds of alcohol problems. This "disaggregated" approach was, in fact, quite successful for men who, after all, experienced more alcohol problems to begin with. But, again, for women, the numbers were too small to create distinct subgroups that could then be analyzed by a number of independent variables.

While surveys were strongly suggesting that heavy drinking and alcohol problems among women were rare in the 1960s, clinical studies of alcohol problems among women increased during this period. In 1974, the National Clearinghouse for Alcohol Information listed 69 U.S. and international publications on the subject of women and alcohol. Review articles of the early 1970s were organized primarily around the same themes of an earlier day with perhaps the added notion that alcoholic women were predominantly housewives "hiding" their drinking (see Corrigan, 1974; Curlee, n.d.; Gomberg, 1974; Lindbeck, 1972). These authors were for the most part conservative in their appraisal of the extent of the problem among women.

Lindbeck (1972) quoted Fox and Lyon (1955) on the sex ratio being 6:1, who in turn quoted Jellinek (1947); however, Lindbeck stated that since the Fox and Lyon publication, "It is suspected that the ratio has changed" (p. 568). Corrigan (1974) pointed out, as did others before her, that the database for the ratio changes from analyses of general populations to analyses of social statistics to analyses of clinical samples. Corrigan drew on data from the 1970 national sample of Cahalan in which there was a 3:1 ratio of symptomatic drinking or psychological dependence and on data from state and county mental hospitals on first admissions and total admissions for alcoholism. (Cahalan, 1970; U.S. Department of Health, Education and Welfare, 1969). She concluded that

> all the available information then points to a progressively lower estimated ratio of males to females as problem drinkers in both the general population and among those who appear for treatment. It would appear reasonable to view the

women problem drinkers as comprising a minimum of one million of the estimated problem drinkers, if five million is accepted as a minimal estimate of the number of problem drinkers in this country. (p. 218)

This tentative statement of Corrigan's in 1974 may still be regarded as one in which alcohol problems among women were minimized or understated epidemiologically. It was perhaps during 1974 through 1976 that alcohol problems among women became "maximized" and were also seen to be growing.

By February 1976, the National Council on Alcoholism (NCA) had created a special office on women and in September of that same year the NCA held its first national conference on women and alcoholism (NCA's *Friday Newsletter*, 1975, 1976a, 1976b). Also in 1976, task forces on female alcoholics had been established in 43 states by NCA. Senate testimony by Antonia D'Angelo of NCA in 1976 reported that the interest in women "was established in response to heavy demands from this growing women's constituency for leadership and guidance" (Committee on Labor and Public Welfare, 1976, p. 10).

The narrative in the Senate hearing on women and alcoholism seemed to revolve around two issues. First, alcoholic women had been ignored in the past and their numbers were growing. Second, female alcoholics comprised a separate but equal group; their troubles were somehow so different from those of male alcoholics that they required separate treatment, separate research directed toward their special needs, and special education and prevention efforts. Chairing the subcommittee on alcoholism and narcotics was Senator Hathaway, himself a recovering alcoholic, who claimed that "Where once we thought women comprised less than 20 percent of our active alcoholics, for example, it appears more and more that they occupy a niche closer to their true representation in the population" (Committee on Labor and Public Welfare, 1976, p. 2). Ernest Noble, then director of the National Institute on Alcohol Abuse and Alcoholism (NIAAA), based the need to address the problems of women on four points: (1) more women are drinking now than 20 years ago; (2) the proportion of young women who drink is higher than in 1953; (3) alcoholic psychoses, alcoholism, and female deaths due to alcohol-related disease increased between 1968 and 1974; and (4) more women came into treatment (Committee on Labor and Public Welfare, 1976, p. 3). We can only guess here where these points came from. No source is cited to support an increase in drinking women between 1956 and 1976, although Gallup surveys in both the United States and Canada do indicate increasing proportions of nonabstaining women during this period (see Ferrence, 1980). The proportion of young women who drank in 1976 as compared to 1953 was probably based on the 1953 publication by Straus and Bacon on drinking among college students. By 1976, a national replication of the Straus and Bacon research had not been performed. The mortality rates cited probably were based on Efron, Keller, and Gurioli's 1974 prevalence update using the Jellinek (1947) formula, which by then had come into disrepute. The alcohol psychosis rates were probably based on working papers of NIAAA's Alcohol Epidemiologic Data System (Coakley, Holland, & Evaul, 1978; Coakley & Johnson, 1979). The increase in the number of women in treatment may be attributed to the increase in treatment facilities stimulated by the growth of NIAAA.

Regardless of the data sources, 1976 could be regarded as "the year of the female alcoholic" in that the Comprehensive Alcohol Abuse and Alcoholism Prevention, Treatment and Rehabilitation Act of 1976 gave special consideration to treatment and prevention grants related to women.

However, epidemiological work going on in the late 1970s and early 1980s did not bear out the claims that heavy drinking and alcohol abuse were increasing among women. Clark et al.'s (1981) trend analysis using eight national samples between 1971 and 1979 and two samples between 1967 and 1979 showed no major differences in female drinking patterns (including problem drinking) over the years under study. Ferrence's (1980) comprehensive review of the evidence on the sex ratio of alcoholism and alcohol problems summarized mortality, morbidity, and survey data from the United States and Canada. She found no evidence to support the convergence hypothesis either for heavy drinking (even when controlling for body weight and composition) or for alcohol problems in either survey or mortality statistics. Morbidity data and drinking and driving data were less conclusive given the lack of complete information over time.

If the accumulation of epidemiological work over a 30-year period indicated that alcohol problems or alcoholism did not seem to be on the increase among women, then one must wonder what factors in the scientific community made it possible to perpetuate the "myth" that the opposite was so. Several methodological issues, possibly in interaction with each other, may have made this possible. One factor relates to the very definitions of alcoholism and alcohol problems, in which varying operational definitions may classify relatively low to relatively high proportions of the population as having drinking problems. Celentano, McQueen, and Chee (1980) note that

> one of the predominant difficulties cited in the alcohol literature is that no standardized procedure exists for distinguishing an "alcoholic" case; there are nearly as many definitions as there are definers (Siegler et al., 1968). There is no systematically used diagnostic nosology; without a clear definition of a "case," it becomes nearly impossible to establish what is not a case, or for that matter what is a control. Thus, one is unable to determine what will be included and excluded in any study concerning alcohol use. (p. 384)

At approximately the same time that alcoholism was seen to be on the rise among women, alcohol problems were also seen to be increasing among other competing interest groups. For instance, by broadening the definition of alcohol problems among the young, a nationwide survey published in

1975 could claim that 34% of the boys and 23% of the girls in a sample of junior and senior high-school students in the United States were problem drinkers (Rachal, Williams, Brehm, Cavanaugh, Moore, & Eckerman, 1975). This meant that the respondent reported being "drunk" four or more times in the past year and/or reported at least minimal problems with school authorities, driving while drinking, problems with friends, or trouble with the police as a result of drinking. A critique of this work suggested these so-called alcohol problems "may not have been problem behavior at all, but behavior well within the normal nonproblem range" (Marden, Zylman, Fillmore, & Bacon, 1976, p. 1357). Thus, by lowering the criteria for problems, the scientific establishment could stand behind the claims that an epidemic of alcohol problems was occurring in some special subgroups of the population. And by distancing themselves from the original alcoholism definition, which was a narrow one concerned with people who experienced a multitude of alcohol-related problems, the epidemic fires could burn (Robinson, 1976).

Several other factors allowed the epidemic fires to burn in the face of existing negative epidemiological evidence. The first was the deeply embedded notion of the "hidden alcoholic," a concept that focused on women. The stereotype of the woman watching soap operas while draining her bottle of sherry or gin has persisted although the evidence for it comes from anecdotes in the literary and clinical literature. Because the hidden alcoholic by definition will not stand up to be counted and because her existence is so strongly embedded in our conceptualization of how female alcoholics drink, the notion of the hidden female drinker challenges the findings of survey research by suggesting that these women may be underreporting their consumption of alcoholic beverages, if not their alcohol problems. However, the evidence to date on sex biases in reporting alcohol consumption as reviewed by Ferrence (1980) indicates that "what evidence there is, though it is by no means conclusive, suggests that women are more likely than men to be included in household surveys and are at least as likely as men to report their consumption accurately" (p. 72).

Another issue has confused the epidemiological findings regarding women. It has been suggested that researchers consistently underestimate the numbers of female alcoholics as a function of the very measures they use to operationalize alcohol problems—measures that were originally derived for men. These biases have been challenged by several researchers. Fillmore, Bacon, and Hyman (1979) in a follow-up of a college population explored a variety of behaviors and consequences of drinking that might be related to the unique roles of women (e.g., neglect of children and spouse, nonfulfillment of domestic and child-raising responsibilities, verbal aggression, and so on). It was reported that "these questions served no useful purpose in increasing the numbers of female problem drinkers; they did provide a more colorful picture of a very few women with obvious alcohol problems" (Fillmore, 1980,

p. 33). Ferrence (1980) points out that the majority of problem-drinking indices include a number of problems that are not subject to sex bias.

> Symptoms of problem drinking such as blackouts or missing meals should occur equally among heavy drinkers of both sexes unless there are sex-linked physiological factors that affect them. In fact, there are a number of symptoms of problem drinking that occur with equal frequency among male and female heavy drinkers (Johnson et al., 1977). For consequences that one would expect to show sex differences, such as job-related problems, one can control for employment status. Johnson et al. (1977) did control in this way and found no difference in the percentage of employed male and female heavy drinkers who had been fired or threatened with dismissal. (p. 74)

Turning from these methodological problems, the more interesting question, when one examines the epidemiological evidence surrounding women's drinking, is why the society at one point in time minimizes or understates the alcohol problems of women while at another point in time it maximizes those problems—when the evidence over time points to consistency in alcohol use and abuse among women. Some tentative answers may be found on several analytical levels. The current maximization of problems may include the following explanations: (1) the relative success of a campaign to change the image of alcohol problems in America; (2) the distance in time from Prohibitionist thinking; (3) the emergence of a federal agency created to address the new image of alcohol problems in America; and (4) the tension brought about in a society when members of one role set take on the habits of another. Each of these is briefly discussed.

In contrast to the 1940s, the 1970s and 1980s in the United States may be regarded as decades in which the earlier efforts of the modern alcoholism movement were finally successful. Although the essence of the disease concept of alcoholism may not have been fully accepted in its pristine form by the American public (Roizen, 1977), the concept of alcoholism as a disease has clearly become a household word. Alcoholism treatment has mushroomed and health insurance for treatment has become a reality (Rodwin, 1982). Room (1978) suggests that the shift from alcohol problem minimization to maximization was a function of the movement's transformation from a voluntary movement to that of an interest group with investments in associating alcohol with a broad range of problems.

The distance from Prohibitionist thinking can be documented by the increase in per capita consumption in this country (Collins, 1980; Room, 1983), which, like Western European countries, has become increasingly "wet" since the Second World War (Makela, Room, Single, Sulkunen, & Walsh, 1981). The tendency also for the "drier" areas of the country to show an increase in per capita consumption as well as in alcohol problems is another indicator that the United States may be characterized as "wet" (Room, 1983). Thus, enough time has passed since the Wet–Dry controversy was the most sensitive alcohol issue in the country that it seems to be a dim piece of history to most Americans. Alcohol researchers of the present day, unlike Jellinek, would not tend to take this issue into consideration when discussing the populations at risk for alcohol problems.

An important political event with implications for alcohol conceptualizations is the emergence of the NIAAA, a bureaucratic agency, governmentally based and funded, centralized around a social problem. With all the difficulties besetting a federal agency struggling for the shrinking dollar, this particular agency, like others, may be seen as one with a product to sell— the product in this case being the treatment and prevention of alcohol problems and alcoholism. To justify its existence among other elite organizations, alcoholism must be seen both to contract in the case of effective treatment and prevention, and to expand in the need for renewed efforts among new populations. During the 1940s, when the modern alcoholism movement was weak and tentative in an era of the Wet–Dry battles of post-Prohibition, it was necessary to conceptualize the problem as being large enough to require attention but small enough to satisfy the politics of both the Wets and the Drys. Never would children be considered alcoholics, and rarely were women seen to be a major subgroup contributing to the problem. In contrast, the current decade represents a time when alcohol problems have grown long tentacles reaching to all members of the society.

The emergence and decline of alcohol as a social problem in our society is not unique, nor is the use of women and children in emphasizing the spread of problems. Other social problems show similar histories. The use of cigarettes in recent decades (Nuehring & Markle, 1974), opiates in the early part of this century (Musto, 1973), and heroin and marijuana in the 1920s and 1930s (Becker, 1963) are all cases in point. Gusfield (1967) states:

> Deviance designations have histories; the public definition of behavior as deviant is itself changeable. It is open to reversals of political power, twists of public opinion, and the development of social movements and moral crusades. What is attacked as criminal today may be seen as sick next year and fought over as possibly legitimate by the next generation. (p. 187)

While Gusfield's observations may explain changing social definitions of problems, which have occurred quite vividly in relation to alcohol use in this country, they do not necessarily explain why claims of problem expansion are made, particularly relating to women and children. Moreover, they do not explain why the use of a drug or a given behavior by women and children should be so threatening to our social order.

A number of authors have interpreted the societal threat of deviant drinking among women as arising from the perception of women as symbolically carrying the moral torch of the society, from women's special obligations of caring for home and hearth, or from the double standard in which drunkenness is expected of men but not women. Sex-role theory, for instance, has become one of the crucial contemporary explanations for excessive or deviant drinking among women (see Beckman, 1975, or Wilsnack, 1973b, as examples). The underlying assumption of this group of theories is that when the carrier of the moral torch and the protector of the home steps into the world of men, this action will produce conflict and is cause for deviant drinking. The remarkable vulnerability attributed to women who step outside of their traditional roles is not confined to the use of alcohol or to contemporary times. In the latter part of the 19th century scientific notions and the ideology of the day combined to use diseases of the womb to keep women in their place. It was thought then that their vulnerability in confronting a man's world would literally make their reproductive organs rise up against them (Stage, 1979).

If it is true that traditional sex roles give men the liberty to drink and consequently to get drunk, but do not give the same right to women, then this may explain why fewer women are deviant drinkers. It may be, however, that the sex-role argument goes much deeper regarding alcohol than its relation to deviant drinking. It is possible that the exaggerated claims of deviant drinking among women actually reflect a societal reaction to *any* drinking among women. While light or moderate drinking has been quite normative for men, it may be that light or moderate drinking for women is still to some extent not culturally acceptable. In an imaginary hearing on the special problems and unmet needs of men who abuse alcohol in the mid-1970s, it is rather unlikely that it would be reported with some drama that more men are drinking now than 20 years ago. In the context of the 1976 Senate hearings on the unmet needs of women (Committee on Labor and Public Welfare, 1976), the term "drinking" brought with it an assocation between women's drinking and sinful, immoral behavior. Gomberg, in response to a literature reporting increases in women's drinking, stated in 1976 that "women engaging in social drinking may involve as little as one occasion a year, e.g., a family gathering. Instead of speaking of the increase in the percentage of American women who drink perhaps we should be speaking of the shrinking percentage of women abstainers" (p. 604).

It is tentatively suggested here that even given the distance from Prohibition, the public's acceptance of alcoholism as some form of a disease, the governmental sanction for treating and preventing alcoholism, and the needs of a federal agency to continually expand a problem, the culture is responding still to any drinking among women as being deviant. Even the scientific literature keeps women's drinking apart in some unique subcategory within the confines of a "disease," which was originally hypothesized to have an underlying common denominator. In a day when women are allegedly going through a social revolution in this country by moving away from what are regarded as traditional female roles, the scientific establishment and the social ideology are clearly warning them that, rather than their wombs retaliating in defiance of this movement, instead their drinking will do so.

THE CONVERGENCE HYPOTHESIS IN A COHORT ANALYSIS

We have pointed out that trend studies since the 1960s have demonstrated little or no change in women's drinking patterns over the last several decades. This does not mean, however, that there may not be changes in drinking patterns between cohorts as they age. Obviously, cross-sectional data can hardly account for changes in a variety of behaviors or attitudes as people age. Because good longitudinal data on multiple cohorts are rare, researchers must often turn to secondary analyses of existing cross-sectional data to gain some information on the aging process across cohorts and the associated behaviors. Unfortunately, as in the case here, the data are not always collected at equal intervals nor are they coded in a manner that would facilitate a straightforward comparison of cohorts from a variety of samples. Nonetheless, we present data from a 1979 national survey of drinking practices and problems (Clark et al., 1981), a 1964 national survey (Cahalan, Cisin, & Crossley, 1969) and a follow-up survey of the 1964 survey in 1967. Our operational definition for heavy–frequent drinking in the following analyses is that the female respondent drinks nearly every day or daily and drinks 5 or more drinks on some occasions.

To the extent that these data are suitable as a crude instrument for examining changes in several cohorts over this 15-year period, we may tentatively test the hypothesis that younger cohorts are exhibiting higher rates of drinking per se and higher rates of heavy–frequent drinking than older cohorts. This reflects the much talked about assumption that as women enter the marketplace or become more liberated from traditional roles, they will abstain less and drink more heavily and frequently. A corollary hypothesis will compare age cohorts of employed and unemployed women, given that employment is often seen as central to the changing roles of women.

Table 1-1 presents the percentage of female respondents who maintained that they currently abstained from alcoholic beverages in five cohorts measured in 1964, 1967, and 1979. The youngest cohort was born between 1935 and 1943 while the oldest was born prior to 1905. These data suggest that abstention is an aging effect as well as a cohort effect. Abstinence increases with age, from the 30s on. These data are essentially in agreement with those of Glenn and Zody (1970), who used Gallup samples between 1945 and 1960. The Glenn and Zody findings for abstention are reproduced in Table 1-2. Although the coded age categories are not the same as ours, these additional data are instructive given the hypothesis that as liberation has steadily increased among women, their use of alcohol has increased as well. Glenn and Zody's youngest cohort in 1945 (the first measurement point) falls somewhere between our two cohorts born between 1905 and 1924. It can be seen that 33% of their youngest cohort abstained, much the same as our own youngest cohort, born 10–32 years later, and that overall both cohorts

TABLE 1-1. Percentage of Female Respondents Who Said They
Were Abstainers, in Five 10-Year Cohorts, 1964, 1967, and 1979

	1964	1967	1979
Cohort 1			
Born 1935–1943	[21–29]	[25–34][a]	[35–44]
	30	29	34
	(n = 258)[b]	(n = 126)	(n = 188)
Cohort 2			
Born 1925–1934	[30–39]	[35–44]	[45–54]
	28	27	40
	(n = 346)	(n = 142)	(n = 130)
Cohort 3			
Born 1915–1924	[40–49]	[45–54]	[55–64]
	35	35	56
	(n = 334)	(n = 136)	(n = 129)
Cohort 4			
Born 1905–1914	[50–59]	[55–64]	[65 +]
	49	44	88
	(n = 266)	(n = 83)	(n = 164)
Cohort 5			
Born in or before 1904	[60 +]	[65 +]	
	56	59	
	(n = 370)	(n = 90)	

[a]Ages (in brackets) are approximate in that the available data were coded in
5-year intervals.

[b]n's are unweighted and percentages weighted in this and remaining tables
using data from the Alcohol Research Group's national samples.

exhibit greater abstention with age. The Glenn and Zody findings, however,
exhibit a drop in female drinking as an historical effect in the 1950s, while
our own data suggest a shift toward abstention in the late 1970s. Overall,
however, these data, in combination, suggest rather strongly that, while at
least two-thirds of the women in all the age cohorts studied between 1945
and 1979 tended to experiment with alcohol to a greater or lesser degree in
youth, the ranks of alcohol users decrease with age.

Table 1-3 and Figure 1-1 present a cohort analysis of percentages of
women who were heavy–frequent drinkers. The overall pattern here suggests
that heavy–frequent intake is rare in youth and old age, with the percentage
drinking in this manner peaking in middle age. The few cross-age, cross-
cohort comparisons that can be made are not conclusive. The percentage of
heavy–frequent drinking in middle age (35–44) is the same for the cohort
born between 1935 and 1943 and that born between 1925 and 1934. However,
a comparison of those born between 1925 and 1934 and those born between
1915 and 1924 measured at roughly the ages of 45–54 would suggest that
heavy–frequent intake as well as abstinence was higher in the younger age
cohort during the middle years. Since the difference for heavy–frequent
drinking is only 4%, these data are certainly less than conclusive, but they

may suggest a shift toward heavy–frequent drinking in the younger cohorts. Overall, these data suggest that the succeeding age cohorts are similar in the relationship of heavy–frequent drinking to aging in that the peak is reached in the middle years.

Data from a cohort analysis cannot, of course, take into account the youngest members of the data set. Figure 1-2 presents a typical cross-sectional analysis that utilizes data from the entire data set by plotting percentage heavy–frequent drinking curves by period of observation and age. Comparison of those 21–29 at each measurement point suggests that this youngest cohort is engaging in higher levels of heavy–frequent drinking than the age cohort born 15 years earlier measured at the same age. If our finding that drinking related similarly to aging across cohorts may be extrapolated to this youngest cohort, then we would expect a higher rate of heavy–frequent drinking to be demonstrated in middle age by the women of this cohort. This, however, is a projection that must be subjected to investigation as this cohort of women and still younger ones age.

A number of hypotheses in the literature on women's drinking relate to the change in occupational roles over the last several decades. While women's roles in the recent past often centered around the home fire and motherhood, the numbers of women in the workplace have increased substantially over

TABLE 1-2. Percentage[a] of Respondents Who Said They Were Abstainers, in Three 15-Year Age Cohorts by Sex

	1945	1950	1955	1960
Cohort 1	[20–34][b]	[25–39]	[30–44]	[35–49]
Males	19.1 (407)[c]	21.7 (198)	21.8 (289)	25.8 (244)
Females	33.2 (530)	45.4 (301)	41.1 (207)	34.9 (195)
Mean	26.1	33.5	31.4	30.3
Cohort 2	[35–39]	[40–54]	[45–49]	[50–64]
Males	23.0 (539)	29.6 (210)	31.8 (212)	34.9 (195)
Females	40.6 (510)	60.2 (170)	50.4 (202)	50.9 (177)
Mean	31.8	44.9	41.1	42.9
Cohort 3	[50–64]	[55–59]	[60–74]	[65–79]
Males	31.7 (371)	45.4 (150)	47.2 (123)	43.5 (138)
Females	53.9 (305)	62.0 (103)	74.5 (84)	66.3 (83)
Mean	42.8	53.7	60.8	54.9

Note. Table based on Glenn, N. D., & Zody, R. E., "Cohort analysis with national survey data," The Gerontologist, 1970, 10 (3), p. 237. Original table indicated percentage of drinkers whereas we present percentage of abstainers.

[a]Percentages for all dates except 1960 are standardized to the educational distribution in the cohort as shown by the 1960 data. The data for 1945 are from Gallup survey 360, those for 1950 are from survey 450, those for 1955 are from survey 543, and those for 1960 are from survey 622.

[b]Ages are in brackets.

[c]n's are in parentheses.

TABLE 1-3. Percentage of Female Respondents Who Were
Heavy–Frequent Drinkers, in Five 10-Year Cohorts, 1964, 1967,
and 1979

	1964	1967	1979
Cohort 1			
Born 1935–1943	[21–29]	[25–34][a]	[35–44]
	2	2	7
	(n = 258)	(n = 126)	(n = 188)
Cohort 2			
Born 1925–1934	[30–39]	[35–44]	[45–54]
	4	7	7
	(n = 346)	(n = 142)	(n = 130)
Cohort 3			
Born 1915–1924	[40–49]	[45–54]	[55–64]
	3	3	2
	(n = 334)	(n = 136)	(n = 129)
Cohort 4			
Born 1905–1914	[50–59]	[55–64]	[65 +]
	1	4	0
	(n = 266)	(n = 83)	(n = 164)
Cohort 5			
Born in or before 1904	[60 +]	[65 +]	
	1	1	
	(n = 370)	(n = 90)	

[a]Ages (in brackets) are approximate in that the available data were coded in
5-year intervals.

the period of measurement points used here. For instance, 35% of women in
the United States were estimated to be working outside the home in 1965,
while in 1979 this figure increased to 45% (U.S. Department of Commerce,
Bureau of the Census, 1979).

One hypothesis relevant to this social change is that when women
occupy the world of men (i.e., the workplace), their drinking will eventually
begin to look like that of men. Interestingly, the converse hypothesis has
never been offered in the alcohol literature to our knowledge—that as more
women invade the workplace, the drinking of men will more closely resemble
that of women. Another hypothesis relates to the change in sex roles, or
more explicitly, the conflict between sex roles, as women enter the workplace
or take on roles that men traditionally occupied alone. This hypothetical
position suggests that when women take on traditional male roles (e.g.,
assertiveness, objectivity) they cannot reconcile these with the roles they
were taught as women (e.g., passivity, subjectivity). A third and related
hypothesis is that women take on too many roles, that is, they suffer from
"role overload" by attempting to be wife, housewife, mother, and worker at
the same time. All these hypotheses suggest that the trend toward increased

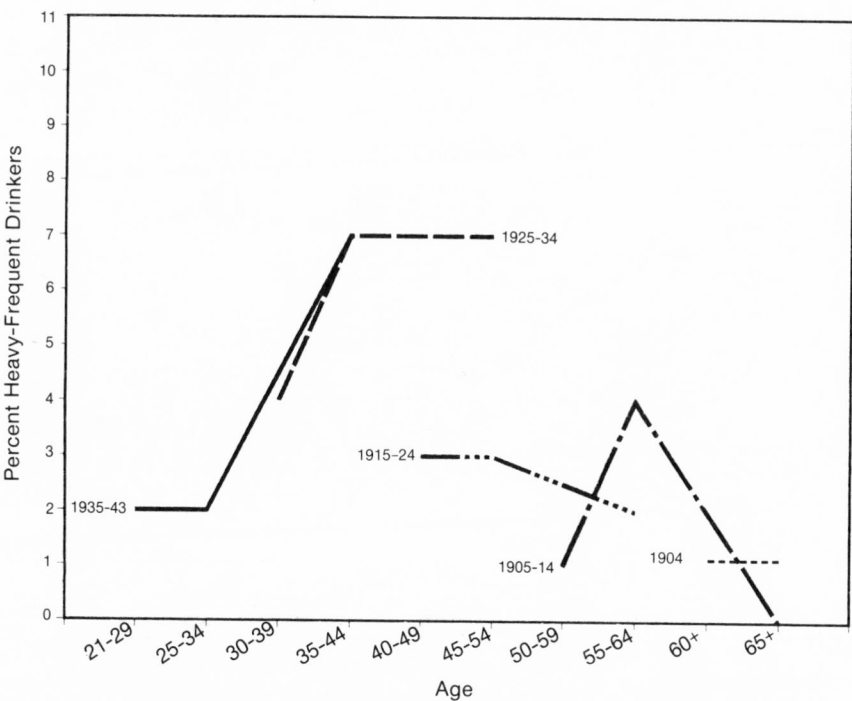

FIGURE 1-1. Percentage of females who were heavy-frequent drinkers, in five 10-year cohorts, 1964, 1967, 1979. Curves indicate date of birth for each cohort.

employment among women will be reflected in a change in their drinking patterns.

Table 1-4 explores this postulation by examining the percentage of abstainers, while Table 1-5 explores it by examining the percentage of heavy-frequent drinkers among employed and unemployed women in five age cohorts. Unemployment here includes women who are housewives as well as those looking for work. While there is a general trend for the unemployed to abstain from alcohol more frequently, this is not a particularly overwhelming finding given the ratio of abstinence to drinking within each cohort. Even among the youngest age cohort (not included in the cohort analysis) who were 21–29 years old in 1979, the difference was not great (19% of the employed abstained and 23% of the unemployed abstained). These data do not support the hypothesis that the employed are much more likely to drink than the unemployed.

Turning to Table 1-5, which compares the percentage of heavy-frequent drinking among employed and unemployed women, we can see that heavy-frequent drinking is uncommon in youth among the unemployed, reaches its

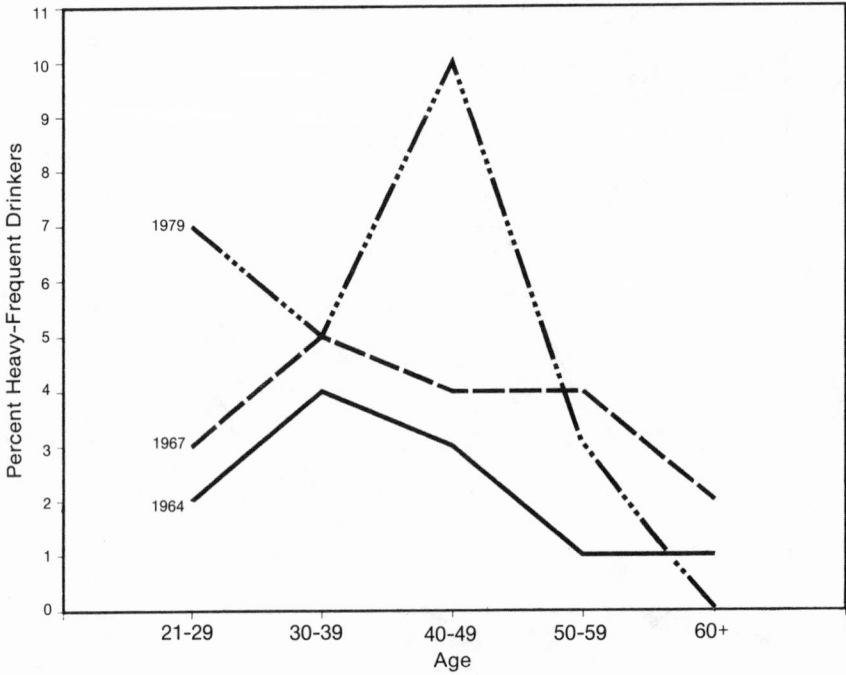

FIGURE 1-2. Percentage of females who were heavy-frequent drinkers by age at date of measurement in 1964, 1967, and 1979. Curves for each period of observation.

peak at ages 35–44 and then decreases at later ages. Among the employed, the peak of heavy–frequent drinking occurs at ages 45–54 and then de- creases. The findings across cohorts by employment status are more erratic than not. The results from the cohort analysis do not suggest that heavy– frequent drinking is more frequent among the succeeding younger cohorts who are employed; however, a period or trend analysis (Figure 1-3) would suggest that this may be the case for the youngest women studied. While the ratio of heavy–frequent drinking between the employed and unemployed was 2:1 among those 21–29 in 1964 and 1967, it rose to 10:3 in 1979. In addition, the period analysis points out that among those measured at 21–29 years of age over the successive years, the rate of heavy–frequent drinking among the unemployed remained around 2–3% while among the employed it increased from 4% to 6% and then to 10% by 1979. Should this trend continue and should this younger age group increase their rate of heavy– frequent drinking with increasing age, we may be seeing the first tendency toward a major period effect in the quantity and frequency of drinking among drinking women who are employed.

TABLE 1-4. Percentage of Employed and Unemployed Female Respondents Who Said They Were Abstainers, in Five 10-Year Cohorts, 1964, 1967, and 1979

	1964		1967		1979	
Cohort 1						
Born 1935–1943	[21–29]		[25–34][a]		[35–44]	
Employed	24	(82)[b]	29	(25)	31	(82)
Unemployed	33	(176)	31	(111)	37	(106)
Cohort 2						
Born 1925–1934	[30–39]		[35–44]		[45–54]	
Employed	30	(94)	20	(29)	41	(56)
Unemployed	28	(252)	28	(113)	39	(73)
Cohort 3						
Born 1915–1924	[40–49]		[45–54]		[55–64]	
Employed	31	(122)	36	(31)	57	(47)
Unemployed	37	(212)	40	(76)	55	(81)
Cohort 4						
Born 1905–1914	[50–59]		[55–64]		[65 +]	
Employed	47	(105)	43	(10)	80	(7)
Unemployed	51	(161)	41	(73)	60	(157)
Cohort 5						
Born in or before 1904	[60 +]		[65 +]			
Employed	41	(43)	—	(1)		
Unemployed	58	(327)	64	(89)		

[a]Ages (in brackets) are approximate in that the available data were coded in 5-year intervals.

[b]n's are in parentheses.

Overall, our findings in this section suggest the possibility that major changes are currently taking place among younger cohorts as they age— heavy–frequent drinking is more common in the younger age groups as compared to older cohorts measured at the same age. These findings must, of course, be interpreted cautiously. First, we are relying on single area– probability samples with their own inherent biases and small cell sizes. Second, the findings of our trend and cohort analyses are limited by the use of only three surveys. Third, it is important to remember that employment– unemployment are not fixed individual characteristics but reflect positions in the life cycle. Fourth, much of our speculation about the younger cohorts requires later samples to trace their drinking over the aging process.

The question of liberation from traditional roles as operationally meas- ured by employment status produced some findings of interest. First, drinking per se does not seem to follow automatically when women leave the home fires for the labor market. Second, among employed drinkers, there is a suggestion of a possible cohort effect of increased heavy–frequent drinking among the youngest cohort.

TABLE 1-5. Percentage of Employed and Unemployed Female Respondents Who Were Heavy–Frequent Drinkers, in Five 10-Year Cohorts, 1964, 1967, and 1979

	1964	1967	1979
Cohort 1			
Born 1935–1943	[21–29]	[25–34][a]	[35–44]
Employed	4 (82)[b]	2 (25)	4 (82)
Unemployed	2 (176)	3 (79)	10 (106)
Cohort 2			
Born 1925–1934	[30–39]	[35–44]	[45–54]
Employed	5 (94)	2 (29)	10 (56)
Unemployed	4 (252)	9 (113)	5 (73)
Cohort 3			
Born 1915–1924	[40–49]	[45–54]	[55–64]
Employed	3 (122)	6 (31)	— (47)
Unemployed	4 (212)	2 (72)	— (81)
Cohort 4			
Born 1905–1914	[50–59]	[55–64]	[65 +]
Employed	2 (105)	— (10)	— (7)
Unemployed	1 (161)	7 (73)	— (157)
Cohort 5			
Born in or before 1904	[60 +]	[65 +]	
Employed	2 (43)	— (1)	
Unemployed	1 (327)	— (89)	

[a]Ages (in brackets) are approximate in that the available data were coded in 5-year intervals.

[b]*n*'s are in parentheses.

CONCLUSION

The first portion of this chapter has dealt with the so-called convergence hypothesis of sex differences in drinking patterns in a historical framework. The point of departure for the paper was to examine the epidemiological evidence concerning drinking among women, which appeared to suggest constancy rather than change over a 40-year period. To achieve this end, the analysis required us to move outside the domain of epidemiological work to examine the cultural and political environment in which these scientists reported their data. Although much of our interpretation of why scientists of different eras reported essentially the same data over the years but in essentially different ways may be regarded as speculation or armchair philosophy, the fact that they minimized or maximized their findings pointedly serves to remind us that scientists, like other members of our society, are subject to cultural biases and assumptions. It would seem almost surprising that this would occur in the area of epidemiology. However, that minimization and maximization of a social problem would take place in any academic area is less of a surprise when it serves as the basis for political enterprise or the work of moral entrepreneurs. Room (1976) has commented that policy

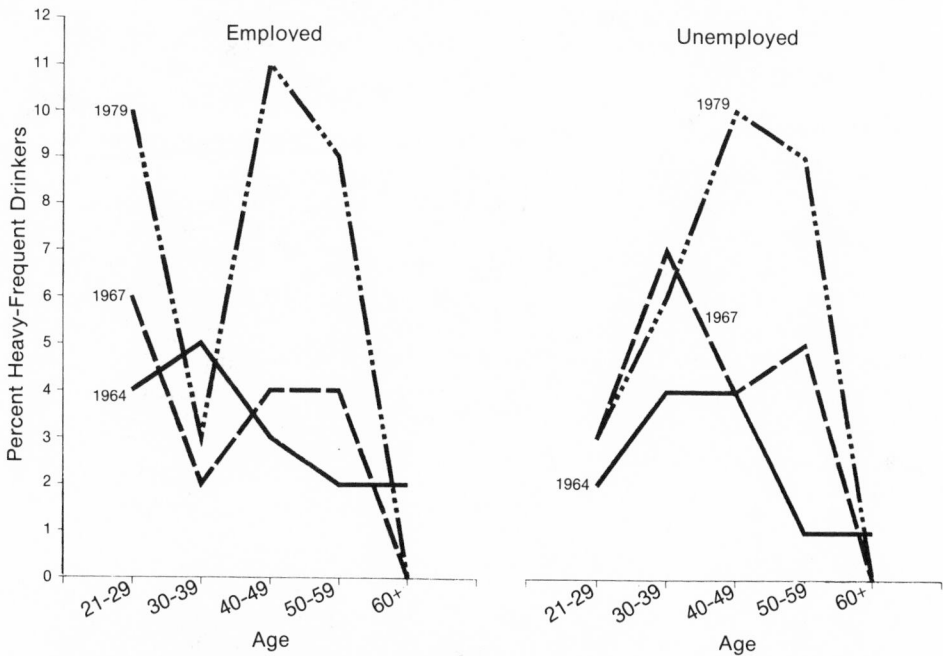

FIGURE 1-3. Percentage of employed and unemployed females who were heavy-frequent drinkers, by age at date of measurement in 1964, 1967, 1979. Curves for each period of observation.

and epidemiology have traditionally made poor bedfellows. While the policymaker regards epidemiology as a simple nose-counting exercise, the epidemiologist is well aware that it is a great deal more complicated than that. Bruun (1970) has suggested to epidemiologists that two or three measures should be used to convince policymakers of the very vagueness of the operational definitions.

The second portion of this chapter dealt with an exploration of the convergence hypothesis by using a cohort analysis in addition to more traditional trend analyses. It was expected that these data would support past data by showing a marked consistency in women's drinking patterns. To a great extent this was true, in that rates of abstinence and heavy–frequent drinking for women demonstrate, like the data for men, an aging effect. However, the youngest cohort, who in 1979 were ages 21–29, seem to show a much higher rate of heavy–frequent drinking than past cohorts measured at the same age, particularly among the employed. Should an aging effect similar to earlier age cohorts take place, in which proportions of heavy–frequent drinkers would rise in middle age, this may in fact indicate a major change in the drinking of these younger cohorts.

It is something of an irony that the first portion of this chapter dealt with the recognition of problem amplification currently ongoing in the alcohol field, while the second portion provided data to support the amplification. One general point that we may draw from this exercise is that major social shifts are slow to show up in nationwide survey data. Essayists and clinicians tend to respond to changes in very small and special social milieus. Often they notice and write of the unusual—the singles bar or the very young alcoholic-type drinker. They may be tapping nascent social changes in the society as a whole, but it takes time for these changes to be noticed in the marginals of a nationwide survey. It would seem to be of some importance to the alcohol field to continue testing the observations in the epidemiological literature of those reporting changes in the culture, for the simple reason that drinking patterns may change rapidly in a society. And it would seem to be of particular importance to continue to monitor the drinking of women in future national probability samples.

ACKNOWLEDGMENTS

Preparation of this chapter was supported by a National Alcohol Center Grant (AA-03524) from the National Institute on Alcohol Abuse and Alcoholism to the Alcohol Research Group, Institute of Epidemiology and Behavioral Medicine, Medical Research Institute of San Francisco.

REFERENCES

Alcoholics Anonymous. New York: Works Publishing, 1939.

Armor, D., Polich, M., & Stambul, H. *Alcoholism and treatment.* Santa Monica, Calif.: Rand Corporation, 1976.

Barrington, A., Pearson, K., & Heron, D. *Eugenics laboratory memoirs XVI: A preliminary study of extreme alcoholism in adults.* London: Dulau, 1910.

Becker, H. S. *Outsiders.* New York: Free Press, 1963.

Beckman, L. J. Women alcoholics: A review of social and psychological studies. *Journal of Studies on Alcohol,* 1975, *36,* 797–824.

Brenner, B. Estimating the prevalence of alcoholism: Toward a modification of the Jellinek formula. *Quarterly Journal of Studies on Alcohol,* 1959, *20,* 255–260.

Brenner, B. Estimating the prevalence of alcoholism from vital rates. *Quarterly Journal of Studies on Alcohol,* 1960, *21,* 140–141.

Bruun, K. Comments. *Drinking and Drug Practices Surveyor,* Spring 1970, *1,* 6.

Cahalan, D. *Problem drinkers.* San Francisco: Jossey Bass, 1970.

Cahalan, D., Cisin, I. H., & Crossley, H. M. *American drinking practices: A national study of drinking behavior and attitudes* (Monographs of the Rutgers Center of Alcohol Studies, No. 6). New Brunswick, N.J.: Rutgers Center of Alcohol Studies, 1969.

Cahalan, D., & Room, R. *Problem drinking among American men.* (Monographs of the Rutgers Center of Alcohol Studies, No. 7). New Brunswick, N.J.: Rutgers Center of Alcohol Studies, 1974.

Celentano, D. D., McQueen, D. V., & Chee, E. Substance abuse by women: A review of the epidemiologic literature. *Journal of Chronic Disease,* 1980, *33,* 383–394.

Clark, W. B. *Sex roles and alcoholic beverage usage* (Working paper No. F.16). Social Research Group, School of Public Health, University of California, Berkeley, 1964.

Clark, W. B., Midanik, L., & Knupfer, G. *Draft report of the 1979 national survey.* Social Research Group, School of Public Health, University of California, Berkeley, April 1981.

Clarke, W. Prostitution and alcohol. *Social Hygiene*, 1917, *3*, 75-90.

Coakley, J. F., & Johnson, S. *Alcohol abuse and alcoholism in the United States: Selected recent prevalence estimates* (Working paper No. 1).Alcohol Epidemiologic Data System, March 27, 1978, updated June 26, 1979.

Coakley, J., Holland, W., & Evaul, J. *Estimates of state prevalence and prevalence rates for male and female alcoholics based on cirrhosis mortality using the Jellinek formula* (Working paper No. 2). Alcohol Epidemiologic Data System, March 24, 1978.

Collins, G. *Aggregate consumption of alcoholic beverages in California: Update of selected tables 1976-1979* (Working paper No. F.124). Social Research Group, School of Public Health, University of California, Berkeley, 1980.

Committee on Labor and Public Welfare, United States Senate, 94th Congress, Second Session. *Alcohol abuse among women: Special problems and unmet needs* (Hearings, September 29, 1976). Washington, D.C.: U.S. Government Printing Office, 1976.

Corrigan, E. M. Women and problem drinking: Notes on beliefs and facts. *Addictive Diseases*, 1974, *1*, 215-222.

Crothers, T. D. Is alcoholism increasing among American women. *The North American Review*, 1892, *155*, 731-736.

Curlee, J. *Women and alcohol.* National Center for Alcohol Education, n.d.

Curran, F. J. Personality studies in alcoholic women. *Journal of Nervous and Mental Disease*, 1937, *86*, 645-667.

Efron, V., Keller, M., & Gurioli, C. *Statistics on consumption of alcohol and on alcoholism* (1974 ed.). New Brunswick, N.J.: Publications Division, Rutgers Center of Alcohol Studies, 1974.

Ferrence, R. G. Sex differences in the prevalence of problem drinking. In O. Kalant (Ed.), *Alcohol and drug problems in women: Research advances in alcohol and drug problems* (Vol. 5). New York: Plenum Press, 1980.

Fillmore, K. M. Discussion summary of "Epidemiology of male/female drinking over the last half century." In *Alcoholism and alcohol abuse among women: Research issues* (NIAAA Research Monograph No. 1, Department of Health, Education and Welfare Publication No. ADM-80-835). Washington, D.C.: U.S. Government Printing Office, 1980.

Fillmore, K. M. *Research as a handmaid of policy: An appraisal of estimates of alcoholism and its cost in the workplace.* Paper presented at the 1981 National Alcoholism Forum of the National Council of Alcoholism, New Orleans, April 1981.

Fillmore, K. M., Bacon, S. D., & Hyman, M. *The 27-year longitudinal panel study of drinking by students in college, 1949-1976* (Final report to the National Institute on Alcohol Abuse and Alcoholism). Social Research Group, School of Public Health, University of California, Berkeley, 1979.

Fillmore, K. M., & Caetano, R. Epidemiology of occupational alcoholism. In *Occupational alcoholism: A review of research issues* (NIAAA monograph, U.S. Department of Health and Human Services Publication No. ADM-82-1182). Washington, D.C.: U.S. Government Printing Office, 1982.

Fox, R., & Lyon, P. *Alcoholism: Its scope, cause and treatment.* New York: Random House, 1955.

Glenn, N. D., & Zody, R. E. Cohort analysis with national survey data. *The Gerontologist*, 1970, *10*, 233-240.

Globetti, G. *The drinking patterns of adults in two Mississippi communities.* (Report No. 12). State College: College of Arts and Sciences, Mississippi State University, 1967.

Gomberg, E. S. Alcoholism in women. In B. Kissin & H. Begleiter (Eds.), *Social aspects of alcoholism.* New York: Plenum Press, 1976.

Gomberg, E. S. Women and alcoholism. In V. Franks & V. Burtle (Eds.), *Women in therapy.* New York: Brunner/Mazel, 1974.

Gusfield, J. R. Moral passage: The symbolic process in public designations of deviance. *Social Problems*, 1967, *15*, 175–188.

Haas, R. M. *Some details of female alcoholism.* Paper presented at the 21st International Institute for the Prevention and Treatment of Alcoholism, Helsinki, June 1975.

Hewitt, C. C. A personality study of alcohol addiction. *Quarterly Journal of Studies on Alcohol*, 1943, *4*, 368–386.

Hultgen, J. F. Four hundred and six cases of alcoholism: Consecutive individual observations. *Quarterly Journal of Inebriety*, 1909, *32*, 117–123.

Jellinek, E. M. Recent trends in alcoholism and alcohol consumption. *Quarterly Journal of Studies on Alcohol*, 1947, *8*, 1–42.

Johnson, P., Armor, D. J., Polich, M. & Stambul, H. *U.S. adult drinking practices: Time trends, social correlates and sex roles.* (Working note prepared for the National Institute on Alcohol Abuse and Alcoholism). Santa Monica, Calif.: Rand Corporation, 1977.

Johnson, S., & Garzon, S. R. *Women and alcoholism: Past imperfect and future indefinite.* Paper presented at the Annual Research Conference of the Association for Women in Psychology, St. Louis, February 3–6, 1977.

Karpman, B. *The alcoholic woman.* Washington, D.C.: Linacre, 1948.

Keller, M., & Efron, V. The prevalence of alcoholism. *Quarterly Journal of Studies on Alcohol*, 1955, *16*, 619–644.

Kerr, N. *Inebriety or narcomania: Its etiology, pathology, treatment and jurisprudence.* London: H. K. Lewis, 1894.

Knupfer, G. Female drinking patterns. In *Selected papers presented at the fifteenth annual meeting of the North American Association of Alcoholism Programs.* Washington, D.C.: North American Association of Alcoholism Programs, 1964.

Knupfer, G., & Room, R. Age, sex and social class as factors in amount of drinking in a metropolitan community. *Social Problems*, 1964, *12*, 224–240.

Lemere, F., O'Hollaren, P., & Maxwell, M. A. Sex ratio of alcoholic patients treated over a 20-year period. *Quarterly Journal of Studies on Alcohol*, 1956, *17*, 437–442.

Lender, M. E. Women alcoholics: Prevalence estimates and their problems as reflected in turn-of-the-century institutional data. *International Journal of the Addictions*, 1981, *16*, 443–448.

Levine, H. G. Temperance and women in 19th-century United States. In O. Kalant (Ed.), *Alcohol and drug problems in women: Research advances in alcohol and drug problems* (Vol. 5). New York: Plenum Press, 1980.

Levine, J. The sexual adjustment of alcoholics: A clinical study of a selected sample. *Quarterly Journal of Studies on Alcohol*, 1955, *16*, 675–680.

Lindbeck, V. L. The woman alcoholic: A review of the literature. *International Journal of the Addictions*, 1972, *7*, 567–580.

Lisansky, E. S. Alcoholism in women: Social and psychological concomitants. I. Social history data. *Quarterly Journal of Studies on Alcohol*, 1957, *18*, 588–623.

Lolli, G. The addictive drinker. *Quarterly Journal of Studies on Alcohol*, 1949, *10*, 404–414.

Makela, K., Room, R., Single, E., Sulkunen, P., & Walsh, B. *Alcohol, society and the state: A comparative study of alcohol control.* Toronto: Addiction Research Foundation, 1981.

Marden, P., Zylman, R., Fillmore, K. M., Bacon, S. D. A critique of "A national study of adolescent drinking behavior, attitudes and correlates" by J. Valley Rachal *et al. Journal of Studies on Alcohol*, 1976, *37*, 1346–1359.

Morelia, C. A. *The female alcoholic in American society.* Unpublished paper, National Center for Alcohol Education, 1974.

Mulford, H. A., & Miller, D. E. Drinking in Iowa. II. The extent of drinking and selected socio-cultural categories. *Quarterly Journal of Studies on Alcohol*, March 1960, *21*, 26–40.

Musto, D. F. *The American disease.* New Haven: Yale University Press, 1973.

National Clearinghouse for Alcohol Information. *Sociocultural aspects of alcohol use and alcoholism. Part B: Cultural groups, women alcohol abusers* (Subject Area Bibliography 1-B- 5). Rockville, Md.: Author, February 1974.

National Council on Alcoholism. *Friday Newsletter*, November 14, 1975.

National Council on Alcoholism. *Friday Newsletter*, February 28, 1976. (a)

National Council on Alcoholism. *Friday Newsletter*, September 24, 1976.(b)

Nuehring, E., & Markle, G. E. Nicotine and norms: The re-emergence of a deviant behavior. *Social Problems*, 1974, *21*, 513–526.

Popham, R. E. The Jellinek alcoholism estimation formula and its application to Canadian data. *Quarterly Journal of Studies on Alcohol*, 1956, *17*, 559–593.

Rachal, J. V., Williams, J. R., Brehm, M. L., Cavanaugh, B., Moore, R. P., & Eckerman, W. C. *Adolescent drinking behavior, attitudes and correlates: A national study* (Final report, Research Triangle Institute, RTI Project No. 23U-891). Research Triangle Park, N.C.: Research Triangle Institute, 1975.

Riley, J. W., & Marden, C. F. The social pattern of alcoholic drinking. *Quarterly Journal of Studies on Alcohol*, 1947, *8*, 265–273.

Robinson, D. *From drinking to alcoholism: A sociological commentary*. New York: John Wiley & Sons, 1976.

Rodwin, V. G. *Health insurance and alcohol treatment services: A strategy for change or a buttress for the status quo?* (Working paper). Alcohol Research Group, Institutes of Medical Sciences, Berkeley, 1982.

Roizen, R., *Barriers to alcoholism treatment* (Working paper No. F.145). Social Research Group, School of Public Health, University of California, Berkeley, 1977.

Roizen, R., Clark, W., & Milkes, J. *The sex-ratio in alcoholism* (Working paper No. F.87). Social Research Group, School of Public Health, University of California, Berkeley, 1979.

Roizen, R., & Milkes, J. The strange case of the Jellinek formula's sex ratio. *Journal of Studies on Alcohol*, 1980, *41*, 682–692.

Room, R. Notes on the spectrum of opiate use. In *The epidemiology of heroin and other narcotics: Use, abuse and addictions: Proceedings of the task force meeting*. Menlo Park, Calif.: Stanford Research Institute, 1976.

Room, R. *Governing images of alcohol and drug problems: The structure, sources and sequels of conceptualizations of intractable problems*. Doctoral dissertation, University of California, Berkeley, 1978.

Room, R. Measurement and distribution of drinking patterns and problems in general populations. G. Edwards, M. M. Gross, M. Keller, J. Moser, & R. Room (Eds.), *Alcohol-related disabilities* (Offset Publication No. 32). Geneva, Switzerland: World Health Organization, 1977.

Room, R. Region and urbanization as factors in drinking practices and problems. In B. Kissin & H. Begleiter (Eds.), *The biology of alcoholism* (Vol. 7). New York: Plenum Press, 1983.

Seeley, J. R., Estimating the prevalence of alcoholism: A critical analysis of the Jellinek formula. *Quarterly Journal of Studies on Alcohol*, 1959, *20*, 245–254.

Siegler, M., Osmond, H., & Newell, S. Models of alcoholism. *Quarterly Journal of Studies on Alcohol*, 1968, *29*, 571–591.

Stage, S. *Female complaints: Lydia Pinkham and the business of women's medicine*. New York: W. W. Norton, 1979.

Straus, R., & Bacon, S. D. *Drinking in college*. New Haven: Yale University Press, 1953.

U. S. Department of Commerce, Bureau of the Census. *Statistical Abstract of the United States* (100th Ed.). In *National Data Book and Guide to Sources*. Washington, D.C.: U.S. Department of Commerce, 1979.

U.S. Department of Health, Education and Welfare. *Inpatient admissions to state and county mental hospitals* (Public Health Service Publication, Statistical Note 49, 1969), 1971.

Van Amberg, R. J. A study of 50 women patients hospitalized for alcohol addiction. *Diseases of the Nervous System*, 1943, *4*, 246–251.

Wechsler, H. Epidemiology of male/female drinking over the last half century. In *Alcoholism and alcohol abuse among women: Research issues* (NIAAA Research Monograph No. 1, U.S. Department of Health, Education and Welfare Publication No. ADM-80-835). Washington, D.C.: U.S. Government Printing Office, 1980.

Wilsnack, S. C. The needs of the female drinker: Dependency, power, or what? In *Proceedings of the Second Annual Alcoholism Conference of the National Institute on Alcohol Abuse and Alcoholism* (U.S. Department of Health, Education and Welfare Publication No. NIH-74-676). Washington, D.C.: U.S. Government Printing Office, 1973. (a)

Wilsnack, S. C. Sex role identity in female alcoholism. *Journal of Abnormal Psychology*, 1973, *82*, 253-261. (b)

2

Drinking and Drinking Problems among Female Adolescents: Patterns and Influences

KEVIN M. THOMPSON
University of Arizona

RICHARD W. WILSNACK
University of North Dakota

INTRODUCTION

Warnings and worries about drinking and alcohol abuse among adolescent girls have gained national attention in the last 10 years. Concern has been aroused by evidence interpreted as showing that the percentage of girls who drink has increased since the 1950s and 1960s, that the percentage of girls with drinking problems has also increased, and that girls' drinking behavior increasingly resembles boys' drinking behavior (Beschner & Treasure, 1979; Biddle, Bank, & Marlin, 1980; Blane & Hewitt, 1977; Downs & Robertson, 1982; Johnston, Bachman, & O'Malley, 1979; Kandel, Single, & Kessler, 1976; Rachal, Williams, Brehm, Cavanaugh, Moore, & Eckerman, 1975; Wechsler, 1980).

These changes have been dramatized on television (e.g., American Broadcasting Company, 1977; National Broadcasting Company, 1975) and publicized in magazine articles (e.g., "Sexes Equal in Alcohol. . . ," 1977; Rooney, 1978; Berman, 1981). Between 1976 and 1981, the *Reader's Guide to Periodical Literature* listed 43 articles dealing with some aspect of drinking among adolescent girls. A recurrent theme in such publicity about adolescent drinking is that girls are approaching boys' levels of drinking and drinking problems.

Concern about girls' drinking can lead people to exaggerate evidence of a crisis (as discussed in Ferrence, 1980) and to single out oversimplified causes. In this chapter, we try to reduce current distortions about girls' drinking in two ways. First, we summarize the best available data on how adolescent girls drink, indicating current patterns of use and abuse, recent trends, and comparisons with boys' drinking. Second, we review a broad range of ideas

37

and evidence about what influences girls to drink and to get into problems related to drinking. Initially, we discuss influences that might affect both sexes—demographic and cultural differences, behavior of parents and peers, and personality characteristics—with attention to how these factors may affect girls and boys differently. We then consider possible gender-specific influences on girls' drinking, such as role orientations, opportunities and settings for drinking, gender-specific drinking norms, and biological differences. Throughout the review, as we deal with particular topics, we comment on the quality and range of available information and on problems of interpreting that information.

PATTERNS OF DRINKING BEHAVIOR

Current Drinking Behavior

To describe how adolescent girls drink there is an abundance of survey data. Unfortunately, the data have two major limitations: The surveys do not all ask similar questions or measure drinking in comparable ways, and many of even the best-designed surveys are local or regional (see, e.g., Blackford, 1977; Downs & Robertson, 1982; Jessor & Jessor, 1977; Kandel et al., 1976; Pandina, 1977; Robles, Martinez, & Moscoso, 1980; Wechsler & McFadden, 1976), which limits the generalizations one can make from the data. Therefore, our general descriptions of current drinking patterns are based on a smaller set of recent national surveys.

A 1983 national survey of high-school seniors (Johnston, Bachman, & O'Malley, 1984) found that 86% of the girls surveyed had used alcohol in the last year, and 64% had used alcohol in the last month. Among high-school girls in the 10th–12th grades, a 1978 national survey (Rachal, Guess, Hubbard, Maisto, Cavanaugh, Waddell, & Benrud, 1980) found that 73% had had at least 1 drink in the past year. Over a wider age range, Fishburne and Cisin (1980) reported that 36% of the 12–17-year-old girls in their 1979 national sample had drunk alcoholic beverages in the month preceding the survey, while Rachal et al. (1975) found that 69% of the 7th–12th-grade girls in their 1974 national sample had drunk alcohol during the preceding year. Although drinking is less common among younger girls, it is safe to conclude that a majority of high-school girls are currently drinking alcoholic beverages.

It may be more important to know how much adolescent girls are drinking, in terms of quantity and frequency. Among high-school seniors surveyed in 1983 (Johnston et al., 1984), nearly half (43%) of the girls had used alcohol on at least 10 occasions in the preceding 12 months, 27% had used alcohol on 20 or more occasions, and 13% had used alcohol 40 or more times. In 1978, 42% of girls in the 10th–12th grades were having several drinks a month (Rachal et al., 1980), and 25% were averaging more than 8 drinks a month. Rachal *et al.* (1980) found that 9% of the 10th–12th-grade girls were reportedly having 5 or more drinks at a time at least once a week, while Johnston *et al.* (1984) reported that 31% of 12th-grade girls in 1983 had consumed 5 or more drinks at a time at least once in the 2 weeks preceding the survey. In short, regular drinking is common among high-school girls, and a sizable minority of these girls engage in at least occasional heavy drinking.

One serious consequence of adolescent drinking is drunkenness. Among the 10th–12th-grade girls surveyed in 1978 (Rachal *et al.*, 1980), reanalyzed data show that 25% reported being drunk or very, very high from drinking at least six times in the preceding year. In 1983, among 12th-grade girls who were drinkers, 39% said that they usually got moderately high or very high whenever they drank alcoholic beverages (Johnston *et al.*, 1984). Drinking also often had adverse consequences for girls' social behavior and relationships. The 1978 data on 10th–12th-grade girls (Rachal *et al.*, 1980) show that among girls who had used any alcohol in the preceding year, 21% reported that they had driven a car at least once after having a "good bit" to drink, 20% had had difficulties with friends because of drinking, and 12% had been criticized by their dates because of drinking. Drinking-related problems with police or school personnel were much less common. However, it is clear that large numbers of high-school girls are at least occasionally drinking in ways that impair their self-control and their relationships with other people.

The recent survey data on adolescent drinking are excellent for estimating how many girls are drinkers, but become less informative as one asks more specific questions about how girls drink and what the consequences are. There is a lack of precise information about when and how often girls engage in episodes of heavy drinking, and how often girls experience specific adverse consequences of drinking. No information is readily available about how rapidly girls drink (as in gulping vs. nursing drinks) or about how gender-specific characteristics (such as metabolism or body fluid levels) may affect intoxication. The description of girls' drinking at present remains a broad outline without many details.

Trends in Girls' Drinking

Conclusions about trends in adolescent girls' drinking depend on the time period and the drinking behavior being studied. From 120 studies of adolescent drinking between 1941 and 1975, Blane and Hewitt (1977) concluded that the percentage of girls (and boys) who were drinkers increased sharply until the mid-1960s, but leveled off after that. Exceptions occurred in some local surveys of urban and suburban populations (e.g., Blackford, 1977, for San Mateo County, California; Smart, Fejer, Smith, & White, 1974, for Toronto, Ontario), which found large increases from the late 1960s to the mid-1970s in the percentages of girls who were drinkers. Blane and Hewitt (1977) themselves noted evidence of a major increase between the mid-1960s and the mid-1970s in the percentage of adolescents who had been drunk at some time.

Since the mid-1970s, the national percentages of adolescent girls who drink or get drunk have not changed much, according to the data summarized in Table 2-1. The percentage of high-school girls who drink may have stopped increasing altogether. (The 1979 increase reported by Fishburne & Cisin, 1980, was related to a change in survey procedure.) However, it is also possible that occasional heavy drinking or drunkenness has become a more common behavior pattern among those high-school girls who drink. Johnston *et al.* (1982, 1984) found a small increase from 1975 to 1981 in the percentage of girls who had very recently had 5 or more drinks at a time (26% in 1975, 31% since 1981), and reanalysis of data from Rachal and his colleagues (1975, 1980) shows that a few more 10th–12th-grade girls in 1978 than in 1974 reported that they had been drunk six or more times in the preceding year (25% vs. 19%).

Recent national changes in girls' drinking behavior have been so small or gradual that they are hard to distinguish from random variations in survey samples and artifactual differences between surveys. It seems reasonable to surmise that major changes in the prevalence of drinking behavior are most likely to occur when people shift from regarding the behavior as deviant to regarding it as normal (or shift in the opposite direction). If drinking has already become ordinary, normal behavior for the majority of adolescent girls, then any further large change in the percentage of girls who drink is not likely immediately. What deserves greater attention in future research is the possibility that occasional episodes of drunkenness or extremely heavy drinking, perhaps as a characteristic of parties or weekend recreation, could become a normal rather than deviant activity involving a majority rather than a minority of adolescent girls.

Comparisons of Girls' and Boys' Drinking

Several investigators have found evidence that girls' and boys' drinking patterns are converging (e.g., Blackford, 1977; Johnston *et al.*, 1982; Rachal *et al.*, 1980), perhaps to the extent that girls are as likely to use alcohol as boys are (e.g., Biddle *et al.*, 1980; Downs & Robertson, 1982; Jessor & Jessor, 1977; Wechsler & McFadden, 1976). Inspection of the data in Table 2-1 shows that national patterns have stabilized in the 1980s, and that boys continue to exceed girls on all measures of drinking behavior. The convergence peaked by the 1978 survey of 10th–12th graders (Rachal *et al.*, 1980), where 73% of the girls and 77% of the boys were drinkers, and 16% of the girls and 19% of the boys drank at moderately heavy levels; and by the 1979 survey of 12–17-year-olds (Fishburne & Cisin, 1980), where 36% of the girls and 39% of the boys had used alcohol in the preceding month.

The convergence is apparently the result of both increases in girls' drinking and decline or stabilization of boys' drinking behavior.

It is also clear in Table 2-1 and from other survey data (see Ferrence, 1980) that girls remain much less likely than boys to drink heavily or to become drunk. In 1978, Rachal *et al.* (1980) found that among 10th–12th graders, 9% of the girls had 5 or more drinks at least once a week, whereas 21% of the boys did; 25% of the girls had felt drunk at least six times in the last year, compared with 36% of the boys. In 1983, Johnston *et al.* (1984) found that 3% of 12th-grade girls were drinking daily, while 8% of boys were doing so.

Gender differences in heavy drinking may result in part from other characteristics of how boys and girls drink. While beer is the typical alcoholic beverage for both girls and boys (Pandina, 1977; Wechsler & McFadden, 1976), there is some evidence that boys are more likely than girls to drink distilled spirits (Margulies, Kessler, & Kandel, 1977), a pattern that could raise boys' ethanol intake and possibly boys' likelihood of becoming intoxicated. There are also indications that boys are more likely to drink with same-sex peers outside the home (Forslund & Gustafson, 1970) and more likely to drink alone (Maddox & McCall, 1964), while girls are more likely to drink at home (Ullman, 1957) or with opposite-sex peers (Harford, 1976). It is plausible that drinking alone or in all-male groups would encourage heavier consumption among boys. Finally, there is the possibility that boys drink faster than girls do, consistent with the finding that gulping drinks is more common among men than among women (Johnson, Armor, Polich, & Stambul, 1977). More rapid drinking by boys could contribute to their heavier consumption per occasion and more frequent intoxication.

Beyond the possible differences in *how* girls and boys drink, there are many possible reasons *why* the two sexes might use alcohol differently, reviewed in the remainder of this chapter. From the descriptive data summarized thus far, we conclude that a majority of girls of high-school age drink alcoholic beverages at least occasionally. Large minorities of these girls have had repeated experiences of intoxication, and have had one or more social problems resulting from drinking. The percentages of adolescent girls using and abusing alcohol have not changed much in recent years, except for a possible increase in the percentage of girls who have episodes of exceptionally heavy drinking. And while adolescent girls are now nearly as likely to drink as adolescent boys are, the boys remain much more likely to use alcohol in extreme ways.

GENERAL INFLUENCES ON GIRLS' DRINKING

Attempts to explain adolescent drinking usually identify variables that could affect both girls and boys: demographic characteristics, influences of parents and peers, personality attributes, and others. Such variables, however, may

TABLE 2-1. *Percentages of Girls and Boys Reporting Use of Alcohol in the Past Month/Year, Heavy Drinking, and Drunkenness, 1974–1983*

Source	Age group	Measure of use	Percentage of girls						
			1974	1975	1976	1977	1978	1979	1980
Johnston et al. (1982, 1984)	Grade 12	Used in the past month		62	62	65	67	67	69
Fishburne & Cisin (1980)	Ages 12–17	Used in the past month	29		29	25		36	
Johnston et al. (1982, 1984)	Grade 12	Used in the past year		82	83	84	86	87	86
Rachal et al. (1975, 1980)	Grades 10–12	Used in the past year[a]	77				73		
Johnston et al. (1982, 1984)	Grade 12	5+ drinks on one or more occasions in preceding two weeks		26	26	29	30	31	30
		Daily use/past month		3	3	4	3	4	4
Rachal et al. (1975, 1980)	Grades 10–12	Moderate/heavy use[b]	16				16		
		Heavy use[c]	8				9		
Rachal et al. (1975, 1980)	Grades 10–12	Drunk six+ times past year	19				25		

[a]Based upon unweighted data.

[b]Drink at least once a week and medium amounts per typical drinking occasion or three to four times a month and large amounts per typical drinking occasion.

[c]Drink at least once a week and large amounts per typical drinking occasion.

affect girls and boys differently (see Ensminger, Brown, & Kellam, 1982). Girls may experience more or less of some conditions than boys do (e.g., drinking by peers). Girls' drinking and boys' drinking may react differently to a given change in some other variable (e.g., age). And the strength of associations with other variables (e.g., parental alcohol use) may be different for girls' and boys' drinking. Unfortunately, relatively few studies of general influences on adolescent drinking differentiate how boys and girls are influenced, and only rarely do studies try to interpret such gender differences.

We review here a wide range of possible causes or conditions for adolescent drinking, causes or conditions that might influence girls as well as boys. Although in many cases the impact of these variables may be the same for both sexes, wherever possible we summarize available information on

				Percentage of boys									
1981	1982	1983	1974	1975	1976	1977	1978	1979	1980	1981	1982	1983	
66	65	64		75	75	78	78	77	77	76	74	74	
			39		36	37		39					
85	85	86		88	88	90	90	90	89	89	88	89	
			84				77						
31	31	31		49	48	50	51	52	52	52	50	50	
3	3	3		9	8	9	8	10	9	8	8	8	
			22				19						
			22				21						
			33				36						

how these variables may have different implications for girls' and boys' drinking. However, it is often necessary to point out merely that research has not determined whether certain influences on adolescent drinking vary with gender.

Demographic or Cultural Influences

AGE

Surveys show a consistent link between drinking and maturation, with both girls and boys increasingly likely to start drinking and to continue drinking regularly as they grow older (Jessor & Jessor, 1975; Kandel et al., 1976; Rachal et al., 1975; Wechsler & Thum, 1973). Rachal et al. (1975) found that 42% of 13-year-old girls were abstainers, but only 21% of the 17-year-old girls abstained. Older adolescents of both sexes are likely to drink at higher quantity–frequency levels (Rachal et al., 1975) and may be more prone to drink in socially inappropriate ways (MacKay, Murray, Haggerty, & Collins,

1963), although at least one study found that young adolescents consume more alcohol per drinking occasion (Harford & Mills, 1978).

Gender differences are evident in how early drinking begins and how much consumption increases over time. Boys are likely to begin drinking before girls do (Johnston et al., 1979; Rachal et al., 1975). Johnston et al. (1984) reported that 38% of boys had tried alcohol by the eighth grade, compared with 25% of girls. Among girls who do start drinking in early adolescence, consumption levels are lower than among boy drinkers of the same age (Rachal et al., 1975; Wechsler, 1979). Among adolescent drinkers, grade level does not seem to affect girls' levels of consumption as much as boys' (Wilsnack & Wilsnack, 1978), nor does it affect girls' problem drinking as much as boys' (Jessor & Jessor, 1977). The later and more gradual development of drinking among girls could have protective consequences for them, given the evidence of a connection between drinking in very early adolescence and later problems with alcohol (MacKay, Phillips, & Bryce, 1967).

SOCIOECONOMIC STATUS

Recent survey research has found no major effects of parental socioeconomic status on adolescent drinking (Donovan & Jessor, 1978; Kandel et al., 1976; Wilsnack & Wilsnack, 1978; Wilsnack, Thompson, & Wilsnack, 1981). This conclusion contrasts with earlier research reporting that heavy and problem drinkers were concentrated among adolescents from lower-status house-holds (Maddox & McCall, 1964; Demone, 1973). No major gender differences in the effects of socioeconomic status have been reported. It appears that any status effects on adolescent drinking are likely to be associated with extreme drinking patterns and the lowest levels of social status (Kandel, 1980). The degree to which status effects on adolescent drinking depend on differing social reactions to drinking behavior, and the degree to which status effects may have declined historically cannot be ascertained from research to date.

REGION AND COMMUNITY

National surveys have repeatedly shown that the percentages of adolescents who drink are higher in the Northeastern and North Central regions of the United States, and lower in the South and West (Fishburne & Cisin, 1980; Johnston et al., 1979, 1984; Rachal et al., 1975). Urff (1982) has noted that these regional patterns are the same for girls and boys.

Adolescent alcohol use has also been common in urban metropolitan areas (Blane & Hewitt, 1977; Fishburne & Cisin, 1980; Johnston et al., 1979, 1984), although Johnston et al. (1984) found that urban-nonurban differences had disappeared by 1983, and found little difference in rates of heavy drinking since 1975 between metropolitan and nonmetropolitan areas. Several studies of nonurban settings with high rates of abstinence have noted a high incidence of drinking-related problems among adolescents who did use alcohol

(Alexander, 1967; Globetti, 1969; Lassey & Carlson, 1980), suggesting that when adolescent drinking violates local norms of abstinence it is particularly likely to have undesirable consequences. However, there is no examination of possible gender differences in the effects of urban versus rural environments, and no research on whether abstinent communities react differently to girls' drinking as distinct from boys' drinking.

ETHNICITY

White adolescents are more likely to use and abuse alcohol than black or Hispanic adolescents are (Rachal et al., 1975, 1980; Thompson, 1982). In the one national survey that included sufficient numbers of Native American teenagers (Rachal et al., 1975), the Native Americans were more likely to be heavy drinkers than respondents from other ethnic groups. Among white adolescents, a recent urban survey (Greeley, McCready, & Thiesen, 1980) found that those with Irish backgrounds were more likely to drink, get drunk, and report drinking problems than adolescents with Italian, English, or Jewish backgrounds. The differences among ethnic groups follow the same pattern for girls and boys, and are reminiscent of adult patterns (e.g., Pittman & Snyder, 1962; Greeley et al., 1980). Such findings run counter to any notion that adolescent drinking can be explained by simple majority–minority, advantaged–disadvantaged, or old generation–new generation dichotomies.

Most research within ethnic groups has found that alcohol use and abuse occur more frequently among boys than among girls. For example, studies of Mexican-American youth (Guinn, 1978; Perez, Padilla, Ramirez, Ramirez, & Rodriguez, 1980) report that drinking occurs disproportionately among boys, and studies of black adolescents show that boys use alcohol more frequently (Higgins, Albrecht, & Albrecht, 1977; Ensminger et al., 1982) and report more complications from use (Alsikafi & Globetti, 1979) than girls do. However, Cockerham (1975), in a study of Arapahoe and Shoshone youngsters, noted no significant differences between boys and girls in drinking frequency or recent drunkenness. National survey data from 1974 (Rachal et al., 1975) indicate that male–female sex ratios for adolescent drinkers and heavy drinkers were highest among Hispanics and lowest among blacks, with ratios for whites and Native Americans falling in between. What is lacking is an explanation of why adolescent drinking is more a male than a female activity across ethnic groups, and an explanation of how and why ethnicity increases or reduces the gender difference.

RELIGION AND RELIGIOSITY

Affiliation with religious groups has long been known to influence whether adolescents drink, and how they drink. Jewish adolescents are likely to use alcohol (Rachal et al., 1975, 1980; Snyder, 1978) but less likely to drink excessively or to develop drinking-related problems than are adolescents of other major religions (Greeley et al., 1980; Rachal et al., 1975, 1980). Being

Catholic increases the likelihood that an adolescent will use alcohol (Maddox & McCall, 1964; Rachal et al., 1980; Zucker, 1976) and will drink heavily (Demone, 1973; Kane & Patterson, 1972; Rachal et al., 1980). Protestant adolescents are less likely to use alcohol than Catholic or Jewish adolescents (Rachal et al., 1980; Zucker, 1976), but this generalization may obscure the fact that adolescents from relatively liberal denominations (e.g., Episcopalians, Lutherans, Presbyterians) more often become drinkers than adolescents from more conservative or ascetic denominations (e.g., Baptists, Methodists; see Nusbaumer, 1981; Rachal et al., 1975; Schlegel & Sanborn, 1979). It has long been argued that adolescents from traditionally abstinent denominations are more likely to experience social problems if they drink, since they lack a context of norms for moderate use of alcohol (Mizruchi & Perrucci, 1970; Mulford, 1964), but recent research has failed to demonstrate this effect (Rachal et al., 1980; Schlegel & Sanborn, 1979).

A deficiency in the research literature is the lack of attention to possible gender differences in the effects of religious affiliation. Catholic affiliation may facilitate girls' heavy drinking more than boys' (Wilsnack et al., 1981); being Jewish may protect girls better than boys against developing drinking problems (Greeley et al., 1980); and conservative Protestantism may make boys and girls equally unlikely to drink heavily (Schlegel & Sanborn, 1979) but may protect girls better than boys against adverse drinking consequences (Rachal et al., 1980). Beyond these patterns, little analysis of gender differences is available.

Paralleling the research on denominational effects, there have been a number of studies about how adolescent drinking is affected by religious commitment, participation, or activism, but few analyses of how such religiosity might affect girls and boys differently. Most of the research on religiosity or religious participation concludes that these characteristics, independent of denomination, make adolescents less likely to become drinkers (Burkett, 1980; Jessor & Jessor, 1975; Larsen, 1978; Potvin & Lee, 1980; Rachal et al., 1975) and moderate the drinking behavior of adolescents who do use alcohol (Rachal et al., 1975; Wechsler & Thum, 1973; Zucker, 1976). Exceptions are that Margulies et al. (1977) found no relationship between adolescent church attendance and use of distilled spirits, and Rachal et al. (1975) found that attending church two to three times per month did not increase abstention more than not attending at all. The only discussion of gender distinctions is in the argument by Jessor and Jessor (1977) that greater involvement of girls in church participation during early adolescence contributes to their much lower likelihood of drinking at this time.

Parental Influence

Parents can influence adolescent drinking in many ways: by making alcohol accessible to their children, by establishing normative patterns for children's drinking or abstention in the household, by modeling drinking behavior, by expressing attitudes toward drinking by their children or other adolescents, and by interacting with children in ways (such as conflicts) that then affect children's use of alcohol. Unfortunately, only a few of these possible influences have been investigated in a way that allows us to specify effects on adolescent girls.

PARENTAL DRINKING

Research has repeatedly found that parents' drinking is positively related to drinking and levels of alcohol consumption of adolescent children (Adler & Lotecka, 1973; Barnes, 1977; Prendergast & Schaefer, 1974; Rachal et al., 1975, 1980; Williams & Klerman, Chapter 10 in this volume). Other studies have concluded that parental alcohol intake is correlated with adolescent problem drinking (Barnes, Benson, & Wilsnack, 1979; Demone, 1973; Glatt & Hills, 1968). Time-simultaneous data analyses (Akers, Krohn, Lanza-Kaduce, & Radosevich, 1979; Thompson & Wilsnack, 1982) suggest that parental drinking has its greatest impact on the initial stages of drinking. However, a time-ordered analysis of 1974 and 1978 national survey data (Thompson & Wilsnack, 1982) shows that 7th and 8th graders' awareness of drinking by the same-sex parent makes these adolescents somewhat more likely to drink in excessive or socially undesirable ways by the 11th and 12th grades.

Research has also found that parental drinking influences drinking behavior of adolescent daughters more than it influences drinking of sons (Forslund & Gustafson, 1970; Greeley et al., 1980; Zucker, 1976). Some studies have found that heavy drinking by girls is related specifically to drinking by their mothers (Widseth & Mayer, 1971; Zucker & Devoe, 1975). Margulies et al. (1977), however, reported that the father's drinking predicted initial use of distilled spirits by girls but not by boys. Time-ordered analysis of national survey data (Thompson & Wilsnack, 1982) revealed that awareness of drinking by both parents in early adolescence (7th–8th grade) influenced girls more than boys to become drinkers by late adolescence (11th–12th grade). Taken together, these findings suggest that girls may be more responsive than boys to how parents behave with alcohol. Given that boys may have more peer models of drinking behavior and at younger ages (Forslund & Gustafson, 1970), a further implication is that parents may have better opportunities to protect daughters than sons against excessive or problem drinking, by the ways that parents themselves drink.

PARENTAL ATTITUDES

Parental approval or disapproval can influence adolescent drinking, but the effects may depend on who receives the approval or disapproval, and what kind of drinking behavior prompts parents to express their views. Broadly speaking, children conform partially to perceived parental attitudes about adolescent drinking, by using alcohol more or less readily (Jessor & Jessor, 1975; Kandel, Kessler, & Margulies, 1978; Rachal et al., 1980) and by becoming more or less likely to develop drinking problems (Braucht, 1974; Kane & Patterson, 1972). However, parental criticism of alcohol use can sometimes have a boomerang effect, leading adolescents who are already drinkers to use and abuse alcohol even more (Globetti, 1978; Jessor, Collins, & Jessor, 1972), possibly as a manifestation of adolescent rebellion or of conflict between parents and peers (Alexander & Campbell, 1967; Britt & Campbell, 1977). The discussion of how parental disapproval of drinking can backfire has unfortunately referred only to data on male drinkers.

Some researchers have found that parental attitudes about alcohol affect daughters' drinking more than sons' drinking (Biddle et al., 1980; Margulies et al., 1977). However, Jessor and Jessor (1977) reported that among drinking adolescents, parental tolerance of drinking was more likely to result in drunkenness among sons than among daughters. Furthermore, Thompson and Wilsnack (1982) found that parental attitudes about boys' drinking mattered more to children of both sexes than attitudes about girls' drinking; specifically, parental tolerance of male adolescent drinking influenced both sons and daughters to start drinking, and encouraged boys who were already drinking to drink more heavily.

PARENT–CHILD INTERACTION

The evidence to date indicates that adolescents are more likely to drink if parents' relations with children are unsupportive, alienated, or hostile (see, e.g., Glatt & Hills, 1968; MacKay, 1961; Wechsler & McFadden, 1976; Zucker & Barron, 1973). Prendergast and Schaefer (1974) noted that adolescents were likely to drink more heavily if they had tense relations with their fathers and felt rejected by their mothers. Potvin and Lee (1980) found that a lack of affection from parents became increasingly associated with drinking by children as the adolescent children grew older. Thompson and Wilsnack (1982) reported that conflict with parents in early adolescence was related to alcohol use and problem drinking by the children 4 years later. Adolescents motivated to avoid parental surveillance and to gain peer support may find it easier to drink in surreptitious and excessive ways, with the alcohol serving as a symbol of rebellion (Alexander, 1967) and/or as medication for the tension and anxiety of life at home (Prendergast & Schaefer, 1974).

The question that cannot be adequately answered is whether troubles with parents encourage both boys and girls to use and abuse alcohol in the same unsupervised, rebellious, and/or medicative ways. The limited evidence suggests that there may be important gender differences in how parent–child interaction affects children's drinking. Jessor and Jessor (1977) reported that parental support and efforts to control children's behavior reduced boys' drunkenness but not girls'. A contrasting finding by Thompson (1982) was that conflict with parents more strongly influenced girls to start drinking. In an urban black sample, Ensminger et al. (1982) found that weakened family bonds increased the likelihood of heavy drinking more among girls than among boys. Time-ordered data analysis (Thompson & Wilsnack, 1982) suggests that tension with parents makes boys more likely to drink in ways that provoke social conflict, perhaps as a way of showing rebellion, while tension with parents makes girls more likely to drink until they feel drunk, perhaps as a way of escaping conflict and its emotional distress.

ISSUES OF INTERPRETATION

Conclusions and hypotheses about parental influences on adolescent drinking must be treated with caution, because they are often stated as oversimplified, bivariate, one-directional relationships. One problem of oversimplification is that parental influences on children's drinking may vary with the children's age. Biddle *et al.* (1980), for example, found that parental norms affected drinking by younger adolescents (age 13–14) and older adolescents (age 17–18), but not drinking by children in middle adolescence (age 15–16). Potvin and Lee (1980) found that a lack of parental affection directly increased alcohol use only in late adolescence (age 17–18), while parental disapproval of children's friends directly increased children's drinking only when the children were 15–16.

Other problems of interpreting parental influences are that certain family conditions often get left out of analyses. One condition frequently neglected is whether the adolescent drinkers are living in single-parent families, or in families reconstituted after divorce, separation, or widowhood. These family characteristics conceivably would affect adolescent drinking and might confound adolescent perceptions of parental behavior. A further neglected aspect of parental influences is that most of the data are based on children's perceptions (for a critique and alternative approach see Kandel, 1978). Thus we are left ignorant about the actual parental behavior that is evaluated by the children, and we cannot be sure what parents do that results in children's increased alcohol use and abuse.

Finally, little work has been done to determine to what extent the relationships between parental behavior and adolescent drinking are two-directional. It is conceivable that drinking and alcohol abuse by adolescents could lead parents to become more hostile or alienated, to change their attitudes about adolescent drinking, or even to modify their own use of alcohol. While there is little available evidence to demonstrate that teenage drinking intensifies parent–child conflict, time-ordered analysis of survey data (Thompson & Wilsnack, 1982) suggests that parents may adapt to children's drinking in early adolescence by becoming more tolerant of adolescent alcohol use.

Peer Influence

Research has shown that adolescent drinking is related to peer modeling of drinking behavior (e.g., Harford, 1976; Margulies *et al.*, 1977; Rachal *et al.*, 1980), peer attitudes toward alcohol use and peer reinforcement of alcohol use (e.g., Akers *et al.*, 1979; Biddle *et al.*, 1980; Rachal *et al.*, 1980), and active peer pressure or enticement to drink (e.g., Alexander & Campbell, 1967; Forslund & Gustafson, 1970). One influence that has not been adequately evaluated is the role of peers in increasing or protecting access to alcohol and opportunities to use it. A second is the effects of interaction with peers, which might lead some teenagers to use alcohol to make social interaction easier and more relaxed, and might lead other teenagers to drink to dull the pain of bad relations with agemates. Some studies have noted differences in the ways that peers influence drinking by girls as distinct from boys, but the reasons for such differences remain largely unexplained.

PEER DRINKING

A consistent finding is that adolescent drinkers are more likely than abstainers to associate with peers who drink (Alexander & Campbell, 1967; Kandel et al., 1976; Rachal et al., 1980; Reister & Zucker, 1968; Wechsler & Thum, 1973). Adolescent drinkers, particularly those who drink heavily, are also likely to perceive alcohol use as exceptionally widespread among acquaintances of their age (Kandel et al., 1978; Rachal et al., 1975; Wechsler & Thum, 1973). Some data analyses indicate that girls are more strongly influenced by peer modeling of drinking than boys are (Jessor, Jessor, & Finney, 1973; Margulies et al., 1977), although Jessor and Jessor (1977) found that peer models facilitated boys' drunkenness more than girls'. In discussing peer modeling as well as other peer influences, it is uncertain to what extent adolescents who drink or who are attracted to alcohol use then choose to associate with like-minded peers, as distinct from the process of friends leading adolescents to use alcohol (see Alexander & Campbell, 1967; Huba, Dent, & Bentler, 1980; Kandel et al., 1978).

PEER ATTITUDES AND NORMS

Researchers have found strong positive relationships between adolescent drinking behavior and perceived peer attitudes toward alcohol use (Britt & Campbell, 1977; Jessor & Jessor, 1975; Larsen, 1978; Rachal et al., 1980). Akers et al. (1979) concluded that peer approval of alcohol use was the most important predictor of adolescent initiation into alcohol use and of subsequent drinking behavior. Biddle et al. (1980), however, found that perceived norms of peers had only an indirect influence on how adolescents drank, but had a direct effect on how adolescents intended to drink as adults.

Attempts to evaluate gender-specific effects of peer attitudes or norms have reached differing conclusions. Thompson's (1982) analysis of 1974 and 1978 national survey data indicated that peer attitudes had less effect on girls' amount of drinking than on boys', but Forslund and Gustafson (1970) reported opposite findings from a smaller study. Biddle et al. (1980) could find no direct relationship between girls' drinking and perceived peer norms, while boys' drinking frequency was likely to go against perceived peer norms. Gender differences may be clearer for more extreme drinking behavior, with survey data (Greeley et al., 1980; Jessor & Jessor, 1977) suggesting that peer attitudes have less impact on girls' excessive or problem drinking than on boys'. Any gender-specific effects of peer attitudes may be complicated by additional unreported variables such as degree of peer consensus, extent of peer contact, and differentiation of influence between same-sex and opposite-sex peers.

PEER PRESSURE

Active pressure from peers (e.g., suggestions, encouragement, persuasion, sanctions) has also been proposed as a factor increasing adolescent use of alcohol. Alexander and Campbell (1967) found that nondrinkers were more likely to try alcohol when they experienced peer pressure to drink. Forslund and Gustafson (1970) found that high-school boys under strong pressure to drink were more likely to begin drinking, regardless of parental drinking behavior, while moderate peer pressure significantly increased the likelihood that girls would drink. However, although peer pressure may help to get adolescents to start drinking, there is no evidence that peer pressure strongly affects how girls or boys use alcohol once they are drinkers.

ISSUES OF INTERPRETATION

Trying to specify how peers affect girls' drinking is difficult for a number of reasons. Data analysis thus far has not been detailed enough to distinguish between differences in the amount of peer-drinking influences that girls and boys experience, and differences in the way that girls and boys react to a given amount of change in peer influences. Furthermore, the influences usually measured (peer drinking, peer attitudes toward alcohol, peer pressure to drink) are likely to be overlapping, mutually reinforcing, and related to other influences (such as drinking opportunities, settings, and supplies). Peer influences are further complicated by variables that typically go unmeasured in studies of adolescent drinking (e.g., how homogenous peer behavior and attitudes are, how extensive a girl's peer relations are, how much a girl depends psychologically on particular or general peer friendships, and how influences differ between male and female peers). And there is usually no way to tell to what extent peer patterns are a consequence of a girl's drinking and not simply a cause of it.

One complication that has been investigated is that peer influences on adolescent drinking may be age-limited. Studies have noted that peers strongly influence adolescents in the mid-teen years (Berndt, 1979; Floyd & South, 1972), and have a strong impact on alcohol use at this stage of adolescence (Margulies et al., 1977). Biddle et al. (1980) reported that adolescents aged 15–16 were influenced by peers' and not parents' drinking norms and behavior, while younger adolescents responded mainly to parental norms, and older adolescents considered the views of both parents and peers. In contrast, Potvin and Lee (1980) found that conformity to peers and the "crowd" had its biggest effects on drinking by 13- and 14-year-olds. The irregularities in peer influences for different age groups support the idea that peers have relatively short-term and immediate effects on adolescent drinking (Brittain, 1963; Forslund & Gustafson, 1970; Glynn, 1980), while parents are more likely to serve as long-term models for the drinking behavior adolescents will engage in as they become adults (Biddle *et al.*, 1980; Maddox & McCall, 1964). Regrettably, no one has determined whether peer influences are age-limited in the same or different ways for girls and boys.

Personality Characteristics

Researchers have tried to identify personality traits or more temporary psychological states that might increase adolescent drinking, either by causing distress that teenagers cope with by drinking, or by making adolescents psychologically unable or unwilling to inhibit their own use of alcohol. Overall, the results of these research efforts suggest that personality characteristics tell us little about who becomes a drinker, but may indicate which adolescent drinkers have higher risks of developing drinking problems (see Cisin, 1978; Jones, 1968; MacKay, 1961). Given that many psychological stresses on adolescent girls may be specific to their transitions to adulthood, and that many adolescent drinking problems are linked to reactions by adults (e.g., in status offenses), the personality variables most relevant to girls' drinking may not have the same relationships to women's drinking and drinking problems later on.

ALIENATION

Alienation does not make adolescents much more likely to start drinking (Potvin & Lee, 1980), presumably because adolescent drinking is so often a part of socially integrated and normative behavior (e.g., parties). Adolescent alienation, however, is associated with drunkenness (Jessor, Young, Young, & Tesi, 1970) and irresponsible use of alcohol (Blane, Hill, & Brown, 1968). Smart and Gray (1979) suggest that social isolation or other aspects of alienation may be important reasons for adolescent problem drinking. At present, research has not distinguished how much feelings of alienation lead adolescents to engage in self-medicative or escape drinking, how much the detachment from other people removes social constraints on drinking behavior, and how much an adolescent's excessive drinking may drive other people away or make the adolescent drinker feel more powerless or socially devalued. There also has been little study of gender differences in the effects of alienation, although Larsen (1978) found that anomie and distrust were related to heavier drinking among adolescent girls, while Jessor and Jessor (1977) found no differences in how alienation increased girls' and boys' drunkenness.

INTERNAL–EXTERNAL LOCUS OF CONTROL

According to Plumb, D'Amanda, and Taintor (1975), adolescents who have relatively little faith in their ability to control their own behavior and its consequences (externals) may be more likely to abuse alcohol in an attempt to assuage feelings of helplessness. Other researchers have found that adolescents who feel they have relatively good control over their own behavior and its consequences (internals) may be as likely to drink as externals are, but are less likely to develop problems related to drinking (Jessor et al., 1970; Oziel, Obitz, & Keyson, 1972). These patterns may apply to both girls and boys; at least one study (Schilling & Carman, 1978) found no gender differences in the internal versus external locus of control of adolescent drinkers, or in the relationships between locus of control and drinking behavior.

Conclusions about locus-of-control effects are tentative for two major reasons. First, no data are provided about how locus of control affects adolescents; some may shrug off feelings of external control as a temporary penalty of being not quite adult, some may be vexed enough by external-control feelings to drink away their discomfort, and some may express a lack of internal control by unrestrained drinking behavior. Second, studies of adolescent drinking have not revealed how much the use or abuse of alcohol may intensify teenagers' feelings that their lives are out of their control, a consequence that could contribute to a "vicious circle" of drinking. In addition, there is no information about whether these possible connections between drinking and locus of control are different for girls and boys.

INDEPENDENCE

Survey data show that the desire to be independent is associated with drinking rather than abstaining among adolescents of both sexes (Donovan & Jessor, 1978; Jessor & Jessor, 1975; Wilsnack & Wilsnack, 1979). The independence symbolized by drinking in defiance of adult authority is evident in Alexander's (1967) finding that adolescents alienated from abstaining fathers were exceptionally likely to use alcohol, and Blane and Chafetz's (1971) finding that among delinquents the drinkers scored higher on measures of independence.

However, Alexander as well as Blane and Chafetz studied boys, and Gorsuch and Butler (1976) reported that rebellion against parental socialization helped explain boys' alcohol abuse but not girls'. The literature on gender-role orientation (e.g., Smith, 1973; Spence & Helmreich, 1978) suggests that the desire to be independent and to defy authority are traditionally masculine characteristics. It is possible that the pursuit of this traditional masculine value might accentuate differences between boys' and girls' drinking, as we discuss under the heading of gender-specific influences on drinking.

CONFORMITY TO EDUCATIONAL GOALS

If adolescent drinking can be a symbolic show of independence, it should not be surprising that adolescents are also more likely to drink if they do not want to do what schools and teachers want them to do. Specifically, adolescents who do not value achievement or success in school are more likely to use alcohol and to drink heavily than adolescents who value academic achievement (Donovan & Jessor, 1978; Jessor & Jessor, 1977; Wilsnack & Wilsnack, 1979). Furthermore, adolescent students apparently use alcohol less the more they have a commitment to education beyond high school (Johnston *et al.*, 1979) and the more they want a successful career (Jessor & Jessor, 1973). It is not clear that the effects of educational aspirations differ for girls and boys. At least two studies have reported that the desire for academic achievement affects the drinking behavior of both sexes (Jessor & Jessor, 1977; Wilsnack & Wilsnack, 1979). However, Margulies *et al.* (1977) found that cutting classes was associated only with girls' initiation into use of liquor, while Jessor and Jessor (1977) found that low *expectations* of academic achievement related to drunkenness only among boys.

Adolescent rejection of academic goals could be accompanied by drinking and alcohol abuse for several reasons relevant to both girls and boys. Besides being a symbolic act of independence, drinking could be used to compensate for any negative feelings or isolation resulting from disliking school or from reduced participation in school. Furthermore, some adolescents may learn a broader set of anti-institutional values that would facilitate both drinking and rejection of formal education. Finally, the effects of drinking could easily impair an adolescent's schoolwork and his or her efforts to succeed in school. Data currently available do not show which of these connections between drinking and antiacademic feelings are most important for adolescent girls.

ANTISOCIAL BEHAVIOR

Adolescent drinking often appears to be one manifestation of a broader tendency to engage in antisocial behavior. Many scholars have noted that excessive and problem drinking among adolescents are strongly associated with fighting, physical aggression, and participation in illegal activities (Blacker, Demone, & Freeman, 1965; Donovan & Jessor, 1978; Jessor & Jessor 1977; Wechsler & Thum, 1973; Widseth & Mayer, 1971; Wilsnack & Wilsnack, 1978; Zucker & Devoe, 1975). Kane and Patterson (1972) found that 45% of adolescents who were frequent drinkers had fought or destroyed property while drinking, and 28% had been arrested or injured because of drinking. Antisocial behavior in adolescence may also be a predictor of or contributor to deviant drinking behavior in adulthood (Robins, Bates, & O'Neal, 1962). However, it may be a mistake to look only for ways that drinking can directly increase delinquency or vice versa (Stacey & Davies, 1970). Adolescent drinking and delinquent activity may be part of a general syndrome of antisocial behavior that is rooted in problems of earlier socialization in the family (Barnes, 1977; Zucker & Devoe, 1975).

Although antisocial behavior among adolescents has been more common among boys than among girls, research has shown that the association between adolescent drinking and antisocial activities is at least as strong for girls as it is for boys. Zucker and Devoe (1975) found similar patterns for both sexes in the relationship of antisocial behavior to several drinking indicators, and Jessor and Jessor (1977) reported that tolerant attitudes toward antisocial behavior influenced girls' and boys' frequency of drunkenness equally. Among delinquent girls studied by Widseth and Mayer (1971), girls who drank excessively were exceptionally likely to have engaged in traditionally masculine forms of delinquency, such as theft (59%), vandalism (40%), and staying out all night without parental permission (79%). Wilsnack and Wilsnack (1978, 1979) found that an index of antisocial activities other than drug use was strongly correlated with drinking quantity–frequency, drinking problems, and symptoms of alcohol dependence among 7th–12th-grade girls. Less is known about gender similarities or differences in the origins of drinking as part of an antisocial behavior pattern, but Zucker and Devoe (1975) found that girls' antisocial behavior and drinking were related to behavior of both parents, while boys' antisocial behavior and drinking were linked only to their fathers. It is not clear whether girls in general gain some protection against alcohol abuse by being less inclined than boys to behave antisocially, although this is implied by gender-role research reviewed in the following section.

GENDER-SPECIFIC INFLUENCES ON GIRLS' DRINKING

Some of the variables that affect adolescent drinking may have diverging or opposite effects on girls and boys. The persisting differences between girls' and boys' drinking may result from influences that specifically encourage boys to drink or discourage girls from drinking. Some of these possible influences are cultural patterns that may make it easier for boys to drink than for girls: gender-specific roles, drinking norms, and opportunities to use alcohol. Biological differences may also be involved. Research on these influences has not been as extensive or thorough as the research on variables that are not gender-specific. Enough is known, however, to indicate some likely reasons why girls and boys have not used alcohol to the same extent, and to suggest why gender differences in adolescent drinking could decline without entirely disappearing.

Gender-Role Orientations

Drinking has not been a part of traditional roles for women and girls. Rather, drinking and drunkenness have often been viewed as a threat to traditional feminine values and role performance, for example, by association with rebelliousness and reduced self-control (see Sandmaier, 1980). Consistent with this viewpoint, several investigators have found that alcohol use is likely to be greater among young women who are hostile or indifferent toward traditionally feminine values or standards of behavior. Parker (1975), in a college sample, found an association between heavy drinking and young women's rejection of traditional feminine roles. Zucker, Battistich, and Langer (1981), also studying college women, found that disagreement with traditionally feminine attitudes was related to drinking rather than abstaining, but was not related to the amount of alcohol use. In contrast, Wilsnack and Wilsnack (1978) reported that among 7th–12th-grade girls in a national sample, rejection of traditionally feminine values did not distinguish between drinkers and nondrinkers, but was related to consumption levels and drinking problems among girls who drank alcoholic beverages. Finally, Larsen (1978) concluded from a study of high-school girls that traditionally feminine girls were more likely to be abstainers, but that the effects of attitudes toward femininity depended on other environmental conditions, such as the availability or unavailability of alcoholic beverages.

Adolescent drinking may be affected most by one particular aspect of traditional femininity: valuing or respecting social obligations, as part of a more general concern for other people and desire to get along with them (see Bakan, 1966). The rejection or denial of social obligations, as a specific opposition to traditionally feminine ideals, is positively related to drinking, levels of alcohol consumption, drunkenness, and drinking problems among both girls and boys, judging from two national surveys (Wilsnack & Wilsnack, 1979; Wilsnack et al., 1981). Since rejection of femininity is easier or more desirable for boys than for girls, the antifeminine denial of social obligations occurs more among boys than among girls and may help to accentuate and sustain the gender differences in adolescent drinking.

There are numerous possible reasons why drinking would accompany adolescent rejection of traditional femininity and specifically the denial of social obligations. Drinking could symbolize rebellion against traditional and obligatory role behavior, and it could be used to reduce the discomforts of psychological and social conflict resulting from violating public and internalized role expectations. Denying obligations could in turn insulate a girl or boy from restraints other people might have imposed on alcohol use, and the effects of alcohol might give a girl or boy an excuse for behaving in an irresponsible way. As yet it is impossible to evaluate the relative importance of these possible explanations.

Gender-Specific Drinking Norms

Norms for appropriate or permissible drinking behavior have traditionally been more restrictive for women and girls than for men and boys (Knupfer, 1964, 1982; Maddox & McCall, 1964). Accordingly, drinking has been integrated into or allowed with a broader range of activities for men than for women (Harford, 1977). Two pieces of evidence suggest that the tradition of gender-specific drinking norms still influences adolescent drinking. Margulies et al. (1977) found that boys were more likely than girls to view use of distilled spirits as a harmless activity, and that this difference contributed to boys' greater likelihood of drinking distilled spirits. Wilsnack and Wilsnack (1978) presented evidence that adolescent girls who felt it was worse for women and girls to drink than for men and boys were less likely to be drinkers themselves, and if they were drinkers, their level of alcohol use was lower than among girls who rejected the traditional gender difference in drinking norms.

Wilsnack and Wilsnack (1978) also found that attitudes toward gender-specific drinking norms were independent of broader orientations toward traditionally feminine ideals and had an independent effect on girls' drinking. However, it is necessary to be cautious about interpreting the impact of gender-specific norms. Drinking experience could lead girls to change their viewpoints, so that drinking could be a cause rather than a consequence of abandoning traditional norms.

Drinking Opportunities

Despite an increase in attention to drinking contexts (e.g., Clark, 1977; Harford, 1977, 1979) there is surprisingly little recent information on how the opportunities to drink differ for girls and boys. There is some evidence that adolescent girls have had less exposure to situations in which alcohol is available (Ullman, 1957), and one study found that adolescent girls with traditional gender-role attitudes encountered fewer drinking opportunities than did girls with less traditional attitudes (Larsen, 1978).

In the past, girls have been more likely than boys to report that they drank in situations where their parents were present (Baur & McCluggage, 1958; Maddox & McCall, 1964; Ullman, 1957), a context in which parental surveillance is likely to produce more restrained adolescent use of alcohol (Rachal et al., 1980). Parents appear to allow boys more freedom than girls to drink in peer-group situations (Clark, 1967), where heavier drinking is more likely in the absence of adult supervision (Rachal et al., 1980). In addition, past studies have concluded that boys are more likely to seek out drinking environments where adults cannot exert control over alcohol use (Maddox & McCall, 1964; Mandell, Cooper, Silberstein, Novick, & Koloski, 1963; Ullman, 1957). It is unfortunate that more recent survey data have not been analyzed for gender differences in drinking opportunities and settings, to determine whether girls still have a lower risk of exposure to occasions of unsupervised drinking.

Biological Differences

If gender differences in adolescent drinking opportunities have been little studied, gender differences in the biology of adolescent drinking have been barely hinted at. One clue that important differences may exist comes from research on the genetics of alcoholism. Among adopted children, biological sons of alcoholic parents (mainly fathers) are more likely to become alcoholics than biological sons of nonalcoholic parents (Goodwin, 1976, 1981). This difference was not found in a parallel study of daughters (Goodwin, Schulsinger, Knop, Mednick, & Guze, 1977). It may be that (1) girls are less likely than boys to inherit a predisposition for alcoholism; (2) the inheritance is somehow sex-linked, perhaps with girls more at risk from alcoholic mothers, as suggested by recent findings by Bohman, Sigvardsson, and Cloninger (1981); (3) the necessary environmental conditions for expressing alcoholic tendencies occur more often for sons than for daughters; or (4) girls are more susceptible than boys to environmental influences that override genetic predispositions for alcoholism, as suggested by Goodwin *et al.* (1977). It is not yet clear which of these explanations is valid.

Gender differences in adolescent drinking may also be related to body weight and body fluids. By mid-adolescence, boys not only weigh more than girls, but also are likely to have a larger percentage of their weight as body fluid (Ray, 1978). Because of these combined characteristics, a given dosage of ethanol should cause a higher blood alcohol concentration in girls than in boys. However, it is not known whether such gender-related differences in blood alcohol levels influence girls to drink less than boys (because girls may experience intoxication from less alcohol intake), or whether the differences make girls more vulnerable than boys to drinking problems, drunkenness, or alcohol dependence from a given pattern of alcohol consumption.

Furthermore, little is known about similarities or differences in the ways that the bodies of adolescent girls and boys absorb, transport, and metabolize ethanol. One can only wonder whether there are any adolescent gender differences in the production of enzymes involved in ethanol metabolism, or in the amounts of ethanol reaching and affecting the brain. Because of the maturation processes going on in adolescence, there may be biological gender differences in the effects of alcohol intake in teenagers that are not the same in adults and that may change in the course of adolescence. However, in raising questions about biological gender differences in adolescent drinking, we are going beyond the scope of the research literature. We have reached the limits of this review.

CONCLUSIONS

People who are alarmed about drinking among adolescent girls can point to evidence that a majority of high-school girls (nearly as many as boys) now use alcohol to some extent, and that large minorities of adolescent girls are experiencing drinking problems and repeated occasions of heavy alcohol consumption and drunkenness. However, there is no evidence that girls' drinking has increased greatly since the mid-1970s, and heavy consumption, drinking problems, and drunkenness remain considerably more likely to occur among boys than among girls. Apparently, public concern has developed as a delayed reaction to earlier changes that are now relatively stabilized.

It may now be more appropriate to watch for changes or deviations in the variables and conditions that influence girls' drinking. Girls may gain some special protection against abusing alcohol by starting to drink at a later age than boys, by adhering to traditionally feminine values (such as caring about other people) and gender-specific drinking norms, by having parents whose behavior and attitudes encourage restraint of drinking, and by encountering fewer opportunities for uncontrolled drinking than boys have. Social changes in these variables (e.g., earlier onset of girls' drinking, more frequent opportunities for girls to drink heavily, a reduced value of concern for other people) could presage general increases in girls' drinking and alcohol abuse. More immediately, girls who begin drinking in early adolescence, who have numerous social opportunities to drink heavily, who live (and perhaps fight) with heavy-drinking parents, and/or who are trying *not* to be traditionally "feminine," may have an exceptionally high risk of becoming excessive or problem drinkers.

Many of the influences on drinking that deserve attention may not be unique to girls. Adolescent girls' drinking, like that of boys, is associated with a desire for independence and with a variety of antisocial behaviors. Girls' use of alcohol may be as responsive as boys' to the effects of alienation from parents or religion and attachment to drinking peers, although there may also be some poorly understood variations related to gender. Generally speaking, any extreme effort by adolescent girls (or boys) to break loose from adult authority and institutions is likely to foreshadow increased drinking.

The information about adolescent girls' drinking reviewed here is modest. Conclusions usually have to be simple comparative statements: that a particular influence makes girls more or less likely to drink in certain ways and affects girls more or less than (or perhaps the same as) boys. People who are trying to help adolescent girls deal with alcohol problems or avoid alcohol problems need much better information. They need to know how much a given improvement in attitudes or in relations with other people is likely to reduce alcohol consumption. They need to know how girls are likely to behave if they have the same opportunities and motives to drink that boys do. They need to know how much girls will vary in their reactions to a given alcohol-related stimulus, such as a mother or a best friend who drinks heavily. And they need to know how influences on girls' use of alcohol may work in combination, as when a girl with drinking friends gets in fights with a heavy-drinking parent. The kinds of knowledge needed for dealing with alcohol problems of adolescent girls are more complex and precise than what the research literature can currently provide. Our hope is that the findings and questions reviewed here will encourage more specific and thorough investigation of drinking among adolescent girls, to aid future prevention and treatment of alcohol problems.

REFERENCES

Adler, P. T., & Lotecka, L. Drug use among high school students: Patterns and correlates. *International Journal of the Addictions*, 1973, *8*, 537–548.

Akers, R. L., Krohn, M. D., Lanza-Kaduce, L., & Radosevich, M. Social learning and deviant behavior: A specific test of a general theory. *American Sociological Review*, 1979, *44*, 636–655.

Alexander, C. N. Alcohol and adolescent rebellion. *Social Forces*, 1967, *45*, 542–550.

Alexander, C. N., & Campbell, E. Q. Peer influences on adolescent drinking. *Quarterly Journal of Studies on Alcohol*, 1967, *28*, 444–453.

Alsikafi, M. H., & Globetti, G. *Black youth drinking and problem drinking in high school: A comparative analysis.* Paper presented at the 42nd Southern Sociological Society Meeting, Atlanta, Georgia, 1979.

American Broadcasting Company. *ABC News Close-up: Minnie's story: The story of a teenage alcoholic*, 1977. (Television show)

Bakan, D. *The duality of human existence.* Chicago: Rand McNally, 1966.

Barnes, G. M. The development of adolescent drinking behavior: An evaluative review of the impact of the socialization process within the family. *Adolescence*, 1977, *48*, 571–591.

Barnes, J. L., Benson, C. S., & Wilsnack, S. C. Psychosocial characteristics of women with alcoholic fathers. In M. Galanter (Ed.), *Currents in alcoholism* (Vol. 6). New York: Grune & Stratton, 1979.

Baur, E. J., & McCluggage, M. M. Drinking patterns of Kansas high school students. *Social Problems*, 1958, *5*, 317–326.

Berman, C. Is your child a secret alcoholic? *Good Housekeeping*, June 1981, pp. 215–216.

Berndt, T. J. Developmental changes in conformity to peers and parents. *Developmental Psychology*, 1979, *15*, 608–616.

Beschner, G. M., & Treasure, K. G. Female adolescent drug use. In G. M. Beschner & A. S. Friedman (Eds.), *Youth drug abuse: Problems, issues, and treatment.* Lexington, Mass.: D. C. Heath, 1979.

Biddle, B. J., Bank, B. J., & Marlin, M. M. Social determinants of adolescent drinking: What they think, what they do and what I think and do. *Journal of Studies on Alcohol*, 1980, *41*, 215–241.

Blacker, E., Demone, H. W., & Freeman, H. E. Drinking behavior of delinquent boys. *Quarterly Journal of Studies on Alcohol*, 1965, *26*, 223–237.

Blackford, L. *Surveys of student drug use, San Mateo County, California: Trends in level of use reported by junior and senior high school students* (Summary report). San Mateo, Calif.: Department of Public Health and Welfare, 1977.

Blane, H. T., & Chafetz, M. E. Dependency conflict and sex role identity in drinking delinquents. *Quarterly Journal of Studies on Alcohol*, 1971, *32*, 1025–1039.

Blane, H. T., & Hewitt, L. *Alcohol and youth: An analysis of the literature, 1960–1975.* (Report prepared for the National Institute on Alcohol Abuse and Alcoholism). Pittsburgh: University of Pittsburgh, 1977. (NTIS No. PB-268-698).

Blane, H. T., Hill, M. J., & Brown, E. Alienation, self-esteem, and attitudes toward drinking in high school students. *Quarterly Journal of Studies on Alcohol*, 1968, *29*, 350–354.

Bohman, M., Sigvardsson, S., & Cloninger, C. R. Maternal inheritance of alcohol abuse. *Archives of General Psychiatry*, 1981, *38*, 965–969.

Braucht, G. N. A psychosocial typology of adolescent alcohol and drug users. In *Proceedings of the Third Annual Alcoholism Conference of the National Institute on Alcohol Abuse and Alcoholism*. (U.S. Department of Health, Education and Welfare Publication No. ADM-75-137). Washington, D.C.: U.S. Government Printing Office, 1974.

Britt, D. W., & Campbell, E. Q. A longitudinal analysis of alcohol use, environmental conduciveness and normative structure. *Journal of Studies on Alcohol*, 1977, *38*, 1640–1647.

Brittain, C. V. Adolescent choices and parent-peer cross-pressures. *American Sociological Review*, 1963, *28*, 385–391.

Burkett, S. R. Religiosity, beliefs, normative standards and adolescent drinking. *Journal of Studies on Alcohol*, 1980, *41*, 662–671.

Cisin, I. H. Formal and informal social controls over drinking. In J. A. Ewing & B. A. Rouse (Eds.), *Drinking: Alcohol in American society–Issues and current research*. Chicago: Nelson-Hall, 1978.

Clark, W. B. *Sex roles and alcoholic beverage use* (Working paper No. 16). Berkeley: Social Research Group, School of Public Health, University of California, Berkeley, 1967.

Clark, W. B. *Contextual and situational variables in drinking behavior*. Berkeley: Social Research Group, School of Public Health, University of California, Berkeley, 1977.

Cockerham, W. C. Drinking attitudes and practices among Wind River Reservation Indian youth. *Journal of Studies on Alcohol*, 1975, *36*, 321–326.

Demone, H. W. The non-use and abuse of alcohol by the male adolescent. In *Proceedings of the Second Annual Alcoholism Conference of the National Institute on Alcohol Abuse and Alcoholism*. (U.S. Department of Health, Education and Welfare Publication No. NIH-74-676). Washington, D.C.: U.S. Government Printing Office, 1973.

Donovan, J. E., & Jessor, R. Adolescent problem drinking: Psychosocial correlates in a national sample study. *Journal of Studies on Alcohol*, 1978, *39*, 1506–1524.

Downs, W. R., & Robertson, J. F. Adolescent alcohol consumption by age and sex of respondent. *Journal of Studies on Alcohol*, 1982, *43*, 1027–1032.

Ensminger, M. E., Brown, C. H., & Kellam, S. G. Sex differences in antecedents of substance use among adolescents. *Journal of Social Issues*, 1982, *38*(2), 25–42.

Ferrence, R. G. Sex differences in the prevalence of problem drinking. In O. J. Kalant (Ed.), *Alcohol and drug problems in women* (Vol. 5 in *Research advances in alcohol and drug problems*). New York: Plenum, 1980.

Fishburne, P., & Cisin, I. H. *National survey of drug abuse: Main findings 1979*. (U.S. Department of Health and Human Services Publication No. ADM-80-976). Washington, D.C.: U.S. Government Printing Office, 1980.

Floyd, H. H., Jr., & South, D. R. Dilemma of youth: The choice of parents or peers as a frame of reference for behavior. *Journal of Marriage and the Family*, 1972, *34*, 627–634.

Forslund, M. A., & Gustafson, T. J. Influences of peers and parents and sex differences in drinking by high school students. *Quarterly Journal of Studies on Alcohol*, 1970, *31*, 868–875.

Glatt, M. M., & Hills, D. R. Alcohol abuse and alcoholism in the young. *British Journal of the Addictions*, 1968, *63*, 183–191.

Globetti, G. The use of beverage alcohol by youth in an abstinence setting. *The Journal of School Health*, 1969, *12*, 179–183.

Globetti, G. Prohibition norms and teenage drinking. In J. W. Ewing & B. A. Rouse (Eds.), *Drinking: Alcohol in American society—Issues and current research*. Chicago: Nelson-Hall, 1978.

Glynn, T. J. *From family to peer: Transitions of influence among drug using youth* (Report prepared for the Research Analysis and Utilization System Meeting). Rockville, Md.: National Institute on Drug Abuse, 1980.

Goodwin, D. W. *Is alcoholism hereditary?* New York: Oxford University Press, 1976.

Goodwin, D. W. Genetic component of alcoholism. *Annual Review of Medicine*, 1981, *32*, 93–99.

Goodwin, D. W., Schulsinger, F., Knop, J., Mednick, S., & Guze, S. B. Alcoholism and depression in adopted-out daughters of alcoholics. *Archives of General Psychiatry*, 1977, *34*, 751–755.

Gorsuch, R. L., & Butler, M. C. Initial drug abuse: A review of predisposing social psychological factors. *Psychological Bulletin*, 1976, *83*, 120–137.

Greeley, A. M., McCready, W. C., & Thiesen, G. *Ethnic drinking subcultures*. New York: Praeger, 1980.

Guinn, R. Alcohol use among Mexican-American youth. *The Journal of School Health*, 1978, *2*, 90–91.

Harford, T. C. Teenage alcohol use. *Postgraduate Medicine*, 1976, *60*, 73–76.

Harford, T. C. *Contextual drinking patterns among men and women*. Paper presented at the National Alcoholism Forum of the National Council on Alcoholism, San Diego, 1977.

Harford, T. C. Ecological factors in drinking. In H. T. Blane & M. E. Chafetz (Eds.), *Youth, alcohol, and social policy*. New York: Plenum, 1979.

Harford, T. C., & Mills, G. S. Age-related trends in alcohol consumption. *Journal of Studies on Alcohol*, 1978, *39*, 207–210.

Higgins, P. C., Albrecht, G. L., & Albrecht, M. H. Black–white adolescent drinking: The myth and the reality. *Social Problems*, 1977, *25*, 215–222.

Huba, G. J., Dent, C., & Bentler, P. M. Causal models of peer and adult support and youthful alcohol use: Tests of a theory. *Psychological Bulletin*, 1980, *13*, 45–66.

Jessor, R., Collins, M. I., & Jessor, S. L. On becoming a drinker: Social-psychological aspects of an adolescent transition. In F. A. Seixas (Ed.), *Nature and nurture in alcoholism*. New York: New York Academy of Sciences, 1972.

Jessor, R., & Jessor, S. L. Problem drinking in youth: Personality, social, and behavioral antecedents and correlates. In *Proceedings of the Second Annual Alcoholism Conference of the National Institute on Alcohol Abuse and Alcoholism*. (U.S. Department of Health, Education and Welfare Publication No. NIH-74-676). Washington, D.C.: U.S. Government Printing Office, 1973.

Jessor, R., & Jessor, S. L. Adolescent development and the onset of drinking: A longitudinal study. *Journal of Studies on Alcohol*, 1975, *36*, 27–51.

Jessor, R., & Jessor, S. L. *Problem behavior and psychosocial development: A longitudinal study of youth*. New York: Academic Press, 1977.

Jessor, R., Jessor, S. L., & Finney, J. A social psychology of marijuana use: Longitudinal studies of high school and college youth. *Journal of Personality and Social Psychology*, 1973, *26*, 1–15.

Jessor, R., Young, H. G., Young E. B., & Tesi, B. Perceived opportunity, alienation, and drinking behavior among Italian and American youth. *Journal of Personality and Social Psychology*, 1970, *15*, 215–222.

Johnson, P., Armor, D. J., Polich, S., & Stambul, H. *U.S. adult drinking practices: Time trends, social correlates and sex roles*. Working note prepared for the National Institute on Alcohol Abuse and Alcoholism. Santa Monica, Calif.: Rand Corp., 1977.

Johnston, L. D., Bachman, J. G., & O'Malley, P. M. *Drugs and the class of 78: Behaviors, attitudes, and recent national trends* (U.S. Department of Health, Education and Welfare Publication No. ADM-79-877). Washington, D.C.: U.S. Government Printing Office, 1979.

Johnston, L. D., Bachman, J. G., & O'Malley, P. M. *Student drug use in America: 1975–1981*. (U.S. Department of Health and Human Services Publication No. ADM-82-1208). Washington, D.C.: U.S. Government Printing Office, 1982.

Johnston, L. D., Bachman, J. G., & O'Malley, P. M. *Drugs and American high school students: 1975–1983*. (U.S. Department of Health and Human Services Publication). Washington, D.C.: U.S. Government Printing Office, 1984.

Jones, M. C. Personality correlates and antecedents of drinking patterns in adult males. *Journal of Consulting and Clinical Psychology*, 1968, *32*, 2–12.

Kandel, D. B. (Ed.). *Longitudinal research on drug use: Empirical findings and methodological issues.* New York: Hemisphere–Halsted Press, 1978.

Kandel, D. B. Drug and drinking behavior among youth. *Annual Review of Sociology*, 1980, *6*, 235–285.

Kandel, D. B, Kessler, R. C., & Margulies, R. Z. Antecedents of adolescent initiation into stages of drug use: A developmental analysis. In D. B. Kandel (Ed.), *Longitudinal research on drug use.* New York: Hemisphere–Halsted, 1978.

Kandel, D. B., Single, E., & Kessler, R. C. The epidemiology of drug use among New York state high school students: Distribution, trends and change in rates of use. *American Journal of Public Health*, 1976, *66*, 43–53.

Kane, R. L., & Patterson, E. Drinking attitudes and behavior of high school students in Kentucky. *Quarterly Journal of Studies on Alcohol*, 1972, *33*, 635–646.

Knupfer, G. *Female drinking patterns.* Paper presented at the Annual Meeting of the North American Association of Alcohol Programs, Washington, D.C., September, 1964.

Knupfer, G. Problems associated with drunkenness in women: Some research issues. In *Special population issues* (NIAAA Alcohol and Health Monograph No. 4, U.S. Department of Health and Human Services Publication No. ADM-82-1193). Washington, D.C.: U.S. Government Printing Office, 1982.

Larsen, B. M. *Female adolescent drinking, problem drinking and sex role orientation: A test of Adler's propositions.* San Francisco: R & E Research Associates, 1978.

Lassey, M. L., & Carlson, J. E. Drinking among rural youth: The dynamics of parental and peer influences. *International Journal of the Addictions*, 1980, *15*, 61–75.

MacKay, J. R. Clinical observations on adolescent problem drinkers. *Quarterly Journal of Studies on Alcohol*, 1961, *22*, 124–134.

MacKay, J. R., Murray, A. E., Haggerty, T. J., & Collins, L. T. Juvenile delinquency and drinking behavior. *Journal of Health and Human Behavior*, 1963, *4*, 276–288.

MacKay, J. R., Phillips, D. L., & Bryce, F. O. Drinking behavior among teenagers: A comparison of institutionalized and non-institutionalized youth. *Journal of Health and Social Behavior*, 1967, *8*, 46–54.

Maddox, G. L., & McCall, B. C. *Drinking among teenagers.* New Brunswick, N.J.: Rutgers Center of Alcohol Studies, 1964.

Mandell, W., Cooper, A., Silberstein, R. M., Novick, J., & Koloski, E. *Youthful drinking, New York State, 1962.* New York: Staten Island Mental Health Society, Wakoff Research Center, 1963.

Margulies, R. Z., Kessler, R. C., & Kandel, D. B. A longitudinal study of onset of drinking among high school students. *Journal of Studies on Alcohol*, 1977, *38*, 897–912.

Mizruchi, E. H., & Perrucci, R. Prescription, proscription and permissiveness: Aspect of norms and deviant drinking behavior. In G. L. Maddox (Ed.), *The domesticated drug: Drinking among collegians.* New Haven, Conn.: College and University Press, 1970.

Mulford, H. A. Drinking and deviant behavior. *Quarterly Journal of Studies on Alcohol*, 1964, *25*, 634–650.

National Broadcasting Company. *Sarah T.: Portrait of a teenage alcoholic.* 1975. (Television Show)

Nusbaumer, M. R. Religious affiliation and abstinence: Fifteen-year changes. *Journal of Studies on Alcohol*, 1981, *42*, 127–131.

Oziel, J., Obitz, L., Keyson, M. General and specific perceived locus of control in alcoholics. *Psychological Reports*, 1972, *30*, 957–958.

Pandina, R. J. *New Jersey survey of alcohol and drug use among adolescents.* Report to the National Institute on Drug Abuse, Rockville, Md., 1977.

Parker, R. B. Sex-role adjustment and drinking disposition of women college students. *Journal of Studies on Alcohol*, 1975, *36*, 1570–1573.

Perez, R., Padilla, A. M., Ramirez, A., Ramirez, R., & Rodriguez, M. Correlates and changes over time in drug and alcohol use within a barrio population. *American Journal of Community Psychology*, 1980, *8*, 621–636.

Pittman, D. J., & Snyder, C. R. (Eds.). *Society, culture and drinking patterns*. New York: Wiley, 1962.

Plumb, M. M., D'Amanda, C., & Taintor, Z. Chemical substance abuse and perceived locus of control. In D. J. Lettier (Ed.), *Predicting adolescent drug abuse: A review of issues, methods, and correlates*. Rockville, Md.: National Institute on Drug Abuse, 1975.

Potvin, R. H., & Lee, C. Multistage path models of adolescent alcohol and drug use. *Journal of Studies on Alcohol*, 1980, *41*, 531–542.

Prendergast, T. J., & Schaefer, E. S. Correlates of drinking and drunkenness among high school students. *Quarterly Journal of Studies on Alcohol*, 1974, *35*, 232–241.

Rachal, J. V., Guess, L. L., Hubbard, R. L., Maisto, S. A., Cavanaugh, E. R., Waddell, R., & Benrud, C. H. *The extent and nature of adolescent alcohol and drug use: The 1974 and 1978 national sample studies*. (Report prepared for the National Institute on Alcohol Abuse and Alcoholism). Research Triangle Park, N.C.: Research Triangle Institute, 1980. (NTIS No. PB81-199267).

Rachal, J. V., Williams, J. R., Brehm, M. L., Cavanaugh, B., Moore, R. P., & Eckerman, W.C. *A national study of adolescent drinking behavior, attitudes, and correlates*. (Final report, Contract No. HSM-42-73-80 (NIA), to the National Institute on Alcohol Abuse and Alcoholism). Research Triangle Park, N.C.: Research Triangle Institute, 1975.

Ray, O. *Drugs, society and human behavior*. Saint Louis, Mo.: Mosby, 1978.

Reister, A. E., & Zucker, R. A. Adolescent social structure and drinking behavior. *Personnel and Guidance Journal*, 1968, *33*, 304–312.

Robins, L. N., Bates, W. M., & O'Neal, P. Adult drinking patterns of former problem children. In D. J. Pittman & C. R. Snyder (Eds.), *Society, culture, and drinking patterns*. New York: Wiley, 1962.

Robles, R. R., Martinez, R. E., & Moscoso, M. R. Predictors of adolescent drug behavior: The case of Puerto Rico. *Youth and Society*, 1980, *11*, 415–430.

Rooney, R. Melody Theodore's crusade against teenage drinking. *Good Housekeeping*, November 1978, pp. 136–139.

Sandmaier, M. *The invisible alcoholics: Women and alcohol abuse in America*. New York: McGraw-Hill, 1980.

Schilling, M. E., & Carman, R. S. Internal-external control and motivations for alcohol use among high school students. *Psychological Reports*, 1978, *42*, 1088–1090.

Schlegel, R. P., & Sanborn, M. D. Religious affiliation and adolescent drinking. *Journal of Studies on Alcohol*, 1979, *40*, 693–702.

Sexes equal in alcohol, drug use. *Science News*, April 30, 1977, pp. 277–278.

Smart, R., Fejer, D., Smith, D., & White, J. *Trends in drug use among metropolitan Toronto high school students, 1968–1974*. Toronto: Addiction Research Foundation, 1974.

Smart, R. G., & Gray, G. Parental and peer influences as correlates of problem drinking among high school students. *International Journal of the Addictions*, 1979, *14*, 905–918.

Smith, M. R. *Measurement of masculinity-femininity in an adolescent population*. Unpublished doctoral dissertation, University of Minnesota, Minneapolis, 1973.

Snyder, C. *Alcohol and the Jews*. Carbondale: Southern Illinois University, 1978.

Spence, J. T., & Helmreich, R. L. *Masculinity and femininity: Their psychological dimensions, correlates, and antecedents*. Austin: University of Texas Press, 1978.

Stacey, B., & Davies, J. Drinking behavior in childhood and adolescence. *British Journal of Addiction*, 1970, *65*, 203–212.

Thompson, K. M. *The combination of parental and ethnic influences on white, black, and Hispanic adolescent drinking*. Master's thesis, University of North Dakota, Grand Forks, 1982.

Thompson, K. M., & Wilsnack, R. W. *Parental influences on adolescent drinking: Modeling, attitudes, or conflict?* Paper presented at the 46th Annual Meeting of the Midwest Sociological Society, Des Moines, Iowa, 1982.

Ullman, A. D. Sex differences in the first drinking experience. *Quarterly Journal of Studies on Alcohol*, 1957, *7*, 229–239.

Urff, D. M. *Sex differences in delinquency: A test of popular explanations.* Master's thesis, University of North Dakota, Grand Forks, 1982.

Wechsler, H. Patterns of alcohol consumption among the young: High school, college, and general population studies. In H. T. Blane & M. E. Chafetz (Eds.), *Youth, alcohol and social policy.* New York: Plenum, 1979.

Wechsler, H. Epidemiology of male/female drinking over the last half century. In *Alcoholism and alcohol abuse among women: Research issues* (NIAAA Research Monograph No. 1, U.S. Department of Health, Education, and Welfare Publication No. ADM-80-835). Washington, D. C.: U.S. Government Printing Office, 1980.

Wechsler, H., & McFadden, M. Sex differences in adolescent alcohol and drug use: A disappearing phenomenon. *Journal of Studies on Alcohol*, 1976, *37*, 1291–1301.

Wechsler, H., & Thum, D. Teen-age drinking, drug use, and social correlates. *Quarterly Journal of Studies on Alcohol*, 1973, *34*, 1220–1227.

Widseth, J. C., & Mayer, J. Drinking behavior and attitudes toward alcohol in delinquent girls. *International Journal of the Addictions*, 1971, *6*, 453–461.

Wilsnack, R. W., Thompson, K. M., & Wilsnack, S. C. *Effects of gender role orientations on adolescent drinking: Patterns over time.* Paper presented at the Annual Meeting of the Society for the Study of Social Problems, Toronto, Canada, 1981.

Wilsnack, R. W., & Wilsnack, S. C. Sex roles and drinking among adolescent girls. *Journal of Studies on Alcohol*, 1978, *39*, 1855–1874.

Wilsnack, S. C., & Wilsnack, R. W. Sex roles and adolescent drinking. In H. T. Blane & M. E. Chafetz (Eds.), *Youth, alcohol and social policy.* New York: Plenum, 1979.

Zucker, R. A. Parental influences upon drinking patterns of their children. In M. Greenblatt & M. A. Schuckit (Eds.), *Alcoholism problems in women and children.* New York: Grune & Stratton, 1976.

Zucker, R. A., & Barron, F. H. Parental behaviors associated with problem drinking and antisocial behavior among adolescent males. In *Proceedings of the First Annual Alcoholism Conference of the National Institute on Alcohol Abuse and Alcoholism.* (U.S. Department of Health, Education and Welfare Publication No. NIH-74-675). Washington, D.C.: U.S. Government Printing Office, 1973.

Zucker, R. A., Battistich, V. A., & Langer, G. B. Sexual behavior, sex-role adaptation and drinking in young women. *Journal of Studies on Alcohol*, 1981, *42*, 457–465.

Zucker, R. A., & Devoe, C. I. Life history characteristics associated with problem drinking and antisocial behavior in adolescent girls: A comparison with male findings. In R. D. Wirt, G. Winokur, & M. Roff (Eds.), *Life history research in psychopathology* (Vol. 4). Minneapolis: University of Minnesota Press, 1975.

3

Alcohol Use and Abuse in Ethnic Minority Women

JOY LELAND
Desert Research Institute
University of Nevada

"DIFFERENT STROKES FOR DIFFERENT FOLKS"

This popular expression neatly summarizes the principle of cultural relativity: Attitudes and behaviors vary among cultures. Such differences are more learned than innate. They occur across the spectrum of human experience: giving birth, child rearing, eating, earning a living, worshiping, governing, playing, dying, and a host of others. It follows that we expect drinking attitudes and behaviors to vary among cultures (Everett, Waddell, & Heath, 1976) and even among subgroups of the same culture (Cahalan, Cisin, & Crossley, 1969).

Women are less likely than men to drink or to experience drinking problems in most cultures and in all modern western societies for which we have data, although the degree of sex differences varies among groups (Bacon, 1976). The evidence about differences in drinking behavior among ethnic groups within the United States is, unfortunately, less abundant for women than for men. The purpose of this chapter is to use the available information, scanty as it is, to describe and analyze differences and similarities among women of the principal American ethnic groups: whites, blacks, Hispanics and, to the degree that the data permit, Asians and Indians (the label used herein, following most of the surveys cited, though "Native Americans" would be preferable).

However, none of these ethnic "groups" is homogeneous; each includes peoples of notable cultural differences. Of equal importance, within each of the ethnic groups there is considerable variation in socioeconomic and other characteristics that tend to be associated with various behaviors, including drinking. Therefore, we should keep in mind that the averages for these five ethnic groups mask a great deal of within-group diversity—a subject that deserves far more study than it has so far received. Nevertheless, such within-group diversity only underscores the importance of any between-group differences that are sufficiently strong to show up in spite of internal variation.

PREVALENCE OF ALCOHOL USE AND ABUSE

Youth

Data on the prevalence of drinking among youth in five ethnic groups, from a large (13,122) national sample surveyed in 1974 (Rachal, Williams, Brehm, Cavanaugh, Moore, & Eckerman, 1975), are shown in Table 3-1. Intermediate drinkers made up the majority of drinkers in all ethnic groups, with nearly equal proportions of the total male and female samples in this category. White girls abstained at a lower rate (28%) than ethnic minority girls, whose rates ranged from 36% among Hispanics to 46% among blacks. Girls who abstained generally outnumbered boys; this was most pronounced among Indians. Among female drinkers, heavy drinking was more prevalent among Indian girls than in any of the other ethnic groups. Heavy-drinking boys outnumbered girls in all five groups, with this difference greatest among Asians (5 to 1) and smallest among Indians (1.9 to 1). Since the youth sample was drawn from school populations, it might be biased by the exclusion of dropouts (among whom heavy drinking rates could be higher than among those who remain in school); however, one attempt to control for this variable found no ethnic-group (white vs. black) differences in propensity for higher dropout rates among problem, as compared to non-problem, drinkers (Santangelo & McCartney, 1981).

Adults

Data on the prevalence of adult drinking are available for blacks, Hispanics and whites (1762 subjects in all) from a 1979 national survey (Clark & Midanik, 1981). This adult sample differentiates fewer ethnic groups and has a smaller total sample than the youth study of Rachal *et al.* (1975). In particular, the sample of Hispanics is uncomfortably small in absolute numbers (35 women, 23 men). The large discrepancy among the white, black and Hispanic sample sizes, resulting from the use of a random sample without oversampling minority groups, distorts tests of significance of the differences among the groups.

We have no comparable national data on Asians or Indians. Some studies have provided information on the prevalence of drinking within individual Indian groups. Unfortunately, these studies are not comparable to the 1979 national survey for various reasons, including lack of sex breakdowns (e.g., Jessor, Graves, Hanson, & Jessor, 1968), use of different age

TABLE 3-1. Prevalence of Drinking in Youth (13–18 Years), U.S. Ethnic Groups[a]: Proportions and Ratios of Total Population (TP) and of Drinkers (D)

	White		Black		Hispanic		Indians		Asians		W/B/H		All groups	
	TP	D	TP	D	TP	D	TP	D	TP	D	TP	D	TP	D
					Proportions (%)									
Females														
Abstainers	28		46		36		38		43		30		32	
Drinkers[b]	72		54		64		62		57		70		68	
Intermediate[c]	66	91	51	93	59	92	51	87	56	95	64	91	62	91
Heavy[d]	6	9	3	7	5	8	11	13	.4	5	6	9	6	9
Males														
Abstainers	21		35		27		17		29		23		24	
Drinkers	79		65		73		83		71		77		76	
Intermediate	64	79	56	85	55	77	61	75	49	75	61	79	60	79
Heavy	15	21	9	15	18	23	22	25	22	25	16	21	16	21
Total sample														
Abstainers	25		41		32		27		35		27		28	
Drinkers	75		59		68		73		65		73		72	
Intermediate	64	85	53	89	57	84	56	80	51	85	62	85	61	85
Heavy	11	15	6	11	11	16	17	20	14	15	11	15	11	15

Ratios

Male/female						
Abstainers	.8	.8	.8	.4	.7	.8
Drinkers[b]	1.1	1.2	1.1	1.3	1.3	1.1
	.9	.9	.9	.9	.8	.9
Intermediate	1.0	1.1	.9	1.2	.9	1.0
Heavy[d]	2.5	3.0	3.6	2.0	55.0	2.7
	2.3	2.1	2.9	1.9	5.0	2.3
Ethnic minority female/white female						
Abstainers	1.6	1.3	1.4	1.5		
Drinkers[b]	.8	.9	.9	.8		
	.8	1.0	.8	.9	1.0	1.0
Intermediate	.8	.9	.8	.9	1.0	
Heavy[d]	.5	.8	.9	.1	.6	

[a] Based on Rachal et al. (1975, p. 50). n = whites, 4348M, 4729F; blacks, 442M, 488F; Hispanics, 721M, 788F; Indians, 407M, 387F; Asians, 110M, 113F; total, 6343M, 6799F.

[b] At least once per year.

[c] Arrived at by combining Rachal et al.'s (1975) "infrequent, light, moderate, and moderate/heavy" categories.

[d] Drinking at least once a week in large amounts (5–12 drinks) per typical drinking occasion.

categories (Whittaker, 1980), or other technical problems (e.g., Burns, Daily, & Moskowitz, 1974; Levy & Kunitz, 1974; Walker, Walker, & Robinson, 1978). In the absence of more appropriate data, we include some information here from a sample (Leland, 1975, 1978) that is relatively large (143 males, 134 females) but is restricted to one small Indian settlement, mainly Northern Paiute and Washo. Although these data are clearly not representative of Indians nationwide, the results are surprisingly similar to the national figures for other ethnic groups.

As shown in Table 3-2, moderate drinkers made up the majority of drinkers in all ethnic group adults of both sexes, except for Hispanic males (44%). Among drinkers in all the ethnic groups, male moderate drinkers are slightly outnumbered by females, yielding similar sex ratios. Adult female abstinence rates were highest among blacks and lowest among Hispanics.

TABLE 3-2. Prevalence of Drinking in Adults (18+ Years), U.S. Ethnic Groups[a]: Proportions and Ratios of Total Population (TP) and of Drinkers (D)

	White		Black		Hispanic		W/B/H		Indian Colony	
	TP	D	TP	D	TP	D	TP	D	TP	D
Proportions (%)										
Females										
Abstainers	39		49		31		40		36	
Drinkers[b]	61		51		69		60		64	
Moderate[c]	56	92	44	86	59	87	55	91	57	89
Heavy[d]	5	8	7	14	10	13	5	9	7	11
Males										
Abstainers	25		30		21		25		22	
Drinkers	75		70		79		75		78	
Moderate	54	72	56	80	36	44	54	72	40	51
Heavy	21	28	14	20	43	56	21	28	38	49
Ratios										
Male/female										
Abstainers	.6		.6		.7		.6		.6	
Drinkers	1.2		1.4		1.1		1.3		1.2	
Moderate	1.0	.8	1.3	.9	.6	.5	1.0	.8	.7	.6
Heavy	4.2	3.5	2.0	1.4	4.3	4.3	4.2	3.1	5.4	4.5
Ethnic minority female/ white female										
Abstainers			1.3		.8				.9	
Drinkers			.8		1.1				1.0	
Moderate			.8	.9	1.1	.9			1.0	1.0
Heavy			1.4	1.8	2.0	1.6			1.4	1.4

[a] Based on Clark and Midanik (1981). n = whites, 640M, 847F; blacks, 66M, 99F; Hispanics, 23M, 35F; total, 757M, 1005F. Indian Colony data from Leland (1975). n = 143M, 134F.

[b] At least 1 drink per month.

[c] Less than 60 drinks per month.

[d] 60+ drinks per month.

Male abstainers were outnumbered by females to a similar degree in all ethnic groups. Among drinkers, heavy drinking by women was most prevalent in blacks (14%) and Hispanics (13%) and least prevalent in whites (8%). Men outnumbered women among heavy drinkers, least in blacks (1.4 to 1), an intermediate amount among whites (3.5 to 1), and most among Hispanics (4.3 to 1) and in the Indian Colony (4.5 to 1).

Black females tended to be concentrated at the extremes of abstinence and heavy drinking, following a pattern noted in an earlier national survey (Cahalan et al., 1969). Ethnic-group differences in proportions of female abstainers, moderate drinkers, and heavy drinkers were not statistically significant in the 1979 study (Clark, 1981), though large ethnic-group differences in sample size may distort the results of significance tests.

Nevertheless, a similar pattern also emerged in a 1974 California survey (Cahalan, 1976), in which black women were nearly absent from the middle drinking categories (3 and 4) of a typology comprised of 7 quantity–frequency classes (Table 3-3). This finding adds to our suspicion that the overrepresentation of black women at drinking extremes would attain statistical significance in a survey that appropriately oversampled black women.

Among women drinkers in the 1979 survey, loss of control or alcohol dependence (defined in Clark & Midanik, 1981, pp. 32–33) was most prevalent among Hispanic women (16%), while proportions in the other ethnic groups were lower: 10% for whites, 11% for blacks (and 11% for women in Leland's (1975) Indian Colony study). However, again the ethnic group differences were not statistically significant (Clark, 1981). More men than women showed either loss of control or alcohol dependence. This pattern was strongest among Hispanics (3.5 to 1) and weaker among whites (1.6 to 1), blacks (2.0 to 1), and Indian Colony residents (2.1 to 1).

Although there are more drinkers in Rachal et al.'s (1975) sample of girls than in Clark and Midanik's (1981) sample of women, the excess is concentrated in the category of intermediate drinkers. The proportions of heavy drinkers are about the same in both groups (Tables 3-1 and 3-2). Furthermore, when we control for abstinence-rate differences between girls and women by looking only at drinkers, rather than the total population, there are identical proportions of heavy (9%) and intermediate or moderate (91%) drinkers in both groups.

Comparisons between girls and adult women are made difficult by differences in definitions for the various categories of abstainers and drinkers (see footnotes b, c, and d, Tables 3-1 and 3-2) and by the absence of a youth measure comparable to the "loss-of-control" measure for adult women. More important, such cross-sectional data provide no indication whether any differences between girls and women are merely age-associated, or portend changes in female drinking behavior in the future. Only longitudinal data could tell us; a 4-year youth follow-up (Wilsnack, Thompson, & Wilsnack, 1981) showed few statistically significant changes between 1974

TABLE 3-3. *Quantity–Frequency Drinking Typology: Proportions and Ratios of Total Population (TP) and of Drinkers (D), for California Women, by Ethnic Group[a]*

Drinking style categories	Whites[b]		Blacks		Hispanics		W/B/H	
	TP	D	TP	D	TP	D	TP	D
Proportions (%)								
Drinkers								
Frequent, heavier (5+ at least weekly)	3	3	4	8	3	5	3	4
Frequent, high-maximum (at least weekly, sometimes 5+)	14	17	13	23	16	23	14	18
Frequent, low-maximum (at least weekly, never 5+)	15	19	—	—	23	32	14	18
Infrequent, high-maximum (less than weekly, sometimes 5+)	11	13	4	8	10	14	10	13
Infrequent, low-maximum (less than weekly, never 5+)	13	16	17	31	7	9	14	16
Infrequent (less than monthly)	27	32	17	31	13	18	25	31
Total drinkers	83	100	55	100	72	100	80	100
Abstainers	18		44		29		20	

Ratios

	C1	C2	C3	C4	C5	C6	C7	C8
Male/female								
Drinkers								
Frequent, heavier (5+ at least weekly)	5.3	6.3	6.8	3.8	4.3	2.8	5.7	4.8
Frequent, high-maximum (at least weekly, sometimes 5+)	2.0	1.9	1.2	.8	2.7	2.0	2.0	1.8
Frequent, low-maximum (at least weekly, never 5+)	1.0	.9	—	—	.4	.3	1.1	1.0
Infrequent, high-maximum (less than weekly, sometimes 5+)	.8	.8	2.8	3.0	2.0	1.4	1.0	.9
Infrequent, low-maximum (less than weekly, never 5+)	.5	.4	.5	.4	—	—	.5	.4
Infrequent (less than monthly)	.4	.4	.3	.3	.8	.6	.5	.4
Abstainers	.7	—	.3	—	.1	—	.6	—
Ethnic minority female/white female								
Drinkers								
Frequent, heavier (5+ at least weekly)	1.3	2.7	1.0	1.7				
Frequent, high-maximum (at least weekly, sometimes 5+)	.9	1.4	1.1	1.4				
Frequent, low-maximum (at least weekly, never 5+)	—	—	1.5	1.7				
Infrequent, high-maximum (less than weekly, sometimes 5+)	.4	.6	.9	1.1				
Infrequent, low-maximum (less than weekly, never 5+)	1.3	1.9	.5	.6				
Infrequent (less than monthly)	.6	1.0	.5	.6				
Abstainers	2.4	—	1.6	—				

[a] Based on Cahalan (1976, Table 1), rounded. Blanks indicate cell size too small for percentage calculations. n = whites, 487F, 348M; blacks, 46F, 37M; Hispanics, 31F, 30M; total, 564F, 415M. Because of rounding, percentages may not add to 100.

[b] Approximate combined rate for four white religious subgroups reported separately in Cahalan (1976), calculated here from rounded percentages. n = Protestants, 296F, 175M; Catholics, 109F, 84M; Jews, 25F, 0M; others, 57F, 89M; total 487F, 348M.

73

and 1978 in drinking among white, Hispanic, or black girls. (See Fillmore, Chapter 1 in this volume, for additional age and cohort analyses of women's drinking.)

ADULT DRINKING PATTERNS

Gross drinking categories, such as "heavy," combine a wide variety of drinking patterns. For example, among women who drink 60 or more drinks per month ("heavy" drinking in the 1979 national survey), it probably makes a big difference in terms of potential consequences and prognosis whether this "dose" is taken at the rate of 2 drinks per day, or concentrated on a few high-maximum occasions. Such information is scarce, even for whites, but especially for the ethnic minorities. None of the sources provide national data comparisons. Most deal with a limited geographical area and only one ethnic group. Those that do compare ethnic groups usually use broad categories, such as "white versus nonwhite." The generalizations made in these reports no doubt apply differentially within the ethnic groups, especially by social class, age, marital status, and urban versus rural residence[1], though such data breakdowns are seldom provided. Except where otherwise indicated, the information on Indians comes from a comprehensive review of the available literature by Leland (1981c). No data at all for Asians were located on this topic.

Data on frequency of drunkenness provide some insight into drinking patterns. Among California women (Cahalan, 1976), about two-thirds of the whites and Hispanics and three-quarters of the blacks report they never get high or tight (See Table 3-4). However, these differences in frequency of drunkenness disappear when we control for ethnic group variations in proportions of abstainers, by considering only the women who drink. Among drinkers, men who claim they never get drunk are outnumbered by women (.6 men per woman); proportions are similar in all three ethnic groups. We have no comparable data for the Indian Colony, but informants mentioned that some Indian women who drink only once a year might get drunk on that occasion. Among women who drink, weekly drunkenness is twice as frequent among blacks (8%) as among whites (3%) and Hispanics (4%), while drunkenness from one to three times per month is much more prevalent among Hispanics (14%) than among whites (7%) and blacks (4%).

We have little solid information about the relative prevalence of daily versus episodic binge drinking among alcohol abusers of either sex by ethnic group. In a mental hospital population, whites, blacks, Hispanics, and Indians did not differ on sustained versus episodic binge drinking (Wanberg, Lewis, & Foster, 1978), but unfortunately the data are not broken down by

1. For example, for blacks: Benjamin (1976), Bourne (1973), Sterne and Pittman (1972), and Vitols (1974); for Hispanics: Dobkin-De-Rios and Feldman (1977) and Lopez-Lee (1979).

TABLE 3-4. Frequency of Drunkenness: Proportions and Ratios of Total Population (TP) and of Drinkers (D), for California Women, by Ethnic Group[a]

	Whites[b]		Blacks		Hispanics		W/B/H	
	TP	D	TP	D	TP	D	TP	D
Proportions (%)								
At least weekly	2	3	4	8	3	4	2	3
1-3 times/month	6	7	2	4	10	14	6	7
Less than monthly, at least yearly	18	22	9	15	3	4	16	21
Less than yearly	11	14	9	15	16	23	12	14
Never[c]	62	54	76	58	68	55	63	54
Not ascertained	1	1	—	—	—	—	1	1
Ratios								
Male/female								
At least weekly	5.0	4.0	3.5	1.9	1.0	.8	5.0	3.7
1-3 times/month	2.0	2.0	15.0	8.3	2.7	2.0	2.5	2.4
Less than monthly, at least yearly	1.1	1.1	1.6	1.0	6.7	5.3	1.3	1.1
Less than yearly	1.5	1.3	.9	.6	.6	.4	1.2	1.2
Never	.7	.6	.4	.4	.4	.5	.6	.6
Ethnic minority female/white female								
At least weekly			2.0	2.7	1.5	1.3		
1-3 times/month			.3	.6	1.7	2.0		
Less than monthly, at least yearly			.5	.7	.2	.2		
Less than yearly			.8	1.1	1.5	1.6		
Never			1.2	1.1	1.1	1.0		

[a]Based on Cahalan (1976, Table 2), rounded. Total population n = whites, 487F, 348M; blacks 46F, 37M; Hispanics, 31F, 30M; total, 564F, 415M. Drinkers n = whites, 403F, 302M; blacks 26F, 33M; Hispanics, 22F, 29M; total 451F, 364M, calculated from Cahalan (1976, Table 1) by subtracting the number of abstainers from the total population; the numbers are approximate because they have been calculated from rounded percentages. Percentages may not add to 100 because of rounding.

[b]Approximate combined rate for four white religious subgroups reported separately in Cahalan (1976), calculated here from rounded percentages. n = Protestants, 296F, 175M; Catholics, 109F, 84M; Jews 25F, 0M; others, 57F, 89M; total 487F, 348M.

[c]For people who never get drunk, n = whites 300F, 140M; blacks 35F, 12M; Hispanics 21F, 9M; total 356F, 161M, calculated by subtracting the total of the four frequency-of-drunkenness categories from the total population (see note a) less those whose drinking style was not ascertained (3F, 8M). For drinkers who never get drunk, n = whites 216F, 93M; blacks, 15F, 8M; Hispanics 12F, 8M; total 243F, 109M, calculated by subtracting total drinkers in the four drunkenness categories from the total population of drinkers (see note a) less those whose drinking style was not ascertained.

sex. In a St. Louis private hospital (Rimmer, Pitts, Reich, & Winokur, 1971), more black women (62%) than white women (39%) were binge drinkers. In a Connecticut public clinic population, episodic drinking was less common in blacks than whites, while daily drinking was more prevalent in blacks than whites. Separate figures by sex are provided for black binge drinkers (18% of females, 4% of males), but not for whites. In a detoxification facility, one-third of the Indian women drank daily (Walker et al., 1978).

Ethnic group beverage choices by sex are thinly documented. Black women are said not to share their men's taste for expensive Scotch (as a status symbol) because it offends their "sweet tooth" (Harper, 1976b); probably this varies among subgroups of black women. Beer is mentioned less frequently in accounts of black than other ethnic groups' drinking, but it is very popular with Indians of both sexes nationwide. Indian Colony women are more apt to take mixed drinks than the men, who tend to eschew such concoctions as "too upper white," particularly the martini. Indians, like blacks, are said to equate "wine" with cheap fortified products fit only for "winos," and to avoid it if other drinks are available. Blacks (sex unspecified) do use such wine, though they are reluctant to admit it, since it occupies the bottom of the beverage status list (Sterne & Pittman, 1976). Puerto Ricans are said to consider wine "unmanly" (Abad & Suarez, 1975). Cubans drink table wines with meals at home (Rodriguez & Rodriguez, 1977), a custom not mentioned for other Hispanic groups, or for blacks or Indians. Social class is no doubt influential for this characteristic.

ADULT DRINKING CONTEXTS

More than among whites, convivial group public drinking (mainly on weekends) is said to predominate among Indians (Leland, 1976; Wanberg et al., 1978), blacks (Benjamin, 1976; Davis, 1975; Harper, 1976b; Sterne & Pittman, 1972; Strayer, 1961) and, to a lesser extent, among Hispanics (Shannon & Shannon, 1973; Wanberg et al., 1978). Although we have no data, a plausible explanation for the predominance of public over private drinking by ethnic minorities is that their housing is less adequate for entertaining than whites' (e.g., for blacks, Benjamin, 1976; Davis, 1975; for Indians, Leland, 1981c). In all three ethnic groups, more men than women are said to take part in public drinking, especially among Hispanics (Alcocer, 1982; Aviles-Roig, 1973; Shannon & Shannon, 1973; Trevino, 1975), but also among Indians (Leland, 1981c) and blacks (Benjamin, 1976; Harper, 1976b; Vitols, 1974). These anecdotal accounts often stress the sex segregation in ethnic-minority public drinking, implying that it is greater than among whites, but the actual relative prevalence of this characteristic among ethnic groups is not known. In all the ethnic groups, private drinking on special occasions or at routine get-togethers is more likely to involve both sexes together than is public drinking.

Bars and taverns that welcome blacks are limited in rural areas, resulting in a pattern of "parking lot" drinking (Benjamin, 1976) as a substitute. Liquor outlets are said to be more numerous in neighborhoods occupied by Hispanics (Alcocer, 1975; Rodriguez & Rodriguez, 1977) and blacks (Gaines, 1976; National Clearinghouse on Alcohol Information, 1977; Sterne & Pittman, 1976) than in white neighborhoods. These are not off limits even to children, a circumstance said to encourage early alcohol use. The same probably applies to Indians in urban settings. On the other hand, liquor still is outlawed by local option on many Indian reservations. These restrictions have not discouraged overall use, but have simply added to the danger of untoward consequences such as accidents, since residents must travel to do their drinking (Leland, 1980).

Discriminatory prohibition for Indians often is implicated as the cause of certain aspects of Indian drinking styles and contexts, such as gulping, because penalties for drunkenness are less severe than those for possession; weak in-group controls, because there has not been enough time since drinking became legal to institutionalize sanctions; and generally uncontrolled behavior reflecting the attraction of the forbidden (see Leland, 1981b). It often is overlooked that blacks, too, have been subjected to official and unofficial efforts to limit alcohol availability, particularly during slavery, but later as well, after a brief interruption during Reconstruction (Gaines, 1976; Morgan, 1981). Yet this common experience does not seem to have produced the same responses in blacks as in Indians, suggesting that the explanation for these peculiarities of Indian drinking may lie elsewhere.

The patterns and contexts of drinking are most thoroughly reviewed for Indians (Leland, 1975, 1976, 1978, 1981c; Weibel, 1981). Harper (1976a) contains the most detail on this subject for blacks. For Hispanics, all of the available data are heavily slanted toward men. The information we do have provides no clear picture of the similarities and differences in drinking patterns and contexts across ethnic groups of women and leaves many questions unanswered about ethnic differences in women's drinking.

CONSEQUENCES OF ADULT DRINKING

Health Consequences

In 1975, the proportion of all deaths that were directly attributed to alcohol (i.e., alcoholic psychosis, alcoholism, liver cirrhosis, and accidental alcohol poisoning) varied greatly among U.S. ethnic groups. Indian women experienced the highest proportion of alcohol deaths (about 8% vs. 2.6% for black and 1.7% for white women) (Malin, Archer, & Munch, 1978; no figures for Hispanics). Proportions for Indian women were also higher than for men of any of the ethnic groups. However, male–female ratios are very similar in all three groups: .9 for Indians, 1.1 for blacks and whites. The high proportion of alcohol deaths among Indian women is all the more striking because their rate of increase from 1966 to 1975 was lower than for Indian men or black women (Malin et al., 1978, Figure 2).

The 1975 cirrhosis death rate per 100,000 Indian women (Table 3-5) is more than six times the rate for white women, while the black female rate is only 1.8 times the white. The relative prevalence nationally of heavy drinking and alcohol dependence in Indian versus white women is unknown, but it is unlikely that Indian rates would be six times those of whites. Heavy drinking

PATTERNS OF ALCOHOL USE

TABLE 3-5. Liver Cirrhosis: Age-Specific Mortality Rates per 100,000 and Ratios by Race, United States, 1975[a]

	15-34	35-54	55-74	75+	All ages[b]
	Mortality rates				
White					
Male	1.6	31.8	67.0	43.6	19.6
Female	0.7	15.0	27.9	17.5	8.6
Black					
Male	9.0	75.4	77.9	29.5	32.9
Female	4.4	37.1	33.5	11.2	15.3
Indian					
Male	19.0	151.6	111.0	—	59.7
Female	25.3	102.7	83.6	—	51.9
	Ratios				
Male/female					
White	2.3	2.1	2.4	2.5	2.3
Black	2.0	2.0	2.3	2.6	2.2
Indian	0.8	1.5	1.3	—	1.2
Ethnic minority female/white female					
Black	6.3	2.5	1.2	0.6	1.8
Indian	36.1	6.8	3.0	—	6.0

[a]From Johnson (1980, Table 4), rounded. Blanks reflect cell size under 20.

[b]From Johnson (1980, Table 6), rounded.

rates for Indian Colony women are only 1.4 times (and alcohol dependence rates only 1.1 times) the national rates for white women. In contrast, the ratio of black to white female cirrhosis deaths is exactly the same as the ratio of heavy drinkers (1.8 black women per white, Table 3-2) and very close to the ratio for alcohol dependence (1.1 black females per white). For Indians, male and female cirrhosis death rates for all ages combined are almost equal (1.2 men per woman), while among blacks and whites, male deaths outnumber female deaths more than 2:1 (Table 3-5).

The cirrhosis death rate for Indian women aged 15-34 is 36 times the white rate, while the corresponding black rate is a little over 6 times the white rate. Ethnic minority female cirrhosis death rates are much closer to those for white females in the higher age categories. If this portends higher rates for minority women relative to whites in the future, as these younger women get older, the prospect is alarming. Alternatively, this may merely be an age-specific phenomenon. In any case, it seems that Indian women are somehow much more cirrhosis prone than white or black women, whether from a genetic predisposition or from environmental influences. Differential autopsy rates do not account for the ethnic group differences in cirrhosis death rates (Johnson, 1980).

Cirrhosis rates in 1970 for socioeconomically deprived Puerto Rican women in New York City were 11 per 100,000 (Aviles-Roig, 1973), lower than the national rates for Indians and blacks. Other regional and local data on the prevalence of cirrhosis in ethnic minority women, including Hispanics, is reviewed by Lopez-Lee (1979).

In his 1974 California study Cahalan (1976) reports that health problems due to drinking were more than twice as prevalent among black women (9%) as among whites (4%, Table 3-6); again, no data are available for Hispanic women. More than twice as many white men as women reported health problems due to drinking, while among blacks the sex ratio was reversed, about twice as many women as men.

Social Consequences

Cahalan's (1976) California study (Table 3-6) provides some ethnic-group breakdowns by type of drinking-related social consequences during the last 3 years: problems with friendships and social life; marriage or home life; and

TABLE 3-6. Problems Associated with Drinking during the Last 3 Years: Proportions and Ratios of Total Population (TP) and of Drinkers (D), California Women, by Ethnic Group[a]

Problems	Whites[b] TP	D	Blacks TP	D	Hispanics TP	D	W/B/H TP	D
Proportions (%)								
Friendship and social life	2	2	4	8	—	—	2	3
Marriage or home life	2	2	—	—	3	2	2	3
Work	1	1	—	—	—	—	1	1
Financial position	2	2	2	4	—	—	2	3
Health	4	4	9	15	—	—	3	4
One or more of the five above	5	6	11	19	3	2	6	7
Ratios								
Male/female								
Friendship and social life	2.0	2.0	—	—	—	—	2.0	1.7
Marriage or home life	3.5	4.0	—	—	6.7	10.5	3.5	2.7
Work	2.0	3.0	—	—	—	—	2.0	2.0
Financial position	2.5	3.0	1.5	.8	—	—	1.5	1.3
Health	2.3	2.8	.6	.4	—	—	3.0	2.5
One or more of the five above	3.0	2.8	.7	.5	7.7	12.0	2.5	2.4
Ethnic minority female/white female								
Friendship and social life			2.0	4.0	—	—		
Marriage or home life			—	—	1.5	1.0		
Work			—	—	—	—		
Financial position			1.0	2.0	—	—		
Health			2.3	3.8	—	—		
One or more of the five above			2.2	3.2	.6	.3		

[a] Based on Cahalan (1976, Table 3), rounded. Blanks indicate cell size too small for percentage calculations. n = whites, 462F, 348M; blacks, 46F, 37M; Hispanics, 31F, 30M; total, 539F, 415M.

[b] Approximate combined rate for three white religious subgroups reported separately in Cahalan (1976), calculated here from rounded percentages. n = Protestants, 296F, 175M; Catholics, 109F, 84M; others, 57F, 89M. Jews (n = 25F, 13M) are omitted because of small cell sizes.

work and financial position. Unfortunately, this study includes health consequences in the combined rates for experiencing one or more problems. This mars comparisons with the national rates for strictly social consequences, which are discussed later. Among California female drinkers, blacks reported one or more problems at about three times the white rate. The excess is commensurate with their higher rate of frequent heavy drinking (2.7 times the white rate in the same study, Table 3-3). In contrast, California Hispanic female drinkers reported problems at only about one-third the rate of their white counterparts, despite a frequent-heavy drinking rate 1.7 times the white rate in the same study (Table 3-3). Perhaps then, for some reason, a given level of drinking creates relatively fewer problems for Hispanic women than for their black or white counterparts. Ethnic-group differences are especially marked in the relative proportions of California men and women drinkers reporting problems: fewer black men than women, more men than women among whites and especially among Hispanics.

Social consequences of drinking were defined in the 1979 national survey (Clark & Midanik, 1981) as experiencing problems in one or more of four areas during the past year. These areas were personal relationships, police, accidents, and employment (for detailed criteria see Clark & Midanik, 1981, p. 32). The combined average (Table 3-7) for whites, blacks, and Hispanics was 4% of female drinkers experiencing at least one problem (vs. 7% in the California survey). Also in contrast to the California study, nationally, drinking consequences were *most* prevalent among Hispanic women (17% of drinkers, nearly six times the white rate). The black female rate (6%) was twice that of whites, who experienced the lowest rate (3%); rates for Indian Colony women lie in between (11%, nearly 4 times the white rate). Larger samples of ethnic women would help clarify whether Hispanic women rank high in drinking consequences, as in the national survey (Table 3-7), or low, as in the California survey (Table 3-6). As in the California survey, black men drinkers in the national survey reported problems at slightly lower rates than black women drinkers, while white and Hispanic men reported problems at over twice the rates of their female counterparts.

ADULT SUPPORT SYSTEMS

Support group involvement is thought to improve treatment outcome for alcohol abusers in general, and for ethnic minorities in particular (e.g., Benjamin & Benjamin, 1975; Davis, 1975; Leland, 1981b; Lopez-Lee, 1979; Rodriguez & Rodriguez, 1977). Some clues about ethnic-group differences in the support systems of alcohol abusers under treatment can be gleaned from data on three special ethnic alcohol treatment programs as compared to data from nonethnic programs, all funded by the National Institute on Alcohol Abuse and Alcoholism (NIAAA) (Leland, 1981b). These data include the proportion of referrals from family and friends, the average

TABLE 3-7. Social Consequences of Drinking, U.S. Ethnic Groups[a]: Proportions and Ratios of Total Population (TP) and of Drinkers (D), Adults

	White		Black		Hispanic		W/B/H		Indian Colony	
	TP	D	TP	D	TP	D	TP	D	TP	D
Proportions (%)										
Male	6	8	3	4	30	39	6	9	18	23
Female	2	3	3	6	10	17	2	4	7	11
Total	4	6	3	5	19	26	4	6	13	18
Ratios										
Male/female	3.0	2.7	1.0	.7	3.0	2.3	3.0	2.3	2.6	2.1
Ethnic minority female/white female			1.5	2.0	5.0	5.7	1.0	1.3	3.5	3.7

[a]Based on Clark and Midanik (1981). n = whites, 640M, 847F; blacks, 66M, 99F; Hispanics, 23M, 35F. Indian Colony data from Leland (1975). n = 143M, 134F.

proportion of nonalcoholics (e.g., family members) to alcoholics who were provided some services, the proportion of nonalcoholic contacts who were successfully involved in treatment, and the rates of intact marriages. On these four measures, the overall picture suggests that support group strength was greatest for Hispanics, followed in order by whites, Indians and blacks (see Leland, 1981b, for a detailed discussion). However, these data mainly reflect support for male drinkers, who predominate in the NIAAA programs; ethnic-group differences in support patterns for female drinkers might be quite different, but they are unknown, since the data are not broken down by sex, either of drinker or of support group members.

In any case, except in the Hispanic program, the NIAAA data do not support anecdotal accounts that depict stronger general support in ethnic minority groups than in whites.[2] Furthermore, in various other programs, there are some specific indications of difficulties in enlisting ethnic-minority families, including Hispanics, into the drinker's treatment.[3] Perhaps existing support simply has been less effectively tapped for alcohol treatment in the minority programs than in the white programs. Maybe support systems are so strong among ethnic minorities that they, more than whites, tend to deal with alcohol problems "in house" (mentioned for rural blacks by Benjamin & Benjamin, 1975), and discourage formal treatment. Support systems no doubt vary greatly within ethnic groups as well as among them, for example, by

2. For example, for blacks: Harper (1979), McAdoo (1980), and Vitols (1974); for Hispanics: Aviles-Roig (1973), Jimenez (1977—Puerto Ricans), Obeso and Bordatto (1979—Puerto Ricans), and Sanchez-Dirks (1978); for Indians: Leland (1976), but counteracted by an aversion to interfering in other people's business, resulting in a pattern of withdrawing from active intervention (Leland, 1978).

3. For example, for Chicanos: Alcocer (1975); for Puerto Ricans: Abad and Suarez (1975); for blacks: Strayer (1961) and Ziegler-Driscoll (1977).

class and urban versus rural residence (mentioned for blacks by Benjamin & Benjamin, 1975; Davis, 1975).

Since alcohol abuse is more common among men than women in all U.S. ethnic groups, it follows that indirect alcohol problems, such as coping with the effects of men's drinking (see review in Ablon, 1976), are faced by more women than direct problems stemming from their own alcohol abuse. However, this relative prevalence is not reflected in the proportions of attention given these two subjects in the literature. Most of the available discussions of female coping are frankly speculative. Only a few are empirically based. The majority deal with the effects of women's behavior on men's drinking only. Few also address the association between women's coping behavior and outcome for themselves and their families. All but one deal with whites only. The exception is a study of women in an Indian settlement by Leland (1975, 1982). Among these Indian women, avoidance and other passive strategies for dealing with male alcohol abuse are far more common than active ones, though the latter are associated with a better outcome both for the drinker and for the coper and her family. These passive avoidance tendencies are similar to those reported for white women (James & Goldman, 1971; Orford, Guthrie, Nicholls, Oppenheimer, Egert, & Hensmen, 1975; Schaffer, 1977), but are far more marked among Indian Colony women. The implications of these findings for Al-Anon advice to wives of alcoholics, which seems to discourage active intervention, are currently being analyzed by Leland.

SEX ROLES

The literature on ethnic-minority female drinkers contains three prominent themes pertinent to the relationship of sex roles to alcohol use and abuse: the double standard for female and male drunkenness (mentioned for Hispanics, blacks, Indians and whites),[4] the alleged "marianismo–machismo" dichotomy among Hispanics, and the claimed "matriarchy" among blacks.

The double standard refers to disproportionate disapproval of female over male alcohol abuse. If the double standard actually were strongest among Hispanics, as anecdotal data suggest, we would expect them to rank highest on the ratio of men to women reporting heavy drinking, and they do (Table 3-2). On the other hand, we might expect Hispanics to rank lowest on the ratio of men to women reporting social consequences of drinking, but they do not (Table 3-7). So the national data do not consistently support the notion of a stronger double standard among Hispanics than among whites or blacks. The California data are similarly equivocal (Tables 3-3, 3-4 and 3-6).

4. For Hispanics: Alcocer (1982), Johnson and Matre (1978), NIAAA (1978), and Sanchez-Dirks (1978); for whites: Clark (1964), Keil (1978), Knupfer (1964), and Morgan (1981); for blacks: Benjamin and Benjamin (1975), who find rural blacks more tolerant of female drinking than urban blacks, and Gaines (1976).

Protection of Hispanic female alcohol abusers may offset any tendency for the double standard to increase social consequences for them (Lopez-Lee, 1979). Accounts of Hispanic drinking often mention that women in these subcultures, more than others, are placed on a pedestal by their families, but are nevertheless markedly subordinate to their husbands who shelter and protect them (Abad & Suarez, 1975; NIAAA, 1978; Obeso & Bordatto, 1979; Sanchez-Dirks, 1978). This role has been labeled as "marianismo" (Abad & Suarez, 1975; Stevens, 1973), which implies, in addition to subordination, overidealization and elements of martyrdom.

How would such a Hispanic female role relate to drinking? Some authors imply that "marianismo" does shape drinking behavior (e.g., NIAAA, 1978; Obeso & Bordatto, 1979), but give little elaboration. Family protectiveness is said to deter acknowledgment of a drinking problem in Hispanic women and hence to discourage seeking help (Alcocer, 1982; Lopez-Lee, 1979; NIAAA, 1978).

The most explicit discussion of traditional Hispanic female sex roles and drinking (Abad & Suarez, 1975) explores the possible effects on men's drinking, rather than women's. The authors note that Hispanic mothers encourage dependence in boys by overindulging them, but expect "macho" behavior from men as adults; the resulting conflict could produce anxiety and consequent alcohol abuse. Conflict or no, many authors say that stringent requirements of the macho code (fearlessness, honor, charisma, leadership) could, either directly or indirectly, encourage male alcohol abuse (Abad & Suarez, 1975; Aviles-Roig, 1973; Dobkin-De-Rios & Feldman, 1977; Meyerson & Associates, 1975; Stevens, 1973) and discourage admitting there is a problem (Abad & Suarez, 1975); others say machismo actually includes elements (dignity, honor, responsibility) that tend to limit alcohol abuse (e.g., Alcocer, 1982; Madsen, 1964; Sanchez-Dirks, 1978; Trevino, 1975). Actually, the relationship, if any, between machismo and male drinking behavior is purely speculative so far (Alcocer, 1982). More importantly, we wonder what the effects of traditional "macho" and "marianismo" sex roles might be on female drinking.

Similarly, the alleged black matriarchy has been invoked as an explanation for alcohol abuse (Bailey, Haberman, & Alksne, 1965; Gaines, 1976; Strayer, 1961), plus a host of other black community pathologies (Moynihan, 1965). Disintegration of the black family makes female-headed households relatively prevalent. This is said to encourage alcohol abuse: in men, by the emasculation resulting from women's economic independence and superior authority; in women, because their male-like role subjects them to stress and eliminates familial constraints, encouraging them to drink like men (see Cahalan *et al.*, 1969; Gaines, 1976; Sterne, 1967; Strayer, 1974). Certainly, it is plausible that these conditions could encourage alcohol abuse by both sexes, but the validity of such an inference depends upon demonstrating that the conditions actually exist among blacks.

Census data do not support main elements of the supposed black matriarchy. Although the proportion of two-parent black families has decreased considerably since 1950, the difference is not accounted for by marital breakup, but by the never married. Black women do not enjoy an economic advantage over men; they are more often unemployed and earn less, despite equal (not superior) educational achievement.

McCray (1980) claims that the notion of the strong, self-sufficient black female, responsible for survival of the black family, is romanticized and no more true than the related myth of the domineering black female. She says the black man's role as provider and protector is underestimated. Leggon (1980) and Davis (1975) suggest that for black women, a career is not optional, but imposed. However, since their work is so clearly necessary to their family's stability, it is a source of pride rather than guilt, as alleged for whites. Hemmons (1980) points out that while white women have been trying to get out of the house, black women have been trying to get back in, but are thwarted by an economic system that is oppressive of black men.

Engram (1980) found that young black and white women with similar economic circumstances have very similar plans and cultural ideals, including the primacy of marital roles. The black females do not have stronger career orientations or weaker homemaking desires. Need, not preference, dictates that more black than white women will work at some time as adults. However, black female labor-market participation has been constant for 50 years while white females have been going to work in increasing numbers, narrowing the ethnic-group differences in these characteristics.

This and other evidence has led many authors to conclude that the black matriarchy and its underlying assumptions are myth. If so, there would seem to be little point in exploring its implications for black drinking, female or male. However, myths die hard, so a few more nails in the coffin provided by the comparative data presented here may be in order.

According to the 1979 national survey data (Clark & Midanik, 1981), heavy drinking tends to be more prevalent among both black and Hispanic female drinkers than among white female drinkers (Table 3-2). It might seem illogical to simultaneously blame heavy drinking on the dominance of the black woman and the subordination of the Hispanic woman, but either is a deviation from the more egalitarian middle ground.

Black female drinkers exhibit loss of control or alcohol dependence at about the same rate (11%) as whites (10%), while Hispanic rates are higher (16%) (Clark & Midanik, 1981). If both ethnic-minority groups actually exhibit sex-role deviations (black female dominance and Hispanic subordination) that influence drinking, we might expect both to outrank whites on this measure of the most severe alcohol abuse.

If independence of spouse is stronger in black women than white women and weaker in Hispanics, we might expect social consequences of drinking to be lower in black and higher in Hispanic women (Table 3-7). In actuality, in the 1979 national survey social consequences were higher in both groups of ethnic-minority women who drink than in whites. Of course it is possible, and even probable, that other factors would cloud any association between social consequences of drinking and independence of spouse.

Data on the individual social consequences measures in the California study are incomplete in many instances, but do provide some opportunities to examine relationships to ethnic-minority sex roles (Table 3-6). Black female drinkers report twice as many financial consequences of drinking as whites, as we would expect if black women were more economically independent of their husbands (no Hispanic data). On the other hand, problems with marriage and home life are equally prevalent among Hispanic and white female drinkers, contrary to our expectations if Hispanic women are, as alleged, less independent of their spouses.

Our indications that black support-system participation in NIAAA treatment programs is lowest of the four ethnic groups is in keeping with the idea of comparatively greater family disorganization in that group. However, the figures may merely reflect the relative failure of treatment programs to enlist black family support overall, rather than any actual weakness therein. In fact, we have cited many contrary anecdotal indications of strong family support among blacks.

To summarize, arguing backward from the dependent to the independent variables, ethnic-group rankings on our measures of drinking and its consequences do not consistently follow those we would expect if the alleged ethnic-group sex-role variations actually exist and influence drinking behavior. However, the proper sequence would be the opposite: test for the existence of sex-role differences first. And, even if empirical support did emerge for the black matriarchy and Hispanic "marianismo," their causal relationship to variations in drinking and its consequences would still remain to be demonstrated.

Although not available for adult women, some ethnic-group comparisons of sex roles and drinking have been reported for a national sample of high-school girls (Wilsnack & Wilsnack, 1978). Traditional femininity was measured by a 6-item scale. Ethnic-group rankings of the girls' desire for traditional femininity from strongest to weakest were: whites, Hispanics, blacks, and Indians (the Oriental ranking was unclear). Among whites, blacks, and Hispanics, rejection of traditional femininity was positively correlated with quantity-frequency of drinking and problem consequences, but was associated with symptomatic drinking only among whites and older blacks. On the other hand, neither the Oriental nor the Indian girls' drinking patterns correlated as predicted with traditional femininity: In the latter, the small coefficients were in the wrong direction. A 1978 follow-up (Wilsnack et al., 1981) showed a continuation of the 1974 propensity for girls to be less likely than boys to drink, drink heavily, get drunk, and get in trouble related to drinking. Nevertheless, there were indications that gender roles are becoming less polarized and are shifting away from orientations that are associated with alcohol abuse. However, these changes were much more widespread and pronounced among white than among black or Hispanic girls.

In summary, we know relatively little about the relationship between sex roles and white female drinking (Leland, 1981a), and even less for Hispanics and other ethnic minorities. Cultural variations in sex roles and in drinking behavior provide an opportunity, so far little exploited, to learn more about the association, if any, between sex roles and alcohol abuse.

ADULT TREATMENT

Blacks, Hispanics, and Indians were overrepresented in NIAAA-supported treatment programs in 1978 (Leland, 1981b), constituting nearly 3 times their proportions in the general population (2 times as many blacks, 3 times as many Hispanics, and over 300 times as many Indians). This overrepresentation is probably due to the special initiatives taken by NIAAA to provide services to minorities, rather than constituting evidence of higher rates of alcohol abuse in ethnic minorities than in the general population. On the other hand, minority groups are reportedly underrepresented in many treatment programs across the country.[5] Characteristics of the treatment program and catchment-area population are among the factors that influence the proportion of ethnic-minority participants.

Only about one-third of the minority NIAAA clients were served by special ethnic programs; the remainder were mainly (67%) sprinkled among the nonethnic programs and a few (2%) were assigned to the "wrong" ethnic program. The nonethnic programs were made up of 70% whites, 18% blacks, 9% Hispanics, and 3% Indians.

Women constituted 15% of the 1978 alcoholic intakes in all NIAAA treatment programs (Leland, 1981b). In all the special ethnic-group programs combined, female proportions (17%) were close to this average. Relative to women in the nonethnic (mostly white) programs, Hispanic women were underrepresented (.7 to 1), blacks were about equally represented (.9 to 1), and Indians were overrepresented (1.4 to 1). In comparison, there were 1.6 Hispanics and 1.1 black and Indian women for every white woman who needed treatment, based on relative ratios of loss of control or alcohol dependence in the 1979 national survey (Clark & Midanik, 1981) discussed earlier. The Hispanic female underrepresentation, though small, is noteworthy in view of the general overrepresentation of ethnic minorities (both sexes combined) in NIAAA treatment programs.

5. For example, among blacks: Argeriou (1978), Benjamin (1976), Lowe and Hodges (1972), Vitols (1974), and Westie and McBride (1979); among Hispanics: Alcocer (1982), Dobkin-De-Rios and Feldman (1977), Flores (1978), Obeso and Bordatto (1979), Rodriguez and Rodriguez (1977), and Westie and McBride (1979).

In non-NIAAA programs where ethnic underrepresentation occurred, lack of child care and fear of losing children are cited as factors inhibiting the participation of Hispanic (Obeso & Bordatto, 1979, Puerto Ricans) and Indian (Frogg, 1977) women. However, though not usually specific to women, by far the most common explanation for underrepresentation of ethnic minorities in treatment is the lack of programs tailored to specific cultural needs (including incorporation of folk medicine and practitioners), accompanied by claims, but rarely any data, that such culture-specific programs produce superior results.[6]

When NIAAA directly supported alcoholism treatment programs, it gathered, but did not routinely publish, data that would allow us to test the hypothesis that culture-specific programs are more successful than routine treatment for ethnic minorities. Although the notion seems plausible, it should be formally tested by comparing treatment outcome measures separately for ethnic-minority men and women treated in the special programs with those treated in the nonethnic programs. Although not broken down by sex, data are available on black clients in six NIAAA program categories in 1977 (NIAAA, 1979). Reductions in impairment between intake and follow-up were greater in the special black program (-50%) than in five nonethnic programs, which ranged from -48% to -31%.

Related to the matter of cultural relevance of program content and methods, there are many indications that ethnic groups vary in their responsiveness to Alcoholics Anonymous (AA). Unless it is drastically modified AA appears to be less popular and effective among the ethnic minorities than among whites. This is especially true among Indians (see summary in Leland, 1980) and blacks (e.g., Bourne, 1973; Scoles & Fine, 1979), but it applies also to Hispanics.[7] Data from the NIAAA special ethnic programs (again, no sex breakdowns) show that, in comparison to the

---

6. For example, for minorities in general: National Council on Alcoholism (1980); for blacks: Benjamin (1976), Davis (1975—not necessarily separate, but culturally relevant), Feagins (1974), Johnson and Garzon (1978), Lowe and Hodges (1972), NIAAA (n.d.), and Zimberg (1974); for Hispanics: Alcocer (1982—but not necessarily separate), Dieppa and Montiel (1979), Flores (1978), Gordon (1981), Jimenez (1977), Johnson and Garzon (1978), Lopez-Lee (1979), Obeso and Bordatto (1979), Rodriguez and Rodriguez (1977—Cuban), and Wanberg et al. (1978); for Indians: Shore (1974), Stevens (1981), Wanberg et al. (1978), and others reviewed in Leland (1980). Gender and ethnic stereotypes often are reported to negatively affect counselors' attitudes and hence outcome, and to influence differential diagnosis and disposition of cases; materials used in prevention, diagnosis, and treatment often contain sex and ethnic bias (evidence summarized in Lopez-Lee, 1979).

7. Indications of low Hispanic participation in Bill C. (1962) and Meyerson and Associates (1975). Lusero (1977) delineates within-group differences associated with differential success of AA affiliation in Chicano males. Lusero asserts that "a Chicano organized and oriented modality, even if it is patterned on such an Anglo entity as AA, would attract Chicanos," and puts particular emphasis on the need for Spanish speaking programs. Alcocer (1982) claims Hispanics are receptive to AA and its abstinence orientation.

nonethnic (mostly white) programs, referral to AA is more common in the Hispanic program, but less common in the Indian and black programs. Of course, relative rates of referral to AA reflect factors other than the desires of clients.

Where underrepresentation of ethnic groups in treatment does occur, differential treatment by law enforcement agencies has been blamed. Several studies report that police are likely to refer whites to treatment, but tend to send minorities to jail (for blacks see Hornstra & Udell, 1973; Lowe & Hodges, 1972; Vitols, 1974; for Indians, Leland, 1980, summarizes the evidence, which is contradictory). Although I have not encountered such an allegation concerning Hispanics, in the 1978 NIAAA programs they had the highest rate of referral from police and the courts (56%), while the black rate (39%) was about the same as the nonethnic program average (37%) and the Indian rate (19%) was far lower. Many factors other than law enforcement attitudes could influence these ethnic-group differences in law enforcement referral to treatment for alcohol abuse, for example, rural versus urban residence.

Ethnic-group differences in participation in treatment may in part reflect differences in follow-up retention rates, estimated here by calculating numbers of clients available for the NIAAA 180-day follow-up, as a percentage of the number of intakes (Leland, 1981b). These follow-up retention rates were above the nonethnic program average (10%) in the black (15%) and Hispanic (12%) programs, but below average in the Indian (7%) program. High black retention rates also have been reported in some non-NIAAA treatment programs (Vitols, 1974), but low rates occur in others (Lowe & Hodges, 1972; Ziegler-Driscoll, 1977). Although Hispanic women are underrepresented relative to white women in NIAAA treatment, their follow-up retention rate is higher, suggesting that the deficit is traceable to low contact rates rather than failure to retain contacts.

In the 1978 NIAAA programs, alcoholic intakes were slightly younger in the ethnic programs (35 years, average) than in the nonethnic programs (38 years), but the Indian program (33 years) accounted for most of the difference; the Hispanic program (36 years) was close to the nonethnic program average, while blacks (40 years) were above the average. However, in the absence of adjustment for ethnic-group differences in age composition of the national population, we can not conclude from these figures[8] that, for example, Indians develop alcohol problems at a younger age than the other groups. Age of presenting for treatment depends on many factors in addition to the age when alcohol abuse actually develops, such as relative willingness to acknowledge that a problem exists. On this topic, it often is pointed out that minority groups are less likely than whites to regard alcohol abuse as

8. Or from scattered claims that minorities present for treatment at a younger age (e.g., blacks: Hornstra & Udell, 1973; blacks and Hispanics: Westie & McBride, 1979).

an illness.[9] This difference is consistent with the reports of their under-representation in general-population programs where the medical model predominates.

In the 1978 NIAAA programs, treatment outcome was poorer in the ethnic programs combined (an impairment index reduction of 23%) than in the nonethnic programs (−30%). However, black program success was above average (−35%), while Hispanic (−26%) and Indian (−16%) programs were below. In the scattered programs reported in the literature, King (1982) found poorer follow-up rates and prognosis among blacks than whites, but better rates among black women than men. Strayer (1961) also found black women more motivated to sobriety than black men, and more motivated than whites of either sex as well. Improvement occurred in twice as many Nevada Indian women as men (Shore & von Fumetti, 1972). In Mexican-Americans, Dobkin-De-Rios and Feldman (1977) present well-documented evidence of poor treatment results, presumably in comparison to the general population, but unfortunately sex differences are not mentioned.

IMPLICATIONS FOR PREVENTION AND TREATMENT

The consequences of drinking appear to be more severe for ethnic-minority women than white women by wider margins than their relative heavy-drinking or alcohol-dependence rates in national surveys would predict. We need to find out why this occurs. Prevention of untoward results of drinking is as worthy a goal as prevention of the alcohol abuse itself. We suspect that culture-specific programs are necessary to attract minority women into treatment. A breakdown by sex and major ethnic groups of data routinely gathered by treatment programs would allow us to test this idea and should have a high priority on the research agenda. In addition, obser-vational studies to determine how programs are actually tailored to each ethnic group and the relative success of different methods are needed to shape prevention and treatment efforts. Ethnic-group rankings on prevalence measures for adults do not always agree with those for youth. Longitudinal data are needed to discover whether the differences are age-specific or portend change in female drinking behavior, including changes in relative standings of ethnic groups.

We need comparable observational and survey data on female drinking patterns and contexts for ethnic minorities and whites to test the validity of anecdotal accounts, such as claims that sex-segregated convivial group public drinking (mainly on weekends) is more prevalent in the ethnic

9. For example, for blacks: King (1982), National Clearinghouse on Alcohol Information (1977), and National Council on Alcoholism (1980); for Hispanics: Galan (1978) and Meyerson and Associates (1975); for Indians: Leland (1975) and Shore (1974).

minorities than in whites. If these are confirmed, what are the implications for prevention and treatment? Would more mixed-sex drinking increase female drinking relative to male, decrease male drinking relative to female, have some other effect or have no effect? Clark (1977) found a strong positive relationship between amount of drinking and tavern patronage in both men and women in San Francisco. If the same were true of ethnic minorities, would measures to encourage private drinking at the expense of public tend to moderate drinking in those groups?

Available data are insufficient to show whether the relatively low Indian and black support group participation in treatment reflects failure of programs to mobilize available support, as anecdotal claims suggest. If so, then it would be appropriate to discover the barriers to recruitment and retention of ethnic support systems in order to counteract them. Data breakdowns by sex are required to discover similarities and differences in support system patterns for women and men.

Sex roles, in the form of the double standard, the claimed Hispanic "marianismo–machismo" dichotomy, and the alleged black matriarchy, have been invoked to explain ethnic-group differences in alcohol use and abuse. Several measures failed to consistently show the ethnic-group rankings that would seem to follow logically if drinking behavior actually were being influenced by these factors. The first order of business is to discover the prevalence and within-group distributions of actual ethnic-group sex-role characteristics. (The three sex-role patterns explored here have been directly challenged as stereotypes and certainly do not exhaust the possibilities.) Only then would it make sense to explore the association between ethnic-minority sex roles and female drinking behavior. Very little is known so far about the relationship between sex roles and drinking—even less for minority women than for whites. Before we seek lessons for prevention and treatment in the realm of sex roles, we need a great deal more information.

Although ethnic minorities are said to be underrepresented in various treatment programs across the country, among women in the 1978 NIAAA programs, only Hispanics had lower participation rates than the average for the nonethnic, that is, mainly white, programs. We would like to know why NIAAA outreach efforts have been more successful with Indian and black women than with Hispanic women. We need to find out what special efforts have been tried and which have succeeded best, so that other programs could benefit from the NIAAA experience.

Treatment outcome was above average in black NIAAA programs, but below average in Hispanic and Indian programs. In this and many other instances, we need detailed program descriptions to flesh out the bare statistics gathered. Such descriptions may help explain variation among and within female ethnic groups as a source of guidance for both prevention and treatment.

Overall, we need a great deal more basic data about the drinking behavior of women of all ethnic groups, with particular attention to within-group variability, as a basis for more definitive suggestions for prevention and treatment.

ACKNOWLEDGMENT

Portions of this research were supported by National Institute on Alcohol Abuse and Alcoholism Grant 3 RO1 AAO3403.

REFERENCES

Abad, V., & Suarez, J. Cross-cultural aspects of alcoholism among Puerto Ricans. In *Proceedings of the 4th Annual Alcoholism Conference of the National Institute on Alcohol Abuse and Alcoholism* (DHEW Publ. No. ADM-76-284). Washington, D.C.: U.S. Government Printing Office, 1975.

Ablon, J. Family structure and behavior in alcoholism: A review of the literature. In B. Kissin & H. Begleiter (Eds.), *The biology of alcoholism* (Vol. 4: *Social aspects of alcoholism*). New York: Plenum, 1976.

Alcocer, A. M. *Chicano alcoholism.* Unpublished paper, California State University, Northridge, 1975.

Alcocer, A. M. Alcohol use and abuse among the Hispanic American population. In *Special population issues* (NIAAA Alcohol and Health Monograph No. 4, DHHS Publ. No. ADM-82-1193). Washington, D.C.: U.S. Government Printing Office, 1982.

Argeriou, M. Reaching problem-drinking blacks: The unheralded potential of the drinking driver programs. *International Journal of the Addictions*, 1978, *13*(3), 433–459.

Aviles-Roig, C. A. Aspectos socioculturales del problema de alcoholismo en Puerto Rico. In E. Tongue, R. T. Lambo, & B. Blair (Eds.), *Report of Proceedings of the International Conference on Alcoholism and Drug Abuse*, San Juan, Puerto Rico, November 1973.

Bacon, M. Alcohol use in tribal societies. In B. Kissin & H. Begleiter (Eds.), *The biology of alcoholism* (Vol. 4: *Social aspects of alcoholism*). New York: Plenum, 1976.

Bailey, M. B., Haberman, P. W., & Alksne, H. The epidemiology of alcoholism in an urban residential area. *Quarterly Journal of Studies on Alcohol*, 1965, *26*, 19–40.

Benjamin, R. Rural black folk and alcohol. In F. D. Harper (Ed.), *Alcohol abuse and black America.* Alexandria, Va.: Douglass Publishers, 1976.

Benjamin, R., & Benjamin, M. Perceptions and management of alcohol-related problems by rural and urban black Mississippians. *Mississippi Geographer*, 1975, *3*, 45–53.

Bill C. The growth and effectiveness of Alcoholics Anonymous in a southwestern city, 1945–1962. *Quarterly Journal of Studies on Alcohol*, 1962, *26*, 279–284.

Bourne, P. G. Alcoholism in the urban Negro population. In P. G. Bourne & R. Fox (Eds.), *Alcoholism; Progress in research and treatment.* New York: Academic, 1973.

Burns, M., Daily, J. M., & Moskowitz, H. *Drinking practices and problems of urban American Indians in Los Angeles* (Preliminary report). Santa Monica Calif.: Planning Analysis and Research Institute, 1974.

Cahalan, D. *Ethnoreligious group differences, 1974 drinking survey.* (Supplement to D. Cahalan et al., *Alcohol problems and their prevention: Public attitudes in California*). Berkeley,

Calif.: Social Research Group, School of Public Health, University of California, Berkeley, 1976.

Cahalan, D., Cisin, I. H., & Crossley, H. M. *American drinking practices: A national study of drinking behavior and attitudes* (Monograph No. 6). New Brunswick, N.J.: Rutgers Center of Alcohol Studies, 1969.

Clark, W. B. *Sex roles and alcohol beverage usage* (Working paper No. 16). Berkeley, Calif.: Social Research Group, School of Public Health, University of California, Berkeley, 1964.

Clark, W. B. *Contextual and situational variables in drinking behavior* (Report to the National Institute on Alcohol Abuse and Alcoholism, Contract No. ADM 281 76 0027). Berkeley, Calif.: Social Research Group, School of Public Health, University of California, Berkeley, 1977.

Clark, W. B., Personal communication, 1981.

Clark, W. B., & Midanik, L. *Alcohol use and alcohol problems among U.S. adults: Results of the 1979 survey* (Working draft). Berkeley, Calif.: Social Research Group, School of Public Health, University of California at Berkeley, 1981.

Davis, F. T., Jr. *Effective delivery of services to black alcoholics.* Washington, D.C.: Roy Littlejohn, 1975.

Dieppa, I., & Montiel, M. Hispanic families: An exploration. In M. Montiel (Ed.), *Hispanic families: Critical issues for policy and programs in human services* (Vols. 1–8). Washington, D.C.: National Coalition of Hispanic Mental Health and Human Services Organizations, 1979.

Dobkin-De-Rios, M., & Feldman, D. J. Southern California Mexican-American drinking patterns: Some preliminary observations. *Journal of Psychedelic Drugs*, 1977, *9*, 151–158.

Engram, E. Role transition in early adulthood: Orientation of young black women. In L. F. Rodgers-Rose (Ed.), *The black woman.* Beverly Hills, Calif.: Sage Publications, 1980.

Everett, M. W., Waddell, J. P., & Heath, D. B. *Cross cultural approaches to the study of alcohol: An interdisciplinary approach.* The Hague, Netherlands: Mouton, 1976.

Feagins, J. L. *A descriptive study of variance in sources of referral pathways to treatment for black and non-black alcoholics.* Doctoral dissertation, University of Pittsburgh, 1974. (University Microfilms No. 75-4089)

Flores, J. L. The utilization of a community mental health service by Mexican Americans. *International Journal of Social Psychiatry*, 1978, *24*, 271–275.

Frogg, W. Women unite to combat alcoholism: An exchange of ideas. In The Do It Now Foundation and the International Council on Alcohol and Addictions, *Alcohol: Use and abuse* (Vol. 1): *Proceedings of the First International Action Conference on Substance Abuse.* Phoenix, Ariz.: Do It Now Foundation, 1977.

Gaines, J. J. Alcohol and the black woman. In F. D. Harper (Ed.), *Alcohol abuse and black America.* Alexandria, Va.: Douglass Publishers, 1976. (NCA1027420)

Galan, F. J. *Alcohol use among Chicanos and Anglos: A cross cultural study.* Doctoral dissertation, Brandeis University, 1978. (University Microfilms No. 78-21699)

Gordon, A. J. The cultural context of drinking and indigenous therapy for alcohol problems in three migrant Hispanic cultures; an ethnographic report. *Journal of Studies on Alcohol*, 1981, Suppl. 9, 217–240.

Harper, F. D. (Ed.). *Alcohol abuse and black America.* Alexandria, Va.: Douglass Publishers, 1976. (a)

Harper, F. D. Etiology: Why do blacks drink? In F. D. Harper (Ed.), *Alcohol abuse and black America.* Alexandria, Va.: Douglass Publishers, 1976. (b)

Harper, F. D. *Alcoholism treatment and black Americans* (DHEW Publ. No. ADM-79-853). Rockville, Md.: National Clearinghouse for Alcohol Information, 1979.

Hemmons, W. M. The women's liberation movement: Understanding black women's attitudes. In L. F. Rodgers-Rose (Ed.), *The black woman.* Beverly Hills, Calif.: Sage Publications, 1980.

Hornstra, R. K., & Udell, B. Psychiatric services and alcoholics. *Missouri Medicine*, 1973, *70*, 103–107.

James, J. E., & Goldman, M. Behavior trends of wives of alcoholics. *Quarterly Journal of Studies on Alcohol*, 1971, *32*, 373–381.

Jessor, R., Graves, T. D., Hanson, R. C., & Jessor, S. L. *Society, personality and deviant behavior: A study of a tri-ethnic community.* New York: Holt, Rinehart & Winston, 1968.

Jimenez, D. R. *A comparative analysis of the support systems of white and Puerto Rican clients in drug treatment programs.* Doctoral dissertation, Brandeis University, 1977. (University Microfilms No. 77-15271)

Johnson, L. V., & Matre, M. Anomie and alcohol use: Drinking patterns in Mexican American and Anglo neighborhoods. *Journal of Studies on Alcohol*, 1978, *39*, 894–909.

Johnson, S. Cirrhosis mortality among American Indian women: Rates and ratios, 1975 and 1976. In M. Galanter (Ed.), *Currents in alcoholism* (Vol. 7). New York: Grune & Stratton, 1980.

Johnson, S., & Garzon, S. R. Alcoholism and women. *American Journal of Drug and Alcohol Abuse*, 1978, *5*(1), 107–122.

Keil, T. J. Sex role variations and women's drinking: Results from a household survey in Pennsylvania. *Journal of Studies on Alcohol*, 1978, *39*, 859–868.

King, L. M. Alcoholism: Studies regarding black Americans: 1977–1980. In *Special population issues* (NIAAA Alcohol and Health Monograph No. 4., DHHS Publ. No. ADM-82-1193). Washington, D.C.: U.S. Government Printing Office, 1982.

Knupfer, G. Female drinking patterns. In *Selected papers presented at the Fifteenth Annual Meeting of the North American Association of Alcoholism Programs.* Washington, D.C.: North American Association of Alcohol Programs, 1964.

Leggon, C. B. Black female professionals: Dilemmas and contradictions of status. In L. F. Rodgers-Rose (Ed.), *The black woman.* Beverly Hills, Calif.: Sage Publications, 1980.

Leland, J. *Drinking styles in an Indian settlement: A numerical folk taxonomy.* Doctoral dissertation, University of California, Irvine, 1975. (University Microfilms 76-13876)

Leland, J. *Firewater myths: Indian drinking and alcohol addiction* (Monograph No. 11). New Brunswick, N.J.: Rutgers Center of Alcohol Studies, 1976.

Leland, J. Women and alcohol in an Indian settlement. *Medical Anthropology*, 1978, *2*(4), 85–119.

Leland, J. Forward and Native American alcohol use: A review of the literature. In P. Mail & D. McDonald (Eds.), *Tulapai to Tokay: A bibliography of alcohol use and abuse among Native Americans of North America.* New Haven, Conn.: Human Relations Area Files, Yale University, 1980.

Leland, J. Sex roles, family organization and alcohol abuse. In J. Orford & J. Harwin (Eds.), *Alcohol and the family.* London: Croom Helm, 1981. (a)

Leland, J. *NIAAA's ethnic alcohol treatment programs: Some comparisons.* Unpublished manuscript, 1981. (b)

Leland, J. The context of Native American drinking: What we know so far. In T. Harford (Ed.), *Social drinking contexts* (National Institute on Alcohol Abuse and Alcoholism Research Monograph 7, U.S. Department of Health and Human Services Publication No. ADM-81-1097). Washington, D.C.: U.S. Government Printing Office, 1981. (c)

Leland, J. *Alcohol in the lives of some Indian women* (Terminal Progress Report, Grant No. 5 ROI AA03403-03). Rockville, Md.: National Institute on Alcohol Abuse and Alcoholism, 1982.

Levy, J. E., & Kunitz, S. J. *Indian drinking: Navajo practices and Anglo-American theories.* New York: Wiley, 1974.

Lopez-Lee, D. Alcoholism among third world women: Research and treatment. In V. Burtle (Ed.), *Women who drink: Alcoholic experience and psychotherapy.* Springfield, Ill.: Charles C. Thomas, 1979.

Lowe, G. D., & Hodges, H. E. Race and the treatment of alcoholism in a southern state. *Social Problems*, 1972, *20*, 240–252.

Lusero, G. T. *Alcoholics Anonymous in a Chicano community: An analysis of affiliation and transferability.* Doctoral dissertation, Brandeis University, 1977. (University Microfilms No. 77-25045)

Madsen, W. The alcoholic agringado. *American Anthropologist*, 1964, *66*, 355–361.

Malin, H. J., Archer, L. D., & Munch, N. E. *A national surveillance system for alcoholism and alcohol abuse.* Paper presented at the 32nd International Congress on Alcoholism and Drug Dependence, Warsaw, Poland, September 3–8, 1978. (Also Alcohol Epidemiologic Data System Working paper No. 8, Rockville, Md.: 1978).

McAdoo, H. P. Black mothers and the extended family support network. In L. F. Rodgers-Rose (Ed.), *The black woman.* Beverly Hills, Calif.: Sage Publications, 1980.

McCray, C. A. The black woman and family roles. In L. F. Rodgers-Rose (Ed.), *The black woman.* Beverly Hills, Calif.: Sage Publications, 1980.

Meyerson, B., and Associates. *Alcohol and alcoholism in Santa Cruz County, San Francisco.* Unpublished paper, 1975.

Morgan, P. *Alcohol, disinhibition and domination: A conceptual analysis.* Paper presented at a conference on Alcohol and Disinhibition. Berkeley, Calif.: Social Research Group, School of Public Health, University of California, Berkeley, 1981.

Moynihan, D. *The Negro family: The case for national action.* Washington, D.C.: U.S. Department of Labor, 1965.

National Clearinghouse on Alcohol Information. *The unseen crisis, blacks and alcohol.* Washington, D.C.: U.S. Government Printing Office, 1977.

National Council on Alcoholism. *A position paper on alcoholism and racial minorities, developed by the Minority Affairs Committee.* Unpublished manuscript, 1980.

National Institute on Alcohol Abuse and Alcoholism. Alcohol and blacks. In *Alcohol topics in brief.* Rockville, Md.: National Institute on Alcohol Abuse and Alcoholism, n.d.

National Institute on Alcohol Abuse and Alcoholism. Alcohol and the Chicano. In *Alcohol topics in brief.* Rockville, Md.: National Institute on Alcohol Abuse and Alcoholism, 1978.

National Institute on Alcohol Abuse and Alcoholism. *Black clients treated in NIAAA funded categorical programs, calendar year 1977.* Rockville, Md.: Program Analysis and Evaluation Branch, National Institute on Alcohol Abuse and Alcoholism, 1979. (NCAI 38708)

Obeso, P., & Bordatto, O. Cultural implications in treating the Puerto Rican female. *American Journal of Drug and Alcohol Abuse*, 1979, *6*(3), 337–344.

Orford, J., Guthrie, S., Nicholls, P., Oppenheimer, E., Egert, S., & Hensman, C. Self-reported coping behavior of wives of alcoholics and its association with drinking outcome. *Journal of Studies on Alcohol*, 1975, *36*(9), 1254–1267.

Rachal, J. V., Williams, J. R., Brehm, M. L., Cavanaugh, B., Moore, R. P., & Eckerman, W. C. *A national study of adolescent drinking behavior, attitudes and correlates* (Final report to the National Institute on Alcohol Abuse and Alcoholism, Contract No. HSM42-73-80). (NTIS NO. PB-246-002; NIAAA/NCALI-75/27)

Rimmer, J., Pitts, F. N., Jr., Reich, T., & Winokur, G. Alcoholism. II. Sex, socioeconomic status and race in two hospitalized samples. *Quarterly Journal of Studies on Alcohol*, 1971, *32*, 942–952.

Rodriguez, A. M., & Rodriguez, L. J. Planning and delivering alcoholism services to the Cubans in America. In R. T. Trotter, 2d, & J. A. Chaviar (Eds.), *El uso de alcohol: A resources book for Spanish speaking communities.* Atlanta, Ga.: Southern Area Alcohol Education and Training Program, 1977.

Sanchez-Dirks, R. D. *Hispanic drinking practices: A comparative study of Hispanic and Anglo adolescent drinking patterns.* Doctoral dissertation, New York University, 1978. (University Microfilms No. 78-18456)

Santangelo, N., & McCartney, D. *Pooled report: A tri-community study of adolescent drinking.* (*Contract No. ADM 281-77-0020*). Rockville, Md.: National Institute on Alcohol Abuse and Alcoholism, Office of Program Policy and Planning, 1981.

Schaffer, J. B. *The relationship between degree of sobriety in male alcoholics and coping styles used by their wives.* Doctoral dissertation, University of North Dakota, 1977. (University Microfilms No. 78-10319)

Scoles, P. E., & Fine, E. W. Introduction to the drinking driver. In M. Galanter (Ed.), *Currents in alcoholism* (Vol. 6: *Treatment and rehabilitation and epidemiology*). New York: Grune & Stratton, 1979.

Shannon, L., & Shannon, M. *Minority migrants in the urban community: Mexican-American and Negro adjustment to industrial society.* Beverly Hills, Calif.: Sage Publications, 1973.

Shore, J. H. Psychiatric epidemiology among American Indians. *Psychiatric Annals*, 1974, *4*(11), 56–66.

Shore, J. H., & von Fumetti, B. Three alcohol programs for American Indians. *American Journal of Psychiatry*, 1972, *128*(11), 1450–1454.

Sterne, M. W. Drinking patterns and alcoholism among American Negroes. In D. J. Pittman (Ed.), *Alcoholism*. New York: Harper & Row, 1967.

Sterne, M. W., & Pittman, D. J. *Drinking patterns in the ghetto*. St. Louis, Mo.: Social Science Institute, Washington University, 1972.

Sterne, M. W., & Pittman, D. J. Alcohol abuse and the black family. In F. D. Harper (Ed.), *Alcohol abuse and black America*. Alexandria, Va.: Douglass Publishers, 1976.

Stevens, E. Machismo and marianismo. *Society*, 1973, *3*(6), 57–63.

Stevens, S. M. Alcohol and world view; a study of Passamaquoddy alcohol use. *Journal of Studies on Alcohol*, 1981, Suppl. No. 9, 122–142.

Strayer, R. A study of the Negro alcoholic. *Quarterly Journal of Studies on Alcohol*, 1961, *22*, 111–123.

Strayer, R. Study of the Negro Alcoholic. In A. Shiloh & I. C. Selavan (Eds.), *Ethnic groups of America: Their morbidity, mortality and behavior disorders* (Vol. 2: *The blacks*). Springfield, Ill.: Charles C Thomas, 1974.

Trevino, M. Machismo alcoholism: Mexican-American machismo drinking. In M. E. Chafetz (Ed.), *Research, treatment and prevention* (Proceedings of the Fourth Annual Alcoholism Conference of the National Institute on Alcohol Abuse and Alcoholism: DHEW Publ. No. ADM 76-284). Rockville, Md.: National Institute on Alcohol Abuse and Alcoholism, 1975.

Vitols, M. M. Culture patterns of drinking in Negro and white alcoholics. In A. Shiloh & I. C. Selavan (Eds.), *Ethnic groups of America: Their morbidity, mortality and behavior disorders* (Vol. 2: *The blacks*). Springfield, Ill.: Charles C Thomas, 1974.

Walker, P. S., Walker, R. D., & Robinson, S. *Female Indian alcoholics: A descriptive comparison of detoxification patients.* Paper presented to the 106th annual meeting of the American Public Health Association, Los Angeles, Calif., October 17, 1978.

Wanberg, K., Lewis, R., & Foster, F. M. Alcoholism and ethnicity: A comparative study of alcohol use patterns across ethnic groups. *International Journal of the Addictions*, 1978, *13*, 1245–1262.

Weibel, J. C. A place for everything and everything in its place: Environmental influences on Indian drinking patterns. In T. Harford (Ed.), *Social drinking contexts* (National Institute on Alcohol Abuse and Alcoholism Research Monograph 7). Washington, D.C.: U.S. Government Printing Office, 1981.

Westie, K., & McBride, D. C. The effects of ethnicity, age and sex upon processing through an emergency alcohol health care delivery system. *British Journal of Addiction*, 1979, *74*, 21–29.

Whittaker, J. O. *Alcohol and the Standing Rock Sioux Tribe: A twenty year follow-up study.* Unpublished manuscript, 1980.

Wilsnack, R. W., Thompson, K. M., & Wilsnack, S. C. *Effects of gender role orientations on* adolescent drinking: Patterns over time. Paper presented at the Annual Meeting of the Society for the Study of Social Problems, Toronto Ontario, August 1981.

Wilsnack, R. W., & Wilsnack, S. C. Sex roles and drinking among adolescent girls. *Journal of Studies on Alcohol*, 1978, *39*, 1855–1874.

Ziegler-Driscoll, G. Family research study at Eagleville Hospital and Rehabilitation Center. *Family Process*, 1977, *16*, 175–189.

Zimburg, S. Evaluation of alcoholism treatment in Harlem. *Quarterly Journal of Studies on Alcohol*, 1974, *35*, 550–557.

4

Multiple Substance Abuse among Women with Alcohol-Related Problems

DAVID D. CELENTANO
The Johns Hopkins University

DAVID V. MCQUEEN
University of Edinburgh

INTRODUCTION

At the end of the 1970s we argued in a review of the literature on substance abuse by women that "little substantive knowledge of the epidemiology of substance abuse among women exists" (Celentano, McQueen, & Chee, 1980). More recently we reviewed the literature on social factors in the etiology of multiple disease outcomes, using the case of blood pressure and alcohol consumption patterns (McQueen & Celentano, 1982) and identifying women as a population requiring further study. We believe that a new approach to substance abuse problems is emerging in the 1980s, namely that there is now a growing appreciation of the fact that multiple, chronic, behaviorally related illnesses and pathophysiological outcomes are often inextricably bound together in the same individual (McQueen & Siegrist, 1982). The multivariate nature of social processes has long been recognized in the methodologies of social scientists, especially with respect to the "independent" variables in a cause–effect equation. However, this phenomenon has often been overlooked in the realm of disease outcomes; that is, it has too often been the case that only a single disease outcome is viewed as a result of many causes. Now we recognize that to talk simply of a woman with a drinking problem is to overlook the role of related and complicating behavioral processes in the individual.

Therefore, this review focuses upon studies that view alcohol-related problems of women within the context of related deleterious outcomes, chiefly multiple drug use. This focus mandates that the chapter have two chief components: (1) a review of the state of the art of current research dealing with multiple substance abuse among adult, problem-drinking women; and (2) a discussion of the issues that should guide research in this area.

BASIC DEFINITIONS

Inherent in such a presentation are definitional considerations. Definitional problems have plagued alcohol research for some time, such that many terms and euphemisms have developed for alcohol-related problems, ranging from "alcoholism" to "drinking problems." There is no consensus about an adequate single label for categorizing alcohol-related problems. It has long been observed that how these problems are defined is strongly related to the vocation of the definer. In fact, there are probably as many definitions as there are definers (Celentano & McQueen, 1978b). Nonetheless, we think it of value to introduce some definitional distinctions here with respect to the area of substance abuse.

Our scope of interest in this chapter is the problem of multiple substance abuse among adult problem-drinking women. We are mainly concerned with those substance-abuse behaviors that lead to chronic pathophysiological outcomes of public-health significance. With this in mind, our bias is to consider multiple substance use and abuse in adolescent women only when there is evidence that it will lead to chronic drug-taking behavior. In general, we think it is premature to concern ourselves with transitory periods of situational abuse during a woman's lifetime, not because these are unimportant for the affected individual—they may even be of clinical significance— but rather because they are less significant for the society as a whole. Therefore, transitional, situational disturbances that do not lead to habitual multiple substance abuse will not be considered in the present review.

Definitions of Substance Abuse

We define multiple substance use as the *habitual* use of two or more mind-state-altering (psychoactive) products, either at the same time or in such a way that the products interact with each other in the individual user. That is, there must be a pattern of regular use of two or more substances, either together or alternately, rather than discontinuation of one in order to use the other. It follows that multiple substance abuse entails usage in which one or more of the products results in deleterious effects for the user. If one goes beyond this rather simplistic definition, one is soon in a quagmire of logical and definitional problems. Once we have more than two mind-state-altering products in use by an individual, the combinations and permutations of these products become very complex, especially when considered in light of the age, weight, and physiological status of the affected individual.

We suggest as a model the following classification schema for multiple substance abuse:

Term	*Definition*
Simple	Two products used producing an abuse pattern in the individual—for example, alcohol and one other drug (a controlled substance), alcohol and one other drug (an uncontrolled substance), two drugs with independent pharmacological effects.
Complex	Two or more products used habitually with a daily pattern of simultaneous use making multiple pharmacological interaction inevitable—for example, daily habitual use of tranquilizers and alcohol, use of several drugs in combination with drinking.

We have purposely created an operationally defined dichotomy, which recognizes that all multiple substance abuse lies on a continuum ranging from "simple" to "complex." Such a continuum should have many components. For example, at the very least one should consider the quantity, frequency, and variability of substance consumption. This would normally lead the investigator to consider in detail the patterns and distribution of multiple substance abuse in individuals and groups. Further, the individual may vacillate markedly from simple to complex usage during a given period of observation. A solid, well-researched picture of such usage patterns does not, to our knowledge, exist in the currently available literature. It is our observation that most of the empirically based epidemiological research has concerned itself with what we have termed simple abuse. On the other hand there exists much anecdotal evidence about the complex pattern. Indeed, the experience of clinicians and social workers who are dealing on a day-to-day basis with problems associated with multiple substance abuse would suggest that this is a rich area for systematic research.

Definitional considerations also relate to what we think are some basic research questions in this field. Figure 4-1 suggests a basic consideration in determining the nature and magnitude of patterns of multiple substance use and abuse. The vertical axis represents the proportion of women in the population engaging in multiple substance use, and the horizontal axis represents our underlying continuum of complexity. Such a figure immediately suggests two interesting aspects. First, we do not have good epidemiological evidence that would provide a consistently adequate description of the proportion of users. Therefore, secondly, we cannot accurately plot curve "a." We have shown curve "a" here as linear, but there is no sound reason to believe that it is not an "L"-shaped curve, similar to curve "b." To ascertain

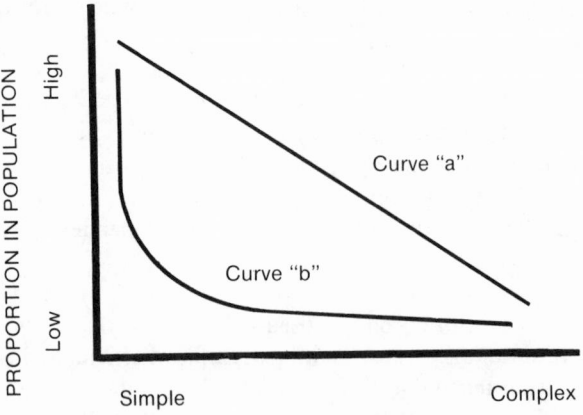

PATTERN OF MULTIPLE SUBSTANCE ABUSE

FIGURE 4-1. Hypothetical relationship between complexity of multiple substance abuse and magnitude of the problem.

the form of the relationship, some basic epidemiological evidence needs to be collected on a population basis. Once such a curve were adequately mapped, we would be able to discuss the seriousness of multiple substance abuse in the overall picture of women's health.

A final definitional consideration is that we do not consider all types of compulsive behavioral abuses involving substances as relevant to this discussion. It may certainly be argued that substance abuse behaviors such as smoking, eating disorders, and obesity are theoretically linked to the substances with which we are concerned here. The difficulty, at this early stage of research, is that we only compound our tasks if we include all of the logical extensions of the construct of substance abuse. First, we need to use limited operational definitions and define the extent of combined use of specific substances. Then, we can more effectively deal with the logical extensions of the multiple substance abuse problem.

MEASUREMENT AND CONCEPTUAL ISSUES

In approaching a discussion of multiple drug use by women with drinking problems, a number of measurement and conceptual issues are immediately apparent. Chief among these is the question of how germane the definitions and labels are to women. It is widely recognized that men constitute the greater portion of the drug abusing population; hence it has been argued that both the definitions of multiple drug abuse (or alcoholism and drug use), addiction, and substance abuse, and also the measures for estimating their prevalence, are severely biased and may not be reflective of the types of problems encountered by women (Celentano *et al.*, 1980). If the definitions themselves focus upon outcomes or behaviors more characteristic of men, how germane are these labels for women? In addition, evidence concerning drug abuse by female problem drinkers in the general population is virtually nonexistent. What is found instead is literature of two types: empirical evidence on drug abuse by women in treatment for alcoholism (or alcohol problems among female narcotics addicts) and anecdotal evidence on licit (prescribed) use of drugs by women who *may* be problem drinkers. While we will draw upon the models or conclusions from these research areas, they will not be the major focus of this review, for it is argued that just such approaches cause confusion concerning the evidence and perpetuate inappropriate paradigms for women. Therefore, the focus will be upon enumerating the evidence for multiple drug use among women who are drinkers, focusing where possible upon those who are defined as having drinking problems.

Biases in Reports of Women's Drinking

There is little agreement on what constitutes a case of problem drinking (Siegler, Osmond, & Newell, 1968). The situation is even more difficult when the population of concern is limited to women. Here, the problem is confounded by numerous biases that are attributable to a number of sources, including gender-differentiated drinking norms, reporting error, and biases in survey measures of drinking problems.

The overall prevalence of problem drinking among women has been assumed to be underestimated because of female "hidden drinking." There is ample anecdotal evidence (Badiet, 1976; Gomberg, 1976; Lisansky, 1958; Rubington, 1972) that stigma is of major relevance to female heavy drinking; hence, hiding the problem minimizes the stigma and allows the female drinker to maintain social appearances. The social norm of abstinence or light drinking for women is powerful in the United States; drunkenness in women can not easily be tolerated, it is asserted, due to women's special roles as guardians of social virtues and socializers of children (Curlee, 1970; Senseman, 1966). If these social norms influence society's (and women's own) ability to recognize female problem drinkers, then the published rates of problem drinking among women are probably gross underestimates.

Several social processes may contribute to the undercounting. There are numerous opportunities for a woman's heavy drinking to be concealed or denied, and it is clear that women as a group are more sheltered from the consequences of their abusive drinking than men (Fraser, 1973; Johnson, DeVries, & Houghton, 1965; Senseman, 1966). Indeed, Lindbeck (1972) suggested that spouses may be the individuals most apt to deny their wives' drinking problems.

It has been argued (Celentano *et al.*, 1980) that one of the major sources of bias in estimating women's rates of problem drinking is that the majority of survey research instruments are geared toward men. For example, the Mulford and Miller (1960a, 1960b) scales of drinking problems, which were the models from which numerous other scales were derived, are directed at enumerating consequences of alcohol consumption that are not relevant, for the most part, for women. Rates of arrest, driving while intoxicated (DWI) experiences, problems with employer, and family financial problems may not be experienced very often by women, even those with high levels of alcohol intake. Indeed, using such a scale, Celentano and McQueen (1978a) found that only .6% of the women in their random sample reported two or more of these problems, whereas 14% were identified as heavy drinkers. Few studies have included questions designed to evaluate consequences of drinking that might be experienced by women; McQueen and Celentano (1982) have recently developed several measures that may fill this void.

Measurement Issues in Drug Use Reporting

As with alcohol abuse, a number of measurement and conceptual issues are involved in acertaining the presence and extent of the abuse of licit and illicit drugs. Since many of the drugs abused by women are illicit or represent nonmedical use of prescription drugs, additional problems are presented, especially with respect to self-reported use and abuse.

While there appears to be some consensus within the alcohol abuse field on what constitutes excessive or abusive alcohol intake, based either upon a measure of quantity–frequency–variability (Q-F-V) of intake or upon associated problems (although cutting points are still subject to considerable debate), in drug abuse research there is no such agreement. Indeed, the National Commission on Marihuana and Drug Abuse (NCMDA, 1973) identified four major classifications of drug abuse commonly used in the field, including: (1) "use" of drugs; (2) "nonmedical" drug use (of psychoactive prescription drugs); (3) "excess" drug use (which was left undefined); and (4) substances which are "addictive." The NCMDA noted that this diversity in definitions has lead to considerable confusion, even among experts, and that the conceptual and policy problems engendered by such usage are detrimental to the field.

A number of alternative concepts of drug abuse have been championed. Smart (1974) suggests that the concept of drug abuse is meaningless, since the pharmacologic effects of abused drugs vary so widely that considering drugs as a single class of abused substances makes little epidemiologic sense. While he is correct from a pathophysiological perspective, such a perspective ignores the broader social meaning of drug abuse. Hence, the NCMDA (1973) suggested that drug abuse generically should be considered as a social problem (as distinct from its medical sequelae), since abuse can be understood most easily from a social normative perspective.

Balter's (1974) definition of drug abuse perhaps most clearly lays out the various conceptual and methodological problems to be addressed. He distinguishes between immediate consequences of use and later implications of abuse. In general, he takes a "short-term" approach, emphasizing the effects of substances upon the central nervous system that, when used in excessive amounts on one occasion or repeatedly, lead to "dependency," mental or personality disturbances, impairment in social functioning, interference in social or personality development, or death. This definition comes quite close to an earlier definition of alcoholism promulgated by the World Health Organization (WHO, 1952).

Multiple Substance Abuse

Morrissey (1981) has recently discussed the general measurement problems that emerge when the term "drug abuse" refers to the use and abuse of multiple drugs, each with its own characteristic pharmacologic action. Indeed, while there is debate concerning generic concepts such as "abuse," "habituation," and "addiction" (Celentano et al., 1980; NCMDA, 1973; Smart, 1974), there is also no agreement as to the definitions and meanings of terms such as "multiple drug abuse" or "polydrug abuse." Sample (1977) defines "polydrug abuse" as "the use of more than one drug, excluding heroin, which are used simultaneously and with a frequency of use of at least once per month" (p. 19). Morrissey (1981) considers this to be a "restrictive" definition (p. 312); to the alcohol researcher, it appears rather flaccid at best. Kaufman (1976) suggests an even looser definition: "Multidrug abuse is the non-medical abuse of more than one drug" (p. 280). Kaufman considers the concept of abuse not as use, but rather in terms of the consequences of use. As Morrissey (1981) suggests, "If such a definition is to be ultimately theoretically meaningful and empirically applicable, one would assume there to be a relationship between observable consequences of use and measures of drug intake" (p. 312).

A number of approaches have been used to measure multiple drug use and abuse. Single, Kandel, and Faust (1974) developed scales for classes of substances. Others have looked at the uses and meanings of drugs (Ferguson, 1974; Gunderson, Russell, & Nail, 1973), and some have considered merely the number and types of drugs used over some distinct period of time (Dodson, 1971; Whitehead, 1974). Classification schemes vary considerably; Morrissey (1981) points to schema as diverse as using the same frequency cutting points for tobacco, alcohol, and medicine (e.g., Hemminki, 1974) to those using the same criteria for marijuana, hallucinogens, and narcotics (e.g., Galli, 1974). Supposedly, the differing pharmacologic actions of these substances and the different short-term consequences of use should lead to differential weighting or frequency counting.

One distinction between the measurement of drug use and abuse and of alcohol use is that many more dimensions of drug use are often considered simultaneously. For example, in alcohol research the quantity, frequency, and variability of alcohol intake are often measured separately and then combined to form one index, such as the Q-F-V or Volume-Variability (V-V) indices of Cahalan, Cisin, and Crossley (1969). In contrast, the Drug Involvement Scale of Gunderson *et al.* (1973) includes such diverse elements as severity of effects, frequency of use, method of administration, and age at first use. Other systems for scoring overall drug use include those of Hughes, Schaps, and Sanders (1973) and Single *et al.* (1974). The scale by Hughes *et al.* (1973) is of interest because it includes the following categories in a continuum: non-users, alcohol users, marijuana users, users of one drug (amphetamines, barbiturates, solvents, and psychedelics), users of any two illicit drugs, users of three illicit drugs, and narcotics users. Each step in the continuum includes the drug(s) mentioned in the former steps. Hence, alcohol use is the first step in the continuum, an ordering with which some alcohol researchers might disagree. While these scales appear to acknowledge more adequately the complexity of multiple drug use, the theory underlying them is often abstruse. Despite the existence of measurement problems, Morrissey (1981) points out that "even though fairly sophisticated indices of multiple drug use are available, it appears as though differences in scoring procedures make little difference in the distributions of overall drug involvement scores" (p. 327).

Given that difficult measurement problems remain, it is perhaps not surprising that the lack of consensus in definitions is mirrored by inadequate data collection and reporting, and unreliable prevalence estimates. Indeed, the literature on multiple drug use by problem drinkers is predominately anecdotal and is relatively unsophisticated. For example, in their introduction to a special issue of the *Journal of Social Issues* on women's use of drugs and alcohol, Marsh, Colten, and Tucker (1982) state: "The use of alcohol, psychotherapeutic drugs and heroin traditionally have been studied separately. However, users of any one substance frequently use at least one other" (p.2). Yet in none of the articles that follow are these multiple drug users so identified even though the editors state that "a number of common themes are apparent" (p. 6).

SOURCES OF DATA

As suggested by the review earlier on definitions and concepts, there is no natural starting point for assessing the evidence on drug use and abuse by women with drinking problems. However, from the clinical and anecdotal literature, it is clear that there is a problem of multiple drug use by alcoholic women, and that there are sources of data, some of which contain separate data on women. However, few of the major data-collection efforts to date have focused primarily upon women. The aim of these efforts is rarely upon substance abuse, but rather upon one or the other of the two main types of substances (alcohol and drugs).

There are four major sources of data on substance abuse by women: (1) treatment-oriented data systems; (2) special population surveys; (3) national surveys; and (4) smaller-scale clinical studies.

Treatment-Oriented Data Systems

Richards (1981) describes two national treatment-oriented data systems that contain data on alcohol use. The Drug Abuse Warning Network (DAWN), developed in 1972 as a collaborative effort of the Drug Enforcement Administration and the National Institute on Drug Abuse (NIDA), collects data from 24 Standard Metropolitan Statistical Areas from episode reports provided by hospital emergency departments, crisis centers, and medical examiners to monitor the consequences of drug abuse. The most recent data available were for the fourth quarter of 1978, when alcohol in combination with other drugs (any mention) was listed as the second most frequent type of episode, with 13% of all mentions. With respect to deaths, 83% of the total of 745 deaths were drug-related; alcohol in combination with other drugs was the most frequently listed cause of death. Unfortunately, the data are not reported separately by sex.

The Client Oriented Data Aquisition Process (CODAP) is a required reporting system for drug abuse programs receiving federal funds for treatment services. The annual data for 1977 (NIDA, 1978) contain information on secondary drug use for those whose primary drug of abuse was alcohol. Of 15,220 such patients in treatment, 34.7% reported at admission that another drug was also a problem for them. The most common secondary drug was marijuana, followed by barbiturates, amphetamines, and tranquilizers. Again, the data were not separately reported by sex. However, since women in the general population outnumber men in their use of prescription sedatives and stimulants (e.g., Ferrence & Whitehead, 1980), these rates are probably not overestimates of secondary drug abuse by female alcoholics.

Special Population Surveys

Special surveys have been conducted on substance abuse in a number of populations, including a major focus on youth and, more recently, on military personnel. A series of studies conducted for the NIDA, the National Household Surveys, has recently been completed. A landmark study (O'Donnell, Voss, Clayton, Slatin, & Room, 1976), *Young Men and Drugs*, provides a unique view of the prevalence of multiple substance abuse; however, as indicated by its title, it sheds no light on the special problems of women. The Drugs and American Youth survey is a longitudinal panel of 2200 males being followed over time; again, the data are limited to men (Johnston, 1973). The final survey is Drug Use Among American High School Students (e.g., Johnston, Bachman, & O'Malley, 1979). This study, part of the Monitoring the Future studies of the University of Michigan, consists of annual surveys of the graduating classes of high school students, including women. However, the data do not show the overlapping use and abuse of the various classes of drugs and alcohol.

National Surveys

National surveys have been the most useful in determining the extent to which drinkers in the general population have problems with multiple drug use. Perhaps the earliest, and most famous, study is the NCMDA study (Abelson, Cohen, Schrayer, & Rappeport, 1973; NCMDA, 1973). This report, *Drug Use in America: Problem in Perspective*, was based upon face-to-face interviews with 2411 adults and 880 adolescents, aged 12–17 years. The study is significant in that concurrent drug use and abuse and alcohol intake were measured; hence, it is one of the very few studies that can be useful in making projections and assertions concerning multiple substance abuse.

Coming from a "drug perspective," NCMDA (1973) reported that "among adults, only a marginal relationship exists between consumption of alcoholic beverages and recent use of ethical or proprietary psychoactive drugs" (p. 59). Somewhat conflicting data are presented in reporting the findings, however, due primarily to unclear definitions. One table (II-14, p. 60) shows that "current users" of beverage alcohol (in the past 7 days) have about the same pattern of recent pill usage (in the past year) as abstainers: 27% and 25%, respectively, have used any "ethical" (prescribed) drug; 12% and 10% have used sedatives, and 16% and 18% report tranquilizer use, while 10% and 5%, respectively, have used stimulants. Aside from the significant difference in the proportions using stimulants, the authors suggest that alcohol users are "no more likely" than abstainers to be involved in multiple substance use. However, given the pharmacologic interactions of these drugs, especially the sedatives and tranquilizers, with alcohol, there are significant public-health implications in these data.

A major difficulty in interpreting the NCMDA data is that current use was measured with very different time intervals (e.g., past 7 days vs. past year in the above analyses). This is even clearer when looking at the report's data on "concurrent multi-drug use." Here no definition of "concurrent" is given, although the implication is that there was close temporal proximity. Table II-18 (p. 62) in the report shows that use of other drugs plus alcohol is differentially distributed across various types of drugs. Concurrent multiple drug use is found for drinkers with the following frequency: 1% report simultaneous use of sedatives and alcohol, 7% use ethical (prescribed) tranquilizers, 20% report stimulant use, and 6% report use of proprietary ("over-the-counter") drugs. Unfortunately, it is not clear precisely what the denominator is for these rates of multiple substance use nor what the exact time intervals for concurrent use are. Further, the percentages are not reported separately by sex. However, given that women are more frequently found to use and abuse prescription sedatives in general (Ferrence & Whitehead, 1980), these rates probably provide conservative estimates of the prevalence of substance use among women drinkers. Regardless of how they are defined, these multiple usages occur differentially by age, with the same peaks in multiple drug use as is the case for heavy drinking in women—at ages 35–49.

Results of another national survey are presented in a provocatively titled work, "Female Polydrug Abusers" (Dammann & Ousley, 1978). Although data regarding all types of drugs and alcohol were collected from a national household sample, only single drugs are presented for frequency counts. While there is rich data on economic conditions, family status, and formal interactions with the substance abuse treatment system for each type of substance separately, there is no discussion of the polydrug abuse problem. Hence, one of the most promising data sets has not been analyzed in a fashion that can answer questions about multiple substance abuse among problem-drinking women.

Clinical Studies

While there is little empirical information concerning multiple substance abuse among women drinkers in the general population, there is some evidence on the use of licit (prescription) drugs by women in treatment for alcoholism. Curlee (1970) suggests that one of the major differences between male and female alcoholics in treatment is their use of medications. In this study, minor tranquilizers and sedatives were found to be commonly used and abused by female patients (43%) at a rate more than twice that reported for male patients (20%). Indeed, 25% of the women were considered to have significant drug problems, as compared to only 10% of the men. From a treatment perspective, these data are important because they raise concern that alcoholic women are at increased risk for accidental overdose (through the drugs' synergistic pharmacologic actions) and for the development of a substitute dependency.

Mulford (1977), reporting on sex differences in alcoholism, has identified women alcoholics as being at higher risk for regular use of drugs other than alcohol and for psychological dependence on drugs. Nearly one woman in four (24%) in this sample of new admissions to alcohol treatment facilities were regular drug users (as compared to 9% of men) and 14% (compared to

4% of men) were considered to be dependent on drugs. Barbiturates and tranquilizers were almost exclusively the drugs of abuse, while the use of drugs other than sedatives in conjunction with alcohol was virtually non-existent (less than 2% of the sample).

A larger, multicenter survey conducted by Tuchfeld, McLeary, and Waterhouse (1975) attempted to ascertain drug-use patterns among persons treated for alcohol problems. Findings showed widespread use of drugs by alcohol clients. For those under 30 years of age, men were three times as likely as women to abuse drugs. For women over the age of 30, minor tranquilizers and other prescription psychotropics were commonly abused. The authors estimated that 30–60% of all clients were abusing other sub-stances at intake, with women more likely to be multiple abusers than men.

These data on the use of prescription drugs by alcoholics in treatment are typical of patterns found in clinical practice. Further, they reflect the sex difference in drug use and abuse in general populations. As Ferrence and Whitehead (1980) have shown, there are major sex differences in psychoactive drug use, with men more likely to use and abuse illicit drugs (especially narcotics, hallucinogens, and inhalants), while women are more frequently found to outnumber men in their use of prescription stimulants, sedatives, and tranquilizers. Various social explanations for these differences have been suggested: Availability, legality, and access appear to account for women's increased use of licit drugs, while deviance paradigms are more frequently used to explain the use of illegal drugs by young men.

While the problem of drug use and abuse among the population seeking treatment for alcohol-related problems is relatively unresearched, the issue of problem drinking among drug abusers has been widely recognized. The Drug Abuse Reporting Program (DARP) data for patients in federal drug abuse treatment programs showed that some 23% consumed the equivalent of more than 8 oz of 80-proof distilled spirits per day (Simpson & Lloyd, 1977). Data from methadone maintenance treatment programs show that alcohol problems characterize from 10–50% of patients (Stimmel, 1981). In a survey of drinking problems among patients being treated for heroin addiction, Goodale, Burton, Carr, LePage, and Orfitelli (1978) reported that 12.5% of the women (as compared to 22% of the men) were problem drinkers.

SUMMARY OF THE STATE OF THE ART

It is abundantly clear that most of the literature relevant to the issue of multiple substance abuse by women is concerned with explanations dealing with only one abusive outcome. That abuse often occurs with two or more substances used concurrently and arising from the same causal processes, has been largely neglected in the research of recent years despite the fact that, for some time now, scientists and agencies have called for research to integrate the related abuse of various substances. Our contention is that this neglect is a direct result, at least in the American experience, of two factors: (1) the separation of funding agencies, which often precludes research or problems from cutting across agency boundaries; and (2) the long tradition of viewing alcohol misuse as a legal–medical problem and drug abuse as an illegal–social problem with medical consequences. Optimistically, we feel that the increasing awareness of the multiple abuse problem will eventually lead to a united effort to understand the issues and problems involved. Pessimistically, we believe that many of the same impediments that kept this kind of research from developing in the 1970s will continue to operate in the 1980s, thus blocking a genuine understanding of the nature of multiple substance abuse. It is also our contention that these impediments to research are particularly problematic for research related to women, because, given women's greater abuse of prescription drugs, multiple substance abuse is in all likelihood a greater problem for women than for men.

In placing much of the blame for the lack of research on multiple substance abuse at the doorstep of funding agencies, we do not wish to ignore the role of researchers themselves in creating this present environment. Past research traditions have largely been dictated by disciplinary considerations. That is, social scientists who have specialized in alcohol use and misuse have largely been unconcerned with drug use and misuse (and vice versa) and have seen the attendant problems as being in separate theoretical domains. For example, in sociology much emphasis has been placed on the outcomes of heavy drug abuse, stressing the criminal effects on society, while in assessing the nature of alcohol abuse much effort has been made to clarify the social contexts of drinking behavior. Similarly, in anthropological writings there have been many monographs on drinking among various ethnic groups, while drug abuse has been seen as coming out of cultures of the "poor."

Given these caveats, we can briefly summarize the state of the art of the research on multiple substance abuse, commenting on three areas of vital importance for the future of this research. These areas are: (1) theory; (2) methodology; and (3) current findings.

Theory

The area that has been written about most consists of theoretical perspectives. Nevertheless, it remains the area with the most pressing need for attention and focus. The theoretical perspectives relevant to multiple substance abuse have come from the distinct fields of drug abuse research and alcohol abuse research. On top of a rather poorly integrated general theoretical perspective, one must add the unique features that apply to multiple substance abuse in women. Our assertion is, however, that we must produce a coherent general theoretical perspective for multiple substance abuse before we can begin to modify it for women in particular.

The most fundamental theoretical questions concern the etiology of multiple substance abuse. Most theoretical positions concerned with the causality of any complex outcome related to health generally isolate four causal sources: (1) the individual; (2) the immediate social environment of the individual; (3) the society; and (4) nature. When dealing with chronic pathophysiological outcomes mediated by behavioral factors, we are concerned with all four of these interacting sources.

With respect to biological nature as a theory base for multiple substance abuse we are not on very firm ground. For example, in the alcohol field the search for a biophysiological basis for abuse has been very elusive. Despite years of debate over whether alcoholism is a disease or whether there is some biological mechanism that underlies loss of control, there remain many skeptics who see the bases for alcohol abuse as lying outside any biochemical model. Similar debates have occurred in the drug abuse area, although the pharmacologically addictive character of many substances has been well documented. The general question of predisposition to multiple substance abuse remains unresolved. The evidence for biological theories consists primarily of retrospective data collected from persons with extensive histories of abuse that has pharmacologically altered basic physiological functions (a result that is undeniable). Thus when one examines the gamut of theories that are concerned with metabolic deficiencies (Dole & Nyswander, 1967), neuropharmacologic effects (Martin, 1970), genetics (Schuckit & Haglund, 1977), and opiate receptors (Lettieri et al., 1980) as explanations of multiple substance abuse, they are primarily theories to explain the outcomes of multiple substance abuse and not the causes. A significant scientific breakthrough, especially in the area of genetics, might alter this conclusion in the future, but we remain skeptical that such a breakthrough will occur.

With respect to a societal-based theory of multiple substance abuse, we are on firmer ground logically but not necessarily in terms of any research findings. It is unquestionable that multiple substance abuse can take place only in societies that allow or encourage its occurrence. Clearly, societies that foster the consumption of alcohol and other drugs through heavy media advertising, emphasis on the good life, positive valuation of "personalities" who abuse substances, tax and economic incentives that encourage production of endangering substances, and emphasis on the joys of escape and getting away from it all should anticipate the creation of a major multiple substance use and abuse problem. The fact that there is not significantly more multiple substance abuse in American society than there appears to be, means that there are still many control mechanisms blocking such a development. Possible explanations of multiple substance abuse from a societal-theoretical perspective include a functional social control viewpoint (Zinberg & Harding, 1979), many general sociological theories related to such concepts as role, achievement norms, adaptation, and social influence

(Antons & Schulz, 1977; Kissin & Begleiter, 1976; Pittman & Snyder, 1962; Robinson, 1976; Wüthrich, 1974), and even broader political and economic explanations. Undoubtedly all of these societal influences are operating in the case of multiple substance abuse. We cannot, however, say at the present time that any of these theories provides a comprehensive understanding of multiple substance abuse, and the methodologies necessary to confirm or deny the societal perspective are lacking at present.

The individual as the locus of an adequate theory of multiple substance abuse is the least satisfactory. In both the drug-abuse literature and the alcohol-abuse literature there has been an extensive search for a "personality type" that will explain abuse (Ausubel, 1952). Any search for a personality type to explain multiple substance abuse in all likelihood will be as fruitless as these other searches. It would, of course, be unfair to characterize all theories of drug and alcohol abuse that center upon the individual as personality-type theories. There are others that are of value, including theories of anxiety and ego defense (Wurmser, 1974, 1978), life scripts, individual coping structures, cognitive control, and so on. The fundamental problem in theories centered upon the individual is their neglect of the fact that the substances abused are products of society; that alcohol, for example, is a commodity produced by the labor market (farmers, manufacturers, distributors, sellers), with powerful economic incentives supporting its use. Among such forces, the individual cannot be held solely responsible for the etiology of such socially induced outcomes.

The immediate social environment of the individual as the locus of a theory of multiple substance abuse is the main bailiwick of most of the theorists who have dealt with the area of drug abuse. Competing theories deal with such items as conditioning (Wikler, 1965, 1973); process, interaction, and drug subcultures (Johnson, 1973); development (Kandel, 1976); the family (Stanton, 1980); poor environment (Rittenhouse, 1977); and various forms of deviance (Kaplan, 1972). The alcohol area also has an extensive literature in this domain (Kissin & Begleiter, 1976). It would seem, then, that this theoretical perspective should be the most fruitful for developing a comprehensive theory of multiple substance abuse firmly based on available literature. Furthermore, this perspective best represents theories of the middle range that combine a societal approach with attention to the individual, encompassing the important person–environment interactions that characterize multiple substance abuse. In our opinion the main theoretical task in the 1980s should be to articulate a sound theory of multiple substance abuse out of theories at this level.

Methodology

From the methodological perspective, it appears that the analytic confusion apparent in the substance-abuse literature reflects the naivete of both drug and alcohol researchers about the other's field. Hence, we have national data sets on women, but the concomitant use of drugs and alcohol is not ascertained (e.g., Dammann & Ousley, 1978; NCMDA, 1973). While the measurement difficulties are acknowledged, including the difficulties of face-to-face interviewing of respondents about potentially nonnormative behavior, it can be argued that the problems have been engendered primarily by researchers who themselves may not be appropriately versed in their fields. Hence, we need a more sophisticated approach to an acknowledged problem and greater collaboration between researchers in the drug- and alcohol-abuse fields. The current Epidemiological Catchment Area studies being funded by the National Institute of Mental Health in a number of large urban areas will provide much data on multiple substance abuse. Given the large numbers of persons interviewed through these studies, an ample number of problem-drinking women should be identified. The extensive drug use histories of this population should provide an in-depth look at the problem of multiple drug use by problem-drinking women, answering many of the data needs identified in this review.

Current Findings

While one might expect that there would be a vast literature on multiple substance abuse, for a number of reasons the literature is quite small. The data suggest that there are some problems of multiple drug use by female heavy drinkers, especially with respect to tranquilizers and barbiturates, and that rates of prescription drug use are relatively high among alcoholic women in treatment. What minimal data exist show little opiate or other illicit drug use by problem-drinking women. While the extent of problem drinking among drug abusers has been well documented, especially with respect to women attending methadone maintenance clinics, drug use is often not assessed among the problem-drinking population.

As is true in much of alcohol research, this topic is one that engenders a great deal of emotional response. Associations of deviance and lack of control enter the picture when drug problems are raised in the alcohol treatment and research community. Yet, the picture appears to be one in which prescribed drugs are abused rather than narcotics and other illicit drugs. However, as we will discuss later, the pharmacologic interactions of the drugs that are abused by problem drinkers create especially important medical and social problems, a reality that needs to be better appreciated and recognized by those in treatment and referral positions.

IMPLICATIONS FOR PREVENTION AND TREATMENT

Recently Room (1981) stated "the case for a problem prevention approach to alcohol, drug, and mental problems" (p. 26). He argued for a wider definition of preventive activities than the conventional one, and called for a systematic process to examine realistic possibilities for prevention efforts. This review of multiple substance abuse among women drinkers is consistent with many of the points made by Room. In particular, the pharmacologic implications of multiple substance abuse must be appreciated as a specific target problem for prevention efforts, given the possibilities for cross-dependence and accidental or intentional overdose of alcohol and other drugs. Persons in the treatment sector need additional training in the pharmacology of multiple drug–alcohol interactions, and both treatment and prevention personnel need to recognize that the two classes of drugs are often used and abused simultaneously.

In our opinion, the development of adequate prevention and treatment efforts in the future will require: (1) a sound delineation of the extent of the multiple substance abuse problem, including basic definitions and epidemiology; (2) an analysis of social influences on women's substance use, including media advertising, marketing and distribution, and physician prescribing practices; (3) an assessment of appropriate health-education strategies and prevention messages targeted to the multiple drug use problem; (4) an evaluation of the adequacy of care provided by institutions that come into initial contact with the drug-abusing female problem drinker; and (5) a thorough analysis of the populations at risk with the notions of primary care and prevention in mind.

This research agenda is easy to state in a hortatorical way. Yet the state of knowledge currently available suggests considerable caution in planning services for both prevention and treatment. At most, one can now call for an increased awareness that in educating or treating a woman with a drinking problem, we must focus on her entire repertoire of behavioral responses. Such a holistic approach can, of course, be recommended for any individual suffering from problems related to dangerous substances. However, a holistic perspective encompassing both alcohol and other drugs may be especially important for problem-drinking women if they are at unusually high risk for multiple abuse of alcohol and prescription psychoactive drugs.

It is probably premature to recommend totally separate and distinct programs for the treatment of multiple substance abusers. Such programs could not be justified given the current state of research. However, combined alcohol–drug treatment programs do exist, consisting primarily of separate programs with separate treatment staffs conducted under a larger organizational umbrella. Moreover, some evidence suggests that such programs may be more effective in attracting women clients than are alcohol-specific treatment agencies (see Beckman & Amaro, Chapter 11 in this volume). Until we learn significantly more about the success of these and other interventions and about the nature and extent of the substance-abuse problem among female problem drinkers and alcoholics, we should proceed cautiously. Our hope is that the pace of research in this area will be greatly accelerated in the coming years, and that in a decade we could finish such a review on a more optimistic note.

REFERENCES

Abelson, H., Cohen, R., Schrayer, D., & Rappeport, M. *Drug experience, attitudes and related behavior among adolescents and adults.* Princeton, N.J.: Response Analysis Corporation, 1973.

Antons, K., & Schulz, W. *Normales Trinken und Suchtentwicklung: Theorie und empirische Ergebnisse interdisziplinaerer Forschung zum sozialintegrierten Alkoholkonsum und suechtigen Alkoholismus.* Gottingen, West Germany: Verlag für Psychologie, 1977.

Ausubel, D. P. *Ego development and the personality disorders.* New York: Grune & Stratton, 1952.

Badiet, P. Women and legal drugs: A review. In A. MacLennan (Ed.), *Women: Their use of alcohol and other legal drugs.* Toronto: Addiction Research Foundation, 1976.

Balter, M. B. Drug abuse: A conceptual analysis and over-view of the current situation. In E. Josephson & E. E. Carroll (Eds.), *Drug use: Epidemiological and sociological approaches.* New York: Wiley, 1974.

Cahalan, D., Cisin, I. H., & Crossley, H. M. *American drinking practices: A national study of drinking behavior and attitudes* (Monograph No. 6). New Brunswick, N.J.: Rutgers Center for Alcohol Studies, 1969.

Celentano, D. D., & McQueen, D. V. Comparison of alcoholism prevalence rates obtained by survey and indirect estimators. *Journal of Studies on Alcohol,* 1978, *39,* 420–434. (a)

Celentano, D. D., & McQueen, D. V. Reliability and validity of estimators of alcoholism prevalence. *Journal of Studies on Alcohol,* 1978, *39,* 869–878. (b)

Celentano, D. D., McQueen, D. V., & Chee, E. Substance abuse by women: A review of the epidemiologic literature. *Journal of Chronic Diseases,* 1980, *33,* 383–394.

Curlee, J. A comparison of male and female patients at an alcoholism treatment center. *Journal of Psychology,* 1970, *74,* 239–247.

Dammann, G., & Ousley, N. Female polydrug abusers. In D. R. Wesson, A. S. Carlin, K. M. Adams, & G. Beschner (Eds.), *Polydrug abuse: The results of a national collaborative study.* New York: Academic, 1978.

Dodson, W. E. Patterns of multiple drug use among adolescents referred by a juvenile court. *Pediatrics,* 1971, *47,* 1033–1036.

Dole, V. P., & Nyswander, M. E. Addiction—a metabolic disease. *Archives of Internal Medicine,* 1967, *120,* 19–84.

Ferguson, L. W. Public-service drug-use scales: Rationale, derivation and norms. *Psychological Reports,* 1974, *34,* 871–876.

Ferrence, R. G., & Whitehead, P. C. Sex differences in psychoactive drug use: Recent epidemiology. In O. J. Kalant (Ed.), *Research advances in alcohol and drug problems* (Vol. 5: *Alcohol and drug problems in women*). New York: Plenum, 1980.

Fraser, J. The female alcoholic. *Addictions,* 1973, *20,* 64–80.

Galli, N. Patterns of student drug use. *Journal of Drug Education,* 1974, *4,* 237–248.

Gomberg, E. S. Alcoholism in women. In B. Kissin & H. Begleiter (Eds.), *The biology of alcoholism* (Vol. 4: *Social aspects of alcoholism*). New York: Plenum, 1976.

Goodale, J. B., Burton, J., Carr, G., LePage, P., & Orfitelli, O. P. Alcohol abuse in a methadone maintenance treatment program. In A. J. Schecter (Ed.), *Drug dependence and alcoholism* (Vol. 1: *Biomedical issues*). New York: Plenum, 1978.

Gunderson, E. K. E., Russell, J. W., & Nail, R. L. A Drug Involvement Scale for classification of drug abusers. *Journal of Community Psychology,* 1973, *1,* 399–403.

Hughes, P. H., Schaps, E., & Sanders, C. R. A methodology for monitoring adolescent drug abuse trends. *International Journal of the Addictions,* 1973, *8,* 403–419.

Hemminki, E. Tobacco, alcohol, medicines and illegal drug taking. *Adolescence,* 1974, *9,* 421–424.

Johnson, B. D. *Marijuana users and drug subcultures.* New York: Wiley, 1973.

Johnson, M. W., DeVries, J. C., & Houghton, M. I. Physicians' views on alcoholism: With special reference to alcoholism in women. *Nebraska State Medical Journal*, 1965, *50*, 378–384.

Johnston. L. *Drugs and American youth*. Ann Arbor: University of Michigan, 1973.

Johnston, L. D., Bachman, J. G., & O'Malley, P. M. *Drugs and the class of '78: Behaviors, attitudes and recent national trends* (DHEW Publ. No. ADM-79-877). Washington, D.C.: U.S. Government Printing Office, 1979.

Kandel, D. B. Adolescent involvement in illicit drug use: A multiple classification analysis. *Social Forces*, 1976, *55*, 438–458.

Kaplan, H. B. Toward a general theory of psychosocial deviance: The case of aggressive behavior. *Social Science and Medicine*, 1972, *6*, 593–617.

Kaufman, E. The abuse of multiple drugs. I. Definition, classification, and extent of problem. *American Journal of Drug and Alcohol Abuse*, 1976, *3*, 279–292.

Kissin, B., & Begleiter, H. (Eds.). *The biology of alcoholism* (Vol. 4: *Social aspects of alcoholism*). New York: Plenum, 1976.

Lettieri, D. J., Sayers, M., & Pearson, H. W. *Theories on drug abuse* (NIDA Research Monograph 20). Rockville, Md.: National Institute on Drug Abuse, 1980.

Lindbeck, V. L. The woman alcoholic; a review of the literature. *International Journal of the Addictions*, 1972, *7*, 567–580.

Lisansky, E. S. The woman alcoholic. *Annals of the American Academy of Political and Social Sciences*, 1958, *315*, 73–81.

Marsh, J. C., Colten, M. E., & Tucker, M. B. Women's use of drugs and alcohol: New perspectives. *Journal of Social Issues*, 1982, *38*, 1–8.

Martin, W. R. Pharmacological redundancy as an adaptive mechanism in the central nervous system. *Federation Proceedings*, 1970, *29*, 13–18.

McQueen, D. V., & Celentano, D. D. Social factors in the etiology of multiple outcomes: The case of blood pressure and alcohol consumption patterns. *Social Science and Medicine*, 1982, *16*, 397–418.

McQueen, D. V., & Siegrist, J. Social factors in the etiology of chronic disease: An overview. *Social Science and Medicine*, 1982, *16*, 353–367.

Morrissey, E. R. The measurement of multiple drug use and its relationship to the patterning of alcohol intake. *American Journal of Drug and Alcohol Abuse*, 1981, *8*, 311–328.

Mulford, H. A. Women and men problem drinkers: Sex differences in patients served by Iowa's community alcoholism centers. *Journal of Studies on Alcohol*, 1977, *38*, 1624–1639.

Mulford, H. A., & Miller, D. E. Drinking in Iowa—II. The extent of drinking and selected sociocultural categories. *Quarterly Journal of Studies on Alcohol*, 1960, *21*, 26–39. (a)

Mulford, H. A., & Miller, D. E. Drinking in Iowa—III. A scale of definitions of alcohol related to drinking behavior. *Quarterly Journal of Studies on Alcohol*, 1960, *21*, 267–278. (b)

National Commission on Marihuana and Drug Abuse. *Drug use in America: Problem in perspective*. Washington, D.C.: U.S. Government Printing Office, 1973.

National Institute on Drug Abuse. *Data from the Client Oriented Data Acquisition Process (CODAP) annual data 1977* (Statistical Series E, No. 7). Rockville, Md.: National Institute on Drug Abuse, 1978.

National Institute on Drug Abuse. *National Drug/Alcohol Collaborative Project: Issues in multiple substance abuse* (DHEW Publ. No. ADM-80-957). Washington, D.C.: U.S. Government Printing Office, 1980.

O'Donnell, J. A., Voss, H. L., Clayton, R. R., Slatin, G. T., & Room, R. G. W. *Young men and drugs—A nationwide survey* (NIDA Research Monograph No. 5). Rockville, Md.: National Institute on Drug Abuse, 1976.

Pittman, D. J., & Snyder, C. R. (Eds.). *Society, culture, and drinking patterns*. Carbondale, Ill.: Southern Illinois University Press, 1962.

Richards, L. G. *Demographic trends and drug abuse, 1980–1995* (DHHS Publ. No. ADM-81-1069). Washington, D.C.: U.S. Government Printing Office, 1981.

Rittenhouse, J. D. *The epidemiology of heroin and other narcotics*. (NIDA Research Monograph 16). Rockville, Md.: National Institute on Drug Abuse, 1977.

Robinson, D. *From drinking to alcoholism: A sociological commentary*. London: Wiley, 1976.

Room, R. The case for a problem prevention approach to alcohol, drug, and mental problems.
Public Health Reports, 1981, *96*, 26–34.

Rubington, E. The hidden alcoholic. *Quarterly Journal of Studies on Alcohol*, 1972, *33*, 667–683.

Sample, C. J. Concept of polydrug use. In L. G. Richards & L. B. Blevens (Eds.), *The
epidemiology of drug abuse: Current issues*. (DHEW Publ. No. ADM-77-432). Washington, D.C.: U.S. Government Printing Office, 1977.

Schuckit, M. A., & Haglund, R. M. J. An overview of the etiologic theories on alcoholism. In
N. Estes & E. Heinemann (Eds.), *Alcoholism: Development, consequences and interventions*. St. Louis, Mo.: Mosby, 1977.

Senseman, L. A. The housewife's secret illness: How to recognize the female alcoholic. *Rhode
Island Medical Journal*, 1966, *49*, 40–42.

Siegler, M., Osmond, H., & Newell, S. Models of alcoholism. *Quarterly Journal of Studies on
Alcohol*, 1968, *29*, 571–591.

Simpson, D. D., & Lloyd, M. R. *Alcohol and illicit drug use* (Institute of Behavioral Research
Report 77-2). Fort Worth, Tex.: Texas Christian University, 1977.

Single, E., Kandel, D., & Faust, R. Patterns of multiple drug use in high school. *Journal of
Health and Social Behavior*, 1974, *15*, 344–357.

Smart, R. G. Addiction, dependency, abuse or use: Which are we studying with epidemiology.
In E. Josephson & E. E. Carroll (Eds.), *Drug use: Epidemiological and sociological
approaches*. New York: Wiley, 1974.

Stanton, M. D. Aspects of the family and drug abuse. In B. Ellis (Ed.), *Drug abuse from the
family perspective*. (DHEW Publ. No. ADM-80-910). Washington, D.C.: U.S. Government Printing Office, 1980.

Stimmel, B. Methadone maintenance and alcohol use. In S. E. Gardner (Ed.), *Drug and alcohol
abuse: Implications for treatment* (DHHS Publ. No. ADM-80-958). Washington, D.C.:
U.S. Government Printing Office, 1981.

Tuchfeld, B. S., McLeary, K. R., & Waterhouse, G. J. *Multiple drug use among persons with
alcohol-related problems*. Springfield, Va.: National Technical Information Service, 1975.
(NTIS No. PB-250380/3SL)

Whitehead, P. C. Multidrug use: Supplementary perspectives. *International Journal of the
Addictions*, 1974, *9*, 185–204.

Wikler, A. Conditioning factors in opiate addiction and relapse. In D. M. Wilner & G. G.
Kassebaum (Eds.), *Narcotics*. New York: McGraw-Hill, 1965.

Wikler, A. Dynamics of drug dependence: Implications of a conditioning theory for research
and treatment. *Archives of General Psychiatry*, 1973, *28*, 611–616.

World Health Organization, Expert Committee on Mental Health, Alcoholism Subcommittee.
Second report (WHO Technical Report Series, No. 48). Geneva, Switzerland: World
Health Organization, 1952.

Wurmser, L. Psychoanalytic considerations of the etiology of compulsive drug use. *Journal of
the American Psychoanalytic Association*, 1974, *22*, 820–834.

Wurmser, L. *The hidden dimension: Psychodynamics of compulsive drug use*. New York:
Aronson, 1978.

Wüthrich, P. *Zur Soziogenese des chronischen Alkoholismus*. Basel, West Germany: S. Karger,
1974.

Zinberg, N. E., & Harding, W. M. Control over intoxicant use: A theoretical and practical
review. *Journal of Drug Issues*, 1979, *7*, 121–143.

BIOLOGICAL AND PSYCHOSEXUAL ASPECTS OF ALCOHOL USE IN WOMEN

The three chapters in this section discuss various biological aspects of women's alcohol use and abuse. The most general of these chapters, Chapter 5 by Hill, reviews the prevalence of biomedical consequences of alcohol abuse in women as compared to men. The two more specific chapters consider the related topics of alcohol use during pregnancy, prior to pregnancy, and during lactation (Chapter 6, Little & Ervin) and relationships between sexual behavior and alcohol use among women (Chapter 7, Wilsnack).

Hill compares morbidity and mortality rates in male and female alcoholics. She concludes that although women in the general population may be less frequently identified as having alcohol-related problems than men, among women with such problems the risks for a variety of biomedical consequences are in most cases equal to or greater than those observed among men. The relative risks for women and men depend upon the group with which they are compared. Hill argues forcefully that the most appropriate comparison group for assessing mortality among alcoholic women is same-age women in the general population rather than men or the population as a whole. Direct comparison of the morbidity of alcoholic men and alcoholic women with similar demographic characteristics and drinking patterns is also recommended.

Morbidity from all causes appears to be as high among women alcoholics as among men alcoholics. Results suggest that the development of some pathological conditions (e.g., cirrhosis of the liver) as a result of excessive drinking may be accelerated in women as compared to men. If nonalcoholic women are used for comparison purposes, alcoholic women appear to have greater mortality from a variety of causes, including liver disease, suicide, and accidents, than do alcoholic men when compared to their nonalcoholic male counterparts.

Hill points out that women may have biological vulnerabilities to developing organ damage as a result of drinking as well as separate biological vulnerabilities to becoming excessive drinkers. Genetic factors may predispose women to alcohol abuse, although findings of genetic studies are somewhat more consistent for men than for women. Recent data also support the idea of a genetic vulnerability to developing organ damage. This type of vulnerability has thus far been investigated primarily with respect to liver diseases, using HLA blood typing and immunological reactions. Reasons for women's greater vulnerability to effects of alcohol on the liver may include differences in drinking patterns, possible adverse effects of estrogen on liver function, and possible differences in autoimmune responses.

Finally, some implications for prevention and treatment are considered. Although research to date cannot yet define safe levels of consumption with respect to risks for particular health consequences, some clues are available. Hill recommends primary prevention efforts that inform women that they may be at risk for health consequences at lower levels of consumption than are men. Specifically, risks for alcoholic cirrhosis and cancers of the head and neck appear to be increased among women who consume more than 2–5 drinks per day. She also notes the need to educate medical practitioners about the health risks of women's drinking, and stresses the value of comprehensive health screening techniques for detecting medical problems that frequently occur in alcoholic women.

In Chapter 6, Little and Ervin present a history of the rediscovery of the fetal alcohol syndrome (FAS) in the early 1970s. This syndrome is characterized by growth deficiency of prenatal onset, characteristic facial dysmorphology, and central nervous system involvement with developmental delay. Far more common than FAS are other fetal alcohol effects linked to maternal alcohol use during pregnancy, including intrauterine growth retardation, morphologic abnormalities, central nervous system involvement, and fetal mortality. Additional questions that remain to be answered include reasons for the aversion to alcohol that develops in pregnant women, and whether other maternal risk factors such as age, habits, genetic predisposition, and life style alter the fetal risk associated with alcohol exposure *in utero*. The effects of the isolated binge, the relative harmfulness of various types of alcoholic beverages, the effects of alcohol use or abuse prior to pregnancy, and the effects of alcohol consumed by lactating mothers also remain to be determined. The authors discuss how determination of "safe" consumption levels for pregnant women is impeded by the questionable validity of some self-report data. They conclude that at present there is no known safe level of alcohol consumption and no safe time during pregnancy in which to drink.

It is to the authors' credit that in this book on women and alcohol they also consider the question of paternal alcohol use. Very little is known about the effects of paternal alcohol consumption on human offspring. Recent animal research, however, has focused on three main issues: (1) a decrease in the number and viability of offspring; (2) changes in the health and development of surviving offspring; and (3) direct evidence of changes in the reproductive material.

A particular strength of this chapter is its discussion of clinical issues related to alcohol and reproduction. An extensive public education program to identify pregnant alcohol abusers is described, including the dissemination of FAS information to health and helping professionals. Once the pregnant alcohol abuser is identified, her guilt and denial may make her initially very difficult to treat. However, she can at the same time be particularly receptive to intervention because of her concern for her developing child. The ambivalence she feels makes this a time of both danger and opportunity for the therapist and the client. A format for the therapeutic encounter with the pregnant alcohol abuser is described, requiring directed yet nonjudgmental action on the part of the therapist. Because clients' children may have longlasting learning and behavior problems, careful neuropsychological evaluation is essential to identify each child's capabilities and to aid the parents in the child's care and management. Little and Ervin discuss in detail the components of such developmental assessment with infants and with older children.

Wilsnack's more psychosocially oriented chapter examines relationships between drinking and sexual behavior in women. Research on the effects of drinking on sexual responsiveness in women presents a striking paradox: Although data from many sources show that women typically perceive alcohol as an aphrodisiac, in experimental studies neither alcohol consumption nor the belief that alcohol has been consumed has any positive effect on women's physiological sexual arousal. In fact, actual alcohol consumption appears to decrease women's physiological sexual arousal while at the same time increasing their self-reported subjective sexual arousal. Wilsnack concludes that although the available research gives little support to a simple physiological disinhibition theory of drinking and sexual arousal, it may be important to study alcohol's disinhibiting effects on women's sexual cognitions and behaviors, including their feelings of subjective sexual arousal and their resulting sexual activity. For women these subjective cognitive effects may play a greater role in reinforcing and maintaining drinking behavior than do changes in objective physiological sexual arousal.

Wilsnack reviews studies showing relatively high levels of sexual dysfunction in alcoholic women and suggests that such women may use alcohol to self-medicate the sexual difficulties they experience. The difficulties of determining causality are discussed: While alcoholism can undoubtedly have negative physiological and psychosocial effects on sexuality, it is also likely that sexual difficulties can precede and contribute to excessive drinking.

An innovative section of this chapter deals with incest and sexual abuse, examining the hypothesis that these experiences may predispose women both to alcohol abuse and to sexual dysfunction. Another section considers drinking and sexual orientation, and finds elevated rates of homosexuality among alcoholic women and high rates of problem drinking among lesbians. Finally, the need for professional training in alcoholism and sexual dysfunction is noted and various treatment approaches suggested by the research literature are discussed. Significant unanswered treatment issues involve the length of preliminary abstinence from alcohol that should precede treatment for sexual dysfunction, and at what point to involve a woman's sexual partner in treatment.

A common emphasis of the chapters in this section is the complexity of the relationships with which they deal. For example, when comparing drinking prior to pregnancy with drinking during pregnancy, Little and Ervin note that the facets of fetal development affected by a history of alcohol abuse may be different than those affected by intrauterine exposure to alcohol, which in turn may vary at different points in the pregnancy. The complexity of these relationships is one reason that the dose-response curve is inexact and the type of fetal alcohol effects associated with a given amount of alcohol vary greatly. Wilsnack considers the interaction of physiological, cognitive, and interpersonal factors in determining the effects of alcohol consumption and alcohol expectations on sexual arousal, while Hill notes the complex relationships mediating male and female alcoholics' risks of various types of disease, and the manner in which psychosocial "life style" variables such as smoking or stress interact with the effects of alcohol consumption to determine risks of biomedical consequences. Taken as a whole, the chapters strongly support the need for complex multifactorial models to guide future research on women and alcohol.

Finally, each author deals sensitively with the therapeutic implications of the research reviewed. Wilsnack notes that a period of abstinence from alcohol may be necessary before treatment of sexual dysfunction, and Hill points out that time should be allowed for recovery from alcohol-induced neuropsychological deficits before intensive psychotherapies are instituted. Little and Ervin recognize the newly recovering woman's need to protect herself and the necessity of temporarily nurturing her defenses and denial regarding her child's problems that are a result of her own drinking during pregnancy.

5

Vulnerability to the Biomedical Consequences of Alcoholism and Alcohol-Related Problems among Women

SHIRLEY Y. HILL
Western Psychiatric Institute and Clinic and
University of Pittsburgh School of Medicine

INTRODUCTION

It has long been assumed that biological factors associated with the causes and consequences of alcohol-related problems can be considered without taking sex into account. Recent evidence suggests, however, that the sexes differ in their risk of developing these biological consequences. This should not be surprising in view of the extensive effects that male and female hormones have on other tissues besides the reproductive systems. In fact, undersecretion or oversecretion of sex hormones such as estrogens, progesterone, and testosterone plays an important role in a variety of diseases. There is reason to believe that alcohol consumption profoundly affects the secretion of these hormones. Furthermore, it is known that the normal breakdown of hormones is impaired in livers damaged by chronic alcohol consumption (Galambos, 1972).

This review discusses the prevalence of biomedical consequences of alcohol-related problems in women and makes comparisons with male alcoholics where data are available. Further, biological factors that may explain why the sexes differ in their vulnerability to alcohol problems are discussed. The topics reviewed include sex differences in morbidity and mortality rates, liver disorders, neuroendocrine changes, cardiovascular effects, risk for development of cancers, and structural and functional changes in the CNS. The discussion of biological vulnerabilities that vary by sex includes a review of the literature on genetic factors that predispose women to abusive drinking and recent data that suggest that there may be a genetic vulnerability to developing organ damage. Finally, new directions for further research into the etiology and consequences of alcoholism as they bear on treatment and prevention in women are discussed.

MORBIDITY AND MORTALITY

Morbidity

Although alcoholics have long been known to have an extremely high morbidity rate, data for comparing morbidity rates in male and female alcoholics have only recently become available, in large part due to a series of investigations by Scandinavian researchers.

Using employment records and records from insurance companies, Swedish investigators (Asma, Eggert, & Hilker, 1971; Lokander, 1962; Lundquist, 1965) found that greater morbidity among alcoholic men caused them to be absent from work more often than nonalcoholic men and to use their insurance benefits more. Other Swedish investigators demonstrated that alcoholic women also have increased morbidity on similar indices as compared to the general female population (Medhus, 1974) as well as greater morbidity when compared to alcoholic men (Dahlgren & Ideström, 1979).

Using Swedish public health insurance data, Medhus (1974) compared disability rates and frequency of sick days among 71 alcoholic women and 71 age-matched control women. The alcoholics were studied for a period lasting from 6 years before their first compulsory treatment by the Swedish Temperance Board until 4 years after. Female alcoholics were only moderately impaired with respect to morbidity 5–6 years prior to their first compulsory treatment; thereafter morbidity increased markedly up to the time of treatment and remained elevated throughout the 4-year observation period following treatment.

Dahlgren and Ideström (1979) determined the frequency of public health insurance use by 66 female and 68 male alcoholics in Sweden over a 15-year period. Morbidity data were obtained for the alcoholics before and after they received treatment for alcoholism, and comparisons were made by age and sex. Women and older patients had higher disability rates, more sick periods, and longer sicknesses during the 6 years before treatment, and their morbidity in these three areas remained elevated after treatment.

Dahlgren and Ideström's results are in agreement with a study completed at Toronto's Addiction Research Foundation. Ashley, Olin, Le-Riche, Kornaczewski, Schmidt, and Rankin (1977) compared physical disease profiles of 135 female and 736 male inpatient alcoholics of similar age, social class, and referral pattern. Although at the time of admission the women had been drinking excessively for fewer years than the men (an average of 14.1 years compared to 20.2 years), the prevalence of most diseases was similar in both sexes, though the women had a higher than expected prevalence of anemia. Particularly noteworthy was the fact that the women showed a significantly shorter average duration of excessive drinking before the first recorded occurrence of fatty liver, hypertension, obesity, anemia, malnutrition, gastrointestinal hemorrhage, or ulcers requiring surgery. These results suggest that the development of complications in relation to excessive drinking may be accelerated in women as compared to men.

Mortality

Excessive death rates in alcoholics of both sexes have been found in investigations in Sweden (Dahlgren & Myrhed, 1977; Medhus, 1975), Norway (Sundby, 1967), Canada (Schmidt & Popham, 1976), England (Nicholls, Edwards, & Kyle, 1974), and the United States (Tashiro & Lipscomb, 1963) (see Table 5-1). While the death rate among male alcoholics has been reported to be two to three times greater than that of men in the general population, the death rate reported for alcoholic women in these studies is 2.7 to 7 times that of women in the general population. Direct comparison of alcoholic men and women with similar demographic characteristics confirms the notion that excess mortality is more pronounced among alcoholic women.

Greater risk for alcoholic women is also evident when mortality by specific causes is examined (see Table 5-2). Mortality from circulatory disorders is 1.7 to 3.0 times greater than normal in alcoholic men, but 1.9 to 10.0 times greater than normal in alcoholic women. For cirrhosis of the liver, the figure are: alcoholic males, 5.0 to 11.5; alcoholic females, 20.0 to 25.0. In the case of digestive disorders mortality is 3.0 to 3.8 times greater than normal in alcoholic men, but 6.7 to 7.8 times greater than normal in alcoholic women. For accidents from all causes: alcoholic males 2.0 to 15.2; alcoholic females, 10.0 to 70.0. Although it has previously been found that women are at greater risk of attempted but uncompleted suicide (Curlee, 1970), Table 5-2 shows that alcoholic women also may be at greater risk for completed suicide than alcoholic men; the mortality ratios for suicide are higher for women than men in three of the four studies. Insufficient data are available to compare mortality from respiratory disorders and cancer of the head and neck by sex.

Except for Schmidt and deLint (1972), the mortality ratios in Tables 5-1 and 5-2 are specific as to age and sex; that is, they were determined by comparing the mortality rates in alcoholics of each sex with those of people of the same sex and age in the general population. Some investigators (Dahlgren & Myrhed, 1977; Schmidt & deLint, 1972) have argued that the excessive mortality of women alcoholics is at least partly attributable to the lower death rates of women in the general population. In other words, it is argued that these findings do not necessarily mean that mortality among female alcoholics is greater than among male alcoholics, but rather that the expected mortality for the female population as a whole is lower. For this reason, some investigators have calculated mortality ratios for women alco-

TABLE 5-1. Ratio of Observed to Expected Mortality among Alcoholics, by Sex

Reference	Sample source	Sample size	Observation period	Source of expected value	Mortality ratio
Brenner (1967)	United States: Alcoholism treatment facilities	258F 1085M	7 years (identified 1954–1957)	Age- and sex-specific mortality, California	5.6F 3.0M
Schmidt & deLint (1972)[a]	Canada: Admission to alcoholism clinics	1119F 5395M	2–14 years (identified 1951–1963)	Age-specific mortality, Ontario	3.2F 2.0M
Pell & D'Alonzo (1973)	United States: Alcoholic employees (one industry)	57F 842M	5 years (identified 1964)	Age-, sex-, payroll-class-matched controls	6.7F 3.1M
Lindelius, Salum, & Agren (1974)	Sweden: Voluntary treatment	118F 139M	5–10 years (identified 1962–1966)	Age-, sex-, and time-period-specific rates, Stockholm	4.0F 2.0M
Nicholls, Edwards, & Kyle (1974)	United Kingdom: Alcoholism admissions—psychiatric hospitals	257F 678M	10–15 years (identified 1953–1957)	Age- and sex-specific rates, United Kingdom	2.7F 3.1M
Medhus (1975)	Sweden: Compulsory treatment by Temperance Board	83F	5–12 years (identified 1961–1968)	Age-, sex-, and time-period-specific rates, Malmo	7.0F
Dahlgren & Myrhed (1977)	Sweden: Treatment at Karolinska Hospital	100F 100M	6–12 years (identified 1963–1969)	Age-, sex-, and time-period-specific rates, Stockholm	5.6F 3.0M

[a]Ratios computed with male life expectancy data.

TABLE 5-2. Ratio of Observed to Expected Mortality among Alcoholics, by Cause and Sex

Reference	Circulatory disorders		Digestive disorders		Cirrhosis		Accidents		Suicide	
	M	F	M	F	M	F	M	F	M	F
Brenner (1967)							6.3	15.8		
Schmidt & deLint (1972)[a]	1.7	4.1	3.6	6.7	11.5	25.0	2.5	12.4	6.0	8.7
Lindelius, Salum, & Agren (1974)									5.0	17.5
Nicholls, Edwards, & Kyle (1974)	1.7	1.9	3.8	7.8			15.2	18.6	26.5	18.4
Medhus (1975)								70.0		30.0
Dahlgren & Myrhed (1977)	3.0	10.0	3.0		5.0	20.0	2.0	10.0	7.0	20.0

[a]Ratios computed with male life expectancy data.

holics on the basis of expected mortality in the male population. Using this method, Dahlgren and Myrhed (1977) found mortality from all causes to be about the same for male and female alcoholics (3.0 for males and 3.1 for females). As may be seen in Table 5-1, using expected death risks for women in the general population, the death rate for alcoholic women in that study is much higher (5.6). Using the expected death risks for men, Schmidt and deLint (1972) also found mortality rates to be similar for alcoholic men (2.0) and women (3.2).

Lower expected mortality for women in the general population does not appear to be a valid reason for dismissing women in the general population as the appropriate comparison group for assessing mortality ratios among alcoholic women. The most appropriate control group for determining mortality ratios is the one that matches the age and sex of the group being examined, and, ideally, the two groups should also be matched by socio-economic status and ethnicity. When what appears to be the most appropriate control population of nonalcoholics is used, the mortality risk for women alcoholics greatly exceeds that for men alcoholics.

SUICIDE

The association between alcoholism and suicide has been well established with reported rates of completed suicide among alcoholics 6 to 20 times that of the general population (Goodwin, 1973). Conclusions regarding differences between the sexes are much less clear. Suicide statistics may be particularly difficult to evaluate since women in the general population have been reported to have a higher rate of attempted suicide than men (Bratfos,

1971), while men in the general population have a higher rate of completed suicide than women (Gibbs, 1966).

Among alcoholic women the incidence of suicide attempts clearly exceeds that for the female population as a whole and that for alcoholic men (Curlee, 1970; Rathod & Thomson, 1971; Rimmer, Pitts, Reich, & Winokur, 1971). Curlee (1970) found attempted suicide rates of 1% for men and 11% for women in a sample of alcoholic patients' case histories, while Rimmer *et al.* (1971) found the rates to be 26% for male alcoholics and 44% for female alcoholics. Rathod and Thomson (1971) reported a similar excess of female attempters, 6% for males and 37% for females. A report based on official U.S. mortality statistics noted lower rates of both alcoholism and suicide among women (Rushing, 1969). However, this investigation did not use alcoholic samples to determine sex differences in suicides; therefore, the sex with the highest rate of alcoholism (males) could be expected to have more suicides in terms of absolute number, though not necessarily in terms of mortality rate.

Although there is no disagreement about alcoholic women having higher rates of attempted suicide, recent data appear to challenge the previous belief that alcoholic women, like women in the general population, have lower rates of completed suicides than alcoholic men. Adelstein and White (1977) indicate that the rate of completed suicide (based on death certificates) among male alcoholics is 22 times the rate for males in the general population, and among females 23 times the population rate. Also, among alcoholic patients studied by Schmidt and deLint (1972), excess suicide was similar for both sexes (frequency of observed suicide/frequency of expected suicide = 6.02 for men and 8.69 for women). However, as mentioned previously, Schmidt and deLint used expected mortality rates for men to calculate these ratios, a somewhat questionable method. Given the lower rates of suicide among women in the general population, their data in fact suggest a greater excess of completed suicide among female alcoholics.

As seen in Table 5-2, two other studies also indicate a preponderance of completed suicides among female alcoholics (Dahlgren & Myrhed, 1977; Lindelius, Salum, & Agren, 1974). The female mortality ratios are presented as the ratio of observed suicides compared to those expected for women in the general population. However, even when the more conservative approach of using the general male population to determine expected suicide rates for alcoholic women was used (Dahlgren & Myrhed, 1977; Schmidt & deLint, 1972), women's risk of completed suicide is at least equal to that of men.

LIVER DISORDERS

The incidence of alcohol-related liver disorders and, in many cases, associated mortality by sex, has now been well documented in the United States (Kramer, Kuller, & Fisher, 1968; Kuller, Kramer, & Fisher, 1969; U.S.

Statistical Bulletin, 1977), Great Britain (Krasner, Davis, Portmann, & Williams, 1977; Morgan & Sherlock, 1977), Sweden (Hallen & Krook, 1963; Hallen & Linne, 1970), and even in Japan (Nakamura, Takezawa, Sato, Kera, & Maeda, 1979) where the incidence of alcoholism in women is low compared to Europe and the United States.

Mortality rates from cirrhosis among white men and women in the general U.S. population and among Metropolitan Life Insurance Company's standard ordinary policyholders are available for the 10-year period between 1963 and 1973 (U.S. Statistical Bulletin, 1977). During that time age-adjusted death rates for white males in the general population increased 29% at all ages combined, while among white females the rates rose by 20%. During that same period increases greater than 40% occurred among men in the 25–44 age group and among women in the 55–64 age group. More recent data suggest that the mortality rate for women may be increasing. For example, four times as many women with alcoholic cirrhosis were admitted to hospitals in England and Wales in 1977 than in 1970 (see Saunders, Davis, & Williams, 1981, for review).

Epidemiological surveys from all over the world indicate a direct relationship between per capita consumption of alcohol and the number of deaths from cirrhosis (Lelbach, 1974; Williams & Davis, 1976). Other variables that can be expected to affect cirrhosis rates are drinking history (length, quantity, and pattern), socioeconomic class, age, and sex. Not all studies that present data by sex include information on these other variables, and some of the variation in prevalence rates in the studies reviewed may be due to these unreported characteristics. Nevertheless, the pattern emerging from the literature suggests that women who drink heavily run a greater risk of liver disorders than men.

Spain (1945) was the first to observe that more women than men developed portal cirrhosis associated with heavy drinking. Also, the women in this study died at an earlier age (average: 48.6 years) than the men (average: 56.3 years). Since then, several studies have indicated sex differences in the incidence of hepatitis and cirrhosis of the liver. These investigations have used a variety of methods to determine the prevalence of liver disease in the populations examined, including large-scale autopsy studies (Hallen & Krook, 1963; Viel, Donoso, Salcedo, & Varela, 1968), analysis of death certificates confirmed by a medical examiner (Kramer et al., 1968; Kuller et al., 1969), follow-up studies of patients who had liver biopsies (Brunt, Kew, Scheuer, & Sherlock, 1974; Krasner et al., 1977; Levi & Chalmers, 1978; Lischner, Alexander, & Galambos, 1971; Mikkelsen, Turrill, & Kern 1968; Morgan & Sherlock, 1977), or both autopsy and biopsy analysis (Phillips & Davidson, 1954; Powell & Klatskin, 1968; Wilkinson, Santamaria, & Rankin, 1969).

In addition to variations in method for determining liver pathology, differing types of samples have been used to identify such cases. Looking only at samples of cirrhotic alcoholic patients, it would appear that more

men than women are affected with liver disorders, in ratios of approximately
1.6 : 1 (Hallen & Krook, 1963; Hallen & Linne, 1970) or 2.7 : 1 (Krasner *et al.*,
1977). However, the relative risk for liver disorders in male and female
alcoholics cannot be determined in studies of this type, because in any
population fewer women than men are alcoholic. A better way to calculate
the relative risk of liver disorders in male and female alcoholics is to
calculate the prevalence of liver disorders in each sex separately.

In order that the incidence of liver disorders among alcoholics could be
determined within each sex, Wilkinson *et al.* (1969) studied 663 male and 137
female alcoholics in Melbourne, Australia. These investigators found 77
cases of alcoholic cirrhosis confirmed by biopsy, representing 16% of the
women and 8% of the men. Among those who had developed cirrhosis,
women reported shorter histories of excessive drinking than did the men (13
years vs. 20 years). Similar excess risk for women has been found in other
studies that used this approach. In an earlier study Phillips and Davidson
(1954) identified histological liver abnormalities in 70% of female alcoholics
but in only 41% of male alcoholics. Viel *et al.* (1968), studying 1079 male and
269 female Chilean alcoholics, found more than twice the rate of cirrhosis
among the women than among the men (29% compared to 11%). Similarly,
Lischner *et al.* (1971) found that 64% of their patients with alcoholic hepatitis
were women, a much higher rate than would be expected on the basis of
male–female ratios of alcoholism in the general population.

Other studies using liver biopsy data confirm these observations. Liver
biopsy is the only reliable method, at this time, for accurately diagnosing
liver disease. Krasner *et al.* (1977) studied 293 cases of alcoholic liver disease
admitted to King's College Hospital Liver Unit by this method and found
significantly higher rates of central sclerosing hyaline necrosis, the most
severe form of alcoholic hepatitis, in the women patients. This disorder
occurred in 11.3% of the women but in only 3.3% of the men.

Morgan and Sherlock (1977) showed that the incidence of chronic
advanced liver disease (hepatitis with or without cirrhosis) in alcoholics was
significantly higher among women (86%) than among men (65%). Analysis
of the socioeconomic status of the patients revealed that more than half were
in the professional and managerial classes; due to the location of the Royal
Free Hospital in London (Hampstead), the sample was selected disproportionately from the higher socioeconomic levels. Since membership in
higher socioeconomic classes can be expected to be advantageous in terms of
both obtaining adequate nutrition and having greater access to the health
care system, these findings are particularly informative. While more women
than men in this sample had liver disorders, the difference was smaller than
in studies employing samples that selected patients from a broader socioeconomic range.

These data are noteworthy in view of reported trends in the incidence of
cirrhosis mortality over the past 20 years, which show that increases have

been greatest among black women, a group that is often found to be socioeconomically disadvantaged. Kramer *et al.* (1968) analyzed death certificates and found a 260% increase in cirrhosis mortality among black women between 1957 and 1966.

A study by Levi and Chalmers (1978) appears to be the only one failing to find sex differences in alcohol-related hepatitis or cirrhosis. This study was conducted in a general hospital rather than an alcoholism treatment unit. Although all subjects could not specifically be labeled "alcoholic," the authors noted that all subjects had consumed at least 80 grams per day of ethanol (about 4½ pints of beer) for at least 1 year.

Recently a number of studies have specifically addressed the question of whether sex differences in the incidence of cirrhosis and hepatitis may be due to differences in quantity of alcohol consumed, pattern of drinking, or number of years of heavy drinking. Three studies reporting that female alcoholics had higher cirrhosis rates (relative to nonalcoholic women) than did male alcoholics (relative to nonalcoholic male controls) interviewed women concerning their daily intake of alcohol (Krasner *et al.*, 1977; Pequignot, Chabert, Eydoux, & Courcoul, 1974; Wilkinson *et al.*, 1969). In all of these, women were found to consume less alcohol than men. Three studies are also available in which duration of drinking was determined by an interview (Ashley *et al.*, 1977; Morgan & Sherlock, 1977; Wilkinson *et al.*, 1969) and in which women were shown to have increased risk for liver disorders. Of these, only the Morgan and Sherlock (1977) investigation failed to find a shorter duration of drinking associated with a higher risk for cirrhosis, hepatitis, or fatty liver in women. Although the quantity of alcohol consumed and the length of history of alcohol abuse were similar for men and women, the incidence of chronic advanced liver disease was higher for women (86%) than men (65%).

Given the substantial evidence that women are more vulnerable to the effects of alcohol, it is critical to begin to ask what mechanism may be responsible for observed differences. A number of theories have been advanced to explain the observed sex differences in liver pathology, including differences in drinking pattern, possible adverse effects of estrogen on liver function, and possible differences in autoimmunity.

The effects of estrogen on liver functioning are well known and have been reviewed by Galambos (1972), who noted that estrogen administration can impair liver function in the absence of liver disease and may worsen liver function when active liver disease is present. The role of estrogen in the increased morbidity and mortality from liver disorders among alcoholic women needs further investigation.

The immunological differences between female and male alcoholics with liver disorders also appear worthy of increased study. In their survey of 293 patients with alcoholic liver disease, Krasner *et al.* (1977) found that women, particularly those under the age of 45, had a significantly higher incidence of alcoholic hepatitis and cirrhosis than men. In addition, auto-antibodies were more common among the women, suggesting that immune mechanisms may play a role in the pathogenesis of alcoholic liver disease in women. Williams and Davis (1976) have also commented on the possible relationship between premenopausal autoimmunity in liver disorders and other inflammatory autoimmune mechanisms that subside after menopause.

NEUROENDOCRINE EFFECTS

Studies have related excessive drinking by women to biological events in their lives. For example, one investigation found that more than half of the women attending an outpatient alcoholism clinic started drinking or in-creased their drinking shortly before menstruation (Belfer, Shader, Carroll, & Harmatz, 1971). Others have attempted to link menopause with excessive drinking in women (Curlee, 1969). Still other studies have found a greater than expected rate of infertility, miscarriages, hysterectomies, and sexual dysfunction among women with alcohol-related problems (Kinsey, 1968; Wilsnack, 1982).

While many references have been made to the presumed relationship between problem drinking and the menstrual cycle, few empirical studies have been done, and all of them have relied on patients' reports rather than on hormone measurements to establish estrual phase. The link between menopause and problem drinking is equally tenuous for lack of empirical data. On the average, alcoholic women come to treatment in their forties (Schuckit, Pitts, Reich, King, & Winokur, 1969; Winokur, Reich, Rimmer, & Pitts, 1970), which is the lower end of the age range for menopause. Further, available data suggest that women who enter treatment at that time have been drinking excessively since their 30s, well before the age of menopause.

A biological explanation may be warranted for clinical observations of excessive rates of infertility, miscarriage, hysterectomy, and sexual dysfunc-tion among women with alcohol-related problems. These changes may be a direct result of the toxic effects of alcohol on the hypothalamic–pituitary–gonadal axis. Recent studies have shown that female rats fed a diet containing 36% of total calories as ethanol over a 50-day period had reduced plasma levels of estradiol and progesterone. These animals also displayed histo-logical evidence of ovarian failure (Van Thiel, Gavaler, Lester, & Sherins, 1978).

While the animal data suggest a direct toxic effect of ethanol on gonadal functioning in female rats, virtually nothing is known about gonadal func-tioning in alcoholic women. Except for three rather small investigations, one in France (Hugues, Perret, Adessi, Cosie, & Modigliani, 1978) and two in the United States (McNamee, Grant, Ratcliffe, Ratcliffe, & Oliver, 1979;

Mendelson, Mello, & Ellingboe, 1981), there is a scarcity of studies of the effects of chronic and acute alcohol intake on circulating gonadotrophin and gonadal steroid concentrations. Hugues *et al.* (1978) have examined hypothalamic–pituitary–gonadal functioning in alcoholic women. Estradiol, follicle-stimulating hormone (FSH), and prolactin levels were measured at baseline in these women and again following administration of synthetic luteinizing hormone releasing hormone (LHRH) and thyrotropin releasing hormone (TRH). This procedure identified two subgroups among the women: those considered to be menopausal and those in menopausal transition. Although the small sample size (11 women) limits the conclusions that can be drawn, the results suggest a normal hypothalamic–pituitary–gonadal axis in postmenopausal alcoholic women. However, the investigators noted that both before and after administration of LHRH and FSH, plasma estradiol levels were somewhat lower in alcoholic women in menopausal transition than in a control group of nonalcoholic women of similar age.

Although only one investigation was specifically of alcoholic women, studies of acutely administered alcohol upon hormone functioning in non-alcoholic women might provide information regarding the mechanism responsible for the gynecological problems observed in women who abuse alcohol. McNamee *et al.* (1979) investigated the effects of acute alcohol administration (2.8 mg per kg of body weight) in young nonalcoholic women. While the conclusions of this study were limited by small sample size (8 women), the findings were essentially negative. Alcohol administration failed to reduce serum testosterone or increase serum luteinizing hormone. No consistent effects were found for progesterone, estradiol, or FSH.

Another study investigated plasma prolactin, luteinizing hormone, and estradiol levels in six normal adult women given alcohol to achieve peak blood alcohol levels of 88 mg per 100 ml (Mendelson *et al.*, 1981). This was a carefully controlled study in which each woman was tested once following ingestion of an isocaloric beverage (equal in calories but without alcohol) and once following alcohol. Measurements were carried out in two consecutive menstrual cycles so that the same point in the menstrual cycle could be sampled (Day 8, 9, 10) once with placebo and once with ethanol. No significant differences were found between alcohol and placebo administration for luteinizing hormone and estradiol. A small but significant elevation in prolactin was found, however, during the descending portion of the blood alcohol curve.

These findings and the negative findings of McNamee *et al.* (1979) depart significantly from those observed for men. Acute alcohol intake in normal men is associated with a sudden and transient reduction of plasma testosterone levels (Mendelson, Mello, & Ellingboe, 1977). In addition, studies of male chronic alcoholics have documented the existence of gonadal dysfunction by the presence of greater than expected infertility rates, hypo-androgenization, and feminization (Van Thiel, Lester, & Sherins, 1974). The only study available (Hugues *et al.*, 1978) that investigated hormonal functioning in alcoholic and nonalcoholic women was essentially negative; no consistent differences in basal levels of estradiol, FSH, or prolactin were found. Although the findings for alcoholic women fail to show significant alteration in hormonal functioning, these results should be considered tentative without confirming evidence from other laboratories.

CARDIOVASCULAR DISORDERS

A variety of possible risk factors for coronary heart disease have been investigated in epidemiological studies, including the sex of the individuals studied. Typically, these studies have used such measures as myocardial infarction and mortality as endpoints in the disease process. Mortality ratios for alcohol-related deaths from circulatory disorders indicate that women have at least the same risk as men (Table 5-2). While sex-specific morbidity data appear to vary with the type of vascular disorder, mortality is typically reported for all cardiovascular disorders combined. Therefore, this review examines risk for selected cardiovascular disorders, specifically, cardiomyopathy and atherosclerosis, where data are available by sex.

Cardiomyopathy refers to disease of the myocardium or middle layer of the heart, which consists of cardiac muscle. The condition, characterized by degeneration of cardiac muscle, is frequently found in alcoholics. Atherosclerosis is characterized by lipid deposits in the inner lining of large and medium-sized blood vessels. The deposits are associated with fibrosis and calcification, which in severe cases can reduce the size of the arterial lumen and predispose the individual to coronary thrombosis. The resulting ischemic manifestations include angina pectoris and myocardial infarction, strokes, and other complications.

Cardiomyopathy

Data on cardiomyopathy associated with alcoholism have consistently indicated that more men than women are affected (Regan, 1973), although this may simply reflect the greater incidence of alcoholism among males. Preclinical abnormalities of cardiac function have also been described for male alcoholics (Spodick, Pigott, & Chirife, 1972). Much less is known about possible preclinical abnormalities in alcoholic women.

One investigation of 22 male and 14 female alcoholics, who were matched for duration and quantity of drinking and were free of heart disease, hypertension, diabetes mellitus, obesity, and pulmonary disease, indicated that women may be less vulnerable to the effects of alcohol on the myocardium (Wu, Sudhakar, Jaferei, Ahmed, & Regan, 1976). After an abstinent period averaging 12 days, the alcoholics' electrocardiograms were obtained for comparison with those of 22 nonalcoholic controls who also were free of heart disease. On the basis of systolic time intervals (spacing of heartbeats), abnormal myocardial function was evident in the men but not in the women, suggesting that women are protected in some manner from the toxic effects of ethanol on the myocardium.

Atherosclerosis and Coronary Occlusions

Recent sex-specific data are available on coronary artery occlusion associated with alcohol intake and other risk factors (Anderson, Barboriak, & Rimm, 1977). While the sample did not specifically include alcoholics, alcohol intake was measured. Coronary arteriography, an accepted procedure for diagnosing coronary artery disease, was used on 1635 male and 371 female heart patients. The degree of coronary occlusion revealed by the procedure was then related to quantitative measurements of blood cholesterol and triglyceride levels, diabetes, age, history of smoking, and alcohol intake. Coronary occlusion was rated on a scale of 0 (no occlusion) to 300 (all three main arteries occluded). The patients were then divided into three groups corresponding to occlusion scores of 0–49, 50–149, and 150–300.

For men in each of these three occlusion groups, increases in age, cholesterol, triglycerides, smoking, and diabetes were found to have a positive correlation to the degree of occlusion. Similar associations were found in the women. However, men showed a negative correlation between alcohol intake and occlusion scores; that is, greater use of alcohol was associated with less occlusion of arteries. In contrast, the women patients did not show significantly different occlusion scores at different levels of alcohol consumption.

It should be noted that alcohol consumption was quite moderate in this group of patients. Even in the group of men that drank most, weekly ethanol consumption was only 201 ml, equivalent to 4 drinks of beverage alcohol a day. Also, among the women, those in the high consumption group (84 ml per week, or between 1 and 2 drinks per day) consumed less alcohol than the lowest consumption group among the men (114 ml per week). Therefore, it is uncertain whether alcohol consumption fails to protect females because of a biological difference or because the average consumption among women in this study was so low. The possible protective effect of low levels of alcohol use among men was also observed in the Framingham Study, a large epidemiological investigation of risk factors associated with cardiovascular disorders (Kannel, 1976).

Results of a number of studies suggest that atherosclerosis is less extensive and myocardial infarctions are less common in people with cirrhosis (Hirst, Hadley, & Gore, 1965; Ruebner, Edin, Miyai, & Keio, 1961). The reason has been assumed to be a protective effect of alcohol against atherosclerosis. One large postmortem study of atherosclerosis among males and females with cirrhosis (Vanacek, 1976) involved analysis of 12,454 autopsies

(6903 males and 5551 females). Liver cirrhosis was found in 507 of the subjects (317 males and 190 females). Although it cannot be assumed that all these cases of liver cirrhosis were alcohol-related, it can be assumed that a significant proportion were. For both males and females, an inverse relationship was found between liver cirrhosis and atherosclerosis (measured by raised lesions of the aorta and coronary arteries and the presence of myocardial lesions).

One more study of coronary disease in women should be mentioned. Talbott, Kuller, Detre, and Perper (1977) examined the relationship between biological and psychosocial risk factors for sudden death in white women. Although the incidence rates of myocardial infarction and sudden death are four to six times higher for men than for women between the ages of 45 and 64, these investigators identified a sample of women between the ages of 25 and 64 without prior history of heart disease who died within 24 hours after the onset of symptoms. Multiple regression analysis revealed that a history of psychiatric illness, cigarette smoking, alcohol consumption, educational incongruity with spouse, and the number of children the woman had given birth to contributed significantly to the differences between the women who died suddenly and a control group of women residing in the same neighborhood. Of the group who died suddenly, 26.5% were heavy drinkers, compared to 6.3% of the control group.

In summary, few studies are available relating excessive alcohol consumption to risk of cardiovascular disorders among women. Preclinical abnormalities suggestive of alcoholic cardiomyopathy appear to be less common among alcoholic women than in alcoholic men, while risk for atherosclerosis may not be significantly worsened by drinking in either sex. It must be emphasized that data suggesting a protective effect of alcohol against atherosclerosis have come primarily from studies of individuals who drink only moderately and are not alcoholic. Further work is needed to determine the relative risk for particular cardiovascular disorders, since mortality data that summarize risk for all such disorders combined suggest that excessive drinking is a risk factor.

Studies are also needed to examine the role of high density lipoprotein (HDL) in male and female alcoholics. Numerous studies have shown that patients with high plasma levels of HDL, a condition associated with drinking alcohol and exercising regularly, have a relatively low risk of developing coronary artery disease (Castelli, Doyle, Gordon, Hames, Hjortland, Hulley, Kagan, & Zukel, 1977). Plasma HDL was found to be about 10% higher in people who consume the equivalent of 1 drink a day than in people who do not drink (Castelli, Gordon, Hjortland, Kagan, Doyle, Hames, Hulley, & Zukel, 1977). Furthermore, the average HDL cholesterol is 45 mg/dl in middle-aged men and 55 mg/dl in middle-aged women, and this 10 mg/dl difference is associated with a twofold difference in risk of developing coronary artery disease (*The Medical Letter*, 1979).

These results suggest that women who drink may be at less risk of developing coronary artery disease than men who drink. However, these risk factors were determined among moderate drinkers, and it is unclear whether the effect of alcohol on HDL gives any protection to women or men who drink excessively or are alcoholic.

CANCERS

The Third National Cancer Survey (Williams & Horm, 1977) provided extensive data on the risk of various kinds of cancer associated with smoking and drinking. A variety of other factors were also taken into account, including socioeconomic status, education, age, and sex. While there is a strong positive association between smoking and drinking, this study analyzed their separate contribution to cancer risk. Thus, the risk of cancer in various sites could be assessed in drinkers of either sex without being confounded by the contribution of smoking. To measure the effect of drinking on the chances of getting a particular kind of cancer, an index of alcohol consumption was used that incorporated daily consumption and duration of alcohol use.

In men, greater use of alcohol was strongly associated with increased risk of oral, pharyngeal, and laryngeal cancers. In women, greater use of alcohol was strongly associated with greater risk of cancer of lip and tongue, pharynx, and esophagus. Of particular importance is the fact that regression analysis of the survey data revealed that in both men and women cancer of the mouth and esophagus were related more to drinking than to smoking. The opposite was true for cancer of the larynx.

The relative importance of smoking and drinking as risk factors for cancer was examined in another retrospective study of 3716 patients with histologically proven cancer of the lung, mouth, esophagus, or bladder (Wynder & Stellman, 1977). Unlike the Williams and Horm (1977) study, this investigation used 18,000 controls who had no history of smoking-related cancers. The risk of mouth, larynx, and esophageal cancers among male smokers increased with the quantity of alcohol consumed. Among nonsmokers, however, alcohol consumption did not result in a significant increase in risk. A similar analysis was not presented for women. The results suggest that heavy alcohol usage interacts with smoking, so that alcohol may be considered to promote tobacco carcinogenesis.

Wynder (1976) had previously suggested that the cancer-promoting effect of alcohol may be due to the nutritional deficiencies associated with alcoholism. Another interpretation is that cancer risk increases with direct exposure to alcohol. Williams and Horm (1977) have noted that the decreasing relative risk of cancers along the digestive tract parallels the progressive dilution of alcohol as it progresses through the tract and the portal circulation. The risk is highest in the oral cavity; lower in the larynx, esophagus, and liver; and lowest in the stomach, pancreas, colon, and rectum.

The role of alcohol and tobacco in multiple primary cancers of the upper digestive system, larynx, and lung was investigated in a prospective study by Schottenfeld, Gantt, and Wynder (1974). Survival rates 5 years after cancer was first diagnosed were significantly higher in women than in men, and the women were less likely to be heavy drinkers or heavy smokers than the men prior to diagnosis. Among patients with single primary cancers, 38% of the men had drunk 7 or more drinks a day before cancer was diagnosed, compared to 14% of the women. Among patients with multiple primary cancers, 62% of the men and 43% of the women had drunk 7 or more drinks daily.

It was found that both men and women reduced their drinking after cancer was diagnosed and in about the same proportion. Among patients with multiple primary cancers, 13% of the men and 14% of the women continued to drink heavily (7 or more drinks a day). Therefore, the greater survival rate noted for women 5 years after diagnosis of the index cancer was related most significantly to the amount of alcohol and tobacco exposure they had experienced before the diagnosis.

Since this study dealt with patients who already had cancer and were admitted to a cancer center for treatment, it does not provide cancer incidence rates (i.e., frequency of new cases) in populations of male and female alcoholics. Nevertheless, the data suggest that individuals who have 7 or more drinks a day are at greater risk of getting cancer than those who drink less. Further, it is not possible to determine the relative vulnerability to development of carcinoma of the oral cavity, pharynx, or larynx in association with drinking by sex, due to the fact that women in this study were distinguished from the men by their less intensive exposure to tobacco and alcohol prior to the index cancer.

EFFECTS ON THE CENTRAL NERVOUS SYSTEM

There has been much debate about the relationship between abuse of psychoactive drugs, including alcohol, and brain damage. Brain damage has been assessed with a variety of psychological tests (see Goodwin & Hill, 1975, and Parsons & Leber, 1982, for reviews), pneumoencephalography (Brewer & Perrett, 1971; Haug, 1968), and electroencephalography (Allen, Wagman, Falliace, & McIntosh, 1971; Johnson, Burdick, & Smith, 1970). More recently, computerized transaxial tomography (CTT) has been used (Bergman, Borg, Hindmarsh, Ideström, & Mutzell, 1980; Cala, Jones, Mastaglia, & Wiley, 1978; Cala, Jones, Wiley, & Mastaglia, 1980; Cala &

Mastaglia, 1980; Epstein, Pisani, & Fawcett, 1977; Fox, Ramsey, Huckman, & Proske, 1976; Hill, 1980; Hill & Mikhael, 1979a; Hill, Reyes, Mikhael, & Ayre, 1979; Ron, Acker, & Lishman, 1980). This technique allows for visualization of brain ventricles and sulci and their measurement.

Unfortunately, few studies have used the controls necessary to pinpoint the location and frequency of morphological cerebral changes among alcoholics. In the studies where structured changes were assessed with CTT, subject selection has often been based on persistent abnormal functioning, neurological signs, or other indicators warranting CTT scans (Epstein et al., 1977; Fox et al., 1976). Although there are studies that appear to fulfill criteria for unbiased sampling techniques, such as those of Bergman et al. (1980) and Hill (1980), these studies included only males.

In general, the reported frequency of ventricular enlargement and cortical atrophy has varied considerably (Parsons & Leber, 1982). This variation is probably due to the heterogeneous selection criteria used by different investigators and the lack of common criteria for assessing CTT scans. Further complicating the picture is the fact that of the dozen or so CTT studies reported in the world literature only five have included women (Cala et al., 1978, 1980; Cala & Mastaglia, 1980; Epstein et al., 1977; Fox et al., 1976).

Conclusions that may be drawn from these five studies are limited because either the number of women included was very small (5 women in the Fox et al. investigation and 16 in the Epstein et al. study), heavy drinking individuals rather than alcoholics were assessed (Cala et al., 1978, 1980), or statistical comparisons between males and females were not made. The one exception is Cala and Mastaglia (1980), which compared males and females and provided a control group of abstainers or light infrequent drinkers.

While the Cala and Mastaglia (1980) study is the first attempt to statistically compare the results obtained for men and women, its conclusions should be interpreted cautiously due to the fact that the sample was obtained from a retrospective case review of more than 14,000 patients who had had a diagnostic CTT scan. This method would be expected to produce an elevated incidence of cerebral atrophy and ventricular enlargement because the available data are based on records of individuals who presumably warranted CTT scans for other reasons such as neurological deficits. Further, though Cala and her colleagues conclude that males may show a greater degree of atrophy at an earlier age, their data were not adjusted for possible differences in mean daily consumption of ethanol or duration of drinking, both of which appear to vary between men and women (e.g., Armor, Polich, & Stambul, 1976). Inspection of the graphs presented by Cala and Mastaglia (1980) indicate that approximately one-third of the male alcoholics studied were below the age of 36, though none of the women studied were below that age. Also, while the age range for the alcoholics was from 17 to 73 years, the control group was between the ages of 15 and 40, a factor that could affect the proportion of alcoholics' scans appearing abnormal when compared to the younger control group.

While the literature on neuropsychological changes in alcoholic men is now abundant (see Parsons & Leber, 1982), neuropsychological investigations of alcoholic women have been rare. To date, these studies in women have been completed in only one laboratory. Hatcher, Jones, and Jones (1977) found alcoholic women to be impaired on both verbal and nonverbal abstracting tasks (Shipley Abstract and Raven's Progressive Matrices) compared to nonalcoholic women. Since male alcoholics have often been reported to show deficits on these and other measures (Goodwin & Hill, 1975; Parsons & Leber, 1982), this study would appear only to show similarities between male and female alcoholics. More recently, Silberstein and Parsons (1980) administered a large battery of neuropsychological tests to alcoholic women to assess cognitive functioning. The subjects were 25 female alcoholics selected from a residential treatment facility and matched for age, education, and vocabulary with 25 nonalcoholic women. This study uncovered deficits for alcoholic women on abstracting tasks (Shipley Abstraction; Raven's Progressive Matrices, Set II; WAIS Digit Symbol and Block Design). However, Silberstein and Parsons found the alcoholic women to be unimpaired on tests measuring verbal abilities (WAIS Comprehension, Similarities, Digit Span, or Picture Completion). This pattern of abstracting deficits coupled with no impairment on verbal tasks is similar to that often found for men. However, unlike the pattern of deficits often reported for male alcoholics, these female alcoholics did not show impairment on either the Category Test or the Wisconsin Card Sorting Test, both of which measure the ability of subjects to display conceptual shifting when asked to sort forms by category.

Two cross validation studies (Fabian, Jenkins, & Parsons, 1981) performed in the same laboratory (University of Oklahoma Health Sciences Center) employed 37 alcoholic and 73 nonalcoholic women in the first study and 35 alcoholic and 35 nonalcoholic women in the second. For the most part, they failed to confirm the previously observed differences in the pattern of neuropsychological deficits noted by Silberstein and Parsons (1980). Whereas Silberstein and Parsons had found alcoholic women without impairment on a variety of tests on which male alcoholics typically show impairment (Category Test, Tactual Performance Test, Raven's Set I, and the Wisconsin Card Sorting Test), the alcoholic women tested by Fabian and colleagues were unimpaired only on the Wisconsin Card Sorting Test, indicating only a minor departure from the typical male alcoholic pattern.

Thus, it may be concluded that while one study (Silberstein & Parsons, 1980) found women alcoholics to be unimpaired on tests of conceptual shifting, a pattern unlike male alcoholics, other studies have shown a pattern of deficits for alcoholic women quite similar to that often observed in male alcoholics (Fabian et al., 1981; Hatcher et al., 1977). It should also be noted that most studies of women alcoholics have employed women alcoholics with shorter histories of heavy drinking than those typically found for male alcoholics employed in neuropsychological studies. For example, Fabian et al. (1981) report their women as having an average history of 6 years of heavy drinking, whereas studies of male alcoholics typically report at least half of their subject population with histories of 10 years or more (Goodwin & Hill, 1975; Parsons & Leber, 1982).

In summary, neuropsychological and neuroradiological data appear to be inconclusive regarding the prevalence of cognitive dysfunction, cerebral atrophy, and ventricular dilatation among alcoholic women when compared to age-matched women who are abstainers or light, infrequent drinkers. Moreover, the expected risk for alcoholic women as compared to alcoholic men is unknown at this time.

BIOLOGICAL VULNERABILITY FOR ALCOHOL ABUSE AND ITS CONSEQUENCES

From a public health perspective, discussion of biomedical consequences of alcohol abuse among women is incomplete without consideration of the vulnerabilities that female individuals have: (1) to drink abusively, and (2) to develop organ damage as a result of drinking. While women's vulnerability to drink abusively can arise because of either biological or psychosocial factors, the present discussion centers on the biological factors. A vulnerability model for alcoholism in women has recently been proposed which takes into account both biological and psychosocial factors (see Hill, 1981).

Genetic Factors and Risk for Alcohol Abuse

Among possible factors that may predispose women to alcoholism and alcohol-related problems is the presence of alcoholism in their families. Several investigators have noticed an increased incidence of alcoholism among the first-degree relatives of female alcoholics (Curlee, 1970; Schuckit et al., 1969; Winokur & Clayton, 1968; Winokur et al., 1970). The fact that a disorder tends to "run in families" does not, of course, indicate that it is inherited. Environmental factors within the family may shape the behavior of its members, possibly across multiple generations, as the work of Wolin, Bennett, and Noonan (1978) indicates.

Evidence suggesting a genetic predisposition to alcoholism can be obtained using a variety of strategies including family history studies, studies of children of alcoholics adopted away before rearing factors come into play, and studies of similarities in drinking patterns of twins. The latter strategy has thus far not been used in studies of alcoholic women.

Family history studies provide a strong suggestion of a genetic predisposition, though the evidence is not conclusive because the contribution of environmental influences is not easily separated from the genetic influence (one lives with an affected parent as well as receiving genes from that parent). Adoption studies can separate the genetic and environmental contributions, while family history studies can only provide definitive evidence that familial transmission occurs. Though more limited than adoption studies, family history studies can provide clues concerning this transmission, particularly when sophisticated tests of transmission are applied to such data. The multifactorial model of disease transmission has been applied to family history data by the Washington University group in order to evaluate the relative contribution of genetic, familial-environmental (influences within the family) and nonfamilial-environmental (influences outside the family, e.g., cultural) factors.

Applying this model to family history data for 365 relatives of male and female alcoholics, Cloninger, Christiansen, Reich, and Gottesman (1978) found that female alcoholics did not have either a greater or a smaller proportion of alcoholic male or female relatives than male alcoholics did, indicating that the male and female alcoholics differed only with respect to nonfamilial-environmental factors, factors beyond the family that may be more cultural in nature (e.g., a greater proportion of one sex being exposed to risk, under greater stress, or more protected than the other sex).

On the basis of one Scandinavian adoption study, a genetic predisposition to alcoholism appeared plausible only for males. Goodwin, Schulsinger, Hermansen, Guze, and Winokur (1973) compared males born to parents with and without alcoholism and found a significantly higher rate of alcoholism in those who had alcoholic parents, even though both groups of offspring had been adopted out before 6 weeks of age and raised by adoptive parents. These results for male offspring of alcoholics were not confirmed in a similar study of daughters of alcoholics who were raised by adoptive parents (Goodwin, Schulsinger, Knop, Mednick, & Guze, 1977). This negative result for daughters whose biological parents were alcoholic should be viewed cautiously, however, because too few cases of alcoholism—only two per group—were found in either group when the daughters were interviewed as adults. More recently Bohman, Sigvardsson, and Cloninger (1981) analyzed data from a variety of sources, including treatment facilities and registration with the Swedish Temperance Board, from 913 Swedish women adopted by nonrelatives at an early age. They concluded that alcoholism in women was genetically transmitted (a threefold increase in daughters of alcoholic mothers) and was passed most often from mothers to daughters; fewer cases of alcoholism developed in daughters of alcoholic fathers than alcoholic mothers, though there was a statistically nonsignificant excess of daughters of alcoholic fathers compared to daughters of nonalcoholic parentage.

If one postulates a genetic factor in alcoholism, then it is of interest to search for the susceptibility that is being inherited. The array of personality "types" represented in the human species may one day provide a clue to the biological vulnerability. Certain aspects of personality appear to have a remarkable stability over the lifetime of an individual, possibly suggesting a genetic influence. Thomas, Chess, and Birch (1968), in a study of children from birth to 10 years, found remarkable consistency in temperament across time. Undoubtedly, the adult personality is acquired through a socialization process that begins in childhood and probably is continued throughout adulthood to some degree. The emphasis here, however, is on the antecedent personality factors that may be biological (genetic) in origin.

There have been a number of attempts to find the "alcoholic" personality but mostly among individuals who have already become alcoholic. The early work of Schuckit *et al.* (1969), which examined the characteristics of 70 female alcoholics, clearly indicates the futility of searching for the "typical alcoholic personality" among men or women who have *already* become alcoholic. Of the 70 alcoholic women, 19 showed preexisting affective disorders, 6 showed sociopathy, 2 schizophrenia, and 6 hysteria.

Few longitudinal studies of personality factors are available, and even fewer involve women who later developed alcohol problems. One exception is the Oakland Growth Study, a prospective study of male and female adolescents who were followed into adulthood. Data from this study revealed different personality characteristics associated with male and female adult drinking patterns. The adult male problem drinkers were described as "under-controlled, impulsive and rebellious" as youth (Jones, 1968, p. 2). On the other hand, the four women who later developed alcohol problems were described as adolescents as being "self-defeating, pessimistic, withdrawn, guilty and depressive" (Jones, 1971, p. 63).

While prospective studies may give some insight into the types of personality structure that give rise to alcoholism, examination of individuals who have already become alcoholic reveals much variability. Nevertheless, the search for the "alcoholic" personality in both men and women remains an intriguing quest, particularly when viewed from a biological (genetic) perspective.

Genetic Factors and Risk for Organ Damage

The possibility that genetic factors may contribute to the risk for developing organ damage has recently been suggested. A genetic vulnerability for developing alcoholic cirrhosis has been demonstrated using HLA blood typing. The HLA histocompatibility genetic locus has been well worked out and employed in the detection of genetic markers for juvenile onset diabetes (Cavender, Orchard, Wagener, LaPorte, Rabin, & Eberhardt, 1982). Melendez, Vargas-Tank, Fuentes, Armas-Merino, Castillo, Wolff, Wegmann, and Soto (1979), studying the distribution of 16 antigens of the HLA-A and 15 antigens of the HLA-B histocompatibility systems in 40 alcoholics with cirrhosis, 18 alcoholics without cirrhosis, and normal control subjects, found the alcoholics with cirrhosis to have a significantly higher frequency of HLA-B13 when compared to normal subjects. The alcoholics without cirrhosis did not show an increase in HLA-B13, indicating that the carriers of HLA-B13 are more susceptible to liver damage. An increased frequency of other HLA antigens has also been found. An increased incidence of HLA-B8 in association with alcoholic cirrhosis was found in one investigation (Bailey, Krasner, Eddleston, Williams, Tee, Doniach, Kennedy, & Batchelor, 1976) and of HLA-B40 in another study (Bell & Nordhagen, 1980). Autoimmune reactions are more common in women and circulating non-organ-specific antibodies have been found more often in women with alcoholic liver disease than in men (Krasner et al., 1977). These investigators also found antinuclear antibodies to be more prevalent in women, and their mean serum IgG and IgM concentrations were higher. These results suggest that in addition to the hepatotoxic effects of alcohol on the liver per se, immunological reactions directed against liver cells may also have a role in the development of alcoholic liver disease.

While the genetic vulnerability to organ pathology associated with alcoholism has thus far been investigated only with respect to liver diseases, results of the cited studies and others suggest that some women may be more susceptible to the adverse consequences of drinking than others. As noted earlier, women appear to run a higher risk overall than men for developing cirrhosis in association with heavy use of alcohol. Further research is needed to determine the relative risks for other organ pathologies such as brain damage.

CONCLUSIONS

Until quite recently it has been assumed that the chronic effects of excessive alcohol consumption could be assessed without regard to the sex of the individual studied. Therefore, it has frequently been the case that women have not been included in these studies, or that too few have been included for meaningful statistical analysis. All too often investigators have failed to report the sex of individuals examined.

Another problem which makes generalizations regarding the effects of chronic alcohol ingestion difficult is the tendency for investigators to label persons as "alcoholic" without regard to the multivariate nature of alcoholism and alcohol-related problems, and particularly without regard to differences seen in men and women. Definitions of "alcoholism" or "alcohol-related problems" are often scanty or missing in the literature. Further, the quantity, frequency, and pattern of alcohol consumption of individuals studied are often ignored.

Given these limitations in much of the existing literature, an attempt has been made to review what is known about the biomedical consequences of chronic alcohol consumption with reference to the sex of the individuals considered. Overall, the conclusions that may be drawn from this review are that even though women may be less frequently identified as suffering from alcohol-related problems in the general population, among women who are so identified the risks for a variety of biomedical consequences are in many cases equal to, if not greater than, those observed in men.

Morbidity from all causes appears to be as prevalent among women as among men who suffer from alcohol-related disorders. Further, there is some indication that morbidity may be accelerated among such women; that is, following a shorter duration of heavy drinking, women present with equal risk of illness in association with alcohol consumption. One notable example is the now demonstrated increased risk for liver disorders among alcoholic women. Such disorders develop at an earlier age, following a shorter duration of heavy drinking, and presumably in association with a lower level of alcohol consumption in women than in men.

Data from the Third National Cancer Survey (Williams & Horm, 1977) as well as other large epidemiological surveys indicate that even when controlling for the effects of smoking, risk for cancers of the head and neck is increased in both men and women as a function of the amount of alcohol consumed. Further, there is some indication that women may have greater risk for these cancers in association with alcohol consumption than do men.

The effects of alcohol consumption on cardiovascular functioning can be considered to be both positive and negative. While chronic and excessive alcohol ingestion appears to be related to the incidence of cardiomyopathy among alcoholics generally, conclusions cannot at present be drawn regarding the relative risk for alcohol-associated cardiomyopathy by sex. Also, while there is some indication that moderate alcohol consumption may be associated with a reduction in coronary artery occlusion in men, women do not appear to be protected by alcohol consumption in this regard. Further, among white women who were victims of sudden death as a result of myocardial infarction, heavy drinking was four times more likely than it was among control group women.

Available data also suggest that alcohol-associated mortality takes its toll equally among women and men. In fact, if nonalcoholic women are used for comparison purposes, alcoholic women appear to run an even greater risk for premature death than do alcoholic men when compared with their nonalcoholic cohorts.

The present chapter has also discussed a number of biological concomitants of alcohol-related problems that might be considered to be more etiological in nature than consequential and were, therefore, discussed as possible biological vulnerabilities for the development of alcohol-related problems. In this section evidence was presented demonstrating that women with alcohol problems often have a family history of alcohol-related problems. However, family history studies only provide evidence that alcoholism tends to run in families but do not specify whether the transmission is genetic, arises from familial environmental factors, or is due to environmental factors outside of the family. Sophisticated analysis of data currently available for families of male and female alcoholics indicates that the transmission of alcoholism within these families is quite similar. The relatively smaller likelihood that women in a given population will develop alcoholism appears to be due to factors that may be considered cultural, and that may mitigate against heavy drinking among women. However, once cultural obstacles are overcome and women become heavy drinkers, the likelihood of becoming alcoholic appears to be as great among women as men. Adoption studies provide the best evidence of a true genetic basis for alcoholism. At present only two studies of adopted daughters of alcoholics are available. One study (Bohman et al., 1981) appears to strongly suggest a genetic factor for women alcoholics, as had been previously found for men alcoholics; specifically, a strong genetic predisposition appears to be passed from mothers to daughters.

If one assumes that genetic factors play a role in the development of alcohol-related problems in women, then a search for these genetic vulnerabilities is in order. The present discussion has emphasized the "trait" aspects of personality as opposed to the "state" aspects, noting the remarkable stability of some personality characteristics throughout the life span. The question has been raised whether or not certain genetically determined personality characteristics or traits could provide the antecedent conditions for development of alcoholism. Few longitudinal prospective studies currently are available to answer this question.

BIOMEDICAL CONSEQUENCES: IMPLICATIONS FOR PREVENTION

The present review has provided evidence that the health consequences of excessive drinking are as serious a problem for women as for men; alcohol-related morbidity and mortality for alcoholic women are as high as, if not higher than, those for alcoholic men. While the greater morbidity reported for women, as measured by the number of sick days taken and the insurance benefits used, could merely indicate differences in attitudes regarding help-seeking, the data for mortality among women as compared to men would appear to argue against that interpretation. Surely, the now abundant data concerning the prevalence of liver disorders and associated mortality among alcoholic women is one instance. Quite possibly women have more health problems as a result of drinking. If this is so, then efforts to prevent such problems for women become increasingly important.

As a result of mass media campaigns women are now much more aware of the hazards of drinking while pregnant. However, the dangers of drinking for the woman herself have not been well publicized beyond those prevention efforts aimed at reducing alcohol-related traffic accidents and associated fatalities. Since women have recently been targeted as a group to which marketing of alcoholic beverages has been aimed (Ratcliffe, 1979; Wilsnack, 1980), it becomes particularly timely to consider prevention efforts that focus on the health consequences of excessive drinking for women.

A number of prevention "models" have been proposed including the proscriptive model, the distribution of consumption model, and the public health model (see Blane, 1976, for review). The proscriptive model sees all use of alcohol as hazardous. With the exception of those religious groups that exercise effective control of their membership with regard to drinking (e.g., Seventh Day Adventists, Latter Day Saints), this model appears not to be feasible, as the repeal of Prohibition in this country attests. The distribution of consumption model (Whitehead, 1972) is based on the notion that increasing the price of alcohol or restricting availability in other ways will reduce per capita consumption to the point where rates of alcoholism in a given population will decrease.

The public health model describes disorders in terms of a host, an agent, and their interactions with environmental factors, using epidemiological techniques for collection and analysis of relevant data. As a prevention model, the public health model distinguishes between primary, secondary, and tertiary prevention. Primary prevention is aimed at removing the causes of the disorder, while secondary prevention consists of early detection to prevent the disorder from becoming fully developed. Tertiary prevention is designed to treat the fully developed disorder to prevent chronic disability, or, if possible, to cure the disorder.

The adequacy of each of these models and others for dealing with alcoholism has been debated for some time (Blane, 1976). Discussion of the pros and cons of each model is beyond the scope of this chapter. However, it should be noted that prevention of alcoholism may require a different strategy than prevention of the health consequences of alcohol consumption. Adoption of the public health model for the purposes of the present discussion appears to best illustrate this point. From the standpoint of preventing alcoholism per se, emphasis on secondary prevention or "nipping it in the bud" appears to have the most favorable cost–benefit ratio, because once cases at high risk have been identified, intervention or lack of it may tip the balance either way. For this reason, most prevention efforts have emphasized the secondary level. Attempting to reach an entire population, many of whom would not be expected to be susceptible, results in a high cost–benefit ratio that renders primary prevention somewhat less attractive. Similarly, tertiary prevention is rarely mentioned in the literature, presumably because prevention and treatment are by definition antithetical (Blane, 1976).

Yet if we look at the literature on the biomedical consequences of alcoholism, it becomes clear that defining safe levels of consumption with respect to the risks for developing particular disorders is not possible, though, of course, we have some clues. The levels associated with the development of liver cirrhosis may well be below those of the average "alcoholic" woman in treatment. Pequignot *et al.* (1974) found when comparing the alcohol consumption of patients with cirrhosis and healthy controls, all of whom lived in one geographic area of France, that women were at greater risk of cirrhosis if their daily intake exceeded 20 gm of ethanol or approximately 2 drinks per day. In contrast, men were at greater risk with intakes of over 60 gm per day (6 drinks).

While risk data by sex and alcohol consumption are not available for risk of cancers of the head and neck, the data presented by Wynder and Stellman (1977) indicate that the risk for developing cancer, independent of cigarette smoking, was increased in men who consumed more than 7 drinks per day. Assuming equal susceptibility between men and women, and adjusting for average body weight differences, it may be assumed that women run an increased risk of developing cancers of the mouth, larynx, and esophagus when they consume more than 4–5 drinks per day (assuming one-third greater body weight in men).

In light of these findings, one can see the value in primary prevention efforts that modify the drinking habits of women who, though they may not be alcoholic, or possibly may never become alcoholic, run a greater risk of developing alcoholic cirrhosis or cancers of the head and neck if they consume more than 2–5 drinks per day. Similarly, tertiary prevention strategies become increasingly important. Women in treatment need to be screened for medical problems and warned of the risks of continued drinking in addition to those attempts to ameliorate the social problems associated with their alcoholism.

BIOMEDICAL CONSEQUENCES:
IMPLICATIONS FOR TREATMENT

If women are at greater risk for health-related problems, then alcoholism treatment facilities have an added responsibility of not only treating the alcohol problem per se, but also providing the most comprehensive screening techniques available for detecting medical problems, particularly those problems that frequently occur in alcoholic women. Every new admission to an alcoholism treatment program, whether inpatient or outpatient, should receive a complete physical examination including routine laboratory screening. Especially important is a full complement of liver enzyme tests including serum glutamic-oxaloacetic transaminase (SGOT), serum glutamic-pyruvic transaminase (SGPT), bilirubin, alkaline phosphatase, and gamma-glutamyl transpeptidase (GGPT).

Many women who drink heavily may be expected to elude alcoholism treatment programs. Alcoholism is defined by its problems (family problems, troubles at work, legal difficulties, signs of physical dependence). Some women, though they meet some of the criteria for alcoholism, fail to reach a treatment facility because they attempt to hide their alcoholism and successfully do so. Others with potential health problems as a result of drinking never enter alcoholism treatment programs because their drinking has not caused social "problems" though they admit to having hangovers, blackouts, or "feeling shaky" after a day of heavy drinking. Strictly speaking, these women would not meet any of the conventional criteria for alcoholism (American Psychiatric Association *Diagnostic and Statistical Manual of Mental Disorders*, 3rd ed., 1980; Feighner, Robins, Guze, Woodruff, Winokur, & Muñoz, 1972; National Council on Alcoholism, 1972). New prevention and intervention strategies are needed for these women through (1) the development of employee assistance programs that provide annual health screening that emphasizes detection of hazardous levels of drinking and provides treatment referral services where needed for both men and women; and (2) development of an increased awareness on the part of general medical practitioners and internists that drinking more than 5 drinks per day may be hazardous to the health of women, whether they are alcoholics or not. Implementation of screening programs through either of these two mechanisms can be aided by the greater use of diagnostic tests measuring mean corpuscular volume (MCV), serum γ glutamyltransferase, and high-density lipoprotein levels, all of which appear to be good indicators of high alcohol intake (Danielsson, Ekman, Fex, Johansson, Kristensson, Nielsson-Ehle, & Wadstein, 1978; Reyes & Miller, 1980; Robinson, Monk, & Bailey, 1979; Sanchez-Craig & Annis, 1981; Saunders *et al.*, 1981; Shaw, Worner, Borysow, Schmitz, & Lieber, 1979).

The presence of neuropsychological and neuroradiological indices of brain dysfunction in male alcoholics is now undisputed. Based on rather few studies, it appears that women alcoholics, too, may be susceptible to alcohol-induced brain pathology. While the complete reversibility of brain dysfunction resulting from alcoholism remains controversial (Carlen, Wortzman, Holgate, & Wilkinson, 1978; Hill & Mikhael, 1979b), it is clear that some improvement in function occurs with increasing abstinence. However, Parsons and Leber (1982), in their review of approximately 20 studies that assessed recovery of function in male alcoholics, concluded that relatively permanent deficits in abstracting and perceptual–motor abilities are typically found. Few of the studies reviewed included alcoholics tested beyond 1 year of sobriety, so that the remaining deficits seen at these points in time must be tentatively considered permanent. Currently, there are no published studies of recovery of functioning in women alcoholics, so the rate of recovery is presently unknown. Nevertheless, from a treatment perspective, it may be useful to screen for neuropsychological deficits in alcoholic women; initiating intensive psychotherapies before some recovery of functioning occurs may be an inefficient use of therapists' time.

While few studies have addressed the efficacy of a variety of therapies for alcoholic women (group vs. individual, inpatient vs. outpatient, insight-oriented therapy vs. cognitive–behavioral therapy), such outcome studies are critically needed (see Blume, 1980; Vannicelli, Chapter 13 in this volume). One promising treatment that has not been systematically explored in women is the use of antabuse in a contingency contracting arrangement with family members. While small numbers of individuals have been reported to have side effects from long-term use of antabuse, certainly the adverse health consequences of continued drinking would appear to outweigh the risk of developing side effects.

In summary, the available literature describing risks for biomedical consequences of alcohol abuse by sex indicates that in many categories women may suffer greater health risks than do men. This review has pointed out the need for further research to determine the extent of organ pathologies for which women may be at risk in association with alcohol abuse. Prevention strategies for women are suggested that point out that "safe" levels of consumption may be lower for women than for men based on data regarding risks for developing liver cirrhosis. Finally, suggestions are offered for more intensive medical screening of women alcoholics in treatment for the purpose of early identification of biomedical consequences of alcohol abuse.

REFERENCES

Adelstein, A., & White, G. Alcoholism and mortality. *Population Trends*, 1977, *6*, 7–13.

Allen, R. P., Wagman, A., Falliace, L. A., & McIntosh, M. Electroencephalographic (EEG) sleep recovery following prolonged alcohol intoxication in alcoholism. *Journal of Nervous and Mental Disease*, 1971, *153*, 425–433.

American Psychiatric Association. *Diagnostic and statistical manual of mental disorders* (3rd ed.). Washington, D.C.: Author, 1980.

Anderson, A. J., Barboriak, J. J., & Rimm, A. A. Risk factors and angiographically determined coronary occlusion. *American Journal of Epidemiology*, 1977, *107*, 8–14.

Armor, D. J., Polich, J. M., & Stambul, H. B. *Alcoholism and treatment* (Report prepared for the National Institute on Alcohol Abuse and Alcoholism, R-1739-NIAAA). Santa Monica, Calif.: Rand Corporation, 1976.

Ashley, M. J., Olin, J. S., Le-Riche, W. H., Kornaczewski, A., Schmidt, W., & Rankin, J. G. Morbidity in alcoholics: Evidence for accelerated development of physical disease in women. *Archives of Internal Medicine*, 1977, *137*, 883–887.

Asma, E. E., Eggert, R. L., & Hilker, R. R. Long-term experience with rehabilitation of alcoholic employees. *Journal of Occupational Medicine*, 1971, *13*, 581–585.

Bailey, R. J., Krasner, N., Eddleston, A. L. W. F., Williams, R., Tee, D. E. H., Doniach, D., Kennedy, L. A., & Batchelor, J. R. Histocompatibility antigens, autoantibodies, and immunoglobulins in alcoholic liver disease. *British Medical Journal*, 1976, *2*, 727–729.

Belfer, M. L., Shader, R. I., Carroll, M., & Harmatz, J. S. Alcoholism in women. *Archives of General Psychiatry*, 1971, *25*, 540–544.

Bell, H., & Nordhagen, R. HLA antigens in alcoholics with special reference to alcoholic cirrhosis. *Scandinavian Journal of Gastroenterology*, 1980, *15*, 453–456.

Bergman, H., Borg, S., Hindmarsh, T., Idestrom, C-M., & Mutzell, S. Computed tomography of the brain and neuropsychological assessment of male alcoholic patients and a random sample from the general male population. *Acta Psychiatrica Scandinavica*, 1980, *62* (Suppl. 286), 47–56.

Blane, H. T. Education and the prevention of alcoholism. In B. Kissin & H. Begleiter (Eds.), *The biology of alcoholism* (Vol. 4: *Social aspects of alcoholism*). New York: Plenum Press, 1976.

Blume, S. B. Clinical research: Casefinding, diagnosis, treatment and rehabilitation. In *Alcoholism and alcohol abuse among women: Research issues* (DHEW Pub. No. ADM-80-835). Washington, D.C.: U.S. Government Printing Office, 1980.

Bohman, M., Sigvardsson, S., & Cloninger, C. R. Maternal inheritance of alcohol abuse. *Archives of General Psychiatry*, 1981, *38*, 965–969.

Bratfos, O. Attempted suicide. *Acta Psychiatrica Scandinavica*, 1971, *47*, 38–56.

Brenner, B. Alcoholism and fatal accidents. *Quarterly Journal of Studies on Alcohol*, 1967, *28*, 517–528.

Brewer, C., & Perrett, L. Brain damage due to alcohol consumption: An air-encephalographic, psychometric and electroencephalographic study. *British Journal of Addiction*, 1971, *66*, 170–182.

Brunt, P. W., Kew, M. C., Scheuer, P. J., & Sherlock, S. Studies in alcoholic liver disease in Britain I. Clinical and pathological patterns related to natural history. *Gut*, 1974, *15*, 52–58.

Cala, L. A., Jones, B., Mastaglia, F. L., & Wiley, B. Brain atrophy and intellectual impairment in heavy drinkers: A clinical psychometric and computerized tomography study. *Australian and New Zealand Journal of Medicine*, 1978, *8*, 147–153.

Cala, L. A., Jones, B., Wiley, B., & Mastaglia, F. L. A computerized axial tomography (CAT) study of alcohol induced cerebral atrophy in conjunction with other correlates. *Acta Psychiatrica Scandinavica*, 1980, *62* (Suppl. 286), 31–40.

Cala, L. A., & Mastaglia, F. L. Computerized axial tomography in the detection of brain damage. I. Alcohol, nutritional deficiency and drugs of addiction. *Medical Journal of Australia*, 1980, *2*, 193–198.

Carlen, P. L., Wortzman, G., Holgate, R. C., & Wilkinson, A. Reversible cerebral atrophy in recently abstinent chronic alcoholics measured by computed tomography scans. *Science*, 1978, *200*, 1076–1078.

Castelli, W. P., Doyle, J. T., Gordon, T., Hames, C. G., Hjortland, M. C., Hulley, S. B., Kagan, A., & Zukel, W. S. HDL cholesterol and other lipids in coronary heart disease: The cooperative lipoprotein phenotyping study. *Circulation*, 1977, *55*, 767–772.

Castelli, W. P., Gordon, T., Hjortland, M. C., Kagan, A., Doyle, J. T., Hames, C. G., Hulley, S. B., & Zukel, W. S. Alcohol and blood lipids: The cooperative lipoprotein phenotyping study. *Lancet*, 1977, *2*, 153–155.

Cavender, D., Orchard, T., Wagener, D., LaPorte, R., Rabin, B., & Eberhardt, M. The development of Type I diabetes in HLA identical siblings of Type I diabetic patients: Associations with specific antigens. *Diabetologia*, 1982, *23*, 379.

Cloninger, C. R., Christiansen, K. O., Reich, T., & Gottesman, I. I. Implications of sex differences in the prevalences of antisocial personality, alcoholism and criminality for familial transmission. *Archives of General Psychiatry*, 1978, *35*, 941–951.

Curlee, J. Alcoholism and the "empty nest." *Bulletin of the Menninger Clinic*, 1969, *33*, 165–171.

Curlee, J. A comparison of male and female patients at an alcoholism treatment center. *Journal of Psychology*, 1970, *74*, 239–247.

Dahlgren, L., & Idestrôm, C-M. Female alcoholics. V. Morbidity. *Acta Psychiatrica Scandinavica*, 1979, *60*, 199–213.

Dahlgren, L., & Myrhed, M. Female alcoholics. II. Causes of death with reference to sex difference. *Acta Psychiatrica Scandinavica*, 1977, *56*, 81–97.

Danielsson, B., Ekman, R., Fex, G., Johansson, B. G., Kristensson, H., Nielsson-Ehle, P., & Wadstein, J. Changes in plasma high density lipoproteins in chronic male alcoholics during and after abuse. *Scandinavian Journal of Clinical and Laboratory Investigation*, 1978, *38*, 113–119.

Epstein, P. S., Pisani, V. D., & Fawcett, J. A. Alcoholism and cerebral atrophy. *Alcoholism: Clinical and Experimental Research*, 1977, *1*, 61–65.

Fabian, M. S., Jenkins, R. L., & Parsons, O. A. Gender, alcoholism, and neuropsychological functioning. *Journal of Consulting and Clinical Psychology*, 1981, *49*, 139–141.

Feighner, J. P., Robins, E., Guze, S. B., Woodruff, R. A., Winokur, G., & Muñoz, R. Diagnostic criteria for use in psychiatric research. *Archives of General Psychiatry*, 1972, *26*, 57–63.

Fox, J. H., Ramsey, R. G., Huckman, M. S., & Proske, A. E. Cerebral ventricular enlargement: Chronic alcoholics examined by computerized tomography. *Journal of the American Medical Association*, 1976, *236*, 365–368.

Galambos, J. T. Alcoholic hepatitis: Its therapy and prognosis. In H. Popper & F. Schaffner (Eds.), *Progress in liver diseases* (Vol. 4). New York: Grune & Stratton, 1972.

Gibbs, J. P. Suicide. In R. K. Merton & R. A. Nisbet (Eds.), *Contemporary social problems* (2nd ed.). New York: Harcourt, Brace & World, 1966.

Goodwin, D. W. Alcohol in suicide and homicide. *Quarterly Journal of Studies on Alcohol*, 1973, *34*, 144–156.

Goodwin, D. W., & Hill, S. Y. Chronic effects of alcohol and other psychoactive drugs on intellect, learning and memory. In J. Rankin (Ed.), *Alcohol, drugs and brain damage*. Toronto: Addiction Research Foundation, 1975.

Goodwin, D. W., Schulsinger, F., Hermansen, L., Guze, S. B., & Winokur, G. Alcohol problems in adoptees raised apart from alcoholic biological parents. *Archives of General Psychiatry*, 1973, *28*, 238–243.

Goodwin, D. W., Schulsinger, F., Knop, J., Mednick, S., & Guze, S. B. Alcoholism and depression in adopted-out daughters of alcoholics. *Archives of General Psychiatry*, 1977, *34*, 751–755.

Hallen, J., & Krook, H. Follow-up studies on an unselected ten-year material of 360 patients with liver cirrhosis in one community. *Acta Medica Scandinavica*, 1963. *173*, 479–493.

Hallen, J., & Linne, I. Cirrhosis of the liver in one community: A study of 768 cases of liver cirrhosis from a city with one hospital: Incidence, etiology and prognosis. In A. Engel & T. Larsson (Eds.), *Alcoholic cirrhosis and other toxic hepatopathias*. Stockholm: Nordiska Bordiska Bokhandelns Forlag, 1970.

Hatcher, E. M., Jones, M. K., & Jones, B. M. Cognitive deficits in alcoholic women. *Alcoholism: Clinical and Experimental Research*, 1977, *1*, 371–377.

Haug, J. O. Pneumoencephalographic evidence of brain damage in chronic alcoholics (A preliminary report). *Acta Psychiatrica Scandinavica*, 1968, Suppl. 203, 135–143.

Hill, S. Y. Comprehensive assessment of brain dysfunction in alcoholic individuals. *Acta Psychiatrica Scandinavica*, 1980, *62* (Suppl. 286), 57–75.

Hill, S. Y. A vulnerability model for alcoholism in women. *Focus on Women: Journal of Addictions and Health*, 1981, *2*, 68–91.

Hill, S. Y., & Mikhael, M. Computerized transaxial tomographic and neuropsychological evaluations in chronic alcoholics and heroin abusers. *American Journal of Psychiatry*, 1979, *136*, 598–602. (a)

Hill, S. Y., & Mikhael, M. Computed tomography scans of alcoholics: Cerebral atrophy? *Science*, 1979, *204*, 1237–1238. (b)

Hill, S. Y., Reyes, R. B., Mikhael, M., & Ayre, F. A comparison of alcoholics and heroin abusers: Computerized transaxial tomography and neuropsychological functioning. In M. Galanter (Ed.), *Currents in alcoholism* (Vol. 5). New York: Grune & Stratton, 1979.

Hirst, A. E., Hadley, G. G., & Gore, I. The effect of chronic alcoholism and cirrhosis of the liver on atherosclerosis. *American Journal of the Medical Sciences*, 1965, *249*, 143–149.

Hugues, J. N., Perret, G., Adessi, G., Cosie, T., & Modigliani, E. Effects of chronic alcoholism on the pituitary-gonadal function of women during menopausal transition and in the post-menopausal period. *Biomedicine Express*, 1978, *29*, 279–283.

Johnson, L. C., Burdick, J. A., & Smith, J. Sleep during alcohol intake and withdrawal in the chronic alcoholic. *Archives of General Psychiatry*, 1970, *22*, 406–418.

Jones, M. C. Personality correlates and antecedents of drinking patterns in adult males. *Journal of Consulting and Clinical Psychology*, 1968, *32*, 2–12.

Jones, M. C. Personality antecedents and correlates of drinking patterns in women. *Journal of Consulting and Clinical Psychology*, 1971, *36*, 61–69.

Kannel, W. B. Some lessons in cardiovascular epidemiology from Framingham. *American Journal of Cardiology*, 1976, *37*, 269–282.

Kinsey, B. A. Psychological factors in alcoholic women from a state hospital sample. *American Journal of Psychiatry*, 1968, *124*, 1463–1466.

Kramer, K., Kuller, L., & Fisher, R. The increasing mortality attributed to cirrhosis and fatty liver, in Baltimore (1957–1966). *Annals of Internal Medicine*, 1968, *69*, 273–282.

Krasner, N., Davis, M., Portmann, B., & Williams, R. Changing pattern of alcoholic liver disease in Great Britain: Relation to sex and signs of autoimmunity. *British Medical Journal*, 1977, *1*, 1497–1550.

Kuller, L. H., Kramer, K., & Fisher, R. Changing trends in cirrhosis and fatty liver mortality. *American Journal of Public Health*, 1969, *59*, 1124–1133.

Lelbach, W. K. Organic pathology related to volume and pattern of alcohol use. In R. J. Gibbins, Y. Israel, H. Kalant, R. E. Popham, W. Schmidt, & R. Smart (Eds.), *Research advances in alcohol and drug problems* (Vol. 1). New York: John Wiley & Sons, 1974.

Levi, A. J., & Chalmers, D. M. Recognition of alcoholic liver disease in a district general hospital. *Gut*, 1978, *19*, 521–525.

Lindelius, R., Salum, I., & Agren, G. Mortality among male and female alcoholic patients treated in a psychiatric unit. *Acta Psychiatrica Scandinavica*, 1974, *50*, 612–618.

Lischner, M. W., Alexander, J. F., & Galambos, J. T. Natural history of alcoholic hepatitis. I. The acute disease. *American Journal of Digestive Diseases*, 1971, *16*, 481–494.

Lokander, S. Sick absence in a Swedish company: A sociomedical study. *Acta Medica Scandinavica*, 1962, *171* (Suppl. 377), 8–169.

Lundquist, G. *Prognosen och forloppet vid alkoholism* (No. 13). Stockholm: Institutet for maltdryckesforskning, 1965.

McNamee, B., Grant, J., Ratcliffe, J., Ratcliffe, W., & Oliver, J. Lack of effect of alcohol on pituitary-gonadal hormones in women. *British Journal of Addiction*, 1979, *74*, 316–317.

Medhus, A. Morbidity among female alcoholics. *Scandinavian Journal of Social Medicine*, 1974, *2*, 5–11.

Medhus, A. Mortality among female alcoholics. *Scandinavian Journal of Social Medicine*, 1975, *3*, 111–115.

Medical Letter on Drugs and Therapeutics, The, January 12, 1979.

Melendez, M., Vargas-Tank, L., Fuentes, C., Armas-Merino, R., Castillo, D., Wolff, C., Wegmann, M. E., & Soto, J. Distribution of HLA histocompatibility antigens, ABO groups and RH antigens in alcoholic liver disease. *Gut*, 1979, *20*, 288–290.

Mendelson, J. H., Mello, N. K., & Ellingboe, J. Effects of acute alcohol intake on pituitary-gonadal hormones in normal human males. *Journal of Pharmacology and Experimental Therapeutics*, 1977, *202*, 676–682.

Mendelson, J. H., Mello, N. K., & Ellingboe, J. Acute alcohol intake and pituitary-gonadal hormones in normal human females. *Journal of Pharmacology and Experimental Therapeutics*, 1981, *218*, 23–26.

Mikkelsen, W. P., Turrill, F. L., & Kern, W. H. Acute hyaline necrosis of the liver. *American Journal of Surgery*, 1968, *116*, 266–272.

Morgan, M. Y., & Sherlock, S. Sex-related differences among 100 patients with alcoholic liver disease. *British Medical Journal*, 1977, *1*, 939–941.

Nakamura, S., Takezawa, Y., Sato, T., Kera, K., & Maeda, T. Alcoholic liver disease in women. *Tohoku Journal of Experimental Medicine*, 1979, *129*, 351–355.

National Council on Alcoholism Criteria Committee. Criteria for the diagnosis of alcoholism. *Annals of Internal Medicine*, 1972, *77*, 127–135.

Nicholls, P., Edwards, G., & Kyle, E. Alcoholics admitted to four hospitals in England. *Quarterly Journal of Studies on Alcohol*, 1974, *35*, 841–855.

Parsons, O. A., & Leber, W. R. Alcohol, cognitive dysfunction and brain damage. In *Biomedical processes and consequences of alcohol use* (NIAAA Alcohol and Health Monograph No. 2, DHHS Publ. No. ADM-82-1191). Washington, D.C.: Government Printing Office, 1982.

Pell, S., & D'Alonzo, C. A. A five-year mortality study of alcoholics. *Journal of Occupational Medicine*, 1973, *15*, 120–125.

Pequignot, G., Chabert, C., Eydoux, H., & Courcoul, M. A. Increased risk of liver cirrhosis with intake of alcohol. *Revue de l'Alcoolisme*, 1974, *20*, 191–202.

Phillips, G. B., & Davidson, C. S. Acute hepatic insufficiency of the chronic alcoholic. *Archives of Internal Medicine*, 1954, *94*, 585–603.

Powell, W. J., & Klatskin, G. Survival of patients with Laennec's cirrhosis. Influence of alcohol withdrawal and possible effects of recent changes in general management of the disease. *American Journal of Medicine*, 1968, *44*, 406–429.

Ratcliffe, M. Catch a woman customer. *Supermarketing*, March 30, 1979, pp. 6–7.

Rathod, N. H., & Thomson, I. G. Women alcoholics: A clinical study. *Quarterly Journal of Studies on Alcohol*, 1971, *32*, 45–52.

Regan, T. J. Alcoholic cardiomyopathy. In N. O. Fowler (Ed.), *Myocardial diseases*. New York: Grune & Stratton, 1973.

Reyes, E., & Miller, W. R. Serum gamma-glutamyl transpeptidase as a diagnostic aid in problem drinkers. *Addictive Behaviors*, 1980, *5*, 59–65.

Rimmer, J., Pitts, F. N., Jr., Reich, T., & Winokur, G. Alcoholism. II. Sex, socioeconomic status and race in two hospitalized samples. *Quarterly Journal of Studies on Alcohol*, 1971, *32*, 942–952.

Robinson, D., Monk, C., & Bailey, A. The relationship between serum gamma-glutamyl transpeptidase level and reported alcohol consumption in healthy men. *Journal of Studies on Alcohol*, 1979, *40*, 896–901.

Ron, M. A., Acker, W., & Lishman, W. A. Morphological abnormalities in the brains of chronic alcoholics: A clinical, psychological and computerized axial tomographic study. *Acta Psychiatrica Scandinavica*, 1980, *62* (Suppl. 286), 41–46.

Ruebner, B. H., Edin, M. D., Miyai, K., & Keio, M. D. The low incidence of myocardial infarction in hepatic cirrhosis. *Lancet*, 1961, *2*, 1435–1436.

Rushing, W. A. Suicide and the interaction of alcoholism (liver cirrhosis) with the social situation. *Quarterly Journal of Studies on Alcohol*, 1969, *30*, 93–103.

Sanchez-Craig, M., & Annis, H. M. Gamma-glutamyl transpeptidase and high density lipoproteins cholesterol in male problem drinkers: Advantages of a composite index for predicting alcohol consumption. *Alcoholism: Clinical and Experimental Research*, 1981, *5*, 540–544.

Saunders, J. B., Davis, M., & Williams, R. Do women develop alcoholic liver disease more readily than men? *British Medical Journal*, 1981, *282*, 1140–1143.

Schmidt, W., & deLint, J. Causes of death of alcoholics. *Quarterly Journal of Studies on Alcohol*, 1972, *33*, 171–185.

Schmidt, W., & Popham, R. E. Heavy alcohol consumption and physical health problems: A review of the epidemiological evidence. *Drug and Alcohol Dependence*, 1976, *1*, 27–50.

Schottenfeld, D., Gantt, R. C., & Wynder, E. L. The role of alcohol and tobacco in multiple primary cancers of the upper digestive system, larnyx and lung: A prospective study. *Preventive Medicine*, 1974, *3*, 277-293.

Schuckit, M., Pitts, F. N., Jr., Reich, T., King, L. J., & Winokur, G. Alcoholism. I. Two types of alcoholism in women. *Archives of General Psychiatry*, 1969, *20*, 301-306.

Shaw, S., Worner, T. M., Borysow, M. F., Schmitz, R. E., & Lieber, C. S. Detection of alcoholism relapse: Comparative diagnostic value of MCV, GGTP, AANB. *Alcoholism*, 1979, *3*, 297-301.

Silberstein, J. A., & Parsons, O. A. Neuropsychological impairment in female alcoholics. In M. Galanter (Ed.), *Currents in alcoholism* (Vol. 7). New York: Grune & Stratton, 1980.

Spain, D. M. Portal cirrhosis of the liver, a review of 250 necropsies with reference to sex differences. *American Journal of Clinical Pathology*, 1945, *15*, 215-218.

Spodick, D. H., Pigott, V. M., & Chirife, R. Preclinical cardiac malfunction in chronic alcoholism: Comparison with matched normal controls and with alcoholic cardiomyopathy. *New England Journal of Medicine*, 1972, *287*, 677-680.

Sundby, P. *Alcoholism and mortality* (National Institute for Alcohol Research, Report No. 6). Oslo: Universitetsforlaget, 1967.

Talbott, E., Kuller, L. H., Detre, K., & Perper, J. Biologic and psychosocial risk factors of sudden death from coronary disease in white women. *American Journal of Cardiology*, 1977, *39*, 858-864.

Tashiro, M., & Lipscomb, W. R. Mortality experience of alcoholics. *Quarterly Journal of Studies on Alcohol*, 1963, *24*, 203-212.

Thomas, A., Chess, S., & Birch, H. *Temperament and behavior disorder in children*. New York: New York University Press, 1968.

U.S. Statistical Bulletin. Recent trends in mortality from cirrhosis of the liver, February 1977.

Van Thiel, D. H., Gavaler, J. S., Lester, R., & Sherins, R. J. Alcohol-induced ovarian failure in the rat. *Journal of Clinical Investigation*, 1978, *61*, 624-632.

Van Thiel, D. H., Lester, R., & Sherins, R. J. Hypogonadism in alcoholic liver disease: Evidence for a double defect. *Gastroenterology*, 1974, *67*, 1188-1199.

Vanacek, R. Atherosclerosis and cirrhosis of the liver. *World Health Organization Bulletin*, 1976, *53*, 567-570.

Viel, B., Donoso, S., Salcedo, D., & Varela, A. Alcoholic drinking habit and hepatic damage. *Journal of Chronic Diseases*, 1968, *21*, 157-166.

Whitehead, P. C. *The prevention of alcoholism: An analysis of two approaches*. Paper presented to the Canadian Sociology and Anthropology Association, May 1972.

Wilkinson, P., Santamaria, J. N., & Rankin, J. G. Epidemiology of alcoholic cirrhosis. *Australasian Annals of Medicine*, 1969, *18*, 222.

Williams, R. R., & Davis, M. Alcoholic liver disease—basic pathology and clinical variants. In G. Edwards & M. Grant (Eds.), *Alcoholism: New knowledge and new responses*. Baltimore, Md.: University Park Press, 1976.

Williams, R. R., & Horm, J. W. Association of cancer sites with tobacco and alcohol consumption and socioeconomic status of patients: Interview study from the third National Cancer Survey. *Journal of the National Cancer Institute*, 1977, *58*, 525-547.

Wilsnack, S. C. Prevention of alcohol problems in women: Current status and research needs. In *Alcoholism and alcohol abuse among women: Research issues* (DHEW Pub. No. ADM-80-835). Washington, D.C.: U.S. Government Printing Office, 1980.

Wilsnack, S. C. Alcohol, sexuality, and reproductive dysfunction in women. In E. L. Abel (Ed.), *Fetal alcohol syndrome* (Vol. 2: *Human studies*). Boca Raton, Fla.: CRC Press, 1982.

Winokur, G., & Clayton, P. J. Family histories. IV. Comparison of male and female alcoholics. *Quarterly Journal of Studies on Alcohol*, 1968, *29*, 885-891.

Winokur, G., Reich, T., Rimmer, J., & Pitts, F. N., Jr. Alcoholism. III. Diagnosis and familial psychiatric illness in 259 alcoholic probands. *Archives of General Psychiatry*, 1970, *23*, 104-111.

Wolin, S. J., Bennett, L. A., & Noonan, D. *Environmental family factors related to alcoholism recurrence.* Paper presented at the National Alcoholism Forum of the National Council on Alcoholism, St. Louis, 1978.

Wu, C. F., Sudhakar, M., Jaferei, G., Ahmed, S. S., & Regan, T. J. Preclinical cardiomyopathy in chronic alcoholics: A sex difference. *American Heart Journal,* 1976, *91,* 281-286.

Wynder, E. L. Nutrition and cancer. *Federation Proceedings: Federation of American Societies for Experimental Biology,* 1976, *35,* 1309-1315.

Wynder, E. L., & Stellman, S. D. Comparative epidemiology of tobacco-related cancers. *Cancer Research,* 1977, *37,* 4608-4622.

6

Alcohol Use and Reproduction

RUTH E. LITTLE
University of Washington

CYNTHIA H. ERVIN
University of Puget Sound

INTRODUCTION

In July 1981, the Surgeon General of the United States advised women who are pregnant or considering pregnancy to abstain from alcoholic beverages, and urged professionals who care for such women to warn them of the risks of drinking during pregnancy (U.S. Department of Health and Human Services, 1981). Thus ended an 8-year debate during which alcohol was identified as hazardous to reproduction, and the dangers of its use were rigorously documented for the first time.

The beginning of the debate was dramatic and unexpected. In spite of an occasional warning of the teratogenic potential of alcohol from scientists in the early part of this century, the prevailing climate of opinion in 1973 was that alcohol use was a social grace, a benign habit that even had therapeutic value. Clinicians advised pregnant women that a glass of wine before bed was better than a sleeping pill; a drink might also obviate the need for pain medication. Alcohol was widely used both orally and intravenously to retard premature labor, a treatment still in use in some areas today. In 1973, there was no reason to suspect that these were not valid therapeutic practices; after all, pregnant women had consumed alcohol for centuries without apparent harm. The general attitude about alcohol use during pregnancy was summed up in a statement by Dr. Ashley Montague, who assured his readers that "no matter how great the amount of alcohol taken by the mother . . . the development of the child will not be affected" (Montague, 1965, p. 114).

Then, in June 1973, Dr. Kenneth L. Jones, representing a research team from the University of Washington in Seattle, reported that a "characteristic pattern of malformation" had been identified in eight children of chronic alcoholics. This report of a new syndrome, originally presented at a scientific meeting, was almost immediately published in the British medical journal *Lancet* (Jones, Smith, Ulleland, & Streissguth, 1973). The pattern of malformation described by Jones and his colleagues in this landmark report is now termed "fetal alcohol syndrome" (FAS).

Shock and disbelief followed the identification and description of the syndrome. Yet additional children with the condition continued to be identified, often without knowledge of the mother's drinking. In early 1977, the National Institute on Alcohol Abuse and Alcoholism acknowledged the growing evidence that alcohol was a teratogen, and sponsored the first gathering of scientists working in the field. The participants at this gathering cautiously concluded that alcohol in high doses was probably teratogenic in humans, and advised women to avoid heavy consumption—defined as 6 or more drinks daily (U.S. Department of Health, Education and Welfare, 1977). Later in 1977, the findings of the first federally funded study of human drinking during pregnancy were published; the study gave the initial indication that moderate maternal alcohol use was hazardous to the developing child (Little, 1977). Reports and studies proliferated, and they were remarkably consistent, whether for humans or animals: High, and perhaps even moderate, doses of alcohol were injurious to the fetus. A "safe" amount of alcohol during pregnancy had not been identified. An inquiry into the hazards of alcohol use was initiated by the President and the Congress of the United States in 1980 (U.S. Department of Treasury & U.S. Department of Health and Human Services, 1980). The result of this inquiry was the warning of the Surgeon General to abstain from alcohol during pregnancy. His warning was not unanimously supported, nor was his recommendation of abstinence necessarily applauded ("Drinking in Pregnancy," 1981). Nevertheless, the message of the Surgeon General was noteworthy because it marked the unequivocal concern of the government of the United States about an issue of increasing public health importance: the role of alcohol use in reproduction.

Reproduction in women touches on many biological areas: menarche, or the first menstrual period; gynecological health, including the ability to bear children; conception and pregnancy; the major postpartum event of lactation; and finally, the menopause. Alcohol has been shown to be a risk factor for dysfunction in some of these areas, while in others the evidence is absent or at best suggestive. The biological effects of alcohol on male reproductive capacity are virtually unknown. In this chapter, we will summarize the risks for reproduction incurred when alcohol is used by either men or women prior to conception, during gestation, or in the lactation period. We will also address a topic far less neatly handled: preventing and dealing with the long-term consequences of heavy maternal drinking during pregnancy. While alcohol use may leave its mark on other areas of reproductive life, nowhere has its tragic effect been documented as fully as on the developing child. The clinical issues involved in helping women who abuse alcohol during pregnancy, and the resources available to them and their children, is a natural complement to a discussion of biological risk. For when risk is incurred, some will be damaged; then the precise world of the researcher must give way to the inexact science of the clinician, if healing is to take place.

RESEARCH FINDINGS AND ISSUES

Pregnancy

The consequences of maternal alcohol use during pregnancy are described elsewhere in several comprehensive reviews (e.g., Abel, 1982; Clarren & Smith, 1978; Little, Graham, & Samson, 1981; Streissguth, Landesman-Dwyer, Martin, & Smith, 1980). The following discussion summarizes the salient points of these reviews, and the reader who desires more detail is encouraged to consult these or the extensive bibliography provided at the end of this chapter.

CLINICAL STUDIES OF FETAL ALCOHOL SYNDROME

The identification of FAS in this country was the result of astute clinical observation and reporting by a team who observed a unique set of features in each of a small group of children. The original clinical report of eight FAS children described the new condition as a concurrent triad of signs consisting of:

- growth deficiency of prenatal onset;
- characteristic facial dysmorphology; and
- central nervous system (CNS) involvement, with developmental delay.

Since the initial report of FAS in 1973, hundreds of individual cases of FAS have been described in the medical literature from many countries and in all ethnic groups and social classes (Clarren & Smith, 1978). The nature of these defects clearly implicates the prenatal period as the time of insult.

The growth deficiency seen in FAS children is usually of prenatal onset and is not accompanied by postnatal catch-up growth. Such children are usually well below the 3rd percentile for height, weight, and head circumference, and this cannot be ascribed to deficiencies in growth hormone, cortisol, and gonadotropins (Root, Reiter, Andriola, & Duckett, 1975; Tze, Friesen, & MacLeod, 1976). Disproportionately decreased adipose tissue results in a thin, waif-like appearance. Failure to thrive has been noted in FAS children since the original eight were identified.

The facial features are an essential element of a diagnosis of FAS. They include a flattened midface, a small chin, and short palpebral fissures (eye slits). Other characteristic facial features are a short, upturned nose with a flattened nasal bridge; an absent or indistinct philtrum (the ridges that form the valley between the nose and mouth); and a thin upper lip.

CNS dysfunction is the most significant effect of prenatal alcohol exposure. Studies of intellectual functioning in children with FAS have demonstrated an average IQ slightly below 70 (in the mildly retarded range) with a wide range of individual IQ scores (Dehaene, Samaille-Villette, Samaille, Crepin, Walbaum, Deroubaix, & Blanc-Garin, 1977; Lemoine, Harousseau, Borteyru, & Menuet, 1968; Majewski, 1978; Olegard, Sabel, Aronsson, Sandin, Johansson, Carlsson, Kyllerman, Iversen, & Hrbek, 1979; Streissguth, Herman, & Smith, 1978a). Increased severity of physical effects tends to be correlated with decreased intellectual performance (Dehaene et al., 1977; Majewski, 1978; Streissguth et al., 1978a). In most cases the IQ scores tend to remain relatively stable (Olegard et al., 1979; Streissguth, Herman, & Smith, 1978b), though one study has indicated some improvement over time for mildly affected children (Dehaene et al., 1977). Other problems also reflect CNS involvement: Microcephaly, altered muscle tone, poor coordination, and hyperactivity are frequently seen (Clarren & Smith, 1978).

Children with FAS exhibit an unusually high rate of other morphologic abnormalities, in addition to their singular facial characteristics. Ear and eye anomalies, altered palmar creases, and cardiac problems are among these abnormalities (Clarren & Smith, 1978).

HUMAN STUDIES OF FETAL ALCOHOL EFFECTS

Alcohol, like other teratogens, gives rise to a spectrum of defects, with much individual variation in both the extent and severity of the damage. This is not surprising, for other birth defects (such as Down's syndrome) also are characterized by varying degrees of impairment. Thus the original term "fetal alcohol syndrome" may be misleading now, for it refers only to the severest end of the spectrum, where the complete triad of growth and mental deficiency, plus specific facial dysmorphism, is expressed. But there is a range of problems much broader than FAS that have been correlated with maternal drinking. For this reason, Dr. David Smith has recommended the use of the term "fetal alcohol effects" in an attempt to answer the diagnostic issue: "Is the child's problem secondary to alcohol exposure in utero?" (Smith, 1979). Fetal alcohol effects are those signs in the offspring that have been linked to alcohol use during pregnancy by the mother.

The major fetal alcohol effects are growth retardation, morphologic abnormalities, CNS involvement, and mortality. The reader will recall that these first three signs, if they are concurrent and severe, define a case of FAS. However, the signs may occur singly or in pairs, and they may range from mild to severe. As long as they are considered secondary to alcohol exposure in utero, they are called fetal alcohol effects.

Alcohol freely crosses the placenta, and blood-alcohol levels in the fetus are approximately equivalent to blood-alcohol levels in the mother (Dilts,

1970; Idapaan-Heikkila, Fritchie, Ho, & McIsaac, 1971). In general, there appears to be a correlation between the severity of the signs and the amount of alcohol to which the fetus is exposed. FAS has been reported only in the children of heavy drinkers (at least 6 drinks daily for some portion of the pregnancy). Outcomes of lesser severity, such as lowered birthweight, have been reported at levels approximating "social" drinking. However, the increased fetal mortality associated with intrauterine alcohol exposure does not fit well into this dose-response model, for this very severe effect is associated with very low levels of alcohol use. Reasons for this will be explored in a subsequent section, after the evidence regarding each of the major fetal alcohol effects has been reviewed.

Intrauterine Growth Retardation. Decreased birthweight and intrauterine growth retardation in children of alcohol abusers has been well documented (e.g., Russell, 1977; Sokol, Miller, & Reed, 1980). Growth deficiency in some degree has also been reported by several investigators in the United States and Europe in unselected samples ranging in size from 264 to 9000 women (Kaminski, Rumeau-Rouquette, & Schwartz, 1976; Little, 1977; Martin, Barr, & Streissguth, 1980; Ouellette, Rosett, Rosman, & Weiner, 1977). Many of these studies controlled for other risk factors, such as maternal smoking, size, age, parity, and socioeconomic status. Significant decreases in birthweight were associated with various levels of alcohol use, beginning at an average of 2 drinks daily in one investigation (Little, 1977).[1] A later investigation (Tennes & Blackard, 1980) was unable to replicate such a finding of decreased birthweight in children of moderate to heavy drinkers, possibly because the number of regular drinkers was very small.

The reported decreases in birthweight are not necessarily due to prematurity, since many studies took gestational age into account. However, prematurity has recently been associated with maternal alcohol use (Berkowitz, 1981; Tennes & Blackard, 1980) although there are conflicting reports from other investigations (Kaminski *et al.*, 1976; Sokol *et al.*, 1980).

Morphologic Abnormalities. In addition to clinical evidence of dysmorphogenesis in children of very heavy drinkers, several studies have examined the relationship between morphogenesis and variable levels of maternal alcohol use. (In all these studies, examination of the infant was made without knowledge of maternal drinking.) Sokol *et al.* (1980) have presented epidemiologic findings documenting greater frequency of malformations in children of alcohol abusers. Ouellette *et al.* (1977) have analyzed results of 322 pregnancies, and described a significantly increased rate of malformation in infants of women who consumed an average of at least 1½ drinks daily, and occasionally had "binges" of at least 5 drinks; however, many women in the group drank more than this. Hanson,

1. In this chapter, a "drink" is .5 oz of ethanol; this is equivalent to a 12-oz bottle of beer, a 4-oz glass of table wine, or 1 oz of 100-proof liquor.

Streissguth, and Smith (1978) report growth retardation and an increased rate of morphologic abnormalities "suggestive of FAS" in a sample of 163 subjects. Among infants born to women ingesting an average of at least 2 drinks daily, 13% were so affected; when the sample was restricted to women consuming 2–3 drinks daily, the frequency was 11%. A 4-year follow-up of a comparable sample found that the abnormalities persisted into childhood (Graham, Darby, Barr, Smith, & Streissguth, 1981). Other investigators have failed to detect any increase in abnormalities at moderate levels of drinking (Kaminski et al., 1976; Tennes & Blackard, 1980).

Central Nervous System Dysfunction. The behavioral abnormalities reported in offspring of moderate to heavy drinkers may be a consequence of CNS involvement. At birth, hypotonia (decreased muscle tone), jitteriness, decreased stimulus habituation, tremulousness, decreased bodily vigor, and other unusual behaviors were all more common in infants whose mothers were moderate to heavy drinkers during pregnancy (Landesman-Dwyer, Keller, & Streissguth, 1978; Ouellette et al., 1977; Streissguth et al., 1980). If heavy smoking accompanied drinking, decreased operant learning was evident (Martin, Martin, Lund, & Streissguth, 1977). One sample of newborns was followed up at 8 months of age; a small but significant decrement in infant mental and motor development was apparent in children whose mothers had drunk regularly or excessively during pregnancy, with the dose–response effect beginning at about 4 drinks per day (Streissguth, Barr, Martin, & Herman, 1980). Follow-up at 4 years of another sample of children whose mothers drank moderately during pregnancy (maximum of 4 drinks daily with mean less than 1 drink) revealed decreased attentiveness and social compliance, and increased fidgetiness (Landesman-Dwyer, Ragozin, & Little, 1981).

Fetal and Perinatal Mortality. The increased risk of perinatal mortality in children of *very* heavy drinkers—alcoholic by any definition—was first noted by Jones and colleagues in 1974 (Jones, Smith, Streissguth, & Myrianthopoulos, 1974). A later report of the outcome of 9000 pregnancies in France revealed a rate of stillbirth among women consuming at least 3 drinks daily that was 2½ times the rate for women drinking less than this; a dose–response trend was evident (Kaminski et al., 1976). Chief cause of death was abruptio placenta. However, not all studies have found increased mortality, even for infants of women abusing alcohol (Sokol et al., 1980).

Of grave concern is a pair of recent reports of significantly increased risk of spontaneous abortion, even at low (self-reported) doses of alcohol. Harlap (Harlap & Shiono, 1980) has reviewed the outcome of over 32,000 pregnancies in California and concluded that the risk of spontaneous abortion in the second trimester is double for women drinking 1–2 drinks daily, compared to nondrinkers; as with the studies previously cited, numerous variables that could have influenced the outcome were taken into account. A clear dose–response effect was evident. Kline (Kline, Shrout, Stein, Susser,

& Warburton, 1980), in New York, compared 616 pregnancies that ended in spontaneous abortion with a control group of pregnancies carried to at least 28 weeks. She estimated that more than 25% of women who drink at least twice weekly are likely to abort, with a "minimum harmful dose" of 1 oz ethanol (2 drinks) per drinking occasion. These latter two reports were cited by the Surgeon General in support of his recommendation of abstinence.

ANIMAL STUDIES OF FETAL ALCOHOL EFFECTS[2]

Animal studies have also documented that ethanol results in teratological consequences for the developing organism. The dosage levels that produce these malformations are in many cases also capable of producing fetal death. Why a given dose is lethal to one fetus while at the same time producing malformations in another within the same uterus may be related to placental structure, differences in placental blood flow, and numbers of possible embryos implanted, which vary for each species. Nevertheless, similar malformations of brain, heart, kidney, and bone structure have been found in mice, dogs, and pigs (Boggan, Randall, DeBeukelaer, & Smith, 1979; Chernoff, 1977; Dexter, Tumbleson, Decker, & Middleton, 1980; Ellis & Pick, 1980; Randall & Taylor, 1979; Randall, Taylor, & Walker, 1977). (Interestingly, the rat has shown resistance to the effects of many agents known to be teratogens in man, including thalidomide and alcohol.)

The evidence from animal studies strongly supports the argument that ethanol exposure *in utero* can result in growth retardation in several species independent of nutrition (Chernoff, 1977; Dexter *et al.*, 1980; Ellis & Pick, 1980; Henderson, Hoyumpa, Rothschild, & Schenker, 1980; Samson, 1981; Sorette, Maggio, Stupoli, Boissevain, & Greenwood, 1980). In some studies, a dose–response curve is apparent. Low doses have not been shown to have permanent effects upon growth, for catch-up may occur (Abel, 1980).

With doses of ethanol that do not result in gross teratology during gestation, smaller but anatomically normal brains have been reported after maternal alcohol exposure (Henderson, Hoyumpa, McClain, & Schenker, 1979): This may be a reflection of growth retardation rather than a specific CNS effect. Other animal studies, however, have examined the effects of ethanol exposure on brain development during the early postnatal period in the rat that corresponds to the later part of human pregnancy. Pronounced effects upon brain growth have resulted from ethanol exposure during this late period (Bauer-Moffett & Altman, 1975, 1977; Diaz & Samson, 1980; Samson & Diaz, 1982). These studies suggest that the developing CNS of the human is vulnerable to ethanol exposure, not only during early stages of pregnancy, but during the latter half of the second and all of the third trimester as well. It is also clear from these studies that ethanol exposure

---

2. This section is based in part on a review of studies of the teratogenic potential of alcohol in animals prepared by Dr. Herman H. Samson of the University of Washington.

during the first few months of life (via breast milk) could have an impact upon brain development in the human infant.

In general, the animal data support several of the human findings. Decreased growth, morphologic abnormalities, central nervous system involvement, and fetal wastage are all correlated with maternal ethanol exposure, with a dose–response effect apparent for some of these outcomes. Investigators have produced models that will hopefully lead to understanding the mechanisms responsible for the human effects of maternal ethanol intake.

ISSUES AND NEW FRONTIERS

"Safe" Doses of Alcohol and the Dose–Response Curve. One of the critical questions facing researchers today is how much alcohol can safely be consumed during pregnancy without impairing fetal development. There are well-done studies linking an average of 1–2 drinks daily to decreased birthweight, growth abnormalities, and behavioral decrements in the newborn and infant (although not all studies report effects at such levels). Increased risk of spontaneous abortion has been found at an even lower dose: 1–2 drinks twice weekly. No risks of alcohol use at lower levels than this have been reported.

However, several caveats should be noted. All of the consumption figures cited are self-reported. The estimate of alcohol use based on such figures is a chancy business at best. There is nothing sacred or absolute about the numbers attached to the statements set out above. The actual dose that corresponds to the noted risk may in fact be double the amount stated, or it may not. Accuracy of self-report appears to vary with the consequences of making the report and the level of drinking reported. Drinking reported to an independent interviewer appears to be of at least satisfactory validity (Kolonel, Hirohata, & Nomura, 1977), while drinking reported to a physician appears far less accurate (Little, 1976; Russell & Bigler, 1979). Retrospective reports may be less valid and reliable than current reports (Klemetti & Saxen, 1967; Little, Mandell, & Schultz, 1977). In any case, the actual consumption corresponding to self-reported amounts is unknown.

If the dose consumed is not accurately known, determination of a dose–response curve is difficult. In general, in humans, there does seem to be greater damage with greater doses of alcohol—with the notable exception of spontaneous abortion. The animal studies support the hypothesis that a dose-response curve exists. However, the lowest dose that elicits a response— and the "safe" level below this dose—is unknown.

Additional Maternal Risk Factors. The outcome of a pregnancy is influenced by numerous factors: the age and reproductive history of the mother; her habits and life-style, including nutrition, smoking and other drug use; her particular metabolic and biochemical make-up; and her genetic heritage. Other factors too numerous to catalog also influence the development of the child. Whether these factors alter the fetal risk experienced with alcohol exposure *in utero* is, in general, unknown.

The work of Brown and colleagues (Brown, Goulding, & Fabro, 1979) indicates a direct deleterious action of alcohol on the developing fetus and suggests that alcohol itself, rather than errors of maternal metabolism or external factors, is responsible, via alteration of cell division and differentiation. However, like many other teratogens, alcohol does not uniformly affect all those exposed to it. What variables mitigate or exacerbate risk is unknown. There is a suggestion that genetic factors in mother or child may influence outcome. Reports exist of differentially affected dizygotic (fraternal) twins who were clearly subject to the same maternal alcohol intake during pregnancy (Christoffel & Salafsky, 1975; Manzke & Grosse, 1975). Animal experiments also indicate the importance of host factors. Resorptions and malformations in mice were more frequent in a strain that metabolizes alcohol slowly (Chernoff, 1977). Severity of fetal effect has also been linked to stage of "alcoholism," independent of dose and years of drinking (Majewski, Bierich, Loser, Michaelis, & Leiber, 1976; Seidenberg & Majewski, 1978); this may reflect a residual risk posed by a history of alcoholism prior to conception.

At present, however, research in this area does not clearly indicate the relative contributions to pregnancy outcome of even the major variables. The investigator can only control for the most obvious factors before the list of potential confounders grows massive. When this minimal control has been effected, alcohol use has still emerged as detrimental to fetal development.

The Endogenous Aversion to Alcohol. In view of the damaging effects of alcohol on the fetus, it is fortunate that most women lose their desire to drink during pregnancy. This curious phenomenon was studied before alcohol was know to be a teratogen, so the reports of decreased drinking cannot be ascribed primarily to denial or conscience.

Drinking decreases substantially, spontaneously, and predictably shortly after conception in all types of human drinkers, from the casual imbiber to the alcoholic (Dickens & Trethowan, 1971; Hook, 1978; Little, Schultz, & Mandell, 1976; Little & Streissguth, 1978; Majewski, 1978; Schwartz, Joujard, Kaminski, & Rumeau-Rouquette, 1972). Such a decrease has also been observed in monkeys, mice, and miniature swine (Elton & Wilson, 1977; Randall, Boggan, & Sutker, 1980; Tumbleson, 1977). The amount that drinking decreases during gestation is directly proportional to the level of drinking before pregnancy. Thus, the heaviest drinkers before pregnancy tend to be the heaviest drinkers after conception, too, and consumption estimates in the two periods are highly rank stable (Little *et al.*, 1976).

The decline in alcohol use in humans appears in the first trimester and levels of consumption remain low throughout the pregnancy (Little *et al.*, 1976). "Binges," or occasions when at least 5 drinks are consumed, are also less frequent in nonproblem drinkers during pregnancy (Little, 1979). But in alcoholic women, an increase in binges may accompany decreased modal drinking, as though the binge were a safety valve utilized when regular alcohol use declines. And even though the frequency of binges may increase during pregnancy for the alcoholic woman, the amount consumed in a binge declines from what it was before conception (Little & Streissguth, 1978).

The reasons for loss of appetite for alcohol are unknown; however, similar endogenous aversions to caffeine and tobacco exist (Hook, 1976, 1978; Little et al., 1976; Streissguth, Martin, Martin, & Barr, 1977). Some investigators have suggested that the aversions are due to a homeostatic mechanism protecting the fetus from embryotoxins (Hook, 1976; Little et al., 1976). Others have hypothesized that the elevation in sex steroids that occurs in pregnancy is responsible; however, one study that administered high doses of estradiol to nonpregnant drinkers failed to detect any change in their alcohol use (Little, Moore, Guzinski, & Perez, 1980). The aversion to alcohol does not appear to be the result of nausea, though nausea may intensify it (Hook, 1976; Little et al., 1976). Conversely, the probability that nausea will occur in early pregnancy appears lower if there is regular drinking and smoking before pregnancy (Little & Hook, 1979). This web of strange relationships may provide a key to one of the mysteries of alcoholism —why one person is indifferent to alcohol, and another craves it. For the present, however, the endogenous aversion to alcohol during pregnancy remains a powerful but unexplained phenomenon.

New Frontiers. Other issues remain to be resolved. Chief among these is the effect of an isolated binge. Clarren has published a very suggestive report describing structural brain abnormalities in a small sample of offspring of binge drinkers (Clarren, Alvord, Sumi, Streissguth, & Smith, 1978). Little else is known about binge-related effects. This is a question of great clinical significance, for obstetricians must frequently advise women who are tempted to terminate a pregnancy because of a heavy drinking episode.

The effect of the binge may depend on its timing. In fact, this is another significant issue to be addressed, for the time-specific consequences of alcohol exposure have not been well explored. Just as there is no known safe dose of alcohol, there does not appear to be a safe time to drink. The first trimester is the vulnerable time of organogenesis; the second trimester brings an increased risk of spontaneous abortion; and alcohol exposure in the third trimester may interfere with the rapid growth that occurs during this time, especially in the brain. Until more is known about "safe" times of pregnancy, the safest course for pregnant women is to abstain.

Finally, some investigators have suggested that one type of beverage may be more harmful than another. A French research team has implicated beer and cider (Kaminski et al., 1976). Others have found no differential effects of the various types of drinks. So there may also be no safe alcoholic beverage, either!

Prior to Pregnancy

Some studies of unselected samples of drinkers have found that a relationship to fetal development exists between alcohol use prior to pregnancy and fetal development. Studies by the Seattle research group that first identified FAS have consistently reported such effects (e.g., Hanson *et al.*, 1978; Little, 1977). However, the investigators note that self-reported drinking "before pregnancy" may actually represent consumption in the very early weeks of gestation, prior to knowledge of pregnancy. Thus what appears to be a relationship with preconception drinking may actually be a reflection of intrauterine alcohol exposure in the period of organogenesis.

A more serious indicator of the detrimental effect of preconception drinking is also reported by the Seattle team (Little, Streissguth, Barr, & Herman, 1980). One hundred women, each with a history of alcoholism prior to conception of a target pregnancy, were studied; half had continued to drink during pregnancy, and the other half were totally abstinent. A control group of nonalcoholic women who drank very little during pregnancy was studied also. When mean birthweights of infants born to the groups of women were compared, the children of the abstinent alcoholic mothers weighed 258 g less than children born to nonalcoholic controls, in spite of their abstinence during pregnancy. Infants of the abstinent alcoholics were, however, heavier than the infants whose alcoholic mothers continued to drink. Differences in birthweights were not due to differences in height, smoking, age, race, parity, gestational age, or sex of child among the groups. The decrement in birthweight in offspring of abstinent alcoholics did not vary with length of abstinence before conception.

This finding suggests that a history of alcohol abuse should be considered a risk factor in pregnancy, independent of maternal alcohol use in gestation. Furthermore, the facets of fetal development affected by a history of alcohol abuse may differ from those affected by intrauterine exposure, or they may be affected in different ways depending on when consumption occurred. The problem of drinking and fetal development is probably not as simple as one might assume; it may be multifactorial in timing and amount of dose, and in the pattern of these factors in the past. If these complex relationships hold, they may be one reason why the dose-response curve is inexact, and why the type of effect linked to given amounts of alcohol use can vary so widely.

In Lactation

Maternal milk serves as a vehicle not only for nutrients, but also for most drugs consumed by the lactating women (Horning, Stillwell, Nowling, Lertratanangkoon, Stillwell, & Hill, 1975; Knowles, 1972; Voherr, 1974;

Worthington, 1979). Alcohol is such a drug, and it occurs in breast milk in similar concentration to that in the maternal peripheral blood (Kesaniemi, 1974). Since alcohol has a profound effect on the growing fetus, especially on the brain, one would reasonably infer that alcohol use by the growing infant (via mother's milk) might have a similar effect. In fact, some of the intellectual deficits ascribed to prenatal alcohol use may be due to its continued use in lactation, when the infant brain is still growing at a very rapid rate. Again, no substantial body of research exists.

A limited number of animal studies of alcoholized lactating dams report decreased body weight (Abel, 1974; DaSilva, Ribiero, & Masur, 1980; Detering, Reed, Ozand, & Karahasan, 1979; Martin, Martin, Sigman, & Radow, 1977; Pilstrom & Kiessling, 1967; Swanberg & Wilson, 1979), decreased viability (Baer & Crumpacker, 1977; Martin, Martin, Sigman, & Radow, 1977; Swanberg & Wilson, 1979), increased emotionality (Abel, 1975), decreased activity (Buckalew, 1978), extensive retardation of brain development (Bursey, 1973), and altered levels of certain neurotransmitters in the brain (Rawat, 1977) in their offspring. In humans, there is one report of pseudo-Cushing syndrome in an infant whose mother nursed and drank heavily (Binkiewicz, Robinson, & Senior, 1978), and another of infant intoxication in the child of a nursing lactating woman (Anderson, 1971). Apparently, no more is known about the consequences for the infant when this powerful drug is taken by a nursing mother.

But there is another dimension to all of this. Pregnancy, lactation, diet, drinking, and smoking are linked together in tantalizing ways. Strong endogenous aversions and cravings for many substances develop in pregnancy, in perhaps half of all pregnant women (Dickens & Trethowan, 1971; Hook, 1978). As noted earlier, alcohol is one of these substances. The immediate question, of course, is whether endogenous maternal cravings and aversions continue into lactation. Food cravings and aversions have been reported to vanish by the end of pregnancy (Harries & Hughes, 1958; Marcus, 1965). However, reports of animal studies indicate that the aversion to alcohol persists in lactating animals (Carver, Nash, Emerson, & Moore, 1953; Emerson, Brown, Nash, & Moore, 1952; Komura, Niimi, & Yoshitake, 1970; Randall et al., 1980). If so, this may further isolate the factors linked to craving; for example, prolactin levels might be a likely candidate for a major link to appetite for alcohol.

Paternal Factors

Why should a book on women and alcohol include a section on the father's role in reproduction? The authors have been involved in considerable public discussion about the impact of a mother's drinking during pregnancy on her offspring. With great regularity, people ask about the role of the father.

Usually they are polite. Occasionally they are angry that the scientific community continues to behave as if mothers were solely responsible for the health and development of their children. We can only agree that the role of the father should be considered too. The effects of parental drinking on children simply cannot be understood if one parent is consistently ignored.

In fact, there have been a number of investigations of the children of alcoholic fathers, but it is hard to say what they amount to, or what can be learned from them. There are several problems that cloud the issue. First, the studies in this area are notorious for their weak methodology, as many writers have noted (el-Guebaly & Offord, 1977; Fox, 1962; Haberman, 1966; Jacob, Favorini, Meisel, & Anderson, 1978; Wilson & Orford, 1978). Control for confounding variables is inadequate or nonexistent. The unique problems of alcoholism, as distinct from other psychosocial traumas, are not addressed. Paternal factors are not separated from maternal ones; some studies simply state that their subjects have "alcoholic parents," while others specify an "alcoholic father" without any information on the mother's drinking habits. Finally, virtually no investigation of humans has attempted to separate the biological influence of the father from his environmental influence after the child is born.

In the first part of the 20th century, a number of investigators conducted animal studies of the alcoholic male's biological influence on offspring. Arlitt and Wells (1917) reported that rats treated with alcohol produced abnormal and deficient sperm as a prelude to becoming completely sterile. Stockard (1913) treated male guinea pigs with alcohol by inhalation for as long as 3 years. When mated with normally fed and housed females, they produced fewer offspring and more stillborns. No obvious or consistent anomalies were noted, though the offspring of alcohol-treated males died soon after birth from various ailments and defects more often than the controls. Several early investigators reported insignificant increases in the percentage of male offspring when the sire was treated with alcohol (MacDowell & Lord, 1927; Pearl, 1917; Stockard & Papanicolaou, 1916). Anderson, Beyer, and Zaneveld (1978) also noted the same finding many years later. It is still not clear whether a sex differential actually exists, but the consistency of the observation at least invites further observation.

Following a substantial hiatus in the study of alcoholic fathering, recent animal researchers have focused on three main issues: (1) a decrease in the number and viability of offspring; (2) changes in the health and development of surviving offspring; and (3) direct evidence of changes in the reproductive material.

A number of studies have recently reported that alcohol-treated male animals produce fewer and less viable offspring than untreated controls (Anderson et al., 1978; Badr & Badr, 1975; Klassen & Persaud, 1976; Pfeiffer, MacKinnon, & Seiser, 1977). The reasons for this are not clear. One possibility is that fewer offspring are conceived. Arlitt and Wells (1917) reported a reduced number of sperm in alcohol-treated rats. Stekhun (1979) reported the same finding in humans, as well as reduced sperm motility. Neither study provides direct evidence of fewer conceptions. In fact, Badr and Badr (1975) reported no reduction in successful matings of mice; Anderson *et al.* (1978) found no decrement in copulation or frequency of conception in the same species. Even if pregnancy does occur, however, the number in the litter could vary, altering the number of offspring.

Another possibility is that fewer offspring initially conceived are brought successfully to term. Stockard (1913) noted increased fetal deaths in offspring of alcohol-treated animals. Badr and Badr (1975) noted increased reabsorption of fetal mice, more dead implants, and correspondingly fewer live embryos. These studies suggest decreased viability of offspring *in utero*.

Given that some of the offspring of alcohol-treated males do survive, what is the outcome? A common finding is that the experimental newborns are actually heavier than those in control groups (Anderson *et al.*, 1978; Klassen & Persaud, 1976; Pfeiffer *et al.*, 1977). The investigators agree that this finding is explained by smaller litter sizes and fewer progeny competing for nutrients and space. One investigator reported that by the ninth day of life, the experimental animals were lighter than the controls (Pfeiffer *et al.*, 1977).

Apparently only one investigator (Pfeiffer *et al.*, 1977) working with animals has looked at behavioral sequelae of paternal alcohol consumption. He found no effect on the ambulation or defecation of rats in an open field. These behaviors are usually used as measures of reaction to stress. Females reared more (a measure of activity in animals) and males reared less than control animals, and female experimentals consumed more alcohol than female controls. Considerably more work needs to be done in this area to determine the behaviors of the progeny of alcohol-treated fathers.

One study of humans has studied the offspring of alcoholic males while controlling for maternal drinking. Dul'nev (1965) studied 22 families with alcoholic fathers and explicitly nonalcoholic mothers. Children conceived before the onset of paternal alcoholism showed normal development. Those conceived during active alcoholism showed intellectual insufficiency, and the degree of insufficiency was associated with the duration of alcoholism. Children born 2–3 years following remission of alcoholism again appeared normal. Dul'nev concluded that paternal alcoholism affects the child's higher nervous-system function. The study was apparently done with no controls for potentially influential demographic variables or for environmental stresses, according to the English abstract.

If alcohol consumption by a father can adversely affect his offspring, how might this effect occur? Soyka and Joffe (1980) suggest several possible physical mechanisms. These could be direct genetic damage contained within the sperm, effects related to the semen, or effects related to changes in the male reproductive organs. There is some evidence for each of these hypotheses in both animal and human research.

Badr and Badr (1975) have been among the foremost proponents of the possibility of genetic change. They interpreted their finding that alcohol-treated sires produced an increase in dead implants as possible evidence for a dominant lethal mutation. Obe, Ristow, and Herha (1977), working with humans, questioned Badr and Badr's interpretation. They found no *in vitro* changes in chromosomes. They did see chromosomal aberrations *in vivo*, but could not rule out the effects of age, nutrition, and other drug use. Furthermore, the kinds of aberrations they saw would not necessarily affect future generations. De Torok (1972) noted chromosomal abnormalities in blood samples of alcoholics; but, again, these abnormalities do not necessarily affect genetic materials. Kohila, Eriksson, and Halkka (1976) found no chromosomal abnormalities in rats exposed to alcohol. Maguire (1975) and Rieger, Michaelis, Schubert, Dobel, and Jank (1975) both found chromosomal changes in vegetable species exposed to alcohol, but one cannot know how to generalize their findings to laboratory animals, to say nothing of human beings. Obe *et al.* (1977) concluded that ethanol has no mutagenic effect: "the question of a mutagenic effect of ethanol at the chromosomal level *in vitro* is at most controversial" (p. 49).

Doepfmer and Hinckers (1965), who have used human subjects, looked directly at the sperm of 5 men who consumed alcohol in the laboratory. They observed sperm oscillation and backward movements, curled tails, broken heads, and distended midsections. The investigators hypothesized damage to the developing sperm. Despite the intriguing quality of their findings, the numbers are small and other investigators have not made similar reports. We are not as skeptical as Obe (Obe *et al.*, 1977), but do conclude that the possibility of any kind of genetic abnormality related to male alcohol consumption is still a very open question.

Effects related to semen have also been considered. Reduced sperm motility in humans is a consistent finding (Doepfmer & Hinckers, 1965, 1966; Molnar & Papp, 1973; Stekhun, 1979). Soyka and Joffe (1980) also suggested that the semen of a man who had been consuming alcohol could have an effect on the uterus or influence the woman's reproduction by absorption through the vaginal walls, though there is apparently no evidence regarding either of these hypotheses.

Soyka and Joffe's (1980) final suggestion is that alcohol consumption may change the male reproductive organs. Indirect evidence of this is supplied by the finding that male alcohol consumption reduces testosterone levels (Badr, Bart, Dalterio, & Bulger, 1977; Klassen & Persaud, 1976; Stekhun, 1979). Semczuk (1978), working with humans, found that male alcoholics had lighter testicles and a decreased diameter of seminal tubules than their nonalcoholic counterparts. He also found relationships between duration of alcohol use and both inhibition of spermatogenesis and degeneration in the periphery of the spermatogenic epithelium. Changes in the male may take place as a result of alcohol use, but, of course, it is not clear if these changes actually affect the offspring.

A plethora of problems has been described in the children of alcoholic parents. Whether these are due to nature or nurture is unknown. Aberrant behavior in older offspring is frequently noted, with an increase in acting out and other behaviors disturbing to authorities. School is a frequently noted arena for trouble (Haberman, 1966; Kammeier, 1971; Hughes, 1977; Miller & Jang, 1977). In our own work we have found a significant decrease in IQ scores of children raised (but not conceived) by alcoholic fathers; all mothers were nonalcoholic light drinkers (Herman, Little, Streissguth, & Beck, 1980). Thus investigations that hope to determine the alcoholic father's impact at conception must take account of the deficiencies linked to his environmental influence.

In summary, very little is known about the effects of paternal alcohol use. Furthermore, there is little evidence of scientific interest in the subject. Most human studies of the possible biological effects have been done in other countries and are not available, except in abstract form, in English. In spite of promising animal work done earlier in this century, only very recently have a few animal researchers taken up this question again. In fact, Kolata (1978) wrote, "The phenomenon of drugs causing birth defects through their action in males alone is unexpected and peculiar" (p. 733). Fathers contribute half of a child's genetic beginnings. Why should one be surprised by the question of whether a father's alcohol use can affect his child? Bosma has noted that "the children of alcoholics are principals in a hidden tragedy" (1972, p. 34). Well controlled human and animal studies are needed to determine if the popular assumption that the father is not a principal player in this tragedy is, in fact, true.

CLINICAL ISSUES IN ALCOHOL AND REPRODUCTION

In the first section of this chapter, we have set out the research evidence that documents the risks of alcohol use for reproduction. That is the easy part, to document risk. In the second section, we describe a more difficult endeavor: prevention of these risks, and treatment of their sequelae if they are incurred.

Treatment of the alcohol abuser has always been challenging at best. When excessive drinking is coupled with reproductive consequences of grave degree, intervening in female alcohol abuse becomes both more difficult and more necessary. And if a child is involved who may have been affected by alcohol, intervention becomes even more imperative in order to avoid the further trauma of being raised by an alcoholic mother.

A demonstration project to develop strategies for intervening in alcohol abuse during pregnancy and preventing the resultant fetal effects was conducted in Seattle during the years 1978–1981 (Little, Streissguth, & Guzinski, 1980). This project was called the Pregnancy and Health Program. All types of pregnant drinkers were treated, from the casual user concerned about an occasional cocktail, to the severely alcoholic woman. Our experience with this program has been helpful in arriving at conclusions about appropriate ways to address the thorny clinical issues involved in treating this population. In this section, these techniques will be reviewed and discussed as they pertain to three types of patients: the pregnant woman, the alcohol-affected child, and the families of affected children.

Identifying and Treating the Pregnant Alcohol Abuser

IDENTIFICATION OF THE ABUSER

There are basically two ways in which an alcohol abuser can be identified by treatment personnel. The abuser can find treatment herself, or she can be referred to treatment by others. Generating self-referrals to treatment is possible if there is extensive awareness among the public, which does not currently exist in most areas. Referral to treatment by others, especially professionals, generally requires heightened knowledge beyond that presently existing. If the pregnant alcohol abuser is to be found, a campaign of both public education and professional training is an essential step.

Heightened public awareness of the risks that alcohol presents to the fetus has been addressed by the Pregnancy and Health Program in three ways: by presentations in the media, by distribution of written and audio-visual materials, and by personal contact with the public by the staff. Media includes television, radio, and newspapers. Public service announcements are particularly effective, especially if the format is changed frequently. The most powerful medium of all appears to be television, but this can be expensive and its effectiveness short-lived. Media messages are vital, but insufficient for a long-term change in public attitudes unless continued over a prolonged period. A less expensive method of public education is distribution of written materials, such as well-designed brochures and posters. These can be very effective, but their usefulness depends on the breadth of their distribution, and on specifying a contact point where the pregnant woman may receive information and be directed to treatment, if that is appropriate. A variant on the theme of written materials is the bus sign, which may be very helpful in an area with good public transportation. Personal contact by knowledgeable professionals on the Pregnancy and Health Program staff has been the least effective of all the public education techniques. It is also cost-ineffective, for the number of people reached by a given presentation is usually limited and personnel costs are high. Contrasting this with the wide range of persons reached by newspapers, radio, and television, one may wish to direct resources in a more economical manner.

The message used in the public education materials must be simple and direct. A scientific treatise, no matter how eloquently presented, will be useless in reaching the majority of the population. The conflict between simple public health messages and the complexity of research issues has caused problems in many fields, and drinking and pregnancy is no exception. Of course, there are a hundred caveats that ideally should be given to qualify the oversimplified presentation that must occur when space and time are limited. But when these qualifications are presented, the message becomes long and diluted, and only those who are vitally interested and well educated will bother to listen. Given the broad range of problems associated with maternal alcohol use, the appropriate message seems to be clear: Women should abstain from alcohol during the entire pregnancy if they wish to be certain that they do not incur risk to their fetus. This message is congruent with the Surgeon General's Advisory on Alcohol and Pregnancy (U.S. Department of Health and Human Services, 1981), and it is the message that was used by the Pregnancy and Health Program in all its public education materials.

An advantage of an extensive public education campaign is that it reaches not only the pregnant woman, but also the friends and family who must support her decision not to drink. A woman who changes her alcohol consumption suddenly may feel social pressures that she did not expect. The fine bottle of French wine for an anniversary, or the beer with the pizza at a local tavern on Friday must be foregone, and those who enjoyed these pleasures with her may resent her decision. For this reason, reaching the family and friends who provide a support system for the pregnant woman is necessary if the message given to her is to be heeded.

Professional identification of the pregnant drinker can easily be achieved, given adequate knowledge and awareness, for pregnancy is a time when women come in contact with a host of care-givers. Foremost is the person providing prenatal care, usually a physician, and his or her staff. Routine screening of every pregnant woman in a prenatal clinic by the Pregnancy and Health Program staff identified 10% of the prenatal patients as drinking at levels possibly detrimental to the welfare of their children. This type of routine screening takes only a minute or two, and is easily incorporated into office procedures. Helping professionals, such as social workers, also see a large number of pregnant women and may serve as key persons in identifying those who are drinking. Both health and helping professionals are in an ideal position to identify and intervene in alcohol abuse. This is fortunate, for the usual techniques by which pressure is exerted on drinkers to obtain treatment are not generally used for the pregnant woman. For example, the pregnant woman is most unlikely to be charged with driving while intoxicated, nor will she be picked out by her employer for referral to an occupational alcoholism program unless her problem is flagrant. All of the protection traditionally given to alcoholics who are female, young, very old, of higher socioeconomic status, or in any other way not typical of the usual stereotype is also afforded to the pregnant woman, except that this protection is even greater for her. We have spoken to such diverse patients as professional women, wives of the clergy, and teenage mothers who admitted to drinking to quiet their developing baby's incessant movements. These young women, apparently in the prime of life and flushed with the bloom of pregnancy, are unlikely to be detected as dedicated drinkers. For this reason, extensive and intensive professional training is essential if the pregnant drinker is to be identified.

Imparting information to health and helping professionals is a very different problem than imparting information to the public. For the public, simplicity and clarity of presentation are paramount needs. For the professional, brevity and credibility are the chief concerns. Most professionals have little time to listen to an involved presentation, and they certainly will not read at great length outside their own discipline. They, like the public, are not interested in the niceties of the scientific question. However, they are themselves well trained, and they will not respond to a message unless it is delivered in familiar language and in a manner that is compatible with their own professional expectations. For this reason, we have found it helpful to have professionals in a specific discipline trained by Program staff of the same discipline: physicians training physicians, nurses training nurses, social workers training social workers, and so forth. Trainers of the same discipline as the audience are able to present the salient points to their group with credibility.

When planning public education or professional training campaigns, one must recall that this is a very new field—only 10 years old. There may be skepticism initially about the risks of alcohol use during gestation, but this is not surprising. The weight of the evidence to date is becoming so great that informing either the public or the professions about alcohol use in pregnancy is not difficult.

TREATMENT[3]

There is probably no person more difficult to treat than the pregnant alcoholic. For her, denial and guilt reach epidemic proportions, blocking attempts to help her. On the other hand, she can be particularly receptive to treatment because of her concern for her developing child. The ambivalence that she feels—so intensely on either side of the question—makes this a time of both danger and opportunity for the therapist and the client.

---

3. We are grateful to the clinical staff of the Pregnancy and Health Program—Rachel Nordin, Randi Campbell, Geraldine Keane, Shari Dunkelman, and Louise Phillips—for discussing these techniques with us and permitting us to present them here.

Clients presenting at the Pregnancy and Health Program represented the entire spectrum of alcohol consumption, from abstinence to severe alcoholism. Our treatment of them changed over the course of the Program, beginning with a very gentle approach that was directed to helping the mother, to a forceful approach directed to protecting the child. The therapeutic encounter has evolved into the following format. The initial encounter begins by taking a reproductive history. The reproductive history is not a threatening subject to the woman, and both the therapist and the client are vitally interested in this area. As noted above, the drinking pregnant woman is at significantly higher risk for fetal loss, and past abortions and terminations may be frequent. There may also be unplanned pregnancies, problems with existing children, and difficulty with the family that compound the client's sense of loss. The reproductive history at the beginning of the first interview sets out the details of one of the two basic areas to be explored.

Once the reproductive history is taken, the drinking history follows. In almost every case, the pregnant alcohol abuser will rationalize and excuse her behavior. Minimizing her drinking is essential if she is to protect herself. The history can begin in the usual way, but it should become quite specific beginning with a month or so before conception. Both frequency and quantity of consumption should be ascertained. The reason for this detail is that it is essential in assessing the dose of alcohol that the fetus has received, and therefore the risk incurred. Binges are important also, although the risk of an isolated binge is not clearly defined. The therapist should not be surprised if low amounts of alcohol use are reported beginning shortly after conception, for the endogenous aversion noted above occurs in well over 50% of women, even those who are severely alcoholic. At some point, it is important to note that the desire to drink will return again after delivery, and any remission of an alcohol problem is probably temporary.

Once the reproductive and drinking histories are taken, the risks associated with the client's particular drinking pattern should be addressed. Clearly no one can predict what will happen in any specific pregnancy, and the vague concept of probability is a difficult one for most people to grasp. Nevertheless, information on risk should be couched in terms of probabilities, rather than certainties. This presentation will make it easier to deal with statements such as "My sister drank very heavily during pregnancy and had a fine baby." It is helpful to explain that risk entails a possibility, and that possibility grows greater as the drinking increases. Risk is not certainty, so the therapist is not predicting the future. Once this qualification is clear, the information on risk can be presented as it is appropriate for the client.

In general, pregnant drinking clients fall into two groups: those who have a choice of whether or not to abstain, and those who have lost that choice. The former group is easier to deal with, for they can accept the information and act on it. There may be apprehension and guilt about past behavior, but future behavior is not a major problem. In contrast, the client with a drinking problem who no longer has reliable control over her drinking will be less responsive. She will deny, prevaricate, and look for loopholes to show that all of this does not really apply to her. At this point a confrontation may be desirable, and an effective question is "Why are you forcing your baby to drink?" This drives home that difficult and sensitive point of placental transfer of alcohol, and makes it possible for the therapist to remind the client that her blood-alcohol levels will be mirrored in the fetus's blood-alcohol levels: In other words, when she drinks a martini, her baby does too.

The pregnancy, like the driving offense or the occupational referral to treatment, may create a crisis that can work for both therapist and client. The welfare of a woman's baby is a powerful weapon to hold over her, and in our experience, this should be done. Including the client's family, friends, and physician or midwife can increase the pressure brought to bear on her to deal with her alcohol problem. In the beginning, we feared that excessive pressure might bring about a spontaneous abortion in clients. That has not proved to be the case. In fact, timid treatment of pregnant women achieves the same results as timid treatment of any alcohol abuser: it enables them to continue their denial and their drinking.

If a client continues to drink, forceful action may be indicated. The legal issues surrounding child abuse *in utero* have not been clarified for alcohol, but the continued drinking of an expectant mother may well be grounds for involuntary commitment.

There are certain characteristics of pregnant alcohol abusers that warrant mention. First is a sense of urgency, a need to get the information on what they have "done" to their child with a minimum of interaction with any therapist. Most clients would like to do it by telephone if possible! It is important to be aware of this sense of urgency, for presenting the information too quickly may result in losing the client before any intervention can take place.

Another issue that generally arises is loss. Past pregnancy loss may need to be resolved. In addition, there will be sorrow at losing the ideal of a perfect pregnancy in the present situation. Anger toward medical personnel in both of these instances is not uncommon. Also, the frequent ambivalence that women feel about having a child is compounded when they realize that this child may not develop to its best potential. This works into feelings of guilt that can be unbearable. The guilt of the client may be so great, and the fear of the therapist in confronting it so extreme, that there can be a conspiracy of silence that is destructive on both sides. In fact, one of the reasons most frequently given for withholding information on risk is that it will "upset" those who receive it. This is a poor excuse for inaction. With almost no exceptions, women seen at the Pregnancy and Health Program have felt guilt long before they were seen by a therapist. Working through these feelings of guilt is essential to the long-term welfare of the client and her child.

The question of termination of a pregnancy marked by drinking is one that will frequently arise. It is a question for which there is no pat answer, for the outcome in a particular pregnancy cannot be predicted. There are many dimensions to the decision: whether or not the pregnancy was wanted, how heavy the drinking has been, the religious and ethical considerations for the woman, and the probability of another conception, should this be desired. If termination is elected, the issue of loss will arise. The guilt felt after such a termination will exacerbate the feelings of loss, and therapeutic intervention may well be needed after the termination as well as before.

In general, women appear to become less amenable to intervention in the later months of pregnancy. Maternal concern seems to be highest in the first trimester. Later, as the pregnancy progresses, the woman turns inward and is less likely to reach out for help. For this reason, as well as because of the crucial importance of the period of organogenesis, pregnant drinkers should be reached as soon as possible after conception.

After the delivery, the stressful postpartum period begins. Whether the urge to drink returns during lactation is not known, but certainly any alcohol consumed passes into the maternal milk. Abstinence, then, continues to be vital to mother and child. If a mother does not lactate, the stresses of a new baby and release from her responsibility of pregnancy make a return to drinking a clear danger, especially as her appetite for alcohol returns to normal. Thus extra support is needed during the postpartum period.

The Alcohol-Affected Child[4]

Only a handful of children seen at the Pregnancy and Health Program were diagnosed by a pediatric dysmorphologist as having the full FAS, even though most of the natural mothers were alcoholic. However, most of the children had learning and/or behavior problems that were disabling to some degree. Furthermore, a majority were diagnosed as having physical signs of fetal alcohol effects, even though they did not have the full syndrome. This is not to say that all children exposed to alcohol *in utero* are affected in some way by alcohol. It does, however, point up the fact that full FAS is only one outcome of alcoholism during pregnancy. Many more children show problems in learning and behavior, perhaps accompanied by only a few, or even one, of the physical signs of alcohol exposure.

Children exposed to alcohol during pregnancy may be difficult to raise because of their learning and behavior problems. A complete developmental evaluation of these children may therefore be advisable. The evaluation

4. See footnote 3.

serves two major purposes: It provides information essential to maximizing the child's growth and development; and it assists the mother in accepting her child's strengths and weaknesses, while providing constructive suggestions for how to deal with them. It puts to rest vague apprehensions and enables the parent(s) to deal constructively with the situation. The developmental evaluation, in almost every instance, has been a positive experience for parents at the Pregnancy and Health Program.

INFANTS

The developmental assessment of infants must take place over time. Judgments about how a baby will function in 5 years cannot be made at birth. Although this is true of all infants, it is particularly true of potentially alcohol-affected children, because of the borderline nature of so many of their difficulties. The basic plan for assessment at the Pregnancy and Health Program reflected the need for testing over time.

At birth, a Brazelton neonatal assessment was used. The Brazelton is one of the few organized methods of looking at an infant's behavioral and reflexive abilities. It also serves as an excellent teaching tool for acquainting new mothers with the wide range of newborn skills and unique qualities of their babies. A pediatric dysmorphology exam was also given. Ideally, the exam should be repeated at about 8 months, because growth measurements obtained during the neonatal period often reflect the impact of maternal size rather than genetic background. This effect is usually diminished by 8 months, when the child approaches his or her true genetic potential for growth. Also, nondysmorphologists may have trouble distinguishing dysmorphic features in the newborn's face. Subtle features can be easier to spot in an older baby. The examination at birth provides a good baseline, and the examination at 8 months serves as an additional measure of validity.

The Bayley Scales of Infant Development (BSID) was the exam of choice at the Pregnancy and Health Program for children between 2 and 30 months. The Mental and Motor Scales were used for evaluations at 4, 8, and 12 months. These ages reflect unique levels of development, and allow the child's growth in motor as well as problem-solving and language skills to be followed. Even if no abnormalities are apparent at birth, follow-up is advisable, for developmental problems can turn up even in the absence of very early signs. Until more is known about the long-term effects of *in utero* alcohol exposure, it is important to follow each child. Many agencies will not have the time or the funding to evaluate each baby so thoroughly every time. In that case, at least one full evaluation is recommended. Screening tools, such as the Denver Developmental Screening Test, can often miss all but the clearest delays. Periodic screening plus one evaluation should be enough for most children.

At the Pregnancy and Health Program, a maternal–infant nurse was responsible for infant assessment. Infants and their mothers are a dyad.

Unless an infant has been completely removed from the custody of his or her mother, the infant should not be seen without the mother's involvement. The maternal–infant nurse balanced the needs of both mother and baby. Although the main goal was, in fact, the welfare of the baby, that goal cannot be isolated from the welfare of the mother.

The maternal–infant nurse's role included assessing the baby's physical growth and skill development, educating the parents about the baby's social and intellectual skills, enhancing the mother–child relationship, providing a supportive and therapeutic relationship for the mother, and intervening in maternal alcoholism when needed.

OLDER CHILDREN

Standard psychological tests were used for the developmental assessment of older children at the Pregnancy and Health Program. Like all tests, these tests are in no way magical, nor are they specifically designed for children with alcohol effects. Rather, information about alcohol-affected children can be obtained from tests that other professionals can use and apply.

Children aged 9 or older were normally given a standard intelligence test (one of the Weschler series or a Stanford–Binet), an academic achievement test (the Wide Range Achievement Test, or WRAT), and the Halstead–Reitan Neuropsychological Test Battery.

Children between the ages of 5–8 were given a standard intelligence test, the WRAT, the Reitan–Indiana Neuropsychological Test Battery (the younger child version of the Halstead–Reitan) and the McCarthy Scales of Children's Abilities. The McCarthy was chosen because it assesses a wider range of skills than a standard intelligence test, including verbal, perceptual-performance, quantitative, memory, and motor skills. Age equivalents, particularly helpful in explaining test results to parents, can be computed for each skill area and subtest. The McCarthy may be especially useful with alcohol-affected children, who sometimes imitate normal talking very well, but do not really understand verbal communication. Because the McCarthy provides separate scores and age equivalents for imitation and comprehension, possible discrepancies in verbal skills can be identified.

For younger children, the McCarthy (down to 2½ years), the Wechsler Preschool and Primary Scale of Intelligence (WPPSI) or Stanford–Binet, and sometimes the Alpern–Boll Developmental Profile are appropriate, depending on the age of the child. The Developmental Profile is administered largely by interviewing the caretaker and can add information both about the child and the parent's perception of the child. If a 2- or 3-year-old is delayed in development, the Bayley can be used to ascertain overall developmental level, even though standard scores cannot be obtained.

In general, the alcohol-affected children who were seen at the Pregnancy and Health Program were easy to test. They usually wanted to please the examiner and were therefore very cooperative. Although a number of the children were hyperactive, they were usually able to work in a structured, one-to-one situation. However, some problems were encountered apart from getting good performance from the child. Alcohol-affected children some-times appear able to do more than they actually can. Examiners may find that the child performs surprisingly poorly on some tasks. If so, the examiner may then: (1) doubt his or her own judgment of the child's task performance; (2) attribute the failure to situational factors, such as fatigue, hunger, and so on; or (3) conclude that the child is not trying. Some children at the Pregnancy and Health Program were tested and retested, with staff not quite believing that they couldn't do a little more. Other problems encountered were typical of any group of children with behavior and learning problems. These include low frustration tolerance, oversensitivity to failure, and short attention span. Ideally, the examiner should have some experience evaluating children with special problems.

As with infants, a pediatric dysmorphology examination is advisable for older children.

After 2 years of evaluating alcohol-affected children at the Pregnancy and Health Program, a clear picture of their potential deficiencies has emerged for the child exposed to alcohol *in utero*. While IQ scores ranged from moderately retarded to above average, the typical child achieved a borderline to low-normal IQ score. Although some of the children showed clear retardation, many functioned intellectually at a confusing, "in-between" level.

Almost all the children evaluated, even those demonstrating normal intelligence, showed learning disabilities of some kind. No one type of learning disability seemed more prevalent than any other. The children showed various combinations of perceptual and spatial deficits, visual–motor incoordination, problem-solving difficulties, and so on. A number of them did show some problem with language, frequently fairly subtle. One group of children seemed to have good verbal skills based on general conversation, but when tested did poorly on verbal comprehension tasks. These children may seem to be understanding more than they are—another potentially confusing characteristic of some alcohol-affected children. Finally, a number of children showed what one parent called mental "short-circuiting." In other words, the child can do a certain task at one time, and then not be able to do the same task at another time. This is another source of confusion.

Behavior problems occurred frequently among the children who came to the Pregnancy and Health Program. The most common problems were hyperactivity and distractibility. Even those who were not hyperactive often showed inappropriate behavior and poor social judgment.

Any learning and behavior problems related to a CNS deficit can, of course, be compounded by a difficult and chaotic home life. Growing up in an alcoholic family can cause just as much trouble as being exposed to alcohol before birth. A number of the children showed emotional as well as learning and specific behavior problems. The confounding of prenatal effects with a difficult environment can be another source of confusion surrounding alcohol-affected children.

Children with subtle alcohol effects often fall between the cracks in the school system. Children with clear FAS are usually identified as handicapped, even though they may be diagnosed incorrectly. FAS children, therefore, tend to get the special help they need, whereas children with fetal alcohol effects often do not. One reason is that children with subtle alcohol effects usually look essentially normal, even if they have some of the characteristic facial features of FAS. Also, they may have undetected or subtle learning disabilities. Academically and intellectually they are frequently not quite behind enough to fit normal criteria for special education. Because they sometimes talk deceptively well and may have a behavior problem, adults can feel that if these children would only settle down, not be so stubborn, or resolve emotional problems, they could do their school work. Finally, it is easy to assume that any learning or behavior problems stem only from a difficult home life. The home life is certainly at least as important as prenatal effects, especially when the prenatal effects are subtle; but the neuropsychological functioning of the child cannot be ignored.

Working with Families of Affected Children[5]

Whenever a child was referred to the Pregnancy and Health Program, a staff member met with the parents, guardian, and/or referring agent before any plan for seeing the child was developed. When an evaluation is requested, the questions to be answered by the evaluation must be clarified first. Preliminary counseling is particularly important for this population because of the many emotional issues that can surround a child affected by a mother's drinking during pregnancy. The issues for a specific child depend on the situation.

Natural mothers were always seen first by counselors with expertise in alcoholism. They assessed whether or not the woman was alcoholic. If so, was she recovering and how solid was her recovery? Was she still drinking? What were her questions about the child? Did she have underlying reasons for wanting the child assessed?

The natural mothers can be divided into three groups for ease of discussion: those who are recovered alcoholics, those who are newly recovering, and those who are still drinking. Specific issues arose with each group.

A mother who is no longer drinking, has a good recovery, and is facing the possible effects of her alcoholism on her child usually feels even more guilty than one can imagine. However, being too afraid or too uncomfortable

---

5. See footnote 3.

to face the issue with her is not helpful. Many women suspected that their drinking was harmful to unborn children even before FAS was identified. As more people become aware of the prenatal effects of alcohol, recovering alcoholic women cannot be shielded from this knowledge. Reluctance to discuss alcohol effects may stem from the therapist's feelings as well as the mother's.

Another distinct group of natural mothers are newly recovering alcoholic women, and the issues may be very different for them. These women often either want to rush in and fix everything immediately, or, on the other hand, deny any possibility of problems with their children. The latter attitude may actually be more functional. The newly recovering woman often needs to protect herself for a while. It can be wise to respect and even to nurture her defenses. In such a case, a conflict may arise between the current needs of the mother and the needs of the child. The mother may need to avoid facing the child's problems, while the child may need evaluation for possible special intervention. Conflicts of this nature have formed the basis for a number of lively discussions between alcohol counselors and child services personnel at the Pregnancy and Health Program. Two conclusions from these discussions are helpful: (1) if the child is not in crisis, meeting the immediate needs of the mother is better for the long-term welfare of both people; and (2) if the child is in crisis, the child's needs must be addressed, in conjunction with sensitive counseling for the mother.

Finally, there are the natural mothers who are still drinking. If a child is living with a drinking alcoholic mother, all the fine evaluation and treatment in the world for this child will be wasted if it is done without addressing the mother's problem. The mother's drinking becomes the main issue. A skillful alcohol counselor or a therapist with expertise in this area can help the woman examine her drinking. To ignore it is to facilitate her alcoholism. If the child has immediate and critical needs which are not being met, a referral to Child Protective Services is appropriate.

Fathers and other relatives who bring in a child for evaluation should also be seen first by a therapist for two reasons. There may be some underlying agenda regarding the natural mother, such as punishment or exoneration. Also, if the natural mother is living and available, she will hear about the evaluation. Because the information can be so threatening, someone needs to meet with her, or at least know where she fits in with the child.

Foster parents can be seen directly by child services personnel, but certain issues still need to be addressed. Even if the natural mother has put the child up for adoption, she may change her mind and suddenly become involved. Thus the natural mother must at least be contacted. The evaluation of the child could provide an opportunity to intervene in her alcoholism; and again, one needs to know how potentially threatening information about her child might be communicated to her. Furthermore, foster parents can sometimes be very angry with the natural mother of an alcohol-affected child, a feeling which may be destructive for the child (and the natural mother) in the long run.

Adoptive parents of alcohol-affected children have to deal with the normal issues of having a handicapped child. In addition, there may be special problems. Because alcohol effects are often not obvious in infancy, adoptive parents may have thought the child was perfectly normal. If the child is unusually thin, caseworkers, new parents, and all concerned may attribute that to postnatal neglect. The parents will, of course, be very disappointed when the child neither gains weight nor develops normally. And anger with the natural mother can be at least as much of an issue for adoptive parents as for foster parents.

SUMMARY

In this chapter, evidence that alcohol is a teratogenic agent has been presented. Intrauterine exposure to alcohol has been linked to growth retardation, abnormalities in physical development, CNS dysfunction, and increased risk of fetal and infant mortality. In surviving infants, FAS is the severest manifestation of this damage. But it is only a fraction of the effects that can occur that are secondary to alcohol exposure *in utero*. There is no known safe dose of alcohol during pregnancy, nor does there appear to be a safe time to drink, from the preconception months through lactation.

There are many questions not yet answered. The father's role, if he is a heavy drinker, remains unexplored. So are the factors that may alter the risk incurred by the alcohol-exposed fetus. The timing, the quantity, the frequency, the beverage—all are variables whose relative impact on fetal development is unknown.

Meanwhile, as researchers search for answers, women drink and become pregnant. If they drink heavily, their treatment is exceedingly difficult. Urgency, guilt, and denial are hallmarks of their behavior. Forceful, yet nonjudgmental action is indicated if they are to be helped. Their children, when they are born, may have learning and behavior problems that are longlasting. They may also have the typical physical signs that have been found in children exposed to alcohol prenatally. The careful neuropsychological evaluation of these children is essential, both to identify their strengths and weaknesses, and to aid the mother in their management.

The pregnant drinker is actually two clients: the mother and the fetus. Intervention in female alcohol abuse can save a life. But for the pregnant woman, it may save two.

ACKNOWLEDGMENTS

This work was supported by the National Institute on Alcohol Abuse and Alcoholism (Grant #AA 03736) and by the Alcoholism and Drug Abuse Institute, University of Washington.

REFERENCES

Abel, E. Alcohol ingestion in lactating rats: Effects on mothers and offspring. *Archives Internationales de Pharmacodynamie*, 1974, *210*, 121-127.

Abel, E. Emotionality in offspring of rats fed alcohol while nursing. *Journal of Studies on Alcohol*, 1975, *36*, 654-658.

Abel, E. L. Fetal alcohol syndrome: Behavioral toxicology. *Psychological Bulletin*, 1980, *87*, 29-50.

Abel, E. L. (Ed.). *Fetal alcohol syndrome* (Vol. 2: *Human studies*; Vol. 3: *Animal studies*). Boca Raton, Fla.: CRC Press, 1982.

Anderson, P. Drugs and nursing. *Drug Interactions and Clinical Pharmacology*, 1971, *11*, 208-223.

Anderson, R. A., Beyer, S. A., & Zaneveld, L. J. D. Alterations of male reproduction induced by chronic ingestion of ethanol: Development of an animal model. *Fertility and Sterility*, 1978, *30*, 193-205.

Arlitt, A. H., & Wells, H. G. The effect of alcohol on the reproductive tissues. *Journal of Experimental Medicine*, 1917, *26*, 769-778.

Badr, F. M., & Badr, R. S. Induction of dominant lethal mutation in male mice by ethyl alcohol. *Nature*, 1975, *253*, 134-136. (Cited in Obe, G., Ristow, H. J., & Herha, J., 1977.)

Badr, F. M., Bart, A., Dalterio, S., & Bulger, W. Suppression of testosterone by ethyl alcohol: Possible mode of action. *Steroids*, 1977, *30*, 647-655.

Baer, D. S., & Crumpacker, D. W. Fertility and offspring survival in mice selected for different sensitivities to alcohol. *Behavior Genetics*, 1977, *7*, 95-103.

Bauer-Moffett, C., & Altman, J. Ethanol-induced reductions in cerebellar growth of infant rats. *Experimental Neurology*, 1975, *48*, 378-382.

Bauer-Moffett, C., & Altman, J. The effects of ethanol chronically administered to preweaning rats on cerebellar development: A morphological study. *Brain Research*, 1977, *119*, 249-268.

Berkowitz, G. S. An epidemiologic study of preterm delivery. *American Journal of Epidemiology*, 1981, *113*, 81-92.

Binkiewicz, A., Robinson, M. J., & Senior, B. Pseudo-Cushing syndrome caused by alcohol in breast milk. *Journal of Pediatrics*, 1978, *93*, 965-967.

Boggan, W. O., Randall, C. L., DeBeukelaer, M., & Smith, R. Renal anomalies in mice prenatally exposed to alcohol. *Research Communications in Chemical Pathology and Pharmacology*, 1979, *23*, 127-142.

Bosma, W. G. Children of alcoholics, a hidden tragedy. *Maryland State Medical Journal*, January 1972, pp. 34-36.

Brown, N. A., Goulding, E. H., & Fabro, S. Ethanol embryotoxicity: Direct effects on mammalian embryos in vitro. *Science*, 1979, *206*, 573-575.

Buckalew, L. W. Effect of maternal alcohol consumption during nursing on offspring activity. *Research Communications in Psychology, Psychiatry and Behavior*, 1978, *3*, 353-358.

Bursey, R. G. *Effect of maternal ethanol consumption during gestation and lactation on the development and learning performance of the offspring.* Doctoral thesis, University of Michigan, 1973. (University Microfilms No. 73-19262)

Carver, J. W., Nash, J. B., Emerson, G. A., & Moore, W. T. Effects of pregnancy and lactation on voluntary alcohol intake of hamsters. *Pharmacology and Experimental Therapeutics*, 1953, *12*, 309.

Chernoff, G. F. The fetal alcohol syndrome in mice: An animal model. *Teratology*, 1977, *15*, 223-230.

Christoffel, K. K., & Salafsky, I. Fetal alcohol syndrome in dizygotic twins. *Journal of Pediatrics*, 1975, *87*, 963-967.

Clarren, S. K., Alvord, E. D., Sumi, S. M., Streissguth, A. P., & Smith, D. W. Brain malformations related to prenatal exposure to ethanol. *Journal of Pediatrics*, 1978, *92*, 64-67.

Clarren, S. K., & Smith, D. W. The fetal alcohol syndrome. *New England Journal of Medicine*, 1978, *298*, 1063–1067.

DaSilva, V. A., Ribiero, M. J., & Masur, J. Developmental, behavioral, and pharmacological characteristics of rat offspring from mothers receiving ethanol during gestation or lactation. *Developmental Psychology*, 1980, *13*, 653–660.

Dehaene, P., Samaille-Villette, C., Samaille, P., Crepin, G., Walbaum, R., Deroubaix, P., & Blanc-Garin, A. P. Le syndrome d'alcoolisme foetal dans le nord de la France. *Revue de l'Alcoolisme*, 1977, *23*, 145–158.

Detering, N., Reed, W. D., Ozand, P. T., & Karahasan, A. Effects of maternal ethanol consumption in the rat on the development of their offspring. *Journal of Nutrition*, 1979, *109*, 999–1009.

de Torok, D. Chromosomal abnormalities in alcoholics. *Annals of the New York Academy of Sciences*, 1972, *197*, 90–100.

Dexter, J. D., Tumbleson, M. E., Decker, J. D., & Middleton, C. C. Fetal alcohol syndrome in Sinclair (S-1) miniature swine. *Alcoholism: Clinical and Experimental Research*, 1980, *4*, 146–151.

Diaz, J., & Samson, H. H. Impaired brain growth in neonatal rats exposed to ethanol. *Science*, 1980, *208*, 751–753.

Dickens, G., & Trethowan, W. H. Cravings and aversions during pregnancy. *Journal of Psychosomatic Research*, 1971, *15*, 259–268.

Dilts, P. V., Jr. Placental transfer of ethanol. *American Journal of Obstetrics and Gynecology*, 1970, *107*, 1195–1198.

Doepfmer, R., & Hinckers, H. J. [On the question of germ-cell damage in acute alcohol intoxication.] *Zeitschrift für Haut- und Geschlechtskrankheiten*, 1965, *39*, 94–107. (CAAAL Abstract 11720, in English)

Doepfmer, R., & Hinckers, H. J. [The effect of alcohol on the motility of human spermatozoa.] *Zeitschrift für Haut- und Geschlechtskrankheiten*, 1966, *40*, 378–382.

Drinking in pregnancy: The danger is disputed. *The New York Times*, September 10, 1981, section 3, p. 14, col. 3.

Dul'nev, V. D. [On the role of paternal alcoholism in the etiology of mental deficiency in offspring] *Pediatriya*, 1965, *44*, 68–69. (Abstract)

el-Guebaly, N., & Offord, D. R. The offspring of alcoholics: A critical review. *American Journal of Psychiatry*, 1977, *134*, 357–365.

Ellis, F. W., & Pick, J. R. An animal model of the fetal alcohol syndrome in beagles. *Alcoholism: Clinical and Experimental Research*, 1980, *4*, 123–134.

Elton, R. H., & Wilson, M. E. Changes in ethanol consumption by pregnant pigtailed macaques. *Journal of Studies on Alcohol*, 1977, *38*, 2181–2183.

Emerson, G. A., Brown, R. G., Nash, J. B., & Moore, W. T. Species variation in preference for alcohol and in effects of diet or drugs on this preference. *Journal of Pharmacology and Experimental Therapeutics*, 1952, *11*, 384.

Fox, R. Children in the alcoholic family. In W. C. Bier (Ed.), *Problems in addiction: Alcohol and drug addiction*. New York: Fordham University Press, 1962.

Graham, J. M., Jr., Darby, B. I., Barr, H. M., Smith, D. W., & Streissguth, A. P. Long-term effects of alcohol consumption during pregnancy. *Teratology*, in press.

Haberman, P. W. Childhood symptoms in children of alcoholics and comparison group parents. *Journal of Marriage and the Family*, 1966, *28*, 152–154.

Hanson, J. W., Streissguth, A. P., & Smith, D. W. The effects of moderate alcohol consumption during pregnancy on fetal growth and morphogenesis. *Journal of Pediatrics*, 1978, *92*, 457–460.

Harlap, S., & Shiono, P. H. Alcohol, smoking, and incidence of spontaneous abortions in the first and second trimester. *Lancet*, 1980, *2*, 173–176.

Harries, J. M., & Hughes, T. T. Enumeration of the "cravings" of some pregnant women. *British Medical Journal*, 1958, *2*, 39.

Henderson, G. I., Hoyumpa, A. M., McClain, C., & Schenker, S. The effects of chronic and acute alcohol administration on fetal development in the rat. *Alcoholism: Clinical and Experimental Research*, 1979, *3*, 99–106.

Henderson, G. I., Hoyumpa, A. M., Rothschild, M. A., & Schenker, S. Effect of ethanol and ethanol-induced hypothermia on protein synthesis in pregnant and fetal rats. *Alcoholism: Clinical and Experimental Research*, 1980, *4*, 165–177.

Herman, C. S., Little, R. E., Streissguth, A. P., & Beck, D. E. *Alcoholic fathering and its relation to child's intellectual development*. Paper presented at the National Council on Alcoholism, Medical Scientific Meetings, Seattle, May 1980.

Hook, E. B. Changes in tobacco smoking and ingestion of alcohol and caffeinated beverages during early pregnancy: Are these consequences, in part, of fetoprotective mechanisms diminishing maternal exposure to embryotoxins? In S. Kelly, E. B. Hook, & P. Janerich (Eds.), *Birth defects: Risks and consequences*. New York: Academic Press, 1976.

Hook, E. B. Dietary cravings and aversions during pregnancy. *American Journal of Clinical Nutrition*, 1978, *31*, 1355–1362.

Horning, M. G., Stillwell, W. G., Nowling, J., Lertratanangkoon, K., Stillwell, R. N., & Hill, R. M. Identification and quantification of drugs and drug metabolites in human breast milk. *Modern Problems in Pediatrics*, 1975, *15*, 73–79.

Hughes, J. M. Adolescent children of alcoholic parents and the relationship of Alateen to these children. *Journal of Consulting and Clinical Psychology*, 1977, *45*, 946–947.

Idapaan-Heikkila, J. E., Fritchie, G. E., Ho, B. T., & McIsaac, W. M. Placental transfer of 14C-ethanol. *American Journal of Obstetrics and Gynecology*, 1971, *110*, 426–428.

Jacob, T., Favorini, A., Meisel, S., & Anderson, C. The alcoholic's spouse, children and family interactions. *Journal of Studies on Alcohol*, 1978, *19*, 1231–1251.

Jones, K. L., Smith, D. W., Streissguth, A. P., & Myrianthopoulos, N. C. Outcome in offspring of chronic alcoholic women. *Lancet*, 1974, *1*, 1076–1078.

Jones, K. L., Smith, D. W., Ulleland, C. N., & Streissguth, A. P. Pattern of malformation in offspring of chronic alcoholic mothers. *Lancet*, 1973, *1*, 1267–1271.

Kaminski, M., Rumeau-Rouquette, C., & Schwartz, D. Consommation d'alcool chez les femmes enceintes et issue de la grossesse. *Revue d'Epidemiologie et de Santé Publique*, 1976, *24*, 27–40. (English translation by Little, R. E., & Schnizel, A. Alcohol consumption in pregnant women and the outcome of pregnancy. *Alcoholism: Clinical and Experimental Research*, 1978, *2*, 155–163.)

Kammeier, M. L. Adolescents from families with and without alcohol problems. *Quarterly Journal of Studies on Alcohol*, 1971, *32*, 364–372.

Kesaniemi, Y. A. Ethanol and acetaldehyde in the milk and peripheral blood of lactating women after ethanol administration. *Journal of Obstetrics and Gynaecology of the British Commonwealth*, 1974, *81*, 84–86.

Klassen, R. W., & Persaud, T. V. N. Experimental studies on the influence of male alcoholism on pregnancy and progeny. *Experimentelle Pathologie*, 1976, *12*, 38.

Klemetti, A., & Saxen, L. Prospective versus retrospective approach in the search of environmental causes of malformation. *American Journal of Public Health*, 1967, *57*, 2071–2075.

Kline, J., Shrout, P., Stein, Z., Susser, M., & Warburton, D. Drinking during pregnancy and spontaneous abortion. *Lancet*, 1980, *2*, 176–180.

Knowles, J. A. Drugs in milk. *Pediatric Currents*, 1972, *21*, 28–32.

Kohila, T., Eriksson, K., & Halkka, O. Goniomitosis in rats subjected to ethanol. *Medical Biology*, 1976, *54*, 150–151.

Kolata, G. B. Teratogens acting through males. *Science*, 1978, *202*, 733.

Kolonel, L. H., Hirohata, T., & Nomura, A. M. Adequacy of survey data collected from substitute respondents. *American Journal of Epidemiology*, 1977, *106*, 476–484.

Komura, S., Niimi, Y., & Yoshitake, Y. Alcohol preference during reproductive cycle in female C57BL mice. *Japanese Journal of Studies on Alcohol*, 1970, *5*, 91–96.

Landesman-Dwyer, S., Keller, L. S., & Streissguth, A. P. Naturalistic observations of newborns: Effects of maternal alcohol intake. *Alcoholism: Clinical and Experimental Research*, 1978, *2*, 171–177.

Landesman-Dwyer, S., Ragozin, A. S., & Little, R. E. Behavioral correlates of prenatal alcohol exposure: A four-year follow-up study. *Neurobehavioral Toxicology and Teratology*, 1981, *3*, 187–193.

Lemoine, P., Harousseau, H., Borteyru, J. P., & Menuet, J. C. Les enfants de parents alcooliques. *Ouest-Medical*, 1968, *21*, 476–482.

Little, R. E. Alcohol consumption during pregnancy as reported to the obstetrician and to an independent interviewer. *Annals of the New York Academy of Sciences*, 1976, *273*, 588–592.

Little, R. E. Moderate alcohol use during pregnancy and decreased infant birthweight. *American Journal of Public Health*, 1977, *67*, 1154–1156.

Little, R. E. Drinking during pregnancy: Implications for public health. *Alcohol Health and Research World*, 1979, *4*(1), 36–42.

Little, R. E., Graham, J. M., & Samson, H. H. Fetal alcohol effects in humans and animals. *Advances in Alcohol and Substance Abuse*, 1982, *1*(3/4), 103–125.

Little, R. E., & Hook, E. G. Maternal alcohol and tobacco consumption and their association with nausea and vomiting during pregnancy. *Acta Obstetrica et Gynecologica Scandinavica*, 1979, *58*, 15–17.

Little, R. E., Mandell, W., & Schultz, F. A. Consequences of retrospective measurement of alcohol consumption. *Journal of Studies on Alcohol*, 1977, *38*, 1777–1780.

Little, R. E., Moore, D. E., Guzinski, G. M., & Perez, A. Absence of effect of exogenous estradiol on alcohol consumption in women. *Substance and Alcohol Actions/Misuse*, 1980, *1*, 551–556.

Little, R. E., Schultz, F. A., & Mandell, W. A. Drinking during pregnancy. *Journal of Studies on Alcohol*, 1976, *37*, 375–379.

Little, R. E., & Streissguth, A. P. Drinking during pregnancy in alcoholic women. *Alcoholism: Clinical and Experimental Research*, 1978, *2*, 179–183.

Little, R. E., Streissguth, A. P., Barr, H. M., & Herman, C. S. Decreased birthweight in infants of alcoholic women who abstained during pregnancy. *Journal of Pediatrics*, 1980, *96*, 974–976.

Little, R. E., Streissguth, A. P., & Guzinski, G. M. Prevention of fetal alcohol syndrome: A model program. *Alcoholism: Clinical and Experimental Research*, 1980, *4*, 185–189.

MacDowell, E. C., & Lord, E. M., 1927. (Cited in Klassen, R. W., & Persaud, T. V. N., 1976.)

Maguire, M. P. Ethanol-induced abnormal meiotic chromosome behavior in maize. *Genetics*, 1975, *80*(3), 54. (Abstract)

Majewski, F. Uber schadigende Einflusse des Alkohols auf die Nachkommen. *Nervenarzt*, 1978, *49*, 410–416.

Majewski, F., Bierich, J. R., Loser, H., Michaelis, R., & Leiber, B. Zur Klinik und Pathogenese der Alkohol-Embryopathie. Bericht uber 68 Falle. *Muenchener Medizinische Wochenschrift*, 1976, *118*, 1635–1642.

Manzke, H., & Grosse, F. R. Inkomplettes und komplettes "Fetal Alkoholsyndrom" bei drei Kindern einer Trinkerin. [Incomplete and complete fetal alcohol syndrome: Three children of a drinker] *Medicinische Welt*, 1975, *26*, 709–712.

Marcus, R. L. Cravings for food in pregnancy. *Manchester Medical Gazette*, 1965, *44*, 16.

Martin, D. C., Barr, H. M., & Streissguth, A. P. Birthweight, birthlength, and head circumference related to maternal alcohol, nicotine, and caffeine use during pregnancy. *Teratology*, 1980, *21*, 54a. (Abstract).

Martin, J., Martin, D. C., Sigman, G., & Radow, B. Offspring survival, development, and operant performance following maternal ethanol consumption. *Developmental Psychobiology*, 1977, *10*, 435–446.

Martin, J., Martin, D. C., Lund, C. A., & Streissguth, A. P. Maternal alcohol ingestion and cigarette smoking and their effects upon newborn conditioning. *Alcoholism: Clinical and Experimental Research*, 1977, *1*, 243–247.

Miller, D., & Jang, M. Children of alcoholics: A 20 year longitudinal study. *Social Work Research and Abstracts*, 1977, *13*, 23–29.

Molnar, J., & Papp, G. [Alcohol as a possible enhancer of mucus in semen.] *Andrologie*, 1973, *5*, 105–106. (CAAAL Abstract 360198)

Montague, A. *Life before birth*. New York: Signet, 1965.

Obe, G., Ristow, H. J., & Herha, J. Chromosomal damage by alcohol in vitro and in vivo. In M. M. Gross (Ed.), *Alcohol intoxication and withdrawal* (Vol. 4: *Experimental studies*). New York: Plenum Press, 1977.

Olegard, R., Sabel, K. G., Aronsson, M., Sandin, B., Johansson, P. R., Carlsson, C., Kyllerman, M., Iversen, K., & Hrbek, A. Effects on the child of alcohol abuse during pregnancy: Retrospective and prospective studies. *Acta Paediatrica Scandinavica*, 1979, *275*, 112–121.

Ouellette, E. M., Rosett, H. L., Rosman, N. P., & Weiner, L. Adverse effects on offspring of maternal alcohol abuse during pregnancy. *New England Journal of Medicine*, 1977, *197*, 528–530.

Pearl, R. The experimental modification of germ cells: The effect of parental alcoholism and certain other drug intoxications upon the progeny. *Journal of Experimental Zoology*, 1917, *22*, 241–310. (Cited in Klassen, R. W., & Persaud, T. V. N., 1976.)

Pfeiffer, W. D., MacKinnon, J. R., & Seiser, R. L. Adverse effects of paternal alcohol consumption on offspring of the rat. *Bulletin of the Psychonomic Society*, 1977, *10*, 246.

Pilstrom, L., & Kiessling, K. H. Effect of ethanol on the growth and on the liver and brain mitochondrial functions in the offspring of rats. *Acta Pharmacologica et Toxicologica*, 1967, *23*, 225–232.

Randall, C. L., Boggan, W. O., & Sutker, P. B. Voluntary consumption of ethanol during pregnancy, lactation, and post-lactation in mice. *Drug and Alcohol Dependence*, 1980, *6*, 47. (Abstract)

Randall, C. L., & Taylor, W. J. Prenatal ethanol exposure in mice: Teratogenic effects. *Teratology*, 1979, *19*, 305–312.

Randall, C. L., Taylor, W. J., & Walker, D. W. Ethanol-induced malformations in mice. *Alcoholism: Clinical and Experimental Research*, 1977, *1*, 219–224.

Rawat, A. K. Developmental changes in the brain levels of neurotransmitters as influenced by maternal alcohol consumption in the rat. *Journal of Neurochemistry*, 1977, *28*, 1175–1182.

Rieger, R., Michaelis, I., Schubert, I., Dobel, P., & Jank, H. W. Non random intrachromosomal distribution of chromated aberrations induced by x-rays, alkylating agents, and ethanol in Vicio Faba. *Mutation Research*, 1975, *27*, 67–79.

Root, A. W., Reiter, E. O., Andriola, M., & Duckett, G. Hypothalamic–pituitary function in the fetal alcohol syndrome. *Journal of Pediatrics*, 1975, *87*, 585–588.

Russell, M. Intra-uterine growth in infants born to women with alcohol related psychiatric disorders. *Alcoholism: Clinical and Experimental Research*, 1977, *1*, 225–231.

Russell, M., & Bigler, L. Screening for alcohol-related problems in an outpatient obstetric-gynecologic clinic. *American Journal of Obstetrics and Gynecology*, 1979, *134*, 4–12.

Samson, H. H. Maternal ethanol consumption and fetal development in the rat: A comparison of ethanol exposure techniques. *Alcoholism: Clinical and Experimental Research*, 1981, *5*, 67–74.

Samson, H. H., & Diaz, J. Effects of neonatal ethanol exposure on brain development in rodents. In E. L. Abel (Ed.), *Fetal alcohol syndrome* (Vol. 3: *Animal studies*.) Boca Raton, Fla.: CRC Press, 1982.

Schwartz, D., Joujard, J., Kaminski, M., & Rumeau-Rouquette, C. [Smoking and pregnancy: Results of a prospective study of 6989 women.] *Revue Européene d'Etudes Cliniques et Biologiques*, 1972, *17*, 867–869.

Seidenberg, J., & Majewski, F. Zur Haufigkeit der Alkoholembryopathie in den Verschiedenen Phasen der mutterlichen Alcoholkrankheit. *Suchtgefahren*, 1978, *24*, 63–75.

Semczuk, M. [Morphological research on the male gonad in long-lasting alcoholization of rats.] *Gegenbrurs Morphologisches Jahrbuch*, 1978, *124*, 546–558. (Abstract)

Smith, D. W. The fetal alcohol syndrome. *Hospital Practice*, 1979, *14*, 121–128.

Sokol, R. J., Miller, S. I., & Reed, G. Alcohol abuse during pregnancy: An epidemiologic study. *Alcoholism: Clinical and Experimental Research*, 1980, *4*, 135–145.

Sorette, M. P., Maggio, C. A., Stupoli, A., Boissevain, A., & Greenwood, M. R. G. Maternal ethanol intake affects rat organ development despite adequate nutrition. *Neurobehavioral Toxicology*, 1980, *2*, 181–188.

Soyka, L. F., & Joffe, J. M. Male mediated drug effects on offspring. In R. H. Schwartz & S. J. Yaffe (Eds.), *Progress in clinical and biological research* (Vol. 36: *Drug and chemical risks to the fetus and newborn*). New York: Alan R. Liss, 1980.

Stekhun, F. I. [Effects of alcohol on male sexual glands.] *Zhurnal Nevropatologii*, 1979, *79*, 192–195.

Stockard, C. R. The effect on the offspring of intoxicating the male parent and the transmission of the defects to subsequent generations. *The American Naturalist*, 1913, *47*, 641–681. (Cited in Klassen, R. W., & Persaud, T. V. N., 1976.)

Stockard, C. R., & Papanicolaou, G. A further analysis of the hereditary transmission of degeneracy and deformities by the descendants of alcoholized mammals (Pts. 1 & 2). *Americal Naturalist*, 1916, *50*, 65–88; 144–177.

Streissguth, A. P., Barr, H. M., Martin, D. C., & Herman, C. S. Effects of maternal alcohol, nicotine and caffeine use during pregnancy on infant mental and motor development at 8 months. *Alcoholism: Clinical and Experimental Research*, 1980, *4*, 152–154.

Streissguth, A. P., Herman, C. S., & Smith, D. W. Intelligence, behavior, and dysmorphogenesis in the fetal alcohol syndrome: A report on 20 patients. *Journal of Pediatrics*, 1978, *92*, 363–367. (a)

Streissguth, A. P., Herman, C. S., & Smith, D. W. Stability of intelligence in the fetal alcohol syndrome: A preliminary report. *Alcoholism: Clinical and Experimental Research*, 1978, *2*, 165–170. (b)

Streissguth, A. P., Landesman-Dwyer, S., Martin, J. C., & Smith, D. W. Teratogenic effects of alcohol in humans and animals. *Science*, 1980, *209*, 353–361.

Steissguth, A. P., Martin, D. C., Martin, J. C., & Barr, H. M. *Alcohol and nicotine ingestion in pregnant women.* Paper presented at the meeting of the Western Psychological Association, Seattle, Washington, April 1977.

Swanberg, K. M., & Wilson, J. R. Genetic and ethanol-related differences in maternal behavior and offspring viability in mice. *Developmental Psychobiology*, 1979, *12*, 61–66.

Tennes, K., & Blackard, C. Maternal alcohol consumption, birthweight, and minor physical anomalies. *American Journal of Obstetrics and Gynecology*, 1980, *138*, 774–780.

Tumbleson, M. E. *FAS in Sinclair (S-1) miniature swine.* Paper presented at the NIAAA Fetal Alcohol Syndrome Workshop, San Diego, February 1977.

Tze, W. J., Friesen, H. G., & MacLeod, P. K. Growth hormone response in fetal alcohol syndrome. *Archives of Disease in Childhood*, 1976, *51*, 703–706.

U.S. Department of Health, Education and Welfare. Press release, June 1, 1977.

U.S. Department of Health and Human Services. Surgeon General's Advisory on Alcohol and Pregnancy. *FDA Drug Bulletin*, July 1981, p. 9.

U.S. Department of Treasury & U.S. Department of Health and Human Services. *Report to the President and the Congress on Health Hazards Associated with Alcohol and Methods to Inform the General Public of These Hazards.* Washington, D.C.: U.S. Government Printing Office, 1980.

Voherr, H. Drug excretion in breast milk. *Postgraduate Medicine*, 1974, *56*, 97–104.

Wilson, C., & Orford, J. Children of alcoholics: Report of a preliminary study and comments on the literature. *Journal of Studies on Alcohol*, 1978, *39*, 121–142.

Worthington, B. S. Nurtition during pregnancy, lactation, and oral contraception. *Nursing Clinics of North America*, 1979, *14*, 269–283.

7

Drinking, Sexuality, and Sexual Dysfunction in Women

SHARON C. WILSNACK
University of North Dakota School of Medicine

INTRODUCTION

Despite recent increases in research on drinking and sexual behavior in men (see, e.g., Lang, Searles, Lauerman, & Adesso, 1980; Lansky & Wilson, 1981; Wilson, 1977, 1981) and increases in research on women and alcohol in general, relatively little attention has been given to relationships between drinking and women's sexuality. A 1980 review of endocrine effects of alcohol on sexual behavior (Greene & Hollander, 1980) found "a surprising paucity of good studies on female animals and virtually no controlled investigations of the effects of alcohol on human females" (p. 2).

Exceptions to this general paucity of research on drinking and sexual behavior in women include fragments of data from several surveys, and four laboratory studies of the effects of alcohol on women's sexual responsiveness. In addition, a number of clinical studies conducted over the past 4 decades contain some information on sexual behavior and various disorders of sexual functioning in problem-drinking and alcoholic women.

The present chapter reviews the state of current knowledge about relationships between alcohol consumption and women's sexuality. The chapter begins with an overview of survey findings on women's drinking and reported levels of sexual activity, followed by a review of self-report and laboratory studies of the effects of drinking on women's sexual responsiveness. Sections that follow summarize findings on sexual behavior and sexual dysfunction in problem-drinking and alcoholic women. The chapter notes methodological limitations of the research reviewed and suggests areas of needed research. A final section considers some possible implications of available findings for the treatment and prevention of alcohol problems and sexual dysfunction in women.

DRINKING AND LEVELS OF SEXUAL ACTIVITY

Drinking and sexual activity are often assumed to be positively associated, as in stereotypes of "playboys," "party girls," and "swinging singles." The limited empirical data appear to support these associations. Two studies of university students conducted in the early 1970s (Arafat & Yorburg, 1973; Curran, Neff, & Lippold, 1973) found that alcohol and other drug use correlated positively with reported levels of past sexual experience and current sexual activity for both men and women. A 1970 national survey of U.S. adults (Klassen, 1970) found positive correlations between an index of potential problem drinking and several indices of more liberal sexual attitudes and behaviors. A recent study of college women (Zucker, Battistich, & Langer, 1981) found that heavy-escape drinkers reported the earliest heterosexual experience and the most frequent sexual activity.

Several interpretations of these findings are possible. Zucker and his colleagues (1981) hypothesize that "disturbed affectional relationships" contribute to both heavier drinking and increased sexual activity. However, these authors' direct measures of interpersonal relationships showed only tenuous connections to drinking and sexual activity. Furthermore, it seems likely that some women would react to disturbed interpersonal relations by reducing rather than increasing their sexual involvement. A second possibility is that certain personality characteristics, such as impulsivity or disregard for conventional social restraints, may increase the likelihood of both heavy drinking and increased sexual activity (see Zucker & Devoe, 1975). Finally, both drinking and sexual activity may be part of a social role or life style in which social expectations and demands to be an enjoyable companion require some willingness both to drink and to be sexually active.

The available data do not favor any single interpretation, but do suggest that the relationships between drinking and sexual activity are of only moderate strength. For example, women's frequency of drinking and their scores on a sexual behavior scale showed a correlation of .39 in Curran et al.'s (1973) college sample, while the correlation between potential problem drinking and an index of unsuppressed sexual activity was only .18 in Klassen's (1970) national adult sample. Other factors may mediate the association between women's drinking and their sexual activity, including women's beliefs about how drinking affects their sexuality, and the actual physiological and psychological effects of drinking on sexual experience.

DRINKING AND SEXUAL RESPONSIVENESS IN WOMEN

The belief that alcohol is an aphrodisiac has apparently been present throughout recorded history, dating at least to the Dionysian and Bacchanalian rites of early Greece and Rome (see Sandmaier, 1980). The prevailing view of *how* alcohol enhances sexual enjoyment is that, as a central nervous system depressant, alcohol progressively depresses higher brain functions that control or inhibit sexual behavior. This "disinhibition" theory is widely held by lay persons and scientists alike, as illustrated in the following statement from a paper describing high rates of drinking among young women seen in a venereal disease clinic (Smithurst & Armstrong, 1975): "The association between alcohol, which lowers or dulls moral and learned restraints, and sexual intercourse is well known and, although there was no evidence deduced from the study that venereal disease was closely tied to drinking, no doubt it was so related in many cases" (p. 342). Such assertions reflect a tendency to accept the disinhibition theory as a self-evident truth despite the lack of conclusive empirical data to support it.

Reported Effects of Drinking on Sexual Responsiveness: Surveys and Clinical Studies

Data from several sources suggest that many contemporary women believe that alcohol enhances sexual pleasure. In a questionnaire survey of approximately 20,000 readers of *Psychology Today* magazine (Athanasiou, Shaver, & Tavris, 1970) 68% of women and 45% of men respondents reported that alcohol increased their sexual enjoyment; 21% of women and 42% of men in this nonrandom sample reported that alcohol decreased sexual enjoyment. Male experience with or fears of alcohol-related loss of erectile function may explain why more men than women reported negative effects of drinking.

Bowker (1977) reported that 48% of men and 56% of women in a college sample of approximately 600 stated they had participated in at least one date where alcohol was used to make one of the partners more sexually willing or responsive. Women in this study were more likely than men to report that drinking alcohol made them feel more sexual. In their laboratory studies of alcohol effects and the menstrual cycle, Jones and Jones (1976) observed that many women social drinkers reported feelings of "sexual excitement" at blood alcohol levels of approximately .04%. Of 103 adult women with no history of alcoholism or other psychiatric disorder (Beckman, 1979), 29% reported that they desired intercourse more when drinking and 32% reported that they enjoyed intercourse more when drinking. And in a 1981 national survey of approximately 1300 adults (Wilsnack, Klassen, & Wilsnack, 1983), 59% of light- and moderate-drinking women and 68% of heavy-drinking women reported that drinking sometimes or usually made them feel less sexually inhibited. Comparable figures for men were 59% and 66%.

In addition to these studies of women in the general population, a few studies have examined the reported effects of drinking on sexual responsiveness in women with alcohol-related problems. Two small clinical studies (Levine, 1955; Wood & Duffy, 1966) found high levels of sexual aversion and inhibition among their alcoholic subjects, with few reports of enhanced sexual pleasure when drinking. One exception was five "promiscuous" women in Levine's sample of 16, who had difficulty becoming sexually aroused when sober and who were sexually active primarily when intoxicated.

When asked how drinking affected their sexual arousal and sexual performance, the alcoholic women studied by Murphy, Coleman, Hoon, and Scott (1980) gave responses that were bimodally distributed. Of 49 sexually active women, 49% indicated that drinking had positive effects on sexual arousal, while 41% reported negative effects. With regard to sexual performance, 46% reported positive effects of drinking and 35% reported negative effects. The authors did not indicate what distinguished women reporting positive effects from those reporting negative effects. Possible differences might include the amount of alcohol consumed, stage of problem drinking or alcoholism, and drinking behavior of the woman's sexual partner.

Rather than focusing on sexual arousal alone, Hammond, Jorgensen, and Ridgeway (1979) asked a sample of 44 alcoholic women how drinking affected various sexual behaviors. Of that sample, 54% reported that they could relate more easily to men after drinking, and 47% reported that they almost always used alcohol before engaging in sexual activity. Drinking seemed to increase the sexual assertiveness of women in this sample: More women reported finding it easy to ask their partner to do things they enjoyed sexually after drinking than before, and more reported initiating sexual activity when drinking than when sober. Despite these socially facilitative effects, drinking also appeared to reduce emotional intimacy: 44% of the alcoholic women felt that drinking diminished some of the closeness that existed between them and their partners. (See Wilmot, 1981, for additional discussion of disruptive effects of drinking on communication and emotional intimacy.)

In a larger, better controlled study, Beckman (1979) compared responses of 120 alcoholic women, 119 "normal" controls, and 118 psychiatric controls to questionnaire items dealing with sexual behavior. Compared to both control groups, the alcoholic women were significantly more likely to report that they desired intercourse most when drinking (57% of alcoholics), enjoyed intercourse most when drinking (55% of alcoholics), and engaged in intercourse most often when drinking (55% of alcoholics). Since alcoholic women in this study also reported significantly lower levels of sexual satisfaction than controls, the findings may suggest that some alcoholic women use alcohol to "treat" sexual problems and enhance sexual pleasure.

The data reviewed in this section indicate that a substantial proportion of women, with and without alcohol problems, view alcohol as an aphrodisiac and report experiencing increased sexual enjoyment when drinking. These subjective data are in sharp contrast to the available evidence on the objective physiological effects of alcohol on women's sexual responsiveness.

Physiological Effects of Drinking
on Sexual Responsiveness: Laboratory Studies

Only in the past 5–10 years have relationships between drinking and sexual responsiveness been the subject of controlled experimental research. Laboratory studies have been made possible in part by the development of procedures for quantitative assessment of physiological sexual arousal, and in part by an increased acceptance of scientific research on sexual behavior in general. Most of the research on drinking and sexual arousal has been done with male subjects. Three studies using female subjects suggest that relationships among alcohol consumption, cognitive mediating variables, and sexual arousal may differ for women and for men.

Most laboratory studies of drinking and sexual responsiveness have used a balanced placebo design in which half the subjects are given an alcoholic beverage and half a nonalcoholic beverage. Taste is generally disguised by adding strong flavoring and/or by floating a small amount of alcohol on the placebo drinks. Half of each group is led to believe that their drinks contain alcohol, the other half that they are drinking a nonalcoholic beverage only. This design allows the pharmacological effects of alcohol on sexual arousal to be separated from the effects of subjects' beliefs that they have consumed alcohol. Subjects are generally young adult, heterosexual volunteers with no history of problem drinking or sexual dysfunction. After receiving the instructional set and drinking either alcohol or a placebo, subjects are exposed to various erotic stimuli such as films, videotapes, audiotapes, or slides. Sexual arousal is measured by self-report, by behavioral indicators such as time spent viewing the erotic materials, and by direct physiological measurement. For males physiological sexual arousal is measured by a mercury strain gauge which monitors penile tumescence. For females changes in vaginal blood volume and pressure pulse are measured by changes in vaginal opacity recorded by a vaginal photoplethysmograph.

Despite some lack of comparability among studies and certain inconsistencies in findings, most studies of men have found a marked alcohol expectation effect. Men who believe they have consumed alcohol show increased sexual arousal on both physiological and behavioral measures, regardless of the actual content of their drinks (e.g., Briddell & Wilson, 1976; Farkas & Rosen, 1976; Wilson & Lawson, 1976b). Actual consumption of alcohol in low to moderate doses has generally had no independent effect on physiological sexual arousal, while at higher blood alcohol levels some studies have found a significant negative linear relationship between consumption and penile tumescence (e.g., Briddell & Wilson, 1976; Farkas & Rosen, 1976). Subsequent studies have found that the alcohol expectation effect—greater sexual arousal in men who believe they have consumed alcohol—is particularly marked when sexual stimuli are deviant (e.g., depicting forcible rape)

(Briddell, Rimm, Caddy, Krawitz, Sholis, & Wunderlin, 1978) and in men who have high levels of sexual guilt (Lang *et al.*, 1980; Lansky & Wilson, 1981). In both cases the belief that they have been drinking alcohol may provide men with an excuse or rationalization for feelings of sexual arousal about which they would normally feel guilty or conflicted.

In contrast to the patterns found for men, studies of women have found no positive effects of either alcohol consumption or alcohol expectations on physiological sexual arousal at any dose level. In a study by Wilson and Lawson (1976a), actual alcohol consumption at four dose levels showed a negative linear relationship to sexual arousal as measured by the vaginal photoplethysmograph. A later study by the same investigators (Wilson & Lawson, 1978) suggested that the negative effects of drinking on sexual arousal were pharmacological rather than expectation effects: Women's beliefs about whether or not their drinks contained alcohol did not influence their level of physiological sexual arousal.

Interestingly, in both of these studies, women's *self-reported* sexual arousal increased with increasing blood alcohol levels, and self-reports of intoxication correlated significantly (correlations were +.48 and +.60 for heterosexual and homosexual films respectively) with reported sexual arousal during erotic films. This enhanced subjective arousal reported by women after drinking was directly opposite to the negative effects of alcohol on physiological sexual arousal.

McCarty, Diamond, and Kaye (1982) recently reported a balanced placebo study of drinking and sexual arousal that included both male and female subjects. These investigators failed to demonstrate alcohol expectation effects on self-reported sexual arousal to conventional (nondeviant) photographic sexual stimuli, for either males or females. However, subjects of both sexes showed a "transfer of excitation" effect (greater sexual arousal when they were unaware that their alcoholic drinks contained alcohol) at moderate levels of sexual arousal. Other findings of this study are difficult to compare directly with earlier studies, due to differences in methodology and data analysis.

While most laboratory investigations have focused on how alcohol affects sexual arousal, Malatesta, Pollack, Crotty, and Peacock (1982) studied alcohol's effects on women's orgasmic responses. In a study of 24 adult women volunteers, drinking significantly reduced the effectiveness of masturbation in response to erotic films. When blood alcohol concentrations of .025%, .05%, and .075% were used, higher levels of intoxication were associated with increased latency to orgasm, increased reported difficulty of attaining orgasm, and decreased reported intensity of orgasm. Nevertheless, increasing intoxication was associated with *increased subjective* sexual arousal and with increased reported pleasurability of orgasm. A parallel study of men (Malatesta, Pollack, Wilbanks, & Adams, 1979) found that alcohol consumption increased latency to orgasm for men as well, but in contrast to the women's findings decreased self-report measures of sexual arousal and pleasurability of orgasm.

These findings raise several questions about gender differences in physiological and subjective alcohol effects. Why do men's beliefs that they have consumed alcohol affect their physiological sexual arousal while such beliefs have no apparent effect on physiological arousal for women? And why do indicators of objective and subjective arousal vary together for men—both decreasing at higher levels of alcohol consumption—but change in opposite directions for women? Answers to both questions may lie in the differential ease with which males and females in this society learn to be sexual. Greater social repression of female sexuality, together with the greater difficulty of self-monitoring and labeling vaginal arousal compared to penile arousal, may cause learned associations between cognitive variables and genital sensations to be weaker for women than for men. Wilson and Lawson (1978) tentatively suggest that for these social and anatomical reasons men may have greater cognitive control over physiological sexual arousal than women, and thus their beliefs about having consumed alcohol mediate their physiological responsiveness to a greater extent than do those of women. It is also possible that women's beliefs about the effects of alcohol on sexuality are weaker than men's, or perhaps more variable due to variations in alcohol effects at different stages of the menstrual cycle (e.g., Jones & Jones, 1976).

The greater ease with which men can monitor physiological sexual arousal may also explain why their subjective and objective measures of arousal show positive correlations. Women, on the other hand, in the absence of clearcut feedback about their "actual" level of physiological sexual arousal, may interpret the nonspecific physiological effects of alcohol more in terms of prevailing environmental cues. In the presence of erotic stimuli, or simply in situations where actual or fantasized sexual partners are available, these nonspecific feeling states may be interpreted by women as feelings of emotional warmth, affection, and sexual arousal (see Wilsnack, 1974).

Discussion

DISINHIBITION THEORY RECONSIDERED

The laboratory findings summarized above led Wilson (1977) to reject a simple disinhibition theory of drinking, in that alcohol had no physiological disinhibiting effects for either women or men.[1] Wilson believes that the data are most consistent with a social learning explanation of how drinking affects sexual behavior. According to this view, a woman (or man) may

---

1. In a later paper, Wilson (1981) discusses a second version of the disinhibition theory, involving psychodynamic concepts of drive and superego control. Neither the psychodynamic version nor the simple physiological disinhibition version gives much attention to the cognitive self-control variables emphasized here.

engage in increased sexual activity after drinking not because her moral inhibitions against sexual behavior have been "dissolved" in alcohol, but rather because she has learned to associate drinking with sexual activity, has come to expect that drinking will enhance her sexual enjoyment, and because drinking frequently occurs in relaxed social settings where sexual partners are more readily available.

In dismissing the notion of disinhibition, Wilson appears to assume that "objective," physiological sexual arousal is more basic, salient, and reinforcing than individuals' subjective cognitive appraisal of their sexual experience. However, it is not clear that women's decreased physiological sexual arousal after drinking affects them more than their increased subjective arousal. Women in Malatesta *et al.*'s (1982) study of orgasmic response described their orgasms following drinking as more pleasurable, even though these orgasms occurred more slowly and less intensely. These findings may indicate that a more prolonged and less overwhelming sexual experience due to drinking is more enjoyable for at least some women, or that drinking helps women to perceive genital sensations and interpret these as pleasurable. Women's subjective feelings of sexual arousal and pleasure may be the more salient in such cases, overriding the physiological depression of arousal caused by alcohol. If so, it may be appropriate to speak of subjective or cognitive sexual disinhibition due to alcohol, even though physiological indices of arousal decrease.

However, the concept of disinhibition by alcohol also implies that previously inhibited sexual feelings and behaviors are somehow released by drinking, presumably by the depressant effects of alcohol on higher brain centers. An increase in women's subjective sexual arousal after drinking may not by itself indicate disinhibition. Subjective sexual arousal may increase simply because drinking causes a state of general physiological arousal which, in the presence of sexual stimuli, women interpret as sexual arousal (see Schachter, 1964; Frieze and Schafer, Chapter 9 in this volume), regardless of prior inhibition. However, certain findings with male subjects suggest that disinhibition may also be involved. As discussed on pp. 193–194, male subjects high in sexual guilt and male subjects viewing deviant sexual stimuli (responses to which are normally inhibited by social restraints) showed the greatest alcohol expectation effects, that is, the greatest increases in sexual arousal when they thought they had consumed alcohol. Since women's sexual feelings and behavior have traditionally been subject to even greater social suppression and psychological inhibition than those of men (e.g., Sherfey, 1973), it seems likely that similar relationships between sexual guilt and alcohol effects would occur in women. However, given the gender differences discussed on pp. 194–195, in women these might be pharmacological effects of actually consuming alcohol rather than the expectation effects found in men. If women with the highest levels of sexual guilt, anxiety, or conflict experienced the greatest increases in subjective arousal after drinking, this might suggest that alcohol was reducing cognitive restraints that normally inhibit sexual behavior. One possible mechanism for such disinhibition would be pharmacological depression by alcohol of higher brain centers that control sexual cognitions and behavior. A second mechanism, not requiring a pharmacological effect, would be women's use of alcohol as an excuse or alibi for feelings or behaviors that would otherwise be unacceptable.

In summary, although the available research gives little support to a simple physiological disinhibition theory of drinking and sexual arousal, it may be useful to study how alcohol may disinhibit women's sexual cognitions and behaviors, including their perceptions of physiological sexual sensations, their interpretation of these as pleasurable, and their resulting sexual activity. If drinking reduces guilt or conflict that otherwise inhibits sexuality, and alters attributions of responsibility in a way that allows a woman greater enjoyment of her physiological sexual sensations, these cognitive effects may play a greater role in reinforcing and maintaining her drinking behavior than the fact that her vaginal pressure pulse is slightly reduced after a drink or two. The possibility that drinking has cognitive disinhibiting effects for women is, of course, not inconsistent with the social learning interpretation advocated by Wilson (1977, 1981). What women have experienced or been told concerning how alcohol disinhibits their sexuality, and their resulting beliefs that drinking will reduce sexual inhibitions, may be important components of the "set" that in social learning formulations helps maintain drinking behavior.

RESEARCH NEEDS

Additional laboratory studies of drinking and sexual responsiveness are needed to replicate and clarify the apparent gender differences in pharmacological versus expectation effects, with studies of women drinkers particularly needed. In the burgeoning literature on alcohol and sexual arousal, only four published studies have used female subjects. It is curious that women's failure to show expectation effects in the two studies that attempted to induce them (McCarty et al., 1982; Wilson & Lawson, 1978) has not caused women to be studied more, as a means of learning more both about the effects of drinking on sexuality and about the nature of alcohol expectation effects.

Studies of pharmacological and expectation effects should include attention to individual differences. Possible mediating variables such as sexual guilt or psychological conservatism should be studied in women, as they have been in men (Barling & Fincham, 1980; Lang et al., 1980). It may be that women with unusually high levels of sexual inhibition experience some physiological, as well as subjective, disinhibition as a result of drinking. By varying alcohol expectations and alcohol content of drinks for subjects with differing levels of sexual guilt, anxiety, or conflict, studies can begin to separate subjective disinhibition due to pharmacological depressant effects of alcohol from that due to expectation effects and altered attributions of responsibility for behavior while drinking.

Consistent with a social learning view of drinking and sexuality, research should investigate relationships between women's drinking behavior and the behavior of their sexual partners. For example, is drinking a culturally stereotyped cue that a woman is sexually available, so that a woman's drinking triggers increased sexual attention and advances by men? Does this attention in turn affect the woman's perception of herself as sexually attractive, and her own feelings of sexual arousal? Under what circumstances does a woman's drinking lead to unwelcome sexual advances? Do unwanted sexual approaches—actual or feared—by men cause some women to cautiously monitor their own behavior while drinking, with resulting effects on their feelings and attributions? Recent findings linking moderate alcohol consumption by women social drinkers with increased social anxiety (Abrams & Wilson, 1979), decreased self-esteem (Konovsky & Wilsnack, 1982), and increased external locus of control (Barling & Bolon, 1981) seem consistent with this last possibility.

In addition to social psychological questions of this sort, studies are needed to determine whether and at what point the physiological depressant effects of alcohol actually impair sexual functioning (e.g., by making intercourse difficult or painful as a result of reduced vaginal lubrication), and whether subjective sexual arousal is also impaired at higher levels of consumption than those studied to date. It will also be important, although difficult, to try to learn how generalizable the findings of laboratory studies of volunteers are to women in general and to more natural settings. Finally, research is needed on how drinking affects sexual responsiveness in women with histories of alcohol abuse, and on ways in which women's beliefs about alcohol and sexuality—for example, that drinking reduces sexual inhibitions and enhances sexual pleasure—may influence the development and maintenance of heavy drinking and drinking-related problems.

DRINKING AND SEXUAL DYSFUNCTION IN WOMEN

Data discussed in earlier sections suggest that acute alcohol intoxication lowers physiological sexual arousal in women social drinkers. To the extent that these effects also occur in problem-drinking women, we might expect chronic excessive drinking to be accompanied by more severe and prolonged disturbances of sexual functioning. Although empirical data are lacking on the acute effects of drinking on sexual responsiveness in women problem drinkers, some data are available on the prevalence of various types of sexual dysfunction in such women. Unfortunately the quality of these data is not high, and considerable caution is necessary in interpreting them.

Most data on sexual dysfunction and problem drinking in women come from small clinical studies of alcoholic women who have drunk excessively for a number of years. Thus it is impossible to separate sexual difficulties that preceded and possibly contributed to women's drinking problems from difficulties which are physiological and/or psychosocial consequences of excessive drinking. Nevertheless, sexual dysfunction in alcoholic samples is often presumed to be primarily a consequence of alcohol abuse. In an unpublished review of clinical studies of alcoholism and sexual dysfunction, Whitfield, Redmond, and Quinn (1979) suggest five physiological mechanisms by which alcohol abuse may affect sexual functioning. These include acute depressant effects of alcohol on physiological sexual arousal, disruption of sex hormone metabolism as a result of vitamin deficiencies and liver damage, interference by alcohol-induced neuropathy with sensory pathways of sexual arousal, organic brain damage resulting in decreased interpersonal and sexual interest, and various medical problems secondary to alcoholism that impair sexual functioning, such as diabetes, hypertension, urinary-tract infections, and vaginitis.

In addition to these physiological mechanisms, intrapersonal and interpersonal aspects of alcoholism may interfere with sexual functioning. For example, intoxication may make the drinker less attractive to his or her partner, resulting in problems of low sexual interest and arousal. Moreover, the isolation, depression, and low self-esteem that characterize many alcoholic persons may seriously impair their ability to form intimate relationships. If these qualities are even more pronounced in women alcoholics than in men, perhaps due in part to a greater social stigma of alcoholism for women, this may imply an even higher risk of sexual dysfunction for problem-drinking women than for their male counterparts (Williams, 1976).

While alcoholism undoubtedly can have detrimental physiological and psychosocial effects on sexuality, it also seems probable that sexual difficulties can precede and contribute to the development of problem drinking. In traditional psychoanalytic theory, psychosexual conflicts, in particular conflicts surrounding suppressed homosexual wishes, were central in the etiology of alcoholism (see Abraham, 1948; Levine, 1955). Even in the absence of psychodynamic conflicts, sexual dysfunction may be a source of life stress that contributes to drinking. Many women alcoholics report marital problems, presumably including sexual difficulties in many cases, as possible precipitants of their problem drinking (Curlee, 1969; Dahlgren, 1979; Sclare, 1970; Tamerin, 1978). It is also possible that certain personality attributes hypothesized to characterize women predisposed to alcoholism, such as low self-esteem or sex-role rigidity, interfere with the formation of satisfying sexual relationships, which in turn increases the women's risk of turning to alcohol for pleasure and relief (see Beckman, 1978; Richardson, 1981; Wilsnack, 1976). Finally, sexual dysfunction may become both cause and consequence of excessive drinking, in a problem-intensifying spiral in which drinking is used to "treat" or cope with sexual difficulties, but only makes the sexual problems and dissatisfaction worse.

In addition to ambiguities of cause and effect, data on sexual dysfunction among problem-drinking women have other methodological limitations. Few studies have used clearcut criteria for either alcoholism or sexual dysfunction. Data for women with different patterns of alcoholism are combined, with little attention to subgroups that may show different types or degrees of sexual disturbance (e.g., women whose alcoholism occurs in combination with antisocial behavior, depression, or hysteria). Categories of sexual dysfunction are rarely defined in behavioral terms. Authors' terminology appears at times to reflect moral judgments and sexual stereotypes more than scientific objectivity. For example, one author (Levine, 1955) describes the same sexual behavior as "frequent extramarital relations" for men and "promiscuity" for women.

A major problem in most studies is the lack of control or comparison groups, making it difficult to know whether the sexual problems described are more common among alcoholic women than among comparable women in the general population. Since sexual difficulties of various sorts are common among women in general (see, e.g., Potter, 1979), we must be cautious about interpreting a specific link between alcoholism and sexual dysfunction on the basis of studies that lack adequate nonalcoholic control groups.

Given these methodological shortcomings, a small number of studies contain some information about sexual behavior in problem-drinking women that permits crude estimates of the prevalence of sexual dysfunction among such women. Table 7-1 summarizes 19 studies from 1937 to 1982, which report quantitative data on sexual behavior in problem-drinking or alcoholic women. The majority describe small samples of women receiving alcoholism treatment; only three include nonalcoholic comparison groups. The table includes one unpublished study (Hammond et al., 1979) that contains unusually rich and detailed information on alcoholic women's sexual functioning, and two (Covington, 1982; Sholty, 1979) that attempt to time-order alcohol abuse and sexual dysfunction. It also includes some unpublished reports that contain information in two areas—incest and rape—where published studies are almost entirely lacking.

Where possible, the table distinguishes among problems of low sexual desire, difficulties in sexual arousal, and failure to reach orgasm (see Kaplan, 1974, 1979). Many reports do not permit such distinctions, using only vague terms such as "frigidity." Since most studies to date have focused on problems of sexual arousal and orgasm, little information is available about alcoholic women's experiences with other sexual dysfunctions, such as vaginismus (vaginal spasms that make intercourse difficult or impossible) or dyspareunia (painful intercourse).

Early Clinical Studies of Alcoholism and Sexual Dysfunction

In an early study of 50 women treated for chronic alcoholism at Bellevue Hospital in New York City (Curran, 1937) 32% of the women reported primary orgasmic dysfunction (never experiencing an orgasm), while another 10% reported reaching orgasm only rarely. Only 40% of the women reported satisfaction with their sexual lives. Curran claimed that "the percentage of frigidity is much greater here than in the general population" (p. 650). His observation would appear valid at least for the 32% of women reporting primary orgasmic dysfunction, a considerably higher percentage than the 10% rate estimated for the general female population (Kinsey, Pomeroy, Martin, & Gebhard, 1953).

Results of a small, frequently cited study by Levine (1955) are generally consistent with Curran's findings. Clinical records of 16 women outpatients in a Connecticut state alcoholism clinic revealed that 8 of the 16 denied any interest or involvement in sexual relations. Of the remaining 8, 5 were described as promiscuous and each of these reported a nearly complete lack of orgasm. The final 3 women were sexually active but frigid, according to therapists' reports. Use of terms like "promiscuous" and "frigid" without further explanation makes it difficult to interpret Levine's findings. A similar problem exists in Wall's (1937) statement that 60% of his sample of alcoholic women engaged in "loose heterosexual activities."

Lisansky (1957) provided additional data on "promiscuous" sexual behavior in alcoholic women, from case records of 46 women outpatients at Connecticut state alcoholism clinics and 37 women alcoholics from the state women's prison farm. Evidence of "sexual promiscuity" associated with drinking was found in the records of 46% of the state farm women but only 11% of the outpatient women. Although promiscuity was not precisely defined, it appeared to mean more or less indiscriminate sexual availability, including prostitution. As in Levine's study, frequency or duration of promiscuous behavior was not specified. Differences in sexual behavior may have been related to differences in drinking patterns (state farm women less frequently drank alone) and differences in economic resources between the higher-socioeconomic-status outpatient women and lower-socioeconomic-status state farm women. To obtain drinks, some lower-status women may need to exchange sex for money or alcohol, while higher-status women do not require this exchange. Data from a study of venereal disease in alcoholic women (Medhus, 1975) support the conclusion that sexual promiscuity, when it occurs, is more common among problem-drinking women of lower socioeconomic status. However, rates of promiscuity among lower-status alcoholic women may not be as high as Lisansky's data would suggest, since many women in her state farm sample may have been sent there for prostitution or related charges.

TABLE 7-1. *Sexual Behavior and Sexual Dysfunction in 19 Studies of Alcoholic Women*

Study/year	Sample	Sexual behavior/dysfunction	Sexual abuse	Sexual preference
		Clinical-descriptive studies		
Curran (1937)	50 lower-SES patients (16% black) in Bellevue Hospital	32% reported primary orgastic dysfunction 10% reported reaching orgasm "rarely" 60% reported lack of sexual satisfaction		4% reported overt homosexual experience
Wall (1937)	50 middle- and upper-SES private hospital patients	60% described as engaging in "loose heterosexual activities"		10% reported history of overt homosexuality
Levine (1955)	16 outpatients in a state alcoholism clinic	50% denied sexual activity or interest 50% sexually active but "frigid" 31% described as promiscuous but nonorgastic		6% described as bisexual with homosexual preference
Massot, Hamel, & Deliry (1956)	64 alcoholic inpatients in a French psychiatric hospital	70% described as "frigid"		
Lisansky (1957)	46 middle-SES outpatients 37 prison farm women	11% of outpatient women, 46% of prison farm women described as sexually promiscuous while drinking		
Kinsey (1966)	46 lower-SES state hospital patients	72% cited "frigidity" as a cause of excessive drinking		7% cited homosexuality as a cause of excessive drinking
Wood & Duffy (1966)	69 middle- and upper-SES outpatients	100% judged to have "poor sexual adjustment" (sexual inhibition and naivete) 3% formed "successive sexual liaisons"		None of subjects reported homosexual relationships
Sclare (1970)	50 lower- and middle-SES Scottish women alcoholics 50 lower- and middle-SES Scottish men alcoholics	28% of women (12% of men) reported "psychosexual difficulty," in particular low sexual interest		

Study	Sample	Findings
Lemere & Smith (1973)	17,000 patients (% female unspecified) in Shadel Hospital	"Few if any" women patients complained of drinking-related sexual inadequacy
Spalt (1975)	36 psychiatric outpatients meeting diagnostic criteria for both alcoholism and affective disorder	14% reported involvement in prostitution 31% reported more than 10 sexual partners
Browne-Mayers, Seelye, & Sillman (1976)	62 middle- and upper-SES private hospital patients	45% judged to have "inadequate sexual response" (low sexual gratification and orgastic dysfunction), additional 11% to have poor sexual adjustment attributable to partner 5% described as promiscuous 3% reported "homosexual conflicts"
Hammond, Jorgensen, & Ridgeway (1979)	44 middle- and late-stage alcoholic outpatients (11% nonwhite)	23% felt sexual interest less than 25% of time during sexual activity with a partner 19% reported primary orgastic dysfunction (never experienced orgasm) 45% reported orgasm 25% of time or less during sexual activity with a partner 12% reported vaginismus on 50% or more of coital opportunities 7% reported dyspareunia 95% of time or more during intercourse 77% indicated interest in receiving sex therapy 50% reported more than 12 sexual partners (21% reported more than 30) 71% of ever-married women reported extramarital sexual involvement 40% reported history of incest 39% reported having been raped 20% reported one or more lesbian relationships since adolescence

(continued)

TABLE 7-1. (Continued)

Study/year	Sample	Sexual behavior/dysfunction	Sexual abuse	Sexual preference
		Clinical–descriptive studies		
Sholty (1979)	30 residents (63% black) of 3 Baltimore halfway houses	43% reported drinking in response to sexual dissatisfaction/inadequacy (27% in response to orgastic dissatisfaction)		
		77% reported deterioration of sexual satisfaction after problem drinking began (47% reported becoming inorgasmic)		
		17% reported improvement in sexual functioning after problem drinking began		
Murphy, Coleman, Hoon, & Scott (1980)	74 lower-middle-SES inpatients and halfway house residents (23% nonwhite)	30% reported little or no sexual desire	54% reported rape as either child or adult	
		28% reported orgasm less than 50% of time during sexual activity with a partner (15% reported orgasm less than 25% of time)		
		Of sexually active women: 19% stated they had a problem with sexual response		
		13% reported lack of sexual arousal more than 50% of time during sexual activity with a partner		
		2% reported vaginismus on more than 50% of occasions		
		6% reported dyspareunia on more than 50% of occasions		
Evans & Schaefer (1980); Schaefer & Evans (1982)	75 outpatients in a women's chemical dependency treatment program in Minneapolis		53% reported incest or other childhood sexual abuse	29% lesbian, 3% bisexual, 7% uncertain

		Control group studies	
Roth, Acker, Petersen, Perry, Shannon, & Anderson (1981)	65 outpatients in a women's alcoholism treatment program in rural Maine		12% reported incest; 29% reported rape
Beckman (1979)	120 alcoholic inpatients and outpatients; 119 normal controls	Alcoholics rated selves significantly less sexually satisfied than normal controls	20% of alcoholics (4% of normal controls, 13% of psychiatric controls) reported 1 or more homosexual experiences
	118 psychiatric controls	Alcoholics more likely than normal or psychiatric controls to report desiring, enjoying, and engaging in intercourse more when drinking than when not drinking	6% of alcoholics (2% of normal and psychiatric controls) considered selves lesbians; 3% of alcoholics (3% of normal and psychiatric controls) considered selves bisexual
Pinhas (1980)	34 alcoholic women (6% black) in early sobriety; 34 nonalcoholic controls	Alcoholics higher on test of sex guilt, lower on test of perceived control of sexual satisfaction	
Covington (1982)	35 middle-SES Caucasian alcoholic women in early sobriety; 35 nonalcoholic controls	79% of alcoholics reported sexual dysfunction prior to alcoholism, 85% during alcoholism, and 74% during the first year of sobriety; 59% of controls reported current or past sexual dysfunction	34% of alcoholics (17% of controls) reported incest; 34% of alcoholics (14% of controls) reported rape; 74% of alcoholics (50% of controls) reported one or more experiences of sexual abuse (incest, rape, molestation)
		64% of alcoholics (44% of controls) reported lack of sexual interest	In early sobriety 17% of alcoholics bisexual, 17% lesbian (Prior to alcoholism 20% bisexual, 3% lesbian; during alcoholism 37% bisexual; 6% lesbian)
		61% of alcoholics (30% of controls) reported lack of sexual arousal or pleasure	
		64% of alcoholics (27% of controls) reported difficulty attaining orgasm	

Five additional clinical studies support earlier findings of sexual inhibition and orgastic dysfunction among problem-drinking women. Massot, Hamel, and Deliry (1956) reported that 70% of their sample of alcoholic women in rural France were sexually "frigid" and experienced feelings of repulsion toward men. Massot *et al.* traced their patients' psychosexual difficulties to disturbed early family relationships, including an ambivalent relationship to a mother who was seen as powerful and severe. In a Minnesota state hospital sample of 46 alcoholic women (Kinsey, 1966), 72% cited frigidity as a cause of their excessive drinking, though "frigidity" was not clearly defined. In a Scottish study of 50 alcoholic women and 50 alcoholic men (Sclare, 1970, 1977), more women (28%) than men (12%) reported sexual problems, in particular a "lack of sexual interest and drive."

Wood and Duffy (1966) studied 69 outpatient alcoholic women of middle to upper socioeconomic status. All were judged to have "poor sexual adjustment" in the form of sexual inhibition and naivete. The authors attributed these problems to conflictual and ungratifying early family relationships (typically involving a rigid, perfectionistic mother and a warmer, often alcoholic father) and "grossly inadequate" sexual instruction. In many cases the women's husbands had introduced their wives to alcohol in order to release the wives' sexual inhibitions. Wood and Duffy, however, found little "promiscuity." In this higher socioeconomic status sample, only 2 of 69 patients reported "successive sexual liaisons," in both cases following a divorce.

In a more recent study of 62 alcoholic women in a private hospital in suburban New York City (Browne-Mayers, Seelye, & Sillman, 1976), 45% of the women were judged to have "inadequate sexual response" due to personal psychodynamic factors. An additional 11% were judged to have poor sexual adjustment for reasons attributable to their sexual partner. Only 5% of the women were described by the authors as promiscuous.

One exception to the general finding of relatively high rates of sexual dysfunction among alcoholic women is Lemere and Smith's (1973) observation that "few if any" women among 17,000 male and female alcoholic patients treated at Shadel Hospital in Seattle complained of drinking-related sexual problems. This claim is made in passing in a paper focusing on male sexual dysfunction. The apparent absence of problems may be due in part to the researchers' or therapists' failure to inquire directly and systematically into the sexual aspects of their women patients' lives. In addition, patients themselves may not recognize that sexual disinterest, lack of arousal, or inorgasmia may be a direct result of the depressant effects of alcohol, or a source of distress that can contribute to excessive drinking.

Improved Definitions of Sexual Dysfunction

The literature reviewed thus far lacks clear operational definitions of various sexual disorders and fails to specify the severity of the disorders. These problems are remedied to a considerable degree in two more recent studies. Both studies use explicit behavioral criteria for the presence and extent of a variety of sexual difficulties.

In the first study, Murphy *et al.* (1980) administered a structured sexual history interview and several standardized questionnaire scales to 74 women inpatients and halfway house residents. These investigators found somewhat lower rates of most sexual difficulties than previous studies had reported (see Table 7-1). While 30% of the women reported lack of sexual desire, less than 15% of the sexually active women reported problems of low arousal, vaginismus, and dyspareunia. Also in this sample, 28% of the women reported reaching orgasm less than 50% of the time and 15% attained orgasm less than 25% of the time. These figures appear low compared with the rates of unspecified orgastic problems reported in earlier clinical studies of alcoholic women.

One possible explanation for the lower rates of sexual dysfunction found by Murphy *et al.* is that the prevalence of sexual dysfunction in the general female population decreased between the 1930s and 1970s. This hypothesis, however, is not supported by any evidence for marked changes in population prevalence rates, nor by any noticeable time trends in rates of sexual dysfunction among alcoholic women in the studies summarized in Table 7-1.

A second possible explanation is that the vague clinical definitions of sexual dysfunction used in previous studies were more inclusive than the quantitative behavioral definitions used by Murphy *et al.* The numerous women described as "frigid" in studies by Levine (1955), Massot *et al.* (1956), Kinsey (1966), and others might not all meet Murphy's criteria for disorders of sexual interest, arousal, or orgasm. It is also unclear how often women described earlier as having orgastic difficulties failed to reach orgasm.

A third possible explanation is that most earlier studies relied on clinicians' judgments or researchers' detection of sexual dysfunction from therapists' case records. This approach may have been less subject to underreporting than were patients' self-reports in Murphy *et al.*'s structured interview and questionnaire, administered upon intake to a treatment program. Whatever the explanation, Murphy *et al.*'s findings suggest that future research should use more explicit criteria for sexual dysfunction, preferably standardized across studies, and should try to quantify the extent and severity of dysfunction.

An unpublished study by Hammond and his associates at the University of Utah (Hammond *et al.*, 1979) provides further detailed information on sexual behavior and sexual dysfunction. Hammond *et al.* gave a self-administered questionnaire to 44 women entering outpatient treatment for alcoholism. The sample was somewhat younger than Murphy *et al.*'s (1980) sample (mean age = 33.0 years and 37.9 years respectively) and included fewer nonwhite women (11% vs. 23%).

Hammond *et al.*'s younger outpatient sample might be expected to have less severe alcohol problems and lower rates of sexual dysfunction than Murphy *et al.*'s older inpatients. In fact, Hammond *et al.*'s outpatients reported more sexual difficulties, particularly in the area of orgastic dysfunction. As shown in Table 7-1, 19% of the women stated they had never had an orgasm, and 45% (as compared with 15% of the women in Murphy *et al.*'s sample) reported they reached orgasm 25% of the time or less. Rates of low sexual interest were approximately the same in the two studies, but Hammond *et al.*'s sample reported more problems with vaginismus. Hammond *et al.*'s subjects reported relatively high numbers of sexual partners (21% reported more than 30), and a majority (71%) of the ever-married women acknowledged extramarital sexual involvement. Compared with Murphy *et al.*'s sample, the women studied by Hammond *et al.* were more likely to label sexuality as a problem area in need of help. In Hammond *et al.*'s sample, 77% indicated that they were possibly interested in receiving treatment for sexual difficulties, while only 19% of Murphy *et al.*'s sample felt they had a problem with sexual response.

Overall, Hammond *et al.*'s findings are more similar than Murphy *et al.*'s to the rates of sexual problems reported in earlier clinical studies. Based on later observation of their subjects in treatment, Murphy and his colleagues concluded that the women had initially underreported the actual extent of their sexual difficulties. One reason for underreporting may have been that Murphy *et al.* administered their sexual history questionnaire as part of a routine treatment intake. This procedure did not allow patients anonymity, and may not have seemed totally confidential. In Hammond *et al.*'s study, on the other hand, women reported on their sexuality in a self-administered questionnaire that they were told was voluntary and confidential and would not become part of their treatment record. Because of these differences in data collection, women in the Hammond study may have felt considerably freer to disclose sensitive information. Future clinical studies of sexual dysfunction should pay careful attention to the probable effects of various data gathering procedures on women's self-disclosure of sexual difficulties. Within the constraints of treatment needs, data collection procedures should assure privacy and confidentiality of information so as to maximize women's valid self-disclosure in an often painful and sensitive area.

Subgroup Comparisons

With the exception of Lisansky's (1957) comparison of outpatient and prison farm women, the studies reviewed thus far have overlooked possible differences in sexual behavior of different subgroups of alcoholic women. One potentially important distinction is between women alcoholics who have no other psychiatric disorders ("primary alcoholics") and those whose alcoholism occurs in combination with other psychiatric illness. Within the latter group, sexual behavior may differ among women whose alcoholism coexists with affective disorders (depression and mania), antisocial personality disorders, and hysteria (see Schuckit, 1972; Schuckit, Pitts, Reich, King, & Winokur, 1969).

No direct comparisons of sexual behavior across such diagnostic subgroups have been reported. Spalt (1975), however, presents some relevant data from a larger study of sexual behavior and affective disorders. Among 36 women meeting diagnostic criteria for both alcoholism and affective disorders, 14% reported personal involvement in prostitution and 31% reported having had more than 10 sexual partners. Much of this "promiscuous" sexual behavior may have occurred among affective disorder-alcoholic women who also had antisocial personality disorders, since diagnoses of antisocial personality and alcoholism overlapped considerably in this sample. Spalt did not present data on problems of low sexual interest and arousal or orgastic dysfunction, which might also differ across diagnostic subgroups, perhaps being more pronounced among alcoholic women with hysterical personality characteristics.

Temporal Sequences of Drinking and Sexual Dysfunction

Most of the studies reviewed here have overlooked not only subgroup differences, but also questions of temporal sequence and cause and effect. While several authors have observed clinically that sexual dysfunction appeared to precede women's excessive drinking, only one study has obtained retrospective time-ordered data: 72% of Kinsey's (1966) alcoholic sample reported that "frigidity" preceded and contributed to their alcohol problems.

More recently, two unpublished studies have gathered retrospective time-ordered data on women's drinking and sexual dysfunction. Sholty (1979) interviewed 30 women residents of three halfway houses in Baltimore. She asked the women about the relevance of sexual difficulties in the development of their problem drinking, and about the effects of drinking and drinking problems on their sexual behavior and satisfaction. Of the women interviewed, 43% reported that feelings of sexual dissatisfaction or sexual inadequacy had contributed to their drinking, and 27% reported that they drank in response to orgastic dissatisfaction. In this study, 77% of the women reported that sexual satisfaction deteriorated after problem drinking began (with 47% becoming inorgasmic), while 17% reported that sexual functioning improved.

Covington (1982) interviewed 35 middle-class alcoholic women in two California counties. Of these, 79% reported experiencing one or more types of sexual dysfunction (including low sexual interest or arousal, painful intercourse, vaginismus, and lack of orgasm) before alcohol became a problem. This increased to 85% during active alcoholism, including two-thirds of the women who had had no sexual problems before alcoholism. (Several women reported sexual dysfunction prior to but not during alcoholism.) In early sobriety (3–12 months), 74% of the women continued to report sexual problems.

Sholty's and Covington's findings are subject to the obvious limitations of retrospective self-reports, including possible failure of memory and conscious or unconscious distortion of temporal sequences to conform to socially desirable patterns. However, the findings tentatively suggest that sexual dysfunction and heavy alcohol consumption may form a mutually reinforcing system in which sexual dissatisfaction contributes to heavy drinking which in turn further reduces sexual satisfaction. As discussed earlier, women's expectancies that drinking will reduce sexual inhibitions and enhance sexual pleasure may be an additional component of this system, serving to initiate and maintain the cycle despite the "objective" deterioration of sexual functioning. Sholty's and Covington's findings also suggest that for a few women, who are perhaps highly inhibited or conflicted about sexuality, heavy drinking may subjectively improve sexual functioning.

Control Group Studies

In the clinical studies of alcoholic women reviewed so far, it is unclear whether rates of sexual dysfunction differ from those in demographically similar nonalcoholic women. Three studies that include matched nonalcoholic control groups address this issue.

In a study by Beckman (1979), 120 women receiving inpatient or outpatient alcoholism treatment had significantly lower ratings of sexual satisfaction than did a sample of 119 nonalcoholic "normals" matched on age, marital status, education, religious preference, and whether or not they had children. Specific problems contributing to sexual dissatisfaction were not reported. As noted earlier, alcoholic women in this study were more likely than normals or psychiatric controls to report that they desired, enjoyed, and engaged in sexual intercourse more when drinking. Alcoholics and psychiatric controls in Beckman's study did not differ on sexual satisfaction, suggesting that sexual problems are not specific to alcoholic women but rather may be characteristic of women with various types of psychiatric disorders. What distinguishes alcoholic women may be their use of alcohol to self-medicate their sexual difficulties.

A second study (Pinhas, 1978, 1980) compared 34 alcoholic women in early sobriety with 34 nonalcoholic women matched on age, marital status, ethnicity, education, religious preference, and socioeconomic status. On a standardized questionnaire, the alcoholic women reported more guilt related to sexual behavior than did the nonalcoholic controls. Group differences were weaker or nonexistent for other forms of guilt, for example, about violation of general moral standards or about aggressive behavior. The alcoholics also reported feeling less control over their opportunities for sexual gratification, for example, in attempts to attract the opposite sex, to intervene in sexual lovemaking to enhance their own pleasure, and to attain orgasm.

A third control group study by Covington (1982) compared 35 middle-class women in early sobriety with 35 nonalcoholic women matched on age, education, marital status, religious preference, and race (white). As noted earlier, 85% of the alcoholic women reported experiencing at least one type of sexual dysfunction during active alcoholism. This rate was significantly higher than the 59% of control women who reported any past or present sexual dysfunction. The most common sexual problems reported by alcoholic women were lack of sexual interest (64% of alcoholics, 44% of controls), lack of sexual arousal or pleasure (61% of alcoholics, 30% of controls), and difficulty attaining orgasm (64% of alcoholics, 27% of controls).

Discussion

RATES OF SEXUAL DYSFUNCTION

What can we conclude about the relationship between alcoholism and sexual dysfunction in women on the basis of the available research? At the least, we can conclude that alcoholic women are not exempt from sexual difficulties. With one exception (Lemere & Smith, 1973), rates of sexual inhibition, low sexual interest, and "frigidity" in studies of alcoholic women ranged from 23% to 100%. In comparison, only 2% of Kinsey et al.'s (1953) female general population sample reported they had never felt sexually aroused, although Kinsey's is almost certainly a more extreme definition of "frigidity" than those used in most alcoholism studies.

Rates of orgastic problems are also somewhat higher in studies of alcoholic women than in Kinsey et al.'s normative sample. Rates of primary orgastic dysfunction in alcoholic women, reported at 19% (Hammond et al., 1979) and 32% (Curran, 1937), exceed Kinsey et al.'s 10% estimate for the general female population. Rates for primary and secondary orgastic dysfunction combined ranged from 15–28% (Murphy et al., 1980) to 64% (Covington, 1982), compared with 28% of women in Kinsey et al.'s (1953) sample who reached orgasm less than 30% of the time after 15 years of marriage (p. 408).

Despite variations in periods of data collection, populations, and definitional criteria, comparisons between Kinsey's (1953) findings and available data on alcoholic women are consistent with three control group studies (Beckman, 1979; Covington, 1982; Pinhas, 1980) in suggesting some excess of sexual dissatisfaction and sexual dysfunction among alcoholic women. In addition, data from Beckman, Sholty, and others suggest that alcoholic women may use alcohol to "treat" or self-medicate the sexual problems they experience. Given that problem-drinking and alcoholic women may be at some increased risk for sexual dysfunction, determining the precise extent of this increased risk will require better controlled studies that compare larger and more representative alcoholic samples to women with other psychiatric disorders and to nonalcoholic women in the general population.

"PROMISCUITY" IN ALCOHOLIC WOMEN

The available data do not support the simple stereotype that alcoholic women have loose sexual morals and are sexually promiscuous. Several studies of women from middle and upper socioeconomic levels (e.g., Browne-Mayers *et al.*, 1976; Wood & Duffy, 1966) found little or no prostitution and little evidence of multiple sexual liaisons. Somewhat higher rates were found in studies of lower socioeconomic status women, possibly due to economic circumstances and more public drinking patterns.

This is not to claim that drinking-related "promiscuity" is extremely rare or occurs only among lower-status women. Wall (1937) speaks of "loose heterosexual activities" in 60% of his private hospital patients, and Lisansky (1957) found that 11% of her middle-class outpatients were sexually promiscuous while drinking. Spalt (1975) reported that 31% of his affective disorder alcoholics had had more than 10 sexual partners, and Hammond *et al.* (1979) found that 50% of their outpatients reported having had more than 12 partners. These figures might be compared with general population estimates from a 1970 national survey, in which only 3% of women age 21–35, and less than 1% of women over 35, reported having had 10 or more sexual partners (Klassen, 1970).

In trying to avoid stereotyping alcoholic women as promiscuous, some researchers may have selectively deemphasized sexual behavior that might seem to fit that stereotype, perhaps particularly among "respectable" middle- and upper-class samples. Regardless of the ambiguities in the research data, many alcoholic women from all socioeconomic backgrounds seem to feel that they have prostituted themselves sexually while drinking. Galbraith (1982) notes that alcoholic women "often consider their sexual behavior as having been 'promiscuous' while drinking, seeking comfort, closeness, and love" (p. 1). Evans and Schaefer (1980) state that a major issue in sexuality groups for alcoholic women involves guilt over indiscriminate choice of sexual partners while drinking and "a high degree of shame from prostituting themselves for drugs, intimacy, emotional and financial security and affection" (p. 39). Future studies of alcoholic women should seek objective information about the number and characteristics of sexual partners during periods of drinking and abstinence. Such information can be presented in a manner that would not reinforce destructive stereotypes about women's drinking, for example, by acknowledging that a woman's choices and options are limited during acute alcoholism. Information on sexual partners might help identify a potentially important treatment and recovery issue for women—guilt and shame regarding "promiscuous" behavior while drinking

—and might stimulate approaches (e.g., changing drinking environments) for preventing drinking-related sexual activity with inappropriate partners.

ALCOHOLIC WOMEN'S SEXUAL PARTNERS

Despite the fact that sexual dysfunction involves two partners, virtually every study of alcoholic women reviewed here has neglected how women's sexual partners may contribute to their sexual dissatisfaction. There are several ways in which information on sexual partners may help in understanding the women's sexual difficulties. Alcoholic women are more likely than women in the general population to be married to or living with heavy-drinking and alcoholic men (Johnson, Armor, Polich, & Stambul, 1977; Mulford, 1977). These men are themselves at increased risk for various forms of sexual dysfunction, including decreased sexual interest and erectile dysfunction (impotence) (e.g., Van Thiel & Lester, 1979). Thus some portion of alcoholic women's sexual dissatisfaction may originate with sexual problems of heavy-drinking partners.

Alcoholic women's sexual partners may also play important roles in reinforcing the women's use of alcohol to cope with sexual dysfunction. Clinicians have observed that husbands of sexually inhibited alcoholic women often encourage their wives to drink as a sexual disinhibitor (see Wood & Duffy, 1966). Such husbands often intentionally or unintentionally sabotage alcoholism treatment efforts, fearing that giving up alcohol will also mean giving up sex (Berenson, 1976). Including sexual partners in future studies of alcoholic women not only may increase our understanding of the etiology of alcohol abuse and sexual dysfunction in women, but also may help in developing more effective interventions for alcohol-related sexual dysfunction. Relationships studied should not be limited to traditional heterosexual marriages but should also include lesbian relationships, quasimarital relationships, and other significant sexual partners of both sexes.

CAUSAL SEQUENCES OF ALCOHOL ABUSE AND SEXUAL DYSFUNCTION

While suggesting that alcoholic women have high rates of unsatisfactory sexual experiences, the available research tells us little about the specific role of alcohol in these experiences, or about whether the sexual problems preceded or followed the onset of excessive drinking. One possibility is that sexual dysfunction in women creates physical, psychological, and interpersonal distress, which alcohol subsequently seems to relieve. Although their recall must be interpreted cautiously, alcoholic women in several studies reviewed earlier (e.g., Covington, 1982; Kinsey, 1966; Sholty, 1979) claimed that sexual difficulties preceded the onset of excessive drinking.

Sexual dysfunction can also be a direct or an indirect consequence of heavy alcohol consumption. Impaired sexual functioning can result from the direct toxic effects of alcohol at gonadal, hormonal, and central nervous system levels (e.g., Greene & Hollander, 1980; Van Thiel & Lester, 1979). Alcohol abuse may also have intrapersonal consequences such as depression and low self-esteem, and interpersonal consequences such as marital tensions and conflicts, that can disrupt sexual functioning. Alcoholic women may be particularly likely to have sexually dysfunctional partners (e.g., problem-drinking men), contributing to further sexual dissatisfaction.

A third causal pattern may be that certain conditions or experiences contribute to both alcohol abuse and sexual problems, for example, child-hood emotional deprivation, deviant parental role models, sexual abuse, or certain physiological predispositions. Finally, there may be reciprocal rela-tionships in which distress due to sexual difficulties contributes to heavy drinking, which in turn produces new or worsens existing sexual problems. Determining the relative importance of these various causal patterns—for distinct groups of alcoholic women—will require more rigorous research designs and more complex data-analysis strategies than studies to date have employed.

INCEST AND SEXUAL ABUSE

Two experiences that may predispose women both to alcohol abuse and to sexual dysfunction are incest and other sexual abuse, including rape. Sexual abuse was apparently too sensitive a topic to include in most earlier clinical studies of alcoholic women, but several recent studies have found that such experiences are rather common among alcohol and drug dependent women. Findings from these studies are summarized in the fourth column of Table 7-1.

Murphy et al. (1980) found that 54% of the women alcoholics in their sample reported having been raped as a child or an adult. The authors do not indicate how many of the women experienced rape as a child and how many as an adult, nor in how many cases the rapist was a relative as compared to a nonrelative. In Covington's (1982) middle-class sample, 34% of the alcoholics reported a history of incest, as compared with 17% of controls, and 34% of the alcoholics, compared with 14% of controls, reported having been raped. Overall, 74% of the alcoholic women, compared with 50% of the nonalcoholic controls, reported one or more experiences of sexual abuse (incest, rape, or molestation). Like most other authors, Covington does not report how many rape experiences preceded and how many occurred during periods of heavy drinking or alcoholism.

More detailed data are provided by Hammond et al. (1979), who found that 39% of their sample reported having been raped and 40% reported a history of incest, defined as "sex play with a relative." The incest partner was most often in the immediate family (brothers, fathers, stepfathers), although 35% of the partners were more distant relatives (e.g., cousins, uncles). A history of rape had significant negative relationships to sexual satisfaction and interest in sexual activity, and a significant positive correlation with vaginismus. Women with a history of incest reported feeling less sexually attractive at age 21, reported fewer positive feelings about sexual activity, and were more likely to report that guilt was one of their usual feelings during lovemaking. A history of incest correlated negatively with ratings of sexual satisfaction when sober but not with sexual satisfaction when intoxicated: Perhaps alcohol helped sedate these women against the negative feelings they associated with sexual activity.

Hayek (1980) also found negative relationships between incest experience and later sexual adjustment. Hayek compared 30 recovering alcoholic women with incest experience and 30 alcoholic women with no history of incest. Compared with the nonincest group, the women with incest experience were more likely to have experienced vaginismus and dyspareunia. The incest subjects had begun drinking alcohol at an earlier age, and more often felt uncomfortable during sexual activity if alcohol was not available.

Other data on incest and sexual abuse are available from women's alcohol and drug abuse treatment programs. Staff members of Chrysalis, an outpatient chemical dependency treatment program in Minneapolis, report that 53% of the 75 women entering treatment over a 2-year period had experienced incest or other sexual abuse prior to age 21 (Evans & Schaefer, 1980; Schaefer & Evans, 1982). The same authors cite earlier surveys of Minnesota chemical dependency treatment centers, in which 40% to 50% of women clients questioned reported they had experienced incest. Of 65 clients entering an outpatient alcoholism treatment program for women in rural Maine (Roth, Acker, Petersen, Perry, Shannon, & Anderson, 1981), 12% reported a history of incest and 29% reported having been raped; additional women acknowledged these experiences later in treatment despite negative answers at intake (Galbraith, 1982). A study of 118 female drug abusers treated in residential therapeutic communities in seven states found that 44% reported incest experience (Benward & Densen-Gerber, 1975). Among these cases, 36% of the partners were age peers (brothers, cousins) and 64% were of the parental generation (uncles, fathers, stepfathers).

Thus, when alcoholic or drug-dependent women are asked about experiences with incest or rape, the rates appear high, ranging from 12% to 53% for incest or other childhood sexual abuse, and up to 74% for all sexual abuse combined (Covington, 1982). The incest rates are much higher than in the general population sample of Kinsey *et al.* (1953), who found that only 5.5% of adult women reported sexual contact with a male relative during childhood. Although not directly comparable, they also appear considerably higher than the American Humane Association's estimate that the annual incidence of incest in the general population is between 40 cases and 1000 cases per million people (National Center on Child Abuse and Neglect, 1978).

Experiencing incest, rape, or other sexual abuse may increase a woman's risk for subsequent alcohol abuse, sexual dysfunction, or both for a variety of reasons. Alcohol or other drugs may be used in an attempt to reduce feelings of guilt, shame, anger, and loss of self-esteem that are common among victims of sexual abuse. Younger victims may express their inner turmoil through antisocial behavior, including alcohol and other drug use and indiscriminate sexual behavior (see Benward & Densen-Gerber, 1975). And the pain and low self-esteem resulting from sexual abuse may drive some women of all ages into overtly self-destructive use of alcohol or other drugs. Heavy use of alcohol or other drugs for any of these reasons may then increase women's vulnerability to further sexual abuse.

Sexual abuse may also cause women to have lasting feelings of fear, anger, and loss of faith in men that can interfere with heterosexual relationships. Ambivalence toward men, together with feelings of guilt and shame surrounding sexuality, may underlie the elevated rates of sexual dysfunction found in alcoholic incest and rape victims (e.g., Hammond et al., 1979; Hayek, 1980).

A final component of this three-way relationship among sexual abuse, alcohol abuse, and sexual dysfunction is the drinking behavior of the perpetrator of the sexual abuse. In a recent review of the literature on alcoholism and incest, Forrest (1983) found that rates of alcohol dependence among incestuous fathers ranged between 20% and 70% in available studies. These studies report that most alcoholic fathers are intoxicated when the incest occurs. In one study (Meiselman, 1978) daughters recalled their fathers' drinking behavior in great detail many years after the incest had taken place. Daughters of intoxicated incestuous fathers may come to associate alcohol with sexuality and thus be predisposed to use alcohol later on to overcome the sexual impediments that develop from early incestuous experience. Additionally, daughters of incestuous alcoholic fathers may have an increased genetic risk for subsequently developing alcoholism themselves.

DRINKING AND SEXUAL ORIENTATION

Several studies of alcoholic women have included information about homosexual experience and self-reported sexual orientation. Unfortunately this information is difficult to interpret, particularly in earlier studies that did not distinguish between single and repeated same-sex experiences, between brief and lasting relationships, or between homosexual and bisexual preferences.

Homosexuality in Alcoholic Women

As shown in the fifth column of Table 7-1, only a small minority of alcoholic women in most clinical studies reported homosexual experience. For example, 4% of Curran's (1937) subjects and 10% of Wall's (1937) subjects reported that they had had at least some overt homosexual experience, but neither author describes the frequency or duration of this experience. In Kinsey's (1966) sample, 7% named homosexuality as a cause of their drinking, and 3% of Browne-Mayers *et al*.'s (1976) subjects reported "homosexual conflicts." Neither study indicates whether additional women had had homosexual experience or considered themselves homosexual without feeling this led to drinking problems or psychological conflicts.

More recent studies have reported somewhat higher rates of homosexual experience and homosexual affectional preference, possibly because both researchers and alcoholic women are able to discuss these experiences more routinely now than in past decades. In Beckman's (1979) study, 20% of the alcoholic women reported at least some homosexual experience, while 6% and 3% considered themselves homosexual and bisexual respectively. The alcoholics were more likely than the nonpsychiatric controls to report homosexual experience. However, the alcoholics did not differ significantly from psychiatric controls. In Hammond *et al*.'s (1979) sample, 20% reported having had one or more lesbian relationships since adolescence, and a study of 75 chemically dependent women receiving outpatient treatment in Minneapolis (Schaefer & Evans, 1982) found that 61% of the clients identified themselves as heterosexual, 29% as lesbians, and 3% as bisexual, with 7% uncertain. During the 5 years prior to treatment, 55% of the women in Schaefer and Evans's sample had experienced sexual relationships with male partners only, 15% with female only, and 30% with both male and female partners. When questioned in early sobriety, 17% of Covington's (1982) 35 middle-class alcoholics described themselves as lesbians and an additional 17% reported a bisexual preference. As shown in Table 7-1, bisexual activity was more than twice as common during active alcoholism as in sobriety, whereas lesbian preference was uncommon prior to and during alcoholism but increased in sobriety.

Rates of homosexual experience in most clinical studies of alcoholic women do not differ greatly from Kinsey *et al*.'s (1953) finding that 19% of women in a general population sample reported having had at least one sexual experience with another woman by age 35. However, Kinsey *et al*.'s finding that only 2–3% of women were exclusively homosexual at the time of the survey may provide a more meaningful comparison. The three studies (Beckman, 1979; Covington, 1982; Schaefer & Evans, 1982) that have approximated a self-definition of exclusive homosexuality—by also including a bisexual preference category—have all found higher rates of lesbian preference than Kinsey *et al*.'s 2–3%.

Alcohol Problems among Homosexuals

Evidence suggesting an increased incidence of homosexuality among alcoholic women is complemented by other data suggesting high rates of problem drinking and alcoholism among lesbians and homosexual men. In two clinical studies (Saghir & Robins, 1973; Swanson, Loomis, Lukesh, Cronin, & Smith, 1972) lesbians exceeded heterosexual women in reported alcohol problems, and in two community surveys—in Los Angeles and four Midwestern cities—rates of alcohol problems among lesbians and homosexual men were estimated at approximately 30%, well above general population rates (Fifield, 1975; Lohrenz, Connelly, Coyne, & Spare, 1978). Although these studies consistently suggest an elevated risk for alcohol problems among lesbians and homosexual men, methodological limitations make it impossible yet to estimate the exact magnitude of the increased risk (see Nardi, 1982b).

One observer (Hastings, 1982) has recently suggested that alcohol abuse may have decreased among lesbians in the past few years. Possible reasons include dissemination of information about lesbians' at-risk status through closely knit communication and peer-pressure networks, statements and role modeling by prominent lesbian recovering alcoholics, some lessening of social oppression of homosexuals, increased alternatives to gay bars for social and romantic interaction, and possible changes in the symbolic meaning of alcohol within some segments of the lesbian community (e.g., from a symbol of rebellion to a symbol of an unhealthy, "unserious" life style or of domination by the larger society). Hastings' provocative observations have hopeful implications for long-term reductions in alcohol problems among lesbians. However, her impressions would be hard to document empirically, given the methodological limitations of the available baseline data on alcohol awareness and alcohol problems within lesbian communities.

Subgroup Differences

It is important to recognize that there may be significant subgroup differences in how lesbians and bisexual women drink and develop alcohol problems. For example, lesbians who are psychologically secure and relatively unconflicted about their sexual orientation may drink primarily for social and cultural reasons. These include the heavy-drinking norms that exist within many gay and lesbian communities, the prominent role of the gay bar as a social and recreational center, and the alienation and isolation experienced by homosexual persons as a result of societal disapproval and rejection (see Burke, 1982; Fifield, 1975; Ziebold, n.d.).

Bisexual women are a second subgroup that, compared with lesbians, has little if any identifiable subculture and few organized political resources or supports. Bisexual women may be more confused about their sexual identity and may feel misunderstood by both lesbians and heterosexual women, from whom they feel pressure to adopt either a lesbian or a heterosexual orientation (see Schaefer & Evans, 1980). Their drinking may be a response to both social-environmental influences and psychological conflicts and stresses. Some women within this subgroup may have a primary lesbian sexual identity, which they try to deny through drinking and heterosexual or bisexual activity (see Covington, 1982).

A third subgroup may consist of heterosexual women who are experiencing confusing feelings of intimacy toward other women. These feelings may arise in the course of treatment and recovery, as women share intimate details of their lives with other women patients and staff. In some cases women may find themselves preferring other women as friends and confidantes after a series of negative experiences with men. Women whose alcoholism begins during adolescence may experience some disruption of psychosexual development, with resulting confusion regarding sexual preference. Although such women may temporarily define themselves as lesbian or bisexual, many may eventually return to a primary heterosexual identity after exploring attractions to other women and clarifying feelings of affection, intimacy, and sexuality (see Schaefer & Evans, 1980).

Unfortunately, virtually no information is available on how alcohol affects the sexual experience of women in any of these three subgroups, nor on possible relationships between drinking and sexual dysfunction in such women. Despite anecdotal reports that lesbians use alcohol as a sexual disinhibitor (e.g., Diamond & Wilsnack, 1978), there is no empirical evidence that this use among lesbians is any more or any less common than among heterosexual women. Studies are needed to compare lesbians and bisexual women with demographically similar heterosexual women on their beliefs about drinking and sexuality, rates of sexual problems, use of alcohol relative to these problems, and subjective and objective effects of alcohol on sexual inhibition, responsiveness, and pleasure. The effects of a lesbian's alcohol abuse upon her intimate relationship with a partner should also be explored and compared with the dynamics observed in heterosexual relationships (see Nardi, 1982a). Information on possible differences in alcohol use and effects related to sexual preference could help treatment and prevention programs for alcohol abuse and alcohol-related sexual dysfunction to be targeted more precisely to the special needs and characteristics—including sexual and affectional preference—of their clients.

CONCLUSIONS: SOME IMPLICATIONS FOR TREATMENT AND PREVENTION

This chapter has stressed the need for more and better research on drinking and sexual functioning. Larger and better-controlled clinical studies are needed to determine what types of sexual disorders women problem drinkers and alcoholics experience, and whether they experience these to a greater extent than comparable women without alcohol problems. Epidemiological research is needed to evaluate risks of sexual dysfunction associated with varying levels of drinking among women in the general population. Impor-

tant questions about temporal relationships between drinking and sexual dysfunction cannot be answered fully without longitudinal data.

Increased scientific knowledge about sexuality and drinking in women
may have important implications for treatment and prevention. The present
section considers some possible implications of existing data, including
training needs of professional care-givers, research on treatment modalities,
and strategies for prevention of alcohol-related sexual dysfunction.

Professional Training in Alcoholism and Sexual Dysfunction

If heavy drinking and alcohol abuse are associated with sexual dysfunction,
then persons who counsel individuals with sexual problems should be sensitive to alcohol abuse as a possible cause and/or consequence of the sexual
problems they are treating. Conversely, professionals who deal with problem-
drinking or alcoholic women should consider the possible presence of sexual
dysfunction as a precipitant of excessive drinking, a consequence of excessive
drinking, or both.

Since most alcoholism therapists have received little training in the
identification or treatment of sexual dysfunction, many may feel personally
uncomfortable and professionally unprepared to deal with patients' sexual
difficulties. Fortunately, alcoholism professionals are becoming increasingly
aware of the need to address their patients' sexual concerns. Articles and
books are beginning to appear that offer clinical guidelines for the assessment
and treatment of sexual dysfunction in alcoholic populations (e.g., Forrest,
1983). Workshops and other training opportunities are increasing, such as
the Family Intimacy Training Program of the University of Minnesota
School of Medicine, which provides training in human sexuality to alcoholism counselors and other human service professionals. Training programs in
alcoholism for sex counselors and therapists have been less evident. However,
these may be forthcoming given the recent encouraging increase in communication between alcoholism professionals and sex therapy professionals
(e.g., Barnes & Schnarch, 1980; Gad-Luther, 1980).

Treatment Programs for Alcohol-Related Sexual Dysfunction

Several approaches have been proposed for addressing sexual issues and
problems in alcoholic women. The Chrysalis outpatient treatment program
for women in Minneapolis (e.g., Evans & Schaefer, 1980; Schaefer, 1980)
uses multiple groups focusing on specific sexuality issues, such as incest,
lesbian support, and alternative life styles (for exploration of affectional
preference). All women in the Chrysalis program also participate in general
sexuality groups that deal with issues such as orgastic problems and loss of
sexual interest, feelings of guilt and shame from indiscriminate sexual activity

while drinking, sexual and sex-role stereotypes, and feelings of anger related to sexual abuse.

Murphy *et al.* (1980) conducted a more structured 12-session Sexual Enhancement Program for 23 alcoholic women. Groups of 4–12 members and 2 leaders participated in didactic presentations, body awareness exercises, guided fantasy, relaxation training, and group discussion. The program had four major stages: sex education, sexual awareness, identification and treatment of specific sexual dysfunctions, and sexual assertiveness. Following the program, participants showed increased scores on a test of general sex education, a Sexual Arousability Inventory, and a Partner Happiness Scale. Murphy *et al.* emphasize sexual enhancement rather than sexual dysfunction, since many women who denied sexual difficulties at intake nonetheless profited from the group, and during treatment some acknowledged problems that had been denied earlier.

A third treatment approach is to involve women alcoholics and their partners in standard sex counseling or therapy, such as the brief sex therapy approaches of Masters and Johnson, Helen Singer Kaplan, or others. Gad-Luther and Dickman (1979) have reported a pilot study using this approach, in which five abstinent male alcoholics and their wives participated in ten three-hour sessions of "psychosexual multiple team therapy." Following treatment, participants showed significant improvements on four dimensions of a Sexual Interaction Inventory. Both Murphy *et al.* (1980) and Gad-Luther and Dickman (1979) limited their assessment of treatment outcome to sexual functioning and sexual satisfaction. A logical next step would be to determine whether alcoholics who have received sexual enhancement training or sex therapy also have better drinking outcomes.

Other Treatment Issues: Preliminary Abstinence
and Significant Other Involvement

Most clinicians recommend not beginning formal treatment for sexual dysfunction until the alcoholic woman has been abstinent from alcohol for some period of time. This allows sexual difficulties due to the acute depressant effects of alcohol, to reversible hormonal effects, or to tensions of early sobriety to be distinguished from more long-term sexual problems that will continue to trouble the abstinent alcoholic. It may also permit a certain amount of natural interpersonal healing to occur, and may enable the alcoholic to develop increased self-esteem and personal coping resources. Clinicians have recommended a period of abstinence ranging from 3–4 months (Forrest, 1983) to 6–12 months or longer (Lewis & Whitfield, 1982). The optimal length of this waiting period is an important empirical question, since delaying help for sexual dysfunction may carry risks of relapse due to chronic sexual tension and dissatisfaction.

A related question is whether and at what point to involve a woman's sexual partner in treatment. Therapists who work with alcoholic women comment on the women's feelings of powerlessness and sexual exploitation and their need to regain feelings of control over their sexual activity and sexual satisfaction (see Evans & Schaefer, 1980; Pinhas, 1980). These considerations might argue for treatment focusing on the woman herself (e.g., in women's groups), independent of any sexual partner. However, many alcoholic women may also have sexually dysfunctional partners (e.g., alcoholic husbands) who contribute to the women's sexual dissatisfaction and reinforce their drinking behavior. Treatment of only the women might accomplish little if it does not also deal with the dysfunction and influence of their partners. In evaluating treatment for alcohol-related sexual dysfunction, future research might compare programs that treat women alone with programs that treat them conjointly with their sexual partners. Possible variables might include treatment sequences (e.g., would individual treatment followed by conjoint therapy be superior to the reverse sequence?) and the relative degrees of dysfunction of the woman and her sexual partner.

Prevention of Alcohol-Related Sexual Dysfunction

To the extent that sexual dysfunction precedes and contributes to heavy drinking, women with sexual problems constitute a high-risk group for alcohol abuse. Treatment of the sexual problem is clearly the strategy of choice for preventing subsequent alcohol abuse. However, where such treatment is not possible or successful, other preventive interventions may help reduce the risk of alcohol problems. Such interventions might include targeted alcohol education, sex education, peer support, and education regarding nonchemical means of coping with sexual frustration and disappointment.

If future research supports an association between a history of incest or rape and later alcohol abuse, women who have experienced these events may be particularly important high-risk target groups for prevention. Providing such women with peer support and with opportunities to express and resolve their feelings about the incest or rape might help decrease their risk of turning to alcohol or other drugs to cope with the painful experiences or their psychosexual consequences.

The reciprocal causal pattern, in which heavy drinking causes or contributes to sexual dysfunction, suggests the need for more widespread and more effective public education concerning the consequences for women of heavy alcohol consumption. Recent education campaigns dealing with the fetal alcohol syndrome are an important step in this direction (see Little & Ervin and Ferrence chapters in this volume). However, as research provides information on other alcohol-related sexual disorders, particularly from studies of women in the general population, this information should be incorporated in broader educational programs to inform women not only about risks to the fetus but also about other risks to women's sexual health and well-being.

ACKNOWLEDGMENTS

Preparation of this chapter was supported in part by Research Grant #AA 04610-02 from the National Institute on Alcohol Abuse and Alcoholism. I am grateful to Richard Wilsnack, Albert Klassen, Sue Evans, and Susan Schaefer for helpful comments on an earlier version of the chapter. This chapter revises and updates the material presented in the chapter "Alcohol, Sexuality, and Reproductive Dysfunction in Women," which appeared in Abel, E. L. (Ed.), *Fetal Alcohol Syndrome* Boca Raton, Fla: CRC Press, 1982.

REFERENCES

Abraham, K. *Selected papers on psychoanalysis.* London: Hogarth, 1948.

Abrams, D. B., & Wilson, G. T. Effects of alcohol on social anxiety in women: Cognitive versus physiological processes. *Journal of Abnormal Psychology*, 1979, *88*, 161–173.

Arafat, I., & Yorburg, B. Drug use and the sexual behavior of college women. *Journal of Sex Research*, 1973, *9*, 21–29.

Athanasiou, R., Shaver, P., & Tavris, C. Sex: A *Psychology Today* report on more than 20,000 responses to 101 questions on sexual attitudes and practices. *Psychology Today*, July, 1970, pp. 39–52.

Barling, J., & Bolon, K. Effects of alcohol, expectancies, sex and social setting on locus of control. *Journal of Studies on Alcohol*, 1981, *42*, 680–684.

Barling, J., & Fincham, F. Alcohol, psychological conservatism, and sexual interest in male social drinkers. *Journal of Social Psychology*, 1980, *112*, 135–144.

Barnes, J. L., & Schnarch, D. M. Sexual dysfunctions of the alcoholic: A response to Gad-Luther. *Sexuality and Disability*, 1980, *3*, 291–293.

Beckman, L. J. Self-esteem of women alcoholics. *Journal of Studies on Alcohol*, 1978, *39*, 491–498.

Beckman, L. J. Reported effects of alcohol on the sexual feelings and behavior of women alcoholics and nonalcoholics. *Journal of Studies on Alcohol*, 1979, *40*, 272–282.

Benward, J., & Densen-Gerber, J. Incest as a causative factor in antisocial behavior: An exploratory study. *Contemporary Drug Problems*, 1975, *4*, 323–340.

Berenson, D. Sexual counseling with alcoholics. In J. Newman (Ed.), *Sexual counseling for persons with alcohol problems: Proceedings of a workshop.* Pittsburgh: Western Pennsylvania Institute of Alcohol Studies, University of Pittsburgh, 1976.

Bowker, L. H. *Drug use among American women old and young: Sexual oppression and other themes.* San Francisco: R & E Research Associates, 1977.

Briddell, D. W., Rimm, D. C., Caddy, G. R., Krawitz, G., Sholis, D., & Wunderlin, R. J. Effects of alcohol and cognitive set on sexual arousal to deviant stimuli. *Journal of Abnormal Psychology*, 1978, *87*, 418–430.

Briddell, D. W., & Wilson, G. T. Effects of alcohol and expectancy set on male sexual arousal. *Journal of Abnormal Psychology*, 1976, *85*, 225–234.

Browne-Mayers, A. N., Seelye, E. E., & Sillman, L. Psychosocial study of hospitalized middle-class alcoholic women. *Annals of the New York Academy of Sciences*, 1976, *273*, 593–604.

Burke, P. *Bar use and alienation in lesbian and heterosexual women alcoholics.* Paper presented at the National Alcoholism Forum of the National Council on Alcoholism, Washington, D.C., April 1982.

Covington, S. S. *Sexual experience, dysfunction, and abuse: A comparative study of alcoholic and nonalcoholic women.* Doctoral dissertation, Union Graduate School, 1982.

Curlee, J. Alcoholism and the "empty nest." *Bulletin of the Menninger Clinic*, 1969, *33*, 165–171.

Curran, F. J. Personality studies in alcoholic women. *Journal of Nervous and Mental Disease*, 1937, *86*, 645–667.

Curran, J. P., Neff, S., & Lippold, S. Correlates of sexual experience among university students. *Journal of Sex Research*, 1973, *9*, 124–131.

Dahlgren, L. *Female alcoholics: A psychiatric and social study.* Stockholm, Sweden: Karolinska Institute, 1979.

Diamond, D. L., & Wilsnack, S. C. Alcohol abuse among lesbians: A descriptive study. *Journal of Homosexuality*, 1978, *4*, 123–142.

Evans, S., & Schaefer, S. Why women's sexuality is important to address in chemical dependency treatment programs. *Grassroots*, 1980, *37*, 37–40.

Farkas, G. M., & Rosen, R. C. Effect of alcohol on elicited male sexual response. *Journal of Studies on Alcohol*, 1976, *37*, 265–272.

Fifield, L. *On my way to nowhere: Alienated, isolated, drunk.* Los Angeles: Gay Community Services Center, 1975.

Forrest, G. G. *Alcoholism and human sexuality.* Springfield, Ill.: Charles C Thomas, 1983.

Gad-Luther, I. Sexual dysfunctions of the alcoholic. *Sexuality and Disability*, 1980, *3*, 273–289.

Gad-Luther, I., & Dickman, D. Psychosexual therapy with recovering alcoholics: A pilot study. *Journal of Sex Education and Therapy*, 1979, *1*(5), 11–16.

Galbraith, S. *Summary of critical sexuality issues observed among alcoholic women in the Skyward Women's Alcoholism Treatment Program.* Unpublished manuscript, Rockland, Maine, 1982.

Greene, L. W., & Hollander, C. S. Sex and alcohol: The effects of alcohol on the hypothalamic-pituitary-gonadal axis. *Alcoholism: Clinical and Experimental Research*, 1980, *4*, 1–5.

Hammond, D. C., Jorgensen, G. Q., & Ridgeway, D. M. *Sexual adjustment of female alcoholics.* Unpublished manuscript, Alcohol and Drug Abuse Clinic, University of Utah, Salt Lake City, 1979.

Hastings, P. Alcohol and the lesbian community: Changing patterns of awareness. *The Drinking and Drug Practices Surveyor*, 1982 (August), *18*, 3–7.

Hayek, M. A. *Recovered alcoholic women with and without incest experience: A comparative study.* Unpublished doctoral dissertation, Reed University, 1980.

Johnson, P., Armor, D. J., Polich, S., & Stambul, H. *U.S. adult drinking practices: Time trends, social correlates and sex roles* (Working Note prepared for the National Institute on Alcohol Abuse and Alcoholism). Santa Monica, Calif.: Rand Corporation, 1977.

Jones, B. M., & Jones, M. K. Women and alcohol: Intoxication, metabolism, and the menstrual cycle. In M. Greenblatt & M. A. Schuckit (Eds.), *Alcoholism problems in women and children.* New York: Grune & Stratton, 1976.

Kaplan, H. S. *The new sex therapy: Active treatment of sexual dysfunctions.* New York: Brunner/Mazel, 1974.

Kaplan, H. S. *Disorders of sexual desire.* New York: Brunner/Mazel, 1979.

Kinsey, A. C., Pomeroy, W. B., Martin, C. E., & Gebhard, P. H. *Sexual behavior in the human female.* Philadelphia: Saunders, 1953.

Kinsey, B. A. *The female alcoholic: A social psychological study.* Springfield, Ill.: Charles C Thomas, 1966.

Klassen, A. D. *Unpublished data from 1970 national survey of sexuality and sexual morality*, Indiana University, Institute for Sex Research, 1970.

Konovsky, M., & Wilsnack, S. C. Social drinking and self-esteem in married couples. *Journal of Studies on Alcohol*, 1982, *43*, 319–333.

Lang, A. R., Searles, J., Lauerman, R., & Adesso, V. Expectancy, alcohol, and sex guilt as determinants of interest in and reaction to sexual stimuli. *Journal of Abnormal Psychology*, 1980, *89*, 644-653.

Lansky, D., & Wilson, G. T. Alcohol, expectations, and sexual arousal in males: An information processing analysis. *Journal of Abnormal Psychology*, 1981, *90*, 35-45.

Lemere, F., & Smith, J. W. Alcohol-induced sexual impotence. *American Journal of Psychiatry*, 1973, *130*, 212-213.

Levine, J. The sexual adjustment of alcoholics: A clinical study of a selected sample. *Quarterly Journal of Studies on Alcohol*, 1955, *16*, 675-680.

Lewis, A. C., & Whitfield, C. L. Alcohol and sexuality. In C. L. Whitfield (Ed.), *The patient with alcoholism and other drug problems*. Chicago: Yearbook Medical Publishers, 1982.

Lisansky, E. S. Alcoholism in women: Social and psychological concomitants. I. Social history data. *Quarterly Journal of Studies on Alcohol*, 1957, *18*, 588-623.

Lohrenz, L. J., Connelly, J. C., Coyne, L., & Spare, K. E. Alcohol problems in several Midwestern homosexual communities. *Journal of Studies on Alcohol*, 1978, *39*, 1959-1963.

Malatesta, V. J., Pollack, R. H., Crotty, T. D., & Peacock, L. J. Acute alcohol intoxication and female orgasmic response. *Journal of Sex Research*, 1982, *18*, 1-17.

Malatesta, V. J., Pollack, R. H., Wilbanks, W. A., & Adams, H. E. Alcohol effects on the orgasmic-ejaculatory response in human males. *Journal of Sex Research*, 1979, *15*, 101-107.

Massot, Hamel, & Deliry. Alcoolisme féminin: Données statistiques et psychopathologiques. *Journal de Medecine de Lyon*, 1956, *37*, 265-269.

McCarty, D., Diamond, W., & Kaye, M. Alcohol, sexual arousal, and the transfer of excitation. *Journal of Personality and Social Psychology*, 1982, *42*, 977-988

Medhus, A. Venereal diseases among female alcoholics. *Scandinavian Journal of Social Medicine*, 1975, *3*, 29-33.

Meiselman, K. C. *Incest: A psychological study of causes and effects with treatment recommendations*. San Francisco: Jossey-Bass, 1978.

Mulford, H. A. Women and men problem drinkers. *Journal of Studies on Alcohol*, 1977, *38*, 1624-1639.

Murphy, W. D., Coleman, E., Hoon, E., & Scott, C. Sexual dysfunction and treatment in alcoholic women. *Sexuality and Disability*, 1980, *3*, 240-255.

Nardi, P. M. Alcohol treatment and the non-traditional "family" structures of gays and lesbians. *Journal of Alcohol and Drug Education*, 1982, *27*(2), 83-89. (a)

Nardi, P. M. Alcoholism and homosexuality: A theoretical perspective. *Journal of Homosexuality*, 1982, *7*(4), 9-25. (b)

National Center on Child Abuse and Neglect. *Child sexual abuse: Incest, assault, and sexual exploitation*. Washington, D.C.: U.S. Government Printing Office, 1978.

Pinhas, V. *Sex guilt and sexual control in the woman alcoholic in early sobriety*. Unpublished doctoral dissertation, Department of Health Education, New York University, 1978.

Pinhas, V. Sex guilt and sexual control in women alcoholics in early sobriety. *Sexuality and Disability*, 1980, *3*, 256-272.

Potter, J. Women and sex—It's enough to drive them to drink! In V. Burtle (Ed.), *Women who drink: Alcoholic experience and psychotherapy*. Springfield, Ill.: Charles C Thomas, 1979.

Richardson, A. M. Androgyny: How it affects drinking practices. *Focus on Women: Journal of Addictions and Health*, 1981, *2*, 116-131.

Roth, P., Acker, C. W., Petersen, R., Perry, W., Shannon, L., & Anderson, J. *Skyward: A rural women's alcoholism project* (Final Report to the National Institute on Alcohol Abuse and Alcoholism.) Rockland, Maine, September, 1981.

Saghir, M. T., & Robins, E. *Male and female homosexuality: A comprehensive investigation*. Baltimore, Md.: Williams & Wilkins, 1973.

Sandmaier, M. *The invisible alcoholics: Women and alcohol abuse in America*. New York: McGraw-Hill, 1980.

Schachter, S. The interaction of cognitive and physiological determinants of emotional state. In

L. Berkowitz (Ed.), *Advances in experimental social psychology*. New York: Academic Press, 1964.

Schaefer, S. Chrysalis: A holistic treatment model for chemically dependent women. *Grassroots*, 1980, *37*, 41–42.

Schaefer, S., & Evans, S. *Affectional preference and chemical dependency: Treatment considerations*. Paper presented at the Conference on Chemical Abuse and Sexuality: Defining the Relationships, University of Minnesota, Minneapolis, September 1980.

Schaefer, S., & Evans, S. *Women's sexuality and alcoholism*. Paper presented at the International Conference on Alcoholism, Oxford, England, April 1982.

Schuckit, M. A. Sexual disturbance in the woman alcoholic. *Medical Aspects of Human Sexuality*, 1972, *6*, 44–65.

Schuckit, M. A., Pitts, F. N., Reich, T., King, L. J., & Winokur, G. Alcoholism. I. Two types of alcoholism in women. *Archives of General Psychiatry*, 1969, *20*, 301–306.

Sclare, A. B. The female alcoholic. *British Journal of Addiction*, 1970, *65*, 99–107.

Sclare, A. B. Alcohol problems in women. In J. S. Madden, R. Walker, & W. H. Kenyon (Eds.), *Alcoholism and drug dependence: A multidisciplinary approach*. New York: Plenum Press, 1977.

Sherfey, M. J. *The nature and evolution of female sexuality*. New York: Vintage Books, 1973.

Sholty, M. J. *Female sexual experience and satisfaction as related to alcohol consumption*. Unpublished manuscript, Alcohol and Drug Abuse Program, University of Maryland, Baltimore, 1979.

Smithurst, B. A., & Armstrong, J. L. Social background of 171 women attending a female venereal disease clinic in Brisbane. *Medical Journal of Australia*, 1975, *1*, 339–343.

Spalt, L. Sexual behavior and the affective disorders. *Diseases of the Nervous System*, 1975, *36*, 644–647.

Swanson, D. W., Loomis, S. D., Lukesh, R., Cronin, R., & Smith, J. A. Clinical features of the female homosexual patient: A comparison with the heterosexual patient. *Journal of Nervous and Mental Disease*, 1972, *155*, 119–124.

Tamerin, J. S. The psychotherapy of alcoholic women. In S. Zimberg, J. Wallace, & S. B. Blume (Eds.), *Practical approaches to alcoholism psychotherapy*. New York: Plenum Press, 1978.

Van Thiel, D. H., & Lester, R. The effect of chronic alcohol abuse on sexual function. *Clinics in Endocrinology and Metabolism*, 1979, *8*, 499–510.

Wall, J. H. A study of alcoholism in women. *American Journal of Psychiatry*, 1937, *93*, 943–952.

Whitfield, C. L., Redmond, A. C., & Quinn, S. J. *Alcohol use, alcoholism, and sexual functioning*. Unpublished manuscript, University of Maryland School of Medicine, 1979.

Williams, K. H. An overview of sexual problems in alcoholism. In J. Newman (Ed.), *Sexual counseling for persons with alcohol problems: Proceedings of a workshop*. Pittsburgh: Western Pennsylvania Institute of Alcohol Studies, University of Pittsburgh, 1976.

Wilmot, R. Sexual drinking and drift. *Journal of Drug Issues*, Winter, 1981, 1–16.

Wilsnack, S. C. The effects of social drinking on women's fantasy. *Journal of Personality*, 1974, *42*, 43–61.

Wilsnack, S. C. The impact of sex roles on women's alcohol use and abuse. In M. Greenblatt & M. A. Schuckit (Eds.), *Alcoholism problems in women and children*. New York: Grune & Stratton, 1976.

Wilsnack, S. C., Klassen, A. D., & Wilsnack, R. W. *Drinking, sexual experience, and reproductive dysfunction among women in a 1981 national survey*. Paper presented at the 14th Annual Medical-Scientific Conference of the National Alcoholism Forum, Houston, Texas, April 1983.

Wilson, G. T. Alcohol and human sexual behavior. *Behaviour Research and Therapy*, 1977, *15*, 239–252.

Wilson, G. T. The effects of alcohol on human sexual behavior. In N. K. Mello (Ed.), *Advances in substance abuse* (Vol. 2). Greenwich, Conn.: JAI Press, 1981.

Wilson, G. T., & Lawson, D. M. Effects of alcohol on sexual arousal in women. *Journal of Abnormal Psychology*, 1976, *85*, 489–497. (a)

Wilson, G. T., & Lawson, D. M. Expectancies, alcohol, and sexual arousal in male social drinkers. *Journal of Abnormal Psychology*, 1976, *85*, 587–594. (b)

Wilson, G. T., & Lawson, D. M. Expectancies, alcohol, and sexual arousal in women. *Journal of Abnormal Psychology*, 1978, *87*, 358–367.

Wood, H. P., & Duffy, E. L. Psychosocial factors in alcoholic women. *American Journal of Psychiatry*, 1966, *123*, 341–345.

Ziebold, T. O. *Alcoholism and the gay community.* Washington, D.C.: Whitman–Walker Clinic, Blade Communications, n.d.

Zucker, R. A., Battistich, V. A., & Langer, G. B. Sexual behavior, sex-role adaptation and drinking in young women. *Journal of Studies on Alcohol*, 1981, *42*, 457–465.

Zucker, R. A., & Devoe, C. I. Life history characteristics associated with problem drinking and antisocial behavior in adolescent girls: A comparison with male findings. In R. D. Wirt, G. Winokur, & M. Roff (Eds.), *Life history research in psychopathology* (Vol. 4). Minneapolis: University of Minnesota, 1975.

ANTECEDENTS AND CONSEQUENCES OF ALCOHOL PROBLEMS IN WOMEN

The first chapter in this section (Chapter 8), by Gomberg and Lisansky, provides a broad overview of biological, psychological, and sociocultural antecedents of female alcoholism. The other two chapters describe specific consequences of alcohol abuse: violence between spouses, generally by the husband toward the wife (Frieze & Schafer, Chapter 9); and effects of female alcohol abuse on the family during different stages of the life cycle (Williams & Klerman, Chapter 10).

Gomberg and Lisansky are interested in antecedent events that increase the probability of alcohol problems among women. Antecedents are defined as life events and responses that occur prior to the beginning of excessive drinking. Various ways of conceptualizing antecedents are discussed, including risk factors, etiology, vulnerability, and motives for drinking. Generalizations and predictions about subpopulations to which an individual belongs are usually considered as risk factors, while the term "vulnerability" generally refers to characteristics of the individual (both biological and psychological) that increase the likelihood of alcohol problems. Within each of three developmental periods (childhood, adolescence, and young adulthood), biological and genetic factors, personality and coping mechanisms, sociocultural factors and roles, and family and peer influences may all be antecedents of alcoholism in women. For instance, adolescent antecedents that occur prior to the development of alcoholism in adulthood possibly include inadequate coping devices; personality characteristics such as distrust of people, maladaptive impulsivity, and depression; and peer pressure.

Gomberg and Lisansky emphasize that there are multiple paths to the onset of alcoholism that include biological, behavioral, and social events that may occur at different points in a person's developmental history. The authors' "prudent conclusion" is that there are similarities and differences in the antecedents, course, and consequences of alcoholism for the two sexes. Since men and women experience different socialization processes and different sanctions for drinking, it is likely that at least some events that lead to onset of alcoholism for men and women will be different. Gomberg and Lisansky's inclusive scheme for analyzing antecedents provides an excellent prototype for future interdisciplinary research in an area that is all too often characterized by a narrow focus on limited sets of antecedent variables.

Because of the lack of information regarding the effects of alcohol on aggressive behavior in women, Frieze and Schafer's chapter concentrates primarily on women as recipients of alcohol-related physical violence by men. The chapter highlights the fact, often neglected in the literature on women and alcohol, that some important "alcohol problems" experienced by women result not from women's own drinking but from that of others. Alcohol use among men is associated with criminal activity, including homicide and assault, and with marital violence in the home. High rates of drinking problems have been reported in the husbands of battered women, and wives of men with drinking problems frequently report that violence is a problem in their marriages. However, the causal role of alcohol use in marital violence is ambiguous: Drinking may serve as an excuse for marital violence rather than being a direct causal factor. Frieze's own research suggests that there are many ways in which alcohol use relates to marital violence. For only one subgroup of the couples she studied did drinking appear to be causal in the violence. Thus, violence can be prevented or reduced by curbing the husband's alcohol use only for this subgroup of violent couples.

While physical aggression is frequently associated with alcohol consumption in men, it is not commonly found in women who drink. Even the few women in Frieze's research who were at least moderately violent toward their spouses when they were drinking appeared to exhibit violence not as a result of their own drinking, but rather in reaction to the alcohol-induced violence of their drinking husbands. A possible explanation for women's being less violent when they drink involves physical size and strength differences that result in women's not being reinforced for violent behavior.

Female and male reactions to alcohol, Frieze and Schafer suggest, can best be explained by a cognitive model that predicts a drinker's reactions based upon the social context in which drinking occurs and the prior expectations of the person about how alcohol will affect him or her. The authors contend that alcohol has physiological effects (e.g., flushing, increased heart rate) that are not readily attributable to the drug and that may be more variable in women than in men due to alcohol's interactions with female hormone levels. Thus, women in particular may have unexplained arousal after drinking, which they may be likely to misattribute as feelings of sexuality and warmth toward their partners. Men, on the other hand, have been socialized to feel strong and powerful and thus may be more likely to interpret alcohol-induced bodily changes as feelings of power or aggression. Frieze and Schafer's cognitive model is consistent with much of the research on drinking and sexual responsiveness in women reviewed by S. Wilsnack in

Chapter 7. The model suggests a number of testable hypotheses for future self-report and behavioral studies of women and men drinkers.

The final chapter of this section, by Williams and Klerman, comprehensively examines the interactions between family relationships and excessive drinking by women during four life stages: adolescence, the childrearing years, the "empty nest" period, and the older years. The authors emphasize that as women move from one life stage to another, change occurs in their roles outside the home as well as in their relationships and responsibilities to both their families of origin and their families of procreation. Therefore, excessive alcohol use may serve different purposes and have different familial impacts at various stages of women's lives.

Studies of adolescence have tended to focus on the impact of parental behavior on adolescent drinking patterns, as discussed also by Thompson and Wilsnack (see Chapter 2). The family life of problem-drinking female adolescents and of women who later become alcoholic shows impaired parent–child relationships and is characterized by separation, neglect, erratic discipline, and poor parenting. There is little research on the effects of excessive adolescent drinking on other family members. Alcohol abuse by young women may impact indirectly on family life through its influence on sexual activity.

Women are more likely than men to cite marital instability and family problems as reasons both for problem drinking and for seeking treatment. There is little empirical information on the effects of a wife's drinking on her husband, his relationship to the children under such circumstances, and the dynamics that perpetuate the wife's drinking or help her to maintain sobriety. Some data are available, however, on alcoholic wives' views of themselves and their marriages and on characteristics of husbands of alcoholic wives. Alcoholic women are more likely to have husbands with drinking problems than are women in general, and such husbands may play an important role in the maintenance of women's problem drinking.

The majority of studies on children of alcoholics have been completed within the last 10 years. Most are exploratory in nature and describe personality characteristics of the children. Parenting patterns, sex-role modeling, and family dynamics have largely been ignored. Most studies involve families with alcoholic fathers, and it is unknown whether such findings are generalizable to families with alcoholic mothers. Williams and Klerman suggest that mother–daughter identification and modeling may have a greater effect on women's drinking patterns than was previously suspected. While sons of alcoholics were heavier drinkers than daughters, irrespective of which parent was alcoholic, daughters in several studies were heavier drinkers specifically if their mothers were heavy drinkers or alcoholics. Because the description of the environment of their family of origin provided by alcoholic parents appears to be similar to those provided by their children, the role of inadequate parenting in the perpetuation of alcohol problems needs to be further explored.

The "empty nest," which occurs when children leave home, has been used to explain later-onset drinking in women, and several studies appear to support this view. However, Williams and Klerman note that changing roles and opportunities for women may decrease the stressful nature of the empty nest period for many women and perhaps reduce the likelihood of excessive drinking at this stage of life. Although elderly female alcoholics have rarely been studied, the composite picture that emerges from available data is that of a widow, living alone or in an institution, often in economic distress, and with limited family contacts.

The difficulty of separating antecedents and effects in this complex area means that the content of the chapters in this section shows some overlap. For instance, when Williams and Klerman discuss the possible implications of demographic trends for female drinking or the effects of parental behavior on adolescent drinking, they are considering antecedents. In reality, many of the variables discussed both by Gomberg and Lisansky and by Williams and Klerman probably have reciprocal relationships to drinking, such that a factor initially contributing to female alcohol abuse (e.g., conflict with parent or spouse) is subsequently intensified as a result of the woman's excessive drinking.

Williams and Klerman's coverage also slightly overlaps that of Frieze and Schafer. Both consider the effects of female alcoholism on child abuse. Both chapters conclude, contrary to popular opinion, that there are no empirical data to support a simple relationship between child abuse and alcoholism in mothers.

All three chapters of this section appear to have important implications for preventing or minimizing women's alcohol problems. Gomberg and Lisansky point out that knowledge of antecedents is essential for defining goals of prevention programs and specifying the groups toward which they are targeted. Williams and Klerman present a number of recommendations for future research and service provision to reduce alcohol problems in women and their negative effects on women's families. And Frieze and Schafer's chapter underscores the need for attention to problems related to others' drinking (such as alcohol-related marital violence, rape, or highway accidents) in comprehensive prevention programming for women.

8

Antecedents of Alcohol Problems in Women

EDITH S. LISANSKY GOMBERG
University of Michigan

JUDITH M. LISANSKY
Rutgers—The State University

INTRODUCTION

Ideally, to demonstrate cause and effect, event A must lead to event B, and, in fact, event B would not occur without the preexistence of A. An acceptable alternative is a sequence in which the earlier event increases the probability that the later event will occur.

In studying the incredibly complex materials of life histories, we are not likely to demonstrate ideal cause-and-effect sequences and we accept an event as causal if it significantly increases the probability of the effect. Robins (1972), discussing life-history research, comments:

> The attribution of cause is one of the most important and perplexing problems facing the researcher. . . . Using either a longitudinal design . . . or a retrospective design . . . the researcher is faced with the problem of interpreting the sequence of events presented. (p. 137)

The more neutral term, "antecedents," which is currently replacing terms like "cause" or "etiology," indicates that the antecedent phenomenon preexisted or came before the behavior under study. It is, perhaps, too broad a term, since it includes everything that has occurred before the phenomenon under study existed: the totality of the individual's biochemical and psychosocial make-up and every event the individual has experienced. The question is, which antecedent events and experiences are relevant and causal? In the present context, which antecedent events and experiences increase the probability of problem drinking and alcoholism?

In an important way, our obeisance in alcohol studies to the multiplicity and complexity of events leading to problem drinking has begged the question and permitted some self-deception. Jellinek (1960) wryly noted that "the etiquette of the American alcoholism literature demands" acknowledgment of the etiological significance of all disciplines. But Jellinek adds:

With few exceptions, however, after having made the prescribed bow, specialists proceed to formulate their etiological theories exclusively in terms of their respective disciplines. (p. 13)

Stating that etiology is complex and multifaceted then permits each investigator to present his or her views as the key to understanding, while still remaining virtuous. A sentence in the introduction of an alcohol paper stating that etiology is complex and includes biological, psychological, and social factors, is sufficient to demonstrate that the researcher really holds a broad view. He or she may then go on to write of factor X or event Y as etiological and have the comfort of having assured the reader that this is only part of the complexity of causation. Few in alcohol research will state an alternative view as openly and frankly as did Goodwin (1976), when reporting his genetic studies. He said:

> Our findings tend to contradict the oft-repeated assertion that alcoholism results from the interaction of multiple causes—social, psychological, biological. This may be true of milder forms of alcoholism, but conceivably severe alcoholism could be relatively uninfluenced by environment, given free access to alcohol. (p. 77)

Some writers, in reviewing the literature about women and alcohol, refer to the "nonspecificity" of antecedent events. It is quite true that many of the antecedents discussed in the alcohol literature, for example, disrupted early family history, also appear significantly often in the histories of persons presenting disordered behaviors other than alcoholism. This observation does not render such antecedents irrelevant to the genesis of alcoholism, but rather it leads to the question: What else must there be besides the nonspecific factors?

It is our assumption that events leading to alcohol problems in adult life are myriad, that causation is indeed complex and interactional. Nonetheless, in spite of its complexity, we assume a lawfulness. It is not random selection or blind fate that determines problem drinking, but events in certain combinations and sequences that lead a person into problem drinking. The fact that defining the events and the sequence is a huge task need not halt the process of research. Scientists are in the early stages of such a process, assembling data about biological, psychological, and social variables so that prediction of problem drinking can be made in the future with greater accuracy.

Events always occur in a chain or sequence. Turmoil in one's family of origin leads to bad feelings, which lead to covering up such bad feelings, which leads to hidden angers, and so on. Furthermore, each chain or sequence is unique just as every human being's life history is unique. However, we do assume a pattern: Certain events and experiences occur in sequence often enough in the lives of alcoholics to be pinpointed as antecedents that increase the probability of problem drinking.

Is there a body of theory about the antecedents of male alcoholism? Most research was, until recently, confined to the male alcoholic (or gender differences were ignored). Thus, there have been a number of psychosocial views espoused: the psychoanalytic view of antecedents of male alcoholism, including concepts of regression, infantile fixation, orality and the like (Lisansky, 1960); a behavioristic view that emphasizes the role of alcohol in reduction of fear, conflict, and tension (Dollard & Miller, 1950); the assumption that psychological dependence is the pivotal concept in the origins of male alcoholism (McCord & McCord, 1960); and, more recently, the view that men drink and develop alcohol problems because alcohol use is tied to power motives and heavy drinking enhances men's feelings of power (McClelland, Davis, Kalin, & Wanner, 1972).

Even if there were a sound body of theory and knowledge about male alcoholism, to what extent could it be generalized to women? That there are gender differences in biological functioning and socialization is evident. We assume, therefore, that there are also important gender differences in the antecedents of alcoholism. At the same time, both sexes experience stress and loss, both sexes manifest depression and other symptomatic behaviors, and, for both sexes, alcohol ingestion affects mind and body. The most prudent conclusion is that there are similarities and differences in the antecedents as well as in the course and consequences of alcoholism for the two sexes. This is, however, an academic matter, since there is a sparse body of information about the antecedents of male alcoholism and even less about the antecedents of female alcoholism.

A Definition and Some Limits

There has been ambiguity in the use of the term "antecedents." One approach to defining antecedents views life stages diagramatically:

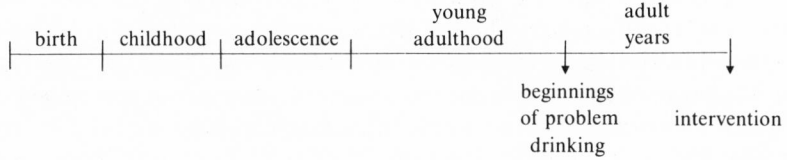

In this diagram, we can define antecedents as life events and responses that occur prior to the beginnings of problem drinking. At that point in the life cycle when the person enters the rehabilitation system, we are dealing with a complicated combination of antecedents that predate the onset of problem drinking, the consequences and effects of excessive drinking, and the drinking itself as the cause of more drinking, increasing isolation and social response, and increasing dependency on alcohol.

No one denies that living and drinking are dynamic processes in which change is recurrent. But as Jellinek (1960) tried to delineate in his description of the "phases" of alcoholism, there are phases and there is a beginning. Such a beginning can be defined in terms of an increase in the amount consumed, behaviors relating to drinking ("sneaking," "gulping"), troubles caused by the drinking, a particular level of dependency, clear indications of continued escape drinking, or whatever—there is a beginning. We define antecedents as the life events and responses that led up to that beginning.

Some Viewpoints about Antecedents of Female Alcoholism

Although information is thin, there have been a number of different approaches to the question of antecedents of problem drinking and alcoholism in women.

RISK FACTORS

A recent review of research findings relating to antecedents of alcoholism divides risk factors quite conventionally into physiological antecedents, psychological vulnerability, drinking behaviors, and social-environmental factors (Gomberg, 1980b). All of these are discussed as antecedent determinants of alcoholism in an individual.

Another way to view risk factors is to look at large segments of the population and to define risk factors in terms of what is known about the distribution of alcoholism in the population. A listing of such risk factors by Goodwin (1981) includes family history, sex, age, school difficulty, occupation, race, ethnicity, religion, geographic region, and income. Thus, there are data to indicate that having a history of alcoholism in the family, being male, being in certain age periods of adult life, and living in an urban community put one at higher risk for developing alcohol problems. Research done some years ago on drinking and alcohol problems among Irish-Americans and other U.S. ethnic and religious groups (e.g., Bales, 1944; Glad, 1947) was similarly directed toward gaining knowledge about high-risk and low-risk ethnic populations, and such studies continue. There are also studies of people in different occupational categories to determine high and low rates of alcohol problems (e.g., Cosper, 1979; Hitz, 1973). Epidemiological data on urban and rural drinking and on drinking behaviors in different regions of the United States contribute to the prediction of high- and low-risk subgroups of the population (Clark & Midanik, 1982).

ETIOLOGY

A "general etiological theory" about the causes of "increasing drinking problems amongst women" has been conceptualized (Cartwright & Shaw, 1978; Shaw, 1980). Shaw states that the evidence demonstrates the etiology of female problem drinking to be "multifactorial." Etiology here includes economic, social, psychological, and physiological variables that determine why, what, and when people drink and the degree of resistance or vulnerability to drinking problems. Economic factors include recent changes in availability of alcoholic beverages, prices, advertising, and increased consumption by women. These authors believe that women manifest physical and psychological vulnerability to drinking problems, but that such vulnerability has in the past been offset by "higher sociological protection."

An etiological theory that deals with psychosocial processes associated with alcoholism has been presented by Kinsey (1966). From this theory Kinsey derived a number of hypotheses, which he tested with a sample of state hospital alcoholic women. In this view, there is a set of "predisposing" factors, a constellation or core of personality traits, and a set of "orienting" factors, such as membership in groups with norms that encourage heavy and hedonistic drinking. Alcohol dependence arises from increasing alienation from normal drinking groups and increasing affiliation with heavy drinking groups.

Roebuck and Kessler (1972) devoted an entire volume to discussion of the etiology of alcoholism and the approaches to explanation by the various disciplines. These authors review the viewpoints of biochemists, psychologists, sociologists, physiologists, and anthropologists about the causes of alcoholism.

VULNERABILITY

Whereas generalizations and predictions about subpopulations are usually subsumed under risk factors, the term "vulnerability" has generally been used to refer to individual factors that increase the likelihood of alcohol problems. Thus, Jellinek (1960) contrasted societal norms about drinking with psychological or physical individual vulnerability:

> In societies which have a low degree of acceptance of large daily amounts of alcohol, mainly those will be exposed to the risk of addiction who on account of high psychological vulnerability have an inducement to go against the social standards. But in societies which have an extremely high degree of acceptance of large daily alcohol consumption, the presence of any small vulnerability, whether psychological or physical, will suffice for exposure to the risk of addiction. (pp. 28–29)

Hill (1981) has proposed "a vulnerability model," which would merge both biological and psychosocial approaches. Her model includes biological vulnerability and psychosocial vulnerability factors unique to women. Alcoholism is viewed as the "joint expression" of such vulnerability, coupled with the occurrence of life events or stressors. Hill diagrams her model as shown in Figure 8-1.

Hill's model is an attempt to account for alcoholism "as an evolving process rather than a static end point," suggesting perhaps that other models view alcoholism as an all-or-none phenomenon. The problem remains as to

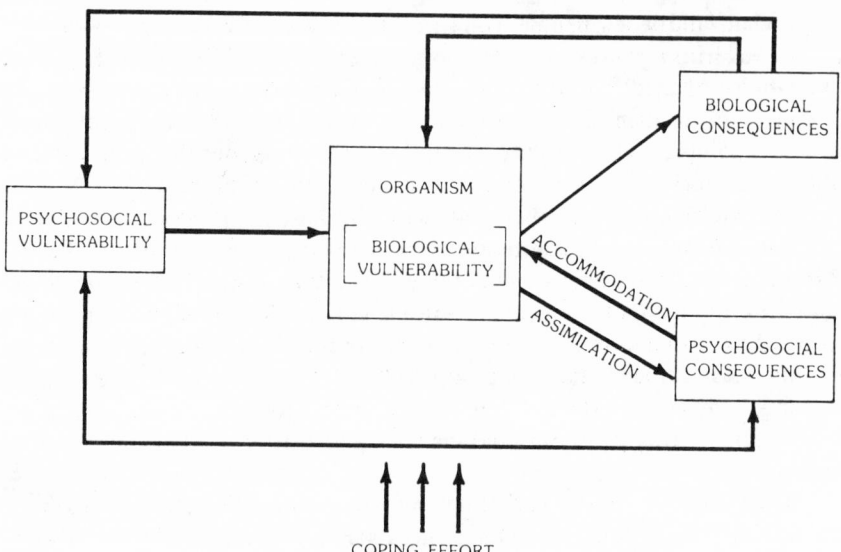

FIGURE 8-1. A vulnerability model for alcoholism in women. From S. Hill, A vulnerability model for alcoholism in women, Focus on Women: Journal of Addictions and Health, 1981, 2, 68–91. Reprinted by permission.

which events this "evolving process" encompasses. There can be no disagreement that, after problem drinking starts, a woman's life is further complicated by the consequences of the drinking. But there remain several questions of significance to the clinician and researcher: Can we determine when the onset of problem drinking occurs or is there no beginning that can be defined? Moreover, once the problem drinking has begun, how are we to separate the prealcoholic "evolving processes" from later events, and how are we to define the early, middle, and later phases of the alcoholic process?

MOTIVES FOR DRINKING AND ALCOHOLISM

Edwards, Hensman, and Peto (1973), in comparing men's and women's motivations for drinking, found that relief of unpleasant feelings and celebration drinking strongly related to the amount women drank, and social pressure to drink was strongly related to problem drinking. Social pressure to drink may come from family members, friends, social networks—in the home, at school, on the job, in the country club, at parties, on dates, and so on.

Fillmore's (1974, 1975) longitudinal study of college drinkers followed into midlife suggests that when young women manifest "psychological dependence" on alcohol for relief of unpleasant feelings, they are more likely to develop drinking problems in adult life.

In a report on "perceived antecedents" of women's alcohol consumption, Beckman (1980) compared alcoholic women with alcoholic men, women in psychiatric treatment for neurotic disorders, and "normal" women. When compared with the nonalcoholic groups, both alcoholic men and women reported being more likely to drink for "escapist" reasons and greater likelihood of experiencing positive affect from drinking. Alcoholic women reported more feelings of powerlessness and inadequacy before drinking than did the other groups. These reported motives for drinking are, it should be noted, motives for current drinking, and whether they are applicable to earlier stages of problem drinking or to prealcoholic drinking is an important question. Are the motives that lead to heavy drinking at the beginning of an alcoholic career the same motives one sees later in that career?

Finally, there is the clinical observation of sex differences in patients' reports of their reasons for problem drinking. Male patients very often relate problem drinking to work-related pressures, and female patients relate it to family problems (Kielholz, 1970). Perhaps these are less motives than rationalizations for drinking: What is sought by both sexes is relief or escape from pressure, tension, and unhappiness generated from different life areas.

To sum up, there is general agreement that predictors should include both biological and psychosocial factors. And although authors use different terms such as "etiology," "vulnerability," and "predisposition," these seem to describe two major kinds of predictors. One set of predictors involves the subgroups to which a person belongs, his or her social identity groups. Thus, one is defined socially as belonging to an age group, a gender group, an ethnic and/or religious group, an occupational group, and so on. Research suggests that not all subgroups of the population are at equally high risk, that is, equally likely to develop alcohol problems. If an individual belongs to subgroups that have high rates of alcoholism, this presumably increases his or her likelihood of alcohol problems. Subgroup predictors should be expanded to include life-event subgroups that may be at increased risk for alcohol problems, for example, the recently divorced, the recently widowed, or the laid off worker. A second set of predictors consists of factors contained within the organism, both biological and psychological. These factors are involved in terms like "vulnerability," and clearly imply a susceptibility or a readiness to develop alcohol problems that the person carries from birth (genetics?), from childhood (ego psychology?), or from recent learning (behaviorism?). Related to this second set of predictors are motives for drinking, or the needs the individual seeks to satisfy with alcohol.

Finally, it would appear that one of the best predictors for problem drinking or alcoholism is the drinking behavior itself. Drinking in particular ways, under particular circumstances, for particular reasons, in earlier life seems to be one of the best ways to predict trouble at a later age.

Why Study Antecedents?

This question is legitimate. When a person appears at a treatment facility, whether it is a detoxification unit for homeless people or a luxurious private facility, that individual is well past the point in his or her life at which the alcoholic drinking began. What facility personnel see is not the beginning of alcoholism but a complicated mixture of prealcoholic antecedents, recent motives for drinking, and consequences of drinking, which often act as triggers or antecedents for more drinking bouts. Family interactions and the attitudes of parents, spouse, children, and other relatives, the self-view of the drinker, the effect of the drinking on work and the response of the employer, police warnings and arrests, negative effects on health—all are part of the admission picture. These characteristics must be given priority because they are the complications of the drinking and are, in a sense, the problem itself and the reason the patient is there. Persons do not enter treatment facilities at the first signs of alcoholism. They come with histories of 2, 5, 10, or 15 years of problem drinking and its complications, and helpers first must deal with the most recent crises and stresses, the here and now.

Nonetheless, antecedents of alcoholism, as we have defined them, are of primary importance in developing effective prevention programs. The work to date in prevention has made it clear that to be effective, prevention programs must have clear goals and be targeted toward specific groups (see Gomberg, 1980a). The knowledge of antecedents of alcoholism is essential for defining these goals and target groups for primary prevention.

An Admission to a Treatment Facility: A History

Louise, a white, 38-year-old woman, is admitted to an alcoholism rehabilitation facility. She has been having some health problems and her concern about those and about her children's problems in school precipitated her coming to the facility. She arrives at the facility with her sister and a concerned friend.

Louise's early history is reasonably positive, but her father was a heavy drinker and there were family quarrels at times about his drinking. Her family of origin was middle-class. Louise's mother was a housewife with few outside interests. Louise attended college for 2 years, but left when she married at age 20. The marriage lasted 10 years and there were two children, a boy now 15 and a girl now 12. After the divorce, Louise worked at several semiskilled clerical jobs, but she is currently unemployed. She says that she began drinking heavily with her husband. Most of her drinking has been at home with a companion or alone, although she has occasionally gone to bars with her ex-husband and, more recently, with her boyfriend. The latter, a few years younger than Louise, moved in with her 2 years ago. He and her children do not get along very well.

Louise has used tranquilizers and other medications. Although she uses marijuana occasionally and, on rarer occasions, cocaine, her first drug of abuse is alcohol. She has been drinking heavily for about 10 years. Despite periods of sobriety which sometimes last for several months, she has always returned to heavy drinking.

The bare outlines of this life story point up some of our problems: It is too late here to talk of primary prevention. But it is not too late to learn what we can about the life events and responses that brought Louise to the beginnings of problem drinking. The question "why?" must be divided into those biological and psychosocial events that contribute to an answer. The question "why?" must also be divided into events and responses as they occur at different stages of the life cycle, for to jumble together events in infancy with events in adolescence and early adulthood makes no sense. We propose then to discuss antecedents to the beginnings of problem drinking in the ways listed in Table 8-1.

CHILDHOOD ANTECEDENTS

Biological and Genetic Factors

In general, researchers agree that alcoholism occurs in the family histories of both men and women alcoholics to a greater extent than is true of the general population. The trend of evidence is that rates of alcoholism are higher in the families of women than men alcoholics (Cotton, 1979; Gomberg, 1980b) although this is occasionally challenged (Hoffman & Noem, 1975). Up to the 1970s, the general view was that alcoholism was learned from heavy-drinking or alcoholic parents. However, a series of studies in the United States and Denmark has had a profound impact on alcohol research (Goodwin, 1976, 1979; Goodwin, Schulsinger, Knop, Mednick, & Guze, 1977). Interestingly, in the studies of adopted children of alcoholic parents, results are much clearer for men than for women. The sons of alcoholics,

TABLE 8-1. Antecedents of Problem Drinking in Women

	Childhood	Adolescence	Young adulthood
Biological and genetic factors	Genetics	Menses	Obstetrical/gynecological events
Personality and coping mechanisms	Learned ways of coping	Inadequate coping devices	Depression, sex-role conflicts
Sociocultural factors and roles	Class and ethnicity	School, religion	Adult roles and stresses
Drinking: family and peer influences	Parents' and family drinking patterns	Parents, peers, and siblings	Drinking of spouse and significant others

raised in nonalcoholic adoptive families, were more likely to be alcoholic in adult life than adopted males whose natural parents were not alcoholic. This difference applies only to the incidence of severe alcoholism. Goodwin (1976) hypothesizes that "severe or 'classic' forms of alcoholism may have mainly a genetic basis, whereas heavy drinking may have mainly psychosocial origins" (p. 79).

Results from a parallel study of adopted daughters are more ambiguous and inconclusive. There is, however, an important finding: Daughters of alcoholics raised in their own families manifested significantly more depression than daughters of alcoholics raised in nonalcoholic families and more than the control adoptive group with no history of family alcoholism (Goodwin *et al.*, 1977). Another finding relative to antecedents is that the sons of alcoholics manifested more childhood hyperactivity, truancy, and school phobia than controls; the daughters showed no such behaviors, but they were described as "more friendless as children."

Some more recently reported work indicates more support for genetic factors in adopted daughters of alcoholic biological parents (Bohman, Sigvardsson, & Cloninger, 1981). Interestingly, alcoholism in daughters was more clearly linked in this study to alcoholism in the biological mother than in the father.

Other research, for example, twin studies and the search for "genetic markers," either has not included women subjects or has yielded inconclusive results.

In addition to genetics, there have been hypotheses about biological antecedents of alcoholism that include enzymatic and nutritional deficiencies (Williams, 1951), presence of a "resentment substance" (Fleetwood, 1955), endocrinopathology (Bleuler, 1955), and vitamin deficiency (Greenberg & Lester, 1957). None of these hypotheses is strongly supported. The most widespread point of view, not held by research scientists, is the "allergy theory," which assumes vaguely that some people are born with an allergy to alcoholic beverages that manifests itself in alcoholism. There is no supporting scientific evidence for this view.

Personality and Coping Mechanisms

In a discussion of psychoanalytic views of alcoholism, Blum (1966) writes of some of the circumstances involved in the failure to grow. The alcoholic's developmental failure is linked to "undue dependency," to love–hate relationships with parents, and to fixation at or regression to oral, anal, or phallic–oedipal levels. This description is limited to male alcoholism and it is unclear how to generalize the theory to women.

There are few clues that delineate the behaviors alcoholic women manifested as young children. Goodwin's comment that the daughters of alcoholic biological parents were "more friendless as children" (Goodwin *et al.*, 1977), and the significant relationship between being raised in an alcoholic family and reported depression as adults, is suggestive. There are few longitudinal data that permit us to see alcoholic women's patterns of behavior as children (Robins, Bates, & O'Neal, 1962; Jones, 1971). Corrigan (1980) suggests that alcoholic women report feelings of deprivation in childhood. She compared alcoholic women with their nonalcoholic sisters and found that the former perceive their parents differently than do their nonalcoholic sisters. They recall receiving less approval from their parents.

The consistent findings of disruption in early family life (alcoholism, death of a parent, divorce, absent parent) suggest that such disruption is a common experience among those who later develop alcohol problems. When men and women who manifest alcoholic behaviors are compared, women more frequently report such disruption (Gomberg, 1980b). Among alcoholic women, there is indication that they see their early childhood experience as one of rejection and deprivation. One may go a step further and hypothesize anger and resentment, negative feelings that are not expressed overtly or constructively.

Sociocultural Factors and Roles

An individual is born into a set of identities or socially defined roles. These identities are formed by the immediate family and the extended family, by the family's church, social groups, organizations, neighborhood, and community. One line of research that has stood up well over the last decades has examined ethnic or subcultural, social-class, geographical, and rural–urban differences in rules and regulations surrounding drinking (e.g., Heath, 1976; Mandelbaum, 1979).

Women and men are socialized as members of a community, social class, ethnic group, and religion, and as such they tend to identify with the norms and attitudes of these groups toward alcohol. Ethnic research has shown that some groups have higher rates and other groups lower rates of alcohol problems, but whether this is generalizable to the women of those groups is uncertain. In some groups, for example, Irish-Americans, the women as well as the men show higher rates of alcoholism than the general population (Stivers, 1976). On the other hand, Hispanic male alcoholism rates are relatively high, but rates appear to be very low among Hispanic women in the United States (Hall, Chaikin, & Piland, 1977).

The norms about drinking vary in clarity, and for some groups drinking norms are quite ambiguous. Ullman (1958) hypothesizes:

> In any group or society in which the drinking customs, values and sanctions—
> together with the attitudes of all segments of the group or society—are well

established, known to and agreed upon by all, and are consistent with the rest of the culture, the rate of alcoholism will be low. (p. 50)

Drinking: Family and Peer Influences

While a child is growing up, there are adult role models, usually parents, who may abstain, drink moderately, become intoxicated occasionally, or drink heavily. Alcohol may play a very insignificant role in the family life: It may either be absent altogether or be used only for family celebrations. Alcohol may, on the other hand, play a very significant role in the family life: There may be frequent incidents of intoxication, quarrels, even violence. And between these two extremes of childhood experience are a myriad of childhood experiences with alcohol.

One of the authors (ESLG) has, for some years now, requested that students enrolled in a university course on substance use and abuse write an autobiography of early memories of alcohol in the family, and their own early and adolescent experiences with alcohol. It is impressive to note the impact of adult behaviors while intoxicated as these are observed by children in the family. This impact appears to be as strong in families where alcohol is not a problem as in families where it is. Whether alcohol has played a minor role or a central role in early family life, most students report some trial and error experience with alcohol in adolescence, usually associated with leaving the family nest. One gets the impression, however, that this trial and error is part of the growing up process for some: a declaration of independence. For others, usually those with a family history of alcohol abuse, the trial and error is filled with affect: conflict and anger.

The question of parental drinking practices as a possible source of intergenerational transmission of alcoholism has been raised in the past (Jackson & Connor, 1953), and recent emphasis on a family systems approach to alcoholism (Ablon, 1976) has reopened the question. Thus, a study by Wolin, Bennett, Noonan, and Teitelbaum (1980), which focused on disrupted family rituals as a factor in intergenerational transmission of alcoholism, suggests that even in families where one or both parents drink alcoholically, there are different effects of such behavior depending on whether family rituals are maintained or disrupted during periods of heaviest parental drinking.

The emphasis of such research on the nature of family life and the greater or lesser impact of the heavy drinking of a parent on family life is welcome. The importance of early perceptions of parental drinking and the influence such perceptions have upon later behavior is a research area that calls for further development. Studies are needed that compare the childhood impact of parental drinking for boys versus girls in families where drinking is heavy, moderate, or infrequent and in families where the heavy drinker is the father, the mother, or both.

ADOLESCENT ANTECEDENTS

Our emphasis here is not on adolescent female problem drinkers but rather on the role of antecedent factors that occur during the adolescence of those women who become problem drinkers as adults. Very little is known about young women who develop drinking problems while still in their teens: Clinical reports suggest that problem drinking in these early years may be linked to other acting out behaviors, such as sexual and antisocial behaviors, and possibly to street-drug abuse. There is also a suggestion in the information available that family response may be greater in the case of the young woman drinking heavily than in the case of the young man doing the same (Gomberg, 1979). It would be hardly surprising if that proved to be true.

Biological and Genetic Factors

The onset of menses occurs during the preadolescent and adolescent years. Attempts to link the menstrual cycle and the effects of alcohol are not new, and reports about this linkage tend to fall into three categories.

First, there are reports that show blood alcohol level varies with phases of the menstrual cycle (Jones & Jones, 1976). While this finding is limited to college women with no apparent alcohol problems, it does suggest a linkage between hormonal status and alcohol effects. Effects of alcohol also are different for those young women who take birth control pills and those who do not (Jones & Jones, 1976; Sutker, 1982).

Second, there are many reports linking the menstrual cycle to variations in mood, affect, symptoms, and suicidal behaviors (Abplanalp, Rose, Donnelly, & Livingston-Vaughan, 1979; Ivey & Bardwick, 1968; Moos, 1969; Sommer, 1978; Wetzel & McClure, 1972). Such research has many methodological problems, not the least of which is the biological and psychological variability of the cycle. Women's belief systems about the menstrual cycle are rarely included in menstruation–mood research, and research reports rarely link mood variations in the menstrual cycle with drinking behaviors.

A third category of studies are those that link the menstrual cycle, usually the premenstruum, to a psychological state, which in turn is linked to drinking. These studies have generally involved alcoholic women. Wall (1937) interpreted dysmenorrhea, reported by 80% of his women alcoholic patients, as "an insult or injury to a narcissistic personality" (p. 944). Lolli (1953) linked the premenstruum and "mild feelings of depression" (p. 10). Podolsky (1963) viewed premenstrual tension as related to the woman alcoholic's acceptance of her femininity or her life situation: Premenstrual tension is a stressful experience particularly for those alcoholic women who are depressed, tense, or lonely. Belfer, Shader, Carroll, & Harmatz (1971) reported that the mood changes of the menstrual cycle appear to have critical implications for the probability of occurrence of a variety of impulse-laden activities, as well as for the probability of active vs. passive coping behavior in response to environmental stress. (p. 543)

And, without defining the mood change of the premenstruum, Beckman (1979) asked alcoholic women and matched controls whether they drank more, less, or the same as usual during the week before the menstrual period. Significantly more alcoholic women reported increased drinking during the premenstruum than did the control group.

As an antecedent condition, the role of the menstrual cycle in female alcoholism needs clarification. The premenstruum and menstrual difficulties and stresses can be antecedent to alcoholic drinking in a very immediate sense; that is, such stress may precipitate or trigger a drinking bout. (Although it has never achieved sound empirical support, some case has been made for a relatively low tolerance for stress as characteristic of prealcoholic and alcoholic persons.) Menstrual difficulties are one of a myriad of stresses that can precipitate a drinking bout—a disappointment, a loss, a quarrel, or even a celebration. But the case for menstrual discomfort as an antecedent condition that brings on alcoholism in adult life remains weak. The effect of sustained, heavy drinking on the menstrual cycle and the role that such effects play in the continuation of drinking is an important area for future research. Another important area that merits investigation is the belief systems of alcoholic and nonalcoholic women about menstruation, about drinking, and about relationships between the two.

Somewhere between biological and psychological antecedents, perhaps a question should be raised about the contribution of adolescent sexual experience. Little is known about the sexual activity and sexual experience of women who develop drinking problems: Is there a high incidence of early sexual activity, a history of sexual abuse, or pregnancy in adolescence among women problem drinkers? And is such sexual activity related to drinking and problem drinking? Some of these questions are considered in detail by S. Wilsnack (Chapter 7) in this volume.

Personality and Coping Mechanisms

Research information about the psychological or behavioral aspects of adolescence that may be antecedent to later alcoholism is sparse. The only description available is by Jones (1971) in her longitudinal research. She followed up a sample of adult women on whom extensive personality and behavioral data had been collected in adolescence. The number of problem drinkers was small but the information—what they were like as adolescent girls—is consistent with clinical findings about adult women problem drinkers and is, at the very least, suggestive of hypotheses about antecedent adolescent behaviors related to later onset of alcohol problems. Jones found that the women who developed problem drinking as adults manifested "inadequate coping devices" in adolescence. She describes these women as they appeared during their adolescent years:

> She fears and rejects life, is distrustful of people, follows a religion which accentuates judgment and punishment. She escapes into ultrafemininity. . . . Problem drinkers of both sexes have in common . . . unstable, unpredictable impulsivity. . . . [Specific to women problem drinkers are] depressive, self-negating, distrustful tendencies. (p. 68)

This description includes a number of behaviors that are mentioned frequently in clinical and research descriptions of alcoholic women: (1) lack of trust; (2) maladaptive impulsivity; (3) low self-esteem; and (4) depression.

Jones states that those women who became problem drinkers as adults were judged, as adolescents, "to suffer profound emotional disturbance and social isolation" (p. 69). This agrees with Goodwin *et al.*'s (1977) description of the daughters of alcoholics as "more friendless [than the control group] as children and shy as adults" (p. 1008). It raises an interesting issue, one that Tracey and Nathan (1976) have explored in a study of four women alcoholics: To what extent is social isolation antecedent to problem drinking or a consequence of problem drinking, or—what is most likely—does the isolation precede the problem drinking and become intensified by it?

Differences between alcoholic women for whom alcohol problems appear relatively early in life and those for whom problems occur in the 30s and 40s have been emphasized (Gomberg, 1979). Both groups of women are seen in treatment facilities, although the latter group make up the largest proportion of women in the facilities. One hypothesis considers the coping mechanisms utilized by these different age groups and suggests that younger women alcoholics will present a history of impulse control problems, acting out, and overt rebelliousness to a greater extent than the older women alcoholics. Older women alcoholics, the hypothesis suggests, will have manifested more submissive behaviors as adolescents, and the current clinical picture will include more depression and guilt. If this hypothesis is supported, the psychological factors and coping mechanisms apparent in adolescence would be different in some ways for the two age-of-onset groups. These differences might be developmental or they might be cohort differences.

Sociocultural Factors and Roles

Adolescence, as we define it in the United States, is an apprenticeship period during which the person prepares to take on adult roles. Most adolescents, particularly the younger ones, are in school: junior high school, senior high school, or college. A sizable number of adolescents, particularly older adolescents, assume adult roles and go to work or enter the military and/or get married. Most authors who write about adolescence distinguish between early, middle, and later adolescent years.

The proportion of adolescents who engage in drinking behavior has risen over the last decades (Rachal, Williams, Brehm, Cavanaugh, Moore, & Eckerman, 1975). This appears to relate to an increase in so-called adult behaviors among adolescents, which includes sexual activity as well as drinking and drug-taking. Although there are still more males than females of high school age who drink, the gap between the sexes has narrowed (Johnston, Bachman, & O'Malley, 1980; Wechsler & McFadden, 1976). This would indicate that young women are probably subjected to more peer pressure to drink than was true a generation ago. Further, there are indications that the role of adult authority in minimizing drinking among young people, be it exercised through school, parents, church, or the law, has weakened over time.

One of the interesting facts that emerges from surveys of high school age students is the significant role of religious involvement. For those who are religiously affiliated and active, the likelihood of the use of substances such as alcohol is less. Relevant here is Jones's (1971) observation about the few women in her longitudinal study who became problem drinkers: She describes them as following "a religion which accentuates judgment and punishment" (p. 68). Such a description makes one wonder if the pious adolescent with overt distrust and denied anger will appear later in the angry, middle-aged, alcoholic woman.

In the later years of adolescence, social roles require many young people to leave the parental nest. They may go to college, find a job, join the military, or get married and establish a new family. Those who find jobs may or may not live with their families of origin, and there are some who decide, with parental financial help (usually middle-class or well-to-do parents), to live on their own even without jobs. What is significant is leaving the home of origin. Many write of "the empty nest," but what about the fledglings?

It is a reasonable hypothesis that there are stages in the leaving-home process and that the initial stage, with its accompanying mixed feelings of freedom and anxiety, very often includes some trial-and-error use of alcohol. Social attitudes toward such trial and error by young women, probably manifested in occasional intoxication, are quite different from social attitudes toward trial and error by young men (Gomberg, 1979). Such episodes, apart from the antipathy they generate and the social response, may indeed be useful prognosticators of future trouble. Fillmore (1975) found "frequent heavy drinking" during college to be the best predictor of later problem drinking among women. Perhaps the key lies in the word "frequent": Trial and error drinking may include one or even two experiences of intoxication, but if the heavy drinking is "frequent" in spite of the consequences, it promises future trouble.

Drinking: Family and Peer Influences

Adolescents, when they are surveyed, differentiate between drinking at home in the presence of parents and relatives, and drinking outside the home with peers. Heavier drinking is more likely to occur outside the home in the presence of other adolescents (Rachal, Maisto, Guess, & Hubbard, 1982). Studies indicate that adolescent drinking becomes more frequent, heavier and more problem-related as the extent of drinking among peers increases (Harford & Spiegler, 1982). Parents and peers are both important influences on adolescent drinking: Research findings show consistency between adolescents' drinking and parental approval or disapproval, and at the same time, peer attitudes and the amount of peer drinking also are very significant influences (Rachal et al., 1982).

On an epidemiological level, the proportion of adolescent girls who drink has moved closer to the proportion of adolescent boys who drink, although girls are still less likely than boys to be heavy drinkers (see Thompson & Wilsnack, this volume). This has led to a "convergence hypothesis": The rates for female alcoholism will eventually be the same as for male alcoholism as this generation of adolescent drinkers grows older. The percentage of adolescent girls who drink and those who drink frequently and/or heavily has increased, and logic dictates that future problem drinkers will be drawn from this population. Indeed, Fillmore's discussion in this volume reports that the female respondents of a 1979 survey who were in their 20s showed a higher rate of heavy drinking than past cohorts and suggests that we may also expect an increase in middle-aged women with drinking problems.

Several studies suggest possible adolescent predictors for individual women. Wilsnack and Wilsnack (1978) found a correlation between heavy drinking and rejection of traditional femininity among adolescent girls, suggesting rebelliousness as one predictor. In a longitudinal study of college women, Fillmore (1975) found the best predictor for female problem drinking in later life to be "frequent heavy drinking." There is also the conclusion drawn by Smart and Gray (1979), who studied the relative importance of parental, peer and demographic variables in predicting problem drinking among high school students: "It was found that problem drinking is best predicted with situational factors and those directly connected with drinking" (p. 912). The three most important variables in predicting adolescent problem drinking were: drinking in cars, not drinking at home, and being male.

YOUNG ADULTHOOD ANTECEDENTS

Biological and Genetic Factors

There are no definitely established biochemical antecedents or markers of alcoholism. It is true that women appear to be more prone than men to some of the complicating medical consequences of heavy drinking but, again, one cannot designate these effects of alcohol as antecedents of alcoholism.

What is unique to women is their gynecological and hormonal make-up and the fact that they experience pregnancy and childbirth. In looking at these biological factors, one finds a curious reversal of interest and attitude in the recent research literature. Studies of women with alcohol problems had suggested, on the basis of self-report from female subjects, that heavy drinking often began in response to obstetrical stress or disappointment. This might include difficulty in conceiving, difficulty in carrying to term, miscarriage, abortion, stillbirth, or hysterectomy. Kinsey's (1966) state hospital women alcoholics reported a very high percentage of "infertility," 28%. Wilsnack (1973) found alcoholic women significantly more likely than control women to report gynecological and obstetrical problems: 26% of her alcoholic sample reported inability to become pregnant or to carry a child to term. Although the alcoholic women queried must have included some women who were engaging in heavy drinking before their infertility occurred, there did seem to be some support for the role of gynecological and obstetrical disappointment and frustration as an antecedent. There was other evidence of such disappointment and frustration; for example, when asked about the number of children they would like to have had, the alcoholic women wished for significantly more than the control women.

Thus, most of the writing about women and alcohol for the last quarter of a century has posited the following sequence:

gynecological/obstetrical events ⟶ alcohol problems

This has been largely reversed in recent years. In the literature on fetal alcohol syndrome and other negative effects on the fetus of heavy drinking, moderate drinking, or any drinking, the emphasis has shifted to the following:

alcohol problems ⎫
any drinking   ⎬ ⟶ gynecological/obstetrical events

It may be, of course, that both views are correct. For those women who begin alcohol abuse relatively early in life and who maintain heavy drinking through a pregnancy, the risk of fetal damage is high. Many heavy-drinking women do stop or reduce their alcohol intake during pregnancy; some do not. For the majority of women seen in treatment facilities, an age group at the end of the childbearing years, the role of gynecological and obstetrical disappointment and frustration could well be antecedent.

Personality and Coping Mechanisms

Two variables have been used as explanations of female alcoholism, or at least as primary antecedent events, and they have dominated the literature on female alcoholism. One of these variables is depression, and the second is sex-role conflict.

DEPRESSION

Schuckit, Pitts, Reich, King, and Winokur (1969) distinguished "two types of alcoholism in women:" primary alcoholism; and secondary alcoholism where depressive features are antecedent. Since practically all the women at treatment centers present with depressive symptoms, it is a matter of distinguishing the two types by their histories. Alcoholic women with preexisting depression have different family histories (e.g., more female relatives with affective disorders), differences in the course of alcoholism and associated behaviors (e.g., more suicide attempts), and may have a better long-term prognosis than primary alcoholic women (Schuckit et al., 1969; Schuckit & Morrissey, 1976).

The incidence of depression among women is high, and significantly higher than it is among men (Gove, 1979). One unanswered question is why some of these depressed women become alcoholic while others do not. Is there a link between alcoholism in the family of origin and depressive symptoms that lead to problem-drinking behaviors?

SEX-ROLE CONFLICT

The literature on sex-role conflict as an etiological agent in female alcoholism is extensive (Beckman, 1978; Greenblatt & Schuckit, 1976; Parker, 1972; Scida & Vannicelli, 1979; Wilsnack, 1973) and will not be reviewed here. A recent comparison of alcoholic women and matched controls showed the alcoholic women to be more anxious and to have a lower opinion of themselves than the controls, but when compared on their views of female roles in contemporary society, differences were small (McLachlan, Walderman, Birchmore, & Marsden, 1979). Work by Wilsnack and Wilsnack (1978) on the sex-role views and drinking behaviors of adolescent girls led them to hypothesize two different age-related antecedents. Among younger women, rejection of traditional femininity seemed more linked to heavy drinking. Among older women, conscious feminine role preference seemed more closely related to heavy drinking.

IMPULSE CONTROL, SOCIAL ISOLATION, AND ANGER

It may well be that young adulthood antecedents need to be differentiated for early-onset and later-onset female alcoholism. One neglected area of research might be the antecedent role of impulse control. Jones (1971) noted that both men and women alcoholics had in common, as adolescents, "unstable, unpredictable impulsivity" (p. 68). Gender and age differences in such impulsivity and its linkage to alcohol problems should be studied.

Another issue is that of social isolation, noted by Jones (1971) and other writers. When a young or middle-aged woman arrives at a treatment facility, the issue of isolation has been compounded and confused by the isolation resulting from her problem drinking. Longitudinal studies, or perhaps retrospective self-report studies, are needed to investigate the social networks of women problem drinkers before they developed problems. No one has reported on the shifts in social networks and social supports that occur as a woman moves from moderate through heavy drinking and into the early signs of alcoholism. Many follow-up studies make the point that rehabilitated female alcoholics restore their social networks and apparently do so to a greater extent than male alcoholics (Kammeier, 1977). Finally, the angers and resentments that precede the onset of alcoholism are too little noted or studied, although we observe clinically the significant role that these play in the drinking bouts and intoxicated behavior of women.

Sociocultural Factors and Roles

There are three aspects of the young adult role that may be examined for antecedents to problem drinking: work role, marital role, and parental role.

WORK ROLE

Studies indicate that the largest proportions of women drinkers are found in professional, semiprofessional, technical, and business jobs, and the lowest proportions are among farm women, laborers, and service workers (Alcohol & Health, 1971). When one looks at heavy drinking, however, the picture changes: The highest percentages are found among service workers, semiskilled workers, laborers, and business women. Blue-collar women and service workers seem to polarize: A high proportion are abstinent, but if they do drink, they seem to drink heavily.

MARITAL ROLE

The relationship between marital status and drinking behaviors is not clear, but a recent report suggests that the incidence of problem drinking is highest for divorced and separated women under 35. This is a significant age and marital status interaction because, for older women, those who are married have higher rates of problem drinking than those who are divorced, separated, or widowed (Johnson, 1982). These statistics suggest that marital disruption is an antecedent more for younger women than for older ones. To complicate matters further, there may be a work status and marital status interaction: Among married women in Johnson's sample, those who did not work outside the home reported a higher percentage of social drinking, but married women working outside the home had significantly higher rates of problem drinking than housewives. There is, then, a complex interplay of age factors, marital status, paid employment outside the home, and occupation, which suggests that some combinations (or, perhaps, life styles) put women more at risk for heavy or problem drinking than other combinations. Although not replicated in a more recent national survey (Wilsnack, Wilsnack, & Klassen, 1984), Johnson's finding that married women employed outside the home manifested higher rates of problem drinking than housewives has led to some hypotheses about dual-role stress as an antecedent to problem drinking among women.

PARENTING ROLE

An early survey of Cahalan, Cisin, and Crossley (1969) found that the peak years for women's heavy drinking occurred in the age groups 21–24 and 45–49. A more recent survey, using somewhat different age categories (Clark & Midanik, 1982), shows the peak of heavy female drinking to occur in the 40s and the peak of problems associated with drinking to occur in the age group 18–25. What is the relationship of these peaks to the childbearing and childraising years? May a case be made for stresses of the parenting role as antecedent? The younger age group, 18–25, is characterized by dating, mating, and childbearing behaviors, and it is possible that young women who drank heavily during the dating and mating periods discontinue the heavy drinking when they become pregnant. But reduction of heavy drinking due to pregnancy is unlikely for the older age group. The peak and decline in heavy drinking among women in their 40s must reflect other influences.

Does the strain of the parenting role in young adulthood act as an antecedent of alcohol problems? There are no clear answers. Bearing and raising children, particularly for women working outside the home, may indeed involve dual-role stress. Possibly relevant are feelings of inadequacy and incompetence in mothering, linked to general feelings of low esteem, and certainly relevant are feelings of abandonment and anger for those young women with young children who experience marital disruption. Some data suggest that poor, nonwhite women who are heads of households and responsible for young children are at high risk for depression (Brown & Harris, 1978) and probably for alcohol problems as well.

There are several major stressors during young adult life that have been pinpointed in research as strong possibilities for antecedents of alcohol problems. These include marital disruption (for younger women), head-of-household responsibility, and, for married women, working outside the home and carrying double responsibilities. The general question of recent stressful events and drinking has been debated for years. In an early study, Lisansky (1957) reported that almost all the alcoholic women studied named a specific recent trauma, such as the loss of a parent, a divorce, or medical problems, which they indicated was linked to the onset of alcoholism. It was cautioned that citing such an event, which occurred more frequently among women alcoholics than among men alcoholics, might indicate women's greater defensiveness and their need to explain their drinking behaviors in terms of a wound inflicted by the social environment. The argument over this issue is unresolved. Recent studies report positive findings (Mulford, 1977) and negative findings (Morrissey & Schuckit, 1978).

One social role that has been little explored is the problem-drinking woman as a medical patient. If women turn to physicians with complaints such as nervousness or insomnia, is this likely to be before or after they have developed drinking problems? What sorts of medical complaints motivate women to turn to physicians? Are the women seeking tranquilization? Such research might explore the question of women's perceptions of alcoholic beverages and the extent to which they are viewed as tranquilizers, sedatives, mood elevators, medicine, and sources of pleasure.

Drinking: Family and Peer Influences

Female alcoholics more often report a heavy drinking or alcoholic spouse than do male alcoholics (Busch & Feuerlein, 1975; Jacob & Lavoie, 1971; Lisansky, 1957; Mulford, 1977; Rosenbaum, 1958). Since there are more male alcoholics, this is not unreasonable. At the same time, there is clinical support for the hypothesis that women often become involved in heavy and alcoholic drinking because they are married to or living with a heavy-drinking or alcoholic man. Transmission of symptomatic drinking behavior often seems to go from man to woman, while we suspect the reverse is far less often true. Male alcoholics will drink alone, with friends, in bars, on the street, at the workplace, almost anywhere. Female alcoholics do most of their drinking at home, either alone or with a significant other. The critical antecedent here may be the existence of a heavy or alcoholic drinker in the woman's home or social environment, whether a husband, lover, parent, sister, or friend. If a woman drinks in company, it usually seems to be with someone close to her.

It has been noted that women working outside the home may emulate male worker patterns of "drinking with the boys" (Sclare, 1975). This kind of adult peer-group social pressure may become a more significant antecedent as larger percentages of women move into the labor force. On-the-job stress and heightened peer pressure to drink would certainly seem to be significant antecedents, particularly for the woman who carries other aspects of vulnerability in her history and experience.

SUMMARY

It seems obvious that there are several, perhaps many, different paths to the onset of alcoholism. These paths include biological, behavioral, and social events which may occur at different points in the life history of the person. We have argued that although the paths are different, all the paths will have some common features. It is these common features that are sought in research on antecedents.

Since men and women are socialized for different roles and behaviors, and there are different sanctions for male and female drinking, it is likely that the events that lead to onset will be different for men and women alcoholics. At the same time, it is likely that both sexes share some antecedents in common, for example, a higher incidence of alcoholism in the family of origin than is true of the general population.

Antecedents of female alcoholism may vary in their importance with the age of onset. Women who show alcoholic behaviors relatively early in life may follow somewhat different pathways into alcoholism than those who begin problem drinking somewhat later.

Finally, pathways to alcoholism may differ for women of different social class and background. An early study (Lisansky, 1957) found that women who came to treatment facilities in the community had different socioeconomic backgrounds than women in a state prison who also manifested alcohol problems. How similar and how different are the pathways to alcoholism for women who have struggled with poverty all of their lives and women who have led middle-class existences?

The fact that there are different pathways to alcoholism should not impede the research seeking knowledge of these pathways. We cannot prevent a given problem until we know more about how people develop it.

REFERENCES

Ablon, J. Family structure and behavior in alcoholism: A review of the literature. In B. Kissin & H. Begleiter (Eds.), *The biology of alcoholism* (Vol. 4: *Social aspects of alcoholism*). New York: Plenum, 1976.

Abplanalp, J. M., Rose, R. M., Donnelly, A. F., & Livingston-Vaughan, L. Psychoendocrinology of the menstrual cycle. II. The relationship between enjoyment of activities, mood, and reproductive hormones. *Psychosomatic Medicine*, 1979, *41*, 605–615.

Alcohol and health: First special report to the U.S. Congress from the Secretary of Health, Education and Welfare (DHEW Publ. No. [HSM] 72-9099). Washington, D.C.: U.S. Government Printing Office, December 1971.

Bales, R. F. *The "fixation factor" in alcohol addiction: An hypothesis derived from a comparative study of Irish and Jewish social norms.* Unpublished doctoral dissertation, Harvard University, 1944.

Beckman, L. J. Sex role conflict in alcoholic women: Myth or reality. *Journal of Abnormal Psychology*, 1978, *87*, 408–417.

Beckman, L. J. Reported effects of alcohol on the sexual feelings and behavior of women alcoholics and nonalcoholics. *Journal of Studies on Alcohol*, 1979, *40*, 272–282.

Beckman, L. J. Perceived antecedents and effects of alcohol consumption in women. *Journal of Studies on Alcohol*, 1980, *41*, 518–530.

Belfer, M. L., Shader, R. I., Carroll, M., & Harmatz, J. S. Alcoholism in women. *Archives of General Psychiatry*, 1971, *25*, 540–544.

Bleuler, M. Familial and personal background of chronic alcoholics. In O. Diethelm (Ed.), *Etiology of chronic alcoholism.* Springfield, Ill.: Charles C Thomas, 1955.

Blum, E. M. Psychoanalytic views on alcoholism. *Quarterly Journal of Studies on Alcohol*, 1966, *27*, 259–299.

Bohman, M., Sigvardsson, S., & Cloninger, C. R. Maternal inheritance of alcohol abuse: Cross-fostering analysis of adopted women. *Archives of General Psychiatry*, 1981, *38*, 965–969.

Brown, G. W., & Harris, T. *Social origins of depression: A study of psychiatric disorder in women.* New York: Free Press, 1978.

Busch, H., & Feuerlein, W. Sozialpsychologische Aspeke in Ehen von Alkoholikerinnen. *Schweizer Archiv für Neurologie*, 1975, *116*, 329–341.

Cahalan, D., Cisin, I. H., & Crossley, H. M. *American drinking practices: A national study of drinking behavior and attitudes.* New Haven, Conn.: College and University Press, 1969.

Cartwright, A. K. J., & Shaw, S. J. Trends in the epidemiology of alcoholism. *Psychological Medicine*, 1978, *8*, 1–4.

Clark, W. B., & Midanik, L. Alcohol use and alcohol problems among U.S. adults: Results of the 1979 national survey. In *Alcohol consumption and related problems* (NIAAA Alcohol and Health Monograph No. 1, DHHS Publ. No. [ADM] 82-1190). Washington, D.C.: U.S. Government Printing Office, 1982.

Corrigan, E. M. *Alcoholic women in treatment.* New York: Oxford University Press, 1980.

Cosper, R. Drinking as conformity: A critique of sociological literature on occupational differences in drinking. *Journal of Studies on Alcohol*, 1979, *40*, 868–891.

Cotton, N. S. Familial incidence of alcoholism: A review. *Journal of Studies on Alcohol*, 1979, *40*, 89–116.

Dollard, J., & Miller, N. E. *Personality and psychotherapy.* New York: McGraw-Hill, 1950.

Edwards, G., Hensman, C., & Peto, J. A comparison of female and male motivation for drinking. *International Journal of the Addictions*, 1973, *8*, 577–587.

Fillmore, K. M. Drinking and problem drinking in early adulthood and middle age. *Quarterly Journal of Studies on Alcohol*, 1974, *35*, 819–840.

Fillmore, K. M. Relationships between specific drinking problems in early adulthood and middle age. *Journal of Studies on Alcohol*, 1975, *36*, 882–907.

Fleetwood, M. F. Biochemical experimental investigations of emotions and chronic alcoholism. In O. Diethelm (Ed.), *Etiology of chronic alcoholism.* Springfield, Ill.: Charles C Thomas, 1955.

Glad, D. D. Attitudes and experience of American-Jewish and American-Irish male youth as related to differences in adult rates of inebriety. *Quarterly Journal of Studies on Alcohol*, 1947, *8*, 406–472.

Gomberg, E. S. L. Problems with alcohol and other drugs. In E. S. L. Gomberg & V. Franks (Eds.), *Gender and disordered behavior: Sex differences in psychopathology.* New York: Brunner/Mazel, 1979.

Gomberg, E. S. L. *Issues in prevention of alcohol problems: A review.* Prepared for the Prevention Issues Panel of the Institute of Medicine Committee on Alcoholism, Alcohol Abuse and Related Problems: Opportunities for Research. Washington, D.C.: National Academy of Sciences, July 1980. (a)

Gomberg, E. S. L. Risk factors related to alcohol problems among women: Proneness and vulnerability. In *Alcoholism and alcohol abuse among women: Research issues* (NIAAA Research Monograph No. 1, DHEW Publ. No. [ADM] 80-835). Washington, D.C.: U.S. Government Printing Office, 1980. (b)

Goodwin, D. W. *Is alcoholism hereditary?* New York: Oxford University Press, 1976.

Goodwin, D. W. Alcoholism and heredity. *Archives of General Psychiatry*, 1979, *36*, 57–61.

Goodwin, D. W. *Alcoholism: The facts.* New York: Oxford University Press, 1981.

Goodwin, D. W., Schulsinger, F., Knop, J., Mednick, S., & Guze, S. B. Psychopathology in adopted and nonadopted daughters of alcoholics. *Archives of General Psychiatry*, 1977, *34*, 1005–1009.

Gove, W. R. Sex differences in the epidemiology of mental disorder: Evidence and explanations. In E. S. L. Gomberg & V. Franks (Eds.), *Gender and disordered behavior: Sex differences in psychopathology.* New York: Brunner/Mazel, 1979.

Greenberg, L. A., & Lester, D. Vitamin deficiency and the etiology of alcoholism. In H. E. Himwich (Ed.), *Alcoholism: Basic aspects of treatment* (Publ. No. 47). Washington, D.C.: American Association for the Advancement of Science, 1957.

Greenblatt, M., & Schuckit, M. A. (Eds). *Alcoholism problems in women and children.* New York: Grune & Stratton, 1976.

Hall, D. C., Chaikin, K., & Piland, B. *A review of the problem drinking behavior literature associated with the Spanish-speaking population group* (Vol. 3) (Final report for the National Institute on Alcohol Abuse and Alcoholism under contract No. ADM 281-76-0025). Menlo Park, Calif.: Stanford Research Institute, 1977.

Harford, T. C., & Spiegler, D. L. Environmental influences in adolescent drinking. In *Special population issues* (NIAAA Alcohol and Health Monograph No. 4, DHHS Publ. No. [ADM] 82-1193). Washington, D.C.: U.S. Government Printing Office, 1982.

Heath, D. B. Anthropological perspective on alcohol: An historical review. In M. W. Everett, J. O. Waddell, & D. B. Heath (Eds.), *Cross-cultural approaches to the study of alcohol.* The Hague, Netherlands: Mouton, 1976.

Hill, S. Y. A vulnerability model for alcoholism in women. *Focus on Women: Journal of Addictions and Health*, 1981, *2*, 68–91.

Hitz, D. Drunken sailors and others: Drinking problems in specific occupations. *Quarterly Journal of Studies on Alcohol*, 1973, *34*, 496–505.

Hoffman, H., & Noem, A. A. Alcoholism among parents of male and female alcoholics. *Psychological Reports*, 1975, *36*, 322.

Ivey, M. E., & Bardwick, J. M. Patterns of affective fluctuation in the menstrual cycle. *Psychosomatic Medicine*, 1968, *30*, 336–345.

Jackson, J. K., & Connor, R. Attitudes of the parents of alcoholics, moderate drinkers and non-drinkers toward drinking. *Quarterly Journal of Studies on Alcohol*, 1953, *14*, 596–613.

Jacob, A. G., & Lavoie, C. *A study of some characteristics of a group of women alcoholics.* Paper presented at the Conference of the North American Association of Alcoholism Programs, Hartford, Conn., June 1971.

Jellinek, E. M. *The disease concept of alcoholism.* New Haven, Conn.: Hillhouse Press, 1960.

Johnson, P. B. Sex differences, women's roles and alcohol use: Preliminary national data. *Journal of Social Issues*, 1982, *38*, 93–116.

Johnston, L. D., Bachman, J. G., & O'Malley, P. M. *Highlights from: Student drug use in America 1975–1980* (DHHS Publ. No. [ADM] 81-1066). Washington, D.C.: U.S. Government Printing Office, 1980.

Jones, B. M., & Jones, M. K. Alcohol effects on women during the menstrual cycle. *Annals of the New York Academy of Sciences*, 1976, *273*, 576–587.

Jones, M. C. Personality antecedents and correlates of drinking patterns in women. *Journal of Consulting and Clinical Psychology*, 1971, *36*, 61–69.

Kammeier, M. L. *Alcoholism is the common denominator: More evidence on the male/female question* (Hazelden Papers No. 2) Center City, Minn.: Hazelden Foundation, 1977.

Kielholz, P. Alcohol and depression. *British Journal of Addiction*, 1970, *65*, 187–193.

Kinsey, B. A. *The female alcoholic: A social psychological study.* Springfield, Ill.: Charles C Thomas, 1966.

Lisansky, E. S. Alcoholism in women: Social and psychological concomitants. *Quarterly Journal of Studies on Alcohol*, 1957, *18*, 588–623.

Lisansky, E. S. The etiology of alcoholism: The role of psychological predisposition. *Quarterly Journal of Studies on Alcohol*, 1960, *21*, 314–343.

Lolli, G. Alcoholism in women. *Connecticut Review on Alcoholism*, 1953, *5*(3), 9–11.

McClelland, D. C., Davis, W. N., Kalin, R., & Wanner, E. *The drinking man: Alcohol and human motivation.* New York: Free Press, 1972.

McCord, W., & McCord, J. *Origins of alcoholism.* Stanford, Calif.: Stanford University, 1960.

McLachlan, J. F. C., Walderman, R. L., Birchmore, D. F., & Marsden, L. R. Self-evaluation, role satisfaction, and anxiety in the woman alcoholic. *International Journal of the Addictions*, 1979, *14*, 809–832.

Mandelbaum, D. G. Alcohol and culture. In M. Marshall (Ed.), *Beliefs, behaviors and alcoholic beverages: A cross-cultural survey.* Ann Arbor, Mich.: University of Michigan, 1979.

Moos, R. H. Fluctuations in symptoms and moods during the menstrual cycle. *Journal of Psychosomatic Research*, 1969, *13*, 37–44.

Morrissey, E. R., & Schuckit, M. A. Stressful life events and alcohol problems among women seen at a detoxication center. *Journal of Studies on Alcohol*, 1978, *39*, 1559–1576.

Mulford, H. A. Women and men problem drinkers: Sex differences in patients served by Iowa's community alcoholism centers. *Journal of Studies on Alcohol*, 1977, *38*, 1624–1639.

Parker, F. B. Sex-role adjustment in women alcoholics. *Quarterly Journal of Studies on Alcohol*, 1972, *33*, 647–657.

Podolsky, E. The woman alcoholic and premenstrual tension. *Journal of the American Medical Women's Association*, 1963, *18*, 816–818.

Rachal, J. V., Maisto, S. A., Guess, L. L., & Hubbard, R. L. Alcohol use among youth. In *Alcohol consumption and related problems* (NIAAA Alcohol and Health Monograph No. 1, Publ. No. [ADM] 82-1190). Washington, D.C.: U.S. Government Printing Office, 1982.

Rachal, J. V., Williams, J. R., Brehm, M. L., Cavanagh, B., Moore, R. P., & Eckerman, W. C. *A national study of adolescent drinking behavior, attitudes and correlates* (Final Report to the National Institute on Alcohol Abuse and Alcoholism). Research Triangle Park, N.C.: Research Triangle Institute, 1975.

Robins, L. N. An actuarial evaluation of the causes and consequences of deviant behavior in young black men. In M. Roff, L. N. Robins, & M. Pollack (Eds.), *Life history research in psychopathology* (Vol. 2). Minneapolis, Minn.: University of Minnesota Press, 1972.

Robins, L. N., Bates, W. M., and O'Neal, P. Adult drinking patterns of former problem children. In D. J. Pittman & C. R. Snyder (Eds.), *Society, culture, and drinking patterns*. New York: Wiley, 1962.

Roebuck, J., & Kessler, R. *The etiology of alcoholism*. Springfield, Ill.: Charles C Thomas, 1972.

Rosenbaum, B. Married women alcoholics at the Washingtonian Hospital. *Quarterly Journal of Studies on Alcohol*, 1958, *19*, 79–89.

Schuckit, M. A., & Morrissey, E. R. Alcoholism in women: Some clinical and social perspectives with an emphasis on possible subtypes. In M. Greenblatt & M. A. Schuckit (Eds.), *Alcoholism problems in women and children*. New York: Grune & Stratton, 1976.

Schuckit, M. A., Pitts, F. N., Jr., Reich, T., King, L. J., & Winokur, G. Alcoholism I. Two types of alcoholism in women. *Archives of General Psychiatry*, 1969, *20*, 301–306.

Scida, J., & Vannicelli, M. Sex-role conflict and women's drinking. *Journal of Studies on Alcohol*, 1979, *40*, 28–44.

Sclare, A. B. The woman alcoholic. *Journal of Alcoholism*, 1975, *10*, 134–137.

Shaw, S. The causes of increasing drinking problems amongst women: A general etiological theory. In Camberwell Council on Alcoholism, *Women and alcohol*. London: Tavistock Publications, 1980.

Smart, R. G., & Gray, G. Parental and peer influences as correlates of problem drinking among high school students. *International Journal of the Addictions*, 1979, *14*, 905–917.

Sommer, B. Stress and menstrual distress. *Journal of Human Stress*, 1978, *4*, 5–10.

Stivers, R. *A hair of the dog: Irish drinking and American stereotype*. University Park: Pennsylvania State University Press, 1976.

Sutker, P. E. *Acute alcohol intoxication: Mood changes and gender*. Paper presented at the 13th Annual Medical-Scientific Conference of the National Alcoholism Forum, Washington, D.C., April 1982.

Tracey, D. A., & Nathan, P. E. Behavioral analysis of chronic alcoholism in four women. *Journal of Consulting and Clinical Psychology*, 1976, *44*, 832–842.

Ullman, A. D. Sociocultural backgrounds of alcoholism. In S. D. Bacon (Ed.), *Understanding alcoholism. Annals of the American Academy of Political and Social Sciences*, 1958, *315*, 48–54.

Wall, J. H. A study of alcoholism in women. *American Journal of Psychiatry*, 1937, *93*, 943–952.

Wechsler, H., & McFadden, M. Sex differences in adolescent alcohol and drug use: A disappearing phenomenon. *Journal of Studies on Alcohol*, 1976, *37*, 1291–1301.

Wetzel, R. D., & McClure, J. N. Suicide and the menstrual cycle: A review. *Comprehensive Psychiatry*, 1972, *13*, 369–374.

Williams, R. J. *Nutrition and alcoholism*. Norman, Okla.: University of Oklahoma Press, 1951.

Wilsnack, R. W., & Wilsnack, S. C. Sex roles and drinking among adolescent girls. *Journal of Studies on Alcohol*, 1978, *39*, 1855–1874.

Wilsnack, R. W., Wilsnack, S. C., & Klassen, A. D. Women's drinking and drinking problems: Patterns from a 1981 national survey. *American Journal of Public Health*, 1984, *74*, 11.

Wilsnack, S. C. Sex-role identity in female alcoholism. *Journal of Abnormal Psychology*, 1973, *82*, 253–261.

Wolin, S. J., Bennett, L. A., Noonan, D. L., & Teitelbaum, M. A. Disrupted family rituals: A factor in the intergenerational transmission of alcoholism. *Journal of Studies on Alcohol*, 1980, *41*, 199–214.

9

Alcohol Use and Marital Violence: Female and Male Differences in Reactions to Alcohol

IRENE HANSON FRIEZE
University of Pittsburgh

PATRICIA COONEY SCHAFER
University of Pittsburgh

INTRODUCTION

Most people can think of at least one occasion when fighting or other aggressive behavior occurred in someone who had been drinking a large quantity of alcohol. Such alcohol-related violence occurs in public as well as in private family situations. There is also a common belief that excessive alcohol use may be a causal factor in wife battering (e.g., Frieze & Knoble, 1980). These experiences suggest that the topic of alcohol and violence is important for understanding issues relating to women and alcohol in at least two ways. First, women may themselves react to alcohol consumption with physical violence. Second, and far more common, women may be the victims of alcohol-related violence by men. Both of these possibilities are explored in this chapter. In order to focus discussion of these complex variables, we will limit the topic under discussion in this chapter in several ways. First, we will not attempt to deal with psychological or other forms of nonphysical aggression. We will consider only the case of overt, physical violence. Second, our major concern is violence in marriage directed either toward the spouse or toward children. It is in this context that women are most exposed to violence and are most violent themselves. Although women may well be victims of other alcohol-induced aggression outside the home (such as rape), research on battered women increasingly supports the idea that it is in the home that the woman is most likely to be assaulted, and that much of this violence is related to alcohol. Therefore, at least for this initial discussion, we will limit ourselves to domestic violence.

Another major concern of this chapter is understanding the differential reactions of men and women to alcohol consumption. In reviewing the literature on alcohol and violence, it is soon evident that physical aggression is a frequent response to alcohol consumption in men, but it is not as commonly found in women who drink. Women may show the opposite pattern and become passive after drinking. The reasons for these differential reactions are not completely clear. In fact, we still do not understand clearly why alcohol produces the effects it does in any type of drinker (e.g., Pernanen, 1981). A cognitive model for understanding the effects of alcohol on the behavior of women and men is proposed, which combines physiological theories and those stressing the social context of the alcohol use. This model assumes that there are definite physiological effects of alcohol, but that these effects are interpreted, and in turn responded to, in light of prior learning and the immediate social setting in which alcohol is consumed.

We will first present an overview of research on alcohol and violence in men, looking at both general findings and those that apply specifically to family settings. Then we turn to the literature on female reactions to alcohol. With this background, a cognitive model of reactions to alcohol is presented in more detail.

ALCOHOL AND VIOLENCE IN MEN

Alcohol has been considered responsible for more aggression and violence than any other drug, especially in men (Kutash, Kutash, Schlesinger, & Associates, 1978). This linkage is found in several types of empirical research. For example, evidence for one of the most serious consequences of alcohol-induced aggression is seen in records of criminal activity. Most alcohol-related murders are impulsive and unplanned, and often involve family members or friends of the aggressor (Mayfield, 1976). Alcohol is also involved in other types of crime. Vanfossen (1979) reports that in 14% of all police calls, there is explicit mention of drinking. He speculates that alcohol may well have been involved in even more crimes, but that this information is not explicitly entered into the police record. Other studies also point to a relationship between alcohol and violence. In a general review of the literature, Nicol, Gunn, Gristwood, Foggitt, and Watson (1973) report that men convicted of violent offenses were often reported to be drinking at the time of the offense and/or to have a general problem with alcohol abuse. They further found in their own research that the most violent of the convicted offenders were more likely to be alcoholics. This group of violent men were also found to be most likely to want to drink in response to stressful social situations. Others have also found that alcohol use is commonly associated with assault (e.g., Mayfield, 1976; Shupe, 1954) and homicide (e.g., Haberman & Baden, 1978; Virkkunen, 1974; Wolfgang & Strohm, 1957) as well as with male criminal behavior in general (Fitzpatrick, 1974; Sobell & Sobell, 1975).

Laboratory research, which typically utilizes college student subjects, has generally supported the idea that alcohol use increases aggressive responses in males. In addition, some studies have sampled a general adult population.

In one such study, which recruited male social drinkers from the general public through advertisements and controlled for a number of potentially confounding experimental effects, Zeichner and Pihl (1979) found that inebriated subjects gave higher levels of shock to fellow subjects than did sober subjects, and that the inebriated subjects were less likely to moderate their aggression in response to pain cues from the shocked subject. Zeichner and Pihl attributed these differences to the disrupting effects of alcohol upon information-processing capabilities.

However, not all laboratory research has been so clear-cut. Specific effects in controlled laboratory situations appear to depend upon the amount of alcohol consumed by the subjects, the type of provocation used to elicit aggressive responses, whether the aggressive subject is able to see the effects of his aggressive behavior, and whether the subject knows how much alcohol he has consumed (Zeichner & Pihl, 1979). Different subject populations may also react differently. Bennett, Buss and Carpenter (1969) did not find increased shock behavior in more inebriated male graduate students, and attributed their lack of differences to the upper-middle-class backgrounds and experiences of their graduate student subjects. It is also possible that graduate students in the physical, biological, and medical sciences in the mid-1960s had personal values that would lead to the inhibition of aggression. Other data would support this idea. In a survey of general attitudes about violence in American men, Blumenthal, Kahn, Andrews, and Head (1972) found that men with more education were generally less tolerant of violence than less educated men. These data may explain the ambiguities in laboratory studies of aggression, most of which sample college students. Such findings support the importance of social factors in understanding male aggression as a response to alcohol.

Other factors may also operate in both laboratory and nonlaboratory aggression. Many people believe that socially unacceptable behavior (such as physical aggression) is more permissable for someone who has been drinking (Goldstein, 1975). In support of this idea, Lang, Goeckner, Adesso, and Marlatt (1975) reported that laboratory subjects who thought that their drinks contained alcohol were more aggressive than subjects who did not think they had been drinking anything alcoholic. These effects were found regardless of the actual alcoholic content of their drinks. Zeichner and Pihl (1979) found that their placebo subjects (who had been given orange juice with a very thin layer of alcohol on the top so that the drink smelled like alcohol) were more verbally aggressive than sober subjects who had not been led to believe that they had been consuming alcohol. These data suggest that prior experiences with alcohol and expectations about the effects of alcohol may influence reactions to alcohol.

Alcohol may also have physiological effects that would lead to increased aggression. Behaviors associated with intoxication include quarrelsomeness, swearing, fighting, and a tendency to break things. Alcohol can impair memory and conceptual abilities, which can cause a misinterpretation of others' actions. Furthermore, individuals who already have aggressive or sociopathic tendencies are especially likely to become violent under the influence of alcohol (Powers & Kutash, 1978). Emotional changes are another commonly reported consequence of alcohol consumption (Schuckit, 1979). However, all of these effects are variable and depend upon the prior emotional state of the person before drinking, the setting in which the alcohol is consumed, the personality of the drinker, the amount of alcohol consumed, the person's previous history of alcohol use, and the drinker's expectancies regarding the effects of alcohol (Rix, 1977).

Alcohol consumption may also indirectly increase the probability of anger and aggression because of the ways in which other people react to someone who is drunk (Pernanen, 1981). For example, a person who is drinking may engage in behavior that makes other people angry (such as dancing too long with someone else's spouse or being too loud). If those who are drinking are told that this behavior is unacceptable, they may in turn become angry. A drinker may also get angry if someone takes away the car keys or otherwise infringes upon his freedom. Pernanen (1981) speculates that the less tolerance there is of drinking, the more likely the drinker is to become violent.

Alcohol and Family Violence

As we have seen, there appears to be some relationship between the use of alcohol and violent behavior in men. This relationship extends to family violence. As mentioned earlier, Mayfield (1976) concludes that murders done under the influence of alcohol chiefly involve acquaintances or family members. In another empirical investigation, Bard and Zacker (1974) found that in 30% of all police calls for family disputes, the violent party (who was typically male) had been drinking. The degree of intoxication was not noted in these police reports. However, data were collected on the level of violence involved. These records indicated that, of all cases where there was clear evidence of physical injury, only 21% showed evidence that one or the other party had been drinking. Thus, alcohol was more rather than less common in the less violent incidents. Bard and Zacker attempted to explain this by hypothesizing that rather than a scenario where the husband was drinking and then beat up his wife who then called the police, a more likely situation was that when the husband was drinking and appeared to be on the verge of becoming violent, the wife called the police to prevent this violence from occurring. Similar data supportive of this reasoning were reported in a later study by the same authors (Zacker & Bard, 1977).

In another study of police records, Gerson (1978) found that there was more marital violence in families where one or both spouses had been drinking. In 44% of the marital assaults where alcohol use was indicated, both spouses had been drinking. In another 44%, only the violent spouse had been drinking. In the remaining 13%, only the victim had been drinking.

Women as Victims of Male Violence in the Home

As discussed, drinking is often associated with marital violence. This typically takes the form of women being the recipients of violence from their husbands. Evidence of this can be found in court records. Byles (1978) analyzed the records of families who had been involved in family court (typically for problems relating to divorce). For these couples, the most frequently cited problem area was violence, usually of the husband against the wife. Alcohol-related problems were the third most common problem. In addition, there was more violence in the alcohol-problem families. Nearly three-fourths of the alcohol-problem families also had problems with violence, while less than a third of the families without alcohol problems reported having difficulties with violence. In the large majority of these families, the wife was the victim of alcohol-related violence.

Similar victimization of women was reported by Orford, Guthrie, Nicholls, Oppenheimer, Egert, and Hensman (1975), who found that the wives of men referred to a clinic for suspected drinking problems frequently reported that violence was a problem in their marriages. Of these women, 45% reported being physically beaten, and another 27% said that their husbands had attempted to inflict serious injuries upon them. In addition, 72% of these wives of suspected alcoholics reported being threatened with violence by their husbands. These percentages are much higher than the generally reported frequencies of violent marriages, which range from one-third to one-half of all marriages (e.g., Frieze, Knoble, Washburn, & Zomnir, 1980; Straus, Gelles, & Steinmetz, 1980). Thus, it does appear that alcohol use by the husband increases the probability that there will also be wife battering.

Research on battered women also finds a high degree of drinking problems in battering husbands. Summarizing across a number of other studies, Langley and Levy (1977) stated that alcohol and other drugs are linked to between 40% and 95% of cases of wife battering. On the basis of their review of the literature, they conclude that there are nine common reasons for wife battering, one of which is alcohol and/or drug use in the batterer. Pizzey (1977) also lists excessive use of alcohol as a defining characteristic of one of the four types of batterers she identifies. Other studies agree that violent husbands are likely to have problems with excessive use of alcohol (e.g., Gelles, 1972; Labell, 1979; Roy, 1977).

Our own research further supports the linkage between wife battering and alcohol use (Frieze & Knoble, 1980). This work involved in-depth interviews with 137 battered women, whom we located in women's shelters, from court records of women who had filed papers to remove a violent spouse from their home, and from volunteers responding to posted notices for participants for a study of violence in marriage. Each of these self-identified "battered" women was matched to a control woman, who was another married woman from the same neighborhood. This allowed for a rough matching on race, ethnicity, and social class (Frieze *et al.*, 1980). About a third of the controls had also experienced violence in their marriages. However, typically these control "battered" women had not been the recipients of extremely severe violence as was common for the battered sample. Questions in the interviews assessed alcohol use in husband and wife as well as asking about the specifics of the violence. Other parts of the structured interviews dealt with power dynamics in the couple, the wife's attributions about the cause of the violence, their childhood backgrounds, and how they handled their own children. Like other researchers, we found that the most severe batterers tended to also be the heaviest drinkers. The heavy-drinking men were especially likely to batter their wives when they had been drinking, so there appeared to be a direct relationship between drinking and violence toward their wives when the sample as a whole was analyzed.

In spite of this general consistency in the literature linking alcohol use and marital violence in men, there is disagreement about the specific role of heavy alcohol use in the actual violence. In one of the classic studies of violent families, Gelles (1972) suggested that alcohol was used by the husband as an excuse for his violence. Gelles argued that behaviors done while drinking elicit less blame than the same behaviors done while sober. Other data support this contention (Richardson & Campbell, 1980). Thus, Gelles suggests that men may drink to give themselves an excuse for violent behavior. Walker (1979) also feels that alcohol serves as a convenient excuse for battering. In her in-depth interview study of battered women, Walker found that although battering men were reported to have drinking problems generally and the most severe violence was done by alcoholic men, the specific incidents of violence in these men did not always involve alcohol.

Given this possibility that alcohol use serves as an excuse for marital violence rather than a direct causal factor, it is interesting to note that a study of the excuses and justifications given by male offenders convicted for crimes of homicide and assault found that men who had assaulted women were the most likely to cite being drunk as an excuse for their actions (Felson & Ribner, 1981). Since there appear to be strong social proscriptions against a man physically attacking a woman, the use of alcohol may be necessary to release these inhibitions or to give these men an excuse for their behavior (Richardson, 1978).

In order to explore the relationship of alcohol and marital violence further, our study of battered women included a factor analysis of questionnaire items relating to alcohol consumption and violence (Frieze & Knoble, 1980). Results are summarized in Table 9-1. As the table shows, five factors emerged that accounted for 51% of the variance. Each of these factors can be interpreted as representing a different type of marriage. In one set of couples

TABLE 9-1. Alcohol, Drug Use, and Violence Patterns

	Factor				
	1	2	3	4	5
Husband's drinking	.67	—	—	—	—
Husband's drinking seen as a problem	.77	—	.29	—	.27
Wife's drinking	—	—	—	.42	—
Wife's drinking seen as a problem	.44	—	—	—	—
Couple has disagreements about drinking	.78	—	.32	—	—
Wife takes drugs	—	—	—	—	—
Wife takes drugs to relieve anxiety	—	—	—	—	−.29
Husband takes drugs	—	—	—	—	.53
Husband takes drugs for pleasure	—	—	.29	.38	—
Husband's overall violence to wife	.34	—	.67	—	—
Husband's overall violence to children	—	—	.47	—	—
Wife's overall violence to husband	—	—	.63	.25	—
Wife's overall violence to children	—	—	.34	—	—
Husband fights in self-defense	—	—	—	.34	−.28
Wife fights in self-defense	—	—	—	—	.30
Husband violent when drunk	.85	—	—	—	—
Husband drunk first time he was violent	.68	.30	—	—	—
Wife drunk—husband's first violence	—	.65	—	—	—
Husband drunk during his worst violence	.79	—	—	—	—
Wife drunk—husband's worst violence	—	.58	—	.35	—
Wife violent when drunk	—	.78	—	.32	—
Wife drunk first time she was violent	—	.79	—	—	—
Husband drunk—wife's first violence	.77	—	—	—	—
Wife drunk when most violent	—	.80	—	.30	—
Husband drunk—wife most violent	.78	—	—	—	—
Husband violent when taking drugs	—	—	—	—	.58
Wife violent when taking drugs	—	—	—	.64	—
Husband pressures wife to have sex	—	—	.60	—	—
Husband rapes wife	—	—	.40	—	—
Wife pressures husband to have sex	—	—	.27	—	—

Note. Loadings over .25. Five factors = 51.4% variance. Minimum eigenvalue = 1.6.
From Frieze and Knoble (1980).

(Factor 1), alcohol use was seen as a problem for both the husband and the wife and the husband was indeed a heavy drinker. In these families, marital violence is almost always associated with being intoxicated. Disagreements over drinking also start many fights. For this group, it appears that the alcohol is causal in the violence. A second group of couples (Factor 2) were characterized by fighting when they had been drinking. However, couples in this group did not drink excessively and they were not especially violent with each other. For another group of couples (Factor 3), there is again a high level of family violence, with the husband being highly violent toward his wife and children and the wife reciprocating this violence. These husbands also display sexual violence. However, in these highly violent couples, there may be little if any problem with heavy drinking in either the husband or the wife. It appears that generally low impulse control (and the resulting violence) is a way of life for these men and that drinking has no direct relationship to the violence. Presumably, if these men do drink heavily, it is yet another example of their difficulties with low impulse control.

These data suggest that there are many ways in which alcohol use relates to marital violence. This may also be true in a more general sense. There may be more than one way in which men react to alcohol consumption. Some of the ambiguities in the literature on alcohol and male aggression may arise from researchers trying to find a single relationship rather than attempting to discover a number of such relationships and the determinants of each.

Women as Victims of Other Alcohol-Related Violence

Battered wives are not the only victims of male alcohol-related violence. Studies of rape have shown that rapists have often been drinking before their assaults and/or they are alcoholic (e.g., Rada, 1975). However, once again the causal connection between alcohol use and sexual assault is not always clear. Groth (1978) points out that about 60% of the rapists in his study reported being under the influence of alcohol or other drugs at the time of their offense. However, alcohol or other drug use occurred frequently in many of these men and may not have been directly related to their rapes. Groth suggests that intoxication did not cause the rapes, but rather that being intoxicated may have led to an impairment of judgment and a loss of impulse control when sexual and aggressive impulses had already been activated by other circumstances. Once again, the exact nature of the relationship between alcohol and violence toward women is unclear.

Similar ambiguities exist in the child abuse literature. Although excessive use of alcohol is often cited as a causal factor in violence of parents against children (e.g., Eberle, 1980; Youcha, 1978), this is not always the case. Black and Mayer (1979) found that although alcoholic parents did indeed abuse their children in some cases, the majority of alcoholic parents did not physically or sexually abuse their children. When abuse did occur, it was more often in the form of neglect rather than physical abuse. Our data further support the idea that alcohol use does not typically lead to child abuse. Returning to the factor analysis of our data presented in Table 9-1, it can be seen that violence directed toward children was typical of neither the husbands nor the wives who were reported to be heavy drinkers in our study. Thus, it appears that even if alcohol use does lead to aggressive impulses in men (or women), they are usually able to control these impulses in certain contexts. Perhaps extremely violent behavior is not seen as appropriate with children and even drunkenness would not be an acceptable justification. Or, if excessive drinking occurs most often at night, children may already be in bed and may not be present to experience the effects of their parents'

drinking. It is also possible that the feelings created by alcohol are not interpreted as aggressive feelings in the presence of children. All of these explanations are plausible. They raise the question of why male alcohol use is more
associated with wife battering than with child abuse and again lead us to
question any simple relationship between alcohol and physical violence in
men (see Hamilton & Collins, 1981).

EFFECTS OF ALCOHOL USE IN WOMEN

The research demonstrates that alcohol has physiological effects in men that
could lead to violent behavior, at least at moderate levels of intoxication.
Although many of the studies providing these data have been done with male
subjects, presumably some of the same effects would exist in women. However, women are not generally as violent as men in our society (e.g., Frodi,
Macaulay, & Thorne, 1977; Johnson, 1972). Women are less likely to
commit violent crimes or to get into physical fights outside the home. Few
women are "husband batterers." Perhaps because of their lower levels of
violence, there is little evidence that women react to alcohol in the same
aggressive way that at least some men do. This raises questions about why
men are more likely to show a violent reaction to alcohol than women are. Is
it a physiological difference or does it relate to other factors? After briefly
reviewing some of the literature on the psychological and behavioral effects
of alcohol use in women, we will suggest a general model that might explain
the differential effects in women and men. Because the available data on
female alcoholics and on alcohol effects in women are limited and often
methodologically flawed (Beckman, 1975; Corrigan, 1980; Smart, 1979),
we must be somewhat speculative in examining the relationships between
family violence and alcohol use in women.

General Effects of Alcohol Use

One of the first questions that arises in studying the physical effects of
alcohol consumption in women is whether these effects are the same for men
and women. At least some research suggests that they are not. Jones and
Jones (1976) report that women become more intoxicated (have higher
blood levels of alcohol) than men, given the same amount of ethanol per
kilogram of body weight. This may be partially attributable to the fact that
because women have higher amounts of body fat and less water in their
bodies, the alcohol is less diluted in the typical female body than in the male
body. However, the degree of intoxication given the same amount of ethanol
consumption is also more variable in women. This is because ethanol metabolism appears to change with the phase of the menstrual cycle. Data from
Jones and Jones (1976) suggest that women become the most intoxicated

just before the onset of the menstrual flow and become least intoxicated after the onset of the menstrual flow. However, these effects are minimized for women taking oral contraceptives. This suggests that there is some direct or indirect effect of estrogen or other female sex-hormone levels on ethanol metabolism. Aside from the general finding that women are likely to become more intoxicated than men even with less actual alcohol consumption (both because of the hormone effects and because they typically have lower body weights), these data also imply that women are less able than men to predict the effects that drinking will have on them, since these effects have been more variable for women than for men.

Along with the differences in level of intoxication, there is some evidence from the same investigators that women may metabolize alcohol faster than men, although these effects too may depend upon the phase of the menstrual cycle and whether the woman is taking oral contraceptives or supplemental estrogen. Thus, men will typically stay intoxicated longer than women. We are not sure what the psychological implications of this difference might be, but whatever psychological effects drinking may have, men will have more time to experience and react to these than women.

Jones and Jones (1976) also report some psychological differences in the reactions of men and women to alcohol. Both sexes show decrements in immediate and delayed memory after drinking. Similarly, both sexes show some decrease in reaction time, although here the effects are greater for men than women. Finally, Jones and Jones found that a number of their female subjects reported increased sexual arousal after moderate amounts of alcohol consumption. This was a spontaneously reported reaction in the female subjects, which did not occur in males. Because this was not part of the original study, complete data were not collected and there was no way of testing if this effect was due to lowered inhibitions or to an actual physiological effect of the alcohol. Increased feelings of sexual arousal after drinking were also reported by Wilson and Lawson (1976a). This study also found that in spite of the women's perceiving themselves as being more aroused, physiological measures of arousal showed *less* evidence of sexual arousal after the women had been drinking. This discrepancy was attributed to the effects of expectations upon sexual feelings (Wilson & Lawson, 1978). Women may believe that they will be sexually aroused after drinking, and these expectations may cause them to actually feel aroused. We will return to this issue later in the chapter, after examining some of the literature on female alcoholism.

Alcohol and the Female Alcoholic

Since there are so few data on the general effects of alcohol in women, we decided to see if the richer literature on female alcoholism might tell us more about women's reactions to alcohol. In looking at this literature, we first had to determine what the appropriate comparison group is for the female alcoholic in order to interpret the data. Should she be compared to non-alcoholic women, to alcoholic men, or to herself when she is sober (see Beckman, 1978a)? All of these comparisons are necessary for understanding the female alcoholic. However, for our purposes of understanding the reactions of men and women to alcohol, the male–female alcoholic comparison is probably the most relevant.

Beckman (1978a) points out that many of the differences between male and female alcoholics parallel the general differences between nonalcoholic men and women. For example, the female alcoholics in her study had a higher need for dependency than the male alcoholics. They also saw themselves as having less control over their lives, had a lower need for power over others, and had less traditional sex-role attitudes. All of these sex differences have also been found in the general population (e.g., Frieze, Parsons, Johnson, Ruble, & Zellman, 1978). Hill (1980) and Gomberg (1979) report that there are more suicides and suicide attempts in female than male alcoholics. Depression has been cited as being especially common in female alcoholics (Curlee, 1969; Schuckit & Morrissey, 1976); once again, we are not sure if these findings are the result of general gender differences or are related to specific effects of alcohol that differ for women and men.

It is also instructive to compare female alcoholics to their nonalcoholic counterparts, in order to gain some ideas about why some women drink to excess. First, there is a general finding that women alcoholics have low self-esteem (e.g., Beckman, 1975). Beyond this, there has been a great deal of concern in the literature about whether female alcoholics have a feminine or masculine sex-role orientation. In one of the first studies to raise this issue, Wilsnack (1973) found that on measures of conscious sex-role identification, both alcoholics and nonalcoholics had feminine orientations, but that the alcoholics were more masculine on measures of unconscious sex role orientation. Other studies have also found that female alcoholics value female roles generally (e.g., Belfer, Shader, Carroll, & Harmatz, 1971; Kinsey, 1966). However, Wilsnack (1974) found that women classified as heavy social drinkers had high power needs. Typically, it is men more than women who have a high need for power. She points out that drinking itself is con-sidered a masculine behavior, and that women who drink heavily may therefore see themselves as being more masculine in their behaviors than nondrinking women.

Finding some support for the idea that female alcoholics are more feminine in their orientations, Beckman (1978b) reports that on independent scales of masculinity and femininity, her sample of women alcoholics were less masculine than controls in sex-role style although they were no more feminine. Other studies have attempted to clarify this issue by noting first that there is more than one type of female alcoholic (e.g., Beckman, 1975, 1978a; Wilsnack, 1976), and second that regardless of whether the female drinkers have conscious feelings of femininity and unconscious masculine feelings or vice versa, some conflict between the conscious and unconscious feelings is typical (Colman, 1975). As Colman points out, most of these women are high either in feminine or in masculine feelings. Few of them are androgynous (accepting of both male and female characteristics in themselves). Anderson (1980) finds that although there is no general pattern of female alcoholics being more feminine or masculine than their nonalcoholic sisters, alcoholic women do show more conflict in their sex-role attitudes and behavior. In another study of this issue, Beckman (1978a, 1978b) found that major sex-role conflicts characterized only about one-fourth of her sample of female alcoholics, although minor conflicts were typical. Thus, the conflict explanation may characterize only some women alcoholics, although this does appear to be a major explanatory factor for the drinking of at least some women. Some data from female social drinkers (Wilsnack, 1974) suggest that drinking may make these women alcoholics feel more feminine.

As mentioned several times, there may well be more than one pattern of female alcoholism and more than one type of reaction to alcohol. Alcohol consumption may have a physiological effect for some women of temporarily relieving depression (Jones & Jones, 1976). Since depression commonly precedes or accompanies female alcoholism, this too may be a major reason for women's drinking. Of course, these factors may also interact. A woman might begin to drink and simultaneously feel warm and loving, more feminine, and less depressed. These feelings might cause her to act in a more stereotypically feminine manner, especially if she also experienced sensations of feeling more sexually aroused. This would be most likely when she was with her husband or with some other person to whom she was attracted. Women tend to act most "feminine" when in the presence of men, especially men whom they find sexually attractive (e.g., Frieze et al., 1978). Warm sexual feelings would in turn tend to interfere with aggressive feelings.

Alcohol and Violence

On the basis of the research that we have reviewed, there is no evidence that women typically become more aggressive after drinking, in the way so many men do. Of course, as with men, the specific effects of alcohol consumption probably depend upon a number of factors. Violence may be a reaction of some women. In our study of battered women and family violence (Frieze & Knoble, 1980), we did find a few cases of women who had drinking problems and who were at least moderately violent toward their husbands when they were drinking. However, factor analyses of the relationships of the violence and drinking variables indicated that these women were not the most violent women in our sample and they were not highly violent toward their children. It was more typical to find high levels of violence in both husband and wife toward each other and toward their children in couples where the husband had the drinking problem, not the wife. And, in these families, the husband tended to be far more violent than his wife. It appears that the violence of these women is not the result of their own drinking, but is in reaction to the alcohol-induced violence of their husbands. Our data do not provide strong evidence that even those women who are violent are being so as a direct result of their own alcohol consumption.

One possible explanation for women's being less violent when they drink centers around the physical size differences between men and women. Men are generally physically stronger as well as taller and heavier than their wives. If a man becomes abusive when he drinks, he can physically force his wife to remain with him and be subjected to his aggression. Most women, even if they did become violent after drinking, could not force their husbands to endure their violence. Thus, women are not reinforced for being violent and they may never have the opportunity to express aggressive feelings. This difference may explain why we found that even those women who became moderately violent when drinking never became very violent. We had no "battered husbands" in our sample. However, it should be kept in mind that the women were not violent to their relatively defenseless children either. Once again, it appears that women do not as commonly display aggression as a reaction to drinking. Other data also support the conclusion that men are more violent than women in the family generally (Frieze *et al.*, 1980), and that women who do drink heavily or are alcoholic are not particularly violent toward their husbands or toward their children (Sandmaier, 1980). Although they may neglect the physical needs of their children because of chronic intoxication, women do not appear to become violent with children after drinking in the way that some men may.

A COGNITIVE MODEL OF MALE AND FEMALE
REACTIONS TO ALCOHOL

As we have seen, it is not always possible to predict the effects of alcohol consumption in either sex (Blum, 1981). Alcohol does have some predictable physiological effects. These include skin flushing due to vasodilation, increased heart rate, and a decreased ability to feel pain. There are also predictable cognitive effects such as memory loss and slower reaction time. There is little if any evidence that there are any major differences in these effects between men and women. However, as we have seen, men are more likely to react to intoxication with aggression, while women typically do not show this pattern. We also know that there are differences in the personalities of male and female alcoholics, but these may simply reflect general sex differences. Whatever their cause, however, they may imply that the two sexes drink for different reasons. Finally, there is also abundant evidence that the social context of drinking is different for men and for women. Drinking is often considered a male activity and more social stigma may be attached to female drinkers than to male drinkers. All this suggests that cognitive processes may be important in understanding the reactions of women and men to alcohol.

In 1962 Schachter and Singer published a classic study in which they demonstrated that people will react to heightened physiological arousal for which they have no prior explanation in a way that is consistent with the environment in which they find themselves. Other studies have found similar effects. For example, Cantor, Zillmann, and Bryant (1975) reported that subjects who had previously exercised but did not realize that they still had a high heart rate reported feeling more sexual arousal after watching an erotic film. Presumably, this was because they misattributed their feelings of arousal to the film instead of correctly identifying the source of their arousal as their previous exercise. Using a similar theoretical model, Berscheid and Walster (1974) suggested that feelings of passionate love may arise in situations in which one feels aroused and is in the presence of a sexually attractive person. In such a situation, people may again misattribute their arousal (from whatever source it really comes) as sexual attraction to the other person.

In order to apply this model to analyzing the effects of drinking, there would have to be a source of unexplained arousal. As discussed earlier, moderate amounts of alcohol cause a number of arousing physiological effects: skin flushing, which results in a feeling of warmth; increased heart rate; and dulling of aches and pains. These effects may not be obviously identifiable as resulting from the alcohol and therefore may be unexplained. This leads to a cognitive interpretation and labeling of one's state of emotional arousal.

A series of studies conducted by McClelland and his colleagues (McClelland, Davis, Kalin, & Wanner, 1972) suggested that these alcohol effects are interpreted by men who are drinking either as sexual feelings or as feelings of strength and power. In fact, McClelland *et al.* speculated that a major reason that men drink is to enhance their feelings of power. They also noted that there is more male drinking in societies around the world that place a high value on self-assertive or "macho" behavior in men.

Other studies have indicated that men report higher sexual arousal after drinking (e.g., Briddell & Wilson, 1976; Wilson & Lawson, 1976b). Using the cognitive model described earlier, one would predict that both aggressive and sexual reactions to alcohol would be possible along with other emotional reactions, depending upon the particular environment in which the alcohol was consumed, and the previous experiences of the drinker. If the drinking occurs in an all-male setting where stereotypical male behavior is stressed, presumably there would be more aggressive than sexual reactions. From a young age, boys are trained to be more aggressive than girls. Being a male in our society means being tough, strong, and aggressive (David & Brannon, 1976). Being a "sissy" means acting like a girl and *not* being aggressive. Children of all ages accept the idea that males are more aggressive and that boys "like to fight" and "throw things" (Tibbets, 1975). Boys are expected to know how to fight and to defend themselves physically if attacked. As they grow older, males are more likely than females to respond to frustration or aggressive provocation with violence (Frodi et al., 1977). On a more general level, men are expected to be assertive and dominant, especially in their relationships with women, and they are more accepting of violence in others (Frieze et al., 1978). Given this background, it is perhaps not surprising that men are more likely to interpret ambiguous physical sensations as feelings of aggression. Women are not trained to be aggressive and therefore may have little experience with aggressive behaviors or feelings. Men, on the other hand, are encouraged to feel and express aggression, at least while they are growing up. They are more likely to know what aggressive feelings are and would have less conflict over their expression.

The effects of alcohol in women may also depend on their cognitive interpretation of the physical sensations they experience as a result of drinking. For example, Wilsnack (1974) argues that women interpret these effects in a manner consistent with their prior sex-role socialization. The sensation of warmth from vasodilation might be interpreted as feelings of emotional warmth by a woman and as feelings of power by a man. Because women are not socialized to feel strong and powerful, nor do they learn to react to feelings of power with aggressive behavior (e.g., Cloward & Piven, 1979), they are probably more likely to interpret these alcohol-induced body changes as being sexual. Wilson and Lawson (1976a) support this argument with data showing that women expect to feel sexual after drinking.

As a further test of this cognitive model, let us briefly review some of the data discussed earlier in the chapter. First, does alcohol have physiological effects that are not readily attributable to the drug? As we have seen, there are a number of physiological effects of alcohol that people may not be aware of. Additionally, these physiological effects are more variable in women than in men due to their interactions with female hormone levels. Thus, women in particular may have unexplained arousal after drinking and we might expect that women would experience a greater variety of reactions than men.

A second question is whether there is a readily available alternative explanation for any unexplained arousal. Again, if one drinks in the presence of one's husband (as women are likely to do), it would be easy to misattribute the alcohol-induced arousal as warm and affectionate feelings for the husband. Of course, any explanation would have to be consistent with one's own self image. Thus, if one sees oneself (or wants to see oneself) as an attractive, feminine woman, such a misattribution of alcohol arousal as sexual interest would be especially likely. Similarily, if a man sees or wants to see himself as a strong, powerful man, he may misinterpret his arousal as in fact indicating that he is feeling strength and power. Once this interpretation is made, behavior consistent with the labeling would be expected. People would then be likely to act in such a way as to reinforce the interpretation that they had made. There may be other more direct effects of alcohol as well. For example, a man who interpreted his arousal as resulting from angry or hostile feelings might feel less concern about acting on these perceived feelings because of alcohol-related deficits in information-processing abilities. And, there would be fewer inhibitions based on fears of retaliation because of the alcohol-induced feelings of power. The cognitive deficits associated with alcohol use also might make it more difficult for the drinker to see that his or her interpretation of the situation was in error.

Of course, not all men become aggressive when drinking (or sober), and some women do get into fights or display physical aggression in other ways. Using the same cognitive model, it is possible to predict other reactions to alcohol than those discussed so far. For example, female alcoholics may interpret the physiological effects of alcohol as indicating that there is something wrong with them. Or, if their feelings of warmth are not recipro-cated by their husbands or lovers, they may feel especially rejected. In either case, they might then become depressed and suicidal. Another reaction reported by male and female alcoholics is to become "belligerent" (Johnson, Armor, Polich, & Stambul, 1977). Some of the same factors that would lead to physical violence after drinking might also cause some men and women to feel angry, even if this is not expressed in actual violence.

Wilsnack (1982) provides some data from a small sample that present an interesting perspective on this question of nonphysical aggression and alcohol. She finds that moderate- and heavy-drinking women are more likely than light-drinking women and men of all drinking levels to want to drink when they are angry and upset, but that these female heavy drinkers are less likely to start a fight with their husbands after drinking than when sober. She also finds that these women never fight with their children when they are drinking. Thus, even though the women do report more (pre-sumably verbal) fights than men do, this tendency is not enhanced by alcohol. In fact, the only situation in her data in which there was more aggression after alcohol consumption was for men, who reported getting into more fights with people outside of the family. It appears that these women may drink to *decrease* aggressive feelings. Whatever the reaction though, it appears to depend on prior expectations and the social context of the drinking.

CONCLUSIONS

The research reviewed in this chapter suggests that male and female reactions to alcohol can best be understood by using a cognitive model that predicts that a drinker's reactions will depend upon the social context in which drinking occurs and the prior expectations of the person about how alcohol will affect him or her. Much of the literature on which this chapter is based uses small and nonrandom samples. There is clearly a need for more and better research about the effects of alcohol that uses this cognitive perspective. Work that goes beyond the limitations of this chapter to marital violence and looks at other forms of physical and nonphysical aggression would be especially useful. Questions that might be asked include such issues as: Do the effects outlined here extend to violence outside the family context? Can we explain nonphysical aggression as a reaction to alcohol using the same theoretical model? Are the sex differences in the same direction when we include arguing and other forms of verbal aggression?

Finally, the data presented in this chapter indicate that women are frequently the victims of alcohol-induced aggression. This is an important, and largely overlooked, problem of the wives and other partners of alcoholics that should receive more attention in designing alcohol prevention and treatment programs. The model proposed here further suggests that, in families in which the wife is the victim of alcohol-induced violence, more attention needs to be given to the specific relationship between alcohol and violence. The violence problems will be solved by attempting to curb the husband's alcohol use in only some of the families. In others, more long-term general therapy will be needed for the men. Reeducation about the effects of alcohol on aggression might also be helpful. Perhaps violent men could be conditioned to react in less hostile ways to the physiological changes that accompany alcohol consumption. Only if these and other steps are taken will women no longer be the victims of male alcohol-induced violence.

REFERENCES

Anderson, S. C. Patterns of sex-role identification in alcoholic women. *Sex Roles*, 1980, *6*, 231–243.

Bard, M., & Zacker, J. Assaultiveness and alcohol use in family disputes. *Criminology*, 1974, *12*, 281–292.

Beckman, L. J. Women alcoholics: A review of social and psychological studies. *Journal of Studies on Alcohol*, 1975, *36*, 797–824.

Beckman, L. J. Psychosocial aspects of alcoholism in women. In F. A. Seixas (Ed.), *Currents in alcoholism* (Vol. 4: *Psychiatric, psychological, social and epidemiological studies*). New York: Grune & Stratton, 1978. (a)

Beckman, L. J. Sex-role conflict in alcoholic women: Myth or reality. *Journal of Abnormal Psychology*, 1978, *87*, 408–417. (b)

Belfer, M. L., Shader, R. I., Carroll, M., & Harmatz, J. S. Alcoholism in women. *Archives of General Psychiatry*, 1971, *25*, 540–544.

Bennett, R. B., Buss, A. H., & Carpenter, J. A. Alcohol and human physical aggression. *Quarterly Journal of Studies on Alcohol*, 1969, *30*, 870–876.

Berscheid, E., & Walster, E. A little bit about love. In T. L. Huston (Ed.), *Foundations of interpersonal attraction*. New York: Academic Press, 1974.

Black, R., & Mayer, J. *An investigation of the relationship between substance abuse and child abuse and neglect.* (Final report to the National Center on Child Abuse and Neglect on Grant No. 90-C-427). Boston: Washingtonian Center for Addictions, 1979.

Blum, R. H. Violence, alcohol, and setting: An unexplored nexus. In J. J. Collins, Jr. (Ed.), *Drinking and crime: Perspectives on the relationships between alcohol consumption and criminal behavior.* New York: Guilford Press, 1981.

Blumenthal, M. D., Kahn, R. L., Andrews, F. M., & Head, K. B. *Justifying violence: Attitudes of American men.* Ann Arbor, Mich.: Institute for Social Research, University of Michigan, 1972.

Briddell, D. W., & Wilson, G. T. Effects of alcohol and expectancy set on male sexual arousal. *Journal of Abnormal Psychology,* 1976, *85,* 225–234.

Byles, J. A. Violence, alcohol problems and other problems in disintegrating families. *Journal of Studies on Alcohol,* 1978, *39,* 551–553.

Cantor, J. R., Zillmann, D., & Bryant, J. Enhancement of experienced sexual arousal in response to erotic stimuli through misattribution of unrelated residual excitation. *Journal of Personality and Social Psychology,* 1975, *32,* 69–75.

Cloward, R. A., & Piven, F. F. Hidden protest: The channeling of female innovation and resistance. *Signs,* 1979, *4,* 651–669.

Colman, C. J. *Problem drinking women: Aspects of their marital interaction and sex role style.* Unpublished doctoral dissertation, Harvard University, 1975.

Corrigan, E. M. *Alcoholic women in treatment.* New York: Oxford University Press, 1980.

Curlee, J. Alcoholism and the "empty nest". *Bulletin of the Menninger Clinic,* 1969, *33,* 165–171.

David, D., & Brannon, R. *The forty-nine percent majority: The male sex role.* Reading, Mass.: Addison-Wesley, 1976.

Eberle, P. A. *Alcohol abusers and non-users: A discriminant analysis of differences between two sub-groups of batterers.* Paper presented at the annual meeting of the National Women's Studies Association, Bloomington, Ind., May 1980.

Felson, R. B., & Ribner, S. A. An attributional approach to accounts and sanctions for criminal violence. *Social Psychology Quarterly,* 1981, *44*(2), 137–142.

Fitzpatrick, J. P. Drugs, alcohol, and violent crime. *Addictive Disorders,* 1974, *1,* 353–367.

Frieze, I. H., Knoble, J. *The effects of alcohol on marital violence.* Paper presented at the Annual Convention of the American Psychological Association, Montreal, Canada, September 1980.

Frieze, I. H., Knoble, J., Washburn, C., & Zomnir, G. *Characteristics of battered women and their marriages.* Unpublished manuscript, University of Pittsburgh, 1980.

Frieze, I. H., Parsons, J. E., Johnson, P. B., Ruble, D. N., & Zellman, G. L. *Women and sex roles: A psychosocial perspective.* New York: W. W. Norton, 1978.

Frodi, A., Macaulay, J., & Thorne, P. Are women always less aggressive than men? A review of the experimental literature. *Psychological Bulletin,* 1977, *84,* 634–660.

Gelles, R. J. *The violent home: A study of physical aggression between husbands and wives.* Beverly Hills, Calif.: Sage Publications, 1972.

Gerson, L. W. Alcohol-related acts of violence: Who was drinking and where the acts occurred. *Journal of Studies on Alcohol,* 1978, *39,* 1294–1296.

Goldstein, J. H. *Aggression and crimes of violence.* New York: Oxford University Press, 1975.

Gomberg, E. S. Problems with alcohol and other drugs. In E. S. Gomberg & V. Franks (Eds.), *Gender and disordered behavior: Sex differences in psychopathology.* New York: Brunner/Mazel, 1979.

Groth, A. N. The older rape victim and her assailant. *Journal of Geriatric Psychiatry,* 1978, *11*(2), 203–215.

Haberman, P. W., & Baden, M. M. *Alcohol, other drugs and violent death.* New York: Oxford University Press, 1978.

Hamilton, C. J., & Collins, J. J., Jr. The role of alcohol in wife beating and child abuse: A review of the literature. In J. J. Collins, Jr. (Ed.), *Drinking and crime: Perspectives on the relationships between alcohol consumption and criminal behavior.* New York: Guilford Press, 1981.

Hill, S. Y. Introduction: The biological consequences. In *Alcoholism and alcohol abuse among women: Research issues* (NIAA Research Monograph No. 1, USDHEW Pub. No. ADM-80-835). Washington, D.C.: U.S. Government Printing Office, 1980.

Johnson, P., Armor, D. J., Polich, S., & Stambul, H. *U.S. adult drinking practices: Time trends, social correlates and sex roles* (Working Note prepared for the National Institute

Johnson, P., Armor, D. J., Polich, S., & Stambul, H. *U.S. adult drinking practices: Time trends, social correlates and sex roles.* (Working Note prepared for the National Institute on Alcohol Abuse and Alcoholism). Santa Monica, Calif.: Rand Corporation, 1977.

Johnson, R. N. *Aggression in man and animals.* Philadelphia: W. B. Saunders, 1972.

Jones, B. M. & Jones, M. K. Women and alcohol: Intoxication, metabolism, and the menstrual cycle. In M. Greenblatt & M. A. Schuckit (Eds.), *Alcoholism problems in women and children.* New York: Grune & Stratton, 1976.

Kinsey, B. A. *The female alcoholic: A social psychological study.* Springfield, Ill.: Charles C Thomas, 1966.

Kutash, I. L., Kutash, S. B., Schlesinger, L. B., & Associates. *Violence: Perspectives on murder and aggression.* San Francisco: Jossey-Bass, 1978.

Labell, L. S. Wife abuse: A sociological study of battered women and their mates. *Victimology,* 1979, *4,* 258–267.

Lang, A. R., Goeckner, D. J., Adesso, V. J., & Marlatt, G. A. Effects of alcohol on aggression in male social drinkers. *Journal of Abnormal Psychology,* 1975, *84,* 508–518.

Langley, R., & Levy, R. *Wife beating: The silent crisis.* New York: Pocket Books, 1977.

Mayfield, D. Alcoholism, alcohol, intoxication, and assaultive behavior. *Diseases of the Nervous System,* 1976, *37,* 288–291.

McClelland, D., Davis, W., Kalin, R., & Wanner, E. *The drinking man.* New York: Free Press, 1972.

Nicol, A. R., Gunn, J. C., Gristwood, J., Foggitt, R. H., & Watson, J. P. The relationship of alcoholism to violent behaviour resulting in long-term imprisonment. *British Journal of Psychiatry,* 1973, *123,* 47–51.

Orford, J., Guthrie, S., Nicholls, P., Oppenheimer, E., Egert, S., & Hensman, C. Self-reported coping behavior of wives of alcoholics and its association with drinking outcome. *Journal of Studies on Alcohol,* 1975, *36,* 1254–1267.

Pernanen, K. Theoretical aspects of the relationship between alcohol use and crime. In J. J. Collins, Jr. (Ed.), *Drinking and crime: Perspectives on the relationships between alcohol consumption and criminal behavior.* New York: Guilford Press, 1981.

Pizzey, E. *Scream quietly or the neighbors will hear.* Short Hills, N.J.: Ridley Enslow Publishers, 1977.

Powers, R. J., & Kutash, I. L. Substance-induced aggression. In I. L. Kutash, S. B. Kutash, L. B. Schlesinger, & Associates, *Violence: Perspectives on murder and aggression.* San Francisco: Jossey-Bass, 1978.

Rada, R. T. Alcoholism and forcible rape. *American Journal of Psychiatry,* 1975, *132*(4), 444–446.

Richardson, D. C., & Campbell, J. L. Alcohol and wife abuse: The effects of alcohol on attributions of blame for wife abuse. *Personality and Social Psychology Bulletin,* 1980, *6,* 51–56.

Richardson, D. R. *The effects of alcohol and verbal provocation on male aggression against female targets.* Unpublished doctoral dissertation, Kent State University, Ohio, 1978.

Rix, K. J. B. *Alcohol and alcoholism.* Montreal, Canada: Eden Press, 1977.

Roy, M. A current survey of 150 cases. In M. Roy (Ed.), *Battered women: A psychological study of domestic violence.* New York: Van Nostrand Reinhold, 1977.

Sandmaier, M. *The invisible alcoholics: Women and alcohol abuse in America.* New York: McGraw-Hill, 1980.

Schachter, S., & Singer, J. E. Cognitive, social, and physiological determinants of emotional state. *Psychological Review,* 1962, *69,* 379–399.

Schuckit, M. A. *Drug and alcohol abuse.* New York: Plenum Medical Book Company, 1979.

Schuckit, M. A., & Morrissey, E. R. Alcoholism in women: Some clinical and social perspectives with an emphasis on possible subtypes. In M. Greenblatt & M. A. Schuckit (Eds.), *Alcoholism problems in women and children.* New York: Grune & Stratton, 1976.

Shupe, L. M. Alcohol and crime: A study of the urine concentration found in 882 persons arrested during or immediately after the commission of a felony. *Journal of Criminal Law, Criminology, and Police Science,* 1954, *44,* 661-664.

Smart, R. G. Female and male alcoholics in treatment: Characteristics at intake and recovery rates. *British Journal of Addiction,* 1979, *74,* 275-281.

Sobell, L. C., & Sobell, M. B. Drunkenness, a "special circumstance" in crime and violence, sometimes. *International Journal of the Addictions,* 1975, *10,* 869-882.

Straus, M. A., Gelles, R. J., & Steinmetz, S. K. *Behind closed doors: Violence in the American family.* Garden City, N.Y.: Anchor Books, 1980.

Tibbets, S. Sex-role stereotyping in the lower grades: Part of a solution. *Journal of Vocational Behavior,* 1975, *6,* 255-261.

Vanfossen, B. E. Intersexual violence in Monroe County, New York. *Victimology,* 1979, *4,* 299-305.

Virkkunen, M. Alcohol as a factor precipitating aggression and conflict behavior leading to homicide. *British Journal of Addiction,* 1974, *69,* 149-154.

Walker, L. E. *The battered woman.* New York: Harper & Row, 1979.

Wilsnack, S. C. Sex role identity in female alcoholism. *Journal of Abnormal Psychology,* 1973, *82,* 253-261.

Wilsnack, S. C. The effects of social drinking on women's fantasy. *Journal of Personality,* 1974, *42,* 43-61.

Wilsnack, S. C. The impact of sex roles on women's alcohol use and abuse. In M. Greenblatt & M. A. Schuckit (Eds.), *Alcoholism problems in women and children.* New York: Grune & Stratton, 1976.

Wilsnack, S. C. *Selected items on drinking and aggression from pretest for national survey of women's drinking.* Unpublished manuscript, University of North Dakota School of Medicine, 1982.

Wilson, G. T., & Lawson, D. M. Effects of alcohol on sexual arousal in women. *Journal of Abnormal Psychology,* 1976, *85,* 489-497. (a)

Wilson, G. T., & Lawson, D. M. Expectancies, alcohol, and sexual arousal in male social drinkers. *Journal of Abnormal Psychology,* 1976, *85,* 587-594. (b)

Wilson, G. T., & Lawson, D. M. Expectancies, alcohol, and sexual arousal in women. *Journal of Abnormal Psychology,* 1978, *87,* 358-367.

Wolfgang, M. E., & Strohm, R. B. The relationship between alcohol and criminal homicide. *Quarterly Journal of Studies on Alcohol,* 1957, *17,* 411-425.

Youcha, G. *A dangerous pleasure.* New York: Hawthorn Books, 1978.

Zacker, J., & Bard, M. Further findings on assaultiveness and alcohol use in interpersonal disputes. *American Journal of Community Psychology,* 1977, *5,* 373-383.

Zeichner, A., & Pihl, R. O. Effects of alcohol and behavior contingencies on human aggression. *Journal of Abnormal Psychology,* 1979, *88,* 153-160.

10

Female Alcohol Abuse:
Its Effects on the Family

CAROL N. WILLIAMS
Brown University

LORRAINE V. KLERMAN
Brandeis University

INTRODUCTION

Any attempt to analyze the impact of female alcohol abuse on the family must consider both the changes that have occurred in women's place in society, particularly within the last 20 years, and the many roles that women currently play within the family depending on their age and stage in the life cycle. This analytic task is made difficult by the inadequacy of research on female alcoholism in general, and on the familial context of women's drinking in particular. This chapter will examine the interactions between family factors and excessive drinking by women during four life stages: adolescence, the child-rearing years, the "empty nest" period, and the older years. The relationships between adolescents and their parents and siblings, wives and their husbands, mothers and their children, and elderly women and their families will be explored. Attention will be paid to the special problems involved when the family has a working mother or when the mother is a single parent. In many of these situations, research data are not available, and these lacunae in current knowledge will be noted.

A life-cycle approach helps to underscore the fact that as women move from one life stage to the next, changes occur in their tasks outside the home, as well as in their relationships and responsibilities to both their families of origin and their families of procreation. Excessive alcohol use may serve different purposes and have different familial impacts at various stages in women's lives. Yet no longitudinal studies exist on the effects of women's alcohol abuse through the entire life cycle, and family studies are scarce.

The deleterious effects that alcohol abuse has on family life and the concern with which it is viewed by the American public are evident from the findings of a Gallup Poll prepared for the 1980 White House Conference on Families. Of the Americans polled, 45% felt that family life had deteriorated in the last 15 years. Also, 59% identified alcohol abuse as the most harmful influence on family life, and 25% reported that alcohol problems had affected their families personally ("Family Life," 1980). A therapist stated it in another way:

> In all the time I have spent working with and observing families, I cannot recall a single, openly communicating, mutually respecting, well-oriented, lovingly close family in which an actively participating member had a serious and lasting drug habit—transient experimentation, occasional booze or pot, yes, but disabling and lasting drug use, no. (Auerswald, 1980, p. 124)

DEMOGRAPHIC TRENDS

The stereotype of a woman alcoholic is that of a homemaker–mother hiding bottles in the laundry hamper and being protected by other members of the family. This picture is incorrect in at least two ways. First, less than half of adult women are non-wage-earning homemakers: working women, single parents and single women who are divorced or separated, widowed, or never married comprise the majority. Second, in recent national surveys, the greatest number of alcohol-related problems were reported by 18–20-year-old women and unemployed women looking for work. This section describes the demographic trends that are probably affecting women's alcohol use, both in more traditional households and in families or households with different compositions and life styles.

Household Composition

Only 28.2% of all American families currently fit the traditional picture of working father, homemaker–mother, and children under 18 years of age. The number of married-couple households declined from 74.8% of all households in 1960 to 65.4% in 1975 and is projected to drop to 54.9% by 1990. The number of female-headed households increased from 17.2% of total households in 1960 to 23.6% in 1975 and is projected to reach 29% by 1990 (Masnick & Bane, 1980). Women 55 years of age and older are the largest age–sex group living alone, but the rate of increase in single-headed households has been fastest among young adults (U.S. Bureau of the Census, 1980).

Marriage and Children

The changes in women's status are associated with new patterns of marriage and childbearing. The decline in marriage is greatest in the late teens and early twenties as young people delay marriage in order to work or complete their education. Moreover, the overall fertility rate has dropped; women are having fewer children and household size is shrinking (U.S. Bureau of the Census, 1980).

Working Women

Among families with children, 60% now have two working spouses (U.S. Department of Labor, 1981). The proportion of families in which only the male is a wage earner is decreasing, and this configuration is lasting for shorter periods of time. The number of households containing two working spouses, single parents with children, and single divorced, separated, widowed, or never-married individuals is increasing dramatically (Masnick & Bane, 1980).

Of all mothers with children under 18 years of age, 58.1% were in the labor force as of March, 1981, which meant that 54% of the nation's children under 18 had working mothers. Divorced mothers were far more likely to be working or looking for work than mothers of any other marital status (U.S. Department of Labor, 1981). In 1978, 19% of all children under 18 lived with a single parent, and this number was projected to reach 25% by 1990. Children in families headed by women were six times more likely than children in families headed by men to be living below the poverty line (U.S. Bureau of the Census, 1978).

Implications

The implications of these demographic trends for female drinking patterns are suggested by several studies. In two national drinking surveys (Cahalan, Cisin, & Crossley, 1969; Johnson, Armor, Polich, & Stambul, 1977), divorced or separated women reported the highest incidence of problem drinking among all women drinkers, with never-married women reporting the second highest incidence. In terms of women and employment, Johnson *et al.* found that the highest rates of problem drinking occurred among unemployed women seeking work, followed closely by employed women. Married working women reported drinking problems twice as often as single working women. Housewives were half as likely to report alcohol problems as employed and unemployed women. Surprisingly, in the 1975 national survey data reanalyzed by Johnson *et al.* the women who reported the greatest number of alcohol problems were the 18–20-year-old group.

A 1981 national survey by Wilsnack, Wilsnack, and Klassen (1984) also discovered that its youngest age group of women (21–34) reported the most drinking problems. However, this survey found that women living in quasi-marital relationships had the highest numbers of drinking problems, followed by women who were divorced/separated, never-married, or unemployed/seeking work. A study of employed women (Volicher, Cahill, & Smith, 1981) positively associated problem drinking with number of children, regardless of age, education, marital status, or income.

Little is known about how women cope with their changing status, and what role alcohol plays as they increasingly enter the work force, become single parents, head their own households, and face economic difficulties. As Wattenberg and Reinhardt (1979) have noted: "In almost every study of female headed households, women mentioned their loneliness, isolation, and overwhelming responsibilities" (p. 464). Women have not been prepared for being single, losing their roles as wives, raising children alone, coping with the absence of support systems, or bearing the economic hardship of these situations. As discussed earlier, several groups sharing these characteristics are known to be at high risk for abusing alcohol: the young, the unemployed, the married jobholder, and the unmarried.

This review of current knowledge concerning women's alcohol abuse and its effect on families begins with adolescence, when the majority of women take their first drink, usually within a family setting (Blane & Hewitt, 1977). See Table 10-1 for a summary of the characteristics of the studies reviewed.

ADOLESCENCE

Studies of adolescence and alcohol abuse tend to focus on the impact of parental behavior on adolescent drinking patterns. Yet it is undoubtedly true that excessive adolescent drinking, perhaps particularly when a daughter is involved, may have significant negative effects on other family members.

Effects of Adolescent Drinking on the Family

A recent study of alcohol use and stress during the family life cycle found that parents drank most when their children were adolescents. Drinking was least frequent during the children's preschool years, increased during the school-age years, peaked in the adolescent years, and sharply declined as children reached maturity (Rouse, 1981). Mental health clinicians report that a family's entrance into therapy is often precipitated by an adolescent daughter's drinking and/or sexual behavior.

Educational films on adolescent drinking often show puzzled and distraught parents trying to deal with an adolescent whose behavior they cannot understand either prior to or after the discovery of the drinking problem. Initially the reaction may be one of denial, but later guilt may emerge or blame may be placed by one parent on the other. Younger children also are clearly affected, either because they are manipulated or influenced by the drinking sibling, or because they are disturbed by the worsening family relationships resulting from the drinking problem. These aspects of adolescent drinking do not appear to have been researched.

TABLE 10-1. Summary of Characteristics of Research Studies

Authors (year)	Sample size and composition	Type of sample	Methods of data collection	Subject of study
Anderson (1976)	30 alcoholic women and 30 non-alcoholic sisters; middle SES[a]	Inpatient and outpatient treatment centers, AA	Interviews, Franck Drawing Completion Test, and questionnaires	Sex-role styles, relationships with parents, and personality characteristics as adolescents
Armor, Polich, & Stambul (1976)	14,000 alcoholic patients and 5300 randomly selected adults; lower and middle SES	44 federally funded alcohol treatment centers and Harris general population drinking surveys	Questionnaires	Characteristics of patients and their treatment outcomes
Baer, Morin, & Gaitz (1970)	52 male and 35 female patients: 15 psychotic, 15 alcoholic, 32 organic brain syndrome, 25 organic brain syndrome and alcoholic; lower SES	County diagnostic centers	Agency rating scale	Patient functioning, family involvement, and attitudes toward patient
Biek (1981)	27 teenage girls and 10 teenage boys	Outpatient clinic	Questionnaire interview	Identification of youth with problem drinking parents
Black & Mayer (1980)	34 alcoholic mothers, 58 alcoholic fathers, and 108 opiate-addicted parents; lower SES	Inpatient detoxification unit	Interviews, MMPI, Survey of Bringing Up Children, and Schedule of Recent Experience	Child care practices, drug use, and family histories
Booz-Allen & Hamilton (1974)	50 adult children aged 19–30 of 46 alcoholic fathers and 10 alcoholic mothers; middle SES	Recruited through agencies and media advertising	Interviews with children	Family background and adult adjustment
Bosma & Jensen (1972–1973)	500 adolescents	Pediatric clinics, mental health clinics, probation and suicide statistics	Survey	Relationship of parental alcoholism to maladjustment in children
Bourgeois, Levigneron, & Delage (1975)	66 children of alcoholics, aged 3–16: 38 alcoholic fathers, 1 alcoholic mother, 27 with 2 alcoholic parents; and 70 children without alcoholic parents; lower SES	Both groups from inpatient children's psychiatric unit	Patients' charts	Family background and child's adjustment

Busch, Kormendy, & Feuerlein (1973)	19 husbands of alcoholics and 19 control husbands; middle SES	Wives in inpatient treatment	Interviews	Comparison of characteristics of husbands with and without alcoholic wives
Cork (1969)	59 male and 53 female children of 53 alcoholic fathers and 19 alcoholic mothers; middle SES	Parents in outpatient treatment	Interviews with children and agency records on parents	Family environment and child's perception of it
Corrigan (1980)	150 alcoholic women, with follow-up on 116 women; 20 husbands, 33 nonalcoholic sisters; all SES	Outpatient, inpatient, and AA treatment settings	Interviews, 2-year follow-up	Etiology of alcoholism in women, effects on self and others, and treatment outcomes
Cutter & Fisher (1980)	76 male and 52 female undergraduates; middle SES	College students	Questionnaires and Definitions of Alcohol Scale	Family experience and purpose of drinking
Dahlgren (1979)	51 husbands of alcoholic women, and 46 married alcoholic men; middle SES	Inpatient treatment unit	6–12-year follow-up with questionnaires and social agency reports	Mortality, marital situations, and psychosocial disturbance
el-Gueblay, Offord, Sullivan, & Lynch (1978)	15 males and 15 females in three groups: alcoholic, schizophrenic, depressive; and 231 children; lower SES	Inpatient hospital unit	Children's medical history, Rutter's Parental Questionnaire, and Randall–McClure Behavior Problem Checklist	Behavioral characteristics and psychological adjustment of children
Fillmore (1975)	109 men and 97 women; middle or upper SES	College students	Questionnaires; 20-year longitudinal follow-up	Relationship of drinking patterns in early and middle adulthood
Hubbard, Santos, & Santos (1979)	50 alcohol-related cases among 250 adult cases	Mental health outreach program to the elderly	Case reports and interviews with case workers and families	Descriptive analysis of overt and covert effects of alcohol on subjects' lives
Human Services Development Institute (1980)	670 children in foster care; lower SES	Foster-care placements in Maine	Questionnaire	Characteristics of children and reasons for placement
Jessor & Jessor (1975)	188 boys and 244 girls; middle and upper-middle SES	Junior high school students	Questionnaire including psychometric scales; 4-year longitudinal study	Psychological and social antecedents to drinking

(continued)

TABLE 10-1. (Continued)

Authors (year)	Sample size and composition	Type of sample	Methods of data collection	Subject of study
Jones (1971)	45 women; middle SES	Berkeley Guidance Study and Oakland Growth Study	Interviews, demographic data, social and psychological testing; 30-year longitudinal study	Antecedent personality characteristics and drinking behavior
Kinsey (1966)	46 alcoholic women; lower SES	State hospital inpatients	Interviews and questionnaire	Demographic, social, and psychological characteristics of women and their families
Krauthamer (1974, 1979)	30 alcoholic mothers, 30 mothers in psychotherapy, and 120 children 8–18; upper-middle SES	Private inpatient alcoholism clinic and private outpatient psychotherapy	Personality and intelligence tests, and life history and maternal attitude questionnaires	Relationships and personality traits of mothers and children
Margulies, Kessler, & Kandel (1977)	Random sample of 1936 students	High school students	Questionnaires, 6-month follow-up	Personal, parental, and peer alcohol use and correlates
McKenna & Pickens (1981)	Adult alcoholic children, 1520 men, 410 women, of alcoholic fathers, alcoholic mothers, two alcoholic parents, and no alcoholic parents; middle SES	Inpatient alcoholism program	Interviews, patient records, 4-, 8-, and 12-month follow-up questionnaires	Rates of alcoholism in parents of alcoholics and characteristics of alcoholics with one, two, or no alcoholic parents
McLachlan, Walderman, & Thomas (1973)	54 13–19-year-old children of alcoholics in four groups: 22 with unrecovered fathers, 6 with unrecovered mothers, 18 with recovered fathers, 8 with recovered mothers, and control group of 54 teenagers without familial alcohol problems; middle SES	Outpatient clinic records, and random selection from community	Intelligence and personality tests and questionnaires on family and drug use	Family relationships, intellectual and emotional development, and drug use
Miller & Jang (1977)	147 children of alcoholics and 112 controls; lower SES	Subgroup of an Oakland, California multiproblem urban sample	Interviews, 20-year follow-up	Family problems, adult adjustment, sex-role identification and antecedents of drinking patterns

Paolino, McCrady, Diamond & Longabaugh (1976)	15 husbands of alcoholic women and Lanyon's normative sample of men; middle SES	Wives in inpatient treatment	Lanyon Psychological Screening Inventory	Husband's psychological adjustment
Rasmussen (1979)	35 couples in which wife is an alcoholic; middle SES	Outpatient clinic	Interviews, Gough Adjective Checklist and Moos Family Environment Scale	Interpersonal characteristics of spouses and perceived family climate
Rathbone-McCuan & Roberds (1980)	25 45–54-year-old women, and 16 women 55 and older; middle and upper-middle SES	Private hospital inpatients	Patient charts	Factors precipitating problem drinking and need for treatment
Rimmer (1974)	25 husbands of alcoholic women; middle and upper SES	Wives in a private psychiatric hospital	Interviews	Husband's psychological adjustment and drinking patterns
Robins, Bates, & O'Neal (1962)	138 girls and 365 boys from child psychiatric clinics, and 100 public school students; lower SES	Child psychiatric clinic and public school	Interviews, agency records; 30-year longitudinal study	Antecedents to drinking and adjustment in adulthood
Rouse (1981)	313 husbands and their wives; lower-middle SES	Framingham Heart Disease Study subsample	Interviews; 15-year longitudinal study	Relationship between family life cycle and drinking
Shyne & Schroeder (1978)	Stratified, weighted national random sample of 9517 children and their families	Public social service agencies	Questionnaires	Description of user and service characteristics
Steinglass (1981)	23 families with alcoholic husband, 8 families with alcoholic wife, and their spouses; middle SES	Recruitment from agencies and general media	Alcoholism and psychological tests, SAAST and SCL-90	Spouse behavior and psychological symptomatology during alcoholic drinking cycles
Tamerin, Tolor, & Harrington (1976)	20 alcoholic females, 20 alcoholic males, and their spouses; middle and upper SES	Private psychiatric hospital inpatients	Katz Adjustment Scale and NIMH Mood Scale	Alcoholics' and spouses' perceptions of the alcoholics' behavior and mood changes when sober and when intoxicated

(continued)

287

TABLE 10-1. (Continued)

Authors (year)	Sample size and composition	Type of sample	Methods of data collection	Subject of study
Van Houten & Golembiewski (1978)	618 runaways and 289 non-runaways; lower-middle and middle SES	Runaway centers and high school classrooms	Questionnaires	Relationship of life stress to adolescent alcohol abuse and runaway behavior
Widseth & Mayer (1971)	104 12–18-year-old girls; lower SES	Division of Youth Services inpatient and halfway house facilities	Interviews	Family background, attitudes, effects of alcohol use, and relation of parental alcohol use to girls' behavior
Williams (1982)	55 alcoholic fathers with no alcoholic mate, 24 alcoholic mothers with no alcoholic mate, and 12 (10 women) alcoholics with alcoholic mates; lower SES	Inpatient detoxification unit	Interview, questionnaire	Child care practices and family stability
Wolin, Bennett, Noonan, & Teitelbaum (1980)	25 families with adult children: 18 with alcoholic father, 5 with alcoholic mother, and 2 with both parents alcoholic; middle and upper SES	Referrals from agencies, private practitioners, AA, advertising, most not presently in treatment	Interviews with parents and children	Effect of different drinking patterns on family rituals and child's subsequent drinking patterns
Wood & Duffy (1966)	69 alcoholic women; middle SES	Outpatient hospital alcohol clinic	Interviews	Etiology of alcoholism
Zucker & Barron (1973) Zucker & Devoe (1975)	75 boys 75 girls	High school students	Interviews, diaries, and questionnaires on alcohol use, parent relationships, and personality; 2-year longitudinal follow-up	Family and social correlates of problem drinking

[a]SES = socioeconomic status.

Alcohol abuse by young females may impact indirectly on family life through its influence on sexual activity. Medical and other professionals who assist pregnant adolescents cite their patients' statements that drinking led to the intercourse that presumably resulted in the pregnancy. These statements are consistent with findings of a study by Bowker (1977): Nearly half of the males in this college sample reported that alcohol was the most commonly used drug for sexual seduction, and the females in the study stated that drinking made them feel more sexual. The role of substance use and abuse, including alcohol and illegal drugs, should be studied by those concerned with reducing the incidence of adolescent pregnancy.

Effects of Parental Behavior on Adolescent and Adult Drinking

Most of the studies of the effects of parental drinking on children are reviewed in the next section on the child-rearing years. This section examines studies that attempt to identify family influences that increase the probability that adolescents will drink excessively or grow up to become alcohol abusers.

Longitudinal studies of adolescents have consistently found that alcohol use by parents increases the chances of alcohol use by both sons and daughters (Jessor & Jessor, 1975; Margulies, Kessler, & Kandel, 1977; Robins, Bates, & O'Neal, 1962; Zucker & Devoe, 1975); and, according to the Jessors, parents have a greater influence on the drinking habits of girls than of boys. Studies, however, that follow children or adolescents into adulthood such as those by Robins et al. (1962), Jones (1971), and Fillmore (1975) have not been very successful in identifying a constellation of behavior and family background that predicts substance abuse by women at a later age. Robins and Smith (1980) concluded from their review of longitudinal studies that substance abuse for both sexes appeared to be associated with peer use, deviant families, and early deviance, but that associations were not as clear for females as for males.

Retrospective self-reports of early family experiences are another method of attempting to identify early family correlates of later problem drinking in adult women. Family relationships, especially with the mother, are most often described in negative terms. In studies by Wood and Duffy (1966) and Kinsey (1966) of alcoholic women in treatment, the women described their mothers as difficult to please, strict, dominant, and emotionally distant, while the fathers were remembered as warmer but weaker. Jones (1971) reported that the mothers of both girls and boys who later become adult alcoholics were viewed as "sour, disagreeable, and dissatisfied." The girls described high levels of family conflict and excessive dependence on their families during adolescence. Anderson (1976) found that alcoholic women, in comparison to their nonalcoholic sisters, reported poorer relationships with and less acceptance by their parents, a report their nonalcoholic sisters corroborated. Both groups perceived their parents similarly, although the nonalcoholic sisters identified with their mothers more closely than did the alcoholic sisters.

Female alcoholics are more likely than other women to have grown up in unstable family environments, with greater disruption occurring as a result of separation and divorce, economic distress, abuse or neglect, or placement of the child outside the home (Corrigan, 1980; Curlee, 1970; Kinsey, 1966; Lisansky, 1957). In general, the quality of child care experienced by these women was poor, discipline was erratic or lax, and demands on the child were inappropriately low or high. In Kinsey's (1966) study, 87% of alcoholic daughters rated their father's child care as inadequate and 75% rated their mother's care similarly. Robins *et al.* (1962) found positive correlations between inadequate child care, which included lax discipline and unmet physical needs, and the development of alcoholism. Problem-drinking adolescents studied by Zucker and Devoe (1975) described their parents as unconcerned, neglectful, and arbitrary in discipline. Girls reported greater distress over lack of affection and nurturance from their parents than did boys. Both Zucker and Devoe and Jessor and Jessor (1975) found relationships between low parent–child interaction, limited responsiveness to the child's needs, high family tension, and heavy or problem drinking in the adolescent.

The picture that emerges of the early family life of problem-drinking adolescents and of women who later become alcoholic is one in which parent–child relationships are impaired and family life is destabilized by separations, neglect, erratic discipline, and poor parenting. This description of the family is quite similar to that given by children of alcoholics in a later section of this chapter. A possible explanation is that female alcoholics' experiences in their families of origin are recreated in their families of procreation, and that the cycle of familial disruption and alcoholism is continued into the next generation. More longitudinal research is needed to trace the effects of the problem-drinking adolescent on the family as well as psychosocial effects of family environment and parenting on the development of alcoholism through several generations of children.

THE CHILD-REARING YEARS

The largest number of studies on the effects of adult female drinking on families examine the child-rearing years, reflecting societal views that the role of the mother is the most important one assigned to adult women and any factor that could lead to disruption in this role should be carefully analyzed. Nevertheless, the impact of adult female alcohol abuse on families is not limited to its effects on the children. Effects may begin before a child is born or even conceived. For example, among the unstudied problems in this area is the effect of excessive drinking on the desirability of a woman either as a sexual or as a marital partner. Does the vulnerability and need for care of the female alcoholic make her more attractive, or does her erratic behavior drive men away? What types of men prefer a woman who has heavy consumption patterns similar to their own and which ones prefer an abstainer or light drinker?

A full analysis of the effects of adult female drinking on the family would include its impact on female sexual interest, ability to conceive, desire for children, and ability to bear children. These studies, however, are reviewed in other chapters, as is the effect of alcohol consumption during pregnancy. In this section, therefore, effects on the family are limited to psychosocial effects on husbands and children. Although the issues of marriage and child-rearing are also important in other stages of the life cycle, for example, adolescent child-rearing and marital relations among the elderly, those issues are addressed primarily in this section, since most women undergo these experiences in early and middle adulthood.

Wife–Husband Relationship

Most studies of marital interactions focus on the wives of drinking husbands, despite the fact that in one national study 44% of ever-married alcoholic women in treatment were divorced or separated, and more female than male patients had alcoholic or problem-drinking spouses (Armor, Polich, & Stambul, 1976). Women are also more likely than men to cite marital instability and family problems as reasons both for problem drinking and for seeking treatment (Beckman, 1976; Curlee, 1970; Lisansky, 1957). There is little empirical information on the husband's effect on his wife's drinking, his relationship to the children under these circumstances, and the dynamics that perpetuate the wife's drinking or help her maintain sobriety.

ALCOHOLIC WIVES' VIEWS OF THEMSELVES AND THEIR MARRIAGES

Tamerin, Tolor, and Harrington (1976) compared alcoholic wives' perceptions of their moods and behavior with the perceptions of their spouses. The women, all of whom were in treatment, were asked how they would describe themselves both when they were sober and when they were intoxicated. Actual behavior during these two states was not observed. Both the wives and their husbands agreed that the women felt depressed and guilty while sober. However, the women paradoxically characterized their behavior when intoxicated both as "full of pep" and "happy" and as depressed and guilty. The husbands' perceptions of their wives' behavior were much more negative. They described their wives as irritable and as evidencing even more guilt and depression when intoxicated than when sober. Husbands were also less critical of their spouses' disturbed moods and behavior when the spouse was sober.

Rasmussen (1979) studied white middle-class couples in which the wife was a recovering alcoholic with an average of 43 months of sobriety. The couples had been married for an average of 18 years. Rasmussen described the wives as dependent, restless, unable to sustain friendships, and married to emotionally distant men. Using the Gough Adjective Checklist and Moos's Family Environment Scale, he found no particular family climate that characterized these families. Rather, climates ranged over Structured, Conflicted, Expressive, Independent, and Moral–Religious.

Corrigan (1980) reported that only 31% of her sample of alcoholic women were currently married. Of those who were divorced or separated, 61% felt that drinking had not been a major factor in their separations or divorces, although 43% acknowledged that signs of drinking problems appeared prior to their breakups. A husband's drinking was given as the reason for the marital dissolution in a number of cases. More women admitted to problems in fulfilling the role of wife than of mother. Of the 20 husbands interviewed, almost all drank with their wives, although they claimed to disapprove of the wives' drinking. Four had been treated for problem drinking. Most had sought help for their wives, but did not realize the problem was alcoholism. More men than women felt the quality of their sexual relations was poor and that the care of the children was suffering as a result of drinking. Among the husbands, 18% stated they wanted to leave their wives, but only 7% did. The reasons given for remaining with their wives were the needs of the children, personal fortitude, and love.

A unique study of couples with one alcoholic spouse (Steinglass, 1981) utilized direct observation as well as alcoholism screening tests and psychiatric symptomatology indices. Couples were observed over a 6-month period, during which some of the alcoholic spouses were drinking, some were sober, and some changed from one status to the other. The investigator found that the greater the degree of alcoholism and the more severe the alcoholic's perception of its consequences, the greater the spouse's distress and psychiatric symptomatology, regardless of the alcoholic's sex. This pattern was observed only in couples with active alcoholism, not where the alcoholic spouse was sober.

CHARACTERISTICS OF HUSBANDS OF ALCOHOLIC WIVES

The clinical literature and the popular media have often portrayed the wife of a male alcoholic as a nagging complainer who contributes to her husband's problem, while viewing the husband of a female alcoholic as deserving of sympathy, often trying to deny or hide his wife's drinking to protect her, rather than contributing to her problem (Chalfant, 1973; Lindbeck, 1972). Research findings do not support this picture. In several studies, female alcoholics described their husbands as domineering, emotionally inaccessible, and rigid (Flintoff, 1963; Myerson, 1966; Rasmussen, 1979; Wood & Duffy, 1966). Fox (1956, 1962) developed one of the earliest clinical typologies of the husbands of alcoholics, using five descriptive categories: suffering martyrs; sadistic; dependent; unforgiving and self-righteous; and dismayed "normals." Husbands of female alcoholics were less patient and accepting and more likely to terminate the marriage than wives of male alcoholics.

A Bavarian study (Busch, Kormendy, & Feuerlein, 1973) compared 19 husbands of alcoholics in treatment to 19 control husbands matched for age and social class. The husbands described the alcoholic marriages as initially not having problems, but gradually deteriorating with the husbands assuming the dominance the wives had originally possessed. The control husbands maintained dominance throughout their marriages. Four of the husbands of alcoholics and three of the control husbands had alcohol problems, but none had psychiatric ones. The husbands of alcoholics displayed less sociability and extraversion and had a more feminine self-concept than the control husbands.

Rimmer (1974) interviewed 25 husbands of alcoholic patients in a private psychiatric hospital and found that five were alcoholic, four were excessive drinkers, and fifteen had psychiatric problems. Most no longer lived with their wives. Paolino, McCrady, Diamond, and Longabaugh (1976) compared the scores of 15 husbands of alcoholics to those of a normative sample of men on the Lanyon Psychological Screening Inventory. Although all scores fell within the normal range, the alcoholics' husbands scored significantly higher than the normative sample on the Defensiveness and Alienation scales, but not the Discomfort scale.

In the only longitudinal study of the marriages of alcoholic females, Dahlgren (1979) compared 51 husbands of alcoholics to a comparison group of male alcoholics over a period of 6–12 years. The alcoholics' husbands tended to be older, 50% were alcoholic, and 14% had psychiatric disturbances. The women's alcohol problems typically started after marriage. While the alcoholic women were not more divorce-prone than the alcoholic men in the comparison group, they were more likely to be widowed. Most of the alcoholic women who reported having sympathetic husbands and no marital disturbances were married to alcoholics. At the end of the observation period, 10 wives and 14 husbands (8 of whom were also alcoholics) in the study group had died; in the comparison group the only alcoholic wife and 8 of the alcoholic men had died.

SUMMARY

Several conclusions can be drawn about the wife–husband relationship. Alcoholic women apparently have a higher prevalence of husbands with drinking problems than do women in general, and their husbands may play an important role in the maintenance of their problem drinking by drinking with them (Corrigan, 1980; Dahlgren, 1979). Some researchers speculate that assortative mating is occurring: Alcoholics and problem drinkers look for those who have family backgrounds and drinking patterns similar to their own (Rimmer & Winokur, 1972). Most studies also report a higher rate of divorce and separation among female than male alcoholics, but the specific contribution of alcoholism to these marital disruptions is unknown (Homiller, 1977).

Mother–Child Relationships

The majority of the studies on children of alcoholics have been completed within the last 10 years. Most are exploratory in nature and primarily describe the personality characteristics of the children. Parenting patterns, sex-role modeling, and family dynamics have been largely ignored, despite their crucial importance to child development. Nor have the siblings who have not developed personality or drinking problems been compared with those who have. Moreover, these studies suffer from many methodological defects. They often lack adequate comparison groups and fail to differentiate between the effects of maternal and paternal drinking on male and female children. The use of varying instruments makes results difficult to compare. Given the fact that in some samples of female alcoholics over half of the subjects were children of alcoholics (e.g., Rathod & Thomson, 1971) and that female alcoholics report higher frequencies of alcoholism and affective disorders in their families than do males (Winokur, 1979), study of the effects of parental alcoholism on children by sex is greatly needed.

GENERAL CHARACTERISTICS OF CHILDREN OF ALCOHOLICS

The problems most commonly found in children of alcoholics regardless of sex of parent are: high risk for developing alcoholism or affective disorder, poor relationship with parent, broken and disrupted homes, and social and psychological deviance (el-Guebaly & Offord, 1977, 1979; Williams, 1981). Unfortunately, most of these findings are based on studies of families with alcoholic fathers. Thus the generalizability of these associations to families with an alcoholic mother or with two alcohol-abusing parents is unknown. Moreover, even for alcoholic fathers, the findings of these studies are suspect, since many of the study groups are drawn from populations in treatment at public institutions or mental health centers and from families of low socio-economic status. The findings might be different if families in private treatment or receiving no treatment had been studied. It is possible that poverty is a cause of the problems uncovered or that it interacts with drinking to cause them. Alcohol abuse per se may not be the most significant factor.

CLINICAL OBSERVATIONS

The clinical literature on alcoholic mothers has had a heavy psychoanalytic orientation. Fox (1963) suggested that an alcoholic mother was more damaging to children than an alcoholic father because of her impairment as a nurturer and care-giver and her overdependency upon her children for her self-esteem as she withdrew from the outside world to hide her drinking. As a result, the children's sex-role development and ability to develop relationships were warped.

Seixas (1977) also felt that alcoholic mothers wreaked more damage than alcoholic fathers, because children's maturation and development through the Eriksonian stages of growth were hindered by the mothers' neuroticism and own lack of ego development. Seixas states, "The infant with an alcoholic mother learns to expect unreliability, inconsistency, ineptitude, and general disorganization" (p. 154). In alcoholic families, roles are never clearly defined and are often reversed, with the children taking on the responsibilities of the parents. They may become either egocentric and exploitive, or compulsive and punctilious in an effort to control and order their chaotic environments. According to Seixas, "In children . . . denial, lack of trust, emotional withdrawal, and lack of respect for authority . . . have helped them survive in a world of alcoholism" (p. 158). Richards (1979) observed that children of alcoholic mothers had problems with reality testing, primitivity in object relations, and pseudomaturity.

EFFECTS DURING CHILDHOOD

In one of the earliest studies of the effects of parental alcoholism, Cork (1969) interviewed "the forgotten children" of alcoholic fathers and alcoholic mothers. The children were described as being easily upset, fearful, and anxious about the future. They felt rejected by both the alcoholic and non-alcoholic parent and were angry and frustrated by the constant quarreling, inconsistency, and unpredictability of each parent. Children viewed an alcoholic mother's drinking more negatively than an alcoholic father's drinking, stating that a mother's drinking was "not nice, not like a mother." Practical reasons were given for disapproving of a father's drinking: He loses jobs, spends all the money, or goes to jail. Cork assessed 97% of the children as being damaged by the effects of a parent's alcoholism. She noted that the children's portrayal of their family life was very similar to the parents' descriptions of their own childhoods, and predicted that the cycle of familial disruption and alcoholism would continue unless intervention occurred.

McLachlan, Walderman, and Thomas (1973) compared four groups of middle-class teenagers from intact families with an alcoholic parent (re-covered and unrecovered mothers and recovered and unrecovered fathers) with a matched comparison group. The effects of an alcoholic mother on the children appeared to be rather benign, regardless of whether the mother was recovered or unrecovered. No significant differences between the recovered and the unrecovered alcoholic mothers groups and the comparison group ap-peared in terms of the teenagers' ratings of their own social competence, mother's personal competence, social distance from the mother, family cohesiveness, parent behavior, or desire for a different mother. On ratings of maternal social competence, unrecovered mothers were perceived as inept, but recovered mothers received the highest ratings of all the groups, including the comparison group. Evidently their children were proud of them!

In contrast, teenage children of unrecovered fathers scored significantly lower than comparison-group teenagers and teenagers with alcoholic mothers in perceptions of their own social competence, their fathers' personal competence, family cohesiveness, and family togetherness and sympathy, and higher in social distance from fathers and desire for a different father. No significant differences were found between the study and comparison groups on measures of personality, intelligence, and academic achievement. Those teenagers who drank were moderate drinkers. The parent–child relationship was more affected by parental drinking than were the personal characteristics of the teenagers, with the mother appearing to have less of an effect, whether drinking or sober, than the father. However, the small number of teenagers with alcoholic mothers ($n = 14$) made these findings very tentative.

Booz-Allen and Hamilton (1974) identified four types of mechanisms by which children attempt to cope with an alcohol-abusing parent of either sex: flight, in which the child withdrew or sublimated feelings; fight, in which he or she became aggressive or delinquent; the perfect child, in which passivity and "being good" were emphasized; and the super-coper, in which the child became dominant caretaker. (Black, 1979, described a similar typology on the basis of her clinical observations.) The most frequently noted outcomes of these mechanisms were difficulties in relations with the opposite sex, over- or underachievement, leaving home and marrying early, and lack of self-confidence.

Both Black (1979) and Booz-Allen and Hamilton (1974) reported that family life did not become significantly better with the recovery of the parent. The former observed that it took years for parents to become healthy role models and the latter found no relationship between recovery of the parent and the type and frequency of problems their adult children faced. In contrast, the study of adolescents by McLachlan *et al.* (1973) found that children of recovered parents felt more loved than children of unrecovered parents, with children of recovered mothers having the highest ratings.

El-Guebaly, Offord, Sullivan, and Lynch (1978) compared the psychosocial adjustment of children with parents diagnosed as alcoholic, depressed, and schizophrenic. Each group had equal numbers of mothers and fathers and all tended to be from lower-middle-class and lower-class settings. When the number of siblings was controlled, no significant differences were found in the children's adjustment among the three diagnostic groups or between children with an ill father or an ill mother. Boys with disturbed fathers were more maladjusted than boys with disturbed mothers, but no other differences were significant. However, 55.9% of the children from all three diagnostic groups were perceived as emotionally disturbed by their parents or were involved with social agencies. Rutter's Parental Questionnaire on Children's Behavior was completed on the children, and 24% scored in the clinically disturbed range; most of these children had disturbed fathers. The authors concluded that the parents' psychiatric diagnoses, regardless of sex, did not differentiate the types of behavior exhibited by their children, at least as it could be measured by the tests used.

Krauthamer (1974, 1979) conducted one of the few research studies exclusively devoted to children of alcoholic mothers. On several scales measuring maternal attitudes, the alcoholic mothers displayed significantly more ambivalent, confused, and inconsistent attitudes toward their children than did nonalcoholic mothers, regardless of social class. Krauthamer concluded, however, that these behaviors were more the result of the drinking than of underlying personality disorders and could be reversed with cessation of excessive alcohol use. The children of alcoholic mothers were found to be more cold, distrustful, rigid, reserved, submissive, and dependent than control children.

Studies of lower-economic-status families, which did not analyze the effects of alcoholic mothers and fathers separately, have found that the children exhibited more antisocial, maladaptive, and aggressive behavior and were lower in school achievement than children from families without alcoholism (Bourgeois, Levigneron, & Delage, 1975; Haberman, 1966; Miller & Jang, 1977). Children from higher-economic-status families with an alcoholic parent did not show emotional, intellectual, or academic impairment, but the children stated that their relationships with their parents were seriously disrupted (Booz-Allen & Hamilton, 1974; Cork, 1969; and McLachlan et al., 1973). These children reported feeling unloved, emotionally neglected, and rejected. They felt strong negative emotion and anger at both the alcoholic parent and the nonalcoholic spouse because they had to assume many of the parents' responsibilities and did not have a "normal" family. The rejection, family conflicts, and inconsistency of their parents' actions often bothered them more than the drinking. In both socioeconomic groups, the children from families with an alcoholic parent experienced more separations from their parents than those in the comparison groups, usually as the result of divorce or separation, removal by the courts, or placement with relatives or foster homes.

A study by Williams (1982) compared the adequacy of child care and family stability among three groups of parents: alcoholic fathers with no alcoholic mate; alcoholic mothers with no alcoholic mate; and alcoholics with alcoholic mates. Most of the respondents in the last group were women. Children in families with two alcoholic parents experienced the greatest incidence of both abuse and neglect, as well as the least adequate child care in terms of inconsistent discipline, and time spent with parent. Children in families with alcoholic mothers were more likely to be neglected and had the least family stability. Three-fourths of the mothers were separated single parents with the lowest income and job skills of the three groups. In comparison, children from families with alcoholic fathers received the most adequate care and had the greatest family stability, probably because the nonalcoholic mother was the primary care-giver. The race of the parent or sex of the child did not affect the adequacy of care or family stability.

Drinking parents are not unaware of their impact on their children. Over 50% of the parents in Black and Mayer's study (1979, 1980) and three-fourths of the 116 mothers in Corrigan's (1980) analysis expressed genuine concern for their children, but admitted that drinking had interfered with the quality of their parenting. Unfortunately, little is known about the mechanisms through which parental drinking affects the adequacy of their child care.

EFFECTS AS ADULTS

Several studies have assessed the impact of parents' alcoholism on their adult children. Hecht (1973) and Black (1979) suggested that even those children who seemed competent, adaptive, and able to survive the vicissitudes of the alcoholic family often develop problems in adulthood. They enter treatment with problems of marital instability, inability to form relationships, despair, and feelings of worthlessness. These children, however, are often unrecognized as casualties of alcoholism because they did not act out as children or develop alcoholism as adults. Their rigid coping skills, which were adequate for childhood, break down before the new challenges of adult passages. Women are especially prone to exhibit these problems, probably because they are more likely to seek treatment for relationship problems and depression than are men.

Wolin, Bennett, Noonan, and Teitelbaum (1980) hypothesized that disruptions in family rituals were associated with the transmission of alcoholism. Twenty-five families, including 5 with alcoholic mothers and 2 with both parents alcoholic, were grouped into transmitter, intermediate, and nontransmitter families, based on the adult child's (average age 24) drinking patterns. Nontransmitter families, in which the adult children showed no sign of alcohol abuse, made a greater effort to prevent the alcoholic's drinking from disrupting special family occasions such as holidays, vacations, dinners, and other special events. In transmitter families, parental drinking resulted in a much higher rate of interference with these rituals, and intermediate families fell between the other two. Families that made a greater effort to protect cohesion, meaning, and stability appeared less likely to perpetuate problems.

PARENTAL INFLUENCES ON CHILDREN'S DRINKING PATTERNS

Studies of the antecedents of alcohol abuse make it clear that children of alcoholic parents are at higher risk for drinking problems than are children from nonalcoholic homes. Although it is difficult to separate possible genetic links from the influence of the home environment, the research evidence seems to suggest that alcohol-abusing parents increase the likelihood that their children will be problem drinkers. Interestingly, in this instance as in several of the other areas described, the influence varies by the sex of the child as well as by the sex of the parent.

A study by McKenna and Pickens (1981) compared four groups of adult alcoholics: male and female adult children of alcoholic fathers, alcoholic mothers, two alcoholic parents, and no alcoholic parents. Adult children with two alcoholic parents reported becoming intoxicated, developing symptoms of alcoholism, and being admitted to treatment at an earlier age and with fewer mean years of drinking than did children in the other three groups. They also had significantly more behavioral problems and arrests. No differences in degree of impairment were found between children of father-only and mother-only alcoholics. None of the groups differed on treatment outcomes. All adult children of alcoholics were more impaired than were children of nonalcoholic parents. The proportion of female alcoholics reporting alcoholism in both biological parents was more than twice that of male alcoholics. The proportions of men and women reporting alcoholism in father only, mother only, or neither parent were approximately equal.

In a 20-year longitudinal study involving a subsample of families with one or two alcohol-abusing parents, Miller and Jang (1977) used path analysis to trace the contributions of various social and psychological factors to the level of functioning and drinking of the adult children in their 30s. They found that sons were heavier drinkers than daughters, irrespective of which parent was alcoholic, but that daughters were heavier drinkers if the mother was alcoholic. Both sons and daughters were significantly heavier drinkers than control children from non-alcohol-abusing families.

Cross-sectional studies have shown similar within- and between-sex relationships. For example, Widseth and Mayer (1971) reported that delinquent adolescent girls who were excessive drinkers generally had drinking mothers, while abstainers had abstinent mothers. No association with the father's drinking patterns was found. The delinquent daughters of problem-drinking mothers were also much more rejecting of them and ran away more frequently than daughters of problem-drinking fathers. In a survey of junior- and senior-high-school girls, Zucker and Devoe (1975) found that heavy drinking in the mother was related to heavy drinking in the daughter. Ambivalence in the mother's attitude toward drinking produced a greater effect on boys' drinking patterns than did the father's drinking pattern (Zucker & Barron, 1973). Heavy-drinking undergraduates were more likely to drink in response to personal problems, rather than for social reasons, if their mothers were heavy drinkers. This relationship did not hold for undergraduates with heavy-drinking fathers (Cutter & Fisher, 1980).

Perhaps the mother's impact is greater because her drinking is perceived as more deviant. Certainly enough evidence exists to warrant continued exploration of the effects of the mother's drinking on the child's drinking and functioning, especially the daughter's. To date, the emphasis has been on the alcoholic father, and the mother's contributions to the children's development, especially the daughter's, have been neglected.

SOCIAL WELFARE STUDIES

The impact of a mother's drinking on her children can be detected in ways other than psychological tests and psychiatric evaluations. In addition to the studies of alcohol-abusing parents and their impact on their children, a separate literature exists that focuses on a variety of social and health problems as the dependent variable and considers, as a possible causal factor, alcohol abuse as reported by the social worker or clinician, the child, or the parent. Unfortunately these studies do not routinely specify family alcohol abuse beyond generalized terms such as "substance abuse," "alcoholism," or "parental drinking," which often makes it difficult to determine which member of the family was drinking and what effect the drinking had on other family members. Knowledge of the dynamics of women's drinking would be enhanced by the integration of studies that specifically delineate female drinking as a dependent and as an independent variable.

A national study of social services to children and their families (Shyne & Schroeder, 1978) revealed that 6.1% of all the reasons for children's services were related to alcoholism in the father and 6.4% to alcoholism in the mother. Alcoholism of the mother was more likely than alcoholism of the father to be the most important reason for services (1.3% compared to .6%).

Based on her review of the literature on alcohol and family violence, Hindman (1979) stated that discipline in alcoholic homes was often lax, inconsistent, and characterized by yelling and threats with very little praise or positive reinforcement. Corrigan (1980) reported that children witnessed or experienced quarrels and fights in two-thirds of her study families. Parental violence required legal intervention in 19 alcoholic homes versus 2 nonalcoholic homes in a study by Bourgeois et al. (1975).

Child abuse and neglect, in particular, have been associated with parental intoxication in studies both of these phenomena (e.g., American Humane Association, 1978; Behling, 1979; Gil, 1970; Young, 1964) and of alcoholic families (e.g., Booz-Allen & Hamilton, 1974; Bourgeois et al., 1975; Cork, 1969; Miller & Jang, 1977). Orme and Rimmer (1981), however, disagree with the conventional wisdom in this field. In their review of the child abuse literature, they concluded that no empirical data supported the association. They believe that inadequate definitions of terms, small and biased samples, limited knowledge of the incidence of child neglect and abuse in the general population, lack of specification of intoxication at the time of abuse, and reliance on clinical and personal judgment and hearsay severely limited the validity of the studies reviewed. Therefore the authors challenged the assumed association between alcoholism and child abuse.

A study of alcoholic and opiate-addicted parents by Black and Mayer (1980), not included in the Orme and Rimmer review, is an exception to the usual practice of not indicating which parent is responsible for the abuse. Personality characteristics and drug of abuse did not differentiate families in which maltreatment of children occurred from families in which it did not. Children were judged to have been mildly neglected in all families and seriously neglected in 30%. Abuse occurred in 23% of the families. Abuse or neglect was more likely to be by the addicted female parent, to involve more than one child, and to be repeated. Women had fewer financial and emotional supports than men, often were single heads of a household, and had the added burden of being primary caretakers of the children despite fewer resources. Other strong predictors of abuse were violence between mates and poverty. Obviously the question of the relationship between child abuse or neglect and parental alcoholism requires further exploration.

Children of alcoholics also experience more separation from their parents than comparison group children (Booz-Allen & Hamilton, 1974; Bourgeois et al., 1975; Chafetz, Blane, & Hill, 1971; Corrigan, 1980; Kammeier, 1971; Miller & Jang, 1977). One factor contributing to this phenomenon is the high rate of divorce and separation among alcoholic families. In addition, however, separation of the child from his or her parents may be effected by outside agents. Two studies reported that over one-third of the children of alcoholic parents were removed from their homes by court order (Bourgeois et al., 1975; Miller & Jang, 1977).

In a study of foster care placement in Maine, 18.7% of the children were placed because of drug and alcohol abuse by the parent. The only reason given more often than substance abuse was mental and emotional illness in the parent, at 21.6% (Human Services Development Institute, 1980). Again, although alcoholic mothers were included in these samples, their effects were not analyzed separately, nor is it known how many were single parents.

Separation from parents may also be accomplished by the child running away. In a study of youth served by runaway centers and a comparison group of nonrunaways, van Houten and Golembiewski (1978) found that 17.2% of the runaways described their mothers as having periods of intoxication; 7.8% (as compared to 4.2% of the nonrunaways) said she was frequently intoxicated. Almost 30% of the runaways' fathers were described as having periods of intoxication, with 17.1% frequently intoxicated, as compared to 2.1% of nonrunaways' fathers. No differences between the drinking patterns of mothers living alone and married mothers were evident. A third of the runaway sample expressed concern about their parents' drinking. Significant correlations existed between parental alcohol abuse and child's alcohol abuse and running away behavior. Girls' drinking was related to both the mother's and the father's alcohol use, while boys' drinking was primarily related to the father's only.

In a study of children with behavior problems in the Baltimore area,

Bosma and Jensen found that over 50% of 2–17-year-old children referred to an inner city pediatric clinic for behavior disorders had an alcoholic parent (cited in Bosma, 1976). Among the adolescent sample, 67% of those referred because of drug problems also had an alcoholic parent, as did many male adolescents on probation and 66% of adolescents who died from suicide.

In a recent study describing a screening test for identifying adolescents adversely affected by a parental drinking problem, Biek (1981) noted that 28 million children nationally are believed to be affected adversely by this problem. The instrument was administered to patients 12 years of age or older at a hospital-based teenage health clinic. Of the respondents, 57% reported that the drinking of one of their parents created problems. These respondents had nearly twice as many somatic complaints and questions about health as did patients who did not report a problem-drinking parent. Unfortunately, neither the study nor the instrument distinguished maternal from paternal alcohol abuse.

SUMMARY

Not enough research has been conducted on the specific effects of an alcoholic mother on her children to be able to draw definitive conclusions. Since children report feeling unloved, rejected by, and angry with their parents as well as rejecting of them, it can be assumed that the parent–child bond has been seriously impaired. Many children of alcoholic parents grow up in family environments disrupted by separations from parents, through the parents' separation and divorce, through their own actions, such as running away, or through agency intervention. There may be a greater association between the mother–daughter identification process and drinking patterns than had previously been suspected. Although no longitudinal studies exist on the family effects of women's drinking through several generations, the descriptions of the family-of-origin environments provided by alcoholic parents appear to be similar to those provided by their children. The role of poor parenting and child care practices in the perpetuation of alcohol problems needs to be explored, especially in terms of the mother–child relationship.

THE EMPTY NEST

As children leave home, many women are faced with a period in which they are still relatively young and vigorous, but their major caretaking role is no longer needed. The resulting "empty nest" has been used to explain later-onset drinking (Curlee, 1969; Sclare, 1970; Wanberg & Knapp, 1970).

In their national study of drinking practices, Cahalan et al. (1969) reported that the highest proportion of heavy drinkers among drinking women was in the 45–49 age group (15%). This proportion dropped to 3% for the 50–54 age group and remained there for older women. At the same time abstinence increased from 36% of 45–49-year-old women to 51% in the 50-plus group. Clark and Midanik (1982) found a similar pattern in results of a 1979 national survey, in which the highest proportion of heavy drinking occurred among women aged 41–50. The middle years appear to be an age of transition in drinking practices for women, as well as transition in family dynamics and other areas of their lives. The same transition in drinking behavior is found in men but at a later age, 65 years and over, when retirement generally occurs (Cahalan *et al.*, 1969).

Overvaluation of the role of mother, loneliness, emptiness, loss of self-esteem, and the onset of menopause contribute to the middle-life crisis. In fact, until recently the majority of alcoholic women seen in treatment have been in their 40s. Many of them have reported that their problem drinking was precipitated by a crisis event involving their marriage, family, or female physiology (Beckman, 1976; Gomberg, 1976; Lindbeck, 1972; Wilsnack, 1976).

Rathbone-McCuan and Roberds (1980) replicated these observations in a study of 45–54-year-old, middle-class alcoholic women, who were compared to alcoholic women 55 years of age and older. The younger women were described as being caught in a larger social and cultural transition. They wanted family stability, yet 40% were divorced. They suffered from boredom and role loss or fear of loss. In this group, 58% worked outside the home. The events most mentioned as precipitating problem drinking were biological: childbirth, breast removal, and hysterectomy. The older women were more likely to mention as precipitating factors family problems or loss through death of husband or children. They were less likely than the younger group to be divorced or working, and more likely to be married or widowed. Given the greater opportunities currently available to women, the number of women experiencing the empty nest syndrome may decline as more women return to work or see this time of life as a chance for enhanced personal fulfillment and self-actualization. As life expectancies expand, women may begin to think in terms of several careers, not just the one of mother.

THE OLDER YEARS

At present relatively little is known about drinking among the elderly generally, and even less about drinking among elderly women and its effects on husbands, children, and grandchildren. Although elderly female alcoholics have rarely been studied, the composite picture that often emerges from fragments of other research is of a widow, living alone or in an institution, often in economic distress, and with limited family contacts.

Prevalence of Alcohol-Related Problems

National cross-sectional surveys consistently report that adults over the age of 65 are more likely to be abstainers than those under 65. Half the abstainers are former drinkers, and the reasons for no longer drinking are related primarily to poor health and lack of interest. Other reasons include less income, fewer social contacts, and a "maturing out" of former drinking problems (Barnes, Abel, & Ernst, 1980). Some do continue to drink, however, and Gomberg (1980) has concluded that "older alcoholics drink to alleviate depression and escape life problems, and their primary alcohol-related problems are with family, health, and the police" (p. 13). It is estimated that as many as 50% of the psychiatric and medical hospital admissions of persons over age 65 may be due to a misdiagnosed primary problem of alcoholism (Barnes *et al.*, 1980).

Given rising life expectancies and the increased prevalence of drinking in American society compared to earlier generations, problem drinkers can be expected to increase among the ranks of the elderly, contributing to the need for intervention with this group. The problems of elderly female drinkers are especially important. If a woman reaches the age of 65, she has a 61% chance of living until age 80, in contrast to men, who have a 40% chance (Masnick & Bane, 1980). Although only 2% of women over 65 are considered to be problem drinkers in comparison to 10% of over-65 men (U.S. Department of Health, Education, and Welfare, 1978), these women are faced with what has been called the triple stigma of sex, age, and alcoholism (Rathbone-McCuan & Triegaardt, 1979).

Wife-Husband Relationship

Few studies focus on the effect of an elderly woman's drinking on her husband or the husband's effect on her drinking. An exception is a study by Hubbard, Santos, and Santos (1979) of elderly alcoholics at a treatment center, which examined the effect of a husband's death on a woman's drinking. Their concept of "team alcoholics" suggests that chronic alcoholic husbands and wives interdependently bolster each other and thus are able to maintain a level of economic and social functioning. Upon the death of the husband, however, the wife declines rapidly and her alcohol use becomes more visible. Her abusive drinking is attributed to reactive loss and perceived as late onset rather than identified as part of a long-term, covert process.

Relationships with Children

The largest number of single-female-headed households (15%) occurs among women over 55 years of age (U.S. Bureau of the Census, 1980), but, fortunately, more than 85% of older persons live less than an hour's distance from a child, and their care is mainly the responsibility of middle-aged daughters and sons (Sussman, 1976). In times of crisis, the elderly are more likely to turn to their daughters than any other family member (Litman, 1971).

Several studies suggest, however, that when the elderly parent is a chronic alcoholic, the attitude of family members tends to be negative and unsupportive. Two studies found that older alcoholics in comparison to patients without alcoholism were living in more debilitated conditions with little or no family support or supervision. Baer, Morin, and Gaitz (1970) described the families of organic brain syndrome patients as much more accepting and sustaining of their parents than families of alcoholics, perhaps because the disease was considered to be out of the patients' control, while alcoholism was perceived as controllable. The families of alcoholics were also less likely to use community resources or to follow through on recommendations made by clinical personnel. Hubbard *et al.* (1979) discovered that late-onset drinkers had moderate family contact, but that families denied the existence of any alcohol problems and tacitly encouraged drinking as a relief and the right of old age.

Summary

The early-onset female alcoholic will probably experience more problems and more severe disruption within the family, as well as the greater chance of losing a symbiotic relationship with a drinking spouse, than the later-onset drinker. But late-onset female drinkers may develop other problems because of the lower tolerance levels of an aging body or the synergistic effect of alcohol with other drugs, since increased prescription drug intake is characteristic of the later years. The misguided encouragement of others to use alcohol medicinally to aid sleep or to deal with the aches and pains of aging may also lead to a drinking problem. Women who have invested themselves in their work as a supplement to or substitute for family activities may suffer a grief process at the loss of role, esteem, and companionship when they retire. Such women may constitute a subgroup of late-onset drinkers.

Older women are as diverse in their needs and characteristics as any other group and this should be reflected in both treatment and research. Involvement of family and strengthening of support networks are greatly beneficial to this group and should be incorporated into treatment. Greater awareness is also needed of the different types of elderly drinkers and of the physiological, economic, interpersonal, and environmental aspects of the interaction between age and alcohol.

RECOMMENDATIONS

This review of the effects of female alcohol abuse on family members has revealed many gaps in research knowledge, as well as problems in service provision. These are summarized in the following sections.

Research

1. Longitudinal research is needed in the alcoholism field generally. Because of their central role in the family and because they have been neglected in previous research, women drinkers in particular should be followed through their life cycle and their use of alcohol observed at various ages. Samples should be stratified by social class, race, and family history (e.g., women from families with alcoholism versus families with affective disorder versus families with no apparent problems). Female problem drinkers should be compared with samples of women with emotional problems only and with women who have no apparent problems.

2. More female subjects should be included in all alcohol studies from childhood through the elderly period. Too often samples include very small numbers of women, if any.

3. The effects of recovery from alcoholism on women and their families should be studied. This should include research on the factors within the family that maintain sobriety.

4. The diversity of female life styles should be recognized, and research should be expanded to examine women in their several roles, changing statuses, and varying family structures. Traditionally, research on female alcoholics has studied women in treatment programs, many in inpatient settings serving those with low incomes. Studies have often been limited to analyses of demographic and personality characteristics or how female alcoholics differ from males. Alternatively, the interest has been on the "hidden" alcoholic woman within an intact family. More in-depth research is needed on divorced and separated women, female heads of households and single parents, married and unmarried career women, and working wives. Little is known about the interaction of these life situations and a woman's excessive use of alcohol.

5. Greater attention should be paid to cross-disciplinary research. Researchers in the field of alcoholism do not make sufficient use of material from other disciplines, such as family theory and research, child development, geriatric research, or feminist theory. Nor do other disciplines adequately study the possible impact of alcohol abuse in their research. It is very difficult to collect information across disciplines, for example, on the role of alcoholism in child abuse or foster-care placement or as a cause of running away, accidents, or marital disruptions. The different record-keeping systems and the varying levels of awareness of issues outside a researcher's area of concern militate against gaining a true perspective on the scope of the problem of alcohol abuse and its effects on many areas of life. This problem might be mitigated by interdisciplinary conferences at which researchers in the areas mentioned learn about alcohol-related issues and provide insights from their fields. Researchers in the field of alcoholism should be encouraged to utilize concepts from other disciplines, and grant applications should be evaluated in these terms.

6. More studies are needed exploring the mechanisms by which children are affected by parental drinking. Since many studies reveal that the impact of parental drinking varies with the sex of the parent and the sex of the child, such studies should collect and analyze data separately by the sex of the parent and child. Not all alcoholic parents are male, and families with alcohol-abusing mothers may need different types of social interventions than those in which the father is the drinker.

Service Provision

1. Additional education of professional personnel in many settings is urgently needed in order to deal adequately with the problems of the female alcoholic who is living in a family setting. This would include personnel in health-care settings, family and marriage counselors, and school and child-guidance personnel, all of whom should be able to recognize signs of alcohol abuse. It would also include alcoholism counselors, who should consider other family members and the family system in their counseling activities.

2. Public education is also essential to achieve greater acceptance of the fact that some women drink excessively, that this fact should not be hidden by families, and that help should be sought. Women and their families should be able to recognize high-risk situations such as marital instability, unemployment, dual responsibilities of family and work, and gynecological crises, all of which can precipitate problem drinking.

3. Women, as well as medical personnel, need to learn how alcohol affects and is affected by their physiology, especially in relation to changes in hormonal levels during the menstrual cycle and with age. Since both women and the elderly have higher levels of prescription drug use than men and younger individuals, public and professional education about alcohol-drug interactions within these groups is needed.

4. Community agencies should encourage the development of a variety of support systems to assist women. These might include parents-without-partners groups, babysitting exchanges, or social activities. One of the major complaints of women who abuse alcohol is their isolation and loneliness. They often need help in making linkages with support systems. This help can come from counselors, business concerns, religious groups, and others. Counseling should be broadened from its present focus on intrapsychic issues to assistance in reaching out to others.

5. Treatment programs for alcoholic wives and mothers should provide individual, group, or family counseling for husbands and children as well. These individuals often must overcome hurt and resentment and learn new methods of interacting with each other and the alcoholic woman if the family is to regain its health.

6. Employment-based alcoholism programs should be alert to the presence of problem drinking in female employees as well as male. When women drinkers are identified, their family situations should be considered as part of

their recovery program. For instance, more flexible hours or ways to share domestic duties to reduce stress might be suggested.

CONCLUSIONS

The role of women in American society has undergone and will continue to undergo major changes. Some women may forego the role of wife and some the role of mother, but more will attempt to combine the activities required by these roles with work outside the home. Even women who choose to be full-time wives and mothers may find their role more stressful because of the changes occurring around them.

These pressures, plus lessening of taboos against female drinking and the increased opportunities to drink, may cause more women to become problem drinkers. Basic research is needed on the interaction between stress and drinking among women. Applied research should test the effectiveness of programs directed at the prevention of problem drinking, at the treatment of those already affected, and at the prevention or amelioration of the impact of problem drinking on the family. Because most women's lives are so intimately entwined with those of other family members and their behaviors have such a significant impact upon their families, this area of alcohol-related research is particularly important and should have high priority.

REFERENCES

American Humane Association. *National analysis of official child neglect and abuse reporting.* Denver, Colo.: Author, 1978.

Anderson, S. C. *Patterns of sex-role identification in alcoholic women.* Unpublished doctoral dissertation, Rutgers University, 1976.

Armor, D. J., Polich, J. M., & Stambul, H. B. *Alcoholism and treatment.* (Report prepared for the National Institute on Alcohol Abuse and Alcoholism). Santa Monica, Calif.: Rand Corporation, 1976.

Auerswald, E. H. Drug use and families—in the context of twentieth century science. In B. G. Ellis (Ed.), *Drug abuse from the family perspective: Coping is a family affair* (DHHS Publ. No. [ADM] 80-910). Washington, D.C.: U.S. Government Printing Office, 1980.

Baer, P. R., Morin, K., & Gaitz, C. M. Familial resources of elderly psychiatric patients: Attitude, capability and service components. *Archives of General Psychiatry,* 1970, *22,* 343–350.

Barnes, G. M., Abel, E. L., & Ernst, C. A. S. *Alcohol and the elderly: A comprehensive bibliography.* Westport, Conn.: Greenwood Press, 1980.

Beckman, L. J. Alcoholism problems and women: An overview. In M. Greenblatt & M. Schuckit (Eds.), *Alcoholism problems in women and children.* New York: Grune & Stratton, 1976.

Behling, D. W. Alcohol abuse as encountered in 51 instances of reported child abuse. *Clinical Pediatrics,* 1979, *18,* 87–88; 90–91.

Biek, J. E. Screening test for identifying adolescents adversely affected by a parental drinking problem. *Journal of Adolescent Health Care,* 1981, *2,* 107–113.

Black, C. Children of alcoholics. *Alcohol Health and Research World,* 1979, 23–27.

Black, R., & Mayer, J. *An investigation of the relationship between substance abuse and child abuse and neglect* (Final report to the National Center for Child Abuse and Neglect). Boston: Washingtonian Center for Addictions, 1979.

Black, R., & Mayer, J. Parents with special problems: Alcoholism and opiate addiction. *Child Abuse and Neglect,* 1980, *4,* 45–54.

Blane, H., & Hewitt, L. *Alcohol and youth: An analysis of the literature, 1960–1975.* (Report prepared for the National Institute on Alcohol Abuse and Alcoholism). Springfield, Va.: National Technical Information Service, March 1977.

Booz–Allen & Hamilton. *An assessment of the needs of and resources for children of alcoholic parents.* (Report commissioned by the National Institute on Alcohol Abuse and Alcoholism). Rockville, Md.: National Institute on Alcohol Abuse and Alcoholism, November 1974.

Bosma, W. G. A., & Jensen, P. Studies of approximately 500 children with behavior problems in the Baltimore area, 1972–1973 (unpublished). (Cited in Bosma, W. G. A. Adolescents and alcohol. In J. R. Gallagher, F. P. Heald, & D. C. Garrell (Eds.), *Medical care of the adolescent.* New York: Appleton-Century-Crofts, 1976.)

Bourgeois, M., Levigneron, M., & Delage, H. [The children of alcoholics: A study of 66 children of alcoholics in a child psychiatry service.] *Annales Médico-Psychologiques,* 1975, *2*(3), 592–609. (Translated by NCALI.)

Bowker, L. H. *Drug use among American women old and young: Sexual oppression and other themes.* San Francisco: R & E Research, 1977.

Busch, H., Kormendy, E., & Feuerlein, W. Partners of female alcoholics. *British Journal of Addiction,* 1973, *68*(3), 179–184.

Cahalan, D., Cisin, I. H., & Crossley, H. M. *American drinking practices: A national study of drinking behavior and attitudes* (Monograph No. 6). New Brunswick, N.J.: Rutgers Center of Alcohol Studies, 1969.

Chafetz, M., Blane, H., & Hill, M. J. Children of alcoholics: Observations in a child guidance clinic. *Quarterly Journal of Studies on Alcohol,* 1971, *32,* 687–698.

Chalfant, H. P. The alcoholic in magazines for women. *Sociological Focus,* 1973, *6*(4), 14–26.

Clark, W. B., & Midanik, L. Alcohol use and alcohol problems among U.S. adults: Results of the 1979 national survey. In *Alcohol consumption and related problems* (NIAAA Alcohol and Health Monograph No. 1, DHHS Publ. No. [ADM] 82-1190). Washington, D.C: U.S. Government Printing Office, 1982.

Cork, R. M. *The forgotten children: A study of children with alcoholic parents.* Toronto, Canada: Paperjacks, 1969.

Corrigan, E. M. *Alcoholic women in treatment.* New York: Oxford University Press, 1980.

Curlee, J. Alcoholism and the "empty nest." *Bulletin of the Menninger Clinic,* 1969, *33*(3), 165–171.

Curlee, J. A comparison of male and female patients at an alcoholism treatment center. *Journal of Psychology,* 1970, *74,* 239–247.

Cutter, H. S. G., & Fisher, J. C. Family experience and the motives for drinking. *International Journal of the Addictions,* 1980, *15*(3), 339–358.

Dahlgren, L. Female alcoholics. IV. Marital situation and husbands. *Acta Psychiatrica Scandinavica,* 1979, *59,* 59–69.

el-Guebaly, N., & Offord, D. R. Offspring of alcoholics: A critical review. *American Journal of Psychiatry,* 1977, *134*(4), 357–365.

el-Guebaly, N., & Offord, D. R. On being the offspring of an alcoholic: An update. *Alcoholism: Clinical and Experimental Research,* 1979, *3,* 148–157.

el-Guebaly, N., Offord, D. R., Sullivan, K. T., & Lynch, G. W. Psychosocial adjustment of the offspring of psychiatric inpatients: The effect of alcoholic, depressive, and schizophrenic parentage. *Canadian Psychiatric Association Journal,* 1978, *23*(5), 281–290.

Family life isn't what it used to be. *Washington Star,* June 3, 1980.

Fillmore, K. M. Relationships between specific drinking problems in early adulthood and middle age: An exploratory 20-year follow-up study. *Journal of Studies on Alcohol*, 1975, *36*(7), 882–907.

Flintoff, W. P. Alcoholism: Community and aftercare aspects. *British Journal of Addiction*, 1963, *59*, 81–91.

Fox, R. The alcoholic spouse. In V. W. Eisensteid (Ed.), *Neurotic interaction in marriage.* New York: Basic Books, 1956.

Fox, R. Children in the alcoholic family. In W. C. Bier (Ed.), *Problems in addictions: Alcohol and drug addiction.* New York: Fordham University, 1962.

Fox, R. *The effects of alcoholism on children.* National Council on Alcoholism, pamphlet, reprinted from *Proceedings of the Fifth International Congress on Psychotherapy, Progress in Child Psychiatry,* 1963.

Gil, D. *Violence against children.* Cambridge, Mass.: Harvard University, 1970.

Gomberg, E. Alcoholism in women. In B. Kissin & H. Begleiter (Eds.), *The biology of alcoholism* (Vol. 4: *Social aspects of alcoholism*). New York: Plenum Press, 1976.

Gomberg, E. *Drinking and problem drinking among the elderly.* Ann Arbor: Institute of Gerontology, University of Michigan, 1980.

Haberman, P. W. Childhood symptoms in children of alcoholics and comparison group parents. *Journal of Marriage and the Family,* 1966, *28,* 152–154.

Hecht, M. Children of alcoholics are children at risk. *American Journal of Nursing,* 1973, *7*(3), 1764–1767.

Hindman, M. H. Family violence: An overview. *Alcohol Health and Research World,* 1979, *4*(1), 2–11.

Homiller, J. D. *Women and alcohol: A guide for state and local decision makers.* Washington, D.C.: Alcohol and Drug Problems Association of North America, 1977.

Hubbard, R. W., Santos, J. F., & Santos, M. A. Alcohol and older adults: Overt and covert influences. *Social Casework,* 1979, *60,* 166–170.

Human Services Development Institute. *State of Maine Foster Care Survey Report.* Portland, Me.: University of Southern Maine, 1980.

Jessor, R., & Jessor, S. L. Adolescent development and the onset of drinking: A longitudinal study. *Journal of Studies on Alcohol,* 1975, *36*(1), 27–51.

Johnson, P., Armor, D. J., Polich, S., & Stambul, H. *U.S. adult drinking practices: Time trends, social correlates and sex roles.* (Report prepared for the National Institute on Alcohol Abuse and Alcoholism). Springfield, Va.: National Technical Information Service, 1977. (NTIS No. PB 294-044/AS)

Jones, M. C. Personality antecedents and correlates of drinking patterns in women. *Journal of Consulting and Clinical Psychology,* 1971, *36,* 61–69.

Kammeier, M. L. Adolescents from families with and without alcohol problems. *Quarterly Journal of Studies on Alcohol,* 1971, *32*(6), 364–372.

Kinsey, B. A. *The female alcoholic: A social psychological study.* Springfield, Ill.: Charles C Thomas, 1966.

Krauthamer, C. The personality of alcoholic mothers and their children: A study of their relationship to birth-order, mother–child attitude, and socioeconomic status. *Dissertation Abstracts International,* 1974, *34,* 5198B. (Abstract)

Krauthamer, C. Maternal attitudes of alcoholic and nonalcoholic upper middle class women. *International Journal of the Addictions,* 1979, *14,* 639–644.

Lindbeck, V. L. The woman alcoholic: A review of the literature. *International Journal of the Addictions,* 1972, *7*(3), 567–580.

Lisansky, E. Alcoholism in women: Social and psychological concomitants. I. Social history data. *Quarterly Journal of Studies on Alcohol,* 1957, *18,* 588–623.

Litman, T. J. Health care and the family: A three generational analysis. *Medical Care,* 1971, *9,* 67–81.

Margulies, R., Kessler, R., & Kandel, D. A longitudinal study of onset of drinking among high school students. *Journal of Studies on Alcohol,* 1977, *38,* 897–912.

Masnick, G., & Bane, M. J. *The nation's families: 1960–1990.* Cambridge, Mass.: Joint Center for Urban Studies of MIT and Harvard University, 1980.

McKenna, T., & Pickens, R. Alcoholic children of alcoholics. *Journal of Studies on Alcohol,* 1981, *42*(11), 1021–1029.

McLachlan, J. F. C., Walderman, R. L., & Thomas, S. *A study of teenagers with alcoholic parents* (Research Monograph No. 3). Toronto, Canada: Donwood Institute, 1973.

Miller, D., & Jang, M. Children of alcoholics: A 20 year longitudinal study. *Social Work Research and Abstracts,* 1977, *13*(4), 23–29.

Myerson, D. J. A therapeutic appraisal of certain married alcoholic women. *International Psychiatry Clinics,* 1966, *3*, 143–157.

Orme, T. C., & Rimmer, J. Alcoholism and child abuse: A review. *Journal of Studies on Alcohol,* 1981, *42*, 273–287.

Paolino, T. J., Jr., McCrady, B. S., Diamond, S., & Longabaugh, R. Psychological disturbances in spouses of alcoholics: An empirical assessment. *Journal of Studies on Alcohol,* 1976, *37*(11), 1600–1608.

Rasmussen, R. K. *Perceived family climate and interpersonal characteristics of alcoholic women and their husbands.* Unpublished doctoral dissertation, California School of Professional Psychology, Berkeley, 1979.

Rathbone-McCuan, E., & Roberds, L. A treatment of the older female alcoholic. *Focus on Women,* 1980, *1*, 104–129.

Rathbone-McCuan, E., & Triegaardt, J. The older alcoholic and the family. *Alcohol Health and Research World,* 1979, *3*(4), 7–12.

Rathod, N. H., & Thomson, I. G. Women alcoholics: A clinical study. *Quarterly Journal of Studies on Alcohol,* 1971, *32*, 45–52.

Richards, T. M. Working with children of an alcoholic mother. *Alcohol Health and Research World,* 1979, *3*(3), 22–25.

Rimmer, J. Psychiatric illness in husbands of alcoholics. *Quarterly Journal of Studies on Alcohol,* 1974, *35*, 281–283.

Rimmer, J., & Winokur, G. The spouses of alcoholics: An example of assortative mating. *Diseases of the Nervous System,* 1972, *33*, 509–511.

Robins, L. N., Bates, W. M., & O'Neal, P. Adult drinking patterns of former problem children. In D. J. Pittman & C. R. Snyder (Eds.), *Society, culture and drinking patterns.* New York: Wiley, 1962.

Robins, L. N., & Smith, E. M. Longitudinal studies of alcohol and drug problems. In O. J. Kalant (Ed.), *Research advances in alcohol and drug problems* (Vol. 5: *Alcohol and drug problems in women*). New York: Plenum Press, 1980.

Rouse, B. A. *Stressful stages in the family life cycle and ethanol intake of husbands and wives.* Paper presented at the National Alcoholism Forum of the National Council on Alcoholism, New Orleans, La., April 1981.

Sclare, A. B. The female alcoholic. *British Journal of Addiction,* 1970, *65*, 99–107.

Seixas, J. Children from alcoholic families. In N. Estes & M. Heinemann (Eds.), *Alcoholism: Development, consequences, and interventions.* St. Louis, Mo.: C. V. Mosby, 1977.

Shyne, A. W., & Schroeder, A. G. *National study of social services to children and their families* (DHEW Publ. No. [OHDS] 78-30150). Washington, D.C.: U.S. Government Printing Office, 1978.

Steinglass, P. The impact of alcoholism on the family: Relationship between degree of alcoholism and psychiatric symptomatology. *Journal of Studies on Alcohol,* 1981, *42*(3), 288–303.

Sussman, M. B. The family life of old people. In R. N. Binstock & E. Shanas (Eds.), *Handbook of aging and the social sciences.* New York: Van Nostrand Reinhold, 1976.

Tamerin, J. S., Tolor, A., & Harrington, B. Sex differences in alcoholics: A comparison of male and female alcoholics' self and spouse perceptions. *American Journal of Drug and Alcohol Abuse,* 1976, *3*(3), 457–472.

U.S. Bureau of the Census. Marital status and living arrangements. *Current population reports* (Series P-20, No. 323). Washington, D.C.: U.S. Government Printing Office, 1978.

U.S. Bureau of the Census. American families and living arrangements. *Current population reports* (Series P-23, No. 104). Washington, D.C.: U.S. Government Printing Office, 1980.

U.S. Department of Health, Education, and Welfare. *Third special report to the U.S. Congress on alcohol and health*. (DHEW Publ. No. [ADM] 81-1080). Washington, D.C.: U.S. Government Printing Office, 1978.

U.S. Department of Labor. *News*. Bureau of Labor Statistics, November 15, 1981.

van Houten, T., & Golembiewski, G. *Adolescent life stress as a predictor of alcohol abuse and/or runaway behavior*. Washington, D.C.: National Youth Alternatives Project, 1978.

Volicher, B. J., Cahill, M. H., & Smith, J. L. Sex differences in correlates of problem drinking among employed males and females. *Drug and Alcohol Dependence*, 1981, *8*, 175-187.

Wanberg, K. W., & Knapp, J. Differences in drinking symptoms and behavior of men and women alcoholics. *British Journal of Addiction*, 1970, *64*, 347-355.

Wattenberg, E., & Reinhardt, H. Female-headed families: Trends and implications. *Social Work*, 1979, *24*(6), 460-467.

Widseth, J. C., & Mayer, J. Drinking behavior and attitudes toward alcohol in delinquent girls. *International Journal of the Addictions*, 1971, *6*(3), 453-461.

Williams, C. N. *Traits in male and female alcoholics' families of origin and families of procreation*. Unpublished manuscript, The Florence Heller Graduate School, Brandeis University, 1981.

Williams, C. N. *Differences in child care practices among families with alcoholic fathers, alcoholic mothers, and two alcoholic parents*. Unpublished doctoral dissertation, The Florence Heller Graduate School, Brandeis University, 1982.

Wilsnack, R. W., Wilsnack, S. C., & Klassen, A. D. Women's drinking and drinking problems: Patterns from a 1981 national survey. *American Journal of Public Health*, 1984, *74*, 11.

Wilsnack, S. C. The impact of sex-roles on women's alcohol use and abuse. In M. Greenblatt & M. A. Schuckit (Eds.), *Alcoholism problems in women and children*. New York: Grune & Stratton, 1976.

Winokur, G. Alcoholism and depression in the same family. In D. W. Goodwin & C. K. Erickson (Eds.), *Alcoholism and affective disorders: Clinical, genetic, and biochemical studies*. New York: SP Medical & Scientific Books, 1979.

Wolin, S. J., Bennett, L. A., Noonan, D. L., & Teitelbaum, M. A. Disrupted family rituals: A factor in the intergenerational transmission of alcoholism. *Journal of Studies on Alcohol*, 1980, *41*, 199-214.

Wood, H. P., & Duffy, E. L. Psychological factors in alcoholic women. *American Journal of Psychiatry*, 1966, *123*, 341-345.

Young, L. R. *Wednesday's children: A study of child abuse and neglect*. New York: McGraw-Hill, 1964.

Zucker, R. A., & Barron, F. H. Parental behaviors associated with problem drinking and antisocial behavior among adolescent males. In *Proceedings of the First Annual Alcoholism Conference of the National Institute on Alcohol Abuse and Alcoholism*. (DHEW Publ. No. [NIH] 74-675). Washington, D.C.: U.S. Government Printing Office, 1973.

Zucker, R. A., & Devoe, C. I. Life history characteristics associated with problem drinking and antisocial behavior in adolescent girls: A comparison with male findings. In R. D. Wirt, G. Winokur, & M. Roff (Eds.), *Life history research in psychopathology* (Vol. 4.). Minneapolis, Minn.: University of Minnesota Press, 1975.

SECTION FOUR

TREATMENT AND PREVENTION OF ALCOHOL PROBLEMS IN WOMEN

The final four chapters of this volume consider how to treat alcohol problems in women and how to prevent their occurrence. In Chapter 11, Beckman and Amaro explore the problems of initially motivating women to enter treatment by breaking down barriers to treatment that may be greater for women than for men. Braiker's chapter on psychotherapeutic issues (Chapter 12) is the most clinically oriented chapter in the volume, based on the author's extensive clinical practice in the treatment of alcoholic women and her analysis of the clinical and research literature. In Chapter 13, Vannicelli considers the outcome of treatment for alcoholic women, looking systematically and critically at available studies of treatment efficacy. Finally, in Chapter 14, Ferrence discusses the rationale for gender-specific approaches to prevention, identifies high-risk groups of women, and describes a variety of strategies for preventing alcohol problems in women.

Beckman and Amaro are interested in the underresearched and underconceptualized area of factors that influence women's access to alcoholism treatment. They present data suggesting that women underuse alcoholism services relative to men, even after correcting for the higher prevalence of alcoholism in men. In their comprehensive theorectical model, characteristics of the individual that affect a person's inclination to use services include individual predisposing factors such as age, ethnicity, or gender; attitudes and beliefs regarding alcohol, treatment, and health; personality characteristics and drinking and treatment history; and current social and situational variables such as social support systems and child care responsibilities. The structural features of the treatment services themselves can also affect entry into and continuation in treatment. These features include types of treatment offered, composition of staff, outreach and referral practices, and attitudes of treatment providers.

The available literature and results of the authors' own research suggest that such socioeconomic factors as employment status and income may serve as greater personal barriers to treatment for women than for men, reflecting the generally disadvantaged position of women in American society. On balance, cognitive factors such as attitudes and beliefs about alcoholism and medical treatment appear to facilitate rather than impede treatment for women. Women alcoholics have more positive attitudes about alcoholism treatment than do men alcoholics. However, women also appear to perceive greater familial, financial, and social costs of seeking treatment than do men. In addition, personal characteristics, particularly those associated with sex-role socialization such as feelings of powerlessness, low self-esteem and lack of competence, may inhibit many women alcoholics from independently seeking treatment. In their own research Beckman and Amaro found that environmental, social, and situational circumstances and characteristics of the treatment delivery system itself generally act as greater barriers to treatment for women than for men. Family and friends are more likely to oppose a woman's entry into treatment, and more problems in relations with others are experienced by women when entering treatment than by men. Support services important for women, such as residential child care and treatment for prescription drug abuse, are only infrequently available. It is suggested that structural characteristics of treatment facilities and attitudes of support network members need to be changed if more women are to be motivated to enter alcoholism treatment facilities.

Although her chapter is of interest to nonclinicians as well, Braiker's major objective is to sensitize clinicians of varying theoretical orientations to some special therapeutic considerations involved in working with alcoholic women. The chapter draws upon available research to characterize alcoholic women as a clinical population and discuss typical therapeutic issues that may arise in their treatment. Given the lack of systematic studies that evaluate the response of different types of female alcoholics to different types of specific treatment interventions, Braiker draws on the literature about male alcoholism, finding it "unwarranted to assert that nothing of what is known about the phenomenon of alcoholism as it is expressed and treated in men can be generalized and applied to women." She does, however, describe some distinctive attributes of alcoholic women that may have treatment relevance, including their early history of deprivation, their sense of social isolation as both adolescents and adults, and their high incidence of primary depression.

Braiker emphasizes the importance of the initial assessment process. The alcoholic woman is likely to have a poor self-concept and to be quite sensitive to possible disapproval and judgment, and may exhibit signs of depression. Therefore, the clinician must convey a nonjudgmental attitude while asking questions in such areas as consumption behavior; symptoms of dependence; social, legal, and physical consequences of alcohol use; and family history of alcoholism and affective disorder. Among other things, the clinician must be alert to the possibility of primary psychiatric disorder and other drug use. The use of a structured assessment protocol, such as those used in several major treatment outcome studies, is recommended, as is self-monitoring of consumption for patients who are still drinking.

Braiker considers three general psychological models that she believes have the greatest relevance to changing self-destructive health behaviors, including excessive alcohol consumption: the rational–cognitive model and its variants, the behavioral model, and the psychodynamic model. Since there is an absence of evidence to support the superiority of any single approach, she recommends a therapeutic flexibility that integrates elements of all three models. The rational–cognitive model is probably most valuable for relatively intelligent women who identify with values such as personal control and independence. Behavioral approaches are particularly useful when the treatment goal is moderation or controlled drinking rather than abstinence. Psychodynamic, insight-oriented therapies may be appropriate when excessive drinking is motivated by underlying conflicts related to aggression or sexuality. In an area where few empirical data exist, Braiker's chapter is an important contribution toward organizing existing clinical knowledge in a way that we hope will stimulate further research on psychotherapy with alcoholic women.

Focusing primarily on outcome rather than therapeutic process, Vannicelli summarizes the state of current knowledge regarding treatment effectiveness by meticulously quantifying and analyzing the treatment outcome literature from 1972 to 1980 and comparing it to earlier reviews. Women have been studied far less frequently than men. During the 9-year period reviewed, women represented only 8% of the subjects in treatment outcome studies; only 45% of the studies included any women at all, and only 12% examined women's data separately. Vannicelli raises the possibility of gender bias by showing that the proportions of women sampled and followed up were considerably larger in female-authored than in male-authored studies. Female authors were also more likely than male authors to specify numbers of women and men in their samples, to report gender differences in treatment outcome, and to specify prognostic characteristics that predicted successful outcomes.

Despite the common belief that female alcoholics have a poorer prognosis and are more difficult to treat than male alcoholics, Vannicelli found no evidence that women have a poorer response to alcoholism treatment than men. Specific treatment modalities have been enthusiastically endorsed in recent years as meeting the special needs of women, but data from the 9-year review provide little information regarding such issues. There appears to be little or no evidence supporting the superiority of any particular treatment for women, and virtually no empirical data are available on the efficacy of treating women separately from men or on the value of a female over a male therapist. Signs of carelessness in the presentation of women's data include the inability to tell if any or how many women were in the samples of some studies, combining a few women with many men in data analysis, lack of control groups or multiple treatment groups, and ignoring subjects who were unreachable for follow-up. Vannicelli calls for carefully designed future studies of female alcoholics and additional meta-analyses of existing studies, as well as studies that examine the effect of therapist expectancies and how they interact with the expectations of patients to influence treatment outcome.

In the book's final chapter, Ferrence discusses a number of recent prevention programs for women that she believes are among the most innovative and well designed in the addictions field. She contends that prevention programs may be more focused, effective, and cost-effective when they take into account gender differences in social and cultural roles, employment patterns, physiology, drinking patterns, and the hazards of excessive consumption.

Until recently most prevention programming was based largely on a sociocultural or socialization model, which assumed that drinking problems can be prevented by instilling appropriate attitudes toward drinking in young people and teaching adults to drink responsibly. Specific programs designed to prevent alcohol problems in women were virtually nonexistent until the last few years. Current programs differ in that target groups tend to be more specific, some programs try to minimize consumption as well as problems, and programs are often oriented toward specific problems such as the fetal alcohol syndrome. Certain high-risk groups of women are considered particularly appropriate target groups for primary prevention or early intervention efforts, including white-collar workers, employed married women, younger women, divorced and separated women, and women with low economic resources.

Ferrence describes several categories of prevention programs for women: mass media campaigns that sometimes have community organization components; alcohol and reproduction programs that may involve media campaigns, community organization, professional education or training, and counseling for pregnant women; alcohol education programs developed primarily for use by small groups of women in the general population; and community-based programs such as training "natural helpers" to identify and deal with problems that may lead to alcohol abuse, and various strategies for reaching women who are at risk for alcohol abuse while in the process of divorce or separation. Ferrence's discussion of prevention goes beyond approaches that address only the behavior of the individual woman drinker to consider additional strategies that address the "agent"—alcohol—and the sociocultural environment in which women's drinking takes place. Consistent with a distribution-of-consumption model of prevention, she proposes reductions in *per capita* consumption of alcohol by such measures as taxation, restrictions on advertising and distribution, and efforts to change drinking norms in the general population. She also advocates the development of prevention constituencies composed of groups having a major concern with health and social issues, including women's organizations, to lobby for specific objectives that would reduce consumption and alcohol problems.

Like many other chapters in this volume, the four chapters of Section IV are all concerned to some extent with gender differences and how they relate to outreach, treatment, and prevention programming. Ferrence discusses differences between women and men in social roles, physiology, drinking patterns, and consequences of excessive consumption, and relates these differences to prevention needs. While recognizing similarities between women and men in motivators toward and away from treatment, Beckman and Amaro are primarily interested in personal characteristics and in structural characteristics of the treatment system that serve as greater barriers to treatment for women than for men. Vannicelli stresses the importance of separating men and women in analyzing data on treatment effectiveness. She implicitly assumes that gender differences may have implications for outcome, while recognizing that to date there is no evidence that the course or outcome of treatment is different for men and women. Braiker appears to assume the fewest gender differences, asserting that much of what is known about alcoholism and its treatment in men may be generalizable also to women. The important empirical question raised by all four chapters is, to what extent (and on what dimensions) men and women are similar—and thus can and should be treated similarly—and in what areas they have different characteristics and different needs that may require gender-specific treatment and prevention programs.

The three chapters on treatment also highlight the importance of clients' and therapists' cognitions and expectations. Beckman and Amaro consider the effect of perceptions regarding treatment, alcoholism, and health on women's use of treatment facilities, and the influence of staff attitudes on women's utilization patterns. Braiker describes rational–cognitive models as one of three main approaches to alcoholism treatment for women. One version of these models, used previously in treatment of depression, helps women identify their negative, self-defeating expectations and subject these to empirical testing. Vannicelli speculates that therapists' beliefs that women do poorly in treatment may be a factor in creating poor outcome, and that beliefs of care providers regarding which modalities work best may influence clients' expectations and ultimately their prognosis. Considering the marked expectation effects found in other areas of psychological research, and given how little variance in alcoholism treatment outcome is accounted for by the client and treatment variables included in most outcome studies, client- and therapist-expectancy variables may be a particularly promising influence to explore in future research on treatment of alcoholic women.

11

Patterns of Women's Use of Alcohol Treatment Agencies

LINDA J. BECKMAN
School of Medicine
University of California, Los Angeles

HORTENSIA AMARO
School of Public Health
Boston University

INTRODUCTION

The assessment of factors that may influence access to treatment programs was recently identified in a report by the Institute of Medicine of the National Academy of Sciences as one major area of "scientific opportunity" for the field of alcohol research (1980, p. 28). Past efforts to determine why some alcohol abusers use treatment services while others do not are sketchy at best, and few studies have focused on alcoholic women's access to treatment services. Yet, evidence suggests that when gender differences in the prevalence of alcohol problems are taken into account, women still may underuse alcohol services relative to men (Furst, Beckman, Nakamura, & Weiss, 1981; Naierman, Savage, Haskins, Lear, Chase, Marvelle, & Lamothe, 1979).

Using a combination of survey data and local census information to estimate prevalence for counties in California, Furst *et al.* (1981) found that even when actual utilization rates were corrected for prevalence, men entered treatment two and one-half times as frequently as did women. And when only public facilities (that is, those supported by government funding) were considered, this picture was much worse: Men were four times as likely to enter treatment as were women.

Discrepancies between estimates of the prevalence of alcohol problems in women and their rates of use of alcohol treatment services suggest that many women in need of services never reach treatment. Of course, many men with alcohol-related problems also never gain access to treatment, but women are even less likely than men to get help for their drinking problems. Women constitute less than 20% of all clients in alcohol treatment on a

319

national level (National Institute on Drug Abuse, 1980), although it has been estimated that they comprise a much higher percentage of the total alcoholic population (e.g., Homiller, 1980; Sandmaier, 1980).

The purpose of this chapter is to examine research regarding barriers to treatment among women with alcohol problems, barriers that can impede both entry into treatment and continuation in treatment. Because of the limited research in these areas, our own data on access to treatment are emphasized. First, an analytic model of the types of variables that serve as environmental and/or personal forces toward or away from help-seeking is presented. Second, the research literature dealing with factors affecting both initial contact with a treatment facility and continuation in treatment after initial contact is explored. Our own research on these topics is presented next. Finally, the implications of these data for prevention and treatment of women's alcohol problems are derived.

Although the relative success of different types of alcoholism treatment has long been debated (for reviews see Baekeland, Lundwall, & Kissin, 1975; Blume, 1978; Emrick, 1975; Noble, 1978; Vannicelli, Chapter 13 in this volume), there is some evidence that treatment programs, regardless of their orientation, produce more positive and lasting outcomes than does doing nothing for the alcohol abuser (Emrick, 1975; Polich, Armor, & Braiker, 1980). Although spontaneous remission has been documented (Boggs, 1967; Kendell & Staton, 1966; Tuchfeld, Simuel, Schmitt, Ries, Kay, & Waterhouse, 1976) and problem drinkers can "mature" out of alcoholism (Cahalan, 1970), there is little agreement as to the extensiveness or permanence of this recovery without formal treatment. It seems reasonable to assume, then, that in order to enter the road to recovery from alcoholism the alcoholic woman or man generally must find help—be it Alcoholics Anonymous (AA), a public alcoholism treatment agency, a private therapist, or a combined alcohol- and drug-abuse treatment service. For this reason, it is important to understand factors influencing treatment use, especially among those groups that currently underuse services. Some potentially effective treatment methods may be characterized by structural barriers to entry (e.g., high cost) or to continuation (e.g., loss of daily contact with one's children). In this chapter we make no claims about the efficacy of various forms of treatment, except to the extent that treatment methods or supportive services impose barriers on women's seeking or continuing in treatment. (The issue of efficacy is discussed by Vannicelli in Chapter 13 of this book.)

FACTORS AFFECTING WOMEN'S USE
OF TREATMENT SERVICES

Perhaps the absence of comprehensive efforts in the past to investigate female alcohol abusers' use of treatment facilities reflects a lack of theoretical understanding of the factors that potentially could influence this process.

Although models that describe use of health-care services are available, they have not previously been adapted to describe use of alcohol-related services. A recent description of factors affecting women's use of alcohol treatment systems (Beckman & Kocel, 1982) has been developed from prior models of health-care services utilization. It incorporates components of both the Andersen *et al.* model of the societal and individual determinants of medical care utilization (e.g., Aday & Andersen, 1974; Andersen & Newman, 1973) and the Becker *et al.* health belief model (e.g., Becker, 1974; Becker, Haefner, Kasl, Kirscht, Maiman, & Rosenstock, 1977; Rosenstock, 1966).

Although the present model was designed to explain causal relationships among groups of variables (see Beckman & Kocel, 1982), the state of the research is such that the combined effects of several factors on women's use of alcohol services have rarely been considered. Therefore, variables are examined individually as they are hypothesized to affect women's use of treatment services.

Potential antecedents of treatment use are listed in Table 11-1. To accept help for an alcohol-related problem, a person generally first must perceive the existence of the problem and be willing to attempt to control the problem through contact with the treatment system. In some cases, when an individual is involuntarily brought to a treatment agency, the person must be willing to remain at the agency if treatment is to occur. Thus, the individual characteristics listed in Table 11-1 can affect personal willingness to take or continue treatment-relevant actions. However, the person also must have the personal resources necessary to secure services. For instance, lack of sufficient information about treatment facilities or lack of sufficient economic resources to secure treatment may act as potential barriers to treatment.

Characteristics related to the individual that affect the person's ability to secure, and inclination to use, services include: (1) individual predisposing factors such as age, ethnicity, or sex; (2) attitudes and beliefs regarding alcohol, treatment, and health; (3) personal enabling traits, that is, personality characteristics, traits, and drinking and treatment history; and (4) social enabling characteristics, that is, current social and situational variables such as child-care responsibilities, social support systems, and access to financial resources.

Predisposing factors are distinguished from the three other types of personal characteristics by their status as sociodemographic or background factors, which act as exogenous (independent) variables in the model of treatment use. Predisposing factors may be either mutable or immutable, although some factors do not clearly fall into one category or the other. The predisposing factors of sex, age, and ethnicity are immutable. Some mutable predisposing factors such as education and income may be changed through both policy and individual efforts, while other mutable predisposing factors, such as religion or marital status, are more often changed through individual decisions.

Individual attitudes and beliefs include those attitudes specific to alco-

TABLE 11-1. Factors Affecting Utilization of Alcoholism Services (Access and Continuation)

I. Individual characteristics
  A. Predisposing factors
    1. Sex
    2. Religion
    3. Age
    4. Ethnicity
    5. Marital status
    6. Education
    7. Offspring
    8. Income
  B. Beliefs about alcohol, treatment, and health
    1. Perceived severity of drinking problem and its consequences
    2. Perceived susceptibility to alcoholism (e.g., presence of alcoholism in family increases perceived susceptibility)
    3. Evaluation of probable efficaciousness of treatment
    4. Perceived possible costs of taking (or continuing) action and their importance:
      a. financial
      b. stigma
      c. job-related
      d. family (e.g., loss of children)
      e. health
      f. legal
    5. Perceived costs of not taking (or continuing) action:
      a. financial
      b. stigma
      c. job-related
      d. family (e.g., loss of children)
      e. health
      f. legal
    6. General beliefs and attitudes concerning:
      a. beliefs in scientific or medical approaches affecting access to treatment
      b. beliefs about the fetal alcohol syndrome
      c. beliefs regarding health services
      d. general health beliefs
    7. Attitudes and knowledge regarding alcoholism and its causes (not considered above)
    8. Consumer satisfaction with prior contact with system
    9. Awareness of treatment alternatives
  C. Personal enabling factors
    1. Personal efficacy
    2. Self-esteem
    3. Alienation
    4. Depression, anxiety, etc.
    5. Treatment and drinking history
    6. Mental health treatment utilization
    7. Sex-role traditionalism
II. Social enabling factors
  A. Child-care responsibilities
  B. Geographic proximity of treatment facilities (travel time, working)
  C. Type of insurance (solo, group practice, public-supported, none)
  D. Ease of care available (travel time, waiting time, etc.)

   E. Attributes of the community one lives in (urban, rural)
   F. Familial support system (network)
   G. Friendship network (level of social support/disapproval)
   H. Events eliciting treatment seeking
III. Treatment service structure characteristics
   A. Access to treatment (cost, e.g., public/private; availability)
   B. Geographic distribution
   C. Attitudes of treatment providers on alcohol abuse in women
   D. Support services available (e.g., child care, transportation)
   E. Type and number of treatment options and aftercare available
   F. Type of outreach procedures
   G. Referral sources (e.g., physicians, agencies)
   H. Composition of staff

holism and alcohol treatment, as well as more general beliefs and attitudes associated with health services and health treatment. This category differs from other individual categories in that it is concerned with cognitive variables, with perceptions, beliefs, knowledge, attitudes, and values. Included in alcohol-specific beliefs are beliefs regarding problem severity, perceived susceptibility, probable efficaciousness of treatment, and the perceived personal costs of seeking (or continuing) in treatment versus not seeking (or discontinuing) treatment. Under this broad category also are knowledge of treatment alternatives and satisfaction with prior contact with treatment agencies.

Personal enabling traits consist primarily, but not exclusively, of personality characteristics such as alienation, depression, sex-role traditionalism, personal efficacy, and self-esteem. Also included in this category are personal history variables related to previous alcoholism and mental health treatment, and drinking history. This second group of variables was placed here rather than under predisposing factors or social enabling factors because they describe neither sociodemographic characteristics nor current situation, yet they are important characteristics of the person.

Social enabling characteristics comprise environmental and interpersonal variables that impinge on the person. They consist of social and situational variables such as child-care responsibilities, geographic proximity to a treatment facility, and insurance coverage. Included in social enabling characteristics are characteristics of the facility as they affect the person (e.g., how distant the facility is from the person), characteristics of the person's family (e.g., familial support system, child-care responsibilities) and characteristics of the person's larger social community (e.g., friendship network, characteristics of the community of residence). It should be noted that some social enabling factors (e.g., insurance coverage) probably are more vulnerable to change through social policy efforts than are predisposing factors or personal enabling traits.

The other major class of characteristics affecting use of treatment services is the structural features of the treatment services themselves. The structural characteristics that can affect entry and continuation in treatment include the type of treatment and support services available, demographic composition of the treatment staff, outreach and referral practices, and attitudes of treatment providers. If a treatment program designed to fit the needs of one cultural, age, or gender group does not satisfy a second group's needs, its members may not use the facility. Also, persons who vary on predisposing factors, such as age or gender, may have different ranges of treatment options available to them. These differences may in turn affect use rates. For instance, the lower mental health care utilization rates of the poor (Glasser, Duggun, & Hoffman, 1975; Rosenblat & Suchman, 1964) have been attributed to the middle-class values of mental health professionals, which dissuade the client from treatment (Lorion, 1973, 1974; Yamamoto, James, & Palley, 1968).

Specific events that elicit treatment-seeking behavior by the alcoholic or her significant others transcend the five broad categories outlined above. Probably most such events are included in social enabling characteristics. Family and friends urging one to seek treatment or a spouse threatening to leave the relationship may well serve as cues to action. But so may changes in personal characteristics, such as a change in mood state or symptom severity, and it is possible that a change in a predisposing factor such as financial status can also serve as a cue to action. A change in a belief or attitude involving alcoholism or alcohol treatment could also elicit help-seeking, as could more knowledge about the types of treatment available. Finally, characteristics of the treatment system such as outreach and referral efforts of agencies (e.g., a television spot) also may facilitate treatment-seeking behavior.

PRIOR RESEARCH ON USE OF TREATMENT SERVICES

The variables influencing women's recognition of their own drinking problems, the determinants of alcoholic women's help-seeking behavior, and others' reactions to such help-seeking are research issues that, despite the growing literature regarding alcoholic women, have largely been ignored. First, the relatively small number of studies that have been conducted on alcoholic women's use of treatment services have several sampling limitations. Ethnic, cultural, class, or religious differences among women alcoholics have not been investigated, due to the small size of these subsamples in most studies. Second, samples of women alcoholics are composed almost entirely of women already in treatment for alcohol-related problems. The omission of problem-drinking women not in treatment prohibits researchers from identifying personal and structural factors that actually differentiate women who enter treatment from those who do not enter treatment.

Research on factors that affect women's entry into treatment needs to overcome the sampling difficulties inherent in studying female alcoholics who are not associated with an institution or organization. A study in progress by Beckman and Bardsley at UCLA is addressing the gap in knowledge about female alcoholics who are not in treatment by using a combination of sampling techniques (e.g., referrals by alcoholics in treatment, media publicity) to identify and interview female alcoholics who are not in treatment. The omission of problem-drinking women not in treatment and of ethnic-group women makes generalizations about women's use of services risky. However, research findings point to a number of differences between men and women that may have implications for early identification and intervention in female alcoholism.

Lack of motivation and high drop-out rates are two major problems identified in the literature on treatment of alcoholism. Silberfeld and Glaser (1978) found that the attrition rate from outpatient alcohol treatment was 83% during the first 3 months; that is, only 17% completed 3 months of treatment. In their review of studies of drop-out rates, Baekeland and Lundwall (1975) report lower drop-out rates for inpatient settings (14-39%) than for outpatient settings (where 52-75% of patients drop out before the fourth session). Even for inpatients, however, a significant proportion leave the treatment program before therapeutic change can be effected. Differences between male and female clients may also have implications for whether treatment, once initiated, is continued. Predisposing, enabling, and structural factors can affect continuation in treatment and different antecedents may influence continuation than influence access to treatment. The structural characteristics of the treatment facility should be particularly important in determining whether women drop out or stay in treatment.

Unfortunately, most studies of drop-out rates and/or treatment duration include only male subjects (e.g., Caster & Parsons, 1977; Dickinson, 1974; Gellens, Gottheil, & Alterman, 1976; Krasnoff, 1977; Lowe & Thomas, 1976; O'Leary, Calsyn, Chaney, & Freeman, 1977; O'Leary, Rohsenow, Schau, & Donovan, 1977; O'Leary, Rohsenow, & Chaney, 1979) or do not specify sex of subjects (Beil & Trojan, 1977; Bowen & Temlow, 1978; Heinemann, Moore, & Gurel, 1976; Reed, Van-Lewen, & Williams, 1971; Smart & Gray, 1978) or, if they include subjects of both sexes, do not consider differences between men and women in variables influencing drop-out rates (e.g., Gertler, Raynes, & Harris, 1973). While there is evidence that women are less likely to use alcohol services than are men, there is no comparable evidence that one gender group is more likely to drop out of treatment than the other. Nevertheless, examination of differences in predisposing factors, beliefs, and enabling factors among clients who do and do not leave treatment, and consideration of the characteristics of agencies with differing drop-out rates, may prove instructive in identifying barriers to women's continuation of alcoholism treatment.

Predisposing Factors

Socioeconomic factors may influence women alcohol abusers to underutilize treatment. Alcoholic women may have lower incomes than have alcoholic men. Some studies have found that female alcoholics are more likely to be divorced than are male alcoholics (Curlee, 1970; Glatt, 1961; Rathod & Thomson, 1971), a characteristic associated with lower family income among women. The lower financial resources of women as compared to men implies that a more limited range of treatment options is available to women. Because of lack of financial resources, and perhaps lack of insurance, they may not be able to select the privately supported facilities that offer the most individually tailored treatment plans and the most intensive treatment experiences.

Low socioeconomic status and social instability appear to be associated with dropping out of treatment. (For a review of these drop-out studies, see Baekeland & Lundwall, 1975.) Completers also have been shown to be somewhat better educated (Patton, 1978). Other studies find drop-outs (sex-unspecified or male) to be younger than non-dropouts (Baekeland & Lundwall, 1975; Cummings, 1975; Kern, Schumelter, & Paul, 1977; Linn, 1978; Schofield, 1978). Since income is one indicator of socioeconomic status, women also may be more likely than men to drop out of treatment because of economic considerations.

Beliefs about Alcohol, Treatment, and Health

Male and female alcoholics report somewhat different attitudes toward alcohol use. Alcoholic women are more likely to report drinking or feeling like drinking when they feel powerless or inadequate than are men (Beckman, 1980). Women perceive their alcohol problems as likely to affect their relationships with their children (Sandmaier, 1980) and therefore may have more guilt regarding their adequacy as parents.

Alcoholic men and women may perceive the social consequences of drinking differently, and indeed the consequences may differ by gender. Alcohol may have different effects on various life domains for women and men because those domains are of different importance to female and male social identities. For instance, since women spend more time in the home caring for children and are more likely to identify this as their primary role, it is to be expected that they perceive greater negative consequences of drinking for the parent–children relationship (or for their children) than do men. In contrast, men as a group may perceive more job-related consequences. In each case, gender differences in perceptions are based on actual gender differences in accepted and acceptable primary roles. Sex-role stereotypes are further discussed under social enabling factors.

Past research on the health behavior and beliefs of men and women (e.g., Blane, Overton, & Chafetz, 1963; Carver, 1977; Hetherington & Hopkins, 1969; Milmoe, Rosenthal, Blane, Chafetz, & Wolf, 1967; Westie & McBride, 1979; Wolf, Chafetz, Blane, & Hill, 1965) suggests that men and women also have different beliefs regarding illness and medical treatment in general. Women generally perceive medical treatment as being more effective than do men and they also evidence greater concern about health matters, hold more favorable opinions regarding health services and providers, and perceive their medical symptoms as being more severe. (The relative accuracy of male versus female perceptions of medical treatment is unclear. For general health problems, level of perceived illness is an important predictor of utilization; see Bice & White, 1969.)

Assuming that differences found for regular medical treatment apply to alcoholism as an illness, women also should perceive alcoholism treatment as more effective and have more favorable opinions about alcoholism services than do men. Also, they might tend to perceive the health-related consequences of their alcohol problems as more severe than do men.

On balance, health-related beliefs and attitudes probably serve as greater motivators toward treatment for women than men. Such factors generally appear to serve as facilitators rather than barriers to entry (and continuation) of treatment for women.

Some data suggest that those with more severe drinking problems (Baekeland & Lundwall, 1975) and those who perceive their drinking problems as severe (Midanik, 1980) will be more likely to drop out of treatment. This is the opposite of what would be expected according to the health belief model for entry into treatment. One explanation for this apparent contradiction is that women's perceptions of health symptoms as more severe, while it may motivate them to enter treatment, might also make them more pessimistic about treatment outcomes, and therefore lead to high drop-out rates.

Some studies imply that negative or ambivalent attitudes toward treatment are associated with dropping out (Baekeland, Lundwall, & Shanahan, 1973; Blane & Meyers, 1963) as is poor motivation (e.g., coercion into treatment; see Baekeland & Lundwall, 1975). It is doubtful that women have poorer motivation or more negative attitudes toward treatment than men. If anything, they should have higher motivation and more positive attitudes. However, if women perceive their symptoms as more severe and they have more favorable opinions about medical treatment and health services than do men, it is possible that their attitudes toward treatment are more ambivalent than are those of male alcohol abusers.

The meager data available regarding male and female attitudes toward specific types of treatment indicate that female alcoholics preferred individual counseling more and group sessions less than did male alcoholics (Curlee, 1971). However, the women involved in this small study did not have the option of women-only groups; the group therapy sessions that they liked less were mixed-gender groups. Research that suggests women are less active in mixed-gender groups (Lockheed & Hall, 1976) also provides indirect support for these data.

Personal Enabling Factors

Female alcoholics have a poorer self-concept and lower self-esteem than do male alcoholics (Beckman, 1978). Women are more likely than men to evidence primary affective disorder, in particular a serious depression that precedes alcohol abuse. As many as 20–30% of women diagnosed as alcoholic evidence this pattern (Schuckit, Pitts, Reich, King, & Winokur, 1969; Schuckit, Rimmer, Reich, & Winokur, 1971). Denial of alcohol problems might also be more frequent among women due to social pressure and the stigma associated with heavy drinking for women. If women with alcohol problems are characterized by severe depression (Curlee, 1970; McLachlan, 1976; Schuckit et al., 1969; Winokur & Clayton, 1968; Zelen, Fox, Gould, & Olson, 1966), low self-esteem (Beckman, 1978), feelings of powerlessness (Beckman, 1980), and high denial of their own drinking problems, these characteristics may serve as barriers to their taking action to initiate treatment.

Studies of the influence of personality variables on dropping out of treatment have produced mixed results. Some studies indicate that inpatient drop-outs depend on alcohol for relief of anxiety and depression (see Baekeland & Lundwall, 1975), and that those (men) who drop out are more socially isolated (Cummings, 1977), introverted (Linn, 1978), depressed (Caster & Parsons, 1977; Linn, 1978), and have more feelings of lack of control (O'Leary, Calsyn, Chaney, & Freeman, 1977; Schofield, 1978) than do male program completers. The Schofield (1978) study compared drop-outs and completers of treatment for each sex, and found that among women the differences in locus-of-control scores, although in the predicted direction, did not reach significance, probably because of the small number of female drop-outs ($n = 5$) involved. One study of men suggested that those who later completed a 1-year treatment program had *higher* levels of denial than did men who later dropped out of treatment (O'Leary, Rohsenow, Schau, & Donovan, 1977). Schuckit and Winokur (1972) suggest that women with both primary affective disorder and alcoholism have a better treatment prognosis (and presumably stay in treatment longer) than do primary alcoholics.

The above discussion suggests that at least some personality traits more characteristic of female alcoholics than male alcoholics are associated with higher drop-out rates. On the other hand, some researchers have found no relationship between personality and dropping out and still others have found personality syndromes more characteristic of men (e.g., psychopathic tendencies) also associated with higher drop-out rates (see Baekeland & Lundwall, 1975; Huber & Danahy, 1975).

Women also report different drinking histories than do men. They are more likely to drink alone, to abuse legal drugs, and to conceal their drinking (Cooperstock, 1971; Horn & Wanberg, 1973; Wanberg & Horn, 1973). The effects of these factors on treatment-use patterns are unclear.

Finally, women's reproductive physiology constitutes a gender-specific personal enabling factor. When body weight is controlled for, women generally reach higher blood alcohol levels on given amounts of alcohol than do men. Also, alcoholic women more frequently report increased alcohol use associated with the premenstruum and with problems related to feminine physiological–reproductive functioning than do nonalcoholic women (Beckman, 1979; Wilsnack, 1982).

One could hypothesize that crises related to female functioning and perhaps biochemical changes that occur with the menstrual cycle may lead to increased alcohol use. This in turn leads to greater symptom severity, which motivates treatment-seeking behavior. The more unpredictable effects of alcohol for women throughout the menstrual cycle may also lead to perception of symptoms at some points of the menstrual cycle as more severe. While the spontaneous cutting back on alcohol use during pregnancy has been documented (see Little & Ervin, Chapter 6 in this volume), it is unclear if women with drinking problems are more likely to seek help for these problems while they are pregnant. The prenatal care associated with the pregnancy presents an excellent opportunity for intervention in women's alcohol abuse problems.

Social Enabling Factors

Familial and nonfamilial social support systems, as well as familial responsibilities regarding children, probably serve as barriers to treatment for women more often than for men. Many previous studies could suggest that female alcoholics are under fewer family and societal pressures to seek help, and thus are less likely to do so (Bates, 1963; Block, 1965; Lisansky, 1958; Wood & Duffy, 1966). Fewell and Bissell (1978), for example, report that other family members play an important protective role in helping the woman to conceal her alcohol problems from outsiders and thereby increase the likelihood of her denial of a drinking problem. Likewise, women's primary responsibilities associated with child raising can act as barriers to treatment. Women may not seek or continue treatment because of the difficulty of finding acceptable alternative child-care arrangements.

Because of societal sex-role ideals and the unique role of women in childbearing and nursing, the family domain is more central to women's lives than to men's. Therefore, women may be more responsive to informal sanctions within the family than are men. The importance of this sort of pressure is suggested by Mulford's results (1977), which indicated that over a quarter of female problem drinkers in treatment felt that their children were most critical of their drinking and exerted pressure on them to stop. Only 10% of men reported similar pressure from children. Men reported feeling more pressure from their spouses to stop drinking than did women, perhaps because alcoholic women are more likely to be married to heavy drinkers or alcoholics, who are less inclined to discourage their wives' drinking (Dahlgren & Myrhed, 1977; Wanberg & Horn, 1970).

Mulford also found that women were apt to become self-critical almost immediately after they became aware that others were critical of their drinking, while men generally became self-critical much later. Women also sought help much sooner after becoming self-critical than did men. Other studies also have shown that female alcoholics are more likely to seek treatment because of familial and interpersonal problems than male alcoholics (Gomberg, 1974), and that they tend to be more sensitive about others' comments about their drinking (Horn & Wanberg, 1969). Thus, it would appear that self-awareness of one's drinking problem, if accompanied by familial criticism of excessive drinking and support for treatment, should facilitate help-seeking behavior by women. However, as outlined above, family obligations and commitments can also act as barriers to women's seeking of treatment.

Women may be more reluctant than men to seek treatment for alcoholism. Presumably alcoholic women are likely to seek help for marital instability, family problems, physical ailments, or emotional problems, but not for their alcoholism (Johnson, 1965; Lindbeck, 1972). This is because alcohol abuse has fewer social consequences, but probably more social stigma, for women than for men (Hanna, 1978). Although they often consult their physicians about drinking-related problems, female problem drinkers may not connect or identify these problems with their drinking habits (Jones & Helrich, 1972; Marden & Kolodner, 1978; Mulford, 1977). Physicians in Nebraska reported that only 11% of their female alcoholic patients appeared with a specific alcohol-identified problem. The remaining 89% presented a variety of related medical and emotional problems (Johnson, 1965). Ferrence, Rush, and Murdock (1980) estimated that close to two-thirds of women with alcohol problems in Ontario go to general agencies rather than those specifically for problem drinkers. Since drinking is not mentioned by women, it more frequently goes unnoticed and unresolved (Lindbeck, 1972).

Not all researchers have found that society places a greater stigma on female than on male alcoholics (e.g., Stafford & Petway, 1977). Differences between female and male alcoholics in treatment-seeking behavior may result, not from society's greater stigmatization of women, but rather from gender-specific responses to stigmatization that are related to differences in the socialization of women and men (Stafford & Petway, 1977).

Service Delivery System Characteristics

In part, women's apparent underutilization of alcohol services is attributable to the service delivery systems. The social context, however, can affect the diagnosis, and treatment, of women's alcohol, mental health, and health problems. For mental health disorders that are congruent with accepted sex-role stereotypes (such as depression), women show higher rates of use of services than do men. In contrast, for problems such as alcoholism that are incongruent with idealized sex-role stereotypes, women show much lower (prevalence-corrected) utilization rates than do men (Russo & Sobel, 1981). Women's needs regarding such incongruent disorders are frequently ignored (Russo & Sobel, 1981) and women with alcohol problems are left untreated or are misdiagnosed more often than are men with similar problems (Gomberg, 1981). Furthermore, national data related to incidence, prevalence, and utilization are aggregated in a way that masks important subgroup differences, and service approaches tend to be based on models describing expectations associated with male roles (Russo & Sobel, 1981; Russo & VandenBos, 1981). Racial and ethnic group differences in sex-role stereotypes and expectations probably are related to different patterns of service use, but such differences have not been satisfactorily investigated.

Treatment for women could be unduly lengthened because of male therapists' sexual curiosity (Abramowitz, Abramowitz, Roback, Corney, & McKee, 1976) and stereotypes about female dependency (Fabrikant, 1974). If this is the case, women may be likely to show longer stays in treatment, not because they need more treatment but because sex-role stereotypes lead to beliefs among therapists that women need more treatment.

Both treatment providers and community gatekeepers (i.e., professionals and paraprofessionals likely to interact with alcohol problems) may differ in their attitudes toward women and men. A double standard of mental health exists in our society. Broverman, Broverman, Clarkson, Rosenkrantz, and Vogel (1970) showed that "normal" women were viewed by clinicians as more submissive, less independent, less adventurous, more easily influenced, more excitable, more emotional, and less objective than "normal" men or "normal" adults. The reluctance of treatment agencies to label a woman as alcoholic (Curlee, 1970; Hanna, 1978) may partially reflect an effort to avoid stigma. Unfortunately, it may also reflect sex-role attitudes of treatment providers whose stereotypes facilitate diagnoses of mental health disorders when in actuality alcoholism is the correct diagnosis.

One key gatekeeper group is physicians. Johnson's (1965) study indicates that physician attitudes toward alcoholic women, in particular, are often highly negative. Female alcoholics are viewed as being "sicker" than male alcoholics, whereas in reality women and men evidence similar levels of "psychopathology" and women may not have as severe behavioral impairment (Beckman, 1975). Knox (1971) and Chappel (1975) have shown that many physicians are unwilling or unable to treat alcoholic patients intensively. In light of this, James (1975) reported that half of her sample of women who were AA members had attempted to discuss their drinking problems with others, including physicians, and had been told that they could not possibly be alcoholic. Physicians are also less likely to believe that women's symptoms indicate underlying physical problems than that men's symptoms indicate physical illness (e.g., McCranie, Horowitz, & Martin, 1978). Thus, one barrier to treatment for women alcoholics may be that their symptoms are not perceived as serious by physicians and other professionals.

Evidence is ambiguous concerning the effects of agency referral and outreach patterns on women's treatment seeking. Several studies have indicated that women usually have relatively high levels of self-referral to treatment agencies (Hoffman & Noem, 1975; Wanberg & Jones, 1973). Such findings are consistent with the results of Corrigan's (1974) evaluation of outreach strategies, which showed that women are more responsive than men to mass media campaigns for alcohol treatment. Other studies have indicated, however, that women are generally pressed into treatment by family and various health and welfare agencies (Browne-Mayers, Seelye & Sillman, 1976; Dahlgren & Myrhed, 1977; Selby, Calhoun, Bass, & Floyd, 1978), while men enter on their own initiative (Dahlgren & Myrhed, 1977). In contrast to being legally coerced into treatment, women indeed may be more likely to be self-referred than men; such "self-referral," however, is often backed by strong informal sanctions.

The goal of alcoholism outreach presumably is to increase motivation to seek treatment and knowledge about treatment resources among alcoholic women and men. A large number of outreach techniques exist, ranging from general appeals to physicians, lawyers, and the courts for help in identifying alcoholics to specific multimedia programs and weekend retreats geared toward women who may be questioning their own use of alcohol. With the exception of Corrigan's (1974) study mentioned above, few outreach techniques for female (or male) problem drinkers have been formally evaluated for their effectiveness in promoting help-seeking behavior or their relative influence on different population subgroups (Sandmaier, 1977). (For a discussion of outreach techniques geared toward prevention, see Ferrence, Chapter 14 in this volume.)

Another barrier that has received almost no research consideration is the lack of supportive services (e.g., child-care arrangements) for women who are undergoing treatment. One report (California Women's Commission on Alcoholism, 1977) indicates that many providers were aware of difficulties posed for their clients by the absence of such services.

Both treatment modalities and support services offered by the majority of alcoholism treatment facilities may be inadequate for female alcohol abusers. A report (Naierman et al., 1979) that examined sex discrimination in health and human development services concluded that alcohol and drug programs were particularly inattentive to women's service needs. Among the service needs identified were treatment for prescription drug use, counseling for incest victims, counseling for battered women, women's support groups, child care, child treatment or counseling, and medical and nutritional care for pregnant women. Only 37% of the coeducational facilities surveyed provided one or more of these services.

With regard to other treatment agency characteristics, studies are needed that directly relate composition of staff, geographic distribution, attitudes of treatment providers and other factors that affect access (e.g., financial cost, availability of beds) to women's patterns of use. It seems likely that structural barriers to seeking treatment for alcohol problems will vary among ethnic and income groups (Milo, 1976), but research evidence regarding ethnic and socioeconomic status differences among women alcoholics is not available.

TREATMENT USE PATTERNS AMONG WOMEN IN CALIFORNIA

Hypotheses

To investigate reasons for the disproportionately low utilization of alcoholism treatment agencies by women, a study of the personal and social characteristics of male and female clients and the structural characteristics of the agencies that they frequent was undertaken. This research was built upon the model of alcoholism treatment utilization previously described.

Gender, a predisposing variable, was hypothesized to affect other personal, environmental and system variables. Because of sex-role norms and the role of women in childbearing and nursing, the family domain is more central to women's lives than men's. We hypothesized that the costs of initially entering treatment, specifically such family-related costs as separation from children or disapproval of spouse, are perceived as greater by women than by men. (These costs probably are perceived as greater by women because in reality they *are* greater for women.) Familial pressures would be of more concern to women, while men would be more affected by legal and job pressures than women would be. Also, women should evidence more favorable opinions regarding treatment services and providers, more satisfaction regarding treatment, and a greater concern about health-related matters, and they should perceive treatment as more effective than do men. (For a more detailed discussion of these predictions, see Beckman & Amaro, 1982.)

Female alcoholics, it was predicted, would score lower on the personal enabling traits of personal efficacy and self-esteem than would men alcoholics. In addition, women would receive less environmental support for a decision to enter treatment from both their families and friends (a social enabling factor). More persons in their social networks should inhibit help-seeking behavior than among men. It was predicted, however, that for women, a familial event would be more likely to elicit treatment-seeking, while for men job-related events and legal events would more frequently prove to be cues to voluntary or involuntary treatment-seeking actions.

Perhaps even more important than individual characteristics that distinguish between women and men are system-provided barriers that differ for the two groups. One of our basic assumptions was that some agencies attract women clients, in part, because they provide the types of facilities and services that satisfy women's needs and/or referral sources believe that, given the facilities available, they provide treatment options that best satisfy women's needs. The outreach procedures and referral sources of an individual treatment facility, as well as its cost and geographic location, can influence a woman's initial entry into treatment. The attitudes of an agency's director and its staff concerning women and alcohol may directly affect whether or not women continue in treatment. Such attitudes, through their influence on the treatment options, support services, and outreach procedures available at the agency, can also indirectly affect entry into treatment for female alcoholics.

Those system-related barriers that may have more impact for women are described in the following hypotheses.

1. The availability and adequacy of child-care facilities have more impact on the utilization rates of women than of men. Women more frequently use facilities that provide child care than facilities without child care.
2. The availability of job counseling, legal aid, and transportation is positively related to the use of facilities by women.
3. The availability and diversity of treatment and support options is positively related to women's utilization rates.
4. Facilities directed by treatment providers with more favorable attitudes toward female alcoholics attract greater proportions of female clients.
5. Women are more likely to utilize facilities that have greater proportions of women on the treatment staff.

Methods

The two data sets discussed here were collected from non-Hispanic Caucasian clients (Anglos) in alcohol treatment facilities and from the directors or co-directors of these treatment agencies located in two California counties, Alameda and Kern.

The client data set consists of information collected in personal interviews with 67 women and 54 men in 46 different alcoholism treatment facilities. Of the women, 46% were inpatients, 34%, outpatients, and 20%, in detoxification programs; the figures for men were 48%, 22%, and 30%, respectively. The data are currently being analyzed from black and Hispanic subsamples, but the present analysis is limited to Anglo clients. Clients were questioned about their beliefs and perceptions concerning alcoholism and barriers to treatment, drinking histories, severity of symptoms, past contacts with alcoholism and mental health treatment agencies and providers (including AA), their current social situations, and background characteristics such as number of children, job status, income, and marital status. They also completed a self-administered questionnaire that measured personal efficacy, self-esteem, social isolation, health beliefs, and health locus of control.

The treatment system data examine the impact of structural characteristics of 53 treatment agencies on female utilization rates (see Beckman & Kocel, 1982). The sample of 53 agencies consists of all the formal treatment agencies for alcoholism in Alameda and Kern counties. Mental health practitioners in private practice (unaffiliated with an agency) who may treat alcoholism, agencies that occasionally see alcoholics, and crisis-intervention programs were not included in the agency sample.

Data on structural characteristics of agencies were obtained through interviews with the directors or assistant directors of each facility. Numbers of clients admitted over a 1-year period and their sociodemographic characteristics (i.e., sex, age, ethnicity) were determined through agency reports and, when necessary, agency directors' estimates. The definition of a "client" probably differs from agency to agency. Most, however, considered a client to be one who has remained in the program for more than 2 days (inpatient) or 2 visits (outpatient). The service delivery system characteristics examined include type of agency (e.g., public vs. private), attitudes of the providers regarding women's needs in treatment, type of support services offered, types of outreach efforts reported, and characteristics of staff members including gender, ethnicity, and professional status.

Individual Characteristics Affecting Utilization

PREDISPOSING FACTORS

As would be expected, given women's generally lower status in our society, women alcoholics had somewhat lower educational levels and income levels than did men alcoholics; however, these differences did not reach significant levels. All clients with the exception of one woman had participated in the work force. Although no differences occurred in prestige of current or usual occupational status as measured by the Duncan Socioeconomic Index, among those who had been employed and were not currently retired women were somewhat less likely than men (27% vs. 47%) to be currently employed ($\chi^2 = 3.92, p < .05$). Contrary to past studies, men and women in this sample did not differ on marital status; the female alcohol abusers were no more likely to be divorced than were their male counterparts. Overall, though, the women's socioeconomic resources appeared somewhat lower than did the men's.

ATTITUDES AND BELIEFS

Women were more optimistic than men regarding the likelihood of successful treatment for alcoholism in general and for their drinking problems specifically. Among the women, 92% believed that there were successful treatments for their own alcohol problems, but only 87% of the men believed this. Among the clients who felt that there were successful treatments, women rated treatments as more successful, although not significantly more successful, than did men. Women also believed that people were somewhat more satisfied with the help obtained from alcoholism treatment agencies than did men. Although women and men did not differ in ratings of the seriousness of their own drinking problems, women reported having a serious drinking problem for fewer years ($t = 2.04, p < .05$). This may be one reason why they were somewhat more optimistic about their own treatment prospects than were men. Such positive attitudes toward alcoholism treatment may motivate women to seek help.

Contrary to predictions, women did not evidence any greater concern about health in general or more favorable attitudes toward getting medical care on the Health Perceptions and Beliefs Scale than did men. Men actually had somewhat higher scores ($t = 1.80, p < .10$) on health worry and concern and had somewhat more favorable attitudes toward going to the doctor ($t = 1.78, p < .10$) than did women. This may occur because of prior negative experiences of women with health professionals, for example, physicians' negative stereotypes of female alcoholics. As was predicted, the perceived costs of entering treatment differed for women and men. Overall, 48% of the women reported experiencing one or more problems due to entering treatment while less than 20% of the men reported experiencing such problems ($\chi^2 = 9.79, p < .01$). Women were more likely than men to report experiencing family problems ($\chi^2 = 4.63, p < .05$), money problems ($\chi^2 = 3.30, p < .10$), and problems involving friends ($\chi^2 = 8.48, p < .01$) because of their decision to enter treatment. Women were somewhat more likely to believe that family problems would have occurred if treatment had not been obtained (72% women vs. 63% men) while a somewhat greater percentage of the men reported problems relating to employment as costs of not obtaining treatment (60% women vs. 74% men). On the other hand, women perceived that more social problems such as conflict with or loss of friends would have occurred if treatment had not been entered (60% women vs. 48% men). None of these differences, however, was statistically significant.

PERSONAL ENABLING FACTORS

The two groups did not differ in scores on generalized expectancy for personal success on the Fibel and Hale Generalized Expectancy of Success Scale (1978) or self-esteem on the Rosenberg Self-Esteem Scale (1965), nor did their scores on the three dimensions of the Wallston and Wallston Multidimensional Health Locus of Control Scale (1978) show any significant differences.

It does not appear that personal traits have acted as greater barriers to treatment for female alcoholics than for male alcoholics. Two cautions are in order, however. First, women's self-esteem and other positive personal traits may have risen more as a result of entering treatment than men's. Second, those with the lowest self-esteem may not have entered treatment precisely because such a personal trait serves as a barrier to treatment-seeking; women still may compose a disproportionate percentage of this not-in-treatment group.

SOCIAL ENABLING FACTORS

It was predicted that there would be less environmental support for women entering treatment than there would be for men. In part this could be due to the stigma attached to alcoholism for women, a factor not directly measured. Nor could environmental support be directly measured. However, the differences (previously discussed) found in the (perceived) costs of entering treatment for men and women provide some support for the greater environmental barriers to women's entering treatment. While family and friends were somewhat more likely to facilitate women's entry into treatment they also were more likely to hinder women from entering treatment than men. These data could indicate a greater salience for women of the opinions held by family members and friends—views that may serve either to hinder or to motivate entry into treatment for women.

The types of consequences or problems experienced from drinking are reflections of the types of threats or sanctions that may be brought against an alcoholic to enter treatment; that is, if an alcoholic does not experience a certain type of consequence of drinking there will be no environmental influence from that area for the alcoholic to correct his or her drinking problem. Women were somewhat (but not significantly) more likely to report problems with children as consequences of excessive drinking while men were somewhat (but again not significantly) more likely to report legal and job problems. No other differences were found in the types of consequences experienced by male and female clients.

Finally, specific events may be differentially likely to serve as cues to the behavior of seeking treatment for women and men. Men were somewhat more likely (60% men vs. 49% women) to report that in the month before they entered treatment a family member or friend suggested that they needed treatment for their drinking problems. Among those who reported a family member or friend suggesting treatment, parents were more likely to suggest treatment for women (41% women vs. 18% men) while for men spouses were more likely to urge treatment (46% men vs. 12% women). Also, children were more likely to suggest treatment for women than they were for men (31% women vs. 9% men), whereas friends were more likely to suggest treatment for men (33%) than for women (25%). More importantly, a significantly greater percentage of women (23%) compared to men (2%) reported experiencing opposition to entering treatment from family and friends ($\chi^2 = 9.47, p < .01$). For women, opposition to treatment came from spouses (27% of women who experienced opposition), other family members (40% of women), and friends (40% of women). Only one male client reported opposition to treatment, which came from a drinking companion.

Approximately 30% of both women and men reported that in the month prior to entering treatment someone outside their family had suggested that they seek treatment. Among this group, more women than men said that their bosses (33% women vs. 20% men) had recommended treatment. Contrary to previous stereotypes, the police or courts were cited by more women (19%) than men (7%) as recommending that they seek treatment for alcohol-related problems. Men reported more frequently than women that the recommendation for treatment had come from a therapist (20% men vs. 5% women).

Although differences frequently were not significant, these results support the contention that family and friends are more likely to function as barriers to treatment for women and to facilitate treatment for men. In cases where the familial environment was supportive it was children and parents who were more likely to motivate women to seek treatment while men were more likely to be motivated because of spouses. Contrary to popular beliefs, employers and the legal systems were no less likely to suggest or mandate treatment for women than for men.

Structural Characteristics Affecting Utilization

Based on our assumption that women clients go to or are referred to agencies that appear to best meet their needs, the analysis examined the relationship between structural variables such as staff composition and the percentage of women in the client population of an agency. The unit of analysis is the treatment agency rather than the individual female client, and the total sample size is 53. In determining the percentage of women in each type of agency, the percentages for each agency were summed and divided by the number of agencies of that type. Each agency was not weighted by its total number of clients served.

AGENCY CHARACTERISTICS

Alcoholic women did not comprise a greater percentage of the client population at private alcohol treatment agencies (29.8%) than at public alcoholism facilities (26.0%). Given the higher prevalence of prescription drug abuse among women (Cooperstock, 1971), we expected that women would be proportionally more likely to utilize the small number of agencies ($n = 11$) that treat both alcohol and drug abuse rather than alcohol-only agencies. Although the difference in the proportion of women in these two agency types (39.4% vs. 24.4%) was in the predicted direction it did not reach significance.

Since initially each agency was not weighted by its number of clients and agencies that served greater proportions of women tended to serve fewer clients ($r = -.34$), percentages were adjusted within each category (e.g., private) by dividing the total number of female clients by the total number of all clients seen by those agencies. The percentage of women served decreases for all four category groups (private $= 22.6\%$, public $= 16.2\%$, alcohol only $= 14.9\%$, alcohol and drug $= 35.9\%$). Public agencies now appear as a group to serve a somewhat, but not significantly, lower proportion of women than do private agencies. Because of the larger client load in the public sector, public alcoholism agencies serve over twice as many female clients yearly in these two counties as private agencies (1500 public vs. 674 private). Of particular concern is the fact that alcohol-only agencies in these two counties have a clientele that is less than 15% female.

The composition of the treatment staff also affected women's use of agencies. A higher proportion of the total clientele was female at facilities with a higher percentage of women on the treatment staff ($r = .256, p < .05$), more professionally trained personnel ($r = .302, p < .05$), and fewer minority staff members ($r = -.424, p < .01$) than at those agencies with contrasting characteristics. When the two agencies treating only female clients were omitted, however, it was found that the relationship between the percent of female treatment staff and the percent of female clients became nonsignificant. In agencies treating both men and women, the presence of women on the treatment staff was not associated with the proportion of female clients.

Women apparently were well represented on the treatment staffs of facilities, composing about 50% of the staff and about 46% of the treatment staff of alcohol treatment agencies. However, figures on female treatment staff may be inflated because many women considered as treatment staff may only be involved in basic medical or custodial care.

TYPES OF SERVICES OFFERED

Agencies that provided (or had available) aftercare services ($t = 2.52, p < .05$) and treatment for children ($t = 2.79, p < .01$) served a significantly greater proportion of women than those that did not provide such services. The number of client support services offered, and the availability of child-care services were positively related to the percentage of female clients, although less strongly ($p < .10$). Neither job counseling, legal counseling, nor transportation was related to the proportion of women who utilized a service.

The complete absence of residential treatment facilities with live-in child-care services in the two counties and the lack of a not-in-treatment sample make it impossible to study the effects of presence versus absence of such services. The need for such services is suggested by the strong relationship between the availability of treatment for children and the proportion of women in facilities that offer this service. The weakness of the association between child-care services and women's use of facilities generally may suggest that the type of child-care services provided (i.e., someone who babysits with the child while the mother is in an outpatient session) is inadequate and that what is needed is a combination child-treatment and residential program with live-in facilities for children. Also, child-care responsibilities and needs probably are lower among women who do eventually reach treatment than among those who do not reach treatment.

ATTITUDES OF TREATMENT PROVIDERS

Each agency director was asked if women are more reluctant to enter treatment than men, if they need different treatment services than men do, if men and women have equal chances for recovery, and if male and female alcoholics differ in any other respects. Contrary to prediction, there were no significant relationships between the providers' self-reported attitudes and use of their agencies by women. It would be important to investigate how the attitudes of treatment providers translate into behaviors and internal policies that affect female clients.

OUTREACH AND REFERRAL

Neither type of outreach method nor total number of outreach techniques was associated with the proportion of women using a treatment facility. Those agencies with higher proportions of female clients were more likely to report that initial referral sources were advertisements and walk-ins ($t = 2.08, p < .05$) and family, friends or word of mouth ($t = 2.10$, $p < .05$). Interestingly enough, approximately one-third of the agencies conducted no outreach at all because they frequently got clients from other agencies or personal referrals and were almost always filled to capacity.

SUMMARY

Predisposing factors, such as employment status and income, may serve as greater personal barriers to entry into and continuation of treatment for women than for men. They reflect the generally disadvantaged position of women in our society. Beliefs about alcohol, treatment, and health generally facilitate women's motivation for treatment; however, women may perceive greater (family, financial, and social) costs of seeking treatment or continuing in treatment. While attitudes about alcoholism and alcoholism-specific treatment were found to be more optimistic in female than in male alcoholics, more general attitudes about health and medical care showed few gender-specific differences among alcoholics. Also, women did not perceive their alcohol problems as any more severe than did men. On balance, however, cognitive factors such as attitudes and beliefs appear to facilitate rather than impede treatment for women. On the other hand, one particular belief set, the perceived cost of seeking (or continuing) treatment, which is likely to be more salient for women because of actual environmental pressure, may be a particularly important cognitive barrier to treatment.

Personal enabling factors, particularly personality characteristics associated with sex-role socialization such as feelings of powerlessness and lack of competence, may inhibit many female alcoholics from independently taking action to seek treatment. In our own recent study, however, women did not appear to have lower self-esteem or higher rates of depression than men. Other research (Chien & Schneiderman, 1975; McKinlay, 1972) suggests that women are more likely than men to take an action toward treatment that is health or mental-health related. In other words, they may be more willing to seek help for alcohol-related health problems than are men, but they also are more likely to deny that the same problems are alcohol-related (Johnson, 1965).

Social enabling factors and treatment service system characteristics generally appear to inhibit women from entry into treatment (relative to men) and also may facilitate women's dropping out of alcoholism treatment. Thus, while individual characteristics on balance may facilitate treatment for women relative to men, in the present study environmental, social, and situational circumstances and characteristics of the treatment delivery system itself generally act as relatively greater barriers to treatment for women. We found that family and friends are more likely to oppose women's entry into treatment and more problems in relationships with others are experienced by women entering treatment than by men entering treatment. Prior literature suggests that support services important for women, such as residential child-care arrangements, counseling for battered women, and treatment for prescription drug use, are only infrequently available at most treatment facilities based on male models of alcoholism (Naierman et al., 1979). The lack of such important supports may cause women to drop out of treatment. Obviously the meager data collected to date do not allow final conclusions regarding the specific nature of treatment barriers. However, patterns in our own data and in past studies clearly indicate that social support networks, societal norms, and the structure of treatment agencies promote inequities in the provision of services to women with alcohol-related problems.

APPLICATION TO PREVENTION AND TREATMENT

Structural characteristics of treatment agencies are particularly important foci for efforts to motivate women to enter treatment earlier in their alcohol abuse careers, because such factors can be directly influenced through changes in social policy. If a woman does not go into an agency she cannot receive help there, even if the treatment and support modalities provided are those most likely to result in remission of alcohol problems. However, the fact that an agency serves large proportions of women relative to men is probably indicative that it is better meeting women's needs than is a facility with a very low proportion of women clients. The literature reviewed, as well as our own data, suggests that alcoholism treatment facilities that provide child treatment, child care, professional treatment staff, and aftercare are best equipped to motivate women to enter treatment. Women's support groups, counseling for battered women and incest victims, and medical and nutritional counseling for pregnant women may also be important. Agencies with a large number of support services and treatment for drugs as well as alcohol abuse may attract women best.

Agency characteristics reflect larger societal attitudes and norms. Alcoholism is a disorder that is incongruent with idealized sex-role stereotypes for women. Because of the lack of congruence and perhaps a tendency among some providers to see women's problems as less serious than men's, alcoholic women's needs are often ignored and their condition misdiagnosed. While this implies that societal stereotypes about sex roles need to be changed before equitable alcohol services will be provided to women, treatment agencies, if designed to satisfy women's needs, also can help to shape community recognition of alcohol problems in women.

Stigmatization and the unwillingness of community gatekeepers such as physicians, mental health professionals, the police, and the courts to label women as "alcoholic" are detrimental to any efforts toward early intervention. Results reported by Chappel (1975), James (1975), Knox (1971), and others suggest that a majority of community gatekeepers need to be educated to identify alcohol problems in women, to make appropriate referrals for such problems and, in some cases, to treat alcohol problems themselves.

Individual and situational characteristics also can sometimes be manipulated to aid secondary and tertiary prevention efforts. Data on family and friends' facilitation of treatment-seeking actions suggest that social support networks composed of family members and friends can be effectively used to facilitate rather than hinder the treatment of women. Particularly important is the education of family members so that they perceive the female alcoholic as having a treatable illness rather than a moral weakness. Often the conspiracy of silence leaves the female alcoholic isolated and alone with no one to talk with about her drinking. For instance, one of our interviewees said, "Everyone knew I had a drinking problem—my ex-husband, my friends, the guy I was living with, my parents—but no one ever mentioned it to me until finally I went to a doctor and when he asked me how much I had been drinking I was honest with him. He told me that if I didn't stop, I would die; he found me a place to go for help."

Though we do not know what cues serve as instigators to treatment, we know that support from parents, children, and other members of one's social network can motivate help-seeking action among women with alcohol problems. Early identification programs will not have optimal effects unless the general public, professionals, and the daughters, sons, parents, siblings, spouses, and friends of alcoholic women are educated to believe that the best way to help a woman with a drinking problem is not by silence but rather by honesty, confrontation, and expression of concern.

Secondary prevention efforts may often fail because of women's lack of economic resources and generally lower status and power in many segments of our society. On the other hand, individual characteristics such as women's self-evaluation and their belief in the efficacy of treatment may facilitate help-seeking behavior among those with alcohol problems. Although our research shows few differences in general health beliefs between women and men, prior research shows more favorable attitudes toward medical treatment among women. If women with such attitudes can be convinced that alcoholism is a disease, these attitudes might also generalize to treatment of alcoholism. In any case, attitudes and beliefs about various illnesses including alcohol abuse can be changed through a combination of public education campaigns and personal contact (e.g., Farquhar *et al.*, 1977; Meyer, Nash, McAlister, Maccoby, & Farquhar, 1980), and the more favorable the opinions women have about alcoholism services and providers and the efficacy of such services, the more likely they will be to continue to use such services.

ACKNOWLEDGMENTS

This research was supported in part by a Research Scientist Development Award from the National Institute on Alcohol Abuse and Alcoholism to the first author and by funding from the State of California Department of Alcohol and Drug Programs to the UCLA Alcohol Research Center.

REFERENCES

Abramowitz, S. I., Abramowitz, C. V., Roback, H. B., Corney, R., & McKee, E. Sex-role related countertransference in psychotherapy. *Archives of General Psychiatry*, 1976, *33*, 71–73.

Aday, L., & Andersen, R. A framework for the study of access to medical care. *Health Services Research*, 1974, *9*, 208–220.

Andersen, R., & Newman, J. P. Societal and individual determinants of medical care utilization in the U.S. *Milbank Memorial Fund Quarterly*, 1973, *51*, 95–124.

Baekeland, F., & Lundwall, L. Dropping out of treatment: A critical review. *Psychological Bulletin*, 1975, *82*(5), 738–783.

Baekeland, F., Lundwall, L., & Kissin, B. Methods for the treatment of chronic alcoholism: A critical appraisal. In R. J. Gibbons, Y. Israel, H. Kalant, R. E. Popham, W. Schmidt, & R. G. Smart (Eds.), *Research advances in alcohol and drug problems* (Vol. 2). New York: Wiley, 1975.

Baekeland, F., Lundwall, L., & Shanahan, T. J. Correlates of patient attrition in the outpatient treatment of alcoholism. *Journal of Nervous and Mental Diseases*, 1973, *157*, 99–107.

Bates, C. R. Clues to the diagnosis of alcoholism. *Journal of the Michigan Medical Society*, 1963, *62*, 977–979.

Becker, M. H. The health belief model and sick role behavior. *Health Education Monographs*, 1974, *2*, 409.

Becker, M. H., Haefner, D. P., Kasl, S. V., Kirscht, J. P., Maiman, L. A., & Rosenstock, I. M. Selected psychosocial models and correlates of individual health-related behaviors. *Medical Care*, 1977, *15*, 27–46.

Beckman, L. J. Women alcoholics: A review of social and psychological studies. *Journal of Studies on Alcohol*, 1975, *36*(7), 797–824.

Beckman, L. J. The self-esteem of women alcoholics. *Journal of Studies on Alcohol*, 1978, *39*(3), 491–498.

Beckman, L. J. The reported effects of alcohol on the sexual feelings and behavior of women alcoholics and nonalcoholics. *Journal of Studies on Alcohol*, 1979, *40*(3), 272–282.

Beckman, L. J. Perceived antecedents and effects of alcohol consumption in women. *Journal of Studies on Alcohol*, 1980, *41*(5), 518–530.

Beckman, L. J., & Amaro, H. *Barriers to treatment among Anglo women alcoholics* (Report prepared for the State of California Department of Alcohol and Drug Programs) Los Angeles, Calif.: University of California at Los Angeles Alcohol Research Center, March 1982.

Beckman, L. J., & Bardsley, P. E. *Barriers to treatment among alcoholic women.* Grant #AA04867 funded by National Institute on Alcohol Abuse and Alcoholism, 1980–1984, UCLA School of Medicine, Los Angeles.

Beckman, L. J., & Kocel, K. M. The treatment-delivery system and alcohol abuse in women: Social policy implications. *Journal of Social Issues*, 1982, *38*(2), 139–151.

Beil, H., & Trojan, A. The use of apomorphine treatment of alcoholism and other addictions: Results of a general practitioner. *British Journal of Addiction*, 1977, *72*, 129–134.

Bice, J. W., & White, K. L. Factors related to the use of health services: An international comparative study. *Medical Care*, 1969, *7*, 124–133.

Blane, H. T., & Meyers, W. R. Behavioral dependence and length of stay in psychotherapy among alcoholics. *Quarterly Journal of Studies on Alcohol*, 1963, *24*, 503–510.

Blane, H. T., Overton, W. F., & Chafetz, M. E. Social factors in the diagnosis of alcoholism. I. Characteristics of the patient. *Quarterly Journal of Studies on Alcohol*, 1963, *24*, 640–663.

Block, M. A. *Alcoholism: Its facets and phases.* New York: John Day, 1965.

Blume, S. B. Diagnosis, casefinding, and treatment of alcohol problems in women: Current status. *Alcohol Health and Research World*, 1978, *3*(1), 10–22.

Boggs, S. L. Measures of treatment outcome for alcoholics: A model of analysis. In D. J. Pitman (Ed.), *Alcoholism.* New York: Harper & Row, 1967.

Bowen, W. T., & Temlow, S. W. Locus of control and treatment dropout in an alcoholic population. *British Journal of Addiction*, 1978, *73*, 51–54.

Broverman, I. K., Broverman, D. M., Clarkson, F. E., Rosenkrantz, P. S., & Vogel, S. R. Sex-role stereotyping and clinical judgments of mental health. *Journal of Consulting and Clinical Psychology*, 1970, *34*, 1–7.

Browne-Mayers, A. M., Seelye, E. E., & Sillman, L. Psychosocial study of hospitalized middle-class alcoholic women. *Annals of the New York Academy of Sciences*, 1976, *273*, 593–604.

Cahalan, D. *Problem drinkers.* San Francisco: Jossey-Bass, 1970.

California Women's Commission on Alcoholism. *A survey of caretakers in California.* Los Angeles: California Women's Commission on Alcoholism, 1977.

Carver, V. The female alcoholic in treatment. *Canadian Psychological Review*, 1977, *18*, 96–103.

Caster, D. U., & Parsons, O. A. Relationship of depression, sociopathy, and locus of control to treatment outcome in alcoholics. *Journal of Consulting and Clinical Psychology*, 1977, *45*, 751–756.

Chappel, J. Physicians' attitudes and effects on the treatment of chemically dependent patients. *Journal of the American Medical Association*, 1975, *237*, 2318–2319.

Chien, A., & Schneiderman, L. J. A comparison of health care utilization by husbands and wives. *Journal of Community Health*, 1975, *1*(2), 118–126.

Cooperstock, R. Sex differences in the use of mood-modifying drugs: An explanatory model. *Journal of Health and Social Behavior*, 1971, *12*, 238–244.

Corrigan, E. M. Women and problem drinking: Notes on beliefs and facts. *Addictive Diseases: An International Journal*, 1974, *1*(2), 215–222.

Cummings, R. E. A study of characteristics of patients who fail to complete a V.A. alcoholic treatment program. *Rehabilitation Literature*, 1975, *36*, 139–141.

Cummings, R. E. A three-year study of a V.A. inpatient alcoholic treatment using demographic and psychological data. *Rehabilitation Literature*, 1977, *38*, 153–156.

Curlee, J. A comparison of male and female patients at an alcoholism treatment center. *Journal of Psychology*, 1970, *74*, 239–247.

Curlee, J. Sex differences in patients' attitudes toward alcoholism treatment. *Quarterly Journal of Studies on Alcohol*, 1971, *32*, 643–650.

Dahlgren, L., & Myrhed, M. Female alcoholics. *Acta Psychiatrica Scandinavica*, 1977, *56*, 39–49.

Dickinson, R. G. *Minnesota Multiphasic Personality Inventory: Alcoholic types and prognostic variables*. Doctoral dissertation, Purdue University, 1974. (University Microfilms No. 75-17181)

Emrick, C. D. A review of psychologically oriented treatment of alcoholism. II. The relative effectiveness of different treatment approaches and the effectiveness of treatment versus no treatment. *Journal of Studies on Alcohol*, 1975, *36*(1), 88–108.

Fabrikant, B. The psychotherapist and the female patient: Perceptions, misperceptions, and change. In V. Franks & V. Burtle (Eds.), *Women in therapy: New psychotherapies for a changing society*. New York: Brunner/Mazel, 1974.

Farquhar, J. W., Maccoby, N., Wood, P. D., Alexander, J. K., Breitrose, H., Brown, B. W., Jr., Haskell, W. L., McAlister, A. L., Meyer, A. J., Nash, J. D., & Stern, M. D. Community education for cardiovascular health. *Lancet*, 1977, *1*(8023), 1192–1195.

Ferrence, R. G., Rush, B. R., & Murdock, W. L. *Services for alcoholics: A study of medical and social service facilities in the Lake Erie region* (Substudy No. 1136). Toronto: Addiction Research Foundation, 1980.

Fewell, C. H., & Bissell, L. Alcoholic denial syndrome: An alcoholic-focused approach. *Social Casework*, 1978, *59*, 6–13.

Fibel, B., & Hale, W. D. The Generalized Expectancy of Success Scale: A new measure. *Journal of Consulting and Clinical Psychology*, 1978, *46*(5), 924–931.

Furst, C. J., Beckman, L. J., Nakamura, C. Y., & Weiss, M. *Utilization of alcoholism treatment services* (Report prepared for the State of California Department of Alcohol and Drug Programs). Los Angeles: University of California at Los Angeles Alcohol Research Center, February 1981.

Gellens, H. K., Gottheil, E., & Alterman, A. I. Drinking outcome of specific alcoholic subgroups. *Journal of Studies on Alcohol*, 1976, *37*(7), 986–989.

Gertler, R., Raynes, A. E., & Harris, N. Assessment of attendance and outcome at an outpatient alcoholism clinic. *Quarterly Journal of Studies on Alcohol*, 1973, *34*, 955–959.

Glasser, M. A., Duggun, T. J., & Hoffman, W. S. Obstacles to utilization of prepaid mental health care. *American Journal of Psychiatry*, 1975, *132*(7), 710–715.

Glatt, M. M. Drinking habits of English (middle-class) alcoholics. *Acta Psychiatrica Scandinavica*, 1961, *37*, 88–113.

Gomberg, E. S. Women and alcoholism. In V. Franks & V. Burtle (Eds.), *Women in therapy: New psychotherapies for a changing society*. New York: Brunner/Mazel, 1974.

Gomberg, E. S. L. Women, sex roles and alcohol problems. *Professional Psychology*, 1981, *12*, 146–155.

Hanna, E. Attitudes toward problem drinkers. *Journal of Studies on Alcohol*, 1978, *39*, 98–109.

Heinemann, E., Moore, B., & Gurel, M. Completion or termination of alcoholism treatment: Toward the development of a predictive index. *Psychological Reports*, 1976, *38*, 1340–1342.

Hetherington, R. W., & Hopkins, C. E. Symptom sensitivity: Its social and cultural correlates. *Health Services Research*, 1969, *4* (Spring), 63–75.

Hoffman, H., & Noem, A. A. Sex differences in a state hospital population of alcoholics on admission and treatment variables. *Psychological Reports*, 1975, *37*, 145–146.

Homiller, J. D. Alcoholism among women. *Chemical Dependencies: Behavioral and Biomedical*, 1980, *4*(1), 1–31.

Horn, J. L., & Wanberg, K. W. Symptom patterns related to excessive use of alcohol. *Quarterly Journal of Studies on Alcohol*, 1969, *30*, 35–58.

Horn, J. L., & Wanberg, K. W. Females are different: On the diagnosis of alcoholism in women. In *Proceedings of the First Annual Alcoholism Conference of the National Institute on Alcohol Abuse and Alcoholism*. (U.S. DHEW No. NIH-74-675). Washington, D.C.: U.S. Government Printing Office, 1973.

Huber, N. A., & Danahy, S. Use of the MMPI in predicting completion and evaluating changes in a long-term alcoholism treatment program. *Journal of Studies on Alcohol*, 1975, *36*, 1230–1237.

Institute of Medicine, Division of Health Promotion and Disease Prevention, National Academy of Sciences. *Alcoholism, alcohol abuse and related problems: Opportunities for research* (Publ. No. 10M 80-04). Washington, D. C.: National Academy Press, 1980.

James, J. E. Symptoms of alcoholism in women: A preliminary study of A.A. members. *Journal of Studies on Alcohol*, 1975, *36*, 1564–1578.

Johnson, M. W. Physicians' views on alcoholism with special reference to alcoholism in women. *Nebraska State Medical Journal*, 1965, *50*, 378–384.

Jones, R. W., & Helrich, A. R. Treatment of alcoholism by physicians in private practice. *Quarterly Journal of Studies on Alcohol*, 1972, *33*, 117–131.

Kendell, R. E., & Staton, M. C. The fate of untreated alcoholics. *Quarterly Journal of Studies on Alcohol*, 1966, *27*, 30–41.

Kern, J. C., Schumelter, W. R., & Paul, S. R. Drinking drivers who complete and drop out of an alcohol education program. *Journal of Studies on Alcohol*, 1977, *38*, 89–95.

Knox, W. J. Attitudes of psychiatrists and psychologists toward alcoholism. *American Journal of Psychiatry*, 1971, *127*, 1673–1679.

Krasnoff, A. Failure of MMPI scales to predict treatment completion. *Journal of Studies on Alcohol*, 1977, *38*, 1440–1442.

Lindbeck, V. L. The woman alcoholic: A review of the literature. *International Journal of the Addictions*, 1972, *7*(3), 567–580.

Linn, M. W. Attrition of older alcoholics from treatment. *Addictive Diseases*, 1978, *3*(3), 437–447.

Lisansky, E. S. The woman alcoholic. *Annals of the American Academy of Political and Social Sciences*, 1958, *315*, 78–81.

Lockheed, M. E., & Hall, K. P. Conceptualizing sex as a status characteristic: Applications to leadership training strategies. *Journal of Social Issues*, 1976, *32*, 111–124.

Lorion, R. P. Socioeconomic status and traditional treatment approaches reconsidered. *Psychological Bulletin*, 1973, *79*, 263–270.

Lorion, R. P. Patient and therapist variables in the treatment of low income patients. *Psychological Bulletin*, 1974, *81*, 344–354.

Lowe, W. C., & Thomas, S. D. Assessing alcoholism treatment effectiveness: A comparison of three evaluative measures. *Journal of Studies on Alcohol*, 1976, *37*, 883–889.

Marden, P. G., & Kolodner, K. *Alcohol abuse among women: Gender differences and their implications for the delivery of services*. Draft manuscript prepared for Division of Special

Treatment and Rehabilitation, National Institute on Alcohol Abuse and Alcoholism, 1978.

McCranie, E. W., Horowitz, A. J., & Martin, R. M. Alleged sex-role stereotyping in the assessment of women's physical complaints: A study of general practitioners. *Social Science and Medicine*, 1978, *12*(2A), 111–116.

McKinlay, J. B. Some approaches and problems in the study of the use of services: An overview. *Journal of Health and Social Behavior*, 1972, *13*, 115–152.

McLachlan, J. F. C. A short adjective checklist for the evaluation of anxiety and depression. *Journal of Clinical Psychology*, 1976, *32*, 195–197.

Meyer, A. J., Nash, J. D., McAlister, A. L., Maccoby, N., & Farquhar, J. W. Skills training in a cardiovascular health education campaign. *Journal of Consulting and Clinical Psychology*, 1980, *48*(2), 129–142.

Midanik, L. *Perceptual variables as factors in dropout from alcoholism treatment*. Paper presented at the 11th Annual Medical–Scientific Conference of the National Council on Alcoholism, Seattle, Wash., May 1980.

Milmoe, S., Rosenthal, R., Blane, H. T., Chafetz, M. E., & Wolf, I. The doctor's voice: Postdictor of successful referral of alcoholic patients. *Journal of Abnormal Psychology*, 1967, *72*, 78–84.

Milo, N. Framework for prevention: Changing health-damaging to health-generating life patterns. *American Journal of Public Health*, 1976, *66*, 435–439.

Mulford, H. A. Women and men problem drinkers: Sex differences in patients served by Iowa's community alcoholism centers. *Journal of Studies on Alcohol*, 1977, *38*, 1624–1639.

Naierman, N., Savage, B., Haskins, B., Lear, J., Chase, H., Marvelle, K., & Lamothe, R. *An assessment of sex discrimination in the delivery of health development services*. Final report submitted to Department of Health, Education, and Welfare, Office of Civil Rights (Contract No. HEW-100-78-0137), June 1979.

National Institute on Drug Abuse. Data from the client-oriented data acquisition process (CODAP): State statistics 1978. *NIDA statistical series* (Series E, No. 13). Washington, D.C.: U.S. Government Printing Office, 1980.

Noble, E. P. (Ed.) *Third special report to the U.S. Congress on alcohol and health* (U.S. Department of Health, Education, and Welfare Publication No. ADM-78-569). Washington, D.C.: U.S. Government Printing Office, 1978.

O'Leary, M. R., Calsyn, D. A., Chaney, E. F., & Freeman, C. W. Predicting alcohol treatment program dropouts. *Diseases of the Nervous System*, 1977, *38*, 993–995.

O'Leary, M. R., Rohsenow, D. J., & Chaney, E. F. The use of multivariate personality strategies in predicting attrition from alcoholism treatment. *Journal of Clinical Psychiatry*, 1979, *40*, 190–193.

O'Leary, M. R., Rohsenow, D. J., Schau, E. J., & Donovan, D. M. Defensive style and treatment outcome among men alcoholics. *Journal of Studies on Alcohol*, 1977, *38*(5), 1036–1040.

Patton, M. Q. *Profile of Hazelden patients discharged in 1977*. Center City, Minn.: Hazelden Literature, 1978.

Polich, J. M., Armor, D. J., & Braiker, H. B. *The course of alcoholism: Four years after treatment* (Report No. R-2433-NIAAA prepared for the National Institute on Alcohol Abuse and Alcoholism). Santa Monica, Calif.: Rand Corporation, January 1980.

Rathod, N. H., & Thomson, I. G. Women alcoholics: A clinical study. *Quarterly Journal of Studies on Alcohol*, 1971, *32*, 45–52.

Reed, A. C., Van-Lewen, A., & Williams, J. H. Effects of progressive relaxation on alcoholic patients. *Quarterly Journal of the Florida Academy of Science*, 1971, *34*, 213–222.

Rosenberg, M. *Society and the adolescent self-image*. Princeton, N.J.: Princeton University, 1965.

Rosenblat, D., & Suchman, E. A. The underutilization of medical care services by blue-collarites.

In A. B. Shostak & W. Gomberg (Eds.), *Blue-collar world*. Englewood Cliffs, N.J.: Prentice Hall, 1964.

Rosenstock, M. Why people use health services. *Milbank Memorial Fund Quarterly*, 1966, *44*, 94–124.

Russo, N. F., & Sobel, S. B. Sex differences in the utilization of mental health facilities. *Professional Psychology*, 1981, *12*(1), 7–19.

Russo, N. F., & VandenBos, G. R. Women in the mental health delivery system. In W. H. Silverman (Ed.), *Community mental health*. New York: Praeger, 1981.

Sandmaier, M. *Alcohol programs for women: Issues, strategies and resources*. Washington, D.C.: National Clearinghouse for Alcohol Information, 1977.

Sandmaier, M. *The invisible alcoholics*. New York: McGraw-Hill, 1980.

Schofield, L. J., Jr. Internal-external control and withdrawal from an alcohol rehabilitation program. *Journal of Clinical Psychology*, 1978, *34*, 571–573.

Schuckit, M. A., Pitts, F. N., Jr., Reich, T., King, L. J., & Winokur, G. Alcoholism. I. Two types of alcoholism in women. *Archives of General Psychiatry*, 1969, *20*, 301–306.

Schuckit, M. A., Rimmer, J., Reich, T., & Winokur, G. The bender alcoholic. *British Journal of Psychiatry*, 1971, *119*, 183–184.

Schuckit, M. A., & Winokur, G. A short-term follow-up of women alcoholics. *Diseases of the Nervous System*, 1972, *33*, 672–678.

Selby, I. W., Calhoun, L. G., Bass, A. E., & Floyd, R. Sex differences among clients of an emergency care unit for alcoholism. *Journal of Clinical Psychology*, 1978, *34*, 567–568.

Silberfeld, M., & Glaser, F. B. Use of the life table method in determining attrition from treatment. *Journal of Studies on Alcohol*, 1978, *39*(9), 1582–1590.

Smart, R. G., & Gray, G. Multiple predictors of dropout from alcoholism treatment. *Archives of General Psychiatry*, 1978, *35*, 363–367.

Stafford, R., & Petway, J. Stigmatization of men and women problem drinkers and their spouses. *Journal of Studies on Alcohol*, 1977, *38*, 2109–2121.

Tuchfeld, B. S., Simuel, J. B., Schmitt, M. L., Ries, J. L., Kay, D. L., & Waterhouse, G. J. *Changes in patterns of alcohol use without the aid of formal treatment*. Research Triangle Park, N.C.: Research Triangle Institute, August 1976.

Wallston, K. A., & Wallston, B. S. Development of the Multidimensional Health Locus of Control (MHLC) scales. *Health Education Monographs*, 1978, *6*(2), 160–171.

Wanberg, K. W., & Horn, J. L. Alcoholism symptom patterns of men and women: A comparative study. *Quarterly Journal of Studies on Alcohol*, 1970, *31*, 40–61.

Wanberg, K. W., & Horn, J. L. Alcoholism syndromes related to sociological classifications. *International Journal of the Addictions*, 1973, *8*, 99–120.

Wanberg, K. W., & Jones, E. Initial contact and admission of persons requesting treatment for alcohol problems. *British Journal of Addiction*, 1973, *68*, 281–285.

Westie, K. S., & McBride, D. C. The effects of ethnicity, age and sex upon processing through an emergency alcohol health care delivery system. *British Journal of Addiction*, 1979, *74*, 21–29.

Wilsnack, S. C. Alcohol, sexuality, and reproductive dysfunction in women. In E. L. Abel (Ed.), *Fetal alcohol syndrome* (Vol. 2: *Human studies*). Boca Raton, Fla.: CRC Press, 1982.

Winokur, G., & Clayton, P. Family history studies. IV. Comparison of male and female alcoholics. *Quarterly Journal of Studies on Alcohol*, 1968, *29*, 885–891.

Wolf, I., Chafetz, M. E., Blane, H. T., & Hill, M. J. Social factors in the diagnosis of alcoholism. II. Attitudes of physicians. *Quarterly Journal of Studies on Alcohol*, 1965, *26*, 72–79.

Wood, H. P., & Duffy, E. L. Psychological factors in alcoholic women. *American Journal of Psychiatry*, 1966, *123*, 341–345.

Yamamoto, J., James, Q. C., & Palley, N. Cultural problems in psychiatric therapy. *Archives of General Psychiatry*, 1968, *19*, 45–49.

Zelen, S. L., Fox, J., Gould, E., & Olson, R. W. Sex-contingent differences between male and female alcoholics. *Journal of Clinical Psychology*, 1966, *22*, 160–165.

12

Therapeutic Issues in the Treatment of Alcoholic Women

HARRIET B. BRAIKER
Los Angeles, California

INTRODUCTION

In recent years, the number of women seeking professional help for problems with alcohol has steadily increased. Some observers view this trend as evidence of a rising rate of alcoholism among the female population generally. Others contend, with more empirical support, that the increases primarily reflect a greater openness to and visibility of problems that have long existed but remained largely hidden due to the strong social sanctions against female drinking (see Cohen, 1981; Fillmore, Chapter 1 in this volume). In any event, the emergence of this new target population has given rise to demands for separate treatment facilities, special approaches, and increased funding for prevention, treatment, and research directed toward women with drinking problems. Reaction to the problem from both the public and private domains has resulted in the establishment of women's treatment programs and the growth of a substantial literature on the topic of female alcoholism.

Notwithstanding these considerable strides, the clinician charged with the responsibility of actually treating individual alcoholic women will find little in the way of sound empirical guidance in the accumulated body of knowledge. It is a literature, sadly, that Annis (1980) has characterized as abounding in myth, rhetoric, speculation, and cliche. Treatment studies are riddled with methodological problems, yielding equivocal and frequently contradictory results. Solid empirical evidence for the effectiveness of any one treatment modality for female alcoholics, or the differential effects of treatment-related factors (e.g., length of treatment, sex of therapist), is essentially absent. Outcome comparisons by sex provide no support for the widespread claim that female alcoholics are harder to treat than their male counterparts (see Vannicelli, Chapter 13 in this volume). And, while a host of prognostic, background, and precipitating factors that differentiate alcoholic women from alcoholic men have been reported, the proportion of variance in treatment outcome explained by such variables is relatively small

(Cronkite & Moos, 1980). Moreover, very little discussion exists as to how these factors might be used to develop treatment intervention procedures specific to women.

In sum, the literature to date on treating female alcoholism points to the gaps rather than the advances in our knowledge of the problem. What does clearly emerge is the imperative need for systematic and careful studies designed to evaluate the response of different types of female alcoholics to a range of specific treatment interventions. It should be noted that this state of affairs is not unique to the treatment of women; unfortunately, the same is largely true for male alcoholics as well. The fault does not lie with inadequate skills or efforts on the part of researchers who study the problem. Alcoholism is a complex, often chronic, probably nonunitary disorder. Alcoholics, male and female, are a widely heterogeneous population for whom no single treatment approach is likely to be uniformly effective or appropriate. As with other complicated disorders that have both organic and functional components, such as schizophrenia or affective illness, empirical knowledge about the causes and amelioration of alcoholism will fit together slowly over time like pieces of a jigsaw puzzle.

And yet, for the clinician who is treating female alcoholics, the exigencies of human suffering cannot await circumspect scientific inquiry and conclusive answers. Research to date does not support the position that female alcoholism is a qualitatively different clinical syndrome than male alcoholism. Indeed, it seems likely that gender differences are superseded by the commonality of self-destructive, abusive use of alcohol. The fact that the overwhelming majority of research on all facets of alcoholism has been done with male samples is certainly a less than desirable circumstance for those interested in women's problems per se. Nonetheless, a voluminous literature does exist on the diagnosis and treatment of alcoholism. It is unwarranted to assert that nothing of what is known about the phenomenon of alcoholism as it is expressed and treated in men can be generalized and applied to women. To do so would be to throw out the baby with the bathwater— simply because the baby is a boy rather than a girl.

Obviously, the life context in which abusive drinking is embedded is different in significant ways for women and for men; physiologically, socially, and psychologically, alcoholism is likely to involve a set of issues for women distinct from those that might typically arise in the course of treatment with men. This chapter attempts to identify the particular patterns and characteristics of female alcoholics as reported in the literature that have utility to the practicing clinician. The intention is to be deliberately nonideological and nondogmatic with respect to definition of treatment goals or prescription of any one intervention strategy. Those decisions are best left to the skilled therapist working in cooperation with his or her patient. Rather, this chapter is intended to sensitize clinicians of varying theoretical orientations to the kinds of therapeutic isssues that work with alcoholic women may entail. It is hoped that such awareness will serve to refine assessment and diagnostic accuracy, stimulate innovative and responsive treatment techniques, and enhance the quality of the therapeutic relationship. We will begin with an overview of those factors that distinguish female alcoholics as a patient population. We will then proceed to a discussion of the clinical assessment of female drinkers. Finally, therapeutic issues as they pertain to women with alcohol problems are considered from the perspective of three broadly construed approaches to changing self-destructive behavior: rational-cognitive, behavioral, and psychodynamic models.

FEMALE ALCOHOLICS: THE PATIENT POPULATION

Obviously, no simple profile can meaningfully or accurately describe the heterogeneous population of women who clinically present as alcohol abusers. Many writers, nevertheless, have attempted to describe common attributes of alcoholic women. While generalizations from this literature must be cautious due to sample biases, inconsistencies of definitional criteria, and imprecise measures, certain impressions emerge concerning the patterns of drinking problems in women, the natural history of the disorder, and the demographic and drinking-context characteristics of female alcoholics.

Gomberg (1976) has profiled the woman at high risk for developing alcohol problems as follows:

> The alcoholism-prone woman begins significantly often with an early history of deprivation, of trouble in early family life in the form of death, desertion, psychiatric disorder, or alcoholism among relatives. She develops into an isolated, distrustful adolescent, fearful of dependence, rather pessimistic and depressed, often unpredictably impulsive and inadequate in frustration tolerance and defense mechanisms for coping with stress. The facade she presents is one of intense femininity and overidentification with the traditional female role. (p. 629)

Another composite picture is offered by Sclare (1970):

> The female alcoholic is about 45 years old, began drinking at about 30 years, has a 50 percent chance of having another psychiatric illness, displays withdrawal symptoms in 50 percent of cases, and has attempted suicide in 33 percent of cases. (p. 123)

Sclare states further that there is a striking incidence (20%) of primary depression (i.e., antedating the onset of alcoholism) in the women studied. In a more recent study, Corrigan (1980) has confirmed the high incidence of depressive symptoms among women entering treatment for alcoholism, including poor concentration, social isolation, feelings of hopelessness, sleep difficulty, and suicide attempts in a significant minority of cases.

Several studies report that the average alcoholic woman drinks alone (Beckman, 1975; Lisansky, 1957; Wanberg & Horn, 1970), hides her drinking problems (Beckman, 1975; Lindbeck, 1972; Senseman, 1966), and is often protected from drinking difficulties by her husband (Curlee, 1968; Senseman, 1966). Not surprisingly then, the typical female alcoholic has a relatively low rate of social problems related to alcoholism and is rarely seen drinking publicly in bars or taverns (Curlee, 1968). At the time of hospitalization for her drinking problem, the average alcoholic woman is between the ages of 40 and 50 (Beckman, 1976; Schuckit, Goodwin, & Winokur, 1972). Disproportionate numbers of Catholics and Irish are described as appearing among female alcoholic samples (Senseman, 1966). Interestingly, several studies have suggested a relationship between female alcohol abuse and sexual dysfunction, although the reason for this is unclear. Schuckit and Morrissey (1976) assert that sexual problems are seen in female alcoholics regardless of socioeconomic class, but that the specific difficulties seem to vary with the samples studied.

Despite repeated attempts to capture the essence of the "female alcoholic personality syndrome," that prototype remains elusive. It appears that the only agreement on what constitutes the female alcoholic personality centers on a poor self-concept and low self-esteem (Beckman, 1978; McLachlan, Walderman, Birchmore, & Marsden, 1979), although it is unclear whether such traits are the result or the cause of problem drinking. Furthermore, on this dimension, it is unclear how female alcoholics differ from women who have other emotional or psychological problems, or indeed *if* they differ in many personality traits from these other groups (Beckman, 1976).

Having recognized the heterogeneity of the female alcoholic population, many researchers have concentrated their efforts on the delineation of discrete diagnostic subtypes among women drinkers. Several such efforts, for example, have focused on the type of psychopathology that is manifested. To a large extent, this emphasis on subtyping female alcoholics according to psychiatric illness arises from a widespread belief among professionals that female alcoholics are more pathological and evidence greater maladjustment and "abnormality" than do their male counterparts (Johnson, 1965; Johnson, DeVries, & Houghton, 1966). Apparently, this argument is based on the assumption that, since excessive drinking is more of a social taboo among women than men, to the extent that women manifest alcoholism they are also evidencing greater pathology by its expression. Beckman (1976), however, has aptly noted the inherent difficulty of separating prealcoholic, predisposing factors from the serious psychological damage that results from a woman's alcoholism once it has been established. A similar discussion of the difficulties involved in unraveling the intricate interplay between societal norms, labeling, and self-perception has been offered by Schuckit and Morrissey (1976):

> Does alcoholism cause more psychiatric disorder in women? Or, does a woman have to be more "ill" to overcome the more intense social stigma against heavy drinking and demonstrate alcoholism? Or, do women displaying alcoholism

more frequently have other major psychiatric disorders of which alcohol problems are symptomatic? Or, is psychiatric disorder in women alcoholics the result of the severe social sanctions taken against women who abuse alcohol? (p. 11)

Although it is somewhat weak, some empirical evidence does exist for the proposition that female alcoholics indeed are more psychologically disturbed than their male counterparts. Such evidence includes the greater amount of psychiatric treatment among women alcoholics (Curlee, 1970; Dahlgren, 1978; Westie & McBride, 1979); more frequent reports by women than men of depressed or sad mood, feelings of inadequacy, low self-esteem, and anxious affect (Belfer, Shader, Carroll, & Harmatz, 1971; Jones, 1971; Mayer, Myerson, Needham, & Fox, 1966; Tamerin, Tolor, & Harrington, 1976; Winokur & Clayton, 1968); and an elevated rate of suicide attempts relative to men (Beckman, 1975; Curlee, 1970; Rathod & Thomson, 1971; Rimmer, Pitts, Reich, & Winokur, 1971). It should be noted that the significance of a higher suicide-attempt rate among alcoholic women is attenuated in light of the higher rates of suicide attempts among women than among men generally (Bratfos, 1971). The complex interweaving of alcohol abuse and depression makes the task of determining primacy for either condition exceedingly difficult. In many studies involving psychiatric symptomatology, it is simply not possible to ascertain whether the women being studied had affective disorders prior to the onset of drinking or, rather, if they demonstrated the transient depressed affect that results from alcohol abuse but disappears after a relatively short period of abstinence (Carrigan, 1978; Corrigan, 1980; Tamerin, Weiner, & Mendelson, 1970). Mello (1980) has cautioned against dismissing alcohol abuse as merely symptomatic of another psychiatric condition. Despite the inherent difficulties, a careful clinical history aimed at disentangling the sequencing of affective and alcoholic symptoms should facilitate a differential diagnosis.

Some authors have raised important questions about whether more psychiatric treatment and more frequent diagnosis of psychiatric illness among female alcoholics as compared with males might, in fact, be artifactual. Women are more likely than men, in general, to report emotional problems (Carrigan, 1978). Moreover, current cultural norms provide more support to women than to men for seeking psychiatric treatment, and women do, in fact, seek such treatment more often than men (Curlee, 1970). Therefore, it is at least arguable that findings of greater psychiatric treatment among female alcoholics reflect societal norms rather than indicating greater individual pathology.

Probably the most successful efforts to subtype alcoholic women based on type of psychopathology have been made by Schuckit and his colleagues (Schuckit & Morrissey, 1976; Schuckit et al., 1972; Schuckit, Pitts, Reich, King, & Winokur, 1969). Schuckit's work has strongly suggested that alcoholism in women is not a unitary disorder. Two major clinical categories have been identified based on evidence of psychological disorder prior to the onset of alcoholism: (1) primary alcoholics (i.e., those having no preexisting major psychiatric disorders); and (2) secondary alcoholics (i.e., those who evidence primary psychiatric disorder with alcoholism as a secondary problem). Schuckit and Morrissey (1976) further identify two categories within the secondary alcoholic type: "affective disorder alcoholics" (women with secondary alcoholism and primary affective disorder); and "sociopathic alcoholics" (women with secondary alcoholism and histories of antisocial life styles antedating their alcohol abuse). This work suggests that clinicians should be particularly sensitive to the possibility of primary psychiatric illness (e.g. depression) in female alcoholics with an accompanying symptomatic abuse of alcohol and/or other drugs. Beckman (1976) has noted the importance of distinguishing women who abuse multiple substances from those who exclusively abuse alcohol. A higher incidence of drug use in addition to alcohol has been reported among female alcoholics than among male alcoholics (Glatt, 1961; Gomberg, 1976; Morrissey, 1978). It is incumbent, therefore, on the prescribing physicians to be knowledgeable about their patients' drinking habits and cognizant of the possibilities of drug cross-dependency and/or dangerous interactions between alcohol and other drugs.

Several other bases for diagnostic subtyping among female alcoholics have been proposed, although the applicability of such groupings to differential treatment approaches is somewhat variable. Mogar, Wilson, and Helm (1970), for example, propose subtyping female alcoholics on the basis of Minnesota Multiphasic Personality Inventory (MMPI) profiles. Among the women studied by these authors, five types were distinguished: normal, depressive, hysterical, psychopathic, and passive-aggressive. Age of onset of heavy or alcoholic drinking has also been proposed as a diagnostic or prognostic distinction. Kinsey (1966) distinguishes among those women with early beginning and slower development of alcoholism, those with early beginning and rapid development, and those with later beginning and rapid development. Several other authors have also argued for the importance of differentiating female alcoholics according to age at onset (Cramer & Blacker, 1963; Curlee, 1967; Gomberg, 1976). However, Schuckit and Morrissey (1976) have noted that "the actual importance of this [later onset of drinking] is unknown, since there is not a close correlation between age of onset of drinking and later alcoholism" (p. 10). On the other hand, length of drinking history has been identified as an important negative prognostic factor among males (Armor, Polich, & Stambul, 1978; Polich, Armor, & Braiker, 1981). This finding may suggest that female alcoholics with relatively short problem-drinking histories also have a better prognosis.

Demographic variables have been mentioned as a basis for subtyping alcoholic women. Schuckit and Morrissey (1976), for example, stress the importance of distinguishing between women of relatively high versus low socioeconomic strata. Ethnicity has also been discussed as a key subtyping variable, with the specific suggestion that black women be treated as a separate category among female alcoholics. This latter assertion is based on the facts that a disproportionately high number of black female alcoholics exist, and that different sociocultural factors may contribute to the development and expression of black women's alcohol problems. There is evidence that black women are at higher risk for alcoholism relative to black men than are white women compared to white men (Roebuck & Kessler, 1972; Leland, Chapter 3, this volume). Several different explanations have been advanced to explain this phenomenon, including a more permissive drinking environment for women within the black culture, and the stresses associated with having to cope with dual roles, such as being the major economic support for the family while also acting as mother–housekeeper (Bailey, Haberman, & Alksne, 1965; Roebuck & Kessler, 1972). A final demographic distinction with important therapeutic implications is marital status. Bromet and Moos (1976) have presented evidence indicating that alcoholism is expressed differently in married as opposed to unmarried women, and therefore have suggested the need for different interventions for the two groups (e.g., adapting the social climate in married households to be more conducive to an abstinent life style).

Still another promising avenue for classification and treatment of alcoholic women concerns the presence of gynecological and endocrine problems. Bourne and Light (1979) have reported elevated rates of such problems among study groups of alcoholic women. The work of Jones and Jones (1976) may suggest that women who experience depression as a consequence of hormonal imbalances and who abuse alcohol as well comprise a distinct subgroup. These authors have proposed the treatment of alcoholic women with estrogen therapy based on the reasoning that both estrogen and alcohol have been demonstrated to inhibit monoamine oxidase, a biochemical associated with depressive illness.

The female alcoholic population has been repeatedly compared to male alcoholics on dimensions of drinking context, pattern, and amount. With respect to context, women are consistently reported to drink alone more often than men and to drink in the privacy of their own homes more frequently than men (Bourne & Light, 1979; Horn & Wanberg, 1969; Sclare, 1970; Wood & Duffy, 1966). This pattern even appears to hold up among skid row women, who maintain more solitary drinking patterns than their male counterparts and remain more sensitive about social disapproval of problem drinking (Garrett & Bahr, 1973). Notwithstanding women's preference for solitary drinking, the frequency of drinking problems among the husbands of alcoholic women is considerably greater than that found either in the general population or in the wives of alcoholic men (Lisansky, 1957).

With respect to patterns and amount of consumption, the most frequently cited differences are that, relative to men, women report less daily drinking, less drinking throughout the entire day, fewer benders or binges, and less frequent drinking (Horn & Wanberg, 1969; Rimmer et al., 1971; Schuckit &

Morrissey, 1976). Compared to men, women report lower weekly consumption and lower consumption per drinking occasion (Morrissey, 1978; Rimmer et al., 1971). In contrast to men, women are reported to prefer liquor (spirits) and wine to beer (Wanberg & Horn, 1970). Clark (1966), while generally conceding that women typically drink less than men, cites some evidence to suggest that when alcohol is used in excess for purposes of dealing with tensions and stress, women may in fact consume as much as men. Moreover, intriguing findings by Jones and Jones (1976) on female alcohol metabolism indicate that women reach higher peak blood alcohol levels than men even when weight differences are taken into account. These authors emphasize the importance of hormonal levels in mediating the rate and effects of ethanol metabolism in women.

In summary, many descriptions of the female alcoholic population have appeared in the literature over several years. Our intention in this section has not been to encourage stereotyping of the individual woman seeking help for drinking problems. Rather, by drawing together the disparate characterizations that exist, we have tried to construct a kind of descriptive landscape of the clinical population of female drinkers so as to prepare the clinician for the type of psychological and practical "terrain" he or she is likely to encounter. Obviously, an accurate diagnostic profile of any individual woman requires a careful and thorough clinical assessment, a topic to which we now turn our attention.

STARTING TREATMENT: THE ASSESSMENT PROCESS

It is by now a dictum of clinical training that therapy begins with the initial interview. In the case of female alcoholics, the assessment process is a matter of both critical importance and great delicacy. The differential diagnosis of female drinkers into appropriate subtype categories functions as a triage point for subsequent treatment interventions. The woman diagnosed as having primary affective illness, for example, who drinks to self-medicate manic or depressive symptoms, will require a different therapeutic protocol than a female business executive who drinks to alleviate work-related stress. In every case, careful assessment of the environmental factors that serve to precipitate and maintain abusive drinking will inform the course of therapeutic intervention and management. Reliable and valid assessment procedures for evaluating consumption patterns and amounts both serve diagnostic purposes and provide important baseline measures against which improvement and change can be gauged.

For purposes of the present discussion, we will assume that the assessment process occurs in an alcoholism treatment facility or comparable context (e.g., a private practitioner specializing in the treatment of alcohol abuse). It must be mentioned, however, that many women with drinking problems do not initially present in such settings. Rather, they appear in medical hospitals, in the offices of private physicians, or in the general mental health care system. Unfortunately, a substantial proportion of alcoholic women remain unidentified and fail to receive help specific to their drinking problems. Liaison arrangements between general medical and mental health facilities and alcoholism treatment centers are needed to train practitioners in the recognition of signs suggestive of a diagnosis of alcoholism. Fine hand tremor, edema of the face, redness of the palms, cigarette burns on the chest (incurred during bouts of intoxication), bruises and fractures, and secondary amenorrhea are among the clinical signs that may suggest presence of an alcohol problem and warrant referral for a comprehensive assessment and evaluation.

The clinical utility of the information collected in the assessment interview will depend, of course, on several factors, including the quality and specificity of the questions asked, the therapist's skill and empathy, the rapport established, and the candor and accuracy with which the patient reports her behavior, thoughts, and feelings. Based on the descriptive information reviewed in the previous section, we may surmise that the alcoholic woman presenting for treatment is likely to have a poor self-concept and low self-esteem. Her drinking probably has been kept hidden, so that the requirement to describe her drinking habits to a "stranger" may be quite threatening and anxiety-producing. Still encumbered by strong social taboos, despite advances of the women's liberation movement, the female alcoholic is likely to be quite sensitive to possible disapproval and judgment. The patient may also exhibit signs of depression such as tearfulness and retarded speech and thought. Organic cognitive deficits (e.g., impaired memory) may also be present as a result of acute or chronic alcohol toxicity. In approaching the assessment situation, therefore, the clinician should convey a nonjudgmental attitude of openness, patience, and ease in asking questions regarding alcohol problems. Acknowledgment by the therapist of the patient's sensitivity and possible embarrassment, accompanied by reassurances of confidentiality and familiarity with these issues (e.g., "I've spoken with many women who feel a bit ashamed or uncomfortable about discussing their drinking, but these feelings usually disappear after we start talking"), may facilitate gaining rapport in the interview.

The assessment begins with a detailed inquiry concerning the core complex of the alcoholism syndrome: consumption behavior, symptoms of dependence, and social, legal and physical consequences of abuse. Several large-scale survey studies of alcoholic populations have utilized carefully designed structured questionnaires for eliciting reliable and valid reports of consumption patterns and amounts (e.g., Armor *et al.*, 1978; Polich *et al.*, 1981). These instruments, often published in the appendices of research reports, will be of great assistance to the clinician in formulating the assessment interview.

The patient should be systematically questioned regarding the type of beverage consumed (including proof), the number of drinks in a typical drinking day (including information on number of ounces per drink), number of drinking days per week, overall pattern of consumption (e.g., daily, weekend, or binge drinking), and temporal pattern within a drinking day (e.g., morning, evening, or continuous). The specificity of these questions will aid the patient in accurately describing the extent and characteristics of her drinking problem. Sometimes, of course, the patient will be unable to accurately report on quantity or other detailed information due to inattention, blackouts, or impaired memory. In these cases, the therapist may use the opportunity to inform the patient about the damaging effects of alcohol on memory and encourage the patient to provide "best estimates."

In addition to the self-reports of consumption, patients who are still drinking when they enter treatment should be asked to keep a record of their consumption during the week (assuming outpatient status). A self-monitoring form that includes entries for date, time of day, amount, and type of beverage will provide useful input in the assessment process. Moreover, the therapeutic effect of self-monitoring in inducing a spontaneous reduction of consumption has been widely noted (see Sobell & Sobell, 1978). The self-monitoring form may also ask the patient to record moods, feelings, and thoughts that preceded the drinking behavior, as well as situations or events that serve as stimulus cues for drinking. This kind of information will be of great utility in planning intervention strategies to change environmental and emotional factors that precipitate and maintain excessive drinking. It is strongly recommended that self-monitoring be incorporated into the treatment process over time, especially when nonabstinence goals (i.e., controlled drinking) are being pursued.

The interpretation of consumption levels for women (i.e., in ascertaining a diagnosis of alcoholism or problem drinking) is a matter of some complexity. One approach to diagnosing alcoholism based on quantity and frequency is the so-called "Lederman curve" of the distribution of alcohol consumption (Brüün, Edwards, Lumio, Mäkelä et al., 1975). Based on that curve, various cutting points have been proposed as diagnostic of alcohol abuse or alcoholism. Some authors have proposed a cutoff of 15 cl of absolute alcohol daily, while others have suggested a cutoff in the area of 20 cl (Blume, 1980). Since consumption curves for men and women in the general population differ markedly, Blume has strenuously argued the invalidity of using equivalent cutoff points for defining alcoholism for men and women. Moreover, the work of Jones and Jones (1976) indicating that women attain higher blood alcohol levels than men do given equivalent amounts of alcohol adjusted for body weight suggests that the metabolism of alcohol may be different for men and women. In addition, Jones and Jones have documented variations in alcohol metabolism within subjects as a function of phases of the menstrual cycle. Use of oral contraceptives has also been reported to alter the rate of alcohol metabolism. While more research is needed to clarify these issues, the clinician should be alert for correlations of drinking level with menstruation, midcycle, and premenstrual periodicity patterns. Mood swings accompanying hormonal changes and their relationship to drinking should be assessed and the patient's history and current use of oral contraceptives should be obtained. Finally, since the effects of alcohol among and within women are highly variable, the patient's subjective evaluation of intoxication at various consumption levels should be recorded. In certain cases, the inclusion of a significant other (e.g., husband, lover, roommate) in the assessment process can be helpful in providing the clinician with a clear and accurate portrait of the patient's consumption patterns.

The assessment of consumption should also include a history of the patient's drinking patterns over time from the onset of heavy drinking. Special attention should be paid to periods of increased drinking as well as to periods of abstinence or reduced or controlled consumption. Sometimes this kind of information can be portrayed by the patient in graphic form with the assistance of a timeline. This assessment tool asks the patient to use present or recent drinking as a baseline against which to compare increases or decreases over the course of a specified period of time (e.g., the last 6 months or the last year). Changes in consumption levels should then be explored by inquiring about the circumstances that precipitated the altered patterns (e.g., breakup of a relationship, children leaving home). A checklist of stressful life events during the preceding 2 years may also be a useful assessment tool in this phase of the interview (see Morrissey & Schuckit, 1978).

In addition to actual consumption behavior, the initial assessment should evaluate the presence and extent of serious dependence symptoms and adverse consequences of drinking. Again, a structured interview approach is advocated. Polich et al. (1981) identified six core symptoms of alcohol dependence that were highly correlated with consumption and significantly prognostic of alcoholic relapse. These six symptoms are tremors (shakes), morning drinking, blackouts, loss of control, missing meals because of drinking, and continuous drinking bouts of 12 hours or more. In an unpublished study by Braiker, Meshkoff, and Armor (1980), these symptoms, with the exception of continuous drinking for 12 hours or more, were found to occur with equal frequency among male and female alcoholic populations. In the assessment, the patient should be asked whether she has ever experienced any of these symptoms, and the frequency with which the symptoms occurred during a typical recent drinking period (e.g., 30 days before her last drink).

Serious adverse consequences of drinking are somewhat more difficult to assess for women than for men. This is probably due to men's greater visibility and harsher treatment by the legal system. Since fewer women than men are in the labor force, job loss or demotions due to drinking are not as common among women. Still, a comprehensive clinical assessment should evaluate the detrimental effects of the patient's drinking in the areas of health, legal difficulties, work, and interpersonal and familial relationships. The latter categories should receive particular emphasis, since women, in general, are most likely to experience the disruptive effects of alcoholism on marital relationships and child-rearing performance (Gomberg, 1976). Because of the dangerous potential of excessive alcohol consumption to the developing fetus, the alcoholic woman should be interviewed as to her intentions regarding pregnancy and her practice of birth control. Any sexually active woman with a drinking problem should be apprised of the reproductive implications of her alcoholism—fetal alcohol syndrome and other fetal alcohol effects—and advised against conceiving until the alcohol problem has abated. This phase of the assessment should also include information about the history of the patient's interpersonal relationships and her current marital and social adjustment. Questions should specifically address sexual orientation or preference, sexual behavior and feelings, and possible sexual dysfunctions. The drinking behavior of her spouse or lover, and her closest friends, should also be examined.

The relatively high incidence of primary affective illness among female alcoholics necessitates an evaluation of family history of unipolar and bipolar affective disorder, as well as a diagnostic appraisal of mood disorder in the patient herself. The therapist should be particularly cognizant of the possibility that alcohol may be used as a self-medication to relieve symptoms, not only of depression, but also of hypomanic or full manic episodes as well. The interview should also include questions about the patient's past and current use of licit and illicit drugs and about their use in combination with alcohol.

Still other important areas for assessment include the patient's subjective understanding of her drinking problems and the role alcohol plays in her life. Career or job functioning as well as educational and career aspirations should be discussed. Because alcoholic women generally suffer from low self-esteem, the interviewer is well advised to provide opportunities for the patient to report positive experiences or aspects of her life in addition to the obvious problems. What, for example, are the things about her life that she is satisfied with or feels good about? What does she feel are her strengths, her best qualities and characteristics?

The assessment process concludes with a discussion and identification of treatment goals. These goals, depending on the therapist's evaluation and orientation, might include either abstention or controlled drinking. Other areas for targeting change should be jointly defined—for example, work or educational goals, marital or family relationships, changes in environments or situations that support drinking, or changes in appearance and self-concept.

In summary, the assessment process should yield a broad informational base from which a sound treatment plan can be constructed. While several purposes are served, perhaps the most important is that the comprehensive clinical assessment conveys the sense that the patient is being viewed and accepted as a whole person, not merely as "an alcoholic," and that her drinking problems are embedded in a complex matrix of the social, emotional, and physiological facts of her life.

THE THERAPEUTIC PROCESS:
CHANGING SELF-DESTRUCTIVE BEHAVIOR

Despite decades of research, the etiology of alcoholism in both men and women remains undetermined. Most sophisticated researchers and writers in the field concur that alcoholism is probably not a unitary disorder with any single cause: Multiple factors—social, physical, and psychological—probably interact in complex sequences to produce the syndrome labeled as alcoholism. While the precise cause remains unclear, little disagreement exists as to the manifestation and expression of the disorder once it is established. Excessive consumption of beverage alcohol over time, with evidence of central nervous system adaptation and tolerance, constitutes addiction to the drug ethanol. The addiction entails sequelae of serious deleterious effects on the individual's health and social and emotional functioning. In short, alcohol abuse is self-destructive behavior.

Henderson, Hall, and Lipton (1979) have identified three general psychological models that have greatest relevance to changing self-destructive health behaviors: the rational model and its variants, the behavioral model, and the psychodynamic model. We now turn to a consideration of the female alcoholic from the perspective of each of these general approaches. In the absence of evidence to support the superiority of any one approach, a therapeutic attitude that allows for integration of elements of all three models is advocated.

Rational and Cognitive Therapies

In its strictest form, the rational model derives from the tradition of 18th-century rationalism. In essence, this model holds that human behavior is governed by objectively logical thought processes. Thus, the rational model would assume that alcohol abuse can be modified by providing appropriate information about the health risks involved and the hazards attendant upon continued future use. More recent developments in the field of cognitive therapy have modified the strict assumptions of the purely rational model. Simply stated, the cognitive model (Beck, 1976) contends that emotional disorders (and, by extension, the self-destructive behaviors that result from them) arise from faulty "automatic" thinking derived from inaccurate, illogical, and negative assumptions. These assumptions are exposed and articulated in the course of treatment and subjected to empirical evaluation and logical analysis. The cognitive model seems particularly relevant to the treatment of alcoholic women since it has been most thoroughly developed in the context of treating depression.

Because of their low visibility and hidden drinking habits, female drinkers probably do have relatively little exposure to direct, personal information about alcohol and its effects on their health. Therapeutic approaches derived from the rational model incorporate explicit, didactic instruction as part of the protocol. Patients may attend group lectures, read literature, and receive personal explanations from their therapists about ethanol addiction and its effects on physical and psychological functioning. The dangerous interaction between alcohol and prescription tranquilizers (e.g., Valium) so widely prescribed to women should be emphasized. Female drinkers should receive detailed information on the fetal alcohol syndrome as well as on the relationship between female physiological functioning and alcohol metabolism.

Surely, no sophisticated therapist would assert that information alone is sufficient to change self-destructive habitual behavior. Variations on the pure information model include more general decision-making models in which the therapist works with the patient in assessing the personal, social, physical, and psychological costs and benefits of her behavior; these models assume that the cost–benefit ratio yielded by such an assessment affects behavior. The approach focuses on the patient's decision to continue drinking the same amount, to cut down, or to abstain altogether as the core therapeutic issue (Janis, 1975). If a decision to change is made but not implemented, the failure is explained by interference from cognitive defenses or rationalizations. Typically, these rationalizations include exaggerated perceptions of withdrawal symptoms or minimization of the self-destructive aspects of drinking. Active cognitive interventions by the therapist are proposed to challenge and counteract the patient's defenses (Reed & Janis, 1974).

Cognitive therapy of depression, as explicated by Beck and his colleagues (Beck, Rush, Shaw, & Emery, 1979), offers a promising approach since, as has been noted repeatedly, depression is so frequently seen as a concomitant problem in alcoholic women. Briefly, this short-term therapeutic model explores the patient's automatic, negative, and self-defeating thoughts, which serve to maintain and enhance depression and symptomatic alcohol abuse. These assumptions are then subjected to empirical testing in a collaborative relationship with the therapist. Women's beliefs and expectations about the role of alcohol consumption in disinhibiting sexuality (e.g., "Without drinking, I can't feel sexy"), social acceptance ("No one will like me if I don't drink"), or tension reduction ("A drink or two helps me to handle my kids better when they get on my nerves") are examples of the kinds of issues this approach addresses.

The rational–cognitive model is probably most appropriate for relatively intelligent women who identify with many of the values embodied in the women's movement ideology, such as personal control, independence, and the exercise of choices and options. Since the therapeutic approaches are relatively short-term and intensive in nature, they require comparably high levels of motivation and concentration.

Behavioral Therapies

Many behavioral therapies have been developed for the treatment of alcoholism, with variable success rates and duration of effect (see Heather & Robertson, 1981). These approaches all derive from the premise that people learn to drink excessively because the behavior has primary and secondary reward value. Behavioral approaches seek to change abusive drinking by changing the stimulus conditions or environmental cues to which drinking has become conditioned and by changing the reinforcement value of drinking itself. The approaches are generally specific and directive. Information obtained in the assessment process concerning the factors that precipitate and maintain drinking behavior is used to formulate treatment plans in order to interrupt and modify learned, habitual patterns.

Behavioral approaches are particularly useful when the specified treatment goal is controlled drinking, or moderation, rather than abstinence. A detailed discussion of the evidence supporting controlled drinking as a valid goal for treatment and of guidelines for such a therapeutic protocol are beyond the scope of the present chapter. The interested reader is referred to Heather and Robertson's (1981) recent volume. In their review of selection criteria for controlled drinking candidates, these authors suggest that the patient's wish to aim for moderation as opposed to abstinence should constitute sufficient grounds for considering such a goal, except where contraindicated by the presence of liver disease or other serious physical problems. Unfortunately, the empirical criteria related to appropriateness of a controlled drinking goal have been established with a population of mainly male alcoholics. These criteria among men are: low to moderate severity of drinking symptoms; relatively younger age; regular employment; and low frequency of contact with Alcoholics Anonymous (Heather & Robertson, 1981). Clear guidelines for the appropriateness of controlled drinking among women must await future research.

The typical behavioral treatment protocol includes teaching the patient to monitor her drinking and to identify the kinds of situations or emotional responses that trigger the desire for a drink. Behavioral records kept by the patient may include time of day, type of beverage, amount in ounces, converted ethanol equivalent, and context of drinking (e.g., situational, emotional). Patients are taught to identify environmental cues for their drinking and to alter their environments to reduce the salience of such cues. For example, women who are unemployed and drink alone at home are encouraged to increase the percentage of time outside the home and to generate a new repertoire of behaviors that is incompatible with drinking. Women whose alcohol consumption increases premenstrually as a coping mechanism for tension may be taught alternative stress management techniques such as deep breathing and relaxation, self-hypnosis, or active physical exercise.

The role of assertiveness training as a specific behavioral technique in the treatment of alcoholic women should be mentioned. Many women lack the skills to deal effectively and assertively in the social world. Excessive drinking may occur in response to feelings of anger, frustration, or helplessness. Assertiveness skills, therefore, may be instrumental in reducing the emotional factors that stimulate the need to drink. Finally, behavioral methods designed to increase success experiences in various areas of a woman's life (e.g., child-rearing practices, job performance) and improve physical appearance are important elements in enhancing the low self-esteem and poor self-concept that characterize most alcoholic women.

Psychodynamic Therapies

Most insight-oriented psychotherapies based on a psychodynamic model view alcoholism as symptomatic behavior that is rooted in unresolved, largely unconscious conflicts thought to develop early in life. Strict adherents of psychodynamic approaches would assert that any approach directed solely at changing the woman's drinking behavior without uncovering and resolving the underlying needs that alcohol fulfills will ultimately be ineffective.

While empirical support for the particular effectiveness of insight-oriented approaches is generally lacking, several etiological models of alcoholism do stress the importance of psychodynamic factors. Since no single causal factor has been found to explain why women become alcoholic, it seems likely that, at least for some subgroup of women, excessive drinking may indeed be motivated by underlying conflicts, especially in the areas of aggression and sexuality.

Interestingly, certain etiological models developed to explain male alcoholism may have particular current relevance to younger women who have been influenced by the sociocultural changes in women's roles over recent years. McClelland's power theory (McClelland, Davis, Kalin, & Wanner, 1972), for example, holds that excessive drinking occurs in men who have strong but unsatisfied needs for personal power. These men, in theory, drink to compensate for doubts generated by a conflict between the need to be strong and powerful on the one hand, and intrapsychic feelings of weakness on the other. The obvious parallels between conflicts experienced by McClelland's "drinking man" and those that have been described as characterizing many of today's upwardly striving women are striking and provocative.

Other therapeutic issues are suggested by dependency models (e.g., Blane, 1968), which attribute the development of alcoholism to strong unsatisfied dependency needs. Anecdotal descriptions of the alcoholic woman's father as warm and alcoholic and her mother as cold and rejecting (e.g., Kinsey, 1968) lend some support to this view. Since women have more socially approved opportunities to express their dependency needs than men, the woman who becomes severely incapacitated due to drinking is generally thought to have conflicts over very intense dependency needs.

Wilsnack's (1974, 1976) work examining the psychological function of alcohol in relation to women's sex-role conflicts raises still another set of therapeutic themes. The so-called "womanliness hypothesis" asserts that the psychological function of excessive drinking is to increase feelings of traditional femininity in women who have been described clinically as expressing "role confusion," "masculine identification," "inadequate adjustment to the adult female role," and "poor feminine identification" (Kinsey, 1966; Wood & Duffy, 1966). According to Wilsnack, empirical evidence that women who drink excessively do so in order to act or feel more like men is lacking. On the contrary, her research findings suggest that alcoholic women consciously value their femininity and want to feel more like traditional women. In summary, underlying conflicts concerning sex-role identity, femininity, dependency, and power are all therapeutic issues that may be amenable to exploration and resolution through the application of insight-oriented therapies based on psychodynamic models.

CONCLUSION

This chapter has sought to conceptualize women alcoholics as a clinical population and to discuss the kinds of therapeutic issues that may arise in the course of their treatment. Obviously, a host of other therapeutic issues also require study. To date, empirical evidence for the beneficial effects of any one treatment modality over any other—group, family, or individual—is absent. Support is similarly lacking for the claim that female alcoholics should work exclusively with female therapists, or for the contention that female alcoholics are more effectively treated in groups that are homogeneous with respect to gender composition. Throughout this chapter, an attempt has been made to draw together the characteristics and problems of female drinkers that have been reported in the clinical and research literature, with the aim of enhancing the quality of assessment protocols, therapeutic relationships, and treatment efficacy. More definitive guidelines for the clinician faced with the emergent new population of female alcoholics seeking help for their dilemma must await future research.

REFERENCES

Annis, H. M. Treatment of alcoholic women. In G. Edwards & M. Grant (Eds.), *Alcoholism treatment in transition*. London: Croom Helm, 1980.

Armor, D. J., Polich, J. M., & Stambul, H. B. *Alcoholism and treatment*. New York: Wiley Interscience, 1978.

Bailey, M. B., Haberman, P. W., & Alksne, H. The epidemiology of alcoholism in an urban residential area. *Quarterly Journal of Studies on Alcohol*, 1965, *26*, 19 40.

Beck, A. T. *Cognitive therapy and the emotional disorders*. New York: International Universities Press, 1976.

Beck, A. T., Rush, A. J., Shaw, B. F., & Emery, G. *Cognitive therapy of depression*. New York: Guilford Press, 1979.

Beckman, L. J. Women alcoholics: A review of social and psychological studies. *Journal of Studies on Alcohol*, 1975, *36*(7), 797-824.

Beckman, L. J. Alcoholism problems and women: An overview. In M. Greenblatt & M. A. Schuckit (Eds.), *Alcoholism problems in women and children*. New York: Grune & Stratton, 1976.

Beckman, L. J. The self-esteem of women alcoholics. *Journal of Studies on Alcohol*, 1978, *39*(3), 491-498.

Belfer, M. L., Shader, R. I., Carroll, M., & Harmatz, J. S. Alcoholism in women. *Archives of General Psychiatry*, 1971, *25*, 540-544.

Blane, H. T. *The personality of the alcoholic: Guises of dependency*. New York: Harper & Row, 1968.

Blume, S. B. Researches on women and alcohol: Casefinding, diagnosis, treatment, and rehabilitation. In *Alcoholism and alcohol abuse among women: Research issues* (NIAAA Research Monograph No. 1, U.S. Department of Health, Education, and Welfare Publication No. ADM-80-835). Washington, D.C.: U.S. Government Printing Office, 1980.

Bourne, P. G., & Light, E. Alcohol problems in blacks and women. In N. K. Mello & J. H. Mendelson (Eds.), *The diagnosis and treatment of alcoholism*. New York: McGraw-Hill, 1979.

Braiker, H. B., Meshkoff, J. E., & Armor, D. J. *A thirty-month follow-up of treated female alcoholics*. Unpublished manuscript, Rand Corporation, Santa Monica, Calif., 1980.

Bratfos, O. Attempted suicide. *Acta Psychiatrica Scandinavia*, 1971, *47*, 38-55.

Bromet, E., & Moos, R. Sex and marital status in relation to the characteristics of alcoholics. *Journal of Studies on Alcohol*, 1976, *37*(9), 1302-1312.

Brüün, K., Edwards, G., Lumio, M., Mäkelä, K., et al. *Alcohol control policies in public health perspective*. Helsinki, Finland: Finnish Foundation for Alcohol Studies, 1975.

Carrigan, Z. H. Research issues: Women and alcohol abuse. *Alcohol Health and Research World*, 1978, *3*(1), 2-9.

Clark, W. Operational definitions of drinking problems and associated prevalence rates. *Quarterly Journal of Studies on Alcohol*, 1966, *27*, 648-668.

Cohen, S. *The substance abuse problems*. New York: Haworth, 1981.

Corrigan, E. M. *Alcoholic women in treatment*. New York: Oxford University Press, 1980.

Cramer, M. J., & Blacker, E. "Early" and "late" problem drinkers among female prisoners. *Journal of Health and Human Behavior*, 1963, *4*, 282-290.

Cronkite, R. C., & Moos, R. H. Determinants of the posttreatment functioning of alcoholic patients: A conceptual framework. *Journal of Consulting and Clinical Psychology*, 1980, *48*, 305-316.

Curlee, J. A. Alcoholic women: Some considerations for further research. *Bulletin of the Menninger Clinic*, 1967, *31*, 154-163.

Curlee, J. A. Women alcoholics. *Federal Probation*, 1968, *32*, 16-20.

Curlee, J. A. A comparison of male and female patients at an alcoholism treatment center. *Journal of Psychology*, 1970, *74*, 239–247.

Dahlgren, L. Female alcoholics. III. Development and pattern of problem drinking. *Acta Psychiatrica Scandinavica*, 1978, *57*, 325–335.

Garrett, G. R., & Bahr, H. M. Women on skid row. *Quarterly Journal of Studies on Alcohol*, 1973, *34*, 1228–1243.

Glatt, M. M. Drinking habits of English (middle-class) alcoholics. *Acta Psychiatrica Scandinavica*, 1961, *37*, 88–113.

Gomberg, E. S. The female alcoholic. In R. E. Tarter & A. A. Sugarman (Eds.), *Alcoholism: Interdisciplinary approaches to an enduring problem*. Reading, Mass.: Addison-Wesley, 1976.

Heather, N., & Robertson, I. *Controlled drinking*. London: Methuen, 1981.

Henderson, J. B., Hall, S. M., & Lipton, H. L. Changing self-destructive behaviors. In G. C. Stone, F., Cohen, & N. E. Adler (Eds.), *Health psychology: A handbook*. San Francisco: Jossey-Bass, 1979.

Horn, J. L., & Wanberg, K. W. Symptom patterns related to excessive use of alcohol. *Quarterly Journal of Studies on Alcohol*, 1969, *30*, 35–58.

Janis, I. L. Effectiveness of social support for stressful decisions. In M. Deutsch & H. Hornstein (Eds.), *Applying social psychology: Implications for research, practice and training*. Hillsdale, N.J.: Lawrence Erlbaum, 1975.

Johnson, M. W. Physicians' views on alcoholism: With special reference to alcoholism in women. *Nebraska State Medical Journal*, 1965, *50*, 378–384.

Johnson, M. W., DeVries, J. C., & Houghton, M. I. The female alcoholic. *Nursing Research*, 1966, *15*, 343–347.

Jones, B. M., & Jones, M. K. Women and alcohol: Intoxication, metabolism and the menstrual cycle. In M. Greenblatt & M. A. Schuckit (Eds.), *Alcoholism problems in women and children*. New York: Grune & Stratton. 1976.

Jones, M. C. Personality antecedents and correlates of drinking patterns in women. *Journal of Consulting and Clinical Psychology*, 1971, *36*, 61–69.

Kinsey, B. A. *The female alcoholic: A social psychological study*. Springfield, Ill.: Charles C Thomas, 1966.

Kinsey, B. A. Psychological factors in alcoholic women from a state hospital sample. *American Journal of Psychiatry*, 1968, *124*, 1463–1466.

Lindbeck, V. The woman alcoholic: A review of the literature. *International Journal of the Addictions*, 1972, *7*, 567–580.

Lisansky, E. S. Alcoholism in women: Social and psychological concomitants: I. Social history data. *Quarterly Journal of Studies on Alcohol*, 1957, *18*, 588–623.

Mayer, J., Myerson, D. J., Needham, M. A., & Fox, M. M. The treatment of the female alcoholic: The former prisoner. *American Journal of Orthopsychiatry*, 1966, *36*, 248–249.

McClelland, D. C., Davis, W. N., Kalin, R., & Wanner, E. *The drinking man: Alcohol and human motivation*. New York: Free Press, 1972.

McLachlan, J. F., Walderman, R. L., Birchmore, D. F., & Marsden, L. R. Self-evaluation, role satisfaction, and anxiety in the woman alcoholic. *International Journal of the Addictions*, 1979, *14*(6), 809–832.

Mello, N. K. Some behavioral and biological aspects of alcohol problems in women. In O. J. Kalant (Ed.), *Research advances in alcohol and drug problems* (Vol. 5: *Alcohol and drug problems in women*). New York: Plenum Press, 1980.

Mogar, R. E., Wilson, W. M., & Helm, S. T. Personality subtypes of male and female alcoholic patients. *International Journal of the Addictions*, 1970, *5*, 99–114.

Morrissey, E. R. Alcohol-related problems in adolescents and women. *Postgraduate Medicine*, 1978, *64*(6), 111–113.

Morrissey, E. R., & Schuckit, M. A. Stressful life events and alcohol problems among women seen at a detoxification center. *Journal of Studies on Alcohol*, 1978, *39*(9), 1559–1576.

Polich, J. M., Armor, D. J., & Braiker, H. B. *The course of alcoholism: Four years after treatment.* New York: Wiley Interscience, 1981.

Rathod, N. H., & Thomson, I. G. Women alcoholics: A clinical study. *Quarterly Journal of Studies on Alcohol*, 1971, *32*, 45–52.

Reed, H., & Janis, I. L. Effects of a new type of psychological treatment on smokers' resistance to warnings about health hazards. *Journal of Consulting and Clinical Psychology*, 1974, *42*, 748.

Rimmer, J., Pitts, F. N., Reich, T., & Winokur, G. Alcoholism: II. Sex, socioeconomic status, and race in two hospitalized samples. *Quarterly Journal of Studies on Alcohol*, 1971, *32*, 942–952.

Roebuck, J. B., & Kessler, R. G. *The etiology of alcoholism: Constitutional, psychological, and sociological approaches.* Springfield, Ill.: Charles C Thomas, 1972.

Schuckit, M. A., Goodwin, D. A., & Winokur, G. A study of alcoholism in half-siblings. *American Journal of Psychiatry*, 1972, *128*, 1132–1136.

Schuckit, M. A., & Morrissey, E. R. Alcoholism in women: Some clinical and social perspectives with an emphasis on possible subtypes. In M. Greenblatt & M. A. Schuckit (Eds.), *Alcoholism problems in women and children.* New York: Grune & Stratton, 1976.

Schuckit, M. A., Pitts, F. M., Reich, T., King, L. J., & Winokur, G. Alcoholism: I. Two types of alcoholism in women. *Archives of General Psychiatry*, 1969, *20*, 301–306.

Sclare, A. B. The female alcoholic. *British Journal of Addiction*, 1970, *65*, 99–124.

Senseman, L. A. The housewife's secret illness. *Rhode Island Medical Journal*, 1966, *49*, 40–42.

Sobell, M. B., & Sobell, L. C. *Behavioral treatment of alcohol problems.* New York: Plenum Press, 1978.

Tamerin, J. S., Tolor, A., & Harringon, B. Sex differences in alcoholics: A comparison of male and female alcoholics' self and spouse perceptions. *American Journal of Drug and Alcohol Abuse*, 1976, *3*, 457–472.

Tamerin, J. S., Weiner, S., & Mendelson, J. H. Alcoholics' expectancies and recall of experiences during intoxication. *American Journal of Psychiatry*, 1970, *126*, 39–46.

Wanberg, K. W., & Horn, J. L. Alcoholism symptom patterns of men and women: A comparative study. *Quarterly Journal of Studies on Alcohol*, 1970, *31*, 40–61.

Westie, K. S., & McBride, D. C. The effects of ethnicity, age, and sex upon processing through an emergency alcohol health care delivery system. *British Journal of Addiction*, 1979, *74*, 21–29.

Wilsnack, S. C. The effects of social drinking on women's fantasy. *Journal of Personality*, 1974, *42*, 43–61.

Wilsnack, S. C. The impact of sex roles on women's alcohol use and abuse. In M. Greenblatt & M. A. Schuckit (Eds.), *Alcoholism problems in women and children.* New York: Grune & Stratton, 1976.

Winokur, G., & Clayton, P. Family history studies: IV. Comparison of male and female alcoholics. *Quarterly Journal of Studies on Alcohol*, 1968, *29*, 885–891.

Wood, H. P., & Duffy, E. L. Psychological factors in alcoholic women. *American Journal of Psychiatry*, 1966, *123*, 341–345.

13

Treatment Outcome of Alcoholic Women: The State of the Art in Relation to Sex Bias and Expectancy Effects

MARSHA VANNICELLI
McLean Hospital and
Harvard Medical School

INTRODUCTION

An exploration of current knowledge regarding treatment outcome with female alcoholics takes us over rough and poorly charted territory. Although much has been written of a speculative nature (often presented with considerable conviction but minimal hard data), with the exception of Annis and Liban (1980) and Gibbs and Flanagan (1977), systematic, empirical reviews of the literature on women's treatment outcome are totally lacking. The absence of systematic study is particularly noteworthy given the number of concerned professionals who have pointed to the dearth of sound empirical studies in this area (Beckman, 1976; Blume, 1980; Corrigan, 1980; Curlee, 1967; Lindbeck, 1972; Lisansky, 1957). Curlee, more than 15 years ago, decried the fact that "studies on alcoholism tend to either ignore women entirely or to simply assume that alcoholism is the same regardless of the sex of the sufferer" (p. 154), and Lindbeck, more than 10 years ago, pointed to the female alcoholic as the "stepchild" in the field of research.

In this chapter an attempt is made to look systematically at what has already been written about women's treatment outcome, the number of women who have been studied, and the circumstances under which they have been investigated, and to set forth a series of questions that need to be answered before reasonable conclusions can be drawn about the outcome of treatment for alcoholic women. Guiding questions that directed this review were the following:

1. How do the outcomes of men and women compare?
   a. What do we know about the specific kinds of programs that produce better outcome in women than in men?

369

    b. Are there enough replications at this point to make us feel confident about the male versus female differences that we do find?
2. Are there prognostic variables that differentiate women who do well from those who do not?
3. What kinds of programs do various subgroups of women do better in?
    a. Do different kinds of women (differentiated by demographic characteristics, drinking history, etc.) get treated in different kinds of settings (e.g., single-sex vs. mixed-sex programs, programs that emphasize one modality as opposed to another); and do the differing treatment settings differentially affect outcome?
4. What consistencies are present across studies (i.e., recurring outcome data about specific subgroups of women in specific kinds of treatment) that are stable and have been replicated; and what are the implications of these data for developing treatment programs for women?
5. What kinds of biases or insufficiencies are present in current studies of treatment outcome that limit the conclusions that can be drawn; and what future research is needed to enable us to make the most effective kinds of clinical, programmatic decisions about treatment for women?

Although the literature review for this chapter was embarked on with keen awareness of the many problems inherent in studies of alcohol treatment outcome (these have been well summarized in excellent reviews by Crawford & Chalupsky, 1977; Hill & Blane, 1967; Mandell, 1979; and Ogborne, 1978), the extent to which these problems have been magnified in the literature on women was not anticipated. Problems around sampling procedures, specification of sample characteristics (particularly sex), and small sample sizes were apparent at the outset and posed a serious challenge in attempting to analyze and interpret an extensive literature. An effort has been made to deal with this confusing array of data, whenever possible, by quantifying and analyzing it—with the hope that the reader will better understand the many caveats in drawing conclusions at this point regarding treatment outcome of alcoholic women.

The time frame selected for the present review covers the period from 1972 to 1980, picking up where the most relevant and extensive prior 20-year review (Emrick, 1974) ends. The present chapter also extends and amplifies the excellent review by Annis and Liban (1980) covering studies from 1950 to 1978, adding more recent studies as well as several studies prior to 1978 that these authors did not include. From time to time throughout this chapter, findings from the present 9-year survey are compared to findings from these two earlier reviews—thus providing a 30-year perspective.

The major data pool for this review consisted of all studies that could be located dealing with treatment outcome of alcoholics and published between 1972 and 1980. This included all English-language documents abstracted by the *Journal of Studies on Alcohol* dealing with outcome, treatment evaluation, prognosis, or follow-up, plus additional references found by examining the bibliographies of every article that was reviewed. Included were all studies that reported on three or more subjects treated with some form of psychological intervention, or with medications if the impact of the medications was measured specifically with respect to subsequent drinking behavior.

Excluded were studies of adolescents, populations that were primarily treated for some other illness (e.g., tuberculosis), studies where the outcome tested was only marginally related to the psychological recovery of the patient (e.g. improvement in specific memory functions following spaced learning trials, increased communications between spouses after playing a couples game), and studies of pharmacological and general medical treatment that examined, for example, effects of antidepressants on depression in alcoholics but did not examine the effects on drinking-related behavior. Studies that looked at drop-out and length of stay as the outcome variable were also omitted, since a clear relationship has not been documented between these variables and outcome. Studies of recidivism, where the only outcome measure was readmission, were omitted for similar reasons. Finally, studies on driving-while-intoxicated (DWI) populations were excluded given their unique characteristics.[1]

A total of 259 studies were found relating to the treatment outcomes of male and female alcoholic patients that met the inclusion criteria above and from which data were available at least from the article abstract.[2] Ninety-five of these studies[3] dealt with female or mixed samples who were followed up for at least 6 months, and these were carefully reviewed. The 6-month criterion was adopted (consistent with the procedures used by Annis & Liban, 1980, and Emrick, 1975) because many researchers have reported a high drinking-relapse rate during the first 6 months after treatment, and because of the instability of significant findings prior to 6 months. The 95 studies that met the 6-month criterion, and in which it was clear that there

---

1. As Chacon *et al.* (1978) point out, court-referred clients, in particular court-referred women, are a special subgroup of persons treated for alcohol problems. Comparison of men and women in this subpopulation are further complicated by the differential probability of men and women's being arrested (and thus entering a DWI population) when stopped for drunk driving.

2. Studies: 1–259 (see boldface numbers following entries in reference section).

3. Studies: 13, 15, 16–19, 24–27, 29–32, 35, 39, 41, 44, 45, 47–49, 52, 54, 55, 57, 60, 61, 64–67, 73, 78, 79, 82–84, 88, 89, 93–98, 111, 112, 122, 124, 126–128, 130, 132, 134, 137, 145, 148, 153–155, 158, 159, 161, 165, 168–170, 173, 174, 188, 192, 201, 202, 207, 208, 211, 214–218, 221, 229, 231, 239–241, 243, 251, 254, 255, 257, 259 (see boldface numbers in reference section).

were at least a few women, were reviewed in their entirety (the articles as well as the abstracts).

The remaining 164 studies of all-male (or sex-unspecified) subjects, or studies of either sex with follow-ups of less than 6 months, were examined in a more limited way—generally by reviewing only the abstract. Data of interest included whether or not sex of subject was specified in the abstract and whether precise male and female sample sizes were given. When this information was not provided in the abstract, the articles themselves were also checked.

Finally, for studies prior to 1972, Chad Emrick provided unpublished data regarding sample size and sex breakdown for 271 of the studies that he reviewed in his exhaustive survey of studies from 1952 to 1971 (Emrick, 1974).

TO WHAT EXTENT HAVE WOMEN BEEN STUDIED (HOW MANY AND UNDER WHAT CIRCUMSTANCES)?

Most current estimates of the ratio of male to female alcoholics in the United States range between 3 : 1, based on Cahalan's (1970) national survey sample of men and women reporting either symptomatic drinking or psychological dependence on alcohol, and 4 : 1 as estimated by the National Institute on Alcohol Abuse and Alcoholism (Noble, 1978). The proportion of women studied in research samples, however, has historically lagged far behind even the more conservative of these ratios (Baekeland, Lundwall, & Kissin, 1975; Costello, 1975; Costello, Biever, & Baillargeon, 1977). The most comprehensive analysis of the sex composition of treatment evaluation studies is provided by Emrick, in his 1974 review. Of the 271 studies on which he had data, 161 (59.4%) included only men or at least did not specify that any women were included. In contrast, only four studies (1.5%) included only women. Only 110 studies (40.6%) included *any* women—and often very few. A further perspective on the actual numbers of women studied is that only 2968 (6.2%) of the 47,492 people studied were women.

Clearly, the representation of women in treatment outcome studies was startlingly low during the era that Emrick reviewed. How has the reseach picture changed in the last decade, given increasing clinical emphasis on the female alcoholic and recent federal initiatives for the funding of research and treatment programs specifically geared to women? In our review of 259 studies we found 143 (55.2%) all-male and sex-unspecified studies[4] and only

4. Studies: 1, 3–12, 14, 22, 23, 28, 34, 36–38, 43, 46, 50, 53, 58, 59, 62, 63, 68, 69, 71, 72, 74, 75, 80, 81, 85–87, 90–92, 94, 99–106, 108–110, 113–115, 117–120, 123, 125, 129, 131, 136, 138–144, 146, 149–152, 156, 157, 160, 162–164, 169, 171, 172, 175, 176–180, 182–184, 186, 187, 189, 190, 193–200, 203–206, 209, 212, 213, 219–228, 232–238, 242, 244–250, 252, 253, 256, 258 (see boldface numbers in reference section).

6 (2.3%) all-female studies.[5] The remaining 110 studies included *some* women.[6] Thus only 116 studies (44.8%) included *any* women; again, often only a handful of women were included. Surprisingly little has changed in this aspect of the research arena. In the current 9-year review period only an additional 5038 women have been studied[7] (out of the total sample of 64,654), and women still represent only 7.8% of all subjects sampled. Combining the entire sample of women from Emrick's 20-year survey and the present 9-year survey, a total of only 8006 women have been included at all in treatment follow-up samples and these women have been scattered over a myriad of treatment modalities, often followed up for very brief periods (less than 6 months), with the outcome data generally embedded within data from men.

The picture is even bleaker when we look at the number of studies where women's data were looked at separately—only 28 studies (10.3%) in Emrick's era and only 30 studies (11.6%) during the past 9 years.[8] Thus, with regard to the number of studies that pay explicit attention to women, things also have not improved. If we talk about the numbers of women rather than the percent of studies, the figures are even more staggering. In terms of the number of women on whom we have 6-month follow-up data that is not indistinguishably combined with male data, we find a maximum of 2459 during the recent review period and 819 during Emrick's period—a grand total of 3278 women over 29 years![9] This failure to distinguish male and female data is a serious problem, since questions about women's treatment outcome can be answered only by looking at those studies where the women's data are presented separately (i.e., in all-female samples or in mixed samples where data from the women and men are analyzed separately).

5. Studies: 33, 44, 47, 64, 161, 207 (see boldface numbers in reference section).

6. Studies: 2, 13, 15–21, 24–27, 29, 32, 35, 39–41, 45, 48, 49, 51, 52, 54–57, 60, 61, 65–67, 70, 73, 76–79, 82–84, 88, 89, 93, 95–98, 107, 111, 112, 116, 121, 122, 124, 126–128, 130, 132–135, 137, 145, 147, 148, 153–155, 158, 159, 165–168, 170, 173, 174, 181, 185, 188, 191, 192, 201, 202, 208, 210, 211, 214–218, 229–231, 239–241, 243, 251, 254, 255, 257, 259 (see boldface numbers in reference section).

7. This figure is probably an overestimate. Sample n's for the 259 studies reviewed included 5242 women. Of these, 3869 were specifically cited as remaining in the follow-up population. In studies that failed to give the n's for women followed up, the sample n was used as the best (but inflated) estimate; and in cases where percent follow-up was known for total sample, but not by sex, follow-up n's were estimated by multiplying the sample n for each sex by total percent followed up. These best estimates of women followed up ($n = 1169$) were then added to the women known to be followed up ($n = 3869$) to provide our figure of 5038 women studied.

8. These studies include the 23 in Table 13-1, the 6 all-women studies referred to in footnote 5, and 1 additional study, which was a duplicate study sample (see reference number 153).

9. This is probably an inflated estimate on two counts: First, Emrick's 819 women were not all followed up for at least 6 months; and second, our figure of 2459 is actually an *estimate* of the number of women followed up for 6 months. Only 1915 women are specifically cited as being included in 6-month follow-ups. For studies that did not give follow-up n's we estimated this by using the original sample n.

Keeping in mind that our total best estimate of the probable sample of women over the past 30 years, studied separately from men and followed up for at least 6 months, is only approximately 3000 women, there are still many additional caveats in the data presented. Data regarding population characteristics (demographic data, subgroups, etc.) were often poorly specified, a definition of alcoholism was given in only 11 of the studies involving women,[10] and the treatments given were often specified in only the vaguest terms. For example, a number of studies examined outcomes across several treatment settings that differed considerably in terms of program format and treatment modalities, but failed to specify how many women were involved in each of these programs, let alone in each of the treatment modalities.

To correct the sad state of affairs regarding research on women's treatment outcome, it is important not only to appeal for more and better studies, but also to understand the factors that have contributed to the problem. Braiker (1982), in a thoughtful but perhaps overly generous attempt to explain the situation, began by saying "without invoking charges of sexist bias against alcoholism researchers, several legitimate explanations can be offered . . ." (p. 112). She, like Blume (1980), pointed to the fact that more men than women are "heavy" or "problem" drinkers or alcoholics— with the result that fewer women enter treatment populations and settings where they might be researched. Both Braiker and Blume also point to the fact that in large scale studies of treatment, women are often excluded because of the relatively small numbers involved and the questionable validity of statistical analyses on small subsets of data (Armor, Polich, & Stambul, 1978; Polich, Armor, & Braiker, 1981). They also cite Hyman (1976) regarding the sheer logistical problems of doing follow-up on women alcoholics who change their names after marriage or divorce and are thus more difficult to locate and interview.

Though the explanations offered by Blume and by Braiker cannot be discounted, data accumulated during the course of this review suggest that issues of sexist bias may, indeed, be a factor. Of interest here are differences in the ways in which male and female investigators have examined and reported data on treatment outcome of alcoholic women. While most studies (78.6%) had male first authors,[11] in those articles where a woman was the first author we found that: (1) the proportion of women in the sample and the proportion of women followed up were considerably larger than in male-authored studies; (2) greater attention was given to specifying male and female sample sizes, both in the original sample and at follow-up; (3) there

10. Studies: 16, 17, 52, 60, 89, 122, 153, 154, 158, 174, 207 (see boldface numbers in reference section).

11. This figure is calculated based on studies in which author sex could be ascertained. It was calculated as number of studies *known* to have male first authors ÷ [number of studies known to have female first authors + number of studies known to have male first authors].

was a greater attempt to try to specify prognostic characteristics that might differentiate good from poor outcome women; and (4) there was a considerably greater likelihood of reporting women's outcome data separately and of examining sex differences in treatment outcome.

More specifically, the data showed that women represented 13.4% of all subjects sampled by female authors, in contrast to only 4.3% of all subjects sampled by male authors ($\chi^2 = 1305$, $p < .001$). Thus, female authors sampled more than three times as many women in proportion to the number of people they studied as did male authors. Women subjects were also more than one and one half times as likely to be followed up by female as by male authors (the percentage of women followed up was 14% in female-authored studies, and 8.7% in male-authored studies; $\chi^2 = 167$, $p < .001$). The same trend occurred in terms of care taken to specify the sample sizes of male and female subjects. When women were the first authors, 72% of the articles specified sex breakdown for the original sample and 48% for the follow-up. In contrast, in male-authored studies specification of male and female sample sizes occurred only 56% of the time in describing the original sample and 38% of the time for follow-up. Finally, 43.5% of female first authors, in contrast to 14.5% of male first authors, looked at women's outcome data separately ($\chi^2 = 6.1$, $p < .01$) and 43.5% of female authors, in contrast to only 12.7% of male authors, examined sex differences ($\chi^2 = 7.3$, $p < .01$). A similar trend occurred with respect to prognostic variables related to women's treatment outcome, with 73.9% of female first authors in contrast to only 52.7% of male first authors reporting relevant data.

Understanding the limitations inherent in the literature reviewed, it is useful at this point to turn our attention to our original set of questions regarding women's treatment outcome.

HOW DO THE OUTCOMES OF MALE AND FEMALE ALCOHOLICS COMPARE?

As Annis and Liban (1980) have pointed out, the paucity of research evidence on the progress of the female alcoholic in treatment has contributed to the development of a sizable body of myth and speculation. Chief among these myths is the belief that female alcoholics are harder to treat and have a poorer prognosis than male alcoholics. Before examining the data relevant to this question, it may be of some interest to explore the possible origins of this belief. Many well-known authorities (e.g., Beckman, 1976; Blume, 1980; Braiker, 1982; Wilsnack, 1982) continue to discuss the poorer prognosis of female alcoholics and find support for this conclusion in limited reviews of the literature. The fact that the limited reviews of knowledgeable, well-meaning investigators consistently lean in one direction (that women do worse) suggests that this belief may have special meaning and importance in the political–social arena within which women alcoholics (and their treaters) are operating. It may be that appeals regarding the greater difficulties in working with women alcoholics, and concerns about the special problems of women and their poorer likelihood of recovery have all been helpful politically in calling attention to a group of patients who were seriously underrepresented in treatment and in need of more attention. It is difficult otherwise to understand the consistent perpetuation of this myth along with the continued tendency to do selective literature reviews that would seem to substantiate it. In tracing back this commonly held belief about women's poorer outcome, one of the earliest references I could find was by deLint (1964) who noted, "Since females are found to be more frequently deprived of one or more parents at an early age than male alcoholics they can be expected to respond less favorably to treatment" (p. 1064). Even earlier is the work by Karpman (1948) who states:

> By clinical observation, alcoholic women are much more abnormal than alcoholic men; in common parlance, when an alcoholic woman goes on a tear, "it is terrific." The reason for the difference probably lies in the fact that even in this sophisticated age women are still subject to more repressions than men, and in attempting to solve their conflicts, they must seek outlets that are still within the limits of conventional social acceptance of their sex. When, therefore, the pressure becomes so great as to make it beyond control, and the usual means fail of their intended purpose, it may break out in the form of alcoholism which naturally must be more vehemently expressed, being in proportion to the tension behind it. And it must be further stated that as alcoholic women are more abnormal than alcoholic men, they are, by the same token, also more difficult to treat. (p. vii)

Karpman was thus suggesting that female alcoholics had to be more abnormal than male alcoholics to break through the more restrictive social norms and cultural barriers against alcoholism in women. Believing this, he concluded that they were more difficult to treat. However, as Lisansky (1957) has pointed out, even if the female alcoholic did appear to be more disturbed than her male counterpart, this might well be the *result* of the greater stigma and more socially punishing consequences of alcoholism in women and not necessarily indicative of greater initial disturbance (prior to the onset of alcoholism). Moreover, even if she did appear to be sicker than her male counterpart at the time she presented for treatment, it would still not follow that she would necessarily do more poorly in treatment.

To the extent that we do fail with some female alcoholics, at this point we do not know much about the factors that contribute to our failure. Certainly premorbid characteristics and problems inherent in adjusting to a socially stigmatizing illness need to be more fully explored. It may be equally important, however, to consider the conscious and unconscious attitudes of treatment personnel toward the alcoholic woman—in terms of both therapists' personal feelings about alcoholism in women and their expectations about the woman alcoholic's potential for recovery.

A Systematic Review of 30 Years of Research Literature

In 1976, Schuckit and Morrissey pointed out that "most information on alcoholism in women is presented not as a primary study of the woman alcoholic, but as a comparison of women to the most frequently utilized yardstick of alcoholism—the male alcoholic" (p. 9). Sadly, when this was written in 1976 and today as well, even comparisons are relatively rare. The relatively few studies in the past 30 years that have distinguished between the outcome rates of men and women are reviewed in the material that follows.

EMRICK'S DATA

Although Emrick did not report sex differences in his 1974 review, he later provided this information as an appendix to Blume's (1980) review of treatment outcome in women. Only 28 of the 271 studies that he reviewed contained outcome data specified by sex. Though the authors did not always test directly for sex differences, when necessary Emrick performed the statistical tests. In terms of drinking-related outcome, he found 25 studies in which there were no differences between men and women, 3 studies in which women had better outcome and 4 in which men had better outcome.[12]

DATA FROM THE CURRENT REVIEW

In the 9-year period that we reviewed, 23 studies (out of 259) were found that contained sex-related outcome information. These studies are outlined in Table 13-1. Statistical comparisons were not made in four of the studies, but the authors provided sufficient information to allow us to perform the necessary statistical tests. In addition, we recalculated tests of significance in three studies, classifying subjects lost to follow-up with the unsuccessful outcome group. This procedure is consistent with the way in which Annis and Liban (1980) handled the 23 studies in their earlier review (9 of which overlap with those presented in the current review). There is considerable evidence to suggest that patients lost to follow-up are a serious source of sampling bias (Hill & Blane, 1967; Vannicelli, Pfau, & Ryback, 1976) and that it is appropriate to handle these cases as treatment failures (Moos & Bliss, 1978). This is particularly important in studies comparing two populations that have differential attrition, as is the case with male and female alcoholics. (Data from the present review of 259 studies indicate that the percentage of women followed up of those originally sampled (75.3%) was considerably higher than the percentage of sampled men who were followed up (55.3%; $\chi^2 = 795$, $p < .001$). Table 13-1 indicates those studies where we calculated or recalculated tests of significance, and, when appropriate, indicates changes in the conclusions drawn.

Of the 23 studies surveyed, 18 (78.3%) showed no significant difference in treatment outcome between male and female alcoholics. Four studies

---

12. These figures add up to more than 28 studies because some studies reported data on more than one sample.

TABLE 13-1. Sex Differences in Treatment Outcome

Authors (year)	Country	Sample	Treatment setting	Treatment modalities
Bateman & Petersen (1972)	United States	T = 719	Inpatient	Therapeutic milieu with: Group Rx Medical care
Beckman (1979)	United States	T = 240 M = 120 F = 120	Inpatient Outpatient	Not specified
Blaney, Radford, & MacKenzie (1975)	Ireland	T = 251 M = 231 F = 20	Inpatient Hospital 1: Alcohol unit Hospital 2: General psychiatric hospital	Hospital 1: Multimodal with: Group Rx AA Antabuse Alcohol education Hospital 2: Not specified
Brisset, Laundergan, Kammeier, & Biele (1980)	United States	T = 352	Inpatient	Multimodal with: Individual Rx Group Rx Family Rx AA Alcohol education Medical care
Bromet & Moos (1977)	United States	T = 494	Inpatient Halfway house (5 facilities)	Program 1: Therapeutic milieu with vocational Rx Program 2: Group medications Program 3: Halfway house (therapeutic community) Program 4: Aversive conditioning Program 5: Therapeutic milieu
Chacon, Rundell, Jones, Gregory, Williams, & Paredes (1978)	United States	T = 1804 M = 1438 F = 366	26 federally funded treatment programs in Oklahoma	Not specified
Crawford (1976)	New Zealand	T = 313 M = 262 F = 51	Inpatient	Multimodal with: Individual Rx Group Rx Family Rx AA Antabuse Alcohol education

Length of program	Follow-up		Outcome	
	Interval	n (%)	Measure	Sex difference
4 weeks	6 months after discharge	T = 517 (72) M = 381 F = 136	Drinking behavior Abstinent Drinking	Not significant
Not specified	1 year	T = 184 (77) M = 91 (76) F = 93 (78)	Drinking behavior Abstinent Heavy drinking Social drinking	Not significant (based on reanalysis of results with unknown Ss included in unsuccessful group)
Not specified	6 months	T = 218 (87)	Drinking behavior Favorable Intermediate Unfavorable	Not significant
38-day average	2 years 3½ years	T = 127 (36)	Drinking behavior Abstinent Drinking without problems Drinking with problems Psychological and social Conception of self and others along 9 dimensions	Not significant
Not specified	6-8 months after discharge	T = 429 (87) M = 360 F = 69	Drinking behavior Subjective rating of drinking problem: 5-point scale ranging from "no problem" to "often a problem" Social, role, and psychological Behavioral impairment Social functioning Psychological well-being	Not significant
Not specified	6, 18 months after admission	T = 1804 (100) M = 1438 (100) F = 366 (100)	Drinking behavior Remission (abstinence or at least 1 month of normal drinking) Nonremission Social and role Employed (yes/no) Monthly earnings Institutionalized in 30 days prior to follow-up (yes/no) Days inactive due to drinking	Significantly higher proportion of women than men in remission
12 weeks	3 months 2 years	T = 208 (66) M = 168 (64) F = 40 (78)	Drinking behavior Abstinent Improved Relapsed	Not significant (based on χ^2 by present author on data provided by Crawford)

(*continued*)

TABLE 13-1. (Continued)

Authors (year)	Country	Sample	Treatment setting	Treatment modalities
Davidson (1976)	Great Britain	T = 100 M = 75 F = 25	Inpatient → outpatient	Multimodal with: Group Rx AA Detox Aftercare
Gillies, Laverty, Smart, & Aharan (1974)	Canada	T = 1388	Inpatient Outpatient (6 facilities)	Multimodal with a few of the following: Individual Rx Group Rx Family Rx Antabuse Drug Rx Occupational Rx
Glover & McCue (1977)	Scotland	T = 94	Inpatient	Aversion therapy compared to conventional therapy
Kammeier (1977)	United States	T = 590 M = 402 F = 188	Inpatient	Multimodal with: Individual Rx Group Rx Family Rx AA Alcohol education Spiritual counseling
Kammeier & Conley (1979)	United States	T = 1291	Inpatient	Not specified (probably same as above)

Length of program	Follow-up			Outcome	
	Interval		n (%)	Measure	Sex difference

12–14 weeks	6 months after discharge	T =
		 M =
		 F =
			82 (82)
			 58 (77)
			 24 (96)
				Drinking behavior
				   Abstinent
				   Mostly abstinent (a few
				     limited relapses)
				   Reported relapse but
				     abstinent for long
				     periods
				   Continuous relapses
					Not significant (based on
					 reanalysis of results with
					 unknown Ss included in
					 unsuccessful group)[a]

Not specified	12 months after intake	T =	968 (70)	Drinking behavior
				   Alcohol involvement
				     scales measuring
				     attitudes and behavior
				     concerned with drink-
				     ing; 4-point continuum:
				     Abstinent
				     Much improved
				     Somewhat improved
				     Not improved
					Not significant

44-day average	6–47 months	T =
		 M =
		 F =
			85 (90)
			 58
			 27
				Drinking behavior
				   Abstinent
				   Controlled drinking
				   Unimproved
					Not significant

38-day average	24 months after treatment	T =	370 (63)	Drinking behavior
				   Drinking frequency: not
				     at all/once/not as
				     often/as often/more
				     often
					Not significant

				Social and health
				   Relationships with
				     others
				   Participation in com-
				     munity affairs
				   Physical health
				   Enjoyment of life
				   Accept and give help
				   (Each of the above
				     measured along a
				     3-point continuum:
				   Improved,
				   The same,
				   Worse)
					Women significantly
					 better outcome than
					 men in all 5 areas

30–35-day average	12 months after admission	Not specified		Drinking behavior
				   Abstinence
				   Infrequent alcohol
				     consumption
				   Frequent alcohol con-
				     sumption
				 Social and role
				   Personal adaptation
				     measure
				   Drinking and adapta-
				     tion combined; 3-point
				     continuum:
				     Strong improvement
				     Some improvement
				     No improvement
					Women significantly
					 better outcome than men

(continued)

[a] Results differ from author's conclusion.

TABLE 13-1. (Continued)

Authors (year)	Country	Sample	Treatment setting	Treatment modalities

Kammeier & Laundergan (1977)	United States	T = 1503
		M = 1083
		F = 420
			Inpatient	Multimodal with:
				  Individual Rx
				  Group Rx
				  Family Rx
				  AA
				  Alcohol education

Levinson (1977)	Canada	T = 154
		M = 120
		F = 34
			Inpatient → outpatient	Multimodal with:
				  Group Rx
				  AA
				  Antabuse
				  Alcohol education
				  Detox
				  Physiotherapy
				  Relaxation Rx
				  Medical care

Madden & Kenyon (1975)	United Kingdom	T = 98 M = 80 F = 18	Outpatient	Alcohol education Group Rx

McCrady, Paolino, Longabaugh, & Rossi (1979)	United States	T = 33
		M = 20
		F = 13
			Inpatient → outpatient	Multimodal with:
				  Group Rx
				  Couples Rx
				  Occupational Rx
				  Recreational Rx
				  Aftercare
				3 groups compared:
				  a. Joint patient-spouse admission
				  b. Alcoholic inpatient, spouse outpatient
				  c. Only alcoholic treated

McLachlan[b] (1978)	Canada	T = 541
		M = 416
		F = 125
			Inpatient → outpatient	Multimodal with:
				  Individual Rx
				  Group Rx

[b]Article not obtainable. Data cited from Annis & Liban (1980).

Length of program	Follow-up		Outcome	
	Interval	n (%)	Measure	Sex difference
33-day average	12 months after treatment	T = 974 (65) M = 712 (66) F = 262 (62)	Drinking behavior Successful (nonuse/ infrequent use) Unsuccessful (frequent use) Social and role Relationship with spouse, family and friends Job performance Self-image Enjoyment of life Health Ability to give and accept help Ability to manage financial affairs (Each of above measured along a 5-point improvement continuum)	Not significant (based on χ^2 by present author on drinking outcome data provided by Kammeier and Laundergan— including unknown Ss in unsuccessful group)
4 weeks	5 years after discharge	T = 115 (75)	Drinking behavior Recovered Significantly improved Moderately improved Unchanged or deteriorated Social, physical, and psychological status Same categories as above, combined with drinking behavior; 3-point global assessment	Not significant
5–15 weeks	6–36 months after discharge	T = 92 (94)	Drinking behavior Recovered (abstinent at least 6 months prior to follow-up) Nonrecovered	Not significant
Not specified	2, 6 months after discharge	T = 26 (79)	Drinking behavior Quantity–frequency index Alcohol impairment index Global drinking categories: Abstinent Normal drinking Problem drinking Social, role, and psychological Number of marriage problems Measures of psychological disturbance and mood along 8 dimensions	Not significant
4 weeks–1 year	12–18 months	T = 519 (96)	Drinking behavior Abstinent Relapsed–recovered	Not significant

(*continued*)

TABLE 13-1. (Continued)

Authors (year)	Country	Sample	Treatment setting	Treatment modalities
				Family Rx AA Alcohol education Relaxation Rx Physiotherapy
Popham & Schmidt (1976)	Canada	T = 150	Outpatient	Group Rx
Ruggels, Mothershead, Pyszka, Loebel, & Lotridge (1977)	United States	T (non DWI) = 1252 M (non DWI) = 1018 F (non DWI) = 234	Inpatient Outpatient Halfway house (8 facilities)	Multimodal with a few of the following: Individual Rx Group Rx Family Rx AA Antabuse Alcohol education Detox Drug Rx Occupational Rx
Seelye (1979)	United States	T = 100 M = 55 F = 45	Inpatient	Multimodal with: Individual Rx Group Rx AA Antabuse Drug Rx
Smart (1979a)	Canada	T = 314 M = 157 F = 157	Inpatient Outpatient (7 facilities)	Multimodal, each with a few of the following: Individual Rx Group Rx Family Rx Drug Rx Occupational Rx
Stinson, Smith, Amidjaya, & Kaplan (1979)	United States	T = 466	Inpatient → outpatient 2 programs: a. intensive care; high staff– patient ratio b. peer-oriented care	Multimodal with: Individual Rx Group Rx Family Rx AA Alcohol education Drug Rx Relaxation Rx Vocational counseling Aftercare
Vannicelli (1978)	United States	T = 100 M = 57 F = 43	Inpatient → outpatient	Therapeutic milieu with: Individual Rx Group Rx Family Rx Antabuse AA Alcohol education Drug Rx Spiritual Rx Aftercare

Length of program	Follow-up		Outcome	
	Interval	n (%)	Measure	Sex difference
			Significantly improved Unimproved	
2 weeks	12 months after entering treatment	T = 96 (64) M = 84 F = 12	Drinking behavior Number of drinking days Volume of alcohol consumed Combined; 3-point continuum Abstinent Moderate More than moderate	Not significant
2–18 months	18 months after entering treatment	T = 714 (57) M = 562 (55) F = 152 (65)	Drinking behavior Quantity–frequency index Impairment index (combined; 2 categories: Recovered Nonrecovered)	Significantly higher proportion of women than men recovered (based on χ^2 by present author on data provided by Ruggels *et al.*)
7–36 weeks	2½–5 years after discharge	T = 100 (100) M = 55 (100) F = 45 (100)	Drinking behavior Much improved Improved Unimproved	Significantly higher proportion of men than women improved (based on χ^2 by present author on Seelye's data)
Not specified	12 months after treatment	T = 314 (100) M = 157 (100) F = 157 (100)	Drinking behavior Abstinence Much improved Somewhat improved Not improved	Not significant
4–6 weeks	3, 6, 12, 18 months after admission	T = 399 (86) M = 336 F = 63	Drinking behavior Decrease or cessation of drinking Social and role Number of days institutionalized Social functioning Vocational functioning Goal attainment	Not significant
4–6 weeks	3, 6 months after discharge	T = 95 (95)	Drinking behavior Number of months since last drink Drinking-related problems: 8-point scale	Not significant

showed superior outcome for women, and one showed superior outcome for men.

As Table 13-1 also indicates, most of the studies in which sex differences were examined involved relatively traditional, multimodal inpatient and outpatient programs. Neither the treatment modalities nor the design features of the studies seemed to be particularly critical in differentiating the four programs in which women did better from the one in which men did better. The only factor that seemed at all noteworthy in the study showing superior outcome for men was the lengthy follow-up interval (2½–5 years).

Overall then, examination of the 51 studies reviewed by Emrick and by the present investigator that provided data on sex differences shows 43 studies in which there were no differences between men and women, 7 studies that show women doing better, and 5 studies in which men have better outcome.[13] The picture that emerges from the combined reviews of Emrick and the present investigator is totally consistent with Annis and Liban's (1980) conclusions based on their analysis of a subset of 23 of these studies. There is no evidence to support the contention that women have a poorer response to treatment than men. If anything, the weight of the evidence seems to lean slightly in the opposite direction.

Before concluding this section, it is important to note that although there is no scientific basis for the belief that women will have a poorer treatment outcome than men, this belief may itself be a factor in creating poor outcome. Voluminous work on experimenter bias (Rosenthal, 1976) suggests that clinicians' characteristics, including their expectations, may have considerable influence on clinical judgments (Alpert, 1970; Robinson & Cohen, 1954; Wooster, 1959), perceptions of behavior (Alpert, 1970; Rapp, 1965) and on actual treatment outcome (Alpert, 1970; Goldstein, 1960; Leake & King, 1977). Perhaps women in treatment would be doing considerably better than men were it not for the presence of negative expectations! Leake and King's (1977) study with alcoholic clients is of particular interest in this regard. In a carefully designed expectancy study, counselors were falsely led to believe at the beginning of the alcohol detoxification period that certain of their clients could be expected to show "remarkable recovery" during the course of counseling. At follow-up, on a number of job and drinking-related outcome measures, patients randomly assigned to the high-expectancy condition (where therapists were given positive expectations) performed significantly better than control subjects. Although this study did not experimentally produce negative expectancies (only positive and neutral, or control, expectancies) it is instructive in highlighting the possible consequences of negative expectancies that therapists may consciously or unconsciously transmit.

13. The number of studies adds up to more than 51 as explained in footnote 12 above.

WHAT KINDS OF PROGRAMS OR TREATMENT MODALITIES ARE MOST EFFECTIVE WITH FEMALE ALCOHOLICS?

The belief that women have a poorer prognosis than men has led to a number of proposals for special treatment modalities and treatment programs that would take account of the unique needs of the female alcoholic. In terms of the most effective forms of special treatment for women, strong opinions have been both plentiful and contradictory. Since disruption of the marital relationship is frequently a major concern among female alcoholics, family therapy has been proposed as an important treatment modality (Meeks & Kelly, 1970; Pattison, 1965). Steinglass (1979b), in contrast, has noted that despite cautious optimism, little hard evidence exists for the effectiveness of family therapy in treating alcoholism. With regard to the relative efficacy of group versus individual therapy, Curlee (1967) writes that women do not relate well in group therapy or in Alcoholics Anonymous (AA). Lindbeck (1975) agrees, stating that female alcoholics utilize individual and family therapy better than group therapy, while the reverse is true for men. On the other hand, Avery (1976) argues for the necessity of group-oriented activities for the female alcoholic, as do Battegay and Ladewig (1970), who state that alcoholic women are more effectively treated in groups. Finally, in the clinical arena there is considerable conviction among many women's program planners that women should be treated separately rather than in mixed-sex treatment programs, and should have female rather than male therapists (Birchmore & Walderman, 1975; Calobrisi, 1976).

Data from the Present 9-Year Review

Despite enthusiastic endorsement of various specific treatment modalities geared to the specific needs of women, very little attention was given to these concerns in the 95 studies that were carefully reviewed for this chapter. Although 18 studies specifically mentioned that family therapy was one of the treatment options offered, 36 mentioned group therapy, and 21 mentioned individual therapy or counseling, little more than this was done to examine these treatment options. Not a single study systematically examined the relative efficacy of family therapy for male versus female alcoholics or compared the effects of family therapy to other modes of treating the female alcoholic. Similarly, not a single study compared the outcomes of patients treated with individual as opposed to group therapy. With regard to the question of separate treatment for women, only three studies[14] reported 6-month follow-up data from programs that had separated residential facilities for women, and three[15] described mixed-sex treatment programs where a special

14. Studies: 33, 44, 126 (see boldface numbers in reference section).

15. Studies: 211, 239, 240 (see boldface numbers in reference section).

women's group was provided. In no instance, however, was a systematic controlled comparison made of single-sex versus mixed-sex treatment.

Finally, in terms of therapist's sex, only nine studies even provided information about this important treatment variable.[16] In one article (Cadogan, 1973) the author, in an attempt to provide the reader with relevant information about the sex of the therapist, wrote "all sessions were conducted by a psychologist with training and experience in groups using problem solving techniques, and by a woman co-therapist experienced in alcoholism counseling. A psychologist and a psychiatric nurse alternated as co-therapists" (p. 1189). (Apparently the reader is to infer that the psychologists were men and the co-therapists women.) Eight of the studies in which therapist sex was specified had both male and female therapists, and one specified that the therapist was a man. Only one of the nine studies (Ruggels, Mothershead, Pyszka, Loebel, & Lotridge, 1977) looked at therapist's sex as a predictor of outcome. In this large scale study of 562 male and 152 female alcoholics treated in federally funded alcoholism treatment centers across the United States, female patients overall showed significantly higher remission rates than male patients. However, no significant relationship was found between therapist's sex and outcome for either male or female alcoholics.

It would thus appear that there is little scientific data supporting (or even examining) (1) the superiority of group versus individual therapy for women; (2) the value of family therapy over other modalities; (3) the need for women to be treated separately; or (4) the value of a female over a male therapist. Moreover, there appears to be little evidence supporting the efficacy of any other particular treatment for women. In the 95 studies that we carefully reviewed, a staggering array of treatment modalities were mentioned—ranging from aversion therapy to traditional individual therapy and including use of medications, AA, Antabuse, group therapy, milieu therapy, occupational therapy, and alcohol education. These therapies, though predominantly delivered in inpatient and outpatient settings, were also described in detoxification facilities and halfway houses. All but 24 of the studies[17] either provided too little description of the treatment modalities used or described multimodal or generic inpatient programs, making it impossible to evaluate the effects of any one specific treatment modality; and in only 18 studies[18] did the experimental design permit controlled comparisons of one kind of treatment versus another or the efficacy of a particular treatment versus no treatment at all. It would appear that the interests of

16. Studies: 29, 32, 35, 45, 126, 165, 188, 201, 229 (see boldface numbers in reference section).

17. Studies: 13, 18, 32, 35, 61, 64, 73, 84, 95, 112, 122, 124, 132, 137, 153–155, 158, 165, 188, 192, 221, 229, 254 (see boldface numbers in reference section).

18. Studies: 25, 35, 41, 57, 95, 112, 130, 158, 165, 173, 188, 207, 221, 231, 240, 243, 254, 255 (see boldface numbers in reference section).

research investigators either lag behind or diverge considerably from those of the care providers faced with setting up treatment programs for women.

Unfortunately, the unsubstantiated, but dearly held, beliefs of care providers carry with them expectations that may well influence their clients' expectations, and ultimately their prognosis. Thus, the female patient who comes to believe that she is getting second-rate treatment because she is in a mixed-sex treatment program, or being treated by a male therapist, or in group rather than in family therapy, may, in fact, do worse because of her own expectations and those of the staff who work with her.

WHAT PROGNOSTIC FACTORS RELATE TO TREATMENT OUTCOME IN FEMALE ALCOHOLICS?

The great majority of studies examining the relationship between patient prognostic factors and treatment outcome have focused on the male alcoholic. As was the case with treatment outcome, study samples examining prognostic variables have most often included only men; when women were included (generally in small numbers) their data were usually combined with the male data so that possible sex differences in prognostic factors were lost. Of the 95 studies that were carefully reviewed for this chapter (studies of female or mixed-sex populations with a minimum of 6-month follow-up), 53 examined outcome in terms of one or more prognostic variables. However, 41 of these looked at prognostic variables without separating men and women (and some of these did not even include sex as one of the prognostic variables). In several other studies sex was looked at as a predictor of outcome—but all other predictors were looked at for both sexes combined. To draw any conclusions from these studies about prognostic indicators for women would be misleading—especially given that the female subsamples were often extremely small (one had only one woman!).

Twelve studies did examine the relationship between prognostic factors and outcome specifically for women.[19] Unfortunately, though sufficient information was generally presented to allow for statistical analysis, in a number of cases significance tests were not reported in the original articles. While it would be of interest to do these analyses and to tabulate the findings of these 12 studies, as Annis and Liban (1980) did in a review covering an earlier period, this task goes beyond the scope of the present chapter. Their review of 13 studies examined 76 specific prognostic variables in 9 major areas. As might be expected, for many variables examined, results from one study to the next were inconsistent, and many of the prognostic variables showed no significant relationship to outcome. Keeping in mind that Annis

19. Studies: 16, 17, 39, 44, 47, 52, 128, 153, 154, 201, 207, 218 (see boldface numbers in reference section).

and Liban's data are based on only 13 studies, the consistent findings (that is, those that were replicated at least once and were not contradicted by other studies) suggest that the following variables are positively related to outcome in women: (1) *demographic and socioeconomic factors* (full time employment at the time of admission, and being married); (2) *social relationships* (number of close friends); (3) *psychiatric diagnosis* (the presence of an underlying neurosis and absence of psychopathy); and (4) *treatment factors* (few treatment variables were positively associated with outcome, and those that were tended to be in poorly controlled studies). Though Annis and Liban's exhaustive survey is certainly a step in the right direction, it is also clear that at this point not a great deal can be said with certainty about prognostic factors in women.

The current review of 12 studies added 8 to the 13 reviewed by Annis and Liban. On the basis of the statistics reported in the 12 studies reviewed here, not a single prognostic variable was found that met our criteria for consistency and replication. Combining the 12 studies reviewed here with the 13 reviewed by Annis and Liban, only one additional prognostic variable emerged—AA referral to treatment, which predicted good outcome in one of the studies Annis and Liban reviewed (Thomas, 1971) and in one from the present review (Corrigan, 1980).

It is of some interest to compare the summary provided by Annis and Liban with the findings of two other comprehensive reviews (both of which were heavily weighted with studies of male subjects). Gibbs and Flanagan (1977), in a review of 45 studies from 1937 to 1974, attempted to isolate the personal characteristics of alcoholics consistently associated with improvement in treatment. They point out that "no stable characteristics were found, but a successful search could hardly have been expected, given the great differences found among the predictor studies . . . [which] investigated the effects of different treatment agents who used different treatments given to different samples measured by different outcome standards over different follow-up periods" (p. 1103). They point to the literature's failure to reveal general predictors, coupled with evidence from Emrick's (1975) exhaustive review which indicates that no treatment has proven superior to others in terms of long-term effects, and suggest that there may be an interaction between the type of treatment given and the personality characteristics of alcoholics receiving each treatment. They somewhat optimistically suggest that if problems of inconsistency in delineating the predictor variables could be eliminated, it might be possible to sort out the interaction between treatment type and personal characteristics of patients.

In a review of more than 60 studies in which client by treatment interactions were examined in relationship to outcome, Ogborne (1978) reached somewhat less optimistic conclusions. Using regression analyses, he found no statistically significant client by treatment interactions; and differences in remission rates between treatments were reduced to minimal significance when client characteristics were controlled. Although social stability, severity of alcoholism, and socioeconomic status were better predictors of outcome than was the type of treatment offered, such characteristics accounted for only 10% of the total variance in remission; and client characteristics and treatment variables together accounted for only 13% of the total variance in remission.

This less than heartening state of affairs, combined with evidence that Ogborne summarizes indicating that particular types of treatment vary in attractiveness for different types of patients, suggests that multimodal treatment programs might be most effective. Such programs offer a cafeteria-style approach, allowing patients to choose for themselves what they believe will work best for them. Emrick (1975) has also suggested this, indicating that "therapists might give attention to matching each alcoholic with the setting and approach which meshes best with his views of the causes, nature and treatment of alcoholism" (p. 95).

HOW WELL HAVE WOMEN BEEN STUDIED? (THE QUALITY OF THE RESEARCH DESIGNS AND ADEQUACY IN REPORTING CRITICAL DATA ABOUT WOMEN)

Carelessness in the Presentation of Women's Data

In addition to the continued promulgation of unsubstantiated beliefs about women alcoholics, the treatment outcome literature continues to abound with carelessness in presenting women as an important subgroup. Problems finding out about women are compounded by the fact that journal articles are frequently presented in a way that makes it difficult to even locate the women. Of the 227 studies for which we had abstracts, 62 studies did not specify in the abstract whether *any* women were in the sample. In the articles themselves, 27 samples remained totally unspecified regarding the presence of women. In 30 additional articles the reader is informed that women were included, but the numbers of women in the sample were not specified, and 58 articles (including two written by this author!) did not specify the numbers of women followed up. As disheartening as this appears, perhaps we should take some encouragement from the fact that current figures are much better than those presented by Hill and Blane (1967), who noted that of 49 studies published between 1952 and 1963 approximately *half* failed to specify the sex composition of their samples.

At this point, to more vividly describe the oversights in the literature, it may be instructive to cite a few examples from the articles reviewed. These examples are cited not for the purpose of pointing to the few that were particularly colorful and flamboyant, but because for each example there were so many other similar instances. Many readers will no doubt recognize, with a twinge of personal discomfort, similar oversights in their own writing, as well as their own failures to notice important oversights when they have been drawing conclusions from the work of others.

As recently as 1980 an article appeared in the *Journal of Studies on Alcohol* (Kish, Ellsworth, & Woody, 1980) in which a population was described as follows: "Although a few women participated, virtually all of the patients were men" (p. 82). Even more disconcerting is a study by Smart (1978c) who described his study population as "our sample of 1091 men" (p. 68). The reader later discovers that the sample of 1091 men contains 47 *housewives* and, we have to guess, other women as well.

In the Kish study the allusion to "a few women" seems to give partial recognition to the fact that the presence of women in the sample cannot be ignored—yet no mention is made in this or similar studies of the precise number of women included. In each case we can assume that it is too few to allow separate analysis, yet these women are combined with men for data analysis as if it would make no difference. This kind of practice (including a small number of women) is in many ways worse than using all male samples, since it treats women as if totally equivalent to men without looking to see if this is so; and may even encourage, incorrectly, inferences to mixed populations. Thus, a study which includes mostly men and a few women generalizes its findings to "alcoholics." While studies that have looked solely at men (for example, the reams of VA studies) also often talk as if they were discussing *all* alcoholics, with these studies the slightly discerning reader is at least aware that the subjects were men only. When some women are included, but not looked at separately, it is much easier for the author to make inferences about all alcoholics, without the reader's picking up the probable fallacy. Still other authors describe their *all male sample* as if it is representative of all people. For example, Polich *et al.* (1981) state (about their exclusively male sample) "in our judgment . . . the ATC population is broadly similar to the general population of persons who enter formal treatment at recognized alcoholism facilities in the United States. Certainly the ATC population is not radically different. For example, it does not include only one socioeconomic group or only a particular range of symptom severity" (p. 18).

Nature and Quality of the Study Designs and Outcome Measures

In the 95 studies that we carefully reviewed, most investigators used either a single group–repeated measures design (i.e., a single treatment group was administered a pretreatment measure and then was given a follow-up measure at some interval after treatment) or a modification of this in which the pretreatment measure was not given but patients (or their evaluators) were asked to indicate perceived improvement at the time of follow-up. Only

18 studies randomly assigned patients to two or more treatment groups or provided matched comparison groups of appropriate controls.[20] Another design problem in these studies involved the handling of data for subjects unreachable for follow-up. In at least a third of the studies this problem was ignored altogether. Unreachable patients, instead of being counted as failures in the outcome results, were simply omitted from the data analysis. (Many studies were so poorly described it was impossible to tell what had been done.)

Several authors (Emrick, 1974; Parker, Winstead, Willi, & Fisher, 1979) have recommended that treatment outcome be evaluated along several dimensions, rather than using drinking-related outcome as the sole criterion of success. Nearly all (96.8%) of the studies reviewed here used some drinking-related index of outcome, with abstinence the most frequently used index (71.5% of the studies used this either as a dichotomous outcome variable or as part of a continuum). However, 50.5% of the studies measured at least one other area of outcome: role or occupational functioning (32.6%), psychological functioning (18.9%), social/interpersonal relations (26.3%), and mood states (9.5%).

SUMMARY AND CONCLUSIONS

It should be clear from the material presented that, strong beliefs notwithstanding, there are relatively few solidly established facts about the outcomes of treated female alcoholics. At this point we can say only that there is little empirical data to substantiate the beliefs that (1) women have poorer prognosis than men, or even that the course or quality of recovery differs for men and women; (2) women need to be treated by women therapists; (3) women need to be treated in separate facilities or with separate kinds of treatment modalities. Only with respect to (1)—differences in male–female prognosis—is there even enough solid data to examine the issue. For issues (2) and (3)—sex of therapist and specific modalities—there are virtually no data available.

Though the present author is certainly among those who call for more and better studies of women, the limited state of current knowledge about the treatment outcomes of alcoholic women—in particular the fact that male–female differences have been demonstrated in neither the course of recovery nor the essential treatment ingredients—suggests that it might be appropriate to at least consider the voluminous literature available on the male alcoholic. As Braiker points out in Chapter 12 of this volume, at this point it would be precipitous, if not irresponsible, to assert that none of what is known

20. See footnote 18.

about the outcomes of treated male alcoholics can be generalized to their female counterparts. Unfortunately, there is reason to believe that little more is known about effective treatment techniques for the male alcoholic than for the female (Annis & Liban, 1980; Emrick, 1975; Ogborne, 1978). It would thus appear that the critical data are still not available that would provide definitive, empirical guidelines for effective treatment of alcoholism in either sex.

It is also important to bear in mind that our conclusions at this point are related specifically to *treatment* outcome. That is, all of our conclusions have to do with those women who have presented for treatment. Since adequate control studies are not available examining treated versus not-treated clients, we do not know, for example, how male and female alcoholics would compare were they given no treatment, or whether the treatment itself made a difference (over no treatment). It is probable, however, that a certain kind of self-selection occurs that differentiates those patients who enter treatment and remain in it (presumably recognizing that they have a problem that they intend to do something about) as opposed to those who do not enter treatment, or drop out soon after. Hence, even in studies with careful outcome measures that do show improvement between pretreatment and posttreatment measures, unless there are adequate control groups it is impossible to know if what is being measured is the therapeutic efficacy of the treatment or merely the motivation of the patient.

Directions for Future Work

While most current investigators (e.g, Annis & Liban 1980; Gibbs & Flanagan, 1977; Ogborne, 1978) who have done large meta-analyses of the treatment outcome literature share this reviewer's pessimism regarding the present state of the art, views regarding the most appropriate next steps vary to some extent. Annis and Liban (1980) point to the need for systematic study of individual differences (including sex of the client) in response to various types of treatment, stating "research addressed to specific patient-treatment combinations should significantly expand our knowledge of the therapeutic modalities most suited to different types of female alcoholics" (p. 418). These authors note that systematic studies of patient-treatment match require: (1) reliable patient assessment procedures; and (2) more carefully specified treatment interventions than are typically found within conventional alcoholism services.

Ogborne (1978) points to an even stickier set of problems—the irrational ways in which patients get recruited for treatment and assigned to specific treatment modalities, both of which severely limit the evaluation of treatment programs and the search for patient by treatment interactions. He cites, for example, the fact that geographical factors are often more likely than any other consideration to determine the kind of treatment given to a particular patient. According to Ogborne, comparative evaluation of such irrationally delivered services would only be possible using multivariate analyses of data from a large data base that included extensive details of program and patient characteristics as well as treatment outcomes. Ogborne concludes that "the poor record keeping, inadequate patient assessment, poorly specified and inconsistent operations that characterize so many of the treatments currently available to alcoholics . . . seriously impede evaluative efforts" (p. 215). The solution he calls for is continuation of large-scale independent studies that are clearly and carefully specified.

The recommendations that follow take account of the concerns of Annis and Liban as well as Ogborne, and specify in some detail the areas that future investigators will hopefully address.

Recommendations for Future Investigators

Investigators should continue to build a base of well-documented studies of women alcoholics that spell out (1) precise treatment given (with components of treatment clearly articulated); (2) population description including demographic description and criteria for excluding patients from treatment[21] or from data analysis; and (3) clearly defined outcome criteria that are presented in a standardized format that can be easily compared from one study to another. This standardized format for outcome data should include the following:

1. Collection of pretreatment measures to which posttreatment outcome can be directly compared (i.e., the same dimension covering the same time frame—for example, number of days abstinent or out of work in the past 6 months should be asked both for the period prior to treatment and for subsequent periods after treatment).
2. Whenever possible, multiple measures of outcome should be used (measures of life functioning, health, and psychological well-being, as well as drinking-related behavior). Not only should the percentage of patients improving on each of these variables be provided, but also the specific criteria for specifying "improved" or "unimproved." (This is equally important for the alcohol-related measures described below.)

21. Costello et al. (1977), on the basis of an extensive review of the literature, indicate that studies showing the best results tend to exclude the relatively large number of poor prognosis cases, whereas studies that show poor outcome appear to employ open door admission policies. Failure to take account of this would be particularly problematic in making comparisons between men and women or between one subgroup of women and another, if exclusion characteristics of the samples differed.

3. Alcohol-related measures should be specified in a more comparable format from one study to another. To increase comparability at least some of the following should be included:
   a. Percentage improved (total sample, males, females) at 6 months and 12 months after discharge.
   b. Percentage of patients abstinent the entire time at 6 and 12 months (again broken down separately for total sample, males, and females).
   c. Percentage of sample abstinent during the past month at 6 and 12 months (specified for total sample, males, and females).
   d. Percentage of subjects whose drinking is "under control" at 6 and 12 months (again, specified by sex, and also clearly defining "under control").

Investigators should provide at least simple tests of statistical significance so that the trends reported (which are often *not significant*, nor even approaching significance) do not get misleadingly quoted, as studies are casually reviewed, adding to the myths that pass for data in the alcohol literature.

Investigators should be encouraged to do meta-analyses on existing studies in which they attempt to draw conclusions across many sets of data—similar to the well-done reviews by Annis and Liban (1980), Costello (1975), Costello *et al.* (1977), Emrick (1974, 1975), and Ogborne (1978).

Authors should take care to specify the precise sex composition (number of men and women) of the initial sample and of the sample followed up (at *each* time period). Outcome results should also be presented separately for men and women, and where subgroups are described, these should be broken down by sex whenever possible. This kind of simple documentation is easily attained by any investigator and would enormously enrich the quality of the data presented. Blume (1980) has suggested that sex composition of the sample be specified in the title of articles. While this would be useful, specification in the abstract and precise breakdowns throughout the article are essential.

Authors should provide enough additional descriptive data about their populations so that it is possible for the reader to know what subgroup is being studied. At a minimum authors should be sure to include data on age of the sample; race; socioeconomic, marital, and employment status; and severity of alcoholism (use of standard measures—possibly the Michigan Alcoholism Screening Test (MAST) (Selzer, 1971) or the Missouri Alcoholism Severity Scale (MASS) (Evenson, Holland, & Cho, 1979)—would be enormously helpful).

Authors should guard against making global conclusions that refer to "alcoholics" (which implies both men and women) or to "male and female alcoholics" when the number of females included is negligible.

Finally, both journal editors and reviewers should be sensitive to the need for this kind of precise specification of data and should require adequate specification prior to accepting manuscripts for publication.

In addition to the above recommendations, the present author would like to see considerably more research devoted to the kinds of motivational issues (including expectancy effects) that have been alluded to throughout this chapter. Additional studies are needed that examine the effect of therapist expectancies, how these interact with the expectations of patients regarding their own recovery, and how both patient and therapist expectancies can be modified through educational and clinical interventions. It would be of particular interest to find out if, in fact, patients who choose a treatment modality in which they have faith, have superior outcomes to those who are given prescribed treatment in a no-choice fashion. Equally important, the therapist's ability to choose what he or she thinks is best for a given client may have significant impact on treatment outcome. Clearly, tremendous uncertainty exists about the treatment and patient characteristics that produce good outcome. Given the small amount of variance that has been accounted for by either of these factors (alone or in combination), at this point it would be of interest to explore the possibility of a larger common denominator—expectancy effects—that might interact with both patient characteristics and treatment factors to account for more of the variance in treatment outcomes.

Despite the fact that many of the critical data regarding alcoholism treatment outcome are still lacking, a desperate need remains for guiding formulations for the programmatic decisions that must be made. To a large extent, our need to "know" has led us to organize and summarize a data base that is so poor that many of our conclusions are as much a reflection of this need to believe as they are statements of reality. Thus, when called upon to organize a highly confusing array of data that has many limitations, the inherent ambiguity in the situation lends itself beautifully to selective review and interpretation of the literature to fit the author's expectations.

No doubt, similar expectancy effects have operated to some extent in the present review. Hopefully, however, greater sensitivity to these potential sources of bias, along with a move toward greater precision and specification in future research, will increase our bank of knowledge regarding the outcomes of treated alcoholic women.

ACKNOWLEDGMENTS

The author wishes to acknowledge with immeasurable appreciation the many hours of assistance and consultation provided by Laurie Nash, MEd. Special thanks also to Chad Emrick, PhD, who generously made available some of his own unpublished data including some laborious calculations done specifically for this chapter.

398   TREATMENT AND PREVENTION OF ALCOHOL PROBLEMS

REFERENCES

Adamson, J. D., Fostakowsky, R. T., & Chebib, F. Measures associated with outcome on one year follow-up of male alcoholics. *British Journal of Addiction*, 1974, *69*, 325-337. **(1)**

Alden, L. Evaluation of a preventive self-management programme for problem drinkers. *Canadian Journal of Behavioral Science*, 1978, *10*, 258-263. **(2)**

Alexander, E. R., Hall, D. J., & Little, J. C. Non-diagnostic prediction of behaviour and outcome in male psychiatric admissions. *British Journal of Psychiatry*, 1974, *124*, 579-587. **(3)**

Alpert, G. *Therapeutic effects of therapist–patient matching and positive therapist expectancies.* Doctoral dissertation, Harvard University, 1970. (University Microfilms No. 72-33398)

Alterman, A. I., Gottheil, E., Gellens, H. K., & Thornton, C. C. Relationships between drinking behavior of alcoholics in a drinking-decisions treatment program and treatment outcome. In P. E. Nathan, G. A. Marlatt, & T. Loberg (Eds.), *Alcoholism: New directions in behavioral research and treatment* (NATO Conference Series: III. Human Factors, Vol. 7). New York: Plenum, 1977. **(4)**

Alterman, A. I., Gottheil, E., Skoloda, T. E., & Thornton, C. C. Consequences of social modification of drinking behavior. *Journal of Studies on Alcohol*, 1977, *38*, 1032-1035. **(5)**

Anderson, W., & Ray, O. Abstainers, non-destructive drinkers and relapsers: One year after a four week in-patient group-oriented alcoholism treatment program. In F. Seixas (Ed.), *Currents in alcoholism* (Vol. 2). New York: Grune & Stratton, 1977. **(6)**

Annis, H. M., & Liban, C. B. A follow-up study of male halfway-house residents and matched nonresident controls. *Journal of Studies on Alcohol*, 1979, *40*, 63-69. **(7)**

Annis, H. M., & Liban, C. B. Alcoholism in women: Treatment modalities and outcomes. In O. Kalant (Ed.), *Research advances in alcohol and drug problems* (Vol. 5: *Alcohol and drug problems in women*). New York: Plenum, 1980.

Annis, H. M., & Smart, R. G. Arrests, readmissions and treatment following release from detoxication centers. *Journal of Studies on Alcohol*, 1978, *39*, 1276-1283. **(8)**

Argeriou, M., & Manohar, V. Relative effectiveness of non-alcoholics and recovered alcoholics as counselors. *Journal of Studies on Alcohol*, 1978, *39*, 793-799. **(9)**

Armor, D. J., Polich, J. M., & Stambul, H. B. *Alcoholism and treatment.* New York: Wiley Interscience, 1978. **(10)**

Athey, G. I., Jr., & Coyne, L. Psychiatric cross-classification and prognosis for alcoholism treatment involvement and benefit. *Alcoholism: Clinical and Experimental Research*, 1980, *4*, 209. **(11)**

Avery, J. Special programs for women. In *Alcohol abuse among women: Special problems and unmet needs*. Washington, D.C.: U.S. Government Printing Office, 1976.

Baekeland, F., & Kissin, B. The clinical use of disulfiram in the treatment of chronic alcoholism. In *Proceedings of the First Annual Alcoholism Conference of the National Institute on Alcohol Abuse and Alcoholism* (U.S. Department of Health, Education, and Welfare Publication No. NIH-74-675). Washington, D.C.: U.S. Government Printing Office, 1973. **(12)**

Baekeland, F., Lundwall, L., & Kissin, B. Methods for the treatment of chronic alcoholism: A critical appraisal. In R. J. Gibbins, Y. Israel, H. Kalant, R. E. Popham, W. Schmidt, & R. G. Smart (Eds.), *Research advances in alcohol and drug problems* (Vol. 2). Toronto, Canada: Wiley, 1975.

Baer, P. R. Aversion and avoidance conditioning as a treatment for alcoholism: Short term effects. In *Proceedings of the First Annual Alcoholism Conference of the National Institute on Alcohol Abuse and Alcoholism* (U.S. Department of Health, Education, and Welfare Publication No. NIH-74-675). Washington, D.C.: U.S. Government Printing Office, 1973. **(13)**

Baker, T. B. Halfway houses for alcoholics: Shelters or shackles? *International Journal of Social Psychiatry*, 1972, *18*, 201–211. **(14)**

Barr, H. L., Rosen, A., Antes, D. E., & Ottenberg, D. J. *Two year follow-up study of 724 drug and alcohol addicts treated together in an abstinence therapeutic community.* Paper presented at the 81st Annual Convention of the American Psychological Association, Montreal, Canada, 1973. **(15)**

Bateman, N. I., & Petersen, D. M. Factors related to outcome of treatment for hospitalized white male and female alcoholics. *Journal of Drug Issues*, 1972, *2*, 66–74. **(16)**

Battegay, V. R., & Ladewig, D. Group therapy and group work with addicted women. *British Journal of Addiction*, 1970, *65*, 89–98.

Beckman, L. J. Alcoholism problems and women: An overview. In M. Greenblatt & M. A. Schuckit (Eds.), *Alcoholism problems in women and children.* New York: Grune & Stratton, 1976.

Beckman, L. J. Treatment prognosis for women and men alcoholics. In M. Galanter (Ed.), *Currents in alcoholism* (Vol. 6). New York: Grune & Stratton, 1979. **(17)**

Beil, H., & Trojan, A. The use of apomorphine in the treatment of alcoholism and other addictions: Results of a general practitioner. *British Journal of Addiction*, 1977, *72*, 129–134. **(18)**

Birchmore, D. F., & Walderman, R. L. The woman alcoholic: A review. *The Ontario Psychologist*, 1975, *7*, 10–16.

Blaney, R., Radford, I. S., & MacKenzie, G. A Belfast study of the prediction of outcome in the treatment of alcoholism. *British Journal of Addiction*, 1975, *70*, 41–50. **(19)**

Blume, S. B. Researches on women and alcohol. In *Alcoholism and alcohol abuse among women: Research issues* (NIAAA Research Monograph No. 1, U.S. Department of Health, Education, and Welfare Publication No. ADM-80-835). Washington, D.C.: U.S. Government Printing Office, 1980.

Boreing, J. L. *Relationship existing between intelligence and successful long-term rehabilitation of alcoholics in a rural setting.* Doctoral dissertation, University of Northern Colorado, 1976. (University Microfilms No. 76-23165) **(20)**

Bowling, A. The relationship between insight and outcome in alcoholic patients. *Australian Journal of Alcoholism and Drug Dependency*, 1977, *4*, 13–15. **(21)**

Bowman, R. S., Stein, L. I., & Newton, J. R. Measurement and interpretation of drinking behavior: I. On measuring patterns of alcohol consumption; II. Relationships between drinking behavior and social adjustment in a sample of problem drinkers. *Journal of Studies on Alcohol*, 1975, *36*, 1154–1172. **(22)**

Braiker, H. B. The diagnosis and treatment of alcoholism in women. In *Special population issues* (NIAAA Alcohol and Health Monograph No. 4, U.S. Department of Health and Human Services Publication No. ADM-82-1193). Washington, D.C.: U.S. Government Printing Office, 1982.

Bresler, M. S. Locus of control as a factor in alcoholism. *Maryland State Medical Journal*, 1975, *24*(11), 88–90. **(23)**

Brissett, D., Laundergan, J. C., Kammeier, M. L., & Biele, M. Drinkers and nondrinkers at three and a half years after treatment: Attitudes and growth. *Journal of Studies on Alcohol*, 1980, *41*, 945–952. **(24)**

Bromet, E., & Moos, R. Environmental resources and the post-treatment functioning of alcoholic patients. *Journal of Health and Social Behavior*, 1977, *18*, 326–338. **(25)**

Bromet, E. J., & Moos, R. Prognosis of alcoholic patients: Comparisons of abstainers and moderate drinkers. *British Journal of Addiction*, 1979, *74*, 183–188. **(26)**

Bromet, E., Moos, R., Bliss, F., & Wuthmann, C. Posttreatment functioning of alcoholic patients: Its relation to program participation. *Journal of Consulting and Clinical Psychology*, 1977, *45*, 829–842. **(27)**

Brown, J., & Lyons, J. P. A progressive diagnostic schema for alcoholism with evidence of clinical efficacy. *Alcoholism: Clinical and Experimental Research*, 1980, *4*, 210. (**28**)

Brown, S., & Yalom, I. D. Interactional group therapy with alcoholics. *Journal of Studies on Alcohol,* 1977, *38*, 426–456. (**29**)

Browne-Mayers, A. N., Gladieux, J. R., Seelye, E. E., & Sillman, L. S. Participation in group therapy: Outcome in treatment of alcoholism. In F. A. Seixas (Ed.), *Currents in alcoholism* (Vol. 4). New York: Grune & Stratton, 1978. (**30**)

Browne-Mayers, A. N., Seelye, E. E., & Brown, D. E. Reorganized alcoholism service: Two years after. *Journal of the American Medical Association*, 1973, *224*, 233–235. (**31**)

Burnum, J. F. Outlook for treating patients with self-destructive habits. *Annals of Internal Medicine*, 1974, *81*, 387–393. (**32**)

Burtle, V., Whitlock, D., & Franks, V. Modification of low self-esteem in women alcoholics: A behavior treatment approach. *Psychotherapy: Theory, Research and Practice*, 1974, *11*, 36–40. (**33**)

Caddy, G. R., Addington, H. J., Jr., & Perkins, D. Individualized behavior therapy for alcoholics: A third year independent double-blind follow-up. *Behaviour Research and Therapy*, 1978, *16*, 345–362. (**34**)

Cadogan, D. A. Marital group therapy in the treatment of alcoholism. *Quarterly Journal of Studies on Alcohol*, 1973, *34*, 1187–1194. (**35**)

Cahalan, D. *Problem drinkers*. San Francisco, Calif.: Jossey-Bass, 1970.

Calobrisi, A. Treatment programs for alcoholic women. In M. Greenblatt & M. Schuckit (Eds.), *Alcoholism problems in women and children*. New York: Grune & Stratton, 1976.

Cameron, D., & Spence, M. T. Lessons from an out-patient controlled drinking group. *Journal of Alcoholism*, 1976, *11*, 44–55. (**36**)

Caster, D. U., & Parsons, O. A. Locus of control in alcoholics and treatment outcome. *Journal of Studies on Alcohol*, 1977, *38*, 2087–2095. (**37**)

Castle, M., & Cornoni, J. C. Follow-up study of patients discharged from an alcohol rehabilitation center. *North Carolina Medical Journal*, 1975, *36*, 292–294. (**38**)

Chacon, C., Rundell, O. H., Jones, R. K., Gregory, D., Williams, H. L., & Paredes, A. Similarities of problem drinking and therapeutic outcome in females and males. *Alcohol Technical Reports*, 1978, *7*, 101–107. (**39**)

Chaucer, N. The brotherhood approach to alcoholism. *Connecticut Medicine*, 1972, *36*(8), 435–436. (**40**)

Chvapil, M., Hymes, H., & Delmastro, D. Outpatient aftercare as a factor in treatment outcome: A pilot study. *Journal of Studies on Alcohol*, 1978, *39*, 540–544. (**41**)

Cicchinelli, L. F., Binner, P. R., & Halpern, J. Output value analysis of an alcoholism treatment program. *Journal of Studies on Alcohol*, 1978, *39*, 435–447. (**42**)

Clark, W. B., & Cahalan, D. Changes in problem drinking over a four-year span. *Addictive Behaviors*, 1976, *1*, 251–259. (**43**)

Cohen, R., Appelt, H., Olbrich, R., & Watzl, H. Alcoholic women treated by behaviorally orientated therapy: An 18-month follow-up study. *Journal of Drug and Alcohol Dependency*, 1979, *4*, 489–498. (**44**)

Cooke, S. E. Project rehab: A progress report. *Maryland State Medical Journal*, 1972, *21*(6), 82–87 (**45**)

Corder, B. F., Corder, R. F., & Laidlaw, N. D. An intensive treatment program for alcoholics and their wives. *Quarterly Journal of Studies on Alcohol*, 1972, *33*, 1144–1146. (**46**)

Corrigan, E. M. *Alcoholic women in treatment*. New York: Oxford University Press, 1980. (**47**)

Costello, R. M. Alcoholism treatment and evaluation: In search of methods. *International Journal of the Addictions*, 1975, *10*, 251–275.

Costello, R. M., Baillargeon, J. G., Biever, P., & Bennett, R. Second-year alcoholism treatment outcome evaluation with a focus on Mexican-American patients. *American Journal of Drug and Alcohol Abuse*, 1979, *6*, 97–108. **(48)**

Costello, R. M., Baillargeon, J. G., Biever, P., & Bennett, R. Therapeutic community treatment for alcohol abusers: A one-year multivariate outcome evaluation. *International Journal of the Addictions*, 1980, *15*(2), 215–232. **(49)**

Costello, R. M ., Bechtel, J. M., & Griffin, M. A community's efforts to attack the problem of alcoholism: II. Base rate data for future program evaluation. *International Journal of the Addictions*, 1973, *8*(6), 875–888. **(50)**

Costello, R. M., Biever, P., & Baillargeon, J. G. Alcoholism treatment programming: Historical trends and modern approaches. *Alcoholism: Clinical and Experimental Research*, 1977, *1*, 311–318.

Costello, R. M., Griffen, M. B., Schneider, S. L., Edgington, P. W., & Manders, K. R. Comprehensive alcohol treatment planning, implementation, and evaluation. *International Journal of the Addictions*, 1976, *11*, 553–570. **(51)**

Crawford, J. J., & Chalupsky, A. B. The reported evaluation of alcoholism treatments, 1968–1971: A methodological review. *Addictive Behaviors*, 1977, *2*, 63–74.

Crawford, R. J. M. Treatment success in alcoholism. *New Zealand Medical Journal*, 1976, *84*, 93–96. **(52)**

Cripe, L. I. *MMPI differences of male alcoholic treatment successes and failures*. Doctoral dissertation, University of Minnesota, 1974. (University Microfilms No. 75-2093) **(53)**

Cronkite, R. C., & Moos, R. H. Evaluating alcoholism treatment programs: An integrated approach. *Journal of Consulting and Clinical Psychology*, 1978, *46*, 1105–1119. **(54)**

Cronkite, R. C., & Moos, R. H. Determinants of the posttreatment functioning of alcoholic patients: A conceptual framework. *Journal of Consulting and Clinical Psychology*, 1980, *48*, 305–316. **(55)**

Cull, J. G., & Hardy, R. E. Program of the Alcoholism Commission of Saskatchewan. In *Organization and administration of drug abuse treatment programs: National and international lecture series*. Springfield, Ill.: Charles C Thomas, 1974. **(56)**

Curlee, J. Alcoholic women: Some considerations for further research. *Bulletin of the Menninger Clinic*, 1967, *31*, 154–163.

Cutter, H. S. G., Boyatzis, R. E., & Clancy, D. D. Effectiveness of power motivation training in rehabilitating alcoholics. *Journal of Studies on Alcohol*, 1977, *38*, 131–141. **(57)**

Dalton, M. S., Chegwidden, M. J., & Duncan, D. Wistaria House: Results of transition of alcoholics—from treatment unit to community house. *International Journal of Social Psychiatry*, 1972, *18*, 213–216. **(58)**

Dalton, M. S., & Duncan, D. W. Physician heal thyself? *Medical Journal of Australia*, 1978, *652*, 406–407. **(59)**

Davidson, A. F. An evaluation of the treatment and after-care of a hundred alcoholics. *British Journal of Addiction*, 1976, *71*, 217–224. **(60)**

Davidson, R. S. Comparative analyses of adversive conditioning in alcoholism. *Current Psychiatric Therapies*, 1973, *13*, 141–148. **(61)**

Davidson, R. S., & Wallach, E. S. Shock facilitation and suppression of alcohol- and coke-maintained behavior. *Psychological Reports*, 1972, *31*, 415–424. **(62)**

Davis, M. A self-confrontation technique in alcoholism treatment. *Quarterly Journal of Studies on Alcohol*, 1972, *33*, 191–192. **(63)**

Davis, T. S., & Hagood, L. A. In-home support for recovering alcoholic mothers and their families: The family rehabilitation coordinator project. *Journal of Studies on Alcohol*, 1979, *40*, 313–317. **(64)**

deLint, J. E. Alcoholism, birth rank and parental deprivation. *American Journal of Psychiatry*, 1964, *120*, 1062–1065.

deLint, J. E., & Levinson, T. Mortality among patients treated for alcoholism: A 5-year follow-up. *Canadian Medical Association Journal*, 1975, *113*, 385–387. **(65)**

DiPaolo, V. Alcohol units up cure rate, census. *Modern Healthcare*, 1978, *8*(12), 30. **(66)**

Duane, W. J., & Norton, F. E., Jr., Description and evaluation of a USAF alcohol rehabilitation center. *British Journal of Alcohol and Alcoholism*, 1978, *13*, 141–147. **(67)**

DuBois, R. L. *Alcoholism treatment follow-up related to staff members' effectiveness.* Master's thesis, North Texas State University, 1978. (University Microfilms No. 13-11557) **(68)**

Dunne, J. A. Counseling alcoholic employees in a municipal police department. *Quarterly Journal of Studies on Alcohol*, 1973, *34*, 423–434. **(69)**

Dwoskin, J., Gordis, E., & Dorph, D. Life-table analysis of treatment outcome following 185 consecutive alcoholism halfway house discharges. *Alcoholism: Clinical and Experimental Research*, 1979, *3*, 334–340. **(70)**

Edwards, G., Orford, J., Egert, S., Guthrie, S., Hawker, A., Hensman, C., Mitcheson, M., Oppenheimer, E., & Taylor C. Alcoholism: A controlled trial of "treatment" and "advice." *Journal of Studies on Alcohol*, 1977, *38*, 1004–1031. **(71)**

Elkins, R. L., & Murdock, R. P. The contribution of successful conditioning to abstinence maintenance following covert sensitization (verbal aversion) treatment of alcoholism. *IRCS Medical Science*, Library Compendium, 1977, *5*, 167. **(72)**

Emrick, C. D. A review of psychologically oriented treatment of alcoholism: I. The use and interrelationships of outcome criteria and drinking behavior following treatment. *Quarterly Journal of Studies on Alcohol*, 1974, *35*, 523–549.

Emrick, C. D. A review of psychologically oriented treatment of alcoholism: II. The relative effectiveness of different treatment approaches and the effectiveness of treatment versus no treatment. *Journal of Studies on Alcohol*, 1975, *36*, 88–108.

Evenson, R. C., Holland, R. A., & Cho, D. W. A scale for measuring the severity of alcoholism and evaluating its treatment. *Journal of Studies on Alcohol*, 1979, *40*, 1077–1081.

Ewing, J. A., & Rouse, B. A. Failure of an experimental treatment program to inculcate controlled drinking in alcoholics. *British Journal of Addiction*, 1976, *71*, 123–134. **(73)**

Faillace, L. A., Flamer, R. N., Imber, S. D., & Ward, R. F. Giving alcohol to alcoholics: An evaluation. *Quarterly Journal of Studies on Alcohol*, 1972, *33*, 85–90. **(74)**

Ferguson, F. N. Stake theory as an explanatory device in Navajo alcoholism treatment response. *Human Organization*, 1976, *35*, 65–78. **(75)**

Ferguson, L. C. *Social competence and prognosis in alcoholism: A one-year, multivariate follow-up study.* Doctoral dissertation, University of Minnesota, 1978. (University Microfilms No. 78-23906) **(76)**

Finlay, D. G. Changing problem drinkers. *Social Work Research Abstracts*, 1977, *13*, 30–37. **(77)**

Finney, J. W., Moos, R. H. Treatment and outcome for empirical subtypes of alcoholic patients. *Journal of Consulting and Clinical Psychology*, 1979, *47*, 25–38. **(78)**

Finney, J. W., Moos, R. H., & Mewborn, C. R. Posttreatment experiences and treatment outcome of alcoholic patients six months and two years after hospitalization. *Journal of Consulting and Clinical Psychology*, 1980, *48*, 17–29. **(79)**

Fischer, J. The relationship between alcoholic patients' milieu perception and measures of their drinking during a brief follow-up period. *International Journal of the Addictions*, 1979, *14*, 1151–1156. **(80)**

Fox, R. P., Graham, M. B., & Gill, M. J. A therapeutic revolving door. *Archives of General Psychiatry*, 1972, *26*, 179–182. **(81)**

Freedberg, E. J., & Johnston, W. E. Effects of various sources of coercion on outcome of treatment of alcoholism. *Psychological Reports*, 1978, *43*, 1271–1278. **(82)**

Freedberg, E. J., & Johnston, W. E. Changes in drinking behavior, employment status and other life areas for employed alcoholics three, six and twelve months after treatment. *Journal of Drug Issues*, 1979, *9*, 523–534. (a) **(83)**

Freedberg, E. J., & Johnston, W. E. Changes in feelings of job satisfaction among alcoholics induced by their employer to seek treatment. *Journal of Occupational Medicine*, 1979, *21*, 549–552. (b) (**84**)

Freedberg, E. J., & Johnston, W. E. Outcome with alcoholics seeking treatment voluntarily or after confrontation by their employer. *Journal of Occupational Medicine*, 1980, *22*, 83–86. (**85**)

Fuller, R. K., & Long, S. Compliance to disulfiram regimen determined by measuring urinary riboflavin. *Alcoholism: Clinical and Experimental Research*, 1980, *4*, 215. (**86**)

Fuller, R. K., & Roth, H. B. Disulfiram for the treatment of alcoholism: An evaluation in 128 men. *Annals of Internal Medicine*, 1979, *90*, 901–904. (**87**)

Gaa'l, C. L., & Freebairn, C. Ear-acupuncture relaxation therapy in alcoholics: Report on a follow-up survey. *Medical Journal of Australia*, 1979, *66*(2), 179–180. (**88**)

Gabrynowicz, J. Hypnosis in a treatment programme for alcoholism. *Medical Journal of Australia*, 1977, *64*, 653–656. (**89**)

Gallant, D. M., Bishop, M. P., Mouledoux, A., Faulkner, M. A., Brisolara, A., & Swanson, W. A. The revolving-door alcoholic: An impasse in the treatment of the chronic alcoholic. *Archives of General Psychiatry*, 1973, *28*, 633–635. (**90**)

Gallen, M., Williams, B., Cleveland, S. E., O'Connell, W. E., & Sands, P. M. A short term follow-up of two contrasting alcoholic treatment programs: A preliminary report. *Newsletter of Research in Mental Health*, 1973, *15*(4), 36–37. (**91**)

Gellens, H. K., Gottheil, E., & Alterman, A. I. Drinking outcome of specific alcoholic subgroups. *Journal of Studies on Alcohol*, 1976, *37*, 986–989. (**92**)

Gertler, R., Raynes, A. E., & Harris, N. Assessment of attendance and outcome at an outpatient alcoholism clinic. *Quarterly Journal of Studies on Alcohol*, 1973, *34*, 955–959. (**93**)

Gibbs, L., & Flanagan, J. Prognostic indicators of alcoholism treatment outcome. *International Journal of the Addictions*, 1977, *12*, 1097–1141.

Gillies, M., Laverty, S. G., Smart, R. G., & Aharan, C. H. Outcomes in treated alcoholics: Patient and treatment characteristics in a one-year follow-up study. *Journal of Alcoholism*, 1974, *9*, 125–134. (**94**)

Glover, J. H., & McCue, P. A. Electrical aversion therapy with alcoholics: A comparative follow-up study. *British Journal of Psychiatry*, 1977, *130*, 279–286. (**95**)

Goby, M. J. A follow-up study of patients over 60 treated at the alcoholism treatment center at Lutheran General Hospital. In M. J. Goby & J. E. Keller (Eds.), *Perspectives on the treatment of alcoholism*. Park Ridge, Ill.: Lutheran General Hospital, 1978. (a) (**96**)

Goby, M. J. A follow-up study of patients referred by employers in 1975 to the alcoholism treatment center of Lutheran General Hospital. In M. J. Goby & J. E. Keller (Eds.), *Perspectives on the treatment of alcoholism*. Park Ridge, Ill.: Lutheran General Hospital, 1978. (b) (**97**)

Goby, M. J. A 40-45 month follow-up study of patients treated at the alcoholic treatment center of Lutheran General Hospital. In M. J. Goby & J. E. Keller (Eds.), *Perspectives on the treatment of alcoholism*. Park Ridge, Ill.: Lutheran General Hospital, 1978. (c) (**98**)

Goby, M. J., Bradley, N. J., & Bespalec, D. A. Physicians treated for alcoholism: A follow-up study. *Alcoholism: Clinical and Experimental Research*, 1979, *3*, 121–124. (**99**)

Goldstein, A. P. Therapist and client expectation of personality change in psychotherapy. *Journal of Counseling Psychology*, 1960, *7*, 180–184.

Gordis, E., Dorph, D., Sepe, V., & Smith, H. Alcoholism treatment outcome among 5578 patients in an urban comprehensive hospital-based program: Application of a computerized data system. *Alcoholism: Clinical and Experimental Research*, 1980, *4*, 216. (**100**)

Gottheil, E. Research on fixed interval drinking decisions in an alcoholism treatment program. In *Proceedings of the Second Annual Alcoholism Conference of the National Institute on Alcohol Abuse and Alcoholism* (U.S. Department of Health, Education, and Welfare Publication No. NIH-74-676). Washington, D.C.: U.S. Government Printing Office, 1973. (**101**)

Gottheil, E., Murphy, B. F., Skoloda, T. E., & Corbett, L. O. Fixed interval drinking decisions: II. Drinking and discomfort in 25 alcoholics. *Quarterly Journal of Studies on Alcohol*, 1972, *33*, 325–340. (**102**)

Gottheil, E., Thornton, C. C., Skoloda, T. E., & Alterman, A. I. Follow-up study of alcoholics at 6, 12, and 24 months. In M. Galanter (Ed.), *Currents in Alcoholism* (Vol. 6). New York: Grune & Stratton, 1979. (**103**)

Grof, S., Soskin, R. A., Richards, W. A., & Kurland, A. A. DPT as adjunct in psychotherapy of alcoholics. *International Pharmapsychiatry*, 1973, *8*, 104–115. (**104**)

Grossman, I., Jr. *The utility of client characteristics as predictors of treatment outcome in alcoholism.* Doctoral dissertation, Bowling Green State University, 1978. (University Microfilms No. 79-07983) (**105**)

Gunderson, E. K. E., & Schuckit, M. A. Prognostic indicators in young alcoholics. *Military Medicine*, 1978, *143*, 168–170. (**106**)

Hallam, R., Rachman, S., & Falkowski, W. Subjective, attitudinal and physiological effects of electrical aversion therapy. *Behaviour Research and Therapy*, 1972, *10*, 1–13. (**107**)

Hamilton, J. R. Evaluation of a detoxification service for habitual drunken offenders. *British Journal of Psychiatry*, 1979, *135*, 28–34. (**108**)

Hart, L. Rehabilitation need patterns of men alcoholics. *Journal of Studies on Alcohol*, 1977, *38*, 494–511. (**109**)

Hart, L., & Stueland, D. An application of the multidimensional model of alcoholism to program effectiveness: Rehabilitation status and outcome. *Journal of Studies on Alcohol*, 1979, *40*, 645–655. (**110**)

Heather, N., Edwards, S., & Hore, B. D. Changes in construing and outcome of group therapy for alcoholism. *Journal of Studies on Alcohol*, 1975, *36*, 1238–1253. (**111**)

Hedberg, A. G., & Campbell, L. M. A comparison of four behavioral treatments of alcoholism. *Journal of Behavior Therapy*, 1974, *5*, 251–256. (**112**)

Hedberg, A. G., Campbell, L. M., Weeks, S. R., & Powell, J. A. Use of the MMPI (Mini-Mult) to predict alcoholics' response to a behavioral treatment program. *Journal of Clinical Psychology*, 1975, *31*, 271–274. (**113**)

Hill, M. J., & Blane, H. T. Evaluation of psychotherapy with alcoholics: A critical review. *Quarterly Journal of Studies on Alcohol*, 1967, *28*, 76–104.

Hoffmann, H., Noem, A. A., & Petersen, D. Treatment effectiveness as judged by successfully and unsuccessfully treated alcoholics. *Drug and Alcohol Dependence*, 1976, *1*, 241–246. (**114**)

Holder, H. D., & Hallan, J. Systems approach to planning alcoholism programs in North Carolina. *American Journal of Public Health*, 1972, *62*, 1415–1421. (**115**)

Humes, C., Cook, D., & Franklin, K. Alcoholic rehabilitation and prevention program. *Rehabilitation Literature*, 1972, *33*(1), 11–13. (**116**)

Hunt, G. M., & Azrin, N. H. A community-reinforcement approach to alcoholism. *Behaviour Research and Therapy*, 1973, *11*, 91–104. (**117**)

Hussain, D. P. M., & Harinath, M. Helping alcoholics abstain: An implantable substance. *American Journal of Psychiatry*, 1972, *129*(3), 363. (**118**)

Hyman, M. M. Alcoholics fifteen years later. In F. A. Seixas & S. Eggleston (Eds.), *Work in progress on alcoholism. Annals of the New York Academy of Sciences*, 1976, *273*, 613–623.

Imber, S., Schultz, E., Funderburk, F., Allen, R., & Flamer, R. The fate of the untreated alcoholic: Toward a natural history of the disorder. *Journal of Nervous and Mental Disorders*, 1976, *162*, 238–247. (**119**)

Intagliata, J. A telephone follow-up procedure for increasing the effectiveness of a treatment program for alcoholics. *Journal of Studies on Alcohol*, 1976, *37*, 1330–1335. (**120**)

Jackson, P., & Oei, T. P. S. Social skills training and cognitive restructuring with alcoholics. *Drug and Alcohol Dependence*, 1978, *3*, 369–374. (**121**)

Jackson, T. R., & Smith J. W. A comparison of two aversion treatment methods for alcoholism. *Journal of Studies on Alcohol*, 1978, *39*, 187–191. **(122)**

Jacobson, N. O., & Silfverskiold, N. P. A controlled study of a hypnotic method in the treatment of alcoholism, with evaluation by objective criteria. *British Journal of Addiction*, 1973, *68*, 25–31. **(123)**

Jindra, N. J., & Forslund, M. A. Alcoholics Anonymous in a western U.S. city. *Journal of Studies on Alcohol*, 1978, *39*, 110–120. **(124)**

Johnston, P. J. *Effects of spouse counseling on the treatment outcome of the problem drinker.* Doctoral dissertation, College of William and Mary, 1979. (University Microfilms No. 80-04431) **(125)**

Kammeier, M. L. *Alcoholism is the common denominator: More evidence on the male/female question.* Center City, Minn.: Hazelden Publications, 1977. **(126)**

Kammeier, M. L., & Conley, J. J. Toward a system for prediction of post-treatment abstinence and adaptation. In M. Galanter (Ed.), *Currents in alcoholism* (Vol. 6). New York: Grune & Stratton, 1979. **(127)**

Kammeier, M. L., & Laundergan, J. C. *The outcome of treatment: Patients admitted to Hazelden in 1975.* Center City, Minn.: Hazelden Publications, 1977. **(128)**

Kanas, T. E., Cleveland, S. E., Pokorny, A. D., & Miller, B. A. Two contrasting alcoholism treatment programs: A comparison of outcomes. *International Journal of the Addictions*, 1976, *11*, 1045–1062. **(129)**

Kaplan, R., Blume, S., Rosenberg, S., Pitrelli, J., & Turner, W. J. Phenytoin, metronidazole and multivitamins in the treatment of alcoholism. *Quarterly Journal of Studies on Alcohol*, 1972, *33*, 97–104. **(130)**

Karpman, B. M. *The alcoholic woman.* Washington, D.C.: Linacre, 1948.

Keehn, J. D., Kuechler, H. A., Oki, G., Collier, D., & Walsh, R. Interpersonal behaviorism and community treatment of alcoholics. In *Proceedings of the First Annual Alcoholism Conference of the National Institute on Alcohol Abuse and Alcoholism* (U.S. Department of Health, Education, and Welfare Publication No. NIH-74-675). Washington, D.C.: U.S. Government Printing Office, 1973. **(131)**

Kern, J. C., & Schmelter, W. R. Result of a low-cost follow-up study of discharged alcoholics. *Alcoholism: Clinical and Experimental Research*, 1979, *3*, 252–254. **(132)**

Kilgus, R. H. *Analysis of prognostic indicators in an alcoholic patient poplation.* Doctoral dissertation (EdD), Northern Illinois University, 1978. (University Microfilms No. 7912486) **(133)**

Kish, G. B., Ellsworth, R. B., & Woody, M. M. Effectiveness of an 84 day and a 60 day alcoholism treatment program. *Journal of Studies on Alcohol*, 1980, *41*(1), 81–85. **(134)**

Klein, J. P. *The Medina Project: Relationships between demographic intake variables and alcoholism rehabilitation outcomes.* Houston, Tex.: University of Texas Health Science Center at Houston, School of Public Health, 1975. **(135)**

Kline, N. S., Wren, J. C., Cooper, T. B., Varga, E., & Canal, O. Evaluation of lithium therapy in chronic and periodic alcoholism. *American Journal of Medical Science*, 1974, *268*, 15–22. **(136)**

Kline, S. A., & Kingstone, E. Disulfiram implants: The right treatment but the wrong drug? *Canadian Medical Association Journal*, 1977, *116*, 1382–1383. **(137)**

Kliner, D. J., Spicer, J., & Barnett, P. Treatment outcome of alcoholic physicians. *Journal of Studies on Alcohol*, 1980, *41*, 1217–1220. **(138)**

Knox, W. J. Four-year follow-up of veterans treated on a small alcoholism treatment ward. *Quarterly Journal of Studies on Alcohol*, 1972, *33*, 105–110. **(139)**

Kolb, D., Gunderson, E. K. E., & Bucky, S. Prognostic indicators for black and white alcoholics in the U.S. Navy. *Journal of Studies on Alcohol*, 1976, *37*, 890–899. **(140)**

Kolb, D., Pugh, W. M., & Gunderson, E. K. E. Prediction of posttreatment effectiveness in Navy alcoholics. *Journal of Studies on Alcohol*, 1978, *39*, 192–196. **(141)**

Kurpiel, R. A. *A follow-up study of black alcoholics.* Doctoral dissertation, University of Virginia, 1979. (University Microfilms No. 80-04605) **(142)**

Lanyon, R. I., Primo, R. V., Terrell, F., & Wener, A. An aversion-desensitization treatment for alcoholism. *Journal of Consulting and Clinical Psychology*, 1972, *38*(3), 394–398. **(143)**

Leake, G. J., & King, A. S. Effect of counselor expectations on alcoholic recovery. *Alcohol Health and Research World*, 1977, *1*(3), 16–22. **(144)**

Levinson, T. Controlled drinking in the alcoholic—a search for common features. In J. S. Madden, R. Walker, & W. H. Kenyon (Eds.), *Alcoholism and drug dependence: A multidisciplinary approach.* New York: Plenum, 1977. **(145)**

Lewis, M. J., Bland, R. C., & Baile, W. Disulfiram implantation for alcoholism. *Canadian Psychiatric Association Journal*, 1975, *20*, 283–286. **(146)**

Liepman, M. R., & Tauriainen, M. E. Factors contributing to success or failure of family coercive interventions on alcoholics. *Alcoholism: Clinical and Experimental Research*, 1980, *4*, 222. **(147)**

Lindbeck, V. The woman alcoholic: A review of the literature. *International Journal of the Addictions*, 1972, *7*(3), 567–580.

Lindbeck, V. *The woman alcoholic* (Public Affairs Pamphlet No. 529). New York: Public Affairs Committee, 1975.

Lisansky, E. S. Alcoholism in women: Social and psychological concomitants. *Quarterly Journal of Studies on Alcohol*, 1957, *18*, 588–623.

Litman, G. K., Eiser, J. R., Rawson, N. S. B., & Oppenheim, A. N. Differences in relapse precipitants and coping behaviour between alcohol relapsers and survivors. *Behaviour Research and Therapy*, 1979, *17*, 89–94. **(148)**

Lowe, W. C., & Thomas, S. D. Assessing alcoholism treatment effectiveness: A comparison of three evaluative measures. *Journal of Studies on Alcohol*, 1976, *37*, 883–889. **(149)**

Lundquist, G. A. R. Alcohol dependence. *Acta Psychiatrica Scandinavica*, 1973, *49*, 332–340. **(150)**

Lysloff, G. O. Anti-addictive chemotherapy—metronidazole and alcohol aversion. *British Journal of Addiction*, 1972, *67*, 239–244. **(151)**

MacDonough, T. S. The relative effectiveness of a medical hospitalization program vs. a feedback-behavior modification program in treating alcohol and drug abusers. *International Journal of the Addictions*, 1976, *11*, 269–282. **(152)**

Madden, J. S. A programme of group counselling for alcoholics. In J. S. Madden, R. Walker, & W. H. Kenyon (Eds.), *Alcoholism and drug dependence: A multidisciplinary approach.* New York: Plenum, 1977. **(153)**

Madden, J. S., & Kenyon, W. H. Group counselling of alcoholics by a voluntary agency. *British Journal of Psychiatry*, 1975, *126*, 289–291. **(154)**

Malcolm, M. T., & Madden, J. S. The use of disulfiram implantation in alcoholism. *British Journal of Psychiatry*, 1973, *123*, 41–45. **(155)**

Mandell, W. A critical overview of evaluations of alcoholism treatment. *Alcoholism: Clinical and Experimental Research*, 1979, *3*(4), 315–323.

Maters, W. The quarter-way house: An innovative alcoholism treatment program. *Maryland State Medical Journal*, 1972, *21*(2), 40–43. **(156)**

McClelland, D. C. Drinking as a response to power needs in man. *Psychopharmacology Bulletin*, 1974, *10*(4), 5–6. **(157)**

McCrady, B. S., Paolino, T. J., Jr., Longabaugh, R., & Rossi, J. Effects of joint hospital admission and couples treatment for hospitalized alcoholics: A pilot study. *Addictive Behaviors*, 1979, *4*, 155–165. **(158)**

McLachlan, J. *Sex differences in recovery rates after one year* (Research Note No. 9). Toronto, Canada: Donwood Institute, 1978. **(159)**

McWilliams, J., & Brown, C. C. Treatment termination variables, MMPI scores and frequencies of relapse in alcoholics. *Journal of Studies on Alcohol*, 1977, *38*, 477–486. **(160)**

Medhus, A. Mortality among female alcoholics. *Scandinavian Journal of Social Medicine*, 1975, *3*, 111–115. **(161)**

Meeks, D. E., & Kelly, C. Family therapy with the families of recovered alcoholics. *Quarterly Journal of Studies on Alcohol*, 1970, *31*, 399–413.

Meyer, J. R. *Dispositional assessment with alcoholics*. Doctoral dissertation, University of Nebraska–Lincoln, 1979. (University Microfilms No. 79-18017) **(162)**

Michaelsson, G. Short-term effects of behaviour therapy and hospital treatment of chronic alcoholics. *Behaviour Research and Therapy*, 1976, *14*, 69–72. **(163)**

Miller, P. M., Hersen, M., Eisler, R. M., & Elkin, T. E. A retrospective analysis of alcohol consumption on laboratory tasks as related to therapeutic outcome. *Behaviour Research and Therapy*, 1974, *12*, 73–76. **(164)**

Miller, W. R. Behavioral treatment of problem drinkers: A comparative outcome study of three controlled drinking therapies. *Journal of Consulting and Clinical Psychology*, 1978, *46*, 74–86. **(165)**

Miller, W. R., & Joyce, M. A. Prediction of abstinence, controlled drinking, and heavy drinking outcomes following behavioral self-control training. *Journal of Consulting and Clinical Psychology*, 1979, *47*, 773–775. **(166)**

Moberg, D. P. Treatment outcome for earlier-phase alcoholics. *Annals of the New York Academy of Sciences*, 1976, *273*, 543–552. **(167)**

Moberg, D. P. Treatment outcome for earlier phase alcoholics. II: Nine month follow-up. In F. A. Seixas (Ed.), *Currents in alcoholism* (Vol. 4). New York: Grune & Stratton, 1978. **(168)**

Moos, R., & Bliss, F. Difficulty of follow-up and outcome of alcoholism treatment. *Journal of Studies on Alcohol*, 1978, *39*, 473–490. **(169)**

Moos, R. H., Bromet, E., Tsu, V., & Moos, B. Family characteristics and the outcome of treatment for alcoholism. *Journal of Studies on Alcohol*, 1979, *40*, 78–88. **(170)**

Moos, R. H., Mehren, B., & Moos, B. S. Evaluation of a Salvation Army alcoholism treatment program. *Journal of Studies on Alcohol*, 1978, *39*, 1267–1275. **(171)**

Moran, M., Watson, C. G., Brown, J., White, C., & Jacobs, L. Systems releasing action therapy with alcoholics: An experimental evaluation. *Journal of Clinical Psychology*, 1978, *34*, 769–774. **(172)**

Mosher, V., Davis, J., Mulligan, D., & Iber, F. L. Comparison of outcome in a 9-day and 30-day alcoholism treatment program. *Journal of Studies on Alcohol*, 1975, *36*, 1277–1281. **(173)**

Murray, R. M. Characteristics and prognosis of alcoholic doctors. *British Medical Journal*, 1976, *2*, 1537–1539. **(174)**

Nelson, P., & Hoffmann, H. Effect of long-term treatment on personality change of high-risk alcoholics. *Psychological Reports*, 1972, *31*, 799–802. **(175)**

Newton, J. R., & Stein, L. I. Implosive therapy, duration of hospitalization, and degree of coordination of aftercare services with alcoholics. In *Proceedings of the First Annual Alcoholism Conference of the National Institute on Alcohol Abuse and Alcoholism* (U.S. Department of Health, Education, and Welfare Publication No. NIH-74-675). Washington, D.C.: U.S. Government Printing Office, 1973. **(176)**

Noble, E. P. (Ed.). *Alcohol and health: Third special report to the U.S. Congress* (U.S. Department of Health, Education, and Welfare Publication No. ADM-78-569). Washington, D.C.: U.S. Government Printing Office, 1978.

Noel, E. C. D.C. Mental Health Administration: Halfway houses. *Medical Annals of the District of Columbia*, 1972, *41*(1), 43–45. **(177)**

Oatsvall, R. D. *Personality factors as predictors of success in an alcoholic treatment program*. Doctoral dissertation, University of Southern Mississippi, 1978. (University Microfilms No. 79-05141) **(178)**

O'Briant, R. G., Lennard, H. L., Allen, S. D., & Ransom, D. C. *Recovery from alcoholism: A social treatment model*. Springfield, Ill.: Charles C Thomas, 1973. **(179)**

Ogborne, A. C. Patient characteristics as predictors of treatment outcomes for alcohol and drug abusers. In Y. Israel, F. B. Glaser, H. Kalant, R. E. Popham, W. Schmidt, & R. G. Smart (Eds.), *Research advances in alcohol and drug problems* (Vol. 4). New York: Plenum, 1978.

Ogborne, A. C., & Wilmot, R. Evaluation of an experimental counseling service for male skid row alcoholics. *Journal of Studies on Alcohol*, 1979, *40*, 129–132. **(180)**

Ogbru, B. A. *Sources of stress, severity of alcoholism, and reported effects of treatment*. Doctoral dissertation, University of Pittsburgh, 1975. (University Microfilms No. 76-7348) **(181)**

O'Leary, M. R., Rohsenow, D. J., Schau, E. J., & Donovan, D. M. Defensive style and treatment outcome among men alcoholics. *Journal of Studies on Alcohol*, 1977, *38*, 1036–1040. **(182)**

Orford, J., Oppenheimer, E., & Edwards, G. Abstinence or control: The outcome for excessive drinkers two years after consultation. *Behaviour Research and Therapy*, 1976, *14*, 409–418. **(183)**

Ornstein, P. The ALCADD test as a predictor of post-hospital drinking behavior. *Psychological Reports*, 1978, *43*, 611–617. **(184)**

Pallone, N., & Tirman, R. Correlates of substance abuse remission in alcoholism rehabilitation: Effective treatment or symptom abandonment? *Offender Rehabilitation*, 1978, *3*(1), 7. **(185)**

Paredes, A., Gregory, D., Rundell, O. H., & Williams, H. L. Drinking behavior, remission, and relapse: The Rand Report revisited. *Alcoholism: Clinical and Experimental Research*, 1979, *3*, 3–10. **(186)**

Parker, M. W., Winstead, D. K., Willi, F. J. P., & Fisher, P. Patient autonomy in alcohol rehabilitation: II. Program evaluation. *International Journal of the Addictions*, 1979, *14*, 1177–1184. **(187)**

Pattison, E. M. Treatment of alcoholic families with nurse home visits. *Family Process*, 1965, *4*, 75–94.

Piorkowski, G., & Mann, E. T. Issues in treatment efficacy research with alcoholics. *Perceptual and Motor Skills*, 1975, *41*, 695–700. **(188)**

Pokorny, A. D., Miller, B. A., Kanas, T., & Valles, J. Effectiveness of extended aftercare in the treatment of alcoholism. *Quarterly Journal of Studies on Alcohol*, 1973, *34*, 435–443. **(189)**

Polich, J. M., Armor, D. J., & Braiker, H. B. Patterns of alcoholism over four years. *Journal of Studies on Alcohol*, 1980, *41*, 397–416. **(190)**

Polich, J. M., Armor, D. J., & Braiker, H. B. *The course of alcoholism four years after treatment*. New York: Wiley Interscience, 1981.

Pomerleau, O., & Adkins, O. *Outcome research on behavioral and traditional treatment for problem drinkers*. Philadelphia: University of Pennsylvania, 1977. (ERIC Document Reproduction Service No. ED 151-625) **(191)**

Popham, R. E., & Schmidt, W. Some factors affecting the likelihood of moderate drinking by treated alcoholics. *Journal of Studies on Alcohol*, 1976, *37*, 868–882. **(192)**

Rae, J. The influence of the wives on the treatment outcome of alcoholics: A follow-up study at two years. *British Journal of Psychiatry*, 1972, *120*, 601–613. **(193)**

Rapp, D. W. *Detection of observer bias in the written record*. Unpublished manuscript, University of Georgia, 1965. (Cited in Rosenthal, R. *Experimenter effects in behavioral research*. New York: Irvington, 1976.)

Ravensborg, M. R. Mood rating in early termination from an alcoholism unit. *Psychological Reports*, 1973, *32*, 1291–1294. **(194)**

Rhead, J. C., Soskin, R. A., Turek, I., Richards, W. A., Yensen, R., Kurland, A. A., & Ota, K. Y. Psychedelic drug (DPT)-assisted psychotherapy with alcoholics: A controlled study. *Journal of Psychedelic Drugs*, 1977, *9*(4), 287–300. **(195)**

Rios, J. P. *Ego structure as a prediction of rehabilitation of the male alcoholic.* Doctoral dissertation, New York University, 1979. (University Microfilms No. 80-10302) (**196**)

Robinson, J., & Cohen, L. Individual bias in psychological reports. *Journal of Clinical Psychology*, 1954, *10*, 333–336.

Rohan, W. P. Follow-up study of problem drinkers. *Diseases of the Nervous System*, 1972, *33*, 196–199. (**197**)

Roscow, J. C. *A study of selected factors affecting alcohol recidivism rates among active duty United States Air Force personnel.* Doctoral dissertation, Saint Louis University, 1977. (University Microfilms No. 78-14631) (**198**)

Rosenberg, H. S. *Differences in coping skills, life events and social support between relapsed and nonrelapsed alcohol abusers.* Doctoral dissertation, Indiana University, 1979. (University Microfilms No. 80-07997) (**199**)

Rosenthal, R. *Experimenter effects in behavioral research.* New York: Irvington, 1976.

Rubington, E. Halfway houses and treatment outcomes: A relationship between institutional atmosphere and therapeutic effectiveness. *Journal of Studies on Alcohol*, 1979, *40*, 419–427. (**200**)

Ruggels, W. L., Mothershead, A., Pyszka, R., Loebel, M., & Lotridge, J. *A follow-up study of clients at selected alcoholism treatment centers funded by NIAAA* (Supplemental Report). Menlo Park, Calif.: Stanford Research Institute, 1977. (**201**)

Savitz, S. A., & Kolodner, G. F. Day hospital treatment of alcoholism. *Current Psychiatric Therapies*, 1977, *17*, 257–263. (**202**)

Scalo, L. *The treatment of alcohol abusers: An evaluation study.* Doctoral dissertation, Indiana University, 1979. (University Microfilms No. 80-03853) (**203**)

Schaefer, H. H., Sobell, M. B., & Sobell, L. C. Twelve month follow-up of hospitalized alcoholics given self-confrontation experiences by videotape. *Behavior Therapy*, 1972, *3*, 283–285. (**204**)

Schlatter, E. K. E., & Lal, S. Treatment of alcoholism with Dent's oral apomorphine method. *Quarterly Journal of Studies on Alcohol*, 1972, *33*, 430–436. (**205**)

Schmitt, A. F., Jr. *A study of personality characteristics as predictors of treatment outcome of young and old alcoholic patients.* Doctoral dissertation, United States International University, 1976. (University Microfilms No. 76-19758) (**206**)

Schuckit, M. A., & Morrissey, E. R. Alcoholism in women: Some clinical and social perspectives with an emphasis on possible subtypes. In M. Greenblatt & M. A. Schuckit (Eds.), *Alcoholism problems in women and children.* New York: Grune & Stratton, 1976.

Schuckit, M. A., & Winokur, G. A short-term follow-up of women alcoholics. *Diseases of the Nervous System*, 1972, *33*, 672–678. (**207**)

Seelye, E. E. Relationship of socioeconomic status, psychiatric diagnosis and sex to outcome of alcoholism treatment. *Journal of Studies on Alcohol*, 1979, *40*, 57–62. (**208**)

Selzer, M. L. The Michigan Alcoholism Screening Test: The quest for a new diagnostic instrument. *American Journal of Psychiatry*, 1971, *127*(12), 89–94.

Shaw, S., Worner, T. M., Borysow, M. F., Schmitz, R. E., & Lieber, C. S. Detection of alcoholism relapse: Comparative diagnostic value of MCV, GGTP, and AANB. *Alcoholism: Clinical and Experimental Research*, 1979, *3*, 297–301. (**209**)

Shore, J. H., & Von Fumetti, B. Three alcohol programs for American Indians. *American Journal of Psychiatry*, 1972, *128*, 1450–1454. (**210**)

Sikic, B. I., Walker, R. D., & Peterson. D. R. An evaluation of a program for the treatment of alcoholism in Croatia. *International Journal of Social Psychiatry*, 1972, *18*, 171–182. (**211**)

Skoloda, T. E., Alterman, A. I., Cornelison, F. S., Jr., & Gottheil, E. Treatment outcome in a drinking-decisions program. *Journal of Studies on Alcohol*, 1975, *36*, 365–380. (**212**)

Skuja, A. T., Wood, D., & Bucky, S. F. Reported drinking among posttreatment alcohol abusers: A preliminary report. *American Journal of Drug and Alcohol Abuse*, 1976, *3*, 473–483. (**213**)

Smart, R. G. Employed alcoholics treated voluntarily and under constructive coercion: A follow-up study. *Quarterly Journal of Studies on Alcohol*, 1974, *35*, 196–209. **(214)**

Smart, R. G. A comparison of recidivism rates for alcoholic detox residents referred to treatment facilities. *Drug and Alcohol Dependence*, 1978, *3*, 218–220. (a) **(215)**

Smart, R. G. Characteristics of alcoholics who drink socially after treatment. *Alcoholism: Clinical and Experimental Research*, 1978, *2*, 49–52. (b) **(216)**

Smart, R. G. Do some alcoholics do better in some types of treatment than others? *Drug and Alcohol Dependence*, 1978, *3*, 65–75. (c) **(217)**

Smart, R. G. Female and male alcoholics in treatment: Characteristics at intake and recovery rates. *British Journal of Addiction*, 1979, *74*, 275–281. (a) **(218)**

Smart, R. G. Young alcoholics in treatment: Their characteristics and recovery rates at follow-up. *Alcoholism: Clinical and Experimental Research*, 1979, *3*, 19–23. (b) **(219)**

Smart, R. G., Finley, J., & Funston, R. The effectiveness of postdetoxication referrals: Effects on later detoxication admissions, drunkenness and criminality. *Drug and Alcohol Dependence*, 1977, *2*, 149–155. **(220)**

Smart, R. G., & Gray, G. Minimal, moderate and long-term treatment for alcoholism. *British Journal of Addiction*, 1978, *73*, 35–38. **(221)**

Sobell, L. C., & Sobell, M. B. Legitimizing alternatives to abstinence: Implications now and for the future. *Journal of Alcoholism*, 1975, *10*, 5–16. **(222)**

Sobell, M. B., & Sobell, L. C. Alcoholics treated by individualized behavior therapy: One year treatment outcome. *Behaviour Research and Therapy*, 1973, *11*, 599–618. (a) **(223)**

Sobell, M. B., & Sobell, L. C. *Evidence of controlled drinking by former alcoholics: A second year evaluation of individualized behavior therapy.* Paper presented at the 81st Annual Convention of the American Psychiatric Association, Montreal, Canada, 1973. (b) **(224)**

Sobell, M. B., & Sobell, L. C. Individualized behavior therapy for alcoholics. *Behavior Therapy*, 1973, *4*, 49–72. (c) **(225)**

Sobell, M. B., & Sobell, L. C. Second year treatment outcome of alcoholics treated by individualized behavior therapy: Results. *Behaviour Research and Therapy*, 1976, *14*, 195–215. **(226)**

Spencer, D. J. A short trial for fenfluramine in alcoholism. *Journal of Alcoholism*, 1972, *7*, 89–90. **(227)**

Stein, L. I., Newton, J. R., & Bowman, R. S. Duration of hospitalization for alcoholism. *Archives of General Psychiatry*, 1975, *32*, 247–252. **(228)**

Steinglass, P. An experimental treatment program for alcoholic couples. *Journal of Studies on Alcohol*, 1979, *40*, 159–182. (a) **(229)**

Steinglass, P. Family therapy with alcoholics: A review. In E. Kaufman & P. N. Kaufman (Eds.), *Family therapy of drug and alcohol abuse.* New York: Gardner Press, 1979. (b)

Stern, B. F. *The effect of an explicit treatment contract in an alcohol inpatient setting.* Doctoral dissertation, Boston College, 1974. (University Microfilms No. 74-21819) **(230)**

Stinson, D. J., Smith, W. G., Amidjaya, I., & Kaplan, J. M. Systems of care and treatment outcomes for alcoholic patients. *Archives of General Psychiatry*, 1979, *36*, 535–539. **(231)**

Thomas, D. A. *A study of selected factors on successfully and unsuccessfully treated alcoholic women.* Unpublished doctoral dissertation, Michigan State University, 1971.

Thornton, C. C., Gellens, H. K., Alterman, A. I., & Gottheil, E. Developmental level and prognosis in alcoholics. *Alcoholism: Clinical and Experimental Research*, 1979, *3*, 70–77. **(232)**

Thornton, C. C., Gottheil, E., Gellens, H. K., & Alterman, A. I. Voluntary versus involuntary abstinence in the treatment of alcoholics. *Journal of Studies on Alcohol*, 1977, *38*, 1740–1748. **(233)**

Thornton, C. C., Gottheil, E., Skoloda, T. E., & Alterman, A. I. Alcoholics' drinking decisions: Implications for treatment and outcome. In E. Gottheil, A. T. McLellan, K. Druley, &

A. Alterman (Eds.), *Addiction research and treatment: Converging trends (Proceedings of the First Annual Coatesville-Jefferson Conference on Addiction)*. New York: Pergamon, 1979. **(234)**

Tomsovic, M. "Binge" and continuous drinkers: Characteristics and treatment follow-up. *Quarterly Journal of Studies on Alcohol*, 1974, *35*, 558–564. **(235)**

Ude, G. R. *Locus of control as both a predictor and outcome measure of therapeutic success in an alcoholic population*. Doctoral dissertation, Emory University, 1977. (University Microfilms No. 77-32394) **(236)**

Uecker, A. E., & Boutilier, L. R. Alcohol education for alcoholics: Relation to attitude changes and posttreatment abstinence. *Journal of Studies on Alcohol*, 1976, *37*, 965–975. **(237)**

Van Dijk, W. K., & Van Dijk-Koffeman, A. A follow-up study of 211 treated male alcoholic addicts. *British Journal of Addiction*, 1973, *68*, 3–24. **(238)**

Vannicelli, M. Impact of aftercare in treatment of alcoholics: A cross-lagged panel analysis. *Journal of Studies on Alcohol*, 1978, *39*, 1875–1886. **(239)**

Vannicelli, M. Treatment contracts in an inpatient alcoholism treatment setting. *Journal of Studies on Alcohol*, 1979, *40*, 457–471. **(240)**

Vannicelli, M., Pfau, B., & Ryback, R. S. Data attrition in follow-up studies of alcoholics. *Journal of Studies on Alcohol*, 1976, *37*, 1325–1330. **(241)**

Vogler, R. E., Compton, J. V., & Weissbach, T. A. Integrated behavior change techniques for alcoholics. *Journal of Consulting and Clinical Psychology*, 1975, *43*, 233–243. **(242)**

Vogler, R. E., Weissbach, T. A., & Compton, J. V. Learning techniques for alcohol abuse. *Behaviour Research and Therapy*, 1977, *15*, 31–38. **(243)**

Wald, H. P. *An examination of the relationship between drinking status after treatment and the self evaluation of the alcoholic*. Doctoral dissertation, University of Pittsburgh, 1978. (University Microfilms No. 79-02801) **(244)**

Waters, W. E., Cochrane, A. L., & Collins, J. Evaluation of social therapy in chronic alcoholism. *British Journal of Preventive Social Medicine*, 1972, *26*, 57–58. **(245)**

Watson, C. G., Herder, J., & Passini, F. T. Alpha biofeedback therapy in alcoholics: An 18-month follow-up. *Journal of Clinical Psychology*, 1978, *34*, 765–769. **(246)**

Webb, N. L., Pratt, T. C., Linn, M. W., & Carmichael, J. S. Focus on the family as a factor in differential treatment outcome. *International Journal of the Addictions*, 1978, *13*, 783–795. **(247)**

Weisz, F., Casacchia, M., Cerbo, R., Meco, G., & Ortigoza, D. Alcoholism: Psychological and therapeutic problems. *Alcoholism*, 1978, *14*, 83–87. **(248)**

Welte, J., Hynes, G., Sokolow, L., & Lyons, J. *Alcoholism treatment effectiveness: An outcome study of New York State operated alcoholism rehabilitation units*. Albany, N.Y.: New York State Division of Alcoholism and Alcohol Abuse, 1979. **(249)**

Westfield, D. R. Two years' experience of group methods in the treatment of male alcoholics in a Scottish mental hospital. *British Journal of Addiction*, 1972, *67*, 267–276. **(250)**

Wiens, A. N., Montague, J. R., Manaugh, T. S., & English C. J. Pharmacological aversive counterconditioning to alcohol in a private hospital: One-year follow-up. *Journal of Studies on Alcohol*, 1976, *37*, 1320–1324. **(251)**

Willems, P. J. A., Letemendia, F. J. J., & Arroyave, F. A two year follow-up study comparing short with long stay inpatient treatment of alcoholics. *British Journal of Psychiatry*, 1973, *122*, 637–648. **(252)**

Williams, R. J. Social stability on admission and success of in-patient treatment for alcoholism. *Drug and Alcohol Dependence*, 1977, *2*, 81–90. **(253)**

Wilsnack, S. C. Alcohol abuse and alcoholism in women. In E. M. Pattison & E. Kaufman (Eds.), *Encyclopedic handbook of alcoholism*. New York: Gardner, 1982.

Wilson, A., Davidson, W. J., Blanchard, R., & White, J. Disulfiram implantation: A placebo-controlled trial with two-year follow-up. *Journal of Studies on Alcohol*, 1978, *39*, 809–819. **(254)**

Wilson, A., White, J., & Lange, D. E. Outcome evaluation of a hospital-based alcoholism treatment programme. *British Journal of Addiction*, 1978, *73*, 39–45. **(255)**

Wilson, L. G., & Shore, J. H. Evaluation of a regional Indian alcohol program. *American Journal of Psychiatry*, 1975, *132*, 255–258. **(256)**

Wooster, H. Basic research. *Science*, 1959, *130*, 126.

Yalom, I. D., Bloch, S., Bond, G., Zimmerman, E., & Qualls, B. Alcoholics in interactional group therapy. *Archives of General Psychiatry*, 1978, *35*, 419–425. **(257)**

Zimberg, S. Evaluation of alcoholism treatment in Harlem. *Quarterly Journal of Studies on Alcohol*, 1974, *35*, 550–557. **(258)**

Zimberg, S. Psychiatric office treatment of alcoholism. In S. Zimberg, J. Wallace, & S. Blume (Eds.), *Practical approaches to alcoholism psychotherapy*. New York: Plenum, 1978. **(259)**

14

Prevention of Alcohol Problems in Women

ROBERTA G. FERRENCE
Addiction Research Foundation
and Queen's University

All along the line, physically, mentally, morally, alcohol is a weakening and deadening force, and it is worth a great deal to save women and girls from its influence.—BEATRICE POTTER WEBB, *Health of Working Girls*, Chapter 10 (1917)

INTRODUCTION

The primary prevention of social as well as medical problems has received increasing attention during the past decade (Fielding, 1978; Klein & Goldston, 1977; Kristein, 1977; Lee & Franks, 1977; McPheeters, 1976). A number of researchers in the field of addictions have pointed to the advantages of primary prevention approaches over the more traditional method of treating casualties (Bacon, 1978; Blane, 1976; Gusfield, 1976; Room & Mosher, 1979/1980; Schmidt & Popham, 1978).

The problems associated with women and alcohol have also received considerable attention during the past 10 years, in part because of increased awareness of the lack of research on this topic (Homiller, 1980). While much has been written on characteristics of female alcoholics, patterns of use, and recommendations for treatment (Greenblatt & Schuckit, 1976; Kalant, 1980; National Institute on Alcohol Abuse and Alcoholism, 1980), literature on prevention strategies for women is just beginning to appear (Ferrence, 1983; Wilsnack, 1980, 1982). Nevertheless, several new women's programs are among the most innovative and well-designed in the field of addictions.

In this chapter, approaches to the prevention of alcohol problems in women are reviewed and assessed in terms of their general efficacy and their suitability for women. Additional strategies that are likely to be effective for women are also presented and evaluated.

414 TREATMENT AND PREVENTION OF ALCOHOL PROBLEMS

RATIONALE FOR SPECIAL APPROACHES
TO PREVENTION FOR WOMEN

The rationale for developing special approaches to prevention for women arises from sex differences in social and cultural roles as well as from differences in physiology. Women's drinking patterns differ considerably from those of men. On the average, women drink less often and in smaller quantities than men do (Clark & Midanik, 1982; Johnson, Armor, Polich, & Stambul, 1977). Their beverage preferences are distributed differently (Harris & Associates, 1975; Health and Welfare Canada, 1973), and they are less likely to drink in public places (Clark, 1977; Johnson et al., 1977). Norms that promote heavy drinking are rare for women, but fairly common among certain groups of men.

There are sex differences in the extent to which women and men are exposed to the hazards of excessive consumption. Aside from differences in actual consumption, women are less likely to drive after drinking, or to drive at those times when drinking is most common—late at night and on weekends (Smith, Wolynetz, & Wiggins, 1976). This applies to a range of vehicles including air and watercraft, heavy equipment, and snowmobiles. Women participate less in a number of other activities linked to alcohol problems. They are less likely than men to smoke, to own weapons, to be employed in hazardous occupations, and to engage in activities where coordination could be adversely affected by alcohol. Women's greater use of prescription psychoactive drugs reduces this disparity, however, because many drugs can potentiate the effects of alcohol (Noble, 1978).

Women's employment patterns and economic situations differ radically from those of men. Women are concentrated in lower-paying jobs and in clerical positions that are largely nonunionized. They are more likely to work part-time or intermittently, so that they often enjoy fewer medical and other benefits. They have fewer opportunities to drink on the job and less money to spend on alcohol during nonworking hours. Their purchasing habits, however, may increase their exposure to alcohol. For example, they regularly shop in supermarkets and grocery stores where sales of liquor are permitted in many jurisdictions.

Women's social patterns restrict them to the home more than men. They are less likely to own a car, or to be able to afford travel. Whether gainfully employed or not, they take major responsibility for child care, cooking, and other homemaking activities that restrict their mobility and reduce their free time. Many women live in suburban or rural areas that are isolated from public drinking facilities. Women are less likely than men to frequent places where liquor is served (Harris & Associates, 1975), and women's organizations are less likely than men's to include drinking as a regular feature of activities.

United States and Canada (Abelson, 1979; Johnson *et al.*, 1977; MacGregor, 1978, 1979). Rates are slightly lower for adolescent women. Rates for males are three to six times higher in adults and two to four times higher in youths. When sex differences in body weight and composition are controlled, sex ratios for heavy drinking are about three to one, men to women (Ferrence, 1980).

Heavy consumption of alcohol is a major risk factor for liver cirrhosis. In Canadian women, the annual rate of all cirrhosis mortality is about 17 per 100,000 population, aged 20 and over (Statistics Canada, 1981a). It is estimated that the annual death rate for alcohol-related cirrhosis in women is about 8 per 100,000 (Ferrence, 1980), approximately half of the total cirrhosis rate for women. The rate increases sharply with age because of the length of time required to develop alcoholic cirrhosis, and is highest among women aged 60 and over (Statistics Canada, 1981a).

Alcohol-related morbidity in women can be measured using hospital admission and discharge statistics. In 1978 in Canada, rates of discharge from nonpsychiatric hospitals were 34 per 100,000 for women with liver cirrhosis, 57 per 100,000 for alcoholism, and 7 per 100,000 for alcoholic psychosis (Statistics Canada, 1982). Total admission rates of women to psychiatric institutions in Canada in 1978 were 29 per 100,000 for alcoholism and 2 per 100,000 for alcoholic psychosis (Statistics Canada, 1981b).

Much higher rates of morbidity are reported in surveys of social and specialized medical agencies. For example, in 1975-76, the annual rate for women entering specialized alcohol and drug treatment agencies in Ontario was 190 per 100,000 women aged 25 and over (Reid, 1977). In another study, Ferrence, Rush, and Murdock (1980) estimate that about two-thirds of problem drinkers who seek help from social agencies go to general agencies, rather than those specifically geared to problem drinkers. They conclude that since women are somewhat underrepresented in alcohol-specific facilities, actual rates of female problem drinkers who seek help may be closer to 1000 per 100,000 women per annum. This includes women who seek help for problems other than those related to alcohol, but are identified as problem drinkers by agency staff.

A number of other conditions are associated with heavy drinking. Alcoholic women (and men) are at increased risk of death from certain types of cancer and heart disease (Schmidt & Popham, 1980; Hill, Chapter 5, this volume). Because these diseases are also associated with smoking, which is as prevalent among alcoholic women as men but less prevalent for women in the general population, female alcoholics are at much greater risk compared to other women than male alcoholics are compared to other men (Schmidt & Popham, 1980).

Women alcoholics experience even greater increased risk of accidental death than that attributable to disease. Accidents account for almost one-third of all deaths among alcoholic women, and these women experience levels of risk that are 10–50 times those of women their age in the general population. A substantial proportion of deaths among alcoholic women are related to the excessive use of drugs (Schmidt & Popham, 1980).

The proportion of pregnant women at risk of fetal damage is difficult to determine. A Canadian study of beverage alcohol consumption that included pregnant women (Health & Welfare Canada, 1973) indicates that women in this group drink only about half as much as women aged 20–39 in general (.23 drinks per day vs. .46 drinks per day). The proportion of women drinking at levels associated with increased risk of fetal damage was also lower for pregnant women. Among pregnant women, the percentages who drank 2 or more drinks of beer, wine, or spirits per day were .1%, .1%, and .3%, respectively. Although this study probably underreports consumption for all groups surveyed, almost identical consumption levels were reported by pregnant women in the Cleveland Alcohol-in-Pregnancy Study (Sokol, Miller, Debanne, Golden, Collins, Kaplan, & Martier, 1981). However, almost 8% of these women fell into the High volume/High maximum category of the Volume–Variability Index (Cahalan, Cisin, & Crossley, 1969). Although pregnant women form only a small portion of the female population at any particular time, most women become pregnant and therefore at risk at some point during their lives.

Drunkenness and Impaired Driving

Legal offenses provide a different measure of alcohol problems. The annual rate of public drunkenness in North American women is about 20 per 100,000 (Kelley, 1976; Statistics Canada, 1972). With increased use of detoxification facilities during the 1970s, it is difficult to assess the usefulness of these data since diversion to these facilities varies among communities.

Impaired driving among women has been largely ignored, probably because women represent only one-fifth of drivers on the road late at night when impairment is most common and most often recorded. Late-night roadside surveys in several countries indicate that about 2% of all women driving are legally impaired, with a blood alcohol concentration (BAC) of .10 or greater (Institute for Road Safety, 1977; Interministerial Committee, 1979; Smith et al., 1976; Wolfe, 1974). This compares to about 5% of men driving. Since women comprise only about 20% of drivers on the road at this time, legally impaired women represent about .4% of all drivers compared to about 4% for men. The sex ratio of impairment among those at risk (i.e., drivers) is similar to that for other alcohol-related problems—2.5 to 1 (Ferrence, 1980). If the proportion of women driving late at night increases, the number of legally impaired women at the wheel would rise considerably.

In a U.S. study (Wilsnack et al., 1984), 7% of women classified as lighter drinkers and 45% of heavier drinkers reported driving while high or drunk during the preceding 12 months. Although women are more conservative than men in their estimates of how much alcohol can safely be consumed before driving, 39% of women in a Vermont survey considered it safe to drive after drinking 3 or more beers (Damkot, Toussie, Akley, Geller, & Whitmore, 1977). Since women drink much less than men and less often on the average, their tolerance to alcohol is generally lower, so that small quantities of alcohol could produce impairment even at BACs that are well below the legal limit.

Determining the nature and extent of alcohol problems in women is a difficult task. Discussion of many areas, including social and economic problems, has been omitted in this chapter because information is lacking or inadequate. Even those data that have been presented may not reflect the true prevalence of various problems in the population. Indexes of problem drinking indicate that 1–21% of women in the general population experience adverse consequences of one type or another from the use of alcohol (Ferrence, 1980). Although these percentages are probably inflated because of the inclusion of very minor or transitory problems, they undoubtedly omit certain types of complications, such as physical and psychological damage, that are not recognized by the respondent.

RISK FACTORS FOR PROBLEM DRINKING

Women in certain social and demographic categories are at increased risk of heavy alcohol consumption and alcohol-related problems. As such they may be important target groups for primary or secondary prevention programs.

Employment

Regular drinking is positively associated with employment status among women. In a 1978–79 Canadian national survey, 22% of female professional and managerial employees and 19% of female white-collar employees drank 7 or more drinks per week, compared to 12% of female blue-collar workers and 11% of housewives (Health & Welfare Canada, 1981b). Among men, there is little variation by status of job, but regular drinking is less common among Canadian men who are unemployed or not in the labor force (Health & Welfare Canada, 1981b).

There are a number of explanations for the female pattern. Women in blue-collar jobs may more often be immigrants who are less likely to drink because of cultural constraints. Parker, Parker, Harford, and Brody (1978) suggest that status inconsistency contributes to more frequent drinking among those with high achieved status and low ascribed status. Women in high-status jobs would fall into this category. Finally, studies of the diffusion of new behaviors and practices indicate that the process occurs earlier among those who have higher social status, are less isolated, and have greater economic resources (Rogers & Shoemaker, 1971). This diffusion model predicts that increases in consumption would occur first among women in the highest socioeconomic status category. Thus, if there is a trend toward higher consumption in women, the present variation among women in different employment categories may be a temporary phenomenon that will decrease with time.

Johnson et al. (1977) report that middle- and upper-class, employed married women are at greater risk of developing alcohol problems than housewives. Based on a U.S. national survey, 8.8 % of married women in the labor force experienced problems with alcohol compared to 3.7% of married women who were not in the labor force and 4.3% of single working women. Employed married women were also more likely to drink heavily (13.2%) than housewives (7.8%) and single working women (9.2%).

Wilsnack et al. (1984) report somewhat different findings. Married women who worked outside the home also had slightly higher rates of problems than those who did not (10% vs. 7%), but 13% of never-married women reported two or more problems, as did 42% of women in quasi-marital partnership.

Women in the labor force are more likely to receive treatment for alcohol problems than housewives. Employment rates for alcoholic women patients in all socioeconomic groups are higher than for women in the general population of the United States (Schuckit & Morrissey, 1976).

It is tempting to speculate that factors such as role conflict or the adoption of male drinking patterns are responsible for the higher rates of alcohol problems among married women in the labor force. This is premature, however, because more detailed information on working and home conditions is required. Such an investigation has been carried out regarding the incidence of coronary heart disease (CHD) among female participants aged 45–65 in the Framingham Heart Study (Haynes & Feinleib, 1980). As with alcohol problems, the incidence of CHD was greater among married women in the labor force. When controls were introduced for number of children and nature of occupation, working women with three or more children who were engaged in clerical jobs experienced much greater risk of CHD than women in other white-collar or blue-collar jobs, or housewives, regardless of family size. (For each factor, the risk was approximately two-fold.) In this study, none of the usual risk factors for CHD, such as age, smoking habits, blood pressure, or cholesterol level, were found to vary by employment status or occupational status. Increased risk was associated with decreased job mobility, having a nonsupportive employer or supervisor, suppressed hostility, and being married to a blue-collar worker (Haynes & Feinleib, 1980).

These findings are relevant to the subject of women and alcohol for several reasons. Both heavy drinking and heart disease have been considered "male" conditions and may, therefore, share some of the same risk factors. The heavy consumption of alcohol is itself a risk factor for CHD. It is commonly believed that stress is a risk factor for both conditions. Contrary to the belief that social change and the resulting conflict that it presents for women is the source of the stress, these findings suggest that lack of autonomy, overwork, and the resulting unresolved frustrations are responsible. Finally, they provide an example of the kind of information that is needed regarding women and alcohol. Greater specification of risk factors would enable program planners to isolate smaller groups of working women who are at excessive risk for alcohol problems.

Metzner (1980) has carried out a pilot investigation of the relationship between women's roles, occupations, role conflict, social support, and drinking practices. Although results are tentative pending the replication of findings with a larger sample, lack of social support, rather than role conflict, appears to be associated with heavier drinking. Kinds of roles and number of roles were not related to amount of drinking or to consuming 14 or more drinks per week. Low social support was most prevalent among women in traditionally female, blue-collar jobs (e.g., operatives, such as garment workers) and those who combined the roles of employed worker and mother.

Metzner's work is an example of the kind of study that may clarify the relationship between sex roles and drinking. The leap from research findings to prevention strategies is difficult, because the direction of causality is not always established; however, the replication of findings using a variety of measures would certainly make this leap more defensible.

Both Haynes and Feinleib (1980) and Metzner (1980) suggest that lack of support of various kinds may be detrimental to women. If the findings for heart disease presented above apply to alcohol-related problems as well, strategies that encourage unionization of clerical workers, for example, and institute employee assistance programs for them would be appropriate. A variety of changes could increase social and economic support for employed mothers. These include improved tax deductions for child care, increased funding for day care, and more generous maternity and sick leave benefits, as found in many countries outside North America.

Age

Young women are more likely to report problems with alcohol than older women (Johnson et al., 1977; Wilsnack et al., 1984). Young women do not report higher levels of consumption (Health and Welfare Canada, 1973; Johnson et al., 1977), nor are they more likely to be classified as heavy drinkers (Cahalan et al., 1969; Clark & Midanik, 1982). Their higher rates of problems appear to result from patterns of drinking that are more likely to involve high-maximum consumption (5 or more drinks per occasion), but not high volume consumption (1.5 or more drinks per day on the average) (Cahalan et al., 1969; Harford & Gerstel, 1981; Wilsnack et al., 1984). This style of drinking is more likely to produce intoxication and is associated with alcohol-related problems that are acute rather than chronic. It is probably related to the life style of young people, which involves a greater concentration of social activity on weekends, more drinking in licensed premises (Clark, 1977), and a greater tolerance for heavy drinking and intoxication.

Longitudinal studies in the United States indicate that the prevalence of alcohol problems in women decreases with age, and that youthful drinking patterns are not highly predictive of adult patterns (see Robins & Smith, 1980). Nevertheless, problems such as impaired driving and intoxication that are associated with acute damage are appropriate targets for prevention programs.

Marital Status

Divorced and separated women also experience increased risk of alcohol problems. This association applies to men as well, and characterizes a range of social, psychological, and physical problems in addition to alcohol use. Johnson et al. (1977) reported that 32% of divorced and separated women drinkers were problem drinkers. Rates of problem drinking were considerably lower among single female drinkers (16%), married female drinkers (10%), and widowed female drinkers (3%). More recent data (Wilsnack et al., 1984) support these findings.

Other Risk Factors

Gomberg (1980) has discussed a number of risk factors associated with alcohol problems in women that could usefully be applied to the development of primary and secondary prevention programs. Research on genetic and physiological factors is just beginning, but there is potential for identifying individuals at high risk. Clearly, pregnant and potentially pregnant women are a high risk category, but this group has already received considerable attention from program planners. Depression and other psychiatric conditions may be additional risk factors for drinking problems (Schuckit & Morrissey, 1976). Certain women appear to be more psychologically vulnerable to such conditions, but for drinking problems to occur, this must be coupled with environmental factors that expose women to alcohol and present drinking as an appropriate way of coping. In addition, depression may result from factors that themselves lead to heavy drinking, such as having an alcoholic parent or spouse.

Until recently, Native American women in some communities and black women who were not abstainers experienced a higher than average rate of many alcohol-related problems, as did women in lower income groups, although rates of heavy drinking were not necessarily higher among these women (Wechsler, 1980). These higher rates of problems may have been related to a lack of social supports and other resources, rather than excessive consumption. More recent evidence suggest that black–white and socio-economic differences in rates of many drinking problems in women have largely disappeared (Wilsnack *et al.*, 1984).

Aase (1981) suggests that some groups of Native American women may experience higher risk of fetal alcohol syndrome (FAS) in their offspring, even though they are more likely than white women to abstain from alcohol. Demographic factors and differences in drinking patterns probably increase the number of pregnancy-years Native American women are exposed to alcohol, even though their consumption of alcohol may be lower than average.

CURRENT APPROACHES TO PREVENTION

Specific programs designed to prevent alcohol problems in women were virtually nonexistent until recently. A number of programs have been developed in the past 5 years. Some are still in progress, while others have been implemented but lack adequate criteria for evaluation. In previous years, women were often included in a larger target group, particularly in mass media programs. Materials were not developed specifically for women, and attempts to assess the impact on women as a group were rarely made, if in fact any evaluation was carried out at all.

Until recently, prevention programming was based largely on a sociocultural or socialization model of drinking behavior (Whitehead, 1975). According to this model, drinking problems could be prevented by instilling appropriate attitudes toward drinking in young people and teaching adults to drink responsibly. It was believed that this could be accomplished by integrating the use of alcohol into daily activities and exposing children to alcohol in an appropriate context (Wilkinson, 1970). Accordingly, prevention programs tried to instill positive attitudes toward moderate social drinking, and emphasized its benefits. Target groups were usually very broad, and the types of problems to be prevented were very general. Finally, prevention programs usually employed a single method or approach.

Current programming efforts differ from those discussed above in several important ways. Target groups tend to be more specific, restricted by age, sex, and employment status or occupation. Some programs try to minimize consumption as well as problems. Others combine various methods, such as mass media, community development, and personal approaches, because there is evidence that such combinations are more effective than simple mass media programs (Maccoby & Farquhar, 1975). Programs tend to be oriented toward specific problems, such as FAS, or life crises that may trigger problem drinking. Some programs attempt to reach their targets directly using education and information, whereas others focus on "gate-keepers" or other community resources to reach their target groups indirectly.

The imperatives of tight money and the increasing emphasis on cost–benefit accountability have led to the incorporation of evaluation components in many programs. The growing recognition that changes in attitudes and knowledge are not necessarily accompanied by corresponding changes in behavior has led to the inclusion of specific behavioral measures of outcome. The addition of control or comparison groups in some projects has substantially improved the quality of the evaluation.

General Prevention Programs for Women

CALIFORNIA PREVENTION DEMONSTRATION PROJECT

This 3-year demonstration project included both mass media and community organization and development components (Wallack & Barrows, 1981). Two experimental sites were chosen in the San Francisco Bay area. One was exposed to both components and the other only to the mass media segment. A control community received no intervention. Cross-sectional surveys of the general population were carried out before, during, and after the inter- vention. Target groups included women aged 25–40 and teenagers and their parents. The general theme of the project was the message "Winners quit while they're ahead" (later changed to "Winners quit drinking while they're ahead"), which emphasized the importance of ceasing to drink before intoxi- cation or impairment develops. Despite recorded increases in recognition, recall, and comprehension of the campaign's messages, and to some extent increased general knowledge about alcohol, no significant changes were found in drinking attitudes or behavior. A small proportion of respondents (9–15%) reported that as a result of the campaign, they drank less or might do so in the future. The lack of any detectable decrease in consumption for the total sample suggests that the reported decrease was either very slight or offset by increases among other respondents.

This project's lack of success in producing behavior change appears to be due largely to its failure to provide a clear prevention message (many viewers believed they had seen a pro-drinking commercial) and to gear this message to the actual drinking habits of the community. Since the majority of adults in North America drink infrequently or not at all, messages aimed at persons who drink to impairment apply to only a small portion of the population. The results of this campaign were not reported separately for women, but since they drink even less than men, it seems unlikely that many female viewers would find the messages relevant to their own drinking patterns. The project evaluators also expressed concern that interference by the alcohol beverage industry weakened the campaign considerably. For example, the broadcast campaign was postponed by the Governor of California and subsequently modified as a result of pressure from the wine industry and certain state legislators (Wallack & Barrows, 1981).

NATIONAL INSTITUTE ON ALCOHOL ABUSE AND ALCOHOLISM (NIAAA)
PUBLIC EDUCATION CAMPAIGN

This large-scale project focuses on clearly identified target groups and uses messages that are geared specifically to those groups (NIAAA, 1981a). There are three overall objectives: to increase public awareness of alcohol problems, to modify attitudes toward the use of alcohol, and to reduce alcohol-related problems by motivating changes in behavior. Messages about FAS are geared to women of child-bearing age and involve direct public service announcements as well as communication with appropriate groups of physicians. Messages about alcohol problems in women are aimed at women who work outside the home. They suggest that heavy or inappropriate use of alcohol can result in a variety of problems. Young people are the target group for information about alternatives that may reduce drinking and driving problems associated with excessive or inappropriate drinking. Messages are also aimed at the general public, which forms the context within which drinking behavior is developed and maintained.

Evaluation of the campaign is comprehensive and involves both process and outcome measures. Evaluation data include surveys of the target audiences and interviews with key observers, such as physicians and counselors, who treat women and youth. We hope that the results will be reported separately for men and women. In addition, data on social indicators, such as the incidence of birth defects and self-referrals of women for treatment, are being collected.

The NIAAA campaign is important for at least two reasons. First, it probably provides a good test of the efficacy of public health campaigns relating to alcohol use. Although this depends to some extent on the messages used, the focus on specific alcohol-related problems will tend to reduce the possibility of misinterpretation by the audience. Whereas previous campaigns have encouraged moderation, a vague term at best, efforts to prevent fetal damage will necessarily stress minimization of drinking or abstinence. Second, the NIAAA campaign should provide information on the kinds of approaches that are best suited to specific target groups, including women of child-bearing age, employed women, and demographic subgroups within these categories.

AWARE PROGRAM

The AWARE public education project was carried out in Saskatchewan, Canada, between 1974 and 1977. Although it was not specifically directed at women, results of the evaluation are reported by sex (Whitehead, 1976, 1978).

A mass media campaign conveyed messages that identified alcohol as a drug, and emphasized moderation in drinking. Survey data collected from a panel of urban and rural subjects before and after the campaign indicate that, in general, women's attitudes toward drinking are more conservative than those of men. Women were initially less tolerant of heavy drinking and less sympathetic toward increasing the number of outlets for the sale of alcoholic beverages. Urban women were more likely than urban men to favor increases in the price of alcohol if it could be shown to produce a decrease in problem drinking, and were more likely to express support for an increase in the legal purchasing age for alcohol (Whitehead, 1976).

These findings suggest that programs geared toward women should take into account the fact that they already drink less than men, are more intolerant of heavy consumption of alcohol, and are more likely to support social control measures that might be implemented to reduce consumption.

Alcohol and Reproduction

The pregnant woman has become a popular target for alcohol problem prevention efforts, for a number of reasons. The problem of alcohol and the fetus is more clear-cut than others. It is more easily viewed as a public rather than an individual health problem, because it is associated with a range of levels of drinking. Its attenuation lies in adopting a behavior—temporary abstinence—that is not greatly at variance with social values, and it cannot be classified as a "victimless crime" as can some other alcohol-related behaviors, such as public drunkenness. Finally, it reflects the trend in our society to direct social programs at those groups that enjoy the least social and economic power—children, women, the poor, minorities, the elderly, and the disabled—and that are believed to experience higher rates of most social and medical problems (cf. Room, 1981).

A number of new programs are geared specifically to the prevention of problems associated with drinking during pregnancy. The evidence that heavy drinking entails substantial risk of fetal damage, and that moderate drinking may also be associated with elevated risk (Little, 1981; Little & Ervin, Chapter 6, this volume; Rosett, 1980) has provided the impetus for at least six programs aimed at women of reproductive age. Four of these are demonstration projects funded by the NIAAA. A precursor of these was a secondary prevention program carried out between 1974 and 1979 at the prenatal clinic of Boston City Hospital (Rosett, Ouellette, Weiner, & Owens, 1977; Rosett, Weiner, & Edelin, 1981). Pregnant women who reported moderate or heavy consumption of alcohol were informed of risks to the fetus. Heavy drinkers were referred to a therapeutic program. Of the more than 1700 women interviewed, about 10% reported heavy drinking. About one-quarter were counseled three or more times. Of these, more than half abstained or reduced their consumption of alcohol before the third trimester of their pregnancies.

The California FAS project is a 3-year project funded in 1978 by NIAAA (NIAAA, 1981b) with a target population of 1.8 million women. There are three components: (1) a community organization project using existing structures to reach two groups of women—high school students and adult women of reproductive age; (2) a medical education project aimed at physicians; and (3) a mass media campaign. The evaluation, an interrupted time-series design, measures increases in knowledge about FAS, changes in beliefs about FAS, decreases in intent to drink during pregnancy, and actual changes in drinking behavior while pregnant. Preliminary results indicate that general knowledge of FAS is high, but there are misconceptions about specific aspects of the problem (Baxter, 1981). Data on behavioral changes are not yet available.

UNIVERSITY OF WASHINGTON PREGNANCY AND HEALTH PROGRAM

The University of Washington Project, also funded by NIAAA in 1978, combined a mass media campaign aimed at the general public in King County, Washington, telephone messages and distribution of brochures to populations of women who were pregnant or potentially pregnant, counseling sessions for pregnant women, and a training program on drinking and pregnancy for appropriate professionals (Little & Ervin, Chapter 6 in this volume; Little, Streissguth, & Guzinski, 1980). Referral services were also provided for pregnant women and mothers with alcohol problems.

Midway through the program, an estimate of program effectiveness was made. Effects of various types of contact on drinking behavior were measured for three groups of women—those who received a brochure and the screening questionnaire, those who were also counseled and had no apparent drinking problem, and those who were counseled and whose drinking was considered to pose a risk of fetal damage (Young, Sanders, Sinclair, Altman, Nordin, Herman, & McIntyre, 1981). Preliminary findings indicate that there was a significant decrease in drinking during pregnancy only among the two groups of women who were counseled, and that increases in drinking after delivery were less pronounced for the women who were counseled than for the group that received the less intensive contact. The training program for professionals also produced positive effects. There were substantial increases over a 2-year period in the proportion of obstetricians who asked patients about current alcohol use and who recommended abstinence or a decrease in drinking during pregnancy (Little, Streissguth, Guzinski, Grathwohl, Blum-hagen, & McIntyre, 1983). A more definitive evaluation of the Pregnancy and Health Program is currently in progress.

NATIONAL COUNCIL ON ALCOHOLISM: GREATER DETROIT AREA
FETAL ALCOHOL SYNDROME PREVENTION PROGRAM

The third NIAAA-funded FAS program involves secondary prevention aimed at reducing the incidence of FAS in Wayne County, Michigan (National Council on Alcoholism, n.d.). The objective of this project is to increase the identification and referral of pregnant women whose drinking puts their unborn children at risk of FAS, by training service providers to perform this function. The program includes training sessions, a seminar, and the circulation of information to the service community. Evaluation involves measuring the effectiveness of presentations, determining the extent to which information is passed on to clients, and establishing what proportion of treatment referrals were made by service providers reached by the program.

CLEVELAND PROSPECTIVE ALCOHOL-IN-PREGNANCY STUDY

In the Cleveland Project, which began in 1979, alcohol use during pregnancy is related to neonatal outcome (Sokol et al., 1981). One goal of the study is to evaluate the effect of abstinence-oriented therapy on fetal outcome. Pregnant women who register for prenatal care are screened for alcohol problems with the Michigan Alcoholism Screening Test (MAST) and a detailed 14-day history of alcohol consumption. Women who are identified as problem drinkers are advised to decrease or eliminate their drinking in order to reduce health risks to their infants, and are referred for abstinence-oriented therapy.

Preliminary results indicate that women with positive MAST scores increased their rate of reported abstinence from 34% to 63% during the course of their pregnancies. Abstinence among women whose MAST scores fell in the nonalcoholic range also increased from 76% to 81%, which was not statistically significant (Sokol et al., 1981). In addition, neonatal outcome will be used to assess the impact of the intervention.

NEW YORK STATE FETAL ALCOHOL SYNDROME PREVENTION PROGRAM

The New York State program combines a public information campaign with a professional education program for physicians (Blume, 1981). A test, which can be self-administered by pregnant women in a physician's waiting room, is included. No formal evaluation of this ongoing program is planned, but organizers have noticed a substantial increase in requests from physicians for information (Burris, 1983). Two other State programs that focus on drinking-related problems, including FAS, involve the training of minority group leaders. Results of the evaluation will be available in 1984.

PREGNANT PAUSE CAMPAIGN

The Division of Drug and Alcohol Services of the New South Wales Health Commission in Australia began a program in 1980 to reduce the hazardous use of alcohol, tobacco, and drugs during pregnancy (Healy, 1980). The project is funded by the Commonwealth Government through the National Drug Education Program. A report and recommendations are planned. The components include a mass media campaign aimed at the general public, a community education campaign, a professional training program for all health care workers involved in prenatal and related areas of care, and the provision of support services such as information, referral, and therapy for pregnant women who wish to reduce their use of alcohol and other drugs. In addition, early prenatal classes that include drug-related information are provided. Evaluation involves a pretest–posttest control group design and includes measures of recall, attitudes, and drinking behavior.

The programs outlined above encourage considerable optimism for the future of primary prevention of FAS. Three of the programs incorporate community development components that reinforce the messages conveyed by the mass media. All include some form of outcome evaluation, and three projects employ quasi-experimental or experimental designs (see Campbell & Stanley, 1963). Results of two studies (Sokol et al., 1981; Young et al., 1981) indicate that it is possible to achieve a significant reduction in drinking among pregnant women who drink heavily.

Of particular interest is the trend away from the disease approach to a public health approach (see Beauchamp, 1980). Integral to this is a shift from an emphasis on individual failings to the promotion of community responsibility for health problems. The Australian project clearly demonstrates this emphasis (Healy, 1980). In an effort to avoid "victim-blaming," most aspects of the campaign are designed to increase knowledge and promote shared responsibility among the family members, friends, and professionals who constitute the pregnant woman's social support system. The community is the focus of prevention, and the campaign attempts to "promote the development of general community and professional beliefs and practices that are conducive to reducing unwise use of psychotropic drugs—including alcohol and tobacco—during pregnancy" (Healy, 1980, p. 211).

General Education Programs

Two education programs, one in Canada and one in the United States, have been developed for use by small groups of women in the general population.

"IT'S JUST YOUR NERVES": A RESOURCE ON WOMEN'S
USE OF MINOR TRANQUILIZERS AND ALCOHOL

This Canadian primary prevention program includes alcohol and drug use as part of a more general focus on women's mental health. The Health Promotion Directorate of Health and Welfare Canada has recently produced a Resource Kit (Health and Welfare Canada, 1981a), consisting of a guidebook, flipchart, and film, which can serve as a basis for discussion among small groups of women. More than 800 Kits, available in both English and

French, are being distributed across Canada. The Directorate trains community facilitators, who in turn implement the program locally, or train other women in the community to do this.

The program was conceived as an educational tool appropriate for a range of users, including those already addicted to drugs and alcohol. The Kit serves as a discussion tool to stimulate the sharing of experiences with drugs and alcohol and the definition of alternatives. The objectives of the program are to increase knowledge and change attitudes related to women's use of alcohol and drugs. The program has been field tested, and according to the organizers, the response was very positive. Evaluation will involve process variables, such as the number and type of groups held and responses of participants to the program.

"REFLECTIONS IN A GLASS"

"Reflections in a Glass" was designed by the National Center for Alcohol Education for adult women who have not been identified as problem drinkers (NIAAA, 1981b). The course is more structured than the Canadian program, and involves eight sessions that cover a range of topics, such as effects of alcohol on the body, drinking and driving, the dangers of combining alcohol with drug use, and the history of women and alcohol. Course materials are designed to be used by a lay facilitator, and include a handbook, cards, visuals, handouts, take-home materials, and films. The objective of the program is to help women make decisions about drinking that will result in a minimization of alcohol-related problems. Beyond initial field testing, no formal evaluation of this program is planned.

These general education programs have the potential to reach large numbers of women, personally, and at low cost. They may also result in benefits, such as increased social integration of group members, that are not specified as objectives. Education programs have not been particularly successful in the past (Schaps, Churgin, Palley, Takata, & Cohen, 1980; Staulcup, Kenward, & Frigo, 1979). However, new strategies that combine affective and peer-oriented techniques with the more traditional information approach may be more likely to provide successful outcomes (Schaps et al., 1980). The "It's Just Your Nerves" and "Reflections in a Glass" programs are clearly of this newer type, but assessing their efficacy will be difficult because the evaluation components are minimal.

Community Programs

NEIGHBORHOOD COUNSELORS PROGRAM

The Neighborhood Counselors Program was initiated in 1977 in Bloomington, Indiana, as a primary prevention program for housewives (Engs & Wilsnack, n.d.; NIAAA, 1981b). Women in the community with natural helping skills were identified and trained to deal with a range of problems that are associated with alcohol. These neighborhood counselors were not expected to function as professional therapists, but as community helpers who could identify problems, help to solve them, and make referrals when appropriate.

Evaluation included measures of the number of persons counseled and referred as well as a pretest–posttest evaluation of counselors' skills. A modest improvement in skills was noted after training.

BREAKTHROUGH

Breakthrough is a primary prevention project aimed at recently divorced, separated, or widowed women. The project, funded by NIAAA in 1980, is being carried out in Ventura County by the California Women's Commission on Alcoholism (California Women's Commission on Alcoholism, 1981). One objective is to determine which of five outreach strategies was most effective in involving members of the target population: generation of referrals from individual helping professionals; generation of referrals from human service agencies; publicity and public speaking; "special events"; and word-of-mouth referrals. The differential appeal of the five strategies to women from different ethnic and socioeconomic backgrounds will be determined. The program itself consists of two courses, one in stress management, the other in life and career planning. These two prevention strategies were chosen because a woman in the process of divorce, separation, or widowhood is generally going through a period of high stress and conflict and also is concerned about planning for her future, which may involve new career decisions. It is assumed that such strategies can increase self-esteem and self-efficacy and decrease dependence on alcohol as a method of coping with stress or feelings of inadequacy.

A sophisticated design for evaluation incorporates both process and outcome variables. The outcome evaluation assesses both the five outreach activities and the two prevention strategies. During the second half of the project, the impact of the two prevention strategies will be tested, using random assignment to no treatment, or to stress management and life and career planning groups. Programs lasting 6 weeks and 12 weeks, for both prevention strategies, will be compared.

ALCOHOLISM CENTER FOR WOMEN PREVENTION PROGRAM

The Alcoholism Center for Women in Los Angeles uses a community-based approach to identify and deliver prevention activities to three groups of adult women at high risk of developing alcoholism: lesbians, incest and battering victims, and adult daughters of alcoholics (Taylor, 1982). Gatekeepers to women's groups, programs for compulsive behavior or relationship problems, lesbian and gay groups, rape counseling and self-defense organizations, and other community-based programs serving women are identified and educated regarding the incidence of alcohol and other drug abuse among their constituents. In order to combat denial and provide group identification for the women, agencies are encouraged to develop speakers' bureaus, which train members of these populations to speak up about themselves and their lives. On the individual level, such activities also build self-esteem and improve assertiveness skills. A variety of other techniques are supported, including workshops for clients on relationships, building a positive support system, conflict resolution and coping skills, and training for professionals on specific dynamics operative in each subpopulation.

The evaluation uses a pretest–posttest design to measure change in knowledge, attitudes, and practices relating to alcohol use and abuse. Positive changes have been reported in knowledge about alcohol use and abuse, attitudes toward personal power, and willingness to seek help. In addition, gatekeepers reported positive change in participants' behavior, such as increased entry into self-help or therapy groups, due to the gatekeepers' intervention.

PROJECT ALERT

Project Alert is an alcohol and drug prevention program for the elderly, the majority of whom are women, that was established in Montgomery County, Pennsylvania, in 1978 (NIAAA, 1981b). A preliminary survey was carried out to determine types of problems encountered by elderly persons and ways of seeking help. On the basis of these data, program goals were delineated. These included helping the elderly to overcome feelings of insecurity, providing health education, and encouraging the elderly to monitor their own health care. With the project staff acting as facilitators, a support group of 20–30 elderly women and men developed and became involved in a range of advocacy and other activities. No formal evaluation was conducted, but staff members believe that positive changes have occurred.

SPECTRUM: ALCOHOL PROBLEM PREVENTION PROJECTS FOR WOMEN BY WOMEN

Spectrum is a manual developed by NIAAA for use by women's organizations in planning and organizing community prevention projects (NIAAA, 1981b). The manual provides information on women and alcohol as well as strategies for developing and evaluating programs. Resources and materials are also included.

Spectrum provides a useful guide for any women's group interested in initiating some sort of prevention activity. Its value lies in the identification of strategies for prevention and in the realistic assessment of the requirements for programming and evaluation. Spectrum emphasizes the advantages of employing networks of women or organizations in developing programs and suggests approaches, such as advocacy, that are appropriate for lay persons and that may be highly effective without incurring great costs.

Some of the suggestions for program content conform to the sociocultural model of drinking behavior, which is no longer considered the most appropriate basis for prevention activities by many researchers in the field (e.g., Beauchamp, 1980; Frankel & Whitehead, 1981). These include the notions that alcohol is not intrinsically good or bad, that safe drinking styles can be acquired through education, and that the decision to drink is solely a personal one that entails individual responsibility.

The community programs discussed in this section are interesting and innovative, and in most cases are conducted at low cost because they utilize community resources. With the exception of Breakthrough, none of the community programs has incorporated any adequate method of assessing outcome. Evaluation components would certainly add to the cost of these programs, but they would provide the basis for deciding whether or not such programs are effective enough to be disseminated to other communities. With increasing budget constraints, the ability to support claims of program effectiveness has become crucial.

ADDITIONAL STRATEGIES AND CONSIDERATIONS

Targets of Prevention

ALCOHOL PROBLEMS AND PER CAPITA CONSUMPTION

To date, most primary prevention programs aimed at reducing alcohol-related problems in women have attempted to reduce intoxication and other problems associated with heavy drinking, and have employed educational and community-development strategies to change individual behavior. Some experts in the field of addictions have suggested that current prevention efforts are too broad and unfocused to be effective. Edwards (1980) recommends that social scientists "address themselves more modestly to more segmented and delineated problems, and . . . get close to other people's realities" (p. 177). In a similar vein, Room (1974) says that "we need to disaggregate 'alcoholism' and talk about the prevention of the specific kinds of problems which are included under that label" (p. 12).

To some extent, current programs for women have focused on specific alcohol-related problems (e.g., FAS) and these programs may be the most likely to result in positive outcomes. However, additional factors need to be considered. The most serious defect in programming is the failure to recognize that the rate of heavy drinking and associated problems in any society is a function of average consumption (Schmidt & Popham, 1978). Efforts to reduce problems without changing drinking norms and behavior in the general population can succeed only if changes are made in other behaviors, for example, reducing impaired driving by reducing all driving. Changes of this type, however, tend to be very difficult to implement. In addition to addressing specific alcohol-related problems, therefore, future programs should also attempt to reduce per capita consumption of alcohol within the total population of women.

This can be accomplished in various ways. Measures aimed at the total population—for example, pricing and taxation policies—are often avoided because they are politically unpopular. There is evidence, however, that a majority of the population would favor such controls, and that a larger proportion of women than men would support them (Whitehead, 1978).

Increased availability of alcoholic beverages in places frequented by women probably promotes greater consumption among women. Communities that do not already permit the sale of alcohol in supermarkets, drug stores, and wine boutiques might prevent increased consumption in women by resisting these changes. Communities that already allow such sales might consider rescinding their regulations.

Another social control measure, increased restrictions on advertising of alcoholic beverages, might have a greater effect on women's drinking than men's. The introduction of new beverages is heavily dependent on massive advertising campaigns directed at prospective markets. In recent years, a number of new light alcoholic drinks have been developed primarily for female drinkers (e.g., "Wine, Spring Water . . . ," 1982). One brewery official has lamented that stricter advertising regulations in Canada make it more difficult to promote new products such as light beer (Hunter, 1982). Increasing these restrictions further might seriously hamper the introduction of products aimed at women and young people, including those who are not yet drinkers.

TARGET GROUPS

For many alcohol problems it is most efficient to direct prevention programs at specific target groups, generally those at risk, or at greatest risk, of experiencing problems. Focusing on a smaller, homogeneous group can be advantageous because the message can be more specific and can include role models that more closely resemble members of the group, and because specific modes of entry to the group (e.g., specialized physicians) may exist that are not appropriate for a diffuse population.

Research to date has not provided program planners with the information needed to make the best decisions about strategies for prevention among specific groups of women. We can, however, apply some general principles that have been effective in other health and social problem areas. Problems associated with acute intoxication among young women, for example, could be addressed as follows: If all jurisdictions were to raise the drinking age to 21 years, as has already been done in some areas, we could expect a decrease in levels of consumption and in alcohol-related collisions among young people under 21 (Wagenaar, 1981). Moreover, social control measures such as this probably have a greater impact on women than men, because women are less likely to break the law.

Higher rates of problem drinking among young single women and divorced and separated women are probably associated with a higher level of social activity, particularly in public places where alcohol is usually served. The predominance of facilities that encourage drinking is not entirely a result of consumer demand; high economic rewards for the sale of alcohol, and the liberalization of drinking legislation, have contributed greatly to the increasing dominance of licensed premises. A reversal of this trend could provide alternative settings for social activity, such as the coffee houses that were popular before the drinking age was lowered. Specific tactics would include the curtailment of drinking at sports complexes, theaters, and other places that are not clearly drinking establishments, and the introduction of measures that would reduce the economic dependence of proprietors on the sale of alcoholic beverages.

Another group at high risk consists of women who are depressed. Such women are particularly prone to cross-addiction because, in addition to their increased risk of alcohol problems, they are very likely to use prescription psychoactive drugs. A number of measures (e.g., physician education, restrictions on prescription refills, price increases, and reduced drug promotion) could be applied to control the use of these drugs, with the potential for a significant decrease among women in cross-addiction, drug overdose while drinking, and impaired driving (Ferrence, 1978).

Confusion may arise regarding the advisability of focusing on certain high-risk groups. Some categories of women experience excessively high rates of alcohol problems, but their actual numbers represent such a small fraction of the general population that prevention programs aimed solely at these groups may not be cost-effective. Analysis of the costs and benefits of using particular strategies with particular target groups can be used to evaluate proposed programs.

For some alcohol problems, it is possible that women should not be treated as a special target group, separate from men. For example, the prevention of impaired driving in women is probably best achieved within the context of programs aimed at the general driving population. However, information about the risk of impairment at low BACs should be directed at women and other groups, such as the young and the elderly, who are likely to experience increased risk of impairment and accidents due to lower body weight, less driving experience, and a lower tolerance for alcohol (Hurst, 1974). In addition, gender differences should be noted in relation to BAC and legal definitions of intoxication. A lean, 150 lb. male would probably require 3–4 drinks within a short period of time to become legally impaired in Canada (BAC $\geq$ .08), whereas a 120 lb. woman, who is likely to have a higher proportion of body fat and less body fluid (Mello, 1980), could reach this limit with only 2–3 drinks (Addiction Research Foundation, 1978).

Prevention Constituencies and Advocacy

Wallack and Barrows (1981) point out the need for a "natural constituency" with a vested interest in decreasing alcohol-related problems. Temperance groups and women's groups were instrumental in bringing about a substantial reduction in the consumption of alcohol before prohibition legislation was enacted. In part, these earlier efforts were effective because they recognized the major role that alcohol plays in the development of alcohol-related problems and because they assumed that everyone who drank was, to some extent, a potential problem drinker. During the past half century, the insistence that the cause of problem drinking is located in problem drinkers themselves has led to the virtual abandonment of primary prevention activities until very recently.

Today, drinking as a moral issue has largely been replaced by health concerns about the effects of alcohol. However, the problems of interest have always been basically social and economic, although the language has changed. The natural constituency for prevention still consists largely of those groups in society that have a major concern with health and social issues—women, the clergy, health practitioners, educators, and politicians. Because most of these groups are less effective politically than business and labor, the successful implementation of prevention policies would require the development of an effective lobby concerned with alcohol problems. There are already a number of women's organizations that have successfully advocated changes in the legal, economic, and social position of women. These organizations, alone or acting in concert with other interested groups, could provide the "natural constituency" for prevention that has been lacking. The support of organizations with a vested interest in decreasing alcohol-related problems could also be sought. These include government and medical agencies and insurance companies.

Objectives of advocacy efforts should be fairly specific and could include the following: the prevention of liquor sales in various locations; increased taxation of alcohol; a reduction in the number of drinking episodes portrayed in the media; and increased restrictions on advertising of alcoholic beverages. Women might specifically advocate reducing the extent to which female drinkers are portrayed in advertisements, and discouraging the promotion of the use of wine with meals and in cooking. Room (1980) suggests that women attempt to change current "business-oriented drinking customs," such as tax deductions for client entertainment, that would promote drinking among women who enter business careers. Rather than warning women that they risk increased health problems by entering traditionally male occupational and social settings, prevention goals might be better served by changing current drinking norms and practices of men so that they are more like those of women.

In the general population, the failure to recognize existing norms and behavior related to abstinence and moderation in drinking, and to provide positive reinforcement for them, has seriously restricted prevention efforts. In Beauchamp's (1980) words, "The overall goal of alcohol policy should be to encourage high rates of minimal or non-use of alcohol, so as to promote low rates of excessive use of alcohol. Frequent but non-problematic use of alcohol would not be defined as harmful or deviant drinking, but it would also not be encouraged as a model for individual adults" (p. 168–169).

There is little evidence that the mass media play a significant role in changing drinking behavior. Nevertheless, they can be instrumental in shaping attitudes and increasing public involvement. They may constitute an important first step in the public education process, particularly because they influence those involved in decision-making (Schankula, 1981). Thus, women might support and attempt to influence the design of mass media prevention programs undertaken by government and industry (cf. Schankula, 1981).

Many prevention activities in the 1980s will have to operate without government funding. Since alcohol programs for women are among the newest, they may be more severely curtailed than those that are more established. Certain strategies can be employed to ensure the continuation of programs for women: increased use of volunteers and self-help programs; collaboration with nonalcohol agencies that have similar objectives (e.g., the teaching of life skills could be conducted jointly with mental health agencies); collaboration with industries, such as insurance companies, that have an interest in prevention; and an increased willingness to promote measures such as legislative changes that are low in cost.

CONCLUSION

This chapter has focused on the primary prevention of problem drinking in women. A number of current programs are reviewed and assessed and additional strategies are suggested. The increased interest in women's issues and women's health over the past few decades is now being translated into programs that focus on alcohol consumption and alcohol problems among specific groups of women.

The design of many of these programs indicates that there is good cause for optimism. Some of these programs may result in decreases in alcohol-related problems in women. Others may provide information that can be used to revise strategies. Future programs that incorporate some of the additional approaches suggested here may ultimately benefit a much broader segment of women in society.

ACKNOWLEDGMENTS

I would like to thank Norma Turner for her very capable assistance and conscientious efforts in preparing the manuscript. Jessica Hill of Health Promotion and Prevention, Health and Welfare Canada, and Ann Baxter of the California Women's Commission on Alcoholism shared their knowledge and opinions regarding current programs for women. I am greatly indebted to Oriana J. Kalant who critically reviewed the manuscript and provided many valuable comments and suggestions.

REFERENCES

Aase, J. M. The fetal alcohol syndrome in American Indians: A high risk group. *Neurobehavioral Toxicology and Teratology*, 1981, *3*, 153–156.

Abelson, H. I. Personal communication, 1979.

Addiction Research Foundation. *Alcohol conversion factors: Information review*. Toronto: Addiction Research Foundation, 1978.

Bacon, S. D. On the prevention of alcohol problems and alcoholism. *Journal of Studies on Alcohol*, 1978, *39*, 1125–1147.

Baxter, A. Personal communication, 1981.

Beauchamp, D. E. *Beyond alcoholism: Alcohol and public health policy*. Philadelphia: Temple University Press, 1980.

Blane, H. T. Issues in preventing alcohol problems. *Preventive Medicine*, 1976, *5*, 176–186.

Blume, S. B. Drinking and pregnancy: Preventing fetal alcohol syndrome. *The New York State Journal of Medicine*, 1981, *81*, 95–98.

Burris, S. Personal communication, 1983.

Cahalan, D., Cisin, I. H., & Crossley, H. M. *American drinking practices: A national study of drinking behavior and attitudes*. New Haven, Conn.: College and University Press, 1969.

California Women's Commission on Alcoholism. *Summary of outreach activities through July 31, 1981: Evaluation of the Breakthrough Project*. Inglewood, Calif.: California Women's Commission on Alcoholism, 1981.

Campbell, D. T., & Stanley, J. C. *Experimental and quasi-experimental designs for research*. Chicago, Ill.: Rand McNally, 1963.

Clark, W. B. *Contextual and situational variables in drinking behavior* (Task 5 Report for NIAAA, Contract ADM-281-76-0027). Social Research Group, School of Public Health, University of California, Berkeley, 1977.

Clark, W. B., & Midanik, L. Alcohol use and alcohol problems among U.S. adults: Results of the 1979 national survey. In *Alcohol consumption and related problems* (NIAAA Alcohol and Health Monograph No. 1, U.S. Department of Health and Human Services Publication No. ADM-82-1190). Washington, D.C.: U.S. Government Printing Office, 1982.

Damkot, D. K., Toussie, S. R., Akley, N. R., Geller, H. A., & Whitmore, D. G. *On-the-road driving behavior and breath alcohol concentration* (U.S. Department of Transportation Report No. DOT HS-802-264). Washington, D.C.: U.S. Government Printing Office, 1977.

Edwards, G. Theoretical synthesis: Discussion. In T. C. Harford, D. A. Parker, & L. Light (Eds.), *Normative approaches to the prevention of alcohol abuse and alcoholism* (NIAAA Research Monograph No. 3, U.S. Department of Health, Education, and Welfare Publication No. ADM-79-847). Washington, D.C.: U.S. Government Printing Office, 1980.

Engs, R. C., & Wilsnack, S. C. *Training "block counselors" as an aid in helping the hidden alcoholic*. Bloomington, Ind.: Bloomington Hospital, n.d.

Ferrence, R. G. Prevention of drug overdosage: Current strategies and implications for policy. *International Journal of the Addictions*, 1978, *13*, 1127–1144.

Ferrence, R. G. Sex differences in the prevalence of problem drinking. In O. J. Kalant (Ed.), *Research advances in alcohol and drug problems* (Vol. 5: *Alcohol and drug problems in women*). New York: Plenum Press, 1980.

Ferrence, R. G. *Drinking, smoking, and women's health: A Canadian perspective.* Toronto: Addiction Research Foundation, 1983.

Ference, R. G., Rush, B. R., & Murdock, W. L. *Services for alcoholics: A study of medical and social service facilities in the Lake Erie Region.* Toronto: Addiction Research Foundation, 1980.

Fielding, J. E. Successes of prevention. *Milbank Memorial Fund Quarterly/ Health and Society*, 1978, *56*, 274–302.

Frankel, B. G., & Whitehead, P. C. *Drinking and damage: Theoretical advances and implications for prevention.* New Brunswick, N.J.: Rutgers Center of Alcohol Studies, 1981.

Gomberg, E. S. Risk factors related to alcohol problems among women: Proneness and vulnerability. In *Alcoholism and alcohol abuse among women: Research issues* (NIAAA Research Monograph No. 1, U.S. Department of Health, Education, and Welfare Publication No. ADM-80-835). Washington, D.C.: U.S. Government Printing Office, 1980.

Greenblatt, M., & Schuckit, M. A. (Eds.) *Alcoholism problems in women and children.* New York: Grune & Stratton, 1976.

Gusfield, J. R. The prevention of drinking problems. In W. J. Filstead, J. J. Rossi, & M. Keller (Eds.), *Alcohol and alcohol problems: New thinking and new directions.* Cambridge, Mass.: Ballinger, 1976.

Harford, T. C., & Gerstel, E. K. Age-related patterns of daily alcohol consumption in Metropolitan Boston. *Journal of Studies on Alcohol*, 1981, *42*, 1062–1066.

Harris, L., & Associates Ltd. *Public awareness of the NIAAA advertising campaign and public attitudes toward drinking and alcohol abuse: Phase IV, winter 1974 and overall summary.* Springfield, Va.: National Technical Information Service, 1975. (NTIS No. PB-244147)

Haynes, S. G., & Feinleib, M. Woman, work and coronary heart disease: Prospective findings from the Framingham Heart Study. *American Journal of Public Health*, 1980, *70*, 133–141.

Health and Welfare Canada. *Special printouts: Nutrition Canada food survey, 1970–1971. Frequency data.* Ottawa: Health and Welfare Canada, 1973.

Health and Welfare Canada. *"It's Just Your Nerves": A resource on women's use of minor tranquillizers and alcohol.* Ottawa: Promotion and Prevention Directorate, 1981. (a)

Health and Welfare Canada. *Special printouts: Canada health survey, 1978–1979. Frequency data.* Ottawa: Health and Welfare Canada, 1981. (b)

Healy, P. The Pregnant Pause campaign: An explanation and an outline. *Focus on Women*, 1980, *1*, 204–213.

Homiller, J. D. Alcoholism among women. *Chemical Dependencies: Behavioral and Biomedical Issues*, 1980, *4*, 1–31.

Hunter, N. Brewers disagree on light beer's future. *The Globe & Mail* (Toronto), February 17, 1982.

Hurst, P. M. Epidemiological aspects of alcohol in driver crashes and citations. In M. W. Perrine (Ed.), *Alcohol, drugs and driving* (U.S. Department of Transportation, Technical Report No. DOT HS-801-096). Washington, D.C.: U.S. Government Printing Office, 1974.

Institute for Road Safety Research (SWOV). *Drinking by motorists.* Voorburg, The Netherlands: Foundation for the Scientific Study of Alcohol and Drug Use, 1977.

Interministerial Committee on Drinking–Driving. *The 1979 Ontario roadside BAC survey: Summary report.* Toronto: Ministry of the Solicitor-General, 1979.

Johnson, P., Armor, D. J., Polich, S., & Stambul, H. *U.S. adult drinking practices: Time trends, social correlates and sex roles* (Report prepared for the National Institute on Alcohol Abuse and Alcoholism). Santa Monica, Calif.: Rand Corporation, 1977.

Kalant, O. J. (Ed.). *Research advances in alcohol and drug problems* (Vol. 5: *Alcohol and drug problems in women*). New York: Plenum Press, 1980.

Kelley, C. M. *Crime in the United States.* Washington, D.C.: U.S. Government Printing Office, 1976.

Kessler, R. C., Brown, R. L., & Broman, C. L. Sex differences in psychiatric help-seeking: Evidence from large-scale surveys. *Journal of Health and Social Behavior*, 1981, *22*, 49–63.

Klein, D. C., & Goldston, S. E. Primary prevention: An idea whose time has come. *Proceedings of the Pilot Conference on Primary Prevention* (U.S. Department of Health, Education, and Welfare Publication No. ADM-77-447). Washington, D.C.: U.S. Government Printing Office, 1977.

Kristein, M. M. Economic issues in prevention. *Preventive Medicine*, 1977, *6*, 252–264.

Lee, P. R., & Franks, P. E. Primary prevention and the executive branch of the federal government. *Preventive Medicine*, 1977, *6*, 209–212.

Little, R. E. Epidemiologic and experimental studies in drinking and pregnancy: The state of the art. *Neurobehavioral Toxicology and Teratology*, 1981, *3*, 163–167.

Little, R. E., Streissguth, A. P., & Guzinski, G. M. Prevention of fetal alcohol syndrome: A model program. *Alcoholism: Clinical and Experimental Research*, 1980, *4*, 185–189.

Little, R. E., Streissguth, A. P., Guzinski, G. M., Grathwohl, H. L., Blumhagen, J. M., & McIntyre, C. E. Change in obstetrician advice following a two-year community educational program on alcohol use and pregnancy. *American Journal of Obstetrics and Gynecology*, 1983, *146*, 23–28.

Maccoby, N., & Farquhar, J. W. Communication for health: Unselling heart disease. *Journal of Communication*, 1975, *25*, 114–126.

MacGregor, B. *Alcohol consumption in Canada—Some preliminary findings of a national survey in Nov.-Dec., 1976* (ERD 78-152). Ottawa: Health and Welfare Canada, 1978.

MacGregor, B. *An assessment of the visibility of phase IIIA of the dialogue on drinking campaign.* Ottawa: Health and Welfare Canada, 1979.

McPheeters, H. L. Primary prevention and health promotion in mental health. *Preventive Medicine*, 1976, *5*, 187–198.

Mello, N. K. Some behavioral and biological aspects of alcohol problems in women. In O. J. Kalant (Ed.), *Research advances in alcohol and drug problems* (Vol. 5: *Alcohol and drug problems in women*). New York: Plenum Press, 1980.

Metzner, H. L. *Role and role conflict in women's drinking practices: Report of the pilot study.* Ann Arbor, Mich.: School of Public Health, University of Michigan, 1980.

Nathanson, A. Sex roles as variables in preventive health behavior. *Journal of Community Health*, 1977, *3*, 142–155.

National Council on Alcoholism: Greater Detroit Area. *Fetal alcohol syndrome: Program abstract.* Unpublished report, n.d.

National Institute on Alcohol Abuse and Alcoholism. *Alcoholism and alcohol abuse among women: Research issues* (NIAAA Research Monograph No. 1, U.S. Department of Health, Education, and Welfare Publication No. ADM-80-835). Washington, D.C.: U.S. Government Printing Office, 1980.

National Institute on Alcohol Abuse and Alcoholism. *NIAAA public education campaign evaluation.* Rockville, Md.: National Institute on Alcohol Abuse and Alcoholism, Division of Prevention, 1981. (a)

National Institute on Alcohol Abuse and Alcoholism. *SPECTRUM: Alcohol problem prevention projects for women by women.* Rockville, Md.: National Institute on Alcohol Abuse and Alcoholism, Division of Prevention, 1981. (b)

Noble, E. P. (Ed.). *Third special report to the U.S. Congress on alcohol and health* (U.S. Department of Health, Education, and Welfare Publication No. ADM-78-569). Washington, D.C.: U.S. Government Printing Office, 1978.

Parker, D. A., Parker, E. S., Harford, T. C., & Brody, J. A. Status inconsistency and drinking patterns among working men and women. *Alcoholism: Clinical and Experimental Research*, 1978, *2*, 101–105.

Reid, A. E. *Alcoholism and drug treatment in Ontario: A review of current programs.* Winnipeg: University of Manitoba, 1977.

Robins, L. N., & Smith, E. M. Longitudinal studies of alcohol and drug problems: Sex differences. In O. J. Kalant (Ed.), *Research advances in alcohol and drug problems* (Vol. 5: *Alcohol and drug problems in women*). New York: Plenum Press, 1980.

Rogers, E. M., & Shoemaker, F. F. *Communication of innovations: A cross cultural approach* (2nd ed.). New York: Free Press, 1971.

Room, R. Minimizing alcohol problems. *Alcohol Health and Research World*, Fall 1974, 12–17.

Room, R. Concepts and strategies in the prevention of alcohol-related problems. *Contemporary Drug Problems*, 1980, *9*, 9–47.

Room, R. The case for a problem prevention approach to alcohol, drug, and mental problems. *Public Health Reports*, 1981, *96*, 26–33.

Room, R., & Mosher, J. F. Out of the shadow of treatment: A role for regulatory agencies in the prevention of alcohol problems. *Alcohol Health and Research World*, 1979/80, *4*, 11–17.

Rosett, H. L. The effects of alcohol on the fetus and offspring. In O. J. Kalant (Ed.), *Research advances in alcohol and drug problems* (Vol. 5: *Alcohol and drug problems in women*). New York: Plenum Press, 1980.

Rosett, H. L., Ouellette, E. M., Weiner, L., & Owens, E. The prenatal clinic: A site for alcoholism prevention and treatment. In F. A. Seixas (Ed.), *Currents in alcoholism* (Vol. 1). New York: Grune & Stratton, 1977.

Rosett, H. L., Weiner, L., & Edelin, K. C. Strategies for prevention of fetal alcohol effects. *Obstetrics and Gynecology*, 1981, *57*, 1–7.

Schankula, H. J. (Chairman). *Alcohol: Public education and social policy* (Report of the Task Force on Public Education and Social Policy). Toronto: Addiction Research Foundation, 1981.

Schaps, E., Churgin, S., Palley, C. S., Takata, B., & Cohen, A. Y. Primary prevention research: A preliminary review of program outcome studies. *International Journal of the Addictions*, 1980, *15*, 657–676.

Schmidt, W., & Popham, R. E. *Alcohol problems and their prevention: A public health perspective.* Toronto: Addiction Research Foundation, 1978.

Schmidt, W., & Popham, R. E. Sex differences in mortality: A comparison of male and female alcoholics. In O. J. Kalant (Ed.), *Research advances in alcohol and drug problems* (Vol. 5: *Alcohol and drug problems in women*). New York: Plenum Press, 1980.

Schuckit, M. A., & Morrissey, E. R. Alcoholism in women: Some clinical and social perspectives with an emphasis on possible subtypes. In M. Greenblatt & M. A. Schuckit (Eds.), *Alcoholism problems in women and children.* New York: Grune & Stratton, 1976.

Smith, G. A., Wolynetz, M. S., & Wiggins, T. R. I. *Drinking drivers in Canada: A national roadside survey of the blood alcohol concentrations in nighttime Canadian drivers.* Ottawa: Road and Motor Vehicle Safety Branch, Transport Canada, 1976.

Sokol, R. J., Miller, S. I., Debanne, S., Golden, N., Collins, G., Kaplan, J., & Martier, S. The Cleveland NIAAA prospective alcohol-in-pregnancy study: The first year. *Neurobehavioral Toxicology and Teratology*, 1981, *3*, 203–209.

Statistics Canada. *Statistics of criminal and other offenses* (Catalogue No. 85-205). Ottawa: Statistics Canada, 1972.

Statistics Canada. *Cause of death: Provinces by sex and Canada by sex and age 1979* (Catalogue No. 84-203, Vital Statistics Catalogue No. 84-202). Ottawa: Statistics Canada, 1981. (a)

Statistics Canada. *Mental health statistics* (Vol. 1: *Institutional admissions and separations*). Ottawa: Health Division, Statistics Canada, 1981. (b)

Statistics Canada. *Hospital morbidity 1978* (Catalogue No. 82-206). Ottawa: Statistics Canada, 1982.

Staulcup, H., Kenward, K., & Frigo, D. A review of federal primary alcoholism prevention projects. *Journal of Studies on Alcohol*, 1979, *40*, 943–968.

Stuart, R. B., & Jacobson, B. Sex differences in obesity. In E. S. Gomberg & V. Franks (Eds.), *Gender and disordered behavior: Sex differences in psychopathology*. New York: Brunner/Mazel, 1979.

Taylor, N. *Alcohol abuse prevention among women: A community approach*. Paper presented at the National Alcoholism Forum of the National Council on Alcoholism, Washington, D.C., April 1982.

Wagenaar, A. C. *Effects of raising the legal drinking age on traffic accident involvement of young drivers*. Paper presented at the 109th Annual Meeting of the American Public Health Association, Los Angeles, November 1981.

Wallack, L. M., & Barrows, D. V. *Preventing alcohol problems in California: Evaluation of the three year "winners" program*. Berkeley, Calif.: Social Research Group, School of Public Health, University of California, 1981.

Wechsler, H. Epidemiology of male/female drinking over the last half century. In *Alcoholism and alcohol abuse among women: Research issues* (NIAAA Research Monograph No. 1, U.S. Department of Health, Education, and Welfare Publication No. ADM-80-835). Washington, D.C.: U.S. Government Printing Office, 1980.

Whitehead, P. C. The prevention of alcoholism: Divergences and convergences of two approaches. *Addictive Diseases: An International Journal*, 1975, *1*, 431–443.

Whitehead, P. C. *Evaluating the AWARE program: Progress and prospects* (Report prepared for the AWARE program). Regina, Canada: Department of Health, Province of Saskatchewan, 1976.

Whitehead, P. C. *Evaluation of a media campaign: The AWARE program and attitudes toward alcohol* (Report prepared for the AWARE program). Regina, Canada: Department of Health, Province of Saskatchewan, 1978.

Wilkinson, P. Sex differences in morbidity of alcoholics. In O. J. Kalant (Ed.), *Research advances in alcohol and drug problems* (Vol. 5: *Alcohol and drug problems in women*). New York: Plenum Press, 1980.

Wilkinson, R. *The prevention of drinking problems: Legal controls and cultural influences*. New York: Oxford University Press, 1970.

Wilsnack, R. W., Wilsnack, S. C., & Klassen, A. D., Jr. Women's drinking and drinking problems: Patterns from a 1981 national survey. *American Journal of Public Health*, 1984, *74*, 11.

Wilsnack, S. C. Prevention of alcohol problems in women: Current status and research needs. In *Alcoholism and alcohol abuse among women: Research issues* (NIAAA Research Monograph No. 1, U.S. Department of Health, Education and Welfare Publication No. ADM-80-835). Washington, D.C.: U.S. Government Printing Office, 1980.

Wilsnack, S. C. Prevention of alcohol problems in women. In *Special population issues* (NIAAA Alcohol and Health Monograph No. 4, U.S. Department of Health and Human Services Publication No. ADM-82-1193). Washington, D.C.: U.S. Government Printing Office, 1982.

Wine, spring water mix introduced by Bright's. *The Globe & Mail* (Toronto), February 17, 1982.

Wolfe, A. C. *1973 U.S. national roadside breathtesting survey: Procedures and results*. Ann Arbor, Mich.: Highway Safety Research Institute, 1974.

Young, A., Sanders, D., Sinclair, L., Altman, G., Nordin, R., Herman, C., & McIntyre, C. *The pregnancy and health program: A demonstration project for strategies of prevention and intervention in drinking during pregnancy*. Presented at Alcoholism and Drug Abuse in the Northwest: Developing Prevention Strategies, University of Washington, Seattle, Washington, 1981.

Author Index

Corrigan, E. M. (continued)
298, 300, 301, 309n, 332, 345n, 351,
353, 366n, 369, 390, 400n.
Cosie, T., 130–132, 151n.
Cosper, R., 236, 256n.
Costello, R. M., 372, 395, 396, 400n.,
401n.
Cotton, N. S., 241, 256n.
Courcoul, M. A., 129, 146, 152n.
Covington, S. S., 200, 205, 209, 211,
213–215, 217, 219, 224n.
Coyne, L., 218, 225n, 398n.
Cramer, M. J., 354, 366n.
Crawford, J. J., 370, 401n.
Crawford, R. J. M., 378, 401n.
Crepin, G., 158, 184n.
Cripe, L. I., 401n.
Cronin, R., 218, 226n.
Cronkite, R. C., 350, 366n, 401n.
Crossley, H. M., 23, 32n, 66, 71, 83,
92n, 104, 114n, 253, 256n, 282, 302,
303, 309n, 418, 421, 438n.
Crothers, T. D., 8, 33n.
Crotty, T. D., 194, 196, 225n.
Crumpacker, D. W., 166, 183n.
Cull, J. G., 401n.
Cummings, R. E., 326, 328, 345n.
Curlee, J., 16, 33n, 101, 107, 114n,
123, 126, 130, 139, 149n, 150n, 199,
224n, 270, 277n, 290, 291, 302,
309n, 326, 328, 331, 345n, 352–354,
366n, 369, 387, 401n.
Curran, F. J., 9, 33n, 201, 202, 211,
216, 224n.
Curran, J. P., 190, 224n.
Cutter, H. S. G., 285, 299, 309n, 401n.

D

Dahlgren, L., 122–126, 150n, 199,
224n, 285, 293, 309n, 330, 332,
345n, 353, 367n.
Daily, J. M., 70, 91n.
D'Alonzo, G. A., 124, 152n.
Dalterio, S., 169, 183n.
Dalton, M. S., 401n.

D'Amanda, C., 52, 64n.
Damkot, D. K., 419, 438n.
Dammann, G., 107, 112, 114n.
Danahy, S., 329, 346n.
Danielsson, B., 147, 150n.
Darby, B. I., 160, 184n.
DaSilva, V. A., 166, 184n.
David, D., 273, 277n.
Davidson, A. F., 378, 401n.
Davidson, C. S., 127, 128, 152n.
Davidson, R. S., 401n.
Davidson, W. J., 411n.
Davies, J., 54, 64n.
Davis, F. T., 76, 80, 82, 84, 87, 92n.
Davis, J., 407n.
Davis, M., 127–130, 142, 147, 151n.,
152n, 153n, 401n.
Davis, T. S., 402n.
Davis, W. N., 235, 257n, 273, 278n.
364, 367n.
Debanne, S., 418, 428, 429, 441n.
DeBeukelaer, M., 161, 183n.
Decker, J. D., 161, 184n.
Dehaene, P., 158, 184n.
Delage, H., 284, 297, 300, 301, 309n.
delint, J. E., 123–126, 152n, 376, 401n.
Deliry, 202, 206, 207, 225n.
Delmastro, D., 400n.
Demore, H. W., 44, 46, 47, 54, 60n.,
61n.
Densen-Gerber, J., 215, 216, 223n.
Dent, C., 50, 62n.
Deroubaix, P., 158, 184n.
Deitering, N., 166, 184n.
deTorok, D., 169, 184n.
Detre, K., 134, 153n.
Devoe, C. I., 47, 54, 55, 65n., 190,
227n, 288, 289, 290, 299, 312n.
DeVries, J. C., 101, 115n., 322, 367n.
Dexter, J. D., 161, 184n.
Diamond, D. L., 219, 224n.
Diamond, S., 287, 293, 311n.
Diamond, W., 194, 197, 225n.
Diaz, J., 161, 184n., 187n.
Dickens, G., 163, 166, 184n.
Dickinson, R. G., 325, 345n.
Dickman, D., 221, 224n.
Dieppa, I., 87, 92n.

Farquhar, J. W., 343, 345n, 347n, 423, 440n.
Faulkner, M. A., 403n.
Faust, R., 103, 104, 116n.
Favorini, A., 167, 185n.
Fawcett, J. A., 137, 150n.
Feagins, J. L., 87, 92n.
Feighner, J. P., 147, 150n.
Feinleib, M., 420, 421, 439n.
Fejer, D., 39, 64n.
Feldman, D. J., 74, 83, 86, 89, 92n.
Felson, R. B., 265, 277n.
Ferguson, F., 402n.
Ferguson, L., 103, 114n, 402n.
Ferrence, R. G., 4, 7, 17-20, 33n, 61n, 105, 107, 108, 114n, 330, 345n, 413, 416-419, 435, 439n.
Feuerlein, W., 254, 256n, 285, 293, 309n.
Fewell, C. H., 329, 345n.
Fex, G., 147, 150n.
Fibel, B., 336, 345n.
Fielding, J. E., 413, 439n.
Fifield, L., 218, 224n.
Fillmore, K. M., 19, 34n, 238, 248, 249, 256n, 285, 289, 310n.
Filmore, K. M., 14, 19, 33n.
Fincham, F., 197, 223n.
Fine, E. W., 87, 95n.
Finlay, D. G., 402n.
Finley, J., 410n.
Finney, J., 50, 62n, 402n.
Fischer, J. C., 285, 299, 309n, 402n.
Fishburne, P., 38, 40, 42, 44, 61n.
Fisher, P., 393, 408n.
Fisher, R., 126, 127, 151n.
Fitzpatrick, J. P., 261, 277n.
Flamer, R., 402n, 404n.
Flanagan, J., 369, 390, 394, 403n.
Fleetwood, M. F., 242, 256n.
Flintoff, W. P., 292, 310n.
Flores, J. L., 86, 87, 92n.
Floyd, H. H., 51, 61n.
Floyd, R., 332, 348n.
Foggitt, R. H., 261, 278n.
Forrest, G. G., 216, 220, 221, 224n.
Forslund, M. A., 41, 47, 50, 51, 52, 61n, 405n.
Fostakowsky, R. T., 398n.

Foster, F. M., 74, 76, 87, 95n.
Fox, J., 328, 348n.
Fox, J. H., 137, 150n.
Fox, M. M., 353, 367n.
Fox, R., 16, 33n, 167, 184n, 292, 294, 310n, 402n.
Frankel, B. G., 433, 439n.
Franklin, K., 404n.
Franks, P. E., 413, 440n.
Franks, V., 400n.
Fraser, J., 101, 114n.
Freebairn, C., 403n.
Freedberg, E. J., 402n, 403n.
Freeman, C. W., 325, 328, 347n.
Freeman, H. E., 54, 60n.
Friesen, H. G., 157, 188n.
Frieze, I. H., 260, 264-266, 270-272, 274, 277n.
Frigo, D., 430, 442n.
Fritchie, G. E., 159, 185n.
Frodi, A., 268, 274, 277n.
Frogg, W., 87, 92n.
Fuentes, C., 142, 151n.
Fuller, R. K., 403n.
Funderburk, F., 404n.
Funston, R., 410n.
Furst, C. J., 319, 345n.

G

Gaa'l, C. L., 403n.
Gabrynowicz, J., 403n.
Gad-Luther, I., 220, 221, 224n.
Gaines, J. J., 76, 77, 82, 83, 92n.
Gaitz, C. M., 284, 305, 308n.
Galambos, J. T., 121, 127, 128n, 129, 150n.
Galan, F. J., 89, 92n.
Galbrarth, S., 212, 215, 224n.
Gallant, D. M., 403n.
Gallen, M., 403n.
Galli, N., 103, 114n.
Gantt, R. C., 136, 153n.
Garrett, G. R., 355, 367n.
Garzon, S. R., 20, 34n, 87, 93n.
Gavaler, J. S., 130, 153n.
Gebhard, P. H., 201, 211, 215n, 217, 224n.

W

Subject Index

E

F